International Monetary Relations

INTERNATIONAL MONETARY RELATIONS

Theory, History, and Policy ✍

Leland B. Yeager

UNIVERSITY OF VIRGINIA

HARPER & ROW, PUBLISHERS, NEW YORK

LIBRARY OF CONGRESS CATALOG CARD NUMBER: *66-10055*

M-P

Contents

Part II. History and Policy

Preface

This book surveys the monetary side of international economics. Its focus is international balance and imbalance and related policies. It does consider some topics that concern the practical merchant and banker (forward exchange and the like), but only insofar as they bear on the main theme. The great emphasis that writings and policy-making in this field have traditionally given to supposed historical "lessons" has prompted a fairly detailed reconsideration here.

My interest in international monetary economics dates back to study years ago at Columbia University under Professors Ragnar Nurkse and James W. Angell, to both of whom I am indebted. The present book incorporates some much-revised sections of a doctoral dissertation written under their guidance, as well as sections adapted from articles of mine appearing in the *Journal of Political Economy, Social Research, Kyklos,* and the *Journal of Finance,* to whose editors or publishers I am indebted for the appropriate permissions. Harcourt, Brace & World, Inc. and D. Van Nostrand Company, Inc. have kindly permitted lengthy quotations from J. M. Keynes, *The Economic Consequences of the Peace,* and B. M. Anderson, *Economics and the Public Welfare,* respectively.

Though trying to be fair in reporting facts and logic both favorable and unfavorable to rival views on exchange-rate policy, I do not try to conceal my own judgments by straddling. Particularly because I take issue with the late Professor Nurkse on some points, I am anxious to make clear how much I admire him and his teaching and many seminal writings.

Thanks go to my colleagues for their courtesies, to the University of Virginia Institute for Research in the Social Sciences and to the Relm Foundation for grants that freed a summer for this project and lightened my teaching load one year, and to several graduate students, most recently Messrs. Marvin Phaup, Gary Lee, and David Tuerck, for assistance with computations and other chores. Although Professor and Mrs. Paul Homan had no actual connection with my work on this book, they helped me see it through in a way that is no less real for their probably not even realizing it. Among the typists who labored over several drafts Mrs. Betty Tillman deserves special thanks.

Only minor revisions could be made in view of developments since the spring of 1964.

LELAND B. YEAGER

Charlottesville, Virginia
June, 1965

Part I

THEORY ∽

The study of international monetary relations (international finance) covers prices, wages, incomes, money supplies, monetary standards, financial policies, international loans, balances of payments, exchange rates, external reserves, and international liquidity. Monetary magnitudes serve as indicators of, and guides to, such underlying "realities" as resource allocation, trade in goods and services, and international transfer of command over resources by way of loans and investment. The chapters of Part I investigate the theory of how the several alternative systems of international monetary relations operate. These chapters include some abstract analysis of policy measures, leaving until Part II a survey of policy in the context of past and current history.

Realities Behind the Veil of Money and Prices

I

The Gain from Trade

A quick review of some leading principles of international economics will introduce our study of the role of money and prices. First, let us recall the sources of gain from trade. Admittedly, the idea of gain for a country as a whole is fuzzy. Relaxing or abolishing restrictions on trade, like any other policy, cannot be proved right or wrong on purely scientific grounds. Appraising any policy whatsoever depends not merely on "positive" propositions, but also on value judgments—personal opinions about how desirable or undesirable various results are. Any supposedly beneficial change in national circumstances harms some people. If a mere act of Congress could abolish hurricanes, some persons would suffer a loss of business, including meteorologists, construction workers, and the present generation of undertakers. The same is true of inventions: people in general gain, but some lose. A vast literature deals with the problem of weighing benefits to some persons against damage to others in assessing social gain or loss. These subtleties concern economic theory and policy in general but do not have an especially strong or direct bearing on international finance in particular. Here, "gain from trade" will mean gain of the same admittedly debatable kind as gain from technological progress or from abolishing hurricanes. Like technological progress, trade widens the range of available ways of transforming labor and other resources into desired goods and services. Technological progress and geographic specialization both make this transformation more "efficient" (to use a loose but convenient word). The basis for specialization and trade among countries of the world is the same as for specialization and trade among states of the United States.[1]

Trade is most obviously beneficial when it bring us goods we could hardly produce at home at all. The gain from cheaper foreign supplies of things we could well make ourselves requires more discussion. Under the conditions of an idealized competitive model, price relations indicate opportunity costs, or how much each product costs in sacrificed production of other things.[2] Suppose we can produce widgets in our country for $5.00. This means, under ideal competitive conditions, that producing a widget costs sacrificing the production of other goods that would also have been worth $5.00 to us.

Suppose, now, that we can buy a widget abroad for only $3.00. If imports and exports pay for each other, an imported widget costs us $3.00 worth of our export products. Supplying these exports means our sacrificing their consumption or the production and consumption of other goods that would also have been worth $3.00 to us. Importing a widget at $3.00 involves only three-fifths as much

---

[1] This is no place to appraise all the various arguments for interference with international trade, such as the argument for protection of defense industries. Valid as these arguments may be, they do not disprove the gain from trade discussed here but merely point out other considerations that must be weighed against it in policy-making.

A convenient way of presenting some pieces of analysis is to apply them to examining and demolishing fallacious arguments. But the use of fallacious arguments in behalf of certain policies does not in itself prove that no valid arguments are available and that the policies themselves must be rejected. On the other hand, analytical *validity* is not the same as *conclusiveness* in policy arguments. Economic analysis is part, but only part, of what is relevant in policy discussions.

[2] See "Realities and Money Prices," p. 7.

sacrifice as making it ourselves at $5.00. Importing a product at a money price below the cost of making it ourselves represents a real saving in the amounts of other desirable things foregone.

Our opportunity for gain is genuine regardless of *why* foreigners sell so cheaply. Perhaps the foreign widgets are cheap because the climate is ideal for their production in foreign countries, or because the land or capital used in widget production is especially abundant there, or because a broad home market there gives scope for cheap mass production, or because the foreign producers have skills stemming from a long tradition of widget production. Perhaps general wage levels in the widget-producing countries are lower than ours or perhaps foreign widget-workers in particular are shamefully underpaid even in relation to the generally low wage levels of their own countries. Perhaps the exchange rate translates prices in the foreign currency at an "unfairly" low value, whatever that might mean. Perhaps foreign governments are subsidizing widget exports. Perhaps widgets grow wild on bushes abroad and need only be gathered at slight expense. What difference does any of this make to us? How can it matter *why* the foreign widgets are so cheap?[3] What matters to us is whether prices *in our own country* correctly indicate realities—whether our prices correctly indicate how much each product costs in required sacrifice of others, given the state of technology and the demands on and scarcity of our resources. The opportunity that foreign prices offer to us is genuine from our point of view, regardless of whether any "distortions" in the foreign price system may be causing foreigners to offer us this opportunity. Refusing this opportunity is the same as refusing any other kind of opportunity for making or getting goods more efficiently or cheaply than before.

---

[3] One possible answer concerns not how genuine but how dependable an opportunity the cheap foreign widgets give us; this is the problem considered in a properly sophisticated version of the "dumping" argument for tariffs. Certain arguments concerning special cases of "external diseconomies" involved in accepting imports or supplying exports could also provide possible answers to the question in the text.

The Principle of Comparative Advantage

Some people who take part in controversies over tariff legislation fail to understand this. They warn about supposed distortions: trade is harmful unless goods of the kinds imported can be produced with greater *absolute* or *physical* efficiency in the foreign country supplying them than in the home country importing them. A reply to this error need not rest on quibbles about how difficult or impossible it is to give a clear meaning to the notion of absolute efficiency. We can assume an extreme case for the sake of analysis; we can imagine one country so inefficient that, in all lines of production, more man-hours of labor, acre-weeks of land, machine-hours of capital goods, etc., are required per unit of final product than elsewhere. Conversely, we can imagine an extremely efficient country where each unit of product requires fewer real inputs of labor and other resources than anywhere else. Yet trade can be beneficial if the country with all-around inferior efficiency specializes in the lines of production where its inferiority is slightest and the country with all-around superior efficiency specializes in the lines of its greatest superiority. International real-cost comparisons are a red herring; what counts is comparing the opportunities available in domestic production and in foreign trade.

This is the *principle of comparative advantage*. It is an "even-if" proposition: it demonstrates how trade can yield benefits *even* in the almost unimaginable situation in which absolute all-across-the-board inferiority and superiority might seem, at first, to rule trade out. Actually, the principle is unnecessary in a demonstration of the gains from trade; elaborating on the example of the $5.00 and $3.00 widgets could provide a satisfactory demonstration. But to accommodate people who persist in supposing that comparisons of absolute efficiency are somehow relevant, the principle accepts their premises for the sake of argument.

The principle of comparative advantage does *not* agree that the gain from specialization comes from having each item produced in the place where it can be produced with the greatest absolute efficiency, i.e., where the inputs of real resources needed per unit of final product are least. Assuming that "absolute efficiency" were meaningful, this misinterpretation of the principle would have an all-around-efficient country produce everything and an all-around-inefficient country produce nothing—in short, there would be no specialization and trade at all (since trade in only one direction could hardly be acceptable to both sides).

A simple variant of traditional examples will help clarify comparative advantage. Considering only two countries and two commodities will suffice to make the point. (Here and in later chapters we adopt the convenient German terminology of naming the home country "Inland" and another country, or all other countries together, "Outland.") Suppose that with a given assortment of labor and other resources (which might be a different given assortment in each country) production possibilities are as shown in the following table.

In Inland, 1 additional bushel of wheat can be had by sacrificing production of ⅓ yard of cloth. In the same sense, the cost of a bushel of wheat in Outland is ½ yard of cloth. As for cloth, producing 1 additional yard costs the sacrifice of 3 bushels of wheat in Inland and only 2 bushels in Outland. These opportunity-cost figures reflect how effectively labor and other resources can shift within each country from one line of production to the other, either directly or in an indirect and complex reallocation.

The conclusions of the example do not depend on any measures of absolute efficiency or absolute real cost in terms of physical quantities of inputs required per unit of output. For all it mattered, we could suppose that the assortment or package of labor and resources necesary to yield the outputs shown in the table is of the same size in Outland as in Inland—or even is much bigger; Outland would be unquestionably less efficient in both lines of production. Still, in the *relative* sense just explained, wheat would be cheaper in Inland and cloth in Outland. Inland gains from trade if it can acquire cloth at a cost per yard any lower than 3 bushels of wheat i.e., if it can get anything more than ⅓ yard of cloth in return for 1 bushel of wheat. Outland gains if it can get anything more than 2 bushels of wheat in return for 1 yard of cloth, i.e., if giving up anything less than ½ yard of cloth will pay for a bushel of wheat. Clearly, terms can be found at which both countries gain[4]—for example, 1 yard of cloth for 2½ bushels of wheat (1 bushel of wheat for ⅖ yard of cloth). By partially or perhaps completely switching out of cloth into wheat production and exporting wheat to pay for imported cloth, Inland can acquire cloth at less sacrifice of wheat than if it produced all its wheat at home. Outland can gain by switching from wheat into cloth production. If consumers so desired, each country could have more of each product for domestic use than in the absence of trade.

There is a further kind of gain that our example does not reveal. *Even if* a country's cloth and wheat production were rigid and unchangeable but if its people could trade on the world market at terms of 1 for 2½, they could gain as long as they were not indifferent

---

[4] This depends on opportunity costs being different in the two countries; otherwise, the international exchange of wheat for cloth would be pointless. If Inland's absolute efficiency exceeded or fell short of Outland's by the same degree in every line of production and if tastes were the same in both countries—unrealistic and almost meaningless conditions—then trade could provide no gain.

Table 1.1 An Example of Comparative Advantage

Country	Output of Wheat (Bushels) or Cloth (Yards)	Opportunity Cost[a]
Inland	90 W *or* 30 C	1 C for 3 W; 1 W for ⅓ C
Outland	40 W *or* 20 C	1 C for 2 W; 1 W for ½ C

[a] How much more of each product could be produced by reallocating labor and resources and cutting back the production of the other product

between having 1 yard of cloth and having 2½ bushels of wheat. (This other kind of gain, not necessarily connected with production, was well illustrated in prisoner-of-war camps, where the prisoners swapped their rations and the contents of their Red Cross packages to get additional satisfactions from fixed total quantities of goods in view of their own differing tastes.) In short, trade permits greater efficiency both in using resources to produce goods and in using goods to "produce" satisfactions.

How much each country gains depends on the terms of trade. These must fall somewhere between the Inland opportunity cost of one cloth for three wheat and the Outland cost of one cloth for two wheat; at terms of trade outside these limits, people in one country would be especially eager for trade but people in the other would refuse. Just where the terms fall depends on supply and demand conditions. Incidentally, the nearer the terms of trade fall to the limit of 1 to 3, the greater is the share of the gain going to Outland; and the nearer to 1 to 2, the greater Inland's share. This is understandable: trade offers gain by providing opportunities different from those already available in domestic production; the farther the terms of trade fall from the domestic opportunity cost, the more significant are the new opportunities offered by trade. The more a country's export products are worth in terms of its import products, the greater is its share of gain.

Gain by a country as a whole is a fuzzy concept, as already admitted. Some producers in each country must cut back their output and switch, if possible, into a relatively more efficient line of production. How do we weigh sectional gains and losses in assessing the national outcome? If the benefited cloth consumers and wheat producers in Inland were considered to be undeserving people whose welfare should count for very little and if the harmed cloth producers and wheat consumers were considered to be especially deserving people whose welfare should count heavily, one might conclude that Inland as a whole lost from trade. On a less special set of judgments about what people deserved, however, we still might say that the country did gain.

Trade would *allow* the country to have more of each product than otherwise. The gainers from trade could more than afford, if necessary, to buy the consent of everyone who would otherwise lose. Actually, of course, the gainers wouldn't bother. Here, however, we may gloss over such problems of welfare economics, since our purpose is only to prepare for describing how wage levels and exchange rates play a part in guiding trade along lines of comparative advantage.

The wheat-and-cloth example is not meant to show how large the volume of trade would be. As long as opportunity costs remain different in the two countries and neither country is yet fully specialized on one product to the exclusion of the other, further specialization and trade would yield further gain. Actually, changes in opportunity cost as specialization went on might prevent complete specialization. As resources shifted out of cloth into wheat production in Inland, still further shifts might become less and less rewarding. Eventually each additional bushel of wheat might cost the sacrifice of perhaps ⅖ rather than only ⅓ yard of cloth. In Outland, cutbacks in wheat and expansion of cloth production might result in each additional yard of cloth costing 2½ rather than only 2 bushels of wheat. But until the two countries' opportunity costs had thus come together, further specialization and trade would be beneficial. (Transportation costs and tariffs—ignored here as irrelevant to showing the nature of the gain—would in reality narrow the scope for beneficial trade.)

Realities and Money Prices

One vital point still remains to be cleared up. Practical businessmen don't know or care anything about comparative advantage and don't need to: they want to buy where *money prices* are lowest and sell where *money prices* are highest. If all lines of production really were less efficient in Outland than in Inland, how could Outland businessmen price any of their goods low enough to capture foreign markets? How could Outland sell anything abroad and earn money to buy abroad? The answer hinges on a generally low level of wages and other incomes in Outland (low, that is, as translated at prevailing rates of exchange and compared with wage and income levels in Inland). Low wage levels—the famous "cheap labor"—are an inevitable result of Outland's inefficient production, but they are also what lets Outland export the products in which it has the smallest disadvantage and so pay for imports that could be produced at home only at still greater disadvantage. Low wages permit Outland to share the benefits of international trade and so be less poor than otherwise.

Inland also gains, even when trading with an inefficient, "cheap-labor" country. Shrinkage of particular Inland industries as a result of trade does not in itself prove otherwise. Shifting labor and resources out of lines of least superior production into lines of most superior production is a key part of the process of reaping the benefits of trade. It would be just as questionable for the Inland government to restrict trade merely on the grounds that Outlanders employed "cheap labor" or had an "unfairly depreciated currency." The difference between Inland and Outland wage levels—wages being translated through the exchange rate into one currency—is necessary to reflect overall differences in efficiency or productivity and so to allow the product price relations that lead profit-seeking businessmen to carry out trade of the sort described by the principle of comparative advantage.

In a competitive economic system no one has to measure directly how much each product costs in terms of the foregone physical output of others. No one has to take these opportunity costs consciously into account. As long as the system works fairly well along the lines of the textbook competitive model, money prices measure them, and people have ordinary profit-and-loss incentives to take them into account. Under competition, if the selling price of a particular commodity happened to exceed or fall short of the change in total cost involved in producing one more or one less unit of it, firms would have a profit incentive to expand or cut back production. Under competition, therefore, the price of a commodity tends to equal the sum of the prices times quantities of the additional ingre-

dients necessary to produce one more unit of it. (These ingredients—resources, factors of production, or factor services—include not only labor and materials but also business enterprise, or whatever the factor receiving profit may be called. So-called "normal" profit thus counts among the payments for ingredients used in making the commodity.)

Under competition, the prices of these ingredients are determined by the bidding for them among various uses. Each firm has a profit incentive to employ each ingredient in such an amount that the effect on the total value of output of employing one more or one less unit of it is equal to its price.

Here we return to the main argument. The price of a product tends to equal the sum of the prices times quantities of the additional ingredients needed to make an additional unit of it. Each ingredient tends to have a price equaling the value of what one unit of it could contribute to production in the various lines employing it. Hence, under competition each product tends to be priced at the additional cost of making an additional unit of it, which in turn tends to equal how much of other products—valued in terms of what consumers were prepared to pay for them— could have been made instead with the necessary ingredients. Prices of $20.00 for a radio and $10.00 for a hat indicate an additional radio costs twice as much as an additional hat in terms of other-products-in-general foregone. The opportunity cost is two hats for one radio.

No doubt reality and the competitive model diverge from one another. But to the extent that the price system does work, the tendencies just outlined, hampered though they may be, do operate.

Prices and Exchange Rates

The argument so far has prepared for showing how a pattern of prices and exchange rates emerges at which businessmen and consumers will have the incentives, under competition, to conduct the trade that yields the gain described by the principle of comparative advantage. Suppose that cloth has a price of $6.00 per yard and wheat a price of $2.00 per bushel in Inland. In Outland, the prices are 36 pesos for cloth and 18 pesos for wheat. (These figures merely illustrate prices reflecting the opportunity costs previously assumed.) To know where they can buy each commodity most cheaply or sell it most dearly, businessmen must consider the dollar-peso exchange rate. At any more than 9 pesos per dollar, both products would be cheaper in Outland than in Inland. Outland would tend to export both and import neither—a situation that could not last if cloth and wheat were the only tradeable products. At the opposite extreme, a rate of fewer than 6 pesos per dollar would make both products cheaper in Inland. A workable exchange rate must fall somewhere between P9 = $1.00 and P6 = $1.00, the exact rate being the one at which each country's exports and imports are equal in total money value.

A more elaborate example will now be instructive. It shows that different patterns of *relative* prices within countries, reflecting different patterns of opportunity costs, set the stage for determining absolute prices at which each country imports some things and exports others. In Inland, according to Table 1.2, a pair of shoes costs 7½ times as much as a bushel of wheat and 15 times as much as a hammer; while in Outland, a pair of shoes costs only 5 times as much as a bushel of wheat and only 7 times as much as a hammer. In Outland a bushel of wheat costs more than a gallon of wine; in Inland it costs less. In Inland a gallon of wine has an opportunity cost of 4 hammers; in Outland a gallon of wine costs only 1⅓ hammers.

These different patterns of relative prices and opportunity cost are translated by the exchange rate into differences in absolute prices (both countries' prices being translated into one currency or the other). At a rate of 1 peso per dollar, *everything* would be cheaper in Inland. (We assume, for simplicity, that the four goods listed are the only ones tradeable.) People would want to buy everthing in Inland and nothing in Outland. Attempts to buy dollars to pay for Inland goods would create lopsided pressure on the foreign-exchange market to exchange pesos for dollars. Unless officially fixed, the exchange rate would move in the direction of more than 1 peso per dollar. At the opposite extreme, a rate of 6 pesos per dollar would make everything cheaper in Outland. As Inlanders eager to buy Outland goods flooded the market with dollars, the rate would move in the direction of fewer pesos per dollar. This shows one of the reasons why the law of demand holds true for foreign exchange as well as for ordinary commodities in ordinary markets. The cheaper one country's currency is in terms of foreign currencies, other things being the same, the wider will be the range of products underselling similar foreign products and the greater will be the quantity of the currency demanded by foreigners to buy that country's relatively inexpensive goods.

Table 1.2 shows that a workable exchange rate must lie somewhere between 1½ and 5 pesos per dollar. At 3 pesos per dollar, for example, Outland would undersell in shoes and wine and Inland in wheat and hammers. The example is not detailed enough to determine the exact exchange rate or export list of each country. These results depend on how strong preferences for the various goods are and on how local prices, reflecting opportunity costs,

Table 1.2. Translation of Relative into Absolute Price Differences

Commodity	Dollar Price in Inland	Peso Price In Outland	Outland Price Converted into Dollars at Rate of					
			P1=$1	P1½=$1	P2=$1	P3=$1	P5=$1	P6=$1
Shoes (pair)	$15.00	P35	$35.00	$23.33	$17.50	$11.67	$7.00	$5.83
Wheat (bushel)	2.00	7	7.00	4.67	3.50	2.33	1.40	1.17
Wine (gallon)	4.00	6	6.00	4.00	3.00	2.00	1.20	1.00
Hammers (each)	1.00	5	5.00	3.33	2.50	1.67	1.00	.83

would change as output changed. In any case, Inland will export hammers and Outland wine, and the exchange rate will be one at which the flows of trade in the two directions pay for each other. (Complications such as international lending are not yet taken into account.) The exchange rate and the international terms of trade are determined together in the interplay of supply and demand.

Trade does not leave local commodity prices unchanged. The Outland demand for hammers, added to the Inland demand, bids the Inland price above $1.00; in Outland, the supply of hammers coming from Inland lowers the price below 5 pesos. Wine shipments from Outland to Inland tend to raise the peso price in Outland and lower the dollar price in Inland. Were it not for transportation costs and other obstacles to trade, prices would move toward being everywhere the same (as translated at the exchange rate emerging from the same process).[5] This equalization of commodity prices would reflect changes in resource allocation and production patterns within countries that made opportunity costs equal among those commodities still produced in at least some amounts in the trading countries. Trade would expand and specialization in production would develop until no further expansion and specialization was worthwhile. But price and cost equalization would not destroy trade. It would destroy incentives for further *expansion* of trade (unless underlying conditions changed, such as population, tastes, technology, etc.). Trade might conceivably wipe out price differences among countries. In a sense, though, the trade would still be motivated or guided by *virtual* price differences—differences that *would have* existed in the absence of

trade and that would appear if trade were cut off or restricted.

The General-equilibrium Theory

The principle of comparative advantage is a proposition in welfare economics; it demonstrates the gain from trade when patterns of opportunity cost differ from country to country. It takes for granted these different patterns and does not try to explain them. A notable attempt at explanation is Bertil Ohlin's general-equilibrium theory of international trade.[6] Ohlin's theory does not necessarily clash with the theory of comparative advantage. Each emphasizes aspects of trade that the other takes for granted. Ohlin's theory, for its part, largely takes the gains from trade for granted and instead tries realistically to describe how and why trade takes place.

We have already seen how differences between countries in opportunity costs and *relative* prices give rise to *absolute* price differences. But what underlies and explains the different patterns of relative prices? What determines a price? The stock answer is "supply and demand." These, however, are categories of influences that in turn needs explaining. *Demand* is the relation between various prices and desired purchases of a commodity and depends on: (1) the needs and preferences of consumers, (2) consumers' incomes, which depend on ownership of and the prices of factors of production, and (3) prices of other commodities. *Supply* is the relation between various prices of the commodity and the quantities offered and reflects the cost of producing and marketing various amounts of the commodity and so depends on: (1) physical conditions of production—climate, the state of technology, and other conditions determining the relation between inputs and output—and (2) the supplies of factors of production actually or potentially used in making the commodity, as well as the bidding for these factors from other uses. Under competition a long-run tendency prevails for the quantity supplied and quantity demanded of each commodity to be equal at a price just covering

---

[5] The translation of comparative advantage into price-and-profit incentives for trade is simplest to explain when exchange rates are flexible. If the monetary systems of various regions and countries are unified, variations in *price and income levels* replace the flexibility of exchange rates. An explanation of this more complicated process appears in Chapter 5.

In the process discussed here exchange rates are not entirely *determined by* the patterns of local-currency prices prevailing in various countries in the absence of trade. On the contrary, exchange rates also *affect* local prices; everything depends on everything else This is not to say that the influence of exchange rates on *general* price levels is anywhere near as strong as the opposite influence.

[6] Bertil Ohlin, *Interregional and International Trade*, Cambridge, Mass.: Harvard University Press, 1933.

cost (counting the "normal" profit of enterprise among the costs). A complete theory must therefore probe into costs and into the prices of factors of production. The price of each factor itself depends on "supply and demand." Demand derives from the technological capacity of the factor to contribute to the production of various goods and from the consumer demands for these goods. Supply, for some factors of production, is a fixed or almost fixed quantity provided by nature (for example, land area). For most factors, supply is a price-quantity relation, with the quantity offered depending on the factor's own price and on other prices. The quantity of electrical engineers, for instance, presumably depends not only on the salaries of electrical engineers but also on the salaries of civil engineers, the fees of doctors, etc. Commodity prices and supplies and demands, factor prices and supplies and demands, incomes—all interact intimately and in complex ways. The various prices and quantities determine one another; no single one is a dominating cause.

All this helps us approach the question: When will internal patterns of relative prices differ from country to country and so set the stage for beneficial trade? In each country some factors of production will be more abundant and cheaper in comparison with other factors than in the outside world; other factors will be relatively scarce and expensive. In the absence of trade, goods produced with relatively large amounts of a country's abundant factors will tend to be relatively cheap; goods requiring large amounts of scarce factors will be expensive. Let us suppose that land is abundant and labor scarce in Inland and that labor is abundant and land scarce in Outland. In Inland high-land-content food is cheap relative to high-labor-content clothing. In Outland the opposite price pattern prevails. As a result, an exchange rate (or a relation between general price levels) can emerge at which Inland will undersell in food and export it and Outland will undersell in clothing and export it.

Just conceivably, different consumer preferences in the two countries might so match the different endowments of factors of production as to keep the internal relative price patterns from diverging. Inlanders might have especially strong preferences for food and Outlanders for clothing. On the other hand, even if the different factors of production were available in the same proportion in both countries, tastes might differ in such a way as to create differences in relative prices. Though both countries had land and labor in the same proportions, Inlanders might so prefer clothing and Outlanders so prefer food that prices would emerge which would promote the exchange of Inland food for Outland clothing.

We shall have to make some qualifications soon. Loosely speaking, meanwhile, it is differences in factor endowments—differences, rather, in the relations of factor supplies to the demands for factors derived from consumer demands for goods and services—that create the patterns of comparative advantage that give rise to international trade. An exchange rate translates international differences in absolute prices (differences that trade itself tends to wipe out). Incidentally, the exchange rate permits comparing absolute factor prices, making it possible to say that a particular kind of labor is cheaper in one country than another. The exchange rate at which a country's imports and exports pay for each other depends largely on reciprocal demand and supply. The more intense the Outland demand for Inland goods and the offer of Outland goods in payment and the weaker the Inland demand for Outland goods and the offer of Inland goods in payment, the stronger will Inland's currency be on the foreign-exchange market and the more favorable Inland's terms of trade.

The general-equilibrium theory suggests the following probable consequences of trade:

1. The price of each commodity traded tends to become the same everywhere except for transportation costs, tariffs, and the like.

2. The same is true for the price of each factor of production. A country tends to export products embodying relatively large amounts of its abundant factors, and the export-derived demand for them lessens their relative abundance and cheapness. Similarly, importing products whose production at home would require relatively large amounts of scarce fac-

tors tends to relieve the relative scarcity and expensiveness of these factors. Trade in goods and services spells trade in the factors of production they embody. The tendency toward factor-price equalization would be complete, however, only under highly restrictive and unrealistic assumptions concerning pure competition, costless transport, internationally identical constant-returns-to-scale production functions, incomplete specialization, identity in kind of the factors in the different countries, substitutability among factors, fewness of factors relative to products, etc. The equalization tendency has almost no chance at all of prevailing in reality. But even if it did, it would in no way imply equalization among countries of relative factor quantities, of real incomes per person, or of standards of living. Equalization of wage rates, in particular, does not mean equalization of average output per person or of average income per person from all factors. Trade would continue to provide a gain even for countries favored with an especially great abundance of natural resources, capital, and entrepreneurial ability in relation to population. Incidentally, if the necessary but almost impossible conditions did hold true and factor prices were equalized among countries, would this not destroy international differences in commodity cost patterns and so destroy the basis for trade? The answer is practically the same as to the earlier question about commodity price equalization. Complete factor-price equalization would destroy the basis not for trade but for its further *expansion*. Assuming costless transport and so forth, a volume of trade any smaller than what would equalize both commodity and factor prices in different countries would leave profit incentives in existence for further expansion of trade. The volume of trade per time period that just accomplishes equalization is motivated by the price differences that *would* exist at any smaller volume; it would be motivated, that is, by *intramarginal* differences.

3. Another consequence of trade and a corollary of the factor-price-equalization tendency is modification of domestic income distributions. Trade tends to reduce the shares going to previously scarce factors of production and to increase the shares of previously abundant factors.

4. A fourth consequence is an *increase* in the international disparity of factor quantities, so far as these respond to price. Opportunities to import fruit may result in maintaining fewer orchards than otherwise. If a country exports chemicals, more chemists may be trained; if it exports automobiles, more capital may be accumulated in factories and heavy machinery. Supplies of natural resources *economically* available may respond to trade through the influence of prices on the rate of discovery or of development for exploitation. Recognizing how trade may increase the factor-supply disparities that cause it does not contradict what has already been said about modification of the scarcity or abundance of factors: a particular factor can become more abundant in absolute amount while less abundant relative to demand or become scarcer absolutely while less scarce relative to demand.

5. Trade affects patterns of demand in several ways: by increasing consumer's real incomes, by modifying domestic income distributions, and by acquainting people with a broader variety of goods and services and thus modifying tastes.

6. The general-equilibrium theory suggest a catch-all category of effects of trade, including broader gains than those from specialization and resource reallocation as described by the principle of comparative advantage. By expanding the markets open to individual producers and entire industries, trade improves opportunities for efficient mass production. Trade and specialization could thus provide an improvement over national self-sufficiency even if countries had otherwise identical conditions. Just as occupational specialization permits individuals to *acquire* comparative advantages, so trade may do the same for countries (as may restrictions on trade). Trade presumably weakens local monopolies. In short, trade does more than merely promote efficient allocation of existing productive resources; it affects industrial structures, tastes, labor supplies, and the types of natural resources and capital equipment in actual use. At best it helps transmit techniques and ideas

as well as goods, promoting modern development. (None of this amounts to claiming that free trade provides the best of all conceivable worlds. Judicious restrictions could conceivably increase a country's gains from trade or promote escape from stultifying overspecialization.)

Recognizing the foregoing effects of international trade undermines the relative-factor-endowment explanation of it. No longer can we simply stress international differences in the relative abundance of various factors. Factor quantities are a result as well as a cause of trade. In reply it might be argued that things such as chemical engineers, factories, hydroelectric sites, and fields prepared for particular crops are not what the theory means by factors of production; instead, these are only intermediate embodiments of the more fundamental factors, whose relative abundance is indeed somehow objectively given apart from the flow of trade. Perhaps so, but then it becomes a problem in metaphysics to specify what the underlying factors of production are and how abundant each is. Consider capital, for example. Its supply is no doubt related to the propensity of the population to save and invest, which is in turn related to attitudes and traditions. But how can these be described as objectively *given* and be quantitively specified? The kinds and quantities of labor available might also be traced back to propensities of the population to absorb training and experience and even to propagate, but this, too, would be a meaningless dodge. A similar problem concerns such things as meteorological, intellectual, social, and political "climates." These profoundly influence possibilities for advantageous international specialization; yet only extreme straining at the accepted meanings of words can assimilate them to "factors of production."

The proposition that a country exports abundant-factor-intensive goods and imports scarce-factor-intensive goods now also appears too simple. Sheer technological necessity does not always make some products inherently labor-intensive, for instance, and others inherently land-intensive. The proportions in which various factors are used depend, among other things, on their prices. Of two products,

A might be the more labor-intensive and *B* the more land-intensive at one ratio of labor and land prices; yet *B* might be the more labor-intensive and *A* the more land intensive at another factor price ratio.[7] Yet factor prices largely result from trade and are not independently given. Apart from the consequences of the very flow of trade to be explained, one cannot always unambiguously say which commodities embody relatively large proportions of which factors of production.

Still another difficulty with the factor-proportions theory is that the absolute scarcity or abundance of factors in a country does not itself determine the flow of trade. What counts is scarcity or abundance relative to the demands for these factors deriving from demands for goods and services embodying them. Yet these demands or tastes, whose role parallels that of factor endowments, themselves largely result from trade. Even if taste patterns were identical from country to country and were left unaffected by changed possibilities of gratification, international trade would raise real incomes and so effect the *marginal* pattern of demand. Even given fixed patterns of consumer preference, consumers' appraisal of the relative importance of various goods at the margin presumably varies with the level of consumers' incomes.

The attempt of the general-equilibrium theory to explain trade in terms of factor endowment thus breaks down when pursued literally.[8] The theory is still useful in discussing some of the most important types of conditions that give rise to comparative advantages and in suggesting the unfathomable complexity of the conditions interacting through the price system in guiding the patterns of geographic specialization and trade.

[7] Evidence that such possibilities are not at all farfetched appears in Bagicha S. Minhas "The Homohypalligic Production Function, Factor-Intensity Reversals, and the Heckscher-Ohlin Theorem," *Journal of Political Economy*, April 1962, pp. 138-156.

[8] The criticisms reviewed above are stressed by Romney Robinson, "Factor Proportions and Comparative Advantage," Parts I and II, *Quarterly Journal of Economics*, LXX, May 1956, pp. 169-192, and August 1956, pp. 346-363. Robinson recognizes that Ohlin takes account of such things as the influence of trade on factor and supplies and tastes; but he thinks that Ohlin is pursuing two separate and rather incompatible theories, one less fully worked out than the other.

In the last analysis, however, there is no single explanation of what *causes* comparative advantage and of *why* trade takes place. We can only illustrate various types of influence. Ultimately we must take different patterns of opportunity cost for granted. We must lamely admit that comparative advantage stems from unfathomably complex differences among countries in climates, resources, populations, tastes, ideologies, and so forth, most of which are consequences as well as causes of trade. But this conclusion need not be disconcerting. The main thing is to recognize that, whatever the reason may be, countries do have comparative advantage in different lines of production and that specialization and trade provide gains like those from technological progress. ". . . the production of one good to exchange for another is an *alternative method of producing* the second commodity. Under competitive conditions, productive resources will not be used in this indirect process of production unless the yield is greater than that obtained by the use of the direct method."[9] Profit incentives lead businessmen to engage in trade yielding the gains the theory describes. Our main interest is in the role of exchange rates, money supplies, and price and wage levels in this working of the international price system. We must now take a closer look at exchange-rate determination.

[9] Frank H. Knight, *The Ethics of Competition*, New York: Kelley, 1951, p. 234.

Foreign Exchange: Rates, Instruments, and Markets

✑ 2

International Remittances

Foreign exchange includes actual foreign coins and banknotes. Mostly it consists of claims on foreign currency, such as bank accounts and negotiable short-term paper. If a merchant in Inland needs foreign funds to pay for goods imported from Outland, he may buy a check drawn by his own bank on its Outland-peso account kept with some Outland bank. (If the merchant's bank does not itself keep funds on deposit abroad, it will presumably have a correspondent relationship with some other Inland bank that does.) The merchant then mails the peso check to the seller in Outland, who deposits or cashes it as he would any other check written in his home currency. Other ways of making payments in foreign currencies will be considered later; meanwhile, it serves our purpose to think of checks drawn by home banks against their accounts kept with foreign banks.

The Inland bank in the example has drawn down its peso balance in Outland. (It has also increased its holdings of Inland dollars, or has reduced its dollars liabilities by deducting the price of the peso check from its customer's balance.) How does the Inland bank now replenish its Outland bank account? (Actually, a bank doesn't have to maintain foreign-currency balances large enough to meet its customers' future demands; it can buy foreign currencies on the market as needed. But we still have to consider how the market is supplied with foreign currencies.) The bank may buy peso checks on Outland banks earned by Inland exporters who have taken payment from their customers in this form. It may also buy peso checks

from Outlanders who need dollars to spend in Inland. If Outlanders paying for purchases in Inland buy dollar checks on their own banks' balances with Inland banks, the Outland banks have to replenish their dollar balances and may do so by buying dollar checks earned by Outland exporters or offered by Inlanders needing pesos to spend in Outland. Foreign-exchange transactions thus basically appear to be exchanges, through the intermediary of banks as dealers, of bank balances in different currencies.

These examples should not be taken to imply bilateral balancing of payments. Each country need not pay to each other country exactly as much as it receives from it. The contrary is more typical. Inland banks replenish their Outland balances by buying pesos not only from Inland exporters to Outland but also from third-country exporters to Outland or from third-country banks holding larger peso balances and smaller dollar balances than they consider convenient.

A country's import trade typically involves exchanging home for foreign bank balances; it involves a demand for foreign exchange to be bought with home money or, in other words, a supply of home money to be sold for foreign exchange. This is true regardless of whether the import goods are priced and payment is required in home or foreign money. If an Inland importer must pay in Outland money, he takes the initiative in exchanging dollars for pesos. If the importer pays in dollars, then the Outland seller must take the initiative in exchanging these dollars for the pesos he wants. Either way, home money demands (is supplied for) foreign money. The currency in which Inland exports are priced is similarly unimportant; it only determines whether the buyer or the seller must take the initiative on the foreign-exchange market. Nor does it much matter if goods are priced and payment is called for in the currency of some third country. The transaction involves an exchange of the importer's home money for foreign money and an exchange of foreign money for the exporter's home money.

Arbitrage

If governments impose no restrictions (as we usually assume until Chapter 7), we hardly need concern ourselves about the nationality of the person taking the initiative in a particular transaction or about the country where particular parts of the transaction take place. Arbitrage links transactors in different countries together into what is in effect a single uniform market. Arbitrage consists of seeking profit from discrepancies between prices prevailing at the same time in different submarkets. Suppose that the pound sterling was quoted at $2.85 in London and $2.75 in New York. In the London part of the market, arbitrageurs would sell pound balances in English banks for dollar balances in American banks, receiving $2.85 for each pound. In New York the arbitrageurs would buy pound balances in English banks with dollar balances in American banks, paying only $2.75 for each pound. The arbitrageurs' eagerness to sell pounds dear in London and buy them cheap in New York bids the exchange rate toward a common level, perhaps $2.80, in both places. Arbitrage quickly destroys the price discrepancies that motivate it.

Arbitrage in unrestricted markets also works to maintain orderly *cross rates* of exchange, that is, to keep exchange rates among numerous currencies consistent or compatible. Exchange rates would be inconsistent or disorderly—cross rates would be "broken"—if at one time, for example, quotations prevailed of 60 Belgian francs per dollar, 3 Belgian francs per Mexican peso, and 10 Mexican pesos per dollar. An arbitrageur could profit by buying 60 Belgian francs

with $1.00, buying 20 Mexican pesos with the 60 Belgian francs, and, finally buying $2.00 with the 20 Mexican pesos. Large-scale attempts to do this would strengthen the franc against the dollar (perhaps toward a rate of 50 francs per dollar), strengthen the peso against the franc (perhaps toward 4 francs per peso), and strengthen the dollar against the peso (perhaps toward $12\frac{1}{2}$ pesos per dollar). This or some such consistent pattern of rates would emerge at which no further arbitrage was profitable.

Large banks conduct most of the arbitrage. Their foreign-exchange traders keep constantly in touch with colleagues at home and abroad by telephone, teletype, and cable and keep constantly alert to the latest quotations. Even small discrepancies of the sort exaggerated in our examples will motivate arbitrage prompt and voluminous enough practically to wipe out the discrepancies literally within minutes. The checks mentioned earlier are written instructions for changing the ownership of deposit claims against banks; instructions of the same kind are commonly transmitted by cable.

The prompt effectiveness of arbitrage justifies assuming that, in the absence of restrictions, traders and institutions scattered all over the world form one single foreign-exchange market. It also justifies assuming that, from the standpoint of an individual country at a given time, foreign exchange is a single uniform commodity. In the absence of restrictions, one foreign currency can be converted into any other foreign currency almost instantly and at a competitively determined rate. Furthermore, changes that affect the foreign-exchange value of the home currency but not the values of foreign currencies among themselves will cause the home currency to appreciate or depreciate by a uniform percentage in relation to all foreign currencies.[1] In a preliminary analysis we may properly express the strength of the home currency by its rate on one foreign currency chosen to represent foreign exchange in gen-

---

[1]This simplification is appropriate here, although, realistically, changes in world-market conditions may require a new pattern of rates of each currency against many others.

eral. We may regard the demand for foreign exchange as arising from imports and other transactions typically involving payments to foreigners and the supply of foreign exchange as arising from exports and other transactions typically involving receipt of payments from foreigners. It hardly matters—as already explained—whether goods are priced in home or in foreign currency.

Supply and Demand

Inland's imports and other transactions involving payments to Outlanders give rise to a demand for Outland pesos to be bought with Inland dollars or, in other words, to a supply of dollars to be sold for pesos. Inland's exports and other transactions involving receipt of payment from Outlanders give rise to a supply of pesos to be sold

for dollars or, in other words, to a demand for dollars to be bought with pesos. We can view the determination of the rate of exchange that clears the market either in terms of supply and demand for pesos and the price of the peso in dollars or, alternatively, in terms of supply and demand for dollars and the price of the dollar in pesos. Table 2.1 illustrates the translation from one viewpoint to the other. The three columns on the left show the demand for and supply of foreign exchange in terms of home money. Columns 1 and 2 reflect the fact that the lower the price of the Outland peso in Inland dollars and the cheaper Outland goods and services appear to Inlanders, the more of them Inlanders want to buy and the more pesos they demand to pay for them. Columns 1 and 3 show that the higher the price of pesos, the more of them are supplied. The reason is that

Table 2.1. Correspondence Between Two Viewpoints in the Foreign-Exchange Market

Pesos Demanded with and Supplied for Dollars			Dollars Demanded with and Supplied for Pesos		
(1) Price of Peso in Dollars	(2) Millions of Pesos Demanded	(3) Millions of Pesos Supplied	(4) Price of Dollar in Pesos	(5) Millions of Dollars Demanded	(6) Millions of Dollars Supplied
$.40	P37.500	P600.000	P2.50	$240.000	$15.000
.35	48.980	459.375	2.857	160.781	17.143
.333	54.000	416.667	3.00	138.889	18.000
.30	66.667	337.500	3.333	101.250	20.000
.25	96.600	234.375	4.00	58.594	24.000
.20	150.000	150.000	5.00	30.000	30.000
.167	216.000	104.167	6.00	17.361	36.000
.15	266.667	84.375	6.667	12.656	40.000
.125	384.000	58.594	8.00	7.324	48.000
.10	600.000	37.500	10.00	3.750	60.000

NOTE: This table was drawn up by assuming two demand functions to start with:

1. The demand for pesos as a function of the price of the peso in dollars (the function represented by Columns 1 and 2). The equation is

$q = \dfrac{6}{p^2}$, where $q =$ the number of millions of pesos demanded and $p =$ the price of the peso in dollars. This demand function has a constant elasticity of 2.

2. The demand for dollars as a function of the price of the dollar in pesos (the function represented by Columns 4 and 5). The equation is

$Q = \dfrac{3750}{P^3}$, where $Q =$ the number of millions of dollars demanded and $P =$ the price of the dollar in pesos. This demand function has a constant elasticity of 3.

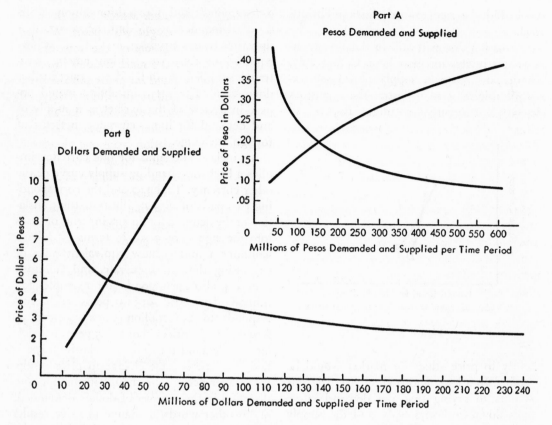

Figure 2.1.

a "high" dollar price of pesos means a "low" peso price of dollars; Inland goods appear cheap to Outlanders and attract a larger volume of peso expenditure on them than would occur if the buying power of the peso over Inland goods were not so high. (A conceivable exception is considered on the next pages.) The three right-hand columns show the same price-quantity relations from the alternative point of view. The cheaper the dollar in pesos, the more dollars are demanded to pay for Outlanders' purchases of the correspondingly cheap Inland goods. The more valuable the dollar in pesos, the more dollars are supplied as Inlanders spend them to buy the correspondingly cheap Outland goods. For any row the prices in Columns 1 and 4 are reciprocals ($.40 per peso is the same as 2.50 pesos per dollar). Columns 2 and 6 correspond: if 37.5 million pesos are being demanded at $.40 each, then 37.5 million × .40 = $15 million are being spent for pesos or in other words, are being supplied

on the foreign-exchange market. If 96 million pesos are being demanded at $.25 each, then 96 million × .25 = $24 million are being supplied in exchange for pesos. Similarly, Columns 3 and 5 correspond: 600 million pesos being supplied at $.40 each amounts to 600 million × .40 = $240 million being demanded; and 37.5 million pesos being supplied at $.10 amounts to $3.75 million being demanded. In Fig. 2.1, part *A* represents the left side and part *B* the right side of Table 2.1; the two sides of the table and the two graphs represent the same conditions. The same equilibrium exchange rate ($.20 per peso, 5 pesos to the dollar) emerges regardless of which point of view is adopted. At a rate "overvaluing" the peso ("undervaluing" the dollar), some suppliers of pesos (demanders of dollars) would be frustrated; at a disequilibrium rate in the opposite direction, the opposite kind of frustration would prevail; and in an unhampered market, competition among frustrated transactors would bid the rate toward the equilibrium level.

A situation that will call for detailed attention later invites mention here. Conceivably, the demand for and supply of foreign exchange might be so inelastic—the quantities demanded and supplied might respond so

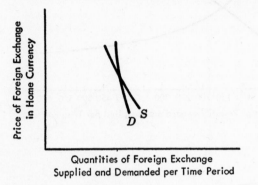

Quantities of Foreign Exchange Supplied and Demanded per Time Period

Figure 2.2.

slightly to price—that the market would be unstable. In a loose and preliminary way this amounts to saying that the demand curve slopes downward so steeply and the supply curve slopes backward so markedly as to intersect as shown in Fig. 2.2. At an above-equilibrium price of foreign exchange, the quantity *demanded* would exceed the quan-

tity *supplied,* and competition among frustrated demanders would bid the rate further upward from equilibrium; at a below-equilibrium rate, competition among frustrated suppliers would bid the rate further downward. The same instability would appear in a view of the market as a supply of and demand for home currency in terms of foreign exchange.

An inelastic demand for one currency implies a backward-bending supply curve of the other currency. Table 2.2 and the corresponding two parts of Fig. 2.3 illustrate the translation of the demand for dollars in terms of pesos into the supply of pesos in terms of dollars. Columns 1 and 3 show equivalent ways of expressing the exchange rate, and Columns 2 and 4 also correspond (for example, $25 million demanded at 10 pesos each corresponds to 250 million pesos supplied at $.10 each). At prices above 17.5 pesos per dollar, the demand for dollars is elastic: a specified small percentage change in price results in a larger percentage change in the opposite direction in the number of dollars demanded, or, in other words, a change in price results in a change in the opposite direction in the total number of pesos that would be spent to buy dollars. This range of elastic demand for dollars corresponds to dollar prices of

Table 2.2. Correspondence Between Demand for One Currency and Supply of the Other

Dollars Demanded with Pesos		Pesos Supplied for Dollars	
(1) Price of Dollar in Pesos	(2) Millions of Dollars Demanded	(3) Price of Peso in Dollars	(4) Millions of Pesos Supplied
P 0	$35	$Infinite	P 0
2	33	.50	66
3	32	.33333	96
5	30	.20	150
10	25	.10	250
15	20	.06667	300
17.5	17.5	.05714	306.25
20	15	.05	300
25	10	.04	250
30	5	.03333	150
32	3	.03125	96
33	2	.03030	66
35	0	.02857	0

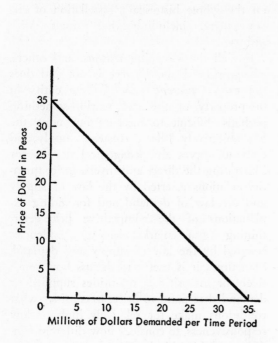

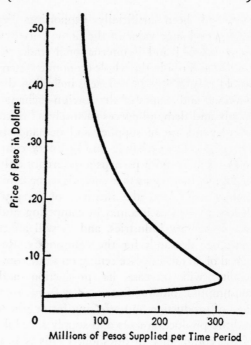

Figure 2.3.

the peso below $.05714; the lower the price of the peso, the fewer pesos would be supplied, as is true of a normally sloping supply curve. The demand for dollars is *inelastic* at prices below 17.5 pesos each: a change in price results in a change in the same direction in the total number of pesos that would be spent to buy dollars. This range corresponds to dollar prices of pesos higher than $.05714. Within it, the higher their price, the fewer pesos would be supplied.[2] Even a backward-bending peso supply curve of this sort might be cut in the normal way by a sufficiently elastic demand curve, yielding a stable equilibrium. For two reasons, though, the unlikely possibility of an unstable market is worth understanding: first, as Chapter 8 will explain, it enters into discussions of the workability of free markets; and second,

applying principles to strange cases as well as ordinary cases is a useful exercise in understanding the principles themselves.

Some warnings are necessary to keep our numerical examples, with their definite schedules and curves, from being misleading. Reality is not that simple. Events that would shift any supply or demand curve would to some extent shift the other curve also. This is notably true of foreign exchange. An export boom that brought more foreign exchange onto the market than before at each exchange rate would presumably raise incomes at home and so raise import demands and the quantity of foreign exchange demanded at that rate. Or a shift in tastes toward imports would not only increase the demand for foreign exchange but also shunt some resources away from producing the commodities now in weakened demand into export production instead, stimulating exports by lowering their prices and so increasing—or if the foreign demand were inelastic, decreasing—the quantity of foreign exchange supplied at a given exchange rate. Even an adjustment from disequilibrium to equilibrium in a particular market shifts the curves that describe the market. If official controls

---

[2] Pondering the relation between Columns 1 and 3 of the table will dispel any momentary puzzlement over the fact that while the inelastic range of the demand-for-dollars curve takes up only half the length of the entire curve, the backward-sloping range of the supply-of-pesos curve takes up much more than half the length The two price scales are different. High pesos-per-dollar rates correspond to low dollars-per-peso rates, and conversely; the equivalents of rates above 17.5 pesos per dollar are squeezed into the range below $.05714 in the dollars-per-peso scale.

that had been artificially supporting the foreign-exchange value of the home currency were dropped and if international trade expanded as a result, the whole economic system would in principle be affected, including the positions and shapes of the foreign-exchange supply and demand curves themselves.[3] Such interdependence of supplies and demands is true of foreign exchange and ordinary commodities alike, with perhaps a difference only in degree. Inventions that cheapen some commodity will affect the incomes of its producers, as well as incomes in competing and complementary industries, and so will affect consumer demands for the commodity. Removal of an official price ceiling on some commodity will increase its production and consumption, bidding factors away from other lines of production and affecting factor prices and the production costs and supply schedule of the commodity in question. (This is just one reason why the total amounts of a commodity that *would be* supplied per time period at various prices depend on what amount is in fact *being* supplied.) In principle, a partial view of the market for foreign exchange or of anything else is incomplete; and it should be supplemented with general-equilibrium considerations whenever they are particularly relevant. But negativistic carping at partial-equilibrium analysis is pointless.

There are still other reasons why a supply curve or a demand curve does not portray a definite price-quantity relation. The amount of something that would be supplied or demanded per time period depends not only on the price supposed to prevail but also on the previous price, on how long this previous price had prevailed, on how long a time actual and potential producers and buyers are considered to have to adjust to the new price, and other such things. The quantity of something supplied or demanded depends not only on tastes, incomes, the prices of other things, and the price of the thing itself but

[3] Svend Laursen hints at some such considerations in his strictures against applying ordinary partial-equilibrium supply-and-demand analysis to foreign exchange as well as to ordinary commodities. See his "The Market for Foreign Exchange," *Economia Internazionale*, **VIII**, November 1955, esp. pp. 762-766.

on the whole historical constellation of circumstances, including the thing's price history.

For all the foregoing reasons, and others, a supply or demand curve is not and does not even *represent* some definite entity in or property of the real world—something perhaps difficult to measure but none the less objectively "there." Instead, supply and demand curves are pedagogical devices for illustrating the direct and inverse price-quantity relations asserted by the law of supply and the law of demand and for aiding explanations of the competitive price-determining and market-clearing tendencies asserted by the law of supply and demand. Sometimes it is useful to discuss how sensitively or insensitively quantities supplied or demanded respond to price, to consider what conditions make for relatively high or low responsiveness, to consider how different conditions of these kinds affect the consequences of particular economic changes, and even to assume definite "elasticities" in numerical or graphical examples. Doing so need not mean really believing in definite supply-and-demand entities having definite numerical elasticities. Supply-and-demand analysis should not suffer discredit because of the emphatically recognized error of taking too literally the simplified pedagogical devices sometimes used in expounding it.

Pegged Rates and the Gold Standard

So far we have assumed an exchange rate freely determined by private supply and demand. Usually, however, rates are officially pegged. Figure 2.4 reflects a policy in one or

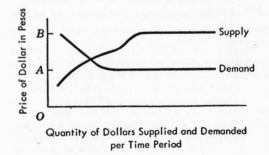

Figure 2.4.

both countries of preventing the exchange rate from going outside the range of *OA* and *OB* pesos per dollar. If the authorities are willing to supply practically unlimited amounts of dollars out of officially held reserves at the price *OB* and are willing to absorb practically unlimited amounts into official reserves at the price *OA,* the supply and demand curves become horizontal at these levels. No matter how the curves shift, their intersection cannot be outside the range of official pegging. By narrowing the spread between the official selling and buying prices of foreign exchange, the authorities could keep the range of possible fluctuation as small as they pleased.

The international gold standard pegs exchange rates indirectly. Under the gold standard a country's monetary authority keeps the national monetary unit and a certain quantity of gold equal in value on free markets by maintaining two-way convertibility. It stands ready both to buy unlimited amounts of gold at a definite price (or to coin all gold brought to the mint by private owners) and also to sell unlimited amounts of gold at the same or very nearly the same price—perhaps by redeeming its paper money in gold coins. (How the authority can remain able to honor these commitments, and the consequences of its doing so, are topics for later chapters.) An *international* gold standard exists among all countries that tie their moneys to gold and allow the unrestricted import and export of gold. If the Inland dollar "contains" 1 gram of gold and the Outland peso ⅕ gram, the so-called mint par between them is 5 pesos per dollar. This par has no more claim to the title of the equilibrium exchange rate, however, than any other rate within a certain narrow range on either side of it. Suppose, for example, that the rate became 5.01 pesos per dollar. Wouldn't arbitrageurs do the following on a huge scale: redeem 5 pesos in 1 gram of gold in Outland, ship the gold to Inland, sell it to the authorities there for $1.00, and sell the dollar on the market at the assumed 5.01 rate for a profit of 0.01 peso? No. This margin would probably be more than eaten up by the expenses of office work, of tele-

phone calls and cables, of perhaps actually melting down one country's coins and refining them into pure gold before delivering it to the monetary authority of the other country, of crating and shipping and insuring the gold, and even of losing interest on capital tied up in gold in transit. If these expenses total 0.05 peso per gram of gold, it would become profitable to ship gold from Outland to Inland only if the peso depreciated to more than 5.05 per dollar. Arbitrage would then tend to check further depreciation.

To clarify the principles of gold arbitrage, let us suppose, at the other extreme, that the peso had strengthened on the market to a rate of only 4.94 per dollar. Arbitrageurs would then redeem $1.00 in 1 gram of gold, ship it to Outland, and receive 4.95 pesos net for it, even after covering the expenses of 0.05 peso. Buying back $1.00 at the assumed 4.94 rate, they would still have 0.01 peso left as profit. Arbitrage of this sort on a large scale would add to the ordinary supply of pesos and demand for dollars and so move the rate toward 4.95, making more arbitrage no longer profitable.

These examples explain why the rates of 5.05 and 4.95 pesos per dollar are known, respectively, as the gold import and export points for Inland and the gold export and import points for Outland. It is also clear why the exchange rate will not go or remain much outside these limits. But the gold points are not absolutely definite and unchanging figures. Since the distance of each gold point from mint par depends on shipping and insurance costs, interest costs, administrative costs, and even the implicit and uncertain costs of diverting the arbitrageurs' time and effort from other activities, the gold points are bound to be somewhat different for different arbitrageurs and to move with changes in interest rates and other conditions. Even the prices at which national monetary authorities buy and sell gold may be subject to some slight fudging. (For historical examples, see pp. 262-263 below.) But the principle remains that exchange rates among gold-standard currencies, while not absolutely rigid, do move within narrow if imprecise limits and that temporary breakouts from these limits set up corrective tendencies.[4]

Gold arbitrage explains how imbalances between ordinary commercial and financial payments into and out of a country or between the amounts of the country's currency being demanded and supplied on the exchange market are "settled" under the international gold standard. No authorities need somehow estimate and deliberately fill any such gap. Given fixed interconvertibility between gold and national moneys and freedom of gold shipments, private parties will undertake the appropriate shipments without any official planning. Weakness or strength pressing the exchange value of a country's currency to one gold point or the other will cause gold movements that tend to shrink or expand the country's money supply. How strongly the money supply responds, and with what further consequences, is something to be examined later.

Even without standing ready to buy and sell practically unlimited amounts of foreign exchange or gold at specified rates, the authorities could conceivably stabilize a country's exchange rate just by rigorously suppressing transactions at rates outside specified narrow limits. The demand curve for foreign exchange would be horizontal at its upper left because no one would be allowed to exercise any effective demand at a higher rate, and the supply curve would be horizontal at its lower left because no one would be allowed to supply foreign exchange at a lower rate.

Such control would of course have wide repercussions.

Methods of International Remittance

Before Chapter 3 introduces the concept of the balance of international payments, it will be helpful to know some factual or "mechanical" details about foreign-exchange and related transactions. A quick survey—too quick to benefit practical merchants and bankers—will furnish a background for the theory and policy discussions still to follow. Institutional facts will prove relevant to such topics as the complexity of international banking and of administering and complying with official controls over it; the comparative complexity and expense of systems of pegged and of free exchange rates; the possibilities of speculation on short-run wobbles and on major adjustments in pegged and in free rates, and the possibilities of speculation by banks, merchants, professional operators, and others; and the influence of official stabilization funds on rates and on the expectations and actions of private operators.

The foreign supplier of an Inland importer may either require payment in advance or require cash on delivery.[5] At the opposite extreme, he may sell on open-book account and wait some weeks or even months for payment. Sooner or later, the importer will have to transfer funds. The simplest method, if not forbidden by the government, is probably to mail an ordinary check written on his regular Inland bank account. The foreign supplier will be able to sell this check to his own bank for Outland currency, since Outland banks can use such checks to replenish their working balances with Inland banks.

But perhaps the Outland supplier will insist on payment in his own currency. If so, the Inland importer may buy a bank draft from

---

[4] Under the gold standard before 1931 and especially before 1914, the dollar rate on the pound sterling almost always kept within a very few cents of the mint par of $4.8665.

In view of the inherent vagueness of the gold points, it is puzzling to see the gleeful iconoclasm with which one student of the gold-standard era reported that exchange rates often did push beyond the gold points, and for long, continuous intervals. See Oskar Morgenstern, *International Financial Transactions and Business Cycles*, Princeton, N.J.: Princeton University Press, for the National Bureau of Economic Research, 1959, *passim*; e.g., p. 567. Morgenstern's remarks are particularly puzzling because he does not say how he knew precisely what the gold points were at each time and does not indicate how big any breakouts of actual exchange rates from the gold points would have to be to discredit standard theory. Morgenstern expresses similar vague doubts about arbitrage tending to maintain orderly cross rates of exchange.

[5] When the terms are C.O.D., the seller will arrange for release of the bill of lading or other documents necessary to obtain the goods from the transportation company only when the buyer makes payment in the agreed way. The seller will send the bill of lading and other shipping documents to an agent of his in the buyer's country (perhaps a foreign branch or correspondent of his own bank), and the agent will release the documents to the buyer at the proper time.

his own bank.[6] This is a check drawn by his bank on a bank balance in Outland. Alternatively, the importer may buy a mail transfer or a telegraphic or cable transfer. There is little difference. Instead of obtaining a draft from his bank and mailing it himself to his foreign supplier, he simply has his bank instruct its foreign branch or correspondent to make the payment to the foreign payee. (What the remitting importer receives from his own bank is not a document to mail abroad but simply a receipt for the Inland money paid for the transfer.) Since the instructions constituting a mail or telegraphic transfer go directly by airmail, telegraph, or cable, they ordinarily arrive sooner than a draft bought and sent by the importer. The deduction from the Inland bank's deposit abroad thus occurs sooner; and to take account of the interest for this difference in time, the price charged for an airmail transfer and especially for a telegraphic transfer may be slightly higher than for a bank draft.

Banks also buy cable transfers from their customers. An American exporter who has received payment in British pounds may sell them for dollars to an American bank, which will have the pounds transferred to its own account by cabling the London bank in which they had been deposited. The telegraphic or cable transfer is the major instrument for effecting payments in the leading exchange markets throughout the world.[7]

For purposes of analysis we have perhaps said enough already about the origin and use of the instruments that actually convey ownership of or claims on foreign currencies and bank accounts. These include various types of checks, drafts, and mailed or cabled instructions, and also, to a small extent, actual foreign coins and banknotes. The appendix gives some further detail and some information about types of document not yet mentioned.

Foreign-exchange Trading

Trading on the foreign-exchange market in the United States takes place: (1) between banks and their customers, who are the ultimate suppliers and demanders of foreign exchange, (2) between different American banks, and (3) between American and foreign banks.[8] About 25 American banks, mostly in New York City, maintain working balances of foreign exchange abroad, though fewer than half of them do most of the business. The New York market also includes some branches and agencies and representative offices of foreign banks and dealers specializing in foreign paper money and coins.

A firm wanting to buy or sell foreign exchange will deal with its bank, ordinarily by telephone. A large firm doing business with several banks will probably shop around for the best rate. If the firm is not located in a major city or for some other reason does not deal with a bank active in the exchange market, its regular bank will act as an intermediary in arranging the transaction with one of its large correspondents. Customers of small outlying banks are more likely to be buying foreign exchange in small amounts than selling it, since they would rarely be drawing drafts or receiving payment in foreign currencies. The city banks list the rates at which the small banks, as agents, may sell exchange. These "retail" rates are high enough to allow some margin of safety and are valid only up to a specified daily total amount and only for a few days, unless altered sooner.

During a day, a large bank will be buying a particular currency from some customers and selling it to others. To some extent these transactions will match, but the chances are that the bank will still be making net purchases or net sales and will want to offset

---

[6] Here, *bank draft* means a check drawn by one bank on another. The term is also used as a synonym for *banker's bill*, that is, a bill of exchange (draft) drawn by a commercial firm on a bank under a letter of credit (as explained in the appendix). The two types of bank draft are alike in both being drawn *on* a bank. Whether the drawer is another bank or a commercial firm is usually clear from the context.

[7] Alan R. Holmes, *The New York Foreign Exchange Market*, New York: Federal Reserve Bank of New York, 1959, p. 18.

[8] The following description draws on Holmes, *op. cit.* (and also the second edition, co-authored by Francis H. Schott, 1965), as well as on Helmut Lipfert, *Devisenhandel*, Frankfurt/Main: Fritz Knapp Verlag, 1958.

them on the interbank "wholesale" market, where banks with a surplus of a particular currency trade with banks short of it. This is an "over-the-counter" market, with no specific location or formal organization in New York. Trading takes place by mail, telegraph, and cable, and above all by telephone. In Germany, however, several foreign-exchange bourses have been organized. Although they are open less than an hour a day and account for only a small fraction of total foreign-exchange turnover in Germany, the rates established on them influence over-the-counter transactions, especially transactions between banks and their business customers. Paris also has a foreign-exchange bourse, which accounts for a larger fraction of total turnover than the German bourses. In London and Zurich, as in New York, all transactions are over-the-counter.[9]

The local banks in New York and in several foreign centers, instead of shopping around among themselves directly, ordinarily deal through brokers. In this way the banks keep their facilities and personnel freer for dealing with their customers. The brokers are in an ideal position to keep themselves and their clients informed about actual exchange rates and about bids and offers. In addition, using these middlemen lets banks remain anonymous as long as possible. Anonymity can be important for large banks whose transactions might be taken as indicating or even determining rate trends; they would risk pushing the rate against themselves when trying to deal directly. Smaller banks known by the kinds of customers they serve to be mainly either buyers or sellers at wholesale might also risk not getting the best possible rates if they dealt directly.

A bank wanting to buy or sell a particular currency phones an inquiry to one of the brokers. The broker phones other banks to seek a counterparty to the transaction. He receives his commission by quoting foreign exchange at a slightly lower price to the selling bank than to the buying bank. Since competition keeps the commission down to a very small fraction of 1 percent, his profit

depends on a large and rapid turnover. As of 1965, eight foreign-exchange brokers were operating in New York (in the 1930s, when the market was more active, there were about 45). Some of the brokers specialize in particular currencies, but all handle the most active ones. Sterling is far in the lead in volume of transactions on the New York market, followed by the Canadian dollar and trailed by Continental European and South American currencies.

The preference of American exporters for quoting prices and receiving payment in dollars limits the commercial supply of foreign exchange on the New York market. And anyway, American banks do not try to offset all imbalances among themselves before dealing with foreign banks; all types of transactions go on at the same time. When an American bank can get a better rate directly from a foreign bank than through a broker from another American bank, it will do so. The foreign banks, for their part, are always alert to chances of advantageously buying or selling dollars in New York.

A bank's market activity centers in its trading room.[10] Each of several traders works with a set of direct telephone connections to the foreign-exchange brokers, the cable companies, and perhaps one or more correspondent banks outside New York. He uses regular telephones for customer contacts and foreign calls. The typical trading room also has a direct teletype link with correspondent banks at home and abroad. At the start of each business day, the traders face the overnight accumulation of mail orders. They learn the latest exchange-rate trends by telephone from London and the Continent, where the markets have been open for several hours. Throughout the day, assistants keep a running record of the bank's short or long position in each currency so that the traders can always judge how eager they should be to buy or sell each currency when quoting rates and when responding to the quotations of others. Profit depends on speed and large volume, since the typical spread between a bank's buying and selling rates for large

[9] Lipfert, *op. cit.*, pp. 53-57, 147-149.

[10] Cf. Holmes, *op. cit.*, chap. VI, and Lipfert, *op. cit.* chap. B.

blocks of a currency is in the range of one-eighth or one-tenth of 1 percent, or even less.[11] The traders also watch for opportunities for arbitrage profit provided by small fleeting discrepancies between rates quoted in New York and elsewhere or between the cross rates of exchange involving two or more foreign currencies. A foreign-exchange trader needs a keen memory, a facility for fast and accurate mental arithmetic, and nerves that can stand the strain of continual decisions involving many thousands of dollars in a few seconds.

In addition, an expert trader needs a "feel" for market trends, an ability to interpret clues about short-run shifts in supply and demand. Although a bank's traders are not deliberate speculators and although they *do* strive for an even balance between their sales and purchases of each currency, they do not immediately offset each individual transaction with a commercial customer by an opposite transaction in the interbank market. Except when the latest transaction has created an uncomfortably large imbalance, they may wait a while to see what offsetting occurs in the course of ordinary business. How willing a trader is to wait depends in part on which way he expects the exchange rate to move over the next few minutes or hours. In fact, his job includes trying to profit from such short-run predictions without running too much risk. How much is "too much" is a matter of opinion. A trader might win compliments if events bore out his judgment and draw criticism for speculating if they did not. Banks have occasionally profited from being short of currencies at the time of large devaluations, as in 1931 and 1949, but some banks have lost heavily on their working balances of foreign exchange.[12]

Foreign-exchange traders must worry not only about their bank's overall long or short position in each currency but also about its time pattern. They must take account of the precise forms of the exchange bought and sold—cable transfers, mail transfers, sight drafts, time drafts, actual currency—since this affects the time when funds sold must be made available and when funds bought become available. Even differences of a day or two matter. Furthermore, banks not only buy and sell currencies "spot" (for deilvery at once or in the next few days) but also make contracts with their customers for purchases and sales some weeks or months later. During a day, a bank may have made net sales of spot sterling matched by net purchases for future delivery. Yet the prospect of a surplus of sterling in the future is no full offset to a deficiency in the present. The bank may therefore want to arrange a "swap" in the interbank market—in this particular example, a sale of "forward" (future) sterling accompanied by a simultaneous spot purchase. Since no two banks are likely to have exactly offsetting patterns of imbalance, some banks have to be satisfied with swaps that meet their needs only roughly; but a clever broker can go a long way toward meeting the exact needs of his clients by working out a set of transactions involving perhaps three or even four or five parties. The participant banks will receive or pay the differences between the spot and forward rates on the currencies involved; these rates are not in general identical. Despite its concern for its net position in each foreign currency in the present and for various future dates, a bank is not determined to keep the time pattern of its position exactly in balance from moment to moment or even from hour to hour. That would be too difficult. If the bank has developed a £100,000 short position in forward sterling and it does not seem about to be offset by further forward or spot transactions with commercial customers, the bank's trader may approximately correct the unbalanced forward position by promptly buying £100,000 spot. The bank now risks a much

[11] Paul V. Horn and Henry Gomez, *International Trade Principles and Practices*, 4th ed., Englewood Cliffs, N.J.: Prentice-Hall, Inc., 1959, p. 314; Charles N. Henning, *International Finance*, New York: Harper & Row, 1958, p. 252. Even if the foreign department of a bank is not profitable in itself, it may be indirectly profitable by helping to attract and retain the deposits and loan business of internationally active corporations.

[12] Henning, *op. cit.*, pp. 252, 252n., 281. On the respectability of not always promptly covering unbalanced positions, see Paul Einzig, "Some Recent Changes in Forward Exchange Practices," *Economic Journal*, **LXX**, September 1960, p. 492, and Einzig, *A Dynamic Theory of Forward Exchange*, London: Macmillan, 1961, pp. 74, 101.

smaller loss from an unfavorable change in the spread between the forward and spot quotations than it would otherwise have risked from an unfavorable move in the dollar quotation on sterling generally (with the forward and spot rates moving approximately together). A closer adjustment of the time pattern of the bank's position can be left for correction by swap transactions later and in less haste. Incidentally, swap transactions (like arbitrage transactions) can be carried out not only by banks but also by commercial firms if they are familiar enough with the market and have the funds available.

Actual trading is similar for both spot and forward exchange. Suppose that a bank wants to cover a £100,000 short position in sterling by a purchase in the interbank market. One of the bank's traders will phone one of the foreign-exchange brokers and inquire, "What's sterling?" He does not reveal at first whether he wants to buy or sell.[13] The answer will be a pair of fractions, perhaps "¼–⁵⁄₁₆" (traders know the prevailing range of the exchange rate so well that only the fractions of a cent need be mentioned). The inquiring bank can sell at the lower rate and buy at the higher rate unless, as a bit more conversation will make clear, these rates are merely the broker's judgment of the market instead of actual bids and offers made by some of his other clients. The bank's trader may decide to accept an actual offer at once. Alternatively, and especially if the broker has quoted mere estimates, the trader may state his bid; and the broker will inquire around among his other clients. In quoting the rate to a potential seller he will deduct a small fraction to allow for his commission. After arranging a deal, the broker identifies each party to the other so that the actual exchange of sterling for dollars may be carried out.

___

[13] In international dealings directly between banks, custom entitles the party initiating and paying for a telephone or teletype conversation to expect the party called to state first his buying and selling rates in the currency inquired about; and the spread should not be "too big." If the party called were then to refuse to back up his rate quotations on a major currency by trading at least a customary sizable minimum amount, his reputation would suffer. Lipfert, *op. cit.*, pp. 66-68.

If the quantity of sterling offered in the interbank market comes to exceed or fall short of the quantity demanded at the then prevailing rate, the brokers will propose some new rate to match desired transactions on the two sides of the market. The rates established in the interbank market influence the rates that banks quote to their commercial customers. At the same time, the interbank rates reflect the banks' transactions with their commercial customers. For example, when sterling would be in excess supply at the previous exchange rate in transactions among banks, the reason probably is that, on balance, commercial customers have been making net sales of sterling to the banks. The exchange rates that emerge in banks' transactions among themselves and with their customers are "administered"; they are proposed and agreed to by definite persons. Yet to all intents and purposes, these rates emerge in sensitive response to competitive pressures and almost as impersonally as the prices on an organized commodity or stock exchange.

It is true that the range within which an exchange rate is freely determined will be narrow if central banks or other authorities are actively making bids and offers in the interbank market to keep the rate within set limits on either side of an official parity. Under an international gold standard, the interconvertibility of gold and national currencies and the operations of gold arbitrageurs had essentially the same effect. In the United States, until some official transactions were begun in 1961, neither the Treasury nor the Federal Reserve Bank of New York intervened directly on the exchange market to influence rates; but they accomplished the same result by keeping dollars and gold interconvertible for foreign monetary authorities at $35.00 per ounce, plus or minus ¼ of 1 percent. Furthermore, the Federal Reserve Bank of New York, whose foreign-exchange trading room is linked by direct wire to the trading rooms of several of the largest banks, will place orders in the New York market on behalf of foreign authorities. Even when these authorities carry out their rate-pegging operations at home, arbitrage of course makes the results felt in New York also.

Whether exchange rates fluctuate freely without any limit or only within narrow limits maintained by official pegging, banks and their large customers must remain alert even to brief and minor fluctuations. Continual interbank trading occurs, and the whole apparatus of foreign-exchange traders and brokers (or alternative arrangements for the same purpose) remains necessary. The persons most directly active in the exchange market devote most of their energies to considering and acting upon hour-by-hour and minute-by-minute fluctuations of small fractions of 1 percent. Their work is necessary, no matter whether the range within which fluctuations *could* occur is limitless or is narrowly limited. Neither the international gold standard nor the sort of official exchange-rate pegging typically practiced nowadays simplifies and cheapens the operation of the market decisively as compared with a system of freely fluctuating rates. This advantage would exist only if continuous official transactions at substantially identical buying and selling rates kept the rates rigid. Banks would then hardly be foreign-exchange dealers in their own right. In practice if not in name, they would be mere intermediaries between their customers and the exchange-pegging authorities. (If the authorities wished to maintain buying and selling rates rigid but with a spread between them, private transactions at other than the two limiting rates would have to be forbidden; and the banks would even more fully have to be mere agents of the authorities.) Nothing short of such official monopoly over the foreign-exchange business would keep rates rigid enough to cut much from the cost of exchange-trading facilities and personnel employed by banks and business firms. But if pegging could hold rates within limits narrow, *permanent,* and *dependable* enough to eliminate substantially all risk of changes, then merchants would no longer need the risk protection that forward-exchange facilities nowadays afford. Elimination of forward exchange would permit some economies in exchange-trading equipment and personnel. Whether or not rates could be pegged permanently and dependably enough to

eliminate the risk of changes, and if so at the cost of what disadvantages, are matters considered in later chapters.

Forward Exchange[14]

Forward-exchange contracts, as already mentioned, specify the purchase and sale of foreign exchange to be delivered some weeks or months later and to be paid for then at an exchange rate agreed on in advance. Readers familiar with futures markets in commodities will recognize forward exchange as futures in foreign exchange. If there were no such facilities, an importer or exporter of goods due to be paid for in foreign currency some time in the future would run the risk of an unfavorable change in the exchange rate in the meanwhile. Since dealing only in terms of one's own currency merely shifts the risk to the foreigner and does not elminate it, insistence on this privilege might rule out some advantageous transactions. Forward exchange is a better answer. By telephoning his bank, an importer or exporter can determine the local-currency equivalent of foreign exchange to be paid or received in the future. A merchant trading in staple commodities at a very small profit margin can obtain a firm forward-rate quotation to guide his final decision about whether or not to agree to a contemplated transaction at a particlular price in foreign currency. He can telephone his bank in advance and arrange for it to keep its rate quotation available for perhaps 30 minutes or an hour.[15]

Forward exchange is also a convenient vehicle for speculation (or would be if banks did not generally shy from forward contracts with persons known to be outright speculators). Instead of buying a foreign currency spot to bet on its rise—a rather amateurish approach—the speculator can buy it forward, take delivery at the agreed time, and then sell at the new spot rate to realize his gain (or

---

[14] The standard reference is Paul Einzig, *The Theory of Forward Exchange,* London: Macmillan, 1937. The 1961 edition is *A Dynamic Theory of Forward Exchange.* Also see Holmes, *op. cit.,* pp. 26-27, 34, 36-54, and Paul Einzig, *Economic Journal,* September 1960, pp. 485-495.

[15] Lipfert, *op. cit.,* pp. 153-154.

loss). Forward sales, conversely, are a convenient method of bear speculation. Finally, forward contracts are used not only for reducing risk in commercial transactions and for speculation but also in interest arbitrage, which will be explained presently.

In the New York foreign-exchange market, pounds sterling and Canadian dollars are the two currencies in which forward contracts are most commonly written. The U.S. dollar is so widely used in international trade that the active markets for forward contracts involving it and minor foreign currencies are located abroad rather than in New York, but American banks can often arrange through their correspondents abroad for forward contracts in these other currencies. Forward rates are commonly quoted for contracts of 30, 60, and 90 days maturity, but banks will tailor the length of contracts to meet the needs of their customers. Rather long maturities are often obtainable. (See p. 223n.)

Banks are able to write forward contracts with little risk to themselves because, for one reason, forward purchases and sales of a particular currency will ordinarily match to a considerable extent. Banks also deal among themselves to even out their individual positions. Even if the overall commercial demand for forward sterling exceeded the overall supply, banks could cover the risk of their excess sales of forward sterling by buying spot sterling and investing it at short term in London until the time for delivery under forward contracts. The willingness of banks to cover unbalanced forward positions by spot transactions, and accordingly the forward rates that the banks are willing to quote, depend on interest rates at home and abroad.

Interest Parities

The principle of *interest parities* explains these interrelations. It gives insight into the costs of covering future receipts of or needs for spot exchange by making contracts in an unrestricted and well-organized forward market. To an importer, the cost of eliminating risk is how much more he must pay for foreign exchange bought forward than he would have had to pay for a spot purchase; to

an exporter, the cost is how much less he receives for foreign exchange sold forward than he would have received for a spot sale. Since forward exchange may be quoted either at a premium above or at a discount from the spot rate, the cost of avoiding exchange risk in a commercial transaction may just as conceivably be negative as positive.

Ordinarily, the forward premium or discount will be slight, corresponding to the difference between short-term interest rates in the two countries concerned. If short-term interest rates were higher in London than in New York by 4 percentage points a year, or by 1 point per three months, then the three-months forward rate for pounds in terms of dollars would stand at about a 1 percent discount from the spot rate. *Interest arbitrage* tends to maintain this relation. To see how, we may suppose that the interest rates are as just mentioned but that the spot and forward exchange rates on the pound were equal. Arbitrageurs (typically banks) would have an incentive to buy pounds spot and at the same time sell them three-months forward at the same rate. During the three months, the funds could be lent in London for more interest than was obtainable in New York, and the risk-free reconversion into dollars would already have been provided for. Arbitrageurs not holding dollars at the start could borrow in New York, convert to spot pounds for relending at higher interest in London, and, under a forward contract made at the start, reconvert capital and interest at the end of the three months into enough dollars to repay capital with interest in New York with profit to spare. The eagerness of arbitrageurs to buy pounds spot and sell them forward would tend to bid up spot pounds and bid down forward pounds, establishing a forward discount in correspondence with the excess of London over New York interest rates. The eagerness to borrow in New York and lend in London would also tend, perhaps only slightly, to narrow the interest-rate differential between the two centers.

Some simple algebra will specify more precisely the conditions in which no one would have incentives either to expand or to shrink the volume of covered interest arbitrage.[16] (Covered interest arbitrage means interest-motivated short-term international transfers of funds protected against exchange risk by forward contracts.) Let

S = spot exchange rate in dollars per pound

F = three-month forward exchange rate in dollars per pound

$p = \dfrac{F - S}{S}$ = premium on the forward pound (a negative p means a discount on the forward pound)

N = short-term interest rate in New York per three months

L = short-term interest rate in London per three months

(p, N and L are understood to be expressed as decimals.)

There is no incentive to expand or shrink the volume of covered interest arbitrage when one dollar plus New York interest for three months just equals one dollar's worth of spot sterling plus London interest for three months reconverted into dollars at the forward rate. In symbols,

$$1 + N = \frac{1}{S}(1 + L) F$$

It follows from the definition of p that $F/S = 1 + p$. Thus the equilibrium condition becomes:

$$1 + N = (1 + p)(1 + L)$$
$$1 + N = 1 + p + L + pL$$
$$p = N - L - pL$$

This equation might be solved for p $\left(= \dfrac{N - L}{1 + L}\right)$ to give the precise interest-parity condition. It is a useful simplification, however, to note that p and L are ordinarily both small decimals, so that their product, pL, is negligibly small. To a close approximation,

[16] The following basically derives from S. C. Tsiang, "The Theory of Forward Exchange and Effects of Government Intervention on the Forward Exchange Market," IMF *Staff Papers*, **VII**, April 1959, pp. 79-80, and John Spraos, "Speculation, Arbitrage and Sterling," *Economic Journal*, **LXIX**, March 1959, p. 2n.

then, the interest-parity condition becomes

$$p = N - L$$

We arrive at the same result if we consider arbitrageurs who want their profit in sterling instead of dollars. There is no incentive to expand or shrink the volume of arbitrage when one pound plus London interest for three months just equals one pound's worth of spot dollars plus New York interest for three months reconverted into pounds at the forward rate. In symbols,

$$1 + L = S(1 + N)\frac{1}{F}$$

By seeing that $S/F = \dfrac{1}{1 + p}$ and recalling that pL is negligibly small, we reach the same result as before.

This approximate equilibrium condition $P = N - L$, which underlay the earlier example, corresponds to the usual verbal statement of the interest-parity condition: the forward premium on the pound expressed as a fraction of the spot dollar rate on the pound corresponds to the excess of New York over London interest rates (or the forward discount corresponds to the excess of London over New York interest rates).

Consider what would happen if this condition were not satisfied. An unrealistically large discrepancy will help make our new example clear: the three-month interest rate is 3 percent in London and 1 percent in New York, while the three-month forward discount on the pound is 4 percent instead of the theoretical 2 percent. Arbitrageurs can profit by borrowing pounds in London, converting them into dollars at the spot rate and at the same time contracting for their later reconversion into pounds at the forward rate, and meanwhile lending them in New York. Although the interest paid in London exceeds the interest earned in New York, this difference is more than outweighed by the opportunity to sell pounds spot and buy them back forward at an abnormally large discount. In their eagerness to do so, arbitrageurs weaken the spot pound and strengthen the forward pound and thus narrow the forward discount into line with the interest rates. (In principle, all these variables are interdependent; and the interest rates themselves would be somewhat affected.)

Departures from Interest Parities

The reasonable simplification of regarding pL in the equilibrium formula as negligibly small is only a minor reason why this interest-parity condition does not describe reality exactly.[17] A more important complication is that the short-term interest rates of the formula cannot be specified unambiguously for each country. Different rates prevail on bank deposits, bank loans, Treasury bills, commercial paper, banker's acceptances, and so forth. Different rates prevail for different "short-term" maturities and for different borrowers. The rate at which arbitrageurs can borrow in a given country may well exceed the rate at which they can lend. (Arbitrageurs such as banks holding balances in various countries, however, may perhaps be considered able to borrow at their own lending rate in the sense that they may use funds for arbitrage which they might otherwise have lent.) Statistical workers may choose some particular interest rate in each country—perhaps the treasury bill rate—as an indicator of short-term interest rates in general; but the chosen rate is hardly "the" rate of the formula.

For these and other reasons, the discrepancy between the actual and the theoretical forward premium or discount on a currency may have to exceed some *minimum sensibile* before arbitrageurs find transactions worth while.[18] Small deviations from interest parity may go uncorrected. Official restrictions on short-term capital movements, or even the fear of their possible imposition, can also impede interest arbitrage. Or not enough funds might be available to arbitrageurs to finance operations

on a large enough scale to wipe out deviations from interest parity. In reality, of course, there is no precise limit to the volume of arbitrage funds available. In principle, arbitrageurs might always borrow additional money by offering high enough rates of interest to bid funds away from other potential borrowers; in principle, interest rates in various countries belong just as fully to a system of mutually determining variables as do the spot and forward rates of exchange. In practice, however, credit rationing and the like do give some reality to the concept of at least a vague and elastic limit to the arbitrage funds available at any particular time and place. For example, banks must not divert so much funds into interest arbitrage that they lose their reputation for taking care of the credit needs of their regular customers. Still another qualification is that short-term investments or cash balances in various currencies yield their holders some intangible benefits of convenience or liquidity in addition to explicit interest. Banks and other potential arbitrageurs presumably tend to distribute their short-term holdings in various forms and in various financial centers so as to equate the marginal yields of interest plus intangible advantages. The interest-parity formula might in principle be adapted for each arbitrageur so as to take into account not only the objectively quoted interest rates and spot and forward exchange rates but also the subjectively appraised convenience yields of short-term assets denominated in various currencies.[19] The parity level of a forward premium or discount would thus become fuzzy, but specified changes in interest rates would still have qualitatively the same effects on arbitrage operations and on forward premiums or discounts as those predicted by the usual simple formula.

The entire preceding discussion assumes that spot exchange rates are flexible or are at least subject to uncertainty. This is a reasonable assumption, for the chief purpose of forward exchange is to enable businessmen to overcome the attendant risk. If perfect confidence prevailed that a spot exchange rate would not move outside definite limits, however, then these limits would pose a fur-

---

[17] Cf. Tsiang, *op. cit.,* pp. 80 ff.

[18] The traditional supposition was that arbitrage would not take place unless motivated by an opportunity for a profit margin of at least 1/2 percent a year. Nowadays, however, 1/16 or 1/32 percent is said often to be enough. In fact, some banks will often conduct arbitrage for no direct profit at all, just to enjoy the prestige of operating on a large scale and so to attract other business. See Paul Einzig, *Economic Journal,* September 1960, pp. 485-488, and *A Dynamic Theory of Forward Exchange,* pp. 50, 167, 169, 170, 201-202.

[19] See Tsiang, *op. cit.,* pp. 81-86.

ther constraint, in addition to the principle of interest parities, on the movements of the forward rate. (A corollary useful in interpreting historical episodes is that a forward rate outside the support limits of a pegged spot rate proves lack of confidence in maintenance of the peg.) Let us assume perfect confidence that spot sterling will stay within the official support limits of $2.78–$2.82. Forward sterling would never rise above $2.82 even if interest rates were very much higher in New York than in London. The interest-rate spread would indeed motivate heavy temporary transfers of funds to New York, but the arbitrageurs would not pay more than $2.82 to get pounds again under forward contracts if they were certain of getting pounds spot for $2.82 or less. They could safely leave their interest-arbitrage funds uncovered. Similarly, the forward pound would never fall below $2.78, no matter how much higher interest rates were in London than in New York. No one would accept less than $2.78 in a forward contract when planning to transfer funds back to New York after temporary investment in London, for at least as favorable a spot rate would certainly be available. (Interest rates and interest arbitrage would still affect just where within the assured spot limits the actual spot and forward rates fell. A very great excess of London over New York interest rates, for example, would tend to put the spot rate at $2.82 and the forward rate at $2.78.)

It follows that if the spot rate were pegged not merely within a range but at one precise figure, and if confidence were absolute that this rigid pegging would continue, then the forward rate would coincide with the spot rate. Or, rather, no forward rate and no forward market would exist. All commercial transactions and all interest-motivated transfers of funds would be uncovered, since, by assumption, no exchange risk would exist to be eliminated.[20]

Paradoxically, strong distrust in a prevailing spot rate of exchange, as well as perfect

confidence in it, could cause the forward premium or discount to deviate from the theoretical interest parity. If a currency were definitely and generally expected to depreciate, merchants would be especially sure to sell scheduled future receipts of it forward but would be inclined to let scheduled future payments in it go uncovered. If they expected an appreciation, merchants would be especially sure to cover scheduled future payments in the currency by forward purchases but would be inclined not to sell future receipts forward. Failure to cover the exchange risk in an ordinary commercial transaction means deliberately bearing the risk in hope of profiting by the expected movement in the rate. In short, this is speculation.[21] Furthermore, quite apart from such passive speculation in connection with commercial transactions, speculators would speculate outright by operating in the forward market or in both the forward and spot markets. Yet even all this passive and outright speculation would not necessarily make the forward-spot relation deviate far from the interest-parities relation; for any sizable discrepancies, almost regardless of their origin, would ordinarily make corrective arbitrage profitable. If spot as well as forward exchange rates were not pegged and could respond freely to supply and demand, arbitarge would tend to press both types of rate into alignment with interest parity. If the spot rate were really free of any official support, at any moment it would correspond to a balance between bullish and bearish opinion; at a free-market rate, expectations would *not* run one-sidedly toward further appreciation or depreciation. In the absence of lopsided expectations about the spot rate, speculation would provide no reason for the forward rate to deviate abnormally from it. Speculation might dominate both spot and forward rates; but even so, the two would tend to move together.

Speculation in itself thus does not create forward premiums or discounts far out of line with interest parity. Such misalignment

[20] The analysis of the two preceding paragraphs derives from Bent Hansen, "Interest Policy, Foreign Exchange Policy and Foreign Exchange Control," *Skandinaviska Banken Quarterly Review*, XL, January 1959, p. 17.

[21] Or rather, it is speculation unless the exchange risk is desired as a hedge against some other risk in the opposite direction, as, for example, of change in the domestic price of an inventory of imported goods.

would typically be due either to interference with the short-term capital movements necessary for interest arbitrage or to heavy speculation based on one-sided expectations of change in an officially *pegged* spot rate. As long as the spot rate stayed pegged, it could not do its share in alignment to the interest-parity relation, and interest arbitrage might be inadequate to achieve alignment through the forward rate alone. History does offer some examples of persistent abnormally large forward discounts on currencies pegged in the spot market but under speculative presure because of fears of impending devaluation. (Some of these examples are mentioned in Chapter 12.)

In summary, the principle of interest-parities describes the relation between spot and forward rates most accurately for a regime of freely fluctuating rates and least accurately for a regime of fixed rates that either are implicitly trusted or are strongly and one-sidedly distrusted. In general—and even for the usual regime in which rates are pegged but are neither implicitly trusted nor overwhelmingly expected to be adjusted in a particular direction—forward premiums and discounts do in fact correspond rather well to the relations between short-term interest rates in the various financial centers. Chapter 12, which compares exchange risk and the possibilities of protection against it under systems of fixed and fluctuating spot rates, will draw some implications from this fact.

Conclusion

This chapter almost defies summarization because its purpose has not been so much to reach conclusions as to introduce concepts needed later on. It explains the supply-and-demand analysis of exchange-rate determination and considers the influences of arbitrage and of rate pegging by direct official operations or indirectly under a gold standard. To provide a background for later inquiry into such matters as exchange controls, exchange risk, speculation, and the administrative feasibility of alternative exchange-rate systems, it surveys some institutional aspects of international remittances and the foreign-exchange market. It distinguishes between spot and forward rates. Perhaps the topic of greatest theoretical interest in the chapter is the interest-parity explanation of forward premium or discount.

✑ Appendix to Chapter 2: Documents of International Finance

International finance involves many documents besides those that directly transfer ownership of existing bank balances. These include other types of bill of exchange or draft. A bill or draft is a negotiable instrument in which one party orders a second to pay a definite sum of money to the order of a third (though the three parties need not all be distinct).[1] The most familiar type is an ordinary check. Other types may originate in various ways. An Inland exporter may arrange to collect payment by drawing a bill on his Outland customer. This document is known as a *commercial* bill or draft, since the drawee is an ordinary business firm rather than a bank. If payable upon presentation, it is known as a *sight draft*. If the seller wishes to grant his customer credit and accordingly draws a bill not payable until some weeks or months in the future, the instrument is known as a *time draft*. If the seller uses a time draft, he may wish to have an agent of his in the buyer's country present it to the buyer for acceptance. By signing the time draft on its face to confirm his obligation to pay it when due, the drawee converts it into an *acceptance,* akin to a promisory note.

If the draft or acceptance is expressed in Outland currency, it is a foreign-exchange instrument from the Inland point of view, and the Inland drawer may wish to sell it on the foreign-exchange market, that is, to his bank. The sale ordinarily is "with recourse": if the drawee fails to pay, the drawer must reimburse the holder. Credit risk may make it difficult to sell the instrument at an advantageously low rate of discount, however, especially if the drawee is not well known and does not enjoy an outstanding reputation. For this reason, it is quite usual to arrange to draw the drafts on the foreign importer's bank rather than on the importer himself.

This introduces the topic of *bankers' bills* (also called *bank drafts*), *bankers' acceptances,* and *letters of credit*. If the reporter wishes to draw his bill of exchange on a bank rather than on his customer directly, he will ask the customer to make the necessary arrangements. The importer's bank agrees to honor a draft or drafts drawn in accordance with specified provisions. The importer agrees to furnish the bank the necessary funds shortly before the draft is to be paid; if all goes as expected, the bank ties up no funds of its own. Instead, it in effect merely sells the use of its good name and credit standing for a moderate commission. If the importer fails to meet his obligation to the bank, the bank must pay the draft anyway and stand the loss itself. The exporter is protected. The bank, for its part, will take precautions to protect itself against default by its customer, the importer. For example, it may insist on receiving the bill of lading or other documents necessary to obtain the goods from the transportation company. Then the bank can withhold these documents from the importer until he pays the money or provides suitable guarantees.

The bill drawn on the bank may be a sight or a time draft. A time draft allows credit to the importer, who will not have to provide the money until shortly before his bank must pay the draft. A time draft will ordinarily be converted into a *banker's acceptance*. An agent of the exporter in the importer's country (typically a foreign branch or correspondent of the exporter's bank) will present the newly drawn bill to the importer's bank. If it is in good order, if the bill of lading and other specified documents accompany it, and if the other stipulated conditions have been met, then the bank will sign, confirming its obligation to pay the draft when due.

---

[1] The first and third parties are the same, for example, when the drawer of the bill names himself as payee. The second party, or drawee, has no legal obligation to honor a draft drawn on him unless it was drawn under an arrangement to which he had already agreed or unless he subsequently accepts an obligation to pay.

The resulting banker's acceptance, as the short-term obligation of a well-known bank, is a prime credit instrument. If the exporter wants cash before the acceptance comes due, he can probably sell it at only the small discount from face value characteristic of high-grade short-term obligations.

The conditions under which the exporter may draw on the importer's bank are specified in a *letter of credit*. This is not in itself a credit instrument or a type of foreign exchange; it is a formal letter from the bank authorizing the exporter to draw a draft or drafts on it up to a specified total amount and promising to honor the drafts provided that all stipulated conditions have been met. Letters of credit typically specify in close detail the time period within which the drafts must be drawn, the amounts of money available, the identifying notations to appear on the drafts, and the documents that must accompany them to evidence shipment of specified goods within a specified time period and by specified means of transport.

The letter of credit is useful to the exporter not only as a set of instructions but also as evidence that a bank has authorized him to draw drafts and has promised to honor them. This evidence greatly improves the salability of a draft. The exporter and anyone who might buy the draft from him can rely on the bank and need not worry about the solvency and trustworthiness of the foreign importer. Even when these are not in doubt, the letter may provide worthwhile assurance: it minimizes the risk that government controls in the importing country may prevent or delay payment, since the importer's bank has presumably taken account of any such problems before issuing the letter and since the government would usually hesitate to force banks to dishonor promises that were permissible when made.[2] Use of a letter of credit benefits the importer as well. The low degree of credit risk helps persuade the exporter to offer his lowest prices and best discounts. Furthermore, the exporter is prodded to ship goods of the qualities

and in the amounts specified in the letter of credit and to ship them on time.

Letters of credit are of many kinds. They may be *revocable* or *irrevocable*. Irrevocable letters are the more usual and are what we have had in mind so far. Such a letter conveys a firm promise that may not be withdrawn or modified without the consent of all parties concerned. Revocable letters, by contrast, convey no firm promise and amount to hardly more than instructions about the preparation and presentation of drafts and documents. Letters of credit may also be classified as *circular* (also called *negotiation*) or *straight* (domiciled). In a circular letter, the opening (issuing) bank mentions no other particular bank through which the drafts are to be negotiated; the exporter may send his drafts directly to the opening bank for payment or may route them through his own bank or any other bank willing to handle them. A straight letter is more usual. It is sent to the beneficiary (the exporter) by way of some other bank, typically a bank in his own city, which is instructed to pay drafts drawn under it on behalf of the opening bank. The latter still has responsibility for providing the necessary funds.

If the exporter wants the second bank's promise to honor his drafts even if the opening bank should fail to do so, the document used is known as a *confirmed* letter of credit. A Brazilian importer might arrange for his local bank to issue a letter of credit in favor of an American exporter. Instead of notifying the American beneficiary directly, the Brazilian bank might ask its New York correspondent to prepare and deliver the letter. Although the Brazilian bank is opening the credit, the letter would provide for the drafts to be drawn on the New York bank, which promises to pay them. The Brazilian bank is supposed to collect from its own customer and pay the New York bank (probably by authorizing a deduction from its balance with the latter); but regardless of what may go wrong, the New York bank binds itself to pay the exporter's drafts if properly drawn and accompanied by the proper documents. The letter issued by the New York bank is known, from the American point of view, as a confirmed irrevocable export letter of credit. Under an alternative arrangement, the New York bank might issue its own letter of credit in favor of the American exporter on behalf of the Brazilian importer, with the Brazilian bank acting as a mere intermediary. Only the New York bank would then be obligated, not both banks. Arrangements in one way or another involving an American bank in the issue of an export

---

[2] The trend in American export business in recent years has been toward less use of letters of credit and more selling on open account and related practices common in domestic business. Reasons for the change include increased competition in foreign trade, better knowledge of foreign buyers and their credit-worthiness, and reductions in risk because of export-credit-guarantee programs and also, presumably, because of dismantling and simplification of foreign government controls over trade and payments. See American Bankers Association, *A Banker's Guide to Financing Exports,* New York: 1963, p. 9.

letter of credit are quite common in U.S. export trade.

A *traveler's letter of credit* is a document carried by the beneficiary on his foreign travels. It authorizes him to write drafts on the opening bank within a specified time period and up to a specified total amount. (He agrees to reimburse the bank. The amounts drawn may be deducted from his regular account with the bank, or he may deposit collateral.) In the letter, the opening bank requests its correspondents throughout the world to cash drafts drawn by the properly identified traveler and to note on the letter itself the amounts drawn so that banks visited later can tell whether the entire amount of the credit has yet been used up. The traveler cashes his drafts on his home bank in the local currency of the country visited at the prevailing exchange rate for bankers' sight drafts. The issuing bank gives the traveler a list of its correspondents. (*Traveler's checks* are in some ways more convenient. They are orders by the issuing company to its paying agencies to pay the indicated sum to the order of the traveler.)

These and still other types and modifications of letters of credit need no detailed discussion here. Neither do the other documents called for in letters of credit or otherwise involved in international business—bills of lading, insurance policies, consular invoices, certificates of inspection, and many more.

The Balance of International Payments

 3

Balance-of-payments Concepts

Transactions that typically involve payments by foreigners to Americans and thus involve supplying foreign money for sale against dollars are classified as "credit" or "plus" transactions. Transactions that typically involve payments by Americans to foreigners and thus involve demanding foreign money with dollars are classified as "debit" or "minus" transactions. Transactions are grouped on the two sides of a statistical record known as the *balance of international payments* of the United States. It summarizes all transactions —buying and selling, borrowing and lending, transfer of investment earnings, and gifts— that have taken place between residents of the United States (including businesses and other institutions) and foreigners during a year or some other definite period. Actually, the term *balance of international payments* is misleading and has nothing to recommend it except long-standing usage; a better term would be *balance of international transactions*.[1] Transactions are not classified according to actual receipts or payments of money that may or may not occur. Instead, they are classified acording to the direction of payment that they would *typically* entail sooner or later, whether or not money is paid in each transaction. Commodity imports, for example, appear on the debit or "payments"-to-foreigners side of a country's balance of international payments not because the act of bringing goods into a country in itself is an outpayment—of course it is *not*—but because commodity imports *typically* have to be paid for. A particular import is still classified this way

[1] Cf. Charles N. Henning, *International Finance*, New York: Harper & Row, 1958, p. 17.

even if it is not paid for (it may come as a gift or as part of a barter deal, or the importer may default on his obligation to make payment). This is just one among many examples of how confusion can arise from the all-too-common practice of referring to transactions as *receipts* or *inpayments* on the one side and *payments* or *outpayments* on the other. These words *seem* so familiar that people are apt to forget the special sense in which they are used. The colorless language of *credits* or *pluses* and *debits* or *minuses* is safer precisely because it lacks any deceptive familiarity and so reminds everyone that the matter under discussion is a technical one. At the cost of repetition, it is worth emphasizing that "credit" items are not in themselves receipts, but simply transactions that ordinarily, but not necessarily, call for payment sooner or later by foreigners to residents of the home country. The way that the words *debit* and *credit* are used here could be reconciled with ordinary accounting language, but the trouble is hardly worth while. We may as well simply accept the fact, without worrying why, that balance-of-payments statisticians use these words as they do.

Table 3.1 is meant to list all categories of items in the balance of payments. There is no single correct list; how many categories appear depends on how broadly or narrowly each is defined. The listing in the table is a convenient one for discussing some balance-of-payments principles, though not necessarily for arranging actual statistics.

Consider items 1, 2, and 3 in the credits lists. Americans are shipping goods, selling transportation, meals, hotel accommodations, and sightseeing tours, and selling shipping services, engineering consultation, legal advice,

Table 3.1. Categories of the Balance of Payments

Credits = Plus Items = Transactions of Kinds Ordinarily Involving Foreign Payments to Americans = Transactions of Kinds Ordinarily Involving a Supply of Foreign Exchange to be Sold for Dollars (A Demand for Dollars to be Bought with Foreign Exchange)

1. Commodity exports from the U.S.
2. Foreign travel in the U.S.
3. Foreign purchases of American services.
4. Receipt by Americans of current earnings on their loans and investments abroad.
5. Gifts, reparations, and other "unilateral transfers" from foreigners to Americans.
6. Capital imports through new loans and investments made in the U.S. by foreigners, including increases in foreign-owned deposits in American banks.
7. Capital imports through recovery by Americans of their loans and investments and bank accounts previously placed abroad.
8. Exports of monetary gold from the U.S.

Debits = Minus Items = Transactions of Kinds Ordinarily Involving American Payments to Foreigners = Transactions of Kinds Ordinarily Involving a Demand for Foreign Exchange to be Bought with Dollars (A Supply of Dollars to be Sold for Foreign Exchange)

1. Commodity imports into the U.S.
2. American travel abroad.
3. American purchases of foreign services.
4. Payment to foreigners of current earnings on their loans and investments in the U.S.
5. Gifts, reparations, and other "unilateral transfers" from Americans to foreigners.
6. Capital exports through new American loans and investments abroad, including increases in American deposits in foreign banks.
7. Capital exports through repayment to foreigners of their earlier loans and investments and bank accounts in the U.S.
8. Imports of monetary gold into the U.S.

banking and brokerage services, insurance protection, and other intangible goods to foreigners. Commodity exports (item 1) are sometimes called *visible exports,* since they consist of tangible goods visibly leaving the country. Item 2 and 3 are sometimes called *invisible exports,* since, while representing sales to foreigners, they do not consist of tangible goods visibly leaving the country. The distinction is a matter of physical detail rather than of economic importance. Visible and invisible exports alike typically (but not always) involve foreigners having to make

payments to Americans and so involve an exchange of foreign money for dollars. (Of course, exchanges of currencies are not themselves the transactions classified under these headings.)

Item 4 might also be described as an invisible export. Americans are making available—are "exporting"—to foreigners the continuing services of American capital that was placed abroad some time in the past through investments in government and private bonds, corporation stocks, American-controlled business enterprises, etc. Item 4 does not refer to new transfers of capital. It comprises interest, dividends, and profits received by Americans on their foreign investments and may be regarded as measuring the value of the services continuing to be currently rendered by capital lent or invested some time ago. This sale of capital services to foreigners appears on the same side of the balance of payments as the sale of the services of American insurance companies, engineers, and lawyers.

Items 1 through 4, taken together, make up the credit side of the so-called *current account* in the U.S. balance of payments. All four types of transaction are of the sort whereby Americans, by *currently* furnishing goods and services (including the continuing services of existing investments) to foreigners, are typically becoming entitled to receive payments from them.

The opposite current-account transactions appear as items 1 through 4 in the debits list. Here Americans are engaging in the types of transactions that ordinarily involve their having to make payment to foreigners: they are importing goods, consuming goods and services as travelers in foreign countries, buying freight carriage and legal advice and other services from foreigners, and continuing to have the use of foreign capital already invested in American securities and in businesses in the United States.

Back in the credits list, we recognize item 5 as the value of foreign gifts and war reparations and other unilateral or unrequited transfers which are being made to the United States.[2] For example, an Englishman might

---

[2] Instead of forming a "unilateral-transfers" account of their own, the credits and debits of item 5 might be

be contributing to the support of a poor relative living in Chicago, or—less plausibly—the United States might be squeezing reparations out of a defeated enemy. Note that the item does *not* refer to the actual transfer of currency or bank deposits from foreign to American ownership. For one thing, the gift or reparations may be made in securities or commodities and not involve money at all. More fundamentally, acceptance of commodities or securities or money has to do with the *form* in which Americans take the gift or reparations transfer, that is, the *use* to which they put its value; and this is something distinct from the *fact* that foreigners are somehow making unilateral transfers of a certain value to the United States. The latter is what item 5 refers to.

More familiar is its counterpart in the debits list: the value of current American donations to foreigners. If someone living in the United States gives money to relatives abroad, the gift involves making a payment to foreigners and so involves a demand for foreign money with dollars (a supply of dollars for foreign money). There is no mystery about why this gift appears on the debit side of the American balance of payments. But the gift itself should be kept in mind, as distinct from the foreigners' acquisition of currency or bank balances or other assets. The very making of the gift is what *typically* involves payment to foreigners and so counts as an American debit; the particular form in which the foreigners receive the gift or the use to which they put its value is something else again. There is still no mystery about the classification even if the donor is the United States government rather than a private person. But a commodity gift instead of a money gift may be confusing. An individual American might send a CARE package or the government might send surplus farm products abroad as a gift. In principle, either of two treatments would conform to the logic of a balance of payments: we could either ignore the commodity gift com-

pletely on the grounds that it gives rise to no international payments or else we could count the actual export of the commodity as an ordinary example of credit item 1 and at the same time count the money value of the gift as a unilateral transfer under debit item 5. The latter is the more usual treatment (except for military goods). In a way, it amounts to pretending that we Americans sell the commodity to foreigners, at the same time giving them the funds with which they immediately pay for it. The commodity-export aspect of the whole operation appears as a credit in the American balance of payments, the gift aspects as a debit.

To clinch the point that credits are not actual receipts and debits not actual payments, let us suppose that Americans give foreigners some ten-dollar bills, which the foreigners simply hoard. The debit in the American balance of payments is *not* the actual transfer of American currency to foreigners. On the contrary, by acquiring American money to hold, the foreigners are investing in short-term claims against the United States (for that is what American money is). As a new foreign loan or investment in the United States —as an example of item 6 in the upper half of the table—this aspect of the transaction is a *credit* in the American balance of payments. The debit aspect consists of the gift abstractly considered, apart from its particular form: Americans are *giving* the foreigners the wherewithal to invest in hoards of American money or to buy American goods or to do anything else with the gift. The particular use to which the foreigners put the gift, such as acquiring a hoard of American currency, does not affect the classification of the gift aspect of the transaction as an undoubted *debit* in the American balance of payments.

Under item 6 in the list of credits, foreigners are making new investments or increasing their investments in American government bonds, American corporation stocks and bonds and other claims against Americans, and in branch offices and factories and other properties in the United States. Accomplishing such transactions typically involves exchanging foreign for American money. These so-called capital imports into the

counted as belonging to the current account. The choice between these two classifications is a matter of plausibility and convenience, not of right or wrong. The case for including item 5 in the current account would be strongest if the unilateral transfers were of a routine and recurrent nature.

United States belong on the same side of the balance of payments as commodity exports. It is helpful to remember that capital imports are typically evidenced by *exports* of stocks, bonds, and title deeds. A type of capital import worth special attention was already mentioned in the last paragraph: increases in foreign holdings of American paper money or coins or deposits in American banks. American currency represents promissory notes issued by the Treasury or the Federal Reserve banks; the foreigners, in acquiring these notes, are investing in or lending to the United States just as if they were acquiring American bonds. The same is true of increased foreign deposits in American banks: since a bank deposit is a debt of the bank to the depositor, increases in foreign-owned bank balances represent foreign lending to American banks.

Item 6 in the debits list consists of American capital exports through purchase ("import") of deeds to properties abroad and of foreign securities and other claims against foreigners. A noteworthy example is acquisition of claims against foreigners in the form of foreign currency or of deposits in foreign banks.

Item 7 in the credits list represents American capital imports through reversal of earlier American capital exports. Americans are engaging in transactions entitling them to receive payment from foreigners: they are re-exporting foreign securities and title deeds previously bought. Similarly, by spending or otherwise drawing down their hoards of foreign currency and by drawing down their balances in foreign banks, Americans are recovering their previous investments in these obligations of foreigners. Under item 7 in the debits list, Americans are exporting capital by discharging some of their previously existing debts to foreigners. In other words, foreigners are selling back their holdings of American securities and properties; Americans are reimporting claims previously sold. In particular, foreigners may be spending their previous holdings of American bank accounts and currency and to that extent ceasing to be creditors of American commercial and Federal Reserve banks and the U.S. Treasury.

For understanding whether particular transactions are classified as debits or credits, it does not matter whether capital movements (headings 6 and 7) are "long-term" or "short-term." The distinction between long- and short-term capital movements is important in analyzing equilibrium and disequilibrium in the balance of payments, but that is another story, to be taken up later.

Under credit item 8, the United States is selling gold to foreigners; such sales would ordinarily call for foreign payments to Americans. In the debit list, the United States is buying foreign gold. Gold exports and imports belong on the same side of the balance of payments, respectively, as commodity exports and imports. In principle, gold transactions could be lumped together with commodity transactions. They are usually shown separately, however, because gold plays a role in intergovernmental settlements and national monetary reserves that makes it something especially interesting to government officials and economists.

The Equality of Credits and Debits

The balance of payments must balance. If full and accurate figures were available, total credits and total debits would have to be equal. Lack of full and accurate figures is a mere practical detail that does not impair this principle. The two sides must have the same total because of the way a balance of payments and the items in it are defined and the way these definitions interlock. A balance of payments must balance for the same general reasons as why a company's balance sheet must balance.

There are two ways of further convincing ourselves that balance is logically necessary. First, we can see the double-entry nature of a balance of payments: each transaction has a debit aspect and a credit aspect of equal size. For example, a commodity export is a credit entry, but it must somehow be paid for or matched. Perhaps the American exporter has engaged in a barter deal, so that a commodity import directly matches the commodity export. Perhaps the American exporter accepts payment in the form of foreign currency or of a deposit in a foreign bank, thus making a loan to foreign monetary authorities or banks, which is a debit in the U.S. balance of payments. Perhaps the foreigner pays for the American goods by drawing on his holding of American currency or on his deposit in an American bank, in which case Americans are discharging debt previously owed to foreigners—again a debit. Perhaps the American exporter sells the goods on credit or gives them to foreigners as a gift; in this case, the loan or gift aspect of the transaction is a balance-of-payments debit, matching the credit aspect consisting of the actual commodity export. Suppose the American exporter expects to get paid but the foreign buyer defaults: it turns out that the American has made an involuntary unilateral transfer, which is an example of debit item 5.

As another example, consider an American gift to foreigners. The gift aspect of the transaction is in itself a debit; the way in which the foreigners take the gift is a credit from the American viewpoint. The gift may actually take the form of a commodity; or the foreigners may immediately use a money gift to buy American commodities. Either way, an export appears in the American balance of payments. The foreigners may use the gift to pay off old debts owed in the United States or else to increase their holdings of American securities, currency, or bank accounts; any of these transactions would represent a capital inflow into the United States and count as a credit.

A second way to see why total debits and credits must be equal is to realize that a country, like an individual or other economic unit, cannot buy goods and services worth more than what it sells unless it draws down its cash reserves (as of gold, foreign money, and bank accounts abroad), sells off some of its investments, receives repayment of debt owed to it, borrows (perhaps by buying on credit), or receives gifts or indemnities or the like. Conversely, a country cannot sell more than it buys in goods-and-services transactions unless it engages in matching debit transactions by accumulating cash reserves, investing, lending, paying off debt, or giving gifts or paying indemnities.

To clinch an understanding of the balance-of-payments concept, it is worth while to draw the analogy between a country and a single family. Examples of credits in the family's balance of payments might be: (1) sales of goods, such as crops grown or cakes and carvings produced by members of the family, (2) provision of lodgings to tourists, (3) work done by wage-earning members of the family, (4) earning of interest and dividends on bank accounts and bonds and stocks, and earning of profit from a family-owned business, (5) receipt of gifts, perhaps from relatives or from public-relief authorities, (6) new borrowing, including the obtaining of credit from sellers of goods bought on the installment plan, (7) undoing loans and investments previously made, including, for example, selling stocks, cashing savings bonds, spending wads of currency kept in the mattress, and drawing down bank accounts, and (8) sale of gold coins from a collection. Debits might include: (1) purchase of groceries and other goods, (2) traveling, staying in hotels, and eating in restaurants, (3) buying medical and legal and repair services, (4) incurring interest on money previously borrowed, (5) making gifts, (6) repayment of borrowings, including payment of installments on credit purchases, (7) purchases of stocks and bonds and increases in bank accounts and hoards of currency, and (8) purchase of gold coins. The family clearly cannot be spending more than it earns on current account (items 1 through 4) without at the same time receiving gifts, borrowing, drawing down bank accounts and hoards of cash otherwise recovering old loans or selling off investments, or selling gold. Conversely, a family cannot be earning more than it spends on current account without lending, investing, making gifts, accumulating cash and bank accounts, or the like.

The necessary balance of debits and credits is a matter of sheer definitions and arithmetic and gives no guarantee of "equilibrium" in any reassuring sense of the word. Total debits would equal total credits even for a family or a country in terrible economic straits.

This necessary equality has a corollary: the *principle of compensating balances*. If the balance-of-payments items are classified into various categories or "accounts," an excess of debits (or credits) in one or more of them must be matched by an equal excess of credits (or debits) in the remaining ones.

Two Examples of Balances of Payments

Tables 3.2 and 3.3 illustrate these principles with actual figures for the United States and Canada. On current or goods-and-services account, Americans in 1963 were exporting merchandise worth more that what they were importing, buying transportation and travel services from foreigners worth more than what they were selling, and earning more on their investments abroad than foreigners were earning on their investments in the United States. The United States was spending

Table 3.2.   U.S. Balance of International Payments for the Calendar Year 1963

	Credits or Plus Items	Debits or Minus Items
	(Millions of Dollars)	
Current Account		
Merchandise	21,902	16,962
Transportation	1,848	2,154
Travel	941	2,071
U.S. military sales and expenditures	632	2,880
Investment income	4,565	1,196
Miscellaneous services	1,715	855
BALANCE ON CURRENT ACCOUNT	5,485	
Unilateral Transfers		
Private remittances (net)		548
Government pensions, nonmilitary grants, and other transfers		2,171
BALANCE ON UNILATERAL TRANSFERS		2,719
Independently Motivated Capital Account		
Private American direct investment abroad (net)		1,799
Private American (including bank) holdings of other long-term foreign assets (net)		1,641
Private American (including bank) short-term capital (net)		642
Foreign direct and long-term portfolio investments other than in U.S. government securities	392	
U.S. government capital, other than special and settlement transactions (net)		1,882
BALANCE ON INDEPENDENTLY MOTIVATED CAPITAL ACCOUNT		5,572
Special U.S. Government Transactions		
Advance repayments of debt to U.S. Government	325	
Advance military payments to U.S. Government	359	
Transactions in nonmarketable, nonconvertible, medium-term securities		43
BALANCE ON SPECIAL U.S. GOVERNMENT TRANSACTIONS	641	
Errors and Omissions		495
Settlement of U.S. Deficit		
Change in U.S. gold and convertible currency holdings and net IMF position	378	
Transactions in nonmarketable, convertible, medium-term securities	702	
Changes in other liquid liabilities to foreigners	1,580	
BALANCE ON SETTLEMENT ACCOUNT	2,660	

NOTES: Transfers of military goods under aid programs are excluded from both merchandise exports and government grants.

Total plus items = total minus items = $35,339 million. In millions of dollars, total plus balances (5,485 on current account, 641 on special U.S. government transactions, and 2,660 on settlement account) = total minus balances (2,719 on unilateral transfers, 5,572 on independently motivated capital, and 495 on errors and omissions) = 8,786.

SOURCE: Department of Commerce figures, rearranged from *Survey of Current Business,* March 1964.

heavily to maintain its military establishment abroad. Earnings exceeded expenditures on miscellaneous services. All in all, the current account showed a surplus of $5½ billion. The net debit on unilateral transfers reflects larger private and governmental gifts and so forth by Americans to foreigners than gifts and so forth in the opposite direction. This is true even though government grants for military purposes are not counted. (The goods constituting the form of transfer of the military grants are likewise left out of the figure for commodity exports. Without disturbing the necessary equality of total debits and total credits, the dollar amount involved could, alternatively, have been included as both a unilateral-transfer debit and a merchandise credit.) Why most of the capital transactions are labeled *independently motivated* and segregated from the capital inflows shown in the special-government-transactions and settlement accounts will be explained later in this chapter. Meanwhile, we notice that more private U.S. capital flowed newly abroad than returned from earlier investment abroad in connection not only with "direct" investment (meaning, for the most part, investment in business properties abroad controlled by U.S. companies) but also with portfolio securities and other long- and short-term assets. Foreign investment in the United States increased. New long- and short-term lending by the U.S. government exceeded regular repayments received. Special U.S. government transactions (explained more fully in Chapter 25) were arranged with foreign governments to keep down the size of the credits that would otherwise have appeared in the ordinary settlement account. (The $43 million debit represents partial reversal of earlier sales of the securities indicated.) The way these and the settlement transactions are classified depends on the *motivation* for them; this is something to keep in mind when we discuss the meaning of a balance-of-payments deficit. In the settlement account, the credit item of $378 million represents sales of gold from the country's monetary reserves, adjusted for smaller changes in other reserve assets (officially held foreign exchange and the country's quasi-automatic drawings rights

in the International Monetary Fund). (The reader should make sure he sees *why* gold exports count as a credit, just as ordinary commodity exports do. Any idea that credit items are necessarily "good" and debit items "bad" causes serious confusion, especially here.) The $702 million represents sales to foreign authorities of special government securities considered practically as liquid as the other liabilities to foreigners whose increases comprise the $1,580 million—other U.S. government securities, bank deposits, and other readily cashable claims on dollars.

"Errors and omissions," finally, is a "cheating item." Its existence and size serves as a warning to regard most figures in all balances of payments as no better than rough approximations. (The way that revisions and reclassifications keep changing published figures underlines this warning, which should be understood even if not actually repeated whenever a balance-of-payments figure is quoted.) Because of inaccuracies and gaps in estimates of other items, total *recorded* debits fell $495 million short of total *recorded* credits, and to make the statement balance, an equivalent debit was entered under "errors and omissions." This item in no way casts doubt on the principle that if all items are fully and accurately stated, their totals *must* balance. It is necessary solely because of practical difficulties in gathering absolutely full and accurate statistics. Tourist spending abroad, for example, must be estimated from information supplied from memory by a sampling of returning travelers. The fact that some people change their residence to or from the United States during the course of a year causes complications. Some smuggled goods go unrecorded. The international lending implied in the shipment of goods that have not been paid for by the end of the year is hard to keep close track of. In some years when errors and omissions is a plus item in the U.S. balance of payments, it may include a considerable hidden transfer of capital into the United States in violation of exchange controls imposed by foreign governments; when it is negative, as in recent years, it presumably includes unrecorded capital outflows.

Finally, as noted at the bottom of the table,

total debits and total credits are equal, and imbalances in one direction in some parts of the statement are matched by opposite imbalances in the remaining parts.

The Canadian balance of payments in Table 3.3 should now be practically self-explanatory.[3] True, the items are grouped rather differently than in the U.S. statement and the Canadian balance classifies items into not several but only two accounts, current and capital (unilateral transfers, for example, are included in the current account). These are

merely differences of arrangement, not of principle.

The errors and omissions item is concealed in "other short-term capital movements." The Canadian statisticians tacitly assume that any discrepancy between debits and credits under all other headings represents a capital movement not directly recorded. Probably the largest type is changes in the balance of commercial indebtedness: capital moves between countries when businessmen of one country in effect make loans to businessmen of another by selling them goods on credit, though changes in the net amount of such debt outstanding are hard to estimate. The net plus of $233 million (Canadian currency) for "other short-term capital movements" suggests that capital was on balance moving into Canada during 1963 by way of Canadian importers running up their debts to foreign suppliers.

---

[3] The item *gold production available for export* calls for comment. Because of the special significance of gold, the Canadian statisticians want to show its current production in the balance of payments even when not all the gold is in fact exported during the year. Production of gold available for export, whether or not it is in fact all exported, is shown as a credit item in the balance of payments, but gold added to official reserves rather than exported is an offsetting debit.

Table 3.3. Canadian Balance of International Payments for the Calendar Year 1963

	Credits or Plus Items	Debits or Minus Items
	(Millions of Canadian Dollars)	
Current Account		
Merchandise trade	7,082	6,579
Travel expenditures	609	589
Interest and dividends	223	869
Freight and shipping	560	641
Inheritance and migrants' funds	149	182
Official contributions		61
Gold production available for export	154	
All other current transactions	449	862
Totals	9,226	9,783
Balance on Current Account		557
Capital Account and Settlement Items		
Direct investment	240	110
Trade in new and outstanding securities (net)	526	
Repayment on Canadian government loans	15	
Subscriptions to international investment agencies		8
Other long-term capital movements (net)		50
Changes in foreign holdings of Canadian short-term assets and in Canadian holdings of foreign short-term assets	112	255
Other short-term capital movements (net)	233	
Change in official holdings of gold and foreign exchange and net position with International Monetary Fund		146
Totals	1,126	569
Balance on Capital Account and Settlement Items	557	

NOTES: Mutual aid to NATO countries is not included in either current credit items or current debit items. Errors and omissions are hidden in "other short-term capital movements."
SOURCE: Figures rearranged from Bank of Canada, *Statistical Summary,* November 1964, pp. 739-740.

But other unrecorded transactions enter into determining this net 233; in fact, it is the figure with which "fudging" occurs.

The Balance of Payments and the National Accounts

The distinction between the current account and other parts of the balance of payments conveniently leads to seeing the relation between a country's foreign transactions and its national income and production. The exact dividing line between what is and what is not included in the current account is rather arbitrary. Despite some exceptions (such as the Canadian inclusion of "official contributions" in the current account), however, the current account generally covers sales and purchases between countries of currently produced goods and services.

In a "closed" economy (without foreign trade),

National Expenditure = National Income
                              or Product

during a given time period. That is to say, total spending to buy all final goods and services produced (including consumption goods and services and investment goods, both private and governmental) equals the total market value of the things produced and so equals the income that this production generates or amounts to.[4] The term *absorption* conveniently covers all private and governmental consumption and real investment (as distin-

guished from mere financial investment in securities and other claims) toward which expenditure is directed. For a closed economy, absorption necessarily equals national income and product: there is no source of consumption goods and services and investment goods except domestic production,[5] and, on the other hand, there is no outlet for what is produced except to consume or invest it at home.

Foreign trade makes the truism slightly more complicated:

National Expenditure − Imports + Exports
         = National Income or
                 Product

The imports and exports are of all currently produced goods and services comprising the current account of the balance of payments. Imports have to be subtracted on the left side of the equation to cancel out the imports that are already included in national expenditure (which mean expenditure *by* the economic units making up the home economy, not necessarily expenditure *on* home production only). This canceling is necessary because imports are part of foreign, not home production; and expenditure on them, though "out of" home income, gives rise to foreign income, so far as its direct impact is concerned. Exports must be added to the left side for the opposite reason: they are part of national production, and expenditure on them gives rise to national income, yet the expenditure on them is foreign, not domestic.

By rearrangement,

Exports − Imports = National Income or
                          Product
                   − National Expenditure

or

Imports − Exports = National Expenditure
                   − National Income or
                          Product

Since national expenditure "absorbs" consumption and investment goods and services, it follows that

---

[4] "Final" goods and services are distinguished from "intermediate" goods that go through further stages of processing and marketing. Counting all values *added* at each stage would be the same thing as counting only final goods and services.

Income and product are measured gross or net according as investment is counted gross or net of depreciation (i.e., without or with subtraction of that part of total investment that simply offsets wear and tear on and damage to capital goods).

Goods and services are valued at market prices, including whatever taxes may go into them. Our purposes permit slurring over this matter of "indirect business taxes."

"Expenditure" is not meant absolutely literally. If a company constructs new capital equipment itself instead of buying it from some other firm, it is still considered to have "spent" money on the equipment (or on everything that went into it). Inventory investment also counts as expenditure. If a commercial farmer diverts some of his crop to his own consumption, he "spends" on these consumer goods.

[5] Consumption plus *new* investment can exceed total production if disinvestment is going on at the same time. But if consumption and investment are added together with the proper negative sign for disinvestment, the statement in the text remains true.

An export surplus = an excess of production over "absorption"

and

An import surplus = an excess of "absorption" over production

An open economy, unlike a closed one, need not always have production and absorption equal. On the one hand, it may be producing goods and services worth more than those it itself consumes or devotes to real capital formation, so that it is building up claims on or paying off debts to foreigners. The claims built up may include foreign securities, business properties and other investments in foreign countries, and foreign currencies and bank deposits and gold. The only other possibility is for the country simply to give the value of its export surplus to foreigners. On the other hand, an open economy may be absorbing into consumption and real investment goods and services worth more than those it itself is producing; it could finance the difference by disposing of its previously acquired foreign investments and gold and foreign exchange or by borrowing from or receiving new investment funds or gifts from foreigners.

What all this means for the behavior of actual persons and business firms and government units is something still to be investigated. We must avoid personifying countries too much and must make it clear who it is that takes decisions and actions. In any case, an imbalance on current account in foreign trade is the same thing as an imbalance between national production and absorption. Nothing said so far implies that this imbalance is necessarily a bad thing.

Equilibrium and Disequilibrium in the Balance of Payments

Discussions about "surpluses," "deficits," "gaps," and "disequilibriums" in balances of payments and about "active" and "passive" and "favorable" and "unfavorable" balances, as well as governmental measures to deal with these troubles, are all too familiar. What can such terms mean, considering that total debits and credits must be equal? Precisely because

it must hold true by definition of the terms involved, this *ex post* equality is hardly reassuring. It no more demonstrates equilibrium than does the fact that actual purchases and sales of any commodity are always equal, even though a shortage caused by a price ceiling may be leaving many would-be buyers unsatisfied. What matters is equality or inequality between the debt and credit totals of certain intentional transactions, or transactions that were considered desirable for their own sakes, as distinguished from other transactions undertaken automatically or passively or without being especially desired and undertaken only as arithmetically necessary counterparts of an imbalance between desired transactions.

We are already familiar with the ideas of a surplus or deficit on *current account*—exports of goods and services in excess of imports or the opposite.[6] We also know how a current-account deficit can be financed—by drawing down foreign assets, borrowing, or receiving gifts. Unless some such transactions on the credit side were available to the country, it could not have a current-account deficit in the first place. A country simply cannot be importing more goods and services than it can pay for in some way or other (at least by getting them on credit).

There may be grounds for worry, however, if a current-account deficit is being financed in a merely stopgap way, as by drawing down bank accounts abroad, selling off gold, receiving stopgap loans from abroad, or receiving gifts granted by foreigners precisely in order to tide the country over the crisis. The worry is that such stopgaps cannot go on forever:

---

[6] The difference in value between exports and imports of *commodities* alone is traditionally called the *balance of trade*. (Some writers, however, use this expression to mean the difference between exports and imports of goods *and services*, making it correspond to what is here called the balance on current account. See, for example, J. E. Meade, *The Balance of Payments*, The Theory of International Economic Policy, Vol. One; London: Oxford University Press, 1951, pp. 7-8, and W. M. Scammell, *International Monetary Policy*, London: Macmillan, 1957, pp. 18-20. An excess of commodity exports over imports is called an "active" or "surplus" or, rather misleadingly, "favorable" balance of trade; the opposite, a "passive" or "deficit" or "unfavorable" balance. Economically, the concept of the balance of commodity trade alone is unimportant, as is the distinction between "visible" trade in commodities and "invisible" trade in services.

eventually, foreign bank accounts and gold and other salable foreign assets will be exhausted, and foreigners will become tired of making bad loans and unrequited gifts. The deficit country may suddenly be caught up by the unpleasant need to live within its income. A persistent current-account deficit may indicate the impending need for sudden unpleasant readjustments.

Financing a current-account deficit in stopgap ways is fundamentally different from financing it by a long-term capital inflow. Long-term international capital movements typically reflect investors' own judgments about where they can lend their money at highest rates of interest or invest it for highest dividends or profits (and borrowers consider where they can borrow most advantageously). The individual investors take account as they themselves see fit of the different degrees of risk on various investments and of marketability of the securities involved and so forth. These profit considerations presumably correlate with the prospective productivity of the capital. Long-term capital entering a country presumably tends to increase the country's capital formation, its productive capacity, and its attainable level of consumption, as well as its ability to provide for transfer of interest and profits on the capital and eventual repayment of the capital sums themselves.

A net inflow of long-term capital of this sort is almost inevitably accompanied by a deficit in the country's current account (gold inflows or short-term capital outflows providing conceivable exceptions). This current-account deficit, far from being grounds for alarm, is the way in which capital in "real" terms comes into the country as the counterpart of the financial transfer. The rise in the country's goods-and-services imports relative to its exports is how additional amounts of real resources become available to the borrowing government units and businesses and even consumers. Machinery and other capital goods may be imported, or increased imports and reduced exports of consumer goods may free domestic resources for real capital formation. To welcome an inflow of long-term investment capital while deploring

a current-account deficit is to fight sheer arithmetic.

A current-account deficit met by *short-term* capital imports, such as stopgap borrowing or use of gold and foreign-exchange reserves, is something quite different. It is but a temporary expedient that may not long be available. Besides, short-term borrowing soon may have to be repaid.

The distinction often drawn between "long-term" and "short-term" capital movements might perhaps better be drawn between *independently motivated* and stopgap or *compensatory* transactions instead.[7] Independently motivated capital movements are typified by long-term international investments made in hope of gain, but short-term private transfers of capital also may sometimes be motivated by different interest rates in different countries and be equally uninfluenced by a desire to finance imbalances in other parts of the balance of payments. Ordinary private trade in goods and services is almost all independently motivated in the present sense. Stopgap or compensatory financing, on the other hand, is officially provided or arranged for, with perhaps some minor exceptions, precisely to cover (and thus permit) an imbalance between other debits and credits.

The distinction between independently motivated and compensatory transactions serves to define a deficit in a country's balance of payments: it is an excess of independently motivated debit over independently motivated credit transactions. In other words, it is an imbalance requiring or permitted by net resort to compensatory credit transactions. Quite conceivably, an independently motivated capital outflow might more than counterbalance a current-account surplus and so produce an overall deficit, as has recently been true of the United States. More typi-

---

[7] J. E. Meade's terms *autonomous* and *accommodating* transactions are often used for essentially the same distinction meant here. Unfortunately, the term *autonomous* has a confusing variety of meanings in economics. In the theory of balance-of-payments adjustment, autonomous changes in imports and exports are those motivated otherwise than by changes in income, yet commodity transactions that Meade would label "autonomous" in the present context might very well be motivated by income changes, though independently of anyone's concern about the overall state of the country's balance of payments.

cally, though, a country in overall deficit will be running a current-account deficit not fully financed or matched by an independently motivated capital inflow. In other words, it will be financing an import balance of goods and services at least in part by stopgap methods.

A balance-of-payments surplus, conversely, is an excess of credits over debits in independently motivated transactions, which typically means net exports of goods and services not fully matched by an independently motivated capital outflow and so matched at least in part by passive official accumulations of gold and foreign exchange or by the granting of stopgap loans and gifts to foreigners. A disequilibrium in this direction poses a less pressing problem for a country's authorities than a deficit. A deficit cannot go on without any limit to its stopgap financing; a painful retrenchment may become necessary; but a country with a surplus faces no equally definite limit to the reserves it can accumulate and the help it can give to foreigners. It may be a waste but it is not a critical problem to continue exporting goods and services worth more than those imported and receiving nothing better for the excess than claims on foreigners that would not have been an attractive investment in their own right.

Balance-of-payments *equilibrium* means the absence of any surplus or deficit as just defined; debits and credits on account of goods-and-services trade together with other independently motivated transactions add up to equal amounts. To avoid tediously long phrases in theoretical discussions, however, it is often convenient to blur the distinction between trade and other independently motivated transactions, such as long-term capital movements, and speak simply of whether or not the country's "trade" is in balance or whether or not the country is "living within its income."

A country may be in equilibrium as far as is shown by the actual statistics, appropriately classified, and yet be in "latent" or "potential" or "suppressed" disequilibrium. The only thing warding off an actual deficit might be import controls or a domestic financial policy resulting in heavy unemployment. The "equilibrium" shown by the statistics might then be described as "artificial," "forced," "precarious," or "unsatisfactory." But though some such adjective may be attached, it does seem simplest to call even this situation an "equilibrium." We might as well define the term without connotations of approval: by *how desirable a method* equilibrium is maintained is a separate matter from *whether* equilibrium prevails. Sometimes it is convenient to refer to actual and to latent or suppressed disequilibrium alike as balance-of-payments "trouble."

Multilateralism and Bilateralism

Related to equilibrium and disequilibrium is the concept of *multilateralism*. By its derivation, the word means "many-sidedness" —here, a many-sided balancing of transactions. Ordinarily, a country's transactions will not balance separately with every other country with which it trades; yet the excess of purchases over sales in transactions with particular countries in no way implies disequilibrium. Balance in total transactions with the rest of the world as a whole is what counts—at least, when currencies can be exchanged for one another without restriction. (When restrictions prevent currency earned by excess sales to one country from being freely exchanged to pay for excess purchases from another country, the story may be different.)

Multilateralism is normal; it characterizes the balance of payments of every family. The opposite would be *bilateralism*—avoiding, as far as possible, purchases in excess of sales in dealing with each particular person or firm. The plumber would try to avoid buying groceries worth more than the plumbing work he sold to the grocer and avoid buying medical care worth more than the plumbing work he sold to the doctor. Such bilateralism interferes with achieving efficiency through specialization. The same misgivings apply to national regulation of imports and exports out of concern for a supposed proper balance in transactions with separate foreign countries. (When foreign countries kept their currencies from being freely exchangeable for one another, however, bilateral policies might conceivably be a necessary evil for a country that would otherwise deplore them.)

Alternative Concepts of Equilibrium and and Disequilibrium

It might seem that one country's deficit or surplus must necessarily be matched by a surplus or deficit of all other countries taken together: Inland and Outland must have equal but opposite balance-of-payments positions. In theoretical discussions this is a convenient assumption, but it does not necessarily hold true of real-world statistics. Certain transactions might be considered independently motivated by the statisticians of one country and compensatory by the statisticians of another. Gold exports might be independently motivated for a gold-producing country, but adding this gold to the official reserves of another country might be compensatory. The authorities of one country might commandeer foreign securities owned by its citizens and sell them abroad to provide compensatory finance, yet people in other countries might buy these securities for ordinary private motives.[8]

As these examples suggest, the distinction between independently motivated and compensatory transactions is not precise. This vagueness cannot be helped; it corresponds to reality. The size and very meaning of a disequilibrium in a country's international transactions depends on just how the line is drawn between their two types. For this reason, incidentally, the distinction is often described —with reference also to the physical arrangement of balances of payments—as a distinction between "above-the-line" and "below-the-line" transactions. A disequilibrium is measured by the difference between the totals of "above-the-line" credits and debits and is "settled" or "financed" by the equal but opposite difference between the two "below-the-line" totals. This neutral language has the advantage of emphasizing the arbitrary element in the distinction between independently motivated and compensatory transac-

tions and therefore in reported figures of surpluses and deficits.

Some further examples may be worth while. If an official agency sells foreign exchange out of its reserves to keep an imbalance between other supply and demand from upsetting the officially desired exchange rate, the balance-of-payments credit that this use of reserves represents is pretty clearly a stopgap or compensatory item. This is true even though the authority does not plan the amount of reserves used and just passively supplies whatever amount may be necessary to keep the exchange rate fixed. If a foreign country simply gives or lends gold or money to a country with alarmingly low reserves precisely in order to tide it over this trouble, the transaction is also clearly compensatory, even though the amount of stopgap financing in this case was planned deliberately instead of determined passively. But suppose a deficit country deliberately raises domestic interest rates to attract funds from abroad. If the policy works, investors will transfer funds for their own advantage and probably with no thought of plugging up any gap. From the private point of view, these transfers are motivated just as independently by private economic advantage as transactions in commodities. Yet the policy that attracted the funds was an emergency measure adopted with the balance-of-payments trouble in mind. How, then, should the capital movement be classified? Or, for another example, suppose that importers build up their indebtedness to foreign suppliers because the government, anxious about its dwindling foreign-exchange reserves, is putting obstacles in the way of its citizens' prompt payment of their external debts. If the foreign exporters acquiesce in the delay because they do not want to lose future business by insisting too obnoxiously on prompt payment and because they are confident of being paid in the end, their extension of the loans may be called voluntary and in accordance with estimates of private advantage. Is the growth of the indebtedness of the deficit country then compensatory or independently motivated? Another example would not even involve any change in government policy. If imports and exports are

---

[8] Meade, *op. cit.*, chap. II.

both habitually bought and sold largely on short-term credit, development of an import surplus (perhaps independently caused by some such development as domestic inflation or foreign depression) would almost automatically be accompanied by a net capital import, since importers are now receiving more total credit than exporters are granting. Are these loans to be classified above or below the line? There are no unequivocal answers to these questions; it is not easy to present statistics of transactions classified by anything so indefinite as motive. But despite all this fuzziness, the distinction between independently motivated and accommodating transactions, and so between equilibrium and disequilibrium, is meaningful.

The definition of disequilibrium introduced in these pages is essentially the same as the third of the "three concepts of the balance of payments" distinguished by Fritz Machlup.[9] This, the *accounting balance,* is the difference between the totals of certain categories of debit and credit items selected from the necessarily balancing complete list of items. It is an *ex post* concept: it uses figures for a period of time that is over and done with and not figures planned or intended for the current period or for the near future. The idea of planned or intended transactions does come into the concept, but only to distinguish independently motivated transactions (which presumably *had been* planned or intended without regard to the country's overall international accounts) from compensatory transactions not undertaken just for those ordinary motives. The accounting balance has an affinity with Machlup's first concept, the *market balance,* which is the difference between the amounts of foreign exchange effec-

tively demanded and supplied over a period of time by buyers and sellers not motivated by a desire to influence the exchange rate. (This distinction between transactions that are and those that are not officially undertaken to influence the exchange rate is probably the most clear-cut example of the distinction between independently motivated and compensatory transactions.) The state of the accounting balance for immediate past time periods may furnish clues to the probable state of the market balance in the immediate future and to the volume of official transactions that would be necessary to keep the exchange rate unchanged. This knowledge can be helpful to the authorities in deciding what if any change in the rate may be advisable, after all, or what other policies they should adopt to head off a prospective market imbalance. The information provided by the accounting balance has only a loose and uncertain relevance, however; too much depends, among other things, on what exchange rates, financial policies, trade and exchange controls, and other economic conditions and policies were affecting the various items in it. The amount and kind of compensatory financing provided also presumably had been affecting the size of some of the supposedly independent items.

Machlup's remaining concept is the *program balance,* the difference between the amount of foreign exchange that some authority considers it necessary or desirable to have available over some future period and the amount that it expects to become available from regular sources. A certain amount of foreign exchange is obviously "necessary" or "desirable" only with reference to some sort of economic plan or program, however vague, and with reference to desired levels of national consumption and investment. An example is the plan drawn up by the West European countries in 1947 to show the excess of foreign-exchange expenditures over foreign-exchange earnings that their postwar reconstruction would "require" in the following few years. More recent examples are the foreign-exchange deficits involved in economic development plans of underdeveloped countries. Serious confusion

---

[9] "Three Concepts of the Balance of Payments and the So-called Dollar Shortage," *Economic Journal,* **LX**, March 1950, pp. 46ff.

The text that follows modifies some details of Machlup's definitions. In particular, his definition of the "market balance" specifies that the amount of foreign exchange demanded is what would-be purchasers would want to buy if "not restricted by specially adopted or discretionary government control measures." This may or may not be the most useful definition. There is something to be said against defining away the very possibility of achieving equilibrium by controls. It may be more useful to recognize this possibility and to discuss separately whether or not controls are preferable to other measures.

(though, one suspects, confusion not always unwelcome to authorities with programs to promote) results from not distinguishing sharply between a "program" balance on the one hand and an "accounting" or a "market" imbalance on the other hand. The latter two refer to what has happened or is happening under certain conditions. But the program balance refers to what is supposedly necessary *to meet certain desires*. If the desired foreign aid is not forthcoming to cover a program deficit, then a deficit of that size cannot materialize in reality; it remains an unsatisfied wish. (To point out confused thought is not necessarily, of course, to condemn the programs whose adoption the confusion might possibly serve.)

Measurement of Disequilibrium in the U.S. Balance of Payments

The only purpose of presenting some actual U.S. and Canadian figures in Tables 3.2 and 3.3 was to emphasize and illustrate the concept of a balance of payments and the necessary equality of debit and credit totals. The later historical chapters discuss actual disequilibria of particular countries. Here, though, it is worth noting the measures of disequilibrium suggested by publications of the U.S. Department of Commerce and usually adopted in the financial press. Probably the most usual of them is the difference between credits and debits on account of all transactions except those listed in the "settlement" account of Table 3.2. The U.S. deficit of recent years is considered to have been settled or financed by net losses of gold and other official reserves plus the growth of foreigners' liquid claims on the United States. These include not only bank accounts, short-term securities, and similar quickly cashable claims but also (because of their ready marketability) ordinary U.S. government securities of *all* maturities. Among these below-the-line" items Table 3.2 also includes transactions in nonmarketable, *convertible,* medium-term special securities sold by the government to foreign monetary authorities. If these transactions were put "above the line" instead, along with transactions in the supposedly less

liquid *nonconvertible* special securities, the overall deficit would shrink from $2,660 million to $1,958 million. On the other hand, recognizing that all the special U.S. government transactions were undertaken to accommodate balance-of-payments disequilibrium and putting them all below the line would raise the deficit to $3,301 million. These alternative figures remind us again of the arbitrary element in all concepts of deficit and surplus.

The concepts corresponding to these three alternatives figures share one notable peculiarity.[10] They implicitly suppose that all increases in American claims on foreigners are independently motivated (even U.S. government acquisition of inconvertible foreign currencies paid for farm products sold on these easy terms to foreign countries as a form of aid, or even the private American transfers of funds abroad in the second half of 1960, when one of the motives for these transfers was concern about a possible devaluation of the dollar). The usual concepts also implicitly suppose, in sharp contrast, that foreign short-term claims on the United States grow only by way of compensatory finance for a U.S. deficit. If a foreigner buys a long-term bond of an American *corporation,* the transaction is considered an independently motivated credit in the U.S. balance of payments and therefore the very opposite of something making for a deficit; if the foreigner buys a U.S. *government* bond, however, whose ready marketability makes it count as a short-term instrument however long its maturity, the transaction is counted among the below-the-line credits that settle and measure a U.S. deficit. For another example, suppose that American imports and exports of goods and services are in balance, that no long-term capital movements or unilateral transfers take place, and that the only other transaction during a particular year is an exchange of balances between American and British banks: a bank in London credits a New York bank with a deposit of £1000, while the New York bank,

---

[10] The following paragraphs have been revised and amplified in the light of Walter R. Gardner, "An Exchange-Market Analysis of the U.S. Balance of Payments," IMF *Staff Papers,* VIII, May 1961, pp. 195-211.

in return, credits the London bank with an equivalent deposit of $2,800. Under the usual definition, the United States would have a deficit of $2,800. A later cancellation of both bank accounts would give the United States a surplus. Only the movement of *foreign* funds counts as compensatory finance. Paradoxically, an inflow of private foreign short-term funds, which in itself would tend to strengthen the dollar on the foreign-exchange market, contributes to what settles and measures a U.S. deficit; and an outflow, which in itself would tend to weaken the dollar on the market, contributes to what settles and measures a U.S. surplus.

It is easy to make fun of the Commerce Department definitions but hard to suggest anything unequivocally better. (The concept of *basic deficit,* explained in Chapter 25, was popular for a while as an attempt to get rid of paradoxes in the classification of short-term capital movements.) Something can even be said for the usual definitions, considering that foreign countries use short-term dollar claims as external reserves, whereas only a very small fraction of short-term claims in foreign currencies count as reserves from the American point of view. The usual concepts focus attention on the ratio between U.S. gold reserves and foreign holdings of U.S. government bonds and short-term claims and thus provide some clue to how adequate the reserves would be in meeting some *future* withdrawal of foreign funds. An inflow of short-term funds that matches a deficit on other items in the balance of payments may be cause for concern because it sets the stage for a possible later withdrawal. But if this concern underlies the usual concepts, it is hard to see why foreign holdings of government securities and short-term dollar claims are so sharply distinguished from foreign holdings of corporate stocks and bonds, since efforts to liquidate these and repatriate the proceeds could be just as disruptive. Even more potentially disruptive, because of the much larger amounts of money involved, would be an attempted run out of *American*-owned liquid assets and securities for fear of devaluation of the dollar.

This discussion is simply a reminder that statistical raw material may be arranged in different ways to yield different measures. Deficits and surpluses do not correspond to definite facts objectively existing in the real world and waiting to be described with precision. What they are depends on definitions that economists and statisticians are free to choose as they think best for various purposes. In work with actual figures, hairsplitting and arbitrariness are necessary because the figures do not automatically fall into neat categories according to the motives underlying the transactions. In abstract analysis, however, rough-and-ready concepts of *deficit* and *surplus* usually suffice.

Personal and National Balances of Payments

The analogy between a country and a family can serve again in analyzing equilibrium and disequilibrium. A family enjoys equilibrium in its balance of payments if its spending on goods and services plus its repayment of old loans and its independently motivated lending and investing are just equal to its sales of goods and services plus its independently motivated disinvestment, recovery of loans previously made, and nonstopgap borrowing. As for borrowing, the key distinction is between borrowing judged worth while in its own right (as to buy a house or to finance an education) and borrowing as an emergency expedient to keep abreast of current bills. If the family is covering expenditure beyond its income only by the temporary expedient of cashing its savings bonds, drawing down its bank account, or otherwise using up its liquid assets, or by emergency borrowing, it has a deficit. The opposite imbalance, matched by passive accumulation of cash, bank accounts, and the like, is a surplus. For a family as for a country, the key conceptual distinctions are a bit fuzzy. (One defect in the analogy will prove important in explaining the possibility of national balance-of-payments crises. For a family, decisions to spend beyond current income and to finance this overspending interlock closely. For a country, an official agency may find itself passively supplying foreign exchange to finance an import surplus that it had no direct part in deciding upon. Related

to this contrast is the fact that a country, unlike a family, has an exchange rate to peg,
alter, or leave free.)

A country's surplus or deficit is an aggregate of the separate imbalances of the
various individuals, families, business firms,
banks, foreign-exchange offices, treasuries,
and other private and government institutions
making up the country's economic system. All
of these are represented in Table 3.4 by

Table 3.4. Individual Balances of Payments

Buyers / Sellers	Jones	Brown	Smith	Outside World	Total Sales
Jones		20	25	0	45
Brown	50		30	10	90
Smith	20	40		5	65
Outside World	15	20	10	—	45
Total Purchases	85	80	65	15	245
Surplus (+) or Deficit (−)	−40	+10	0	+30	

Table 3.5. Consolidation of Individual Balances of Payments

Buyers / Sellers	Jones + Brown + Smith	Outside World	Total Sales
Jones + Brown +Smith		15	15
Outside World	45		45
Total Purchases	45	15	60
Surplus (+) or Deficit (−)	−30	+30	

just three men. The numbers show their
transactions among themselves and with outsiders in goods and services and in claims
and investments bought and sold for nonstopgap motives. For example, during the period
covered, Smith buys $25.00 worth of such
things from Jones; Smith sells $5.00 worth to
the outside world; Brown's sales exceed his
purchases by $10.00. Table 3.5 washes out the
three men's transactions with each other and
shows only the group's transactions with the
outside world. The group's balance (−30)
equals the total of the balances of each mem-

ber with all other transactors, fellow-country-
men and outsiders alike (−40, +10, and 0).

The point illustrated is obvious but important. If a country is making purchases and
independently motivated loans, investments,
repayments, and gifts abroad in excess of its
independently motivated transactions in the
opposite direction—if it is resorting to compensatory or stopgap finance—then some of
the economic units composing it must be
doing the same. If all of its units were "operating within their means" (in the sense just
implied by contrast), or if the surpluses of
some just balanced the deficits of others, the
country as a whole could not have an external
deficit.

There should now be no mystery about
what tends to prevent persistent disequilibrium in a country's balance of payments:
individual economic units strive to keep their
own affairs in order. In a country with a
deficit, some economic units must be having
financial troubles. Troubled individuals and
firms will try to expand their sales or cut
their purchases, and some transactions with
the outside world will be affected. Not even
careless spendthrifts can go ever deeper into
debt, if only because their creditors will get
tired of making bad loans.

Any mystery, then, is not about equilibrating tendencies but about how they could fail
as often as they apparently do. Sometimes
the trouble might seem to be the aftermath
of war. Ruritania's industries have been
ruined by the fighting; her import "needs"
are great, her balance-of-payments deficit is unavoidable. But this argument falls into the
"fallacy of misplaced concreteness." Ruritania,
an abstraction, cannot be impoverished; it is
the *Ruritanians* who are impoverished. If they
had used up their external reserves and could
not get help abroad, they could not possibly
keep on running a deficit. They might starve,
but they would starve with their balance of
payments in equilibrium. Foreign aid permits and in a sense *is* their deficit. It is illogical to argue that they should receive aid *because* they have a deficit. Rather, they should
be permitted a deficit because they are impoverished and deserve help in gratitude for
their wartime sacrifices.

The inhabitants of Geneva, as Professor Röpke explains,[11] found themselves comparatively poor at the end of World War II. The League of Nations had been liquidated. Trade with the French hinterland had been impeded. Income from tourists had declined. The inhabitants had suffered losses on their foreign investments. Yet nobody worried about Geneva's balance of payments. Not the city, but rather its inhabitants, had been impoverished. People had to refrain from buying more goods and services than they could afford, and this behavior took care of the city's balance of payments.

This apparent denial of the very possibility of balance-of-payments trouble can be reconciled with experience. A country with a deficit must contain individuals or institutions that are living beyond their means, dissipating their resources in a stopgap way, to a greater extent than others are doing the reverse. Even if the national government were creating money to cover a yawning budget deficit, however, the country as a whole would not necessarily have a balance-of-payments deficit (though it could have if foreigners were acquiring some of the inflated currency, thereby in effect making loans or perhaps ultimately gifts to the inflating government). By inflation, amounting to a tax on money and government securities, the government might be wresting real wealth from the public and forcing it to absorb less than its current production. We must look further for the institution whose deteriorating finances would explain a country's balance-of-payments deficit. This would be the central bank or other official agency selling foreign exchange to peg the rate. If this agency is being

[11] Wilhelm Röpke, *Internationale Ordnung*, Erlenbach-Zürich: Rentsch, 1945, pp. 227-230.

called upon to sell more foreign exchange than is being offered to it—in other words, if it could not replenish its foreign-exchange reserves in a free market at the same price at which it is selling them—this very fact shows that it is dealing in foreign exchange at a below-equilibrium price in home currency. In so doing, it is dissipating its assets—"operating beyond its means"—since only nominally, but not at free-market values, is the home currency it takes in fully worth the foreign exchange it pays out.

Foreign loans or gifts, if obtained, could explain a country's continuing deficit. The argument still stands: a country as a whole can have an external deficit only if individuals and institutions are, on balance, using up assets or going into debt as a stopgap—behaving without ordinary financial prudence. If the country has mere balance-of-payments "trouble" because various *ad hoc* import and exchange controls are suppressing a latent deficit, an exchange-pegging agency is in corresponding trouble. It would be dissipating its assets (or incurring debt to foreigners), were not the controls choking off the demand for the foreign exchange being sold unduly cheap.

As a matter of analysis, though not necessarily as a policy recommendation, it is worth while to remember that a country could avoid balance-of-payments trouble (though not all economic trouble) simply by not having any agency dealing in foreign exchange in ways that ran counter to its own financial self-interest. Either of two extremes would satisfy this condition: complete international monetary unification or complete national monetary independence. These extremes and intermediate arrangements will be considered next.

Monetary Systems and International Adjustment

 4

The 100 Percent Gold Standard

When different countries shared a common monetary system to the fullest conceivable extent, no agency could be dealing in foreign exchange to influence rates because no exchange rates would exist. All members of the system would use the same single kind of money. No national authority could have the slightest independence in creating money and determining the local money supply. Even fractional-reserve banking would be ruled out: no one could issue demand deposits or any other means of payment unless they were backed unit-for-unit by the sole standard money. Monetary unification would thus be even more complete than it is at present between Switzerland and Liechtenstein or among the states of the United States. The sole money might conceivably be fiat money issued by a single international authority, but it is even simpler to suppose that nothing but actual gold serves as a medium of exchange. The system would not really be different, though, if some or all of the money in circulation consisted not of actual gold coins but of more convenient fully backed gold certificates in the form of subsidiary token coins, paper currency, or demand deposits. The total quantity of money would still coincide with the total quantity of monetary gold. In redeeming other kinds of money in gold, a bank or other issuing agency would not be *pegging* them to gold but simply honoring them as claim checks on gold actually held in storage. For the same reason, no issuing agency could ever be in danger of running out of gold reserves.

As a practical matter, such complete monetary unity is of course impossible. It is worth analyzing because of the way it highlights, by contrast, some crucial features of more realistic systems. Under complete unity, each country's money supply—its share of the total quantity of monetary gold in all countries —would be determined solely by the concern of individual persons and institutions not to let their cash balances shrink or expand to sizes that they themselves considered inappropriate to their own circumstances.

Suppose that the Outland demand for Inland goods declines or that some Inland demand switches from domestic to foreign products. Inlanders in the affected export or import-competing industries, with their sales reduced and their cash dwindling, have clear incentives to push their own sales at home and abroad (perhaps by cutting prices) and to retrench on their purchases. They will retrench on buying Outland goods and on buying from fellow Inlanders. These others, also seeing their incomes and cash dwindle, will in turn push their sales and limit their purchases, again partly affecting exports and imports. Individual families and firms have adequate incentives to try to keep solvent and hold enough cash; beyond this, there is no distinct problem for the country as a whole. Of course, the underlying shift of demand away from their products does worsen the Inlanders' terms of trade, but this in an inexorable "real" development, not avoidable by mere financial devices. One of the things Inlanders may economize on in view of their changed circumstances is the holding of cash balances. They will draw down their cash while figuring out how to rearrange their purchases and sales; this is one of their reasons for holding cash in the first place—to have it as a buffer to draw on while making orderly adjustments to changed circumstances. Meanwhile, their own (and the country's) balances of payments are temporarily in deficit. But private incentives effectively limit the size and duration of their deficit. This is one key feature of the 100-percent gold standard.

The same incentives work in the opposite direction to prevent opposite initial changes from causing a troublesome balance-of-payments surplus. Individuals will not accumulate cash without limit.

Fractional Reserves and the Reinforcement of Drains

The automaticity of adjustment under a 100-percent monetary system is easier to understand if we contrast it with a fractional-reserve system. An official agency has issued fiduciary money amounting to several times as much as its gold reserve. Ordinarily it has no trouble honoring the relatively few demands for redemption that actually are made. But now an initial shift in home or foreign demand causes Inlanders to buy more than they sell. They may be willing to pay for excess purchases for a while by drawing down their cash balances. But since Outlanders are not willing to accept final settlement in Inland currency, it must be redeemed in gold. The resulting drain is a bigger fraction of the agency's gold reserves than of the cash balances of individuals. If the gold reserves had amounted to only 10 percent of the total money supply, a drain equaling only 5 percent of this total would amount to fully *half* of the reserves. The drain can pose a serious problem for the agency pegging its monetary liabilities to gold—a serious problem for "the country," as is commonly said. Yet the drain can be so small in relation to cash balances of ordinary Inland money that people are willing to draw their balances down that far and even farther. Since cash balances are swollen with fiduciary money (and since the price level is correspondingly high), a drain of an absolute size (that is, size measured in dollars rather than as a percentage) that might have been ample to make people pull

their expenditures and receipts back into balance under a 100-percent gold standard might not be big enough under the fractional system. An otherwise large enough drain would be too small in relation to all the money pyramided onto a fractional gold base and in relation to the corresponding price level. Partial-reserve money *dilutes* the otherwise adequately corrective cash-balance effect.[1]

The problem is not that the deficit might continue forever. Dwindling cash balances would strengthen people's incentives to retrench on their purchases or push their sales. Unfortunately, adjustment might not be complete before the agency ran out of reserves and had to stop pegging the exchange rate. How can it undo the dilution of the cash-balance effect and make individuals behave so that, as under the 100-percent standard, what is financially sound for themselves is financially sound for itself also? It must make the cash balances of individuals vary not merely by the same absolute amount as its own gold reserve, but by roughly the same *percentage*. Then, since individuals simply will not draw down their cash balances to anywhere near zero, the gold reserve cannot run out either. Complete safety requires complete proportionality. A $1-billion gold drain must make the money supply shink by $2 billion under a 50-percent reserve system, by $10 billion under a 10-percent reserve system, and so forth. This "reinforcement" of the money-supply effects of a gold drain conforms to the so-called "rules of the game" of the fractional-reserve gold standard. (For discussion in a historical context, see Chapter 14.) Reinforcement corrects for the above-mentioned "dilution" inherent in a fractional-reserve system. The country's central bank can contract the money supply by reducing its loans and investments and thus its monetary liabilities; the government can get money out of circulation by collecting taxes in excess of its expenditures.

This centralized reinforcement is not auto-

---

[1] To speak of a cash-balance effect is not to assert that an excess demand for or excess supply of money necessarily has its main impact *directly* in the markets for goods and services. Direct impacts may occur mainly in the markets for securities and other investment assets, with the markets for currently produced goods and services being affected through a chain of repercussions.

matic. To those who are denied loans or loan renewals or government services that they had been counting on or who must pay higher taxes, the deflationary policies must seem arbitrary. Under the 100-percent standard, people see their cash balances shrinking in obvious relation to their increased purchases or reduced sales and independently of any deliberate policy. Under the fractional standard, the shrinkage of cash balances is not in such close and obvious relation to people's own overspending. It comes, instead, from identifiable acts of the monetary or fiscal authorities. Even people not directly affected by the deflationary policies as borrowers or taxpayers are affected indirectly by reduced sales to the first group. In a sense soon to be examined more fully, the reinforcement necessary to safeguard a fractional-reserve standard makes correction of a balance-of-payments deficit objectionably harsh and rapid.

Could the necessary reinforcement work more satisfactorily if the only money issued on a fractional-reserve basis were the demand deposits of private banks? The only reserve requirements might be those that banks themselves individually adopted to compromise prudently between safety and immediate earnings. If depositors demanded gold to pay foreigners for an excess of imports over exports, the banks would have to protect their reserve ratios by shrinking their loans and investments and their deposit liabilities by probably several times as much as their loss of gold reserves. This magnified shrinkage in individuals' cash balances would stop them from overspending before the gold reserves were gone. To persons denied new bank loans and pressed for repayment of old ones, the deflation would seem almost as arbitrary as if it had been imposed by a central authority. The process is more automatic only in minor respects. First, the decisions to deflate are made decentrally, by dozens or hundreds or thousands of individual bankers rather than by a single authority. Secondly, bankers are less likely than an authority to avoid or delay reinforcing the gold drain in hope that the underlying balance-of-payments disturbance will soon reverse itself of its own accord and without corrective action. The individual

banker may not even be aware of the rather indirect connection between the country's balance-of-payments deficit and the drain on his own reserves. In any case, he cannot wait to see how things work out. He must avoid insolvency. If he lags behind other banks in deflating, a disproportionate fraction of the national gold drain will impinge on his reserves. He has no recourse to the controls over trade, the legal suspension of gold payments, and the excuses ultimately available to a governmental authority. The contrast holds for a gold gain, too; while a non-profit-seeking official agency might refrain from expanding its money issues in full proportion, growing excess reserves of unprofitable gold would soon prod a laggard banker into step with a general expansion. But the similarities between systems of officially issued and privately issued fractional-reserve money are normally more basic than the contrasts.

The contrast is greater between 100-percent money on the one hand and fractional-reserve money, by whomever issued, on the other. With 100-percent money, to repeat, the concern of individuals to maintain cash balances that they consider adequate but not excessive in the light of their real incomes and wealth is all that is necessary to avoid national balance-of-payments trouble. Furthermore, cash-balance changes fully sufficient to correct over- or underspending are inseparably linked with that over- or underspending. It is unnecessary to draft innocent parties into the adjustment process, contracting or expanding their cash balances in an apparently arbitrary way by measures of banking or fiscal policy. Adjustment need proceed no faster or more harshly than individuals see fit in the light of their own unmanipulated circumstances.

Offsetting the Impact of Reserve Changes

The 100 percent standard seems appealing because the internal adjustments to an external disturbance of any given size can proceed more impersonally and slowly than under fractional reserves. But even setting aside quibbles about whether "slower" adjustment has a precise and unambiguous meaning, one might ask whether a slower adjustment is necessarily preferable, after all.

If slowing down is always desirable, even apart from detailed knowledge about the particular circumstances, then why aren't 200 percent reserves better than 100 percent, and so on indefinitely?[2] A 200 percent standard would mean a monetary gold stock twice as large as the ordinary money supply. Inflows and outflows of gold would expand and contract the money supply by only half as much. When an export surplus draws in gold, the country's authorities adopt restrictive banking and fiscal policies in order to acquire half of the gold for themselves and cut down the growth of the money supply in the hands of the public. When an import surplus draws gold out, expansionary policies cut down the shrinkage of the money in the hands of the public. The cash-balance incentives for individuals to bring their sales and purchases back into equality are weakened.

In analyzing such policies, it is convenient to recall the term *absorption,* introduced in Chapter 3. It means the total of private and public consumption and capital accumulation in the country. An export surplus of goods and services is the same thing as an excess of the value of current production over the value of current absorption; an import surplus is this difference in reverse. Now, policies that partially offset any addition of gold to the money supply amount to taxing absorption. Open-market sales of securities or other contractionary central-bank operations make credit more expensive and less readily available, while "overcharging" for public services through a government budget surplus is an even more obvious tax on absorption. Credit-cheapening operations and a government budget deficit, conversely, subsidize absorption and put gold into circulation in partial replacement of the outward drain. By operating a 200 percent gold standard, the authorities are apparently not just slowing down the correction of external surpluses and deficits but are eliminating part of the correction.

[2] J. E. Meade, *The Balance of Payments,* London: Oxford University Press, 1951, p. 185, presents the slower-adjustment argument for 100-percent reserves. Milton Friedman, *Essays in Positive Economics,* Chicago: University of Chicago Press, 1953, p. 186, questions the necessary superiority of slower adjustment and mentions the idea of 200-percent reserves.

Actually, this distinction is empty. Over the fullness of time and apart from gifts and loans and so forth, a country's imports and exports, like its absorption and production, must be equal. (Admittedly, authorities may occasionally suffer the embarrassment of running out of fractional reserves.) The policies of alternately taxing and subsidizing absorption under a 200 percent standard keep absorption and production from matching each other as closely in each individual month or year as they otherwise would. The time pattern of absorption is partially smoothed out in the face of fluctuations in production. (These can be fluctuations in the real value of production, corresponding to changes in the terms of trade and caused by changes in supplies and demands, rather than fluctuations in the physical level of output. For that matter, absorption is smoothed out in the face of fluctuations not only in output but also in the *propensity* to absorb.) The authorities accumulate gold reserves when restraining absorption and decumulate gold reserves when subsidizing it. Even under a mere 100 percent standard, some smoothing takes place, but only in accordance with the decisions of private individuals and firms, who use temporary spurts in their real incomes partly to build up cash balances and who draw down their cash balances to maintain absorption when their real incomes slump temporarily. The most obvious conceivable justification for official policies to accomplish still more smoothing—in effect, for building up and drawing down additional reserves *on behalf of* the private economy—is that the authorities either know better how much smoothing is proper or know better what the future holds in store and how likely various developments are to prove temporary.

Perhaps a more realistic reason for *offsetting* the monetary effects and adjustment incentives that gold gains and losses would produce is to save the home economy from disruptive *reinforcement* occurring through the profit-and-safety-motivated decentralized responses of a private banking system. But this danger means that the monetary system was not based on at least 100 percent gold reserves after all. Marginally, however—that is, in the face of gold movements that are small in relation to the total gold reserve—the authorities can operate *as if* they were on a 100-percent-or-more standard: they can keep gold gains and losses from swelling or shrinking the ordinary money supply several times as much or just as much or even at all. The authorities can absorb or disgorge gold, allowing their reserve ratio, even if it is only a fractional ratio, to go up or down. They have comparatively little difficulty absorbing a gold *inflow* by restrictive central-bank and fiscal operations and may have ample motive. Unless it were thus kept out of the reserves of the commercial banks, the new gold would serve as the basis of a multiple bank-credit and bank-deposit expansion. A resulting inflation of prices and money incomes might be unwanted both because of its immediate consequences and because of the difficulties that a gold drain would later involve in view of well-known resistances to downward adjustments in incomes and prices. Contraction imposed by a drain of gold from the reserves of the commercial banks, even when not set against a background of recent inflation, can have unpleasant domestic consequences, and the authorities may well want to offset it by expansionary central-bank and budget operations.[3] They may consider the risk of an excessive drain on their reserves well worth taking in view of the deflationary difficulties thereby avoided, especially if they believe that the underlying balance-of-payments disturbance responsible for the country's gold loss is temporary and likely to reverse itself soon even without any corrective process or action.

The Dilemma of a Fractional-reserve System

This last proviso is important, for the policy just outlined does fully or partially destroy equilibrating incentives. The authorities are in a dilemma under a fractional-reserve system. Suppose they aim at balance-of-payments

equilibrium and so reinforce the monetary impact of gold inflows and outflows, either by themselves creating and destroying fiduciary money or by permitting or causing the banking system to do so. This means using fiscal and banking policies to manipulate the cash balances even of persons who had not been "absorbing" more or less than their incomes. Suppose, on the other hand, that the authorities "offset" domestic monetary responses, impeding external adjustment. A continuing surplus implies taxing away domestic income or wealth to build up gold reserves that hardly represent an attractive national investment in their own right. A continuing deficit endangers the gold reserves and threatens to force departure from the gold standard.

Whatever the authorities do under a fractional-reserve standard, their behavior is incompatible with a fully automatic gold standard. They cannot even pursue a meaningful "passive" policy, for if they neither promote nor prevent certain responses, they at least *permit* responses different from those that would have occurred under a 100-percent standard. "There is . . . a fundamental conflict between the principles of central banking and the principles of the gold standard." "A so-called managed gold standard is . . . not a gold standard at all. . . ."[4]

Further Comparison of 100 Percent and Fractional Standards

The distinctiveness of the 100 percent gold standard does stand up well, after all, despite

---

[3] An "offsetting" policy is not always and necessarily domestically stabilizing; it depends on what the initial disturbance to the balance of payments was. If it was an inflation originating at home, the resulting balance-of-payments deficit would exert deflationary influences as a partial counterweight. Offsetting these deflationary influences would actually mean perpetuating the original inflation.

[4] The two quotations (though not the details of this analysis) are from John H. Williams, *Postwar Monetary Plans and Other Essays,* New York: Knopf, 1944, pp. 183-184, and Frank D. Graham, *Fundamentals of International Monetary Policy,* Essays in International Finance, No. 2, Princeton, N. J.: Princeton University, 1943, p. 12. Williams seems to mean only that passivity or "offsetting" is incompatible with gold-standard principles. Triffin shows that "reinforcement" in accordance with the traditional "rules of the game" is also a great departure from the mechanism of the pure gold standard; see his "National Central Banking and the International Economy" in Lloyd A. Metzler, Robert Triffin, and Gottfried Haberler, *International Monetary Policies,* Postwar Economic Studies, No. 7, Washington: Board of Governors of the Federal Reserve System, 1947, pp. 48-54.

questions whether its supposed superiority over fractional reserves does not imply the still greater superiority of more than 100-percent reserves. It safely allows private parties alone to decide how far to finance temporary imbalances by building up or drawing down their cash reserves. Local money supplies go up or down in each time period only by the absoluate amount of a voluntarily accepted temporary surplus or deficit.[5] And since the world money supply remains constant, with transfers of money between residents of different countries having no basically different impact than transfers between residents of a single country, overall levels of demand do not change, so far as they depend on the quantity of money. The pattern of demand changes as tastes and technology change, of course, and so do relative prices. But even changes in *national* price levels and terms of trade are hardly more than statistical fabrications, less significant than changes in the relative prices paid and received by the particular groups affected by the underlying real changes. The relevant groupings are not mainly by nationality. Even the concept of each country's local money supply is unimportant. The absence of national fractional-reserve system avoids most of the difficulties blamed on the gold standard of historical experience, under which currencies were largely fiduciary and only imperfectly international.

But not even a 100 percent gold standard guarantees completely smooth adjustment to all economic changes. Because of various price inflexibilities and frictional resistances to sudden rearrangements of spending patterns, a sudden shift in demand is likely to impose transitional losses radiating beyond the persons first affected by the underlying changes in tastes or technology.[6] Even within countries, the existence of "depressed areas" illustrates the difficulties of reallocating resources promptly when patterns of demand alter. Perhaps little can be done about these frictions within countries. Internationally, however, any arrangements that could improve effective price flexibility and also preserve balance-of-payments equilibrium without shrinkage in national money supplies should score a point in comparison with even a 100 percent gold standard.

What scores decisively is practical considerations. The 100 percent standard can be nothing more than a theoretical extreme useful for understanding, by comparison, the characteristics of other systems. One difficulty is that its full logic would require all countries to adhere to it. If some countries were on 100-percent and others on fractional reserves, payments disequilibria and gold movements would affect the total world volume of money (gold plus fiduciary money pegged to it). No longer would adjustments take place against the background of an approximately stable average world purchasing power of gold; instead, price levels must change. The burden of making these changes falls unevenly among countries, depending largely on their different gold reserve ratios. Furthermore, the need for larger and more pervasive price changes under mixed standards than under a universal pure gold standard gives more scope for wage and price inflexibilities to make adjustments inefficient and burdensome. In practice, not even a single country can maintain the 100 percent standard, let alone all countries together. Not only central banking but also commercial banking as we know it would have to be suppressed. All the obstacles familiar from discussions of the 100 percent reserve-banking proposal would have to be overcome. The authorities would have to be vigilant against strong private profit incentives to invent money substitutes and devices for "economizing" on money in ingenious new forms as soon as older forms had been suppressed. (Nevertheless, a few economists do argue that the benefits of a 100 percent standard would be worth the efforts necessary to attain and maintain it. Their arguments are summarized in Chapter 28.)

---

[5] This paragraph, as well as almost the entire discussion of 100 per cent versus partial-reserve gold standards, abstracts from new gold production, withdrawal of gold into nonmonetary uses, and secular economic growth.

[6] For hypothetical examples, see Philip H. Wicksteed, *The Common Sense of Political Economy,* London: Macmillan, 1910, p. 643, or Wilhelm Röpke, *Die Lehre von der Wirtschaft,* 4th ed. Erlenbach-Zürich: Rentsch, 1946, pp. 94-96.

Types of Gold and Foreign-exchange Standard

The gold standard of historical experience was a fractional-reserve standard. Various types are distinguishable. Under a *gold-coin standard,* all other kinds of money are convertible on demand into gold coin. The actual circulation of gold coins, together with at least short-run stability in the public's preferred ratio of gold coins to other types of money held, is supposed to provide a fairly stable and not-too-highly geared connection between a country's monetary gold stock and its total money supply. One advantage claimed for this system is that the threat of drains on their gold reserves will restrain the government and the central and commercial banks from following inflationary policies. They must take care not to alarm the man in the street, who, by demanding or not demanding redemption of his money in gold coin, can exercise control over financial policies.

Under a *gold-bullion standard,* the authorities stand ready to buy and sell uncoined gold at a fixed price, but only in large minimum amounts.[7] The absence of gold coins from circulation and the obstacle this poses to redemption and gold hoarding by the ordinary citizen permit "economies" in the use of gold, that is, a smaller and probably more flexible gold reserve ratio.

A *gold-exchange standard* permits still further "economies." The monetary authority of a country ties its currency to gold not directly but by dealing on the foreign-exchange market to maintain a substantially fixed exchange rate with some foreign currency that *is* on a

gold-coin or gold-bullion standard. The authority holds its reserves as bank deposits and other liquid claims in the foreign currency. The opportunity to earn interest is one reason for holding reserves in this form rather than in actual gold. The gold reserves of the country on the actual gold standard—the so-called center country—do double duty: they "back up" its own currency directly and the currencies of one or more "members" of the system at one remove. The total money supplies of the member countries are pyramided onto a smaller and presumably more variable percentage of actual gold than would be in effect if each held its own gold reserve. Still, the authorities of each country must pay some attention to the relative sizes of their monetary liabilities and their foreign-exchange reserves so they can keep domestic money redeemable *de facto* in foreign exchange.

A *foreign-exchange standard* need not be a *gold*-exchange standard: the foreign money held as reserves and to which the home currency is pegged need not be a gold-standard currency, after all. The most notable example is the system maintained by members of the Sterling Area during the 1930s, when the British pound was not linked to gold. As long as a country is anxious to keep its exchange rate fixed, maintain an adequate reserve of foreign exchange in relation to its domestic money supply, and allow gains and losses of foreign exchange to expand and contract the latter, it limits its monetary independence in the same general way as it would under an actual gold standard.

Intermediate positions are conceivable between being on a gold standard and being on an exchange standard. The national monetary authority might hold its reserves partly in gold and partly in foreign currencies tied to gold and deal on the foreign-exchange market to keep the exchange rate so close to par that private gold arbitrageurs would seldom if ever find it worthwhile to operate. Even if the authority stood ready to buy and sell actual gold at a fixed price, it might seldom be called on to do so.

Except for major restrictions on the right of domestic private parties to demand inter-

---

[7] The monetary system of the United States since 1934 is sometimes called a "limited gold bullion standard." The Treasury will buy gold from anyone at $34.9125 per fine ounce and will sell it at $35.0875, but only to licensed industrial users and foreign monetary authorities. Private ownership and export of gold are severely restricted. The total money supply is not geared automatically or even significantly to the gold stock (though in recent years the U.S. government has been deciding its financial policies partly with an eye on its gold losses). The system thus lacks the essential characteristics of a gold standard as it used to be understood, except for the stability of exchange rates with other currencies also defined in gold—and even this stability does not command as much confidence as formerly.

convertibility at a fixed rate between the local currency and either gold or foreign exchange, many countries are on some such intermediate standard nowadays. Practically all members of the International Monetary Fund define their currency units in gold. To maintain its exchange parity, each country must take care not to get too far out of step with monetary conditions and price levels in other countries; yet balance-of-payments surpluses and deficits are not allowed to have any close and automatic effect on domestic money supplies. Today's compromise system is often called a gold-exchange standard, though the little-used term *gold-par standard* seems more descriptive.[8]

There is no clear-cut line between being on and being off a gold or exchange standard. International monetary linkage is a matter of degree, to be judged by how large or small and how variable the ratio is between a country's gold or foreign-exchange reserves and its domestic money supply and by how closely the money supply responds to the balance of payments. The linkage is largely window-dressing if fixed exchange rates are maintained by controls over imports and other expenditures abroad and if the money supply is insulated from balance-of-payments developments.

At the opposite extreme from the 100 percent gold standard stands complete national monetary independence. Each country's money then has its total supply determined solely by domestic considerations, is not pegged to or backed by or redeemable in gold or anything else, and has its rates of exchange against foreign currencies determined by the free play of private supply and demand. As later chapters will try to show, either extreme system may have a logic and coherence not found in any compromise arrangement.

Palliatives of Disequilibrium

Before considering further how balance-of-payments disequilibriums are corrected under different monetary arrangements, we

may mention some temporary *palliatives* of disequilibrium. Most of what is said about a deficit will apply in reverse to a surplus. Most obviously, the authorities can draw upon their external reserves to peg the exchange rate, but perhaps this is less a palliative of a deficit than a means of financing and therefore perpetuating it.

A more genuine palliative operates under an international gold standard of unquestioned permanence. As the foreign-exchange value of the home currency falls near the gold export point, people will realize that depreciation cannot go much further and that if the exchange rate moves at all it must bounce back from the limit. A practically risk-free opportunity prompts speculators to sell foreign exchange and buy the home currency. This "equilibrating" inflow of short-term capital covers the deficit and checks the drain on the gold reserves that would otherwise occur. Speculation is similarly equilibrating even under a nongold foreign-exchange standard when full confidence prevails that the authorities will maintain the pegged exchange rates within narrow predetermined limits.

Speculators respond quite differently when they suspect that the gold parity or the official support limits may collapse. If they see that only the drawing down of limited gold or foreign-exchange reserves is staving off the depreciation of the currency, they will want to get rid of it while it is still enjoying artificial support. An outflow of short-term private capital then compounds instead of palliates the deficit from ordinary transactions.

Palliative, or "equilibrating," speculation is not necessarily confined to a fully trusted gold or exchange standard; it may even occur under freely fluctuating exchange rates. A depreciation that is expected to prove only temporary will attract purchases of the currency—in other words, an inflow of short-term funds that helps cover a temporary deficit. Whether this or destablizing speculation is more likely is an important question for later chapters.

A second genuine palliative involves short-term capital movements motivated by dif-

---

[8] Cf. Henrik Åkerlund, *Guldparistandarden,* Stockholm: Grafiska Konstanstalten Tryckeri, 1959.

ferences in interest rates at home and abroad. A deficit in the goods-and-services account itself suggests that people and institutions of a country are in the aggregate spending beyond their incomes; voluntary domestic saving has fallen short of intended investment. Unless the external deficit is associated with a continuing domestic cheap-money policy, interest rates are likely to rise as a result of an excess demand for loanable funds that would otherwise prevail. Higher interest rates not only keep some short-term funds invested in the country that would otherwise have moved abroad but perhaps even attract some funds from abroad. The authorities of the deficit country may strengthen this automatic palliation by actively promoting a rise in domestic interest rates. Short-term funds are presumably more likely to respond to interest rates in this helpful manner when exchange rates are fixed and trusted than when they are subject to change.

These palliatives can at best provide time for adjustments affecting trade and long-term capital movements; they can hardly stave off the need for adjustments indefinitely. Reserves cannot hold out forever. Speculators will not go on acquiring a weak currency if the causes of its weakness prove more than temporary. Short-term investors will not continue pouring funds into a deficit country in response to a mere interest-rate advantage if a persistent disequilibrium in other transactions threatens the value of its currency.

Balance-of-payments Correctives

There are three ways in which a balance-of-payments disequilibrium can be cured "automatically," that is, without direct orders from some authority but rather through appropriate incentives to private economic units, concerned as they are with their own incomes and cash balances and expenditures.[9] To cor-

rect a deficit (and conversely for a surplus), each of these three involves a fall in the ratio of total home money income to total foreign money income. This ratio is not, of course, an indicator by which persons and firms govern their decisions and actions. Mentioning it is simply a device for organizing a comparison of the three mechanisms: (1) The ratio could conceivably fall without any decline in the physical volume of domestic production and employment; home money income could fall simply through cuts in the prices and wages at which goods and services were valued; (2) Home income and its ratio to foreign income could fall through a shrinkage in the physical volume of goods and services produced, with prices and wages unchanged; and (3) The ratio could fall through a change in the exchange rate used in making home and foreign money incomes comparable. Or the ratio could fall through changes partly in prices, partly in real income, and partly in exchange rates.

Which mechanism or combination of these three mechanisms operates depends on the monetary relations among the various countries. Under a gold standard or a foreign-exchange standard requiring governments to conduct their domestic monetary and fiscal policies so as to keep fixed exchange rates workable without direct controls over international trade and payments, the first and second mechanisms operate together. Their relative importance depends on how frictionlessly price and wage levels adjust up and down. If the countries have independent fiat moneys free to fluctuate against one another, the third mechanism operates. If exchange rates are not free to fluctuate and yet national monetary and fiscal policies do not operate enough in parallel to keep fixed rates workable without controls, the combination of mechanisms at work depends on the exact nature of monetary and fiscal and exchange-rate policies. If these policies prevent any of the three "automatic" mechanisms from operating, direct controls over international trade and payments appear necessary.

---

[9] These three possibilities should perhaps be counted *in addition to* the cash-balance effect, which plays a role in all of them but may deserve mention as a separate corrective mechanism in its own right. The cash-balance effect is discussed in the early pages of this chapter and again in the next chapter.

International Adjustment under Fixed Exchange Rates

 5

This chapter describes balance-of-payments adjustment when national monetary systems are closely linked, though linked less completely than under a 100-percent gold standard. (Adjustment under that standard is too simple to need further explanation.) Several sections of the chapter give attention to aspects of the adjustment process that dominate standard treatments of the topic.

The Price-level Mechanism

Though adjustments involving price levels and production-and-employment levels actually operate together, considering each separately at first will contribute to clarity. In explaining adjustment under the gold standard, economists until the 1930s traditionally emphasized a theory based on the price-specie-flow mechanism of Richard Cantillon and David Hume. Developments making for a deficit in Inland's balance of payments push its exchange rate to the gold export point. Outward gold shipments by arbitrageurs shrink the reserve base and in turn shrink the home money supply. Inland's general price and wage levels fall accordingly. Opposite developments take place in Outland, where a balance-of-payments surplus corresponds to Inland's deficit: gold flows in, the money supply expands, and prices and wages rise.

Since Outland is the entire rest of the world, these effects of trade with Inland will probably be diluted almost to imperceptibility over its entire vast economy. The important thing, however, is that Inland's price level falls and Outland's rises, each *relatively* to the other's. Now consider some Inlanders who have been hesitating between buying certain goods from their fellow Inlanders and importing similar goods from Outland. The relative cheapening of Inland goods will tip their decisions in favor of *not* importing. Similarly, Outlanders will have reason to buy the relatively cheapened Inland goods.

How sensitively these responses to price occur depends on how closely substitutable for each other Inland and Outland goods are in the minds of consumers in both countries and how readily factors of production in each country can shift from one line of production into another. These conditions of substitutability in consumption and production underlie the elasticities of import and export supply and demand. To understand why proper operation of the gold-flow and price-level mechanism depends on high enough elasticities, let us consider the most unfavorable case conceivable. Both demand elasticities are zero: Inlanders will buy a certain physical quantity of imports and Outlanders will buy a certain physical quantity of Inland's exports, no more and no less, regardless of price. Now, when the gold drain lowers the prices of Inland goods (and their prices go down in terms of both Inland and Outland money, since both moneys are tied to gold), Inlanders will receive a smaller total amount of money than before for their physically unchanged exports. Furthermore, Inland's total expenditure on its imports of Outland goods rises slightly, since the physical volume of trade remains unchanged and the expansion of Outland's money supply raises Outland prices slightly. The worsened balance-of-payments deficit results in bigger gold flows, greater price deflation in Inland and inflation in Outland, more of the perverse response that brings a still bigger disequilibrium, and so on in a vicious circle. And this perverse result could still occur even if export and import quantities did respond to price in the normal way to *some* extent, provided this response was very slight. This perversity could not last indefinitely, however: the limited sizes of their incomes and their concern not to let their cash balances fall dangerously low would ultimately *make* Inlanders behave with enough price-sensitivity to assure a normal corrective effect. The bothersome question under a fractional-reserve standard (but not under a 100-percent standard) is whether the monetary authority might not run out of gold reserves before Inlanders had finished drawing down their cash balances to the extent they individually saw fit.

Sufficient price-elasticity of demand makes the adjustment successful rather than perverse. Even though the price per unit of Inland's imports rises slightly because gold gains have increased Outland's money supply and prices, imports might fall enough in quantity to reduce their total money value. And even though the price per unit of Inland's exports falls, exports might rise enough in quantity to increase their total money value. One or both of these adjustments must occur. Just how much demand elasticity is "enough" is a complicated matter and will be considered in Chapter 8 in connection with the effectiveness of exchange-rate variation. There we shall see that the requirements for normal balance-of-payments adjustment are not very stringent and are almost certain to be satisfied in reality. The theory of unduly low elasticities is mentioned here only as a basis for emphasizing later on how similar the gold standard and variable exchange rates are in this respect: it is not the exchange-rate mechanism alone whose proper working depends on high enough demand elasticities.

The Role of Cash-balance Management

Our example of what happens to countries' general price levels, while illuminating in a preliminary way, is crude. The relative shift in national price levels is not the only influence to motivate the appropriate shift in flows of trade: a more direct influence is the monetary developments to which the shift in price levels is itself a response. In the gold-losing deficit country, the cash balances of individuals and business firms shrink. They become and remain smaller than before not only in nominal money amount but also in terms of real purchasing power, at least until (and probably even after[1]) prices and wages have fully responded to the monetary deflation. Out of concern not to let their cash balances shrink too far, people in the deficit country become less eager than before to buy capital assets and consumption goods alike. Decisions about buying and selling and managing cash balances interlock. It is strange that this adjustment effect should have been so widely overlooked even in the traditional analysis relying on the quantity theory of money; for anything better than a purely mechanical version of the quantity theory must emphasize how the money supply interacts with demands for cash balances so as to affect people's market behavior and *thereby* —rather than in some direct magical way— affect prices. This "absorption"-depressing cash-balance effect is part of the answer to the skeptical question sometimes asked: How can mere changes in price levels correct a country's tendency, evidenced by its external deficit, to consume and invest in overall excess of its current production?

This effect need not be entirely lost even if a palliative inflow of short-term capital postpones a gold outflow. For Inland cash balances may go into the possession of speculators motivated by confidence that Inland's

---

[1] In the new position, with the price level reduced and balance-of-payments equilibrium restored in the former deficit country, individuals and businesses, from their own points of view, find their real incomes smaller than they were while the deficit was furnishing a net inflow of desired goods and services. The drawing down of the country's gold reserves in paying for this net inflow had represented a kind of subsidy to the incomes or absorption of individual economic units. Its discontinuance now represents a fall in real incomes from private points of view, tending to deter people from as much consumption and investment—and as much holding of real cash balances—as before. Later pages and chapters give further explanation.

currency will rebound from the gold export point. Ordinary persons and businesses in Inland still see their own cash dwindling as they spend in excess of their incomes, and this gives them incentives to retrench on consumption and investment. The resulting decline in spending accompanies a decline in the money supply available to ordinary Inland residents or—which is the same thing here—a decline in the average velocity of the entire Inland money supply held by all holders (since the balances acquired by speculators presumably have an unusually low velocity). This cash-balance effect probably imposes less correction of Inland's balance of payments than a gold outflow would, however, since the palliative inflow of short-term capital postpones or avoids the multiple contraction of currency and deposits that a drain of gold reserves would otherwise have imposed on a fractional-reserve monetary and banking system.

Adjustments in Relative Prices and in Subsidization

Besides the cash-balance effect and movements of general price levels, shifts in *relative* prices also tend to restrain absorption in the deficit country. Our preliminary assumption that export prices fall and rise along with general price levels in the deficit and surplus countries is an oversimplification. The prices of each country's imports and exports —the very prices supposed to be decisive in adjusting flows of trade—tend to move by smaller percentages than countries' general price levels because they are determined by supplies and demands on the world market rather than by money supplies of individual countries. The monetary contraction in a gold-losing deficit country does not lower all prices in the same proportion. The relevant distinction is between international goods and services, which are imported and exported, and domestic goods and services, like houses and haircuts and labor, which do not typically move in international trade. Of course, the dividing line is fuzzy and shiftable: even local services can be "exported" by sale to visiting foreigners, and large enough spreads between foreign and domestic prices could motivate trade in goods ordinarily too bulky in relation to value. Still, the distinction is meaningful. As for the goods belonging most fully to the "international" category, their prices are determined largely by worldwide supply and demand and are not much affected by monetary contraction in the gold-losing deficit country. Monetary contraction there has its main impact, instead, on prices of domestic goods and factors of production.

Because domestic goods become relatively cheaper, Inlanders have reason to shift their buying away from imports and exportable goods onto domestic goods and to concentrate their production and sales efforts on the more favorable foreign market. Corresponding but opposite price shifts and incentives in Outland may slightly reinforce the balance-of-payments adjustment. These substitution effects are important and deserve attention far out of proportion to the space needed to state them.

Among the most "domestic" of a country's noninternational goods and services are labor, land, and other factors of production. Wage rates, land rents, and other factor prices fall as gold losses deflate the money supply of a deficit country,[2] while prices of international goods fall little if at all. This implies a fall in the real purchasing power of productive factors and in the real incomes of their owners. Their worsened situation joins with and perhaps even overshadows the cash-balance effect already mentioned in restraining overabsorption. Neither this change nor the response of individuals in reducing their consumption and investment necessarily means that overall production and employment drop. Nor is the change identical to a worsening of the terms of trade in the ordinary sense of the ratio of export to import prices.

The fall in the real value of individuals' incomes in the adjustment process may be traced to discontinuance of what had amounted to a subsidy. This subsidy is best

---

[2] If frictions keep factor prices from responding to monetary deflation, unemployment develops and real-income aspects of balance-of-payments adjustment come into play.

explained with examples of the sort of disturbance that might have originally caused a deficit in Inland's balance of payments. Consider first a "real" (as distinguished from a monetary) disturbance: the world demand for Inland's exports declines because of changes in tastes or technology or in competition from other suppliers. (A depression in Outland would also count as a real disturbance from Inland's point of view; the unemployment and the drop in production make Outland a less effectively eager trading partner. This is true even though the depression in Outland stemmed from monetary causes there.) The consequent worsening of the terms of trade is quite the same for Inland as a deterioration in technology: the process of converting Inland factors into Inland exports and then into imports from Outland now gives a reduced "yield." Inevitably, Inland's real national income has fallen. Yet this fact escapes being fully brought to bear on the decisions of individuals and businesses as long as corrective tendencies are somehow kept from working (in particular, as long as domestic factor prices do not fall relative to international-goods prices in the way just described) and as long as shipments of gold abroad continue to pay for imports in excess of the value of exports. In effect, sale of gold from the reserves at a fixed price too low to equate private supply and demand subsidizes the incomes of and absorption by individuals and businesses. The fall in factor prices relative to international-goods prices, when it finally occurs as the domestic money supply shrinks, represents an offset to or a discontinuation of this subsidy. The country's worsened real economic position comes to bear on the decisions of individual economic units. The unchanged price of gold again becomes an equilibrium price. The overabsorption that constituted the external deficit is restrained and the gold shipments that had been associated with the income subsidy shrink or cease.

One related development also offsets the subsidy represented by gold outflows in the face of not-yet-adjusted price relations. This offset is the very process of reinforcing the monetary contraction imposed by gold losses under a fractional-reserve standard. In the process of getting more money out of circulation, credit becomes more expensive and less readily available, or a government budget surplus overcharges the public for government services. These policies impede absorption. They need not continue or be pushed further after they have ended the subsidy to absorption by raising the equilibrium value of the currency up to its pegged level.

Next consider a monetary (rather than real) disturbance to balance-of-payments equilibrium—monetary inflation in Inland. If the money supply expands through a government budget deficit, undercharging the public for government services subsidizes absorption. So does putting new money into circulation by making credit artificially cheap and abundant. The rise in the money supply also directly stimulates absorption. Since under fixed exchange rates the domestic monetary inflation has a lesser upward impact on the prices of goods and services supplied and demanded in world markets than on the prices of domestic goods and services, the real incomes of workers and other owners of factors of production rise. Although the real economic position of the country as a whole has not improved (except perhaps to a minor extent through improved terms of trade), the positions of individual economic units have improved because their incomes and absorption are being subsidized by sale at a bargain price of gold from the official reserves.

Any correction of the resulting overabsorption and balance-of-payments deficit involves bringing to the attention of the decision-making economic units the fact that the country's real economic position has *not* improved. The disinflation imposed by gold losses reverses the subsidization of incomes and absorption just described. In particular, the lowering of the temporarily increased prices of domestic factors of production, relative to the prices of internationally traded goods, brings the real incomes of owners of productive factors back into correspondence with the real economic position of the country. (In so far as factor prices are on a ratchet and will not fall again once they have risen, unemployment develops; and a fall in employment and in real income produced comes to the aid of balance-of-payments adjustment in the unpleasant manner still to be described.)

Real and monetary disturbances to the balance of payments require comparison. A failure of cash balances and the ratio of domestic factor prices to international-goods prices to go down in response to a real disturbance, together with the drain on gold reserves, subsidizes the *maintenance* of previous levels of absorption despite real economic deterioration from the national point of view.[3] When domestic monetary inflation expands cash balances and raises the ratio of domestic factor prices to international-goods prices, a failure of these changes to reverse themselves, together with gold outflows, subsidizes an increase in absorption, even though the country's real economic position has not improved. The actual mechanism of balance-of-payments adjustment—money-supply shrinkage and a fall of domestic factor prices relative to international-goods prices—remedies either of these failures.

The Income Mechanism

In the 1920s Professor Frank Taussig and some of his graduate students at Harvard studied historical examples of balance-of-payments adjustment under the gold standard before World War I. The process seemed to have worked surprisingly well—too well and too promptly for traditional theory to explain everything. Traditional theory, as usually presented, had emphasized gold flows and price-level shifts in the light of too mechanical a version of the quantity theory;

it had not adequately shown the role of cash-balance or purchasing-power effects on consumption and investment. In reality, Taussig and his students sometimes found disturbances met without appreciable gold flows and price shifts.[4] Of course, to the very extent that trade did respond sensitively and promptly to even slight changes in cash balances and prices, no sizable disequilibrium would develop in the first place and no conspicuous gold flows and price shifts would be necessary. But this did not seem to be the full explanation. Some unknown equilibrating mechanism also must have been at work. But what? The application of modern income theory to international trade, following publication of Keynes's *General Theory of Employment, Interest and Money* in 1936, helped solve Taussig's puzzle.[5] Ironically

---

[3] A long-term independently motivated capital outflow is an example of a real disturbance. It is true that this response to attractive investment opportunities abroad does not spell a worsening of the country's real economic position, but the quantity of resources available for *current* absorption at home is reduced. This fact must be brought to bear on the decisions of individual economic units, and absorption must not be subsidized, if the country is to escape an overall balance-of-payments deficit. Independently motivated capital movements are the most typical examples in the literature of balance-of-payments disturbances; but here, adjustment to them is considered separately in the appendix.

[4] See F. W. Taussig, *International Trade,* New York: Macmillan, 1927, pp. 239-244, 260-262; and Harry D. White, *The French International Accounts 1880–1913,* Cambridge: Harvard University Press, 1933, esp. chap. 1, which reviews several earlier studies. While not rejecting the classical mechanism of gold flows and sectional price adjustments, White was more inclined to stress that international transfers of purchasing power and consequent shifts in demand schedules could take place without large net shipments of gold. His purchasing-power-transfer and demand-shift effect seems loosely related to the cash-balance effect of the present chapter.

[5] A recent commentator on the "smoothness of the transfer process under the gold standard that puzzled Taussig and his students" argues that variations in employment and real income of the sort envisaged in Keynesian theory could not have played an important role; these variations were not large, and their effects could have operated only with too much delay. Nor could price effects have accomplished the necessary variations in real absorption relative to real income at substantially full employment. The smooth adjustments historically experienced must have been due to the influence on total absorption of interest-rate changes (upward in deficit and downward in surplus countries). Saving and investment must be (or, in the days of the gold standard, must have been) sufficiently responsive to interest rates in the ways supposed by classical theory. (As for actual gold movements, they were supposedly kept small by equilibrating speculation based on confidence in the existing gold parities.) See Egon Sohmen, *Flexible Exchange Rates: Theory and Controversy,* University of Chicago Press, 1961, pp. 35-38, 60-64.

Especially in the light of how casual the evidence offered is, Sohmen's emphasis on interest rates as the key element in the adjustment process seems strained indeed. The present text puts the emphasis, instead, on interrelations between cash balances and propensities to save or spend and on the role of prices and exchange rates in conveying to individual economic units right or wrong information about the sizes of real incomes

enough, this neo-Keynesian theory of international adjustment is more relevant to the pre-1914 era of close international monetary linkage than to the era of independent national full-employment policies that has followed its own development. Still, the theory holds an important place in present-day literature, affords valuable insights, if only partial ones, and is definitely worth considering at length.

For a preliminary view of the income-adjustment mechanism, consider a disturbance to the trade of New England, whose monetary system is of course tied to that of the rest of the United States. Whether competition from other sources has weakened the outside demand for New England textiles or New Englanders themselves have switched some purchases from local to outside goods does not much affect the example: in either case, a slump in the demand for local goods causes a deficit in the region's balance of payments. Businessmen and workers who had been making these goods now find their profits and wages smaller than before. Production and employment decline. Those who first suffer drops in income now must cut back their spending on goods and services, causing a second "round" of New Englanders to lose sales and jobs, profits and wages. As poverty spreads, New Englanders cut their purchases not only of each other's goods and services but also, incidentally, of imports from outside the region. This cut in imports in response to a fall in income reduces the deficit by partially matching or offsetting the initial export slump or import spurt.

An initial disturbance in the opposite direction causes an external surplus and touches off a chain reaction of rising production, employment, profits, and wages. (For real income to rise in this way, some labor and resources must have previously been idle, available to meet demands for increased output.) Prosperity spreads as New Englanders

buy more than before of each other's goods and services. Incidentally they also tend to buy more from outside the region, thus partially correcting the balance-of-payments surplus.

A Quick Review of Income Theory for a Closed Economy

To prepare for a closer look at how home income and foreign trade interact, we shall review in a simplified way the Keynesian theory of income determination in a closed economy. Persons earn income by selling labor and other productive factors. The demand for these factors depends on a flow of spending to buy the goods and services made from them. Incomes thus arise from spending and at the same time are the main source of people's spending. The two big categories of private spending are *consumption* and *investment*. (*Investment* means purchases not of stocks and bonds but of newly produced capital goods and inventories.) *Saving* is defined as the difference between income and consumption. Considering how much of their incomes people save is an indirect but convenient way to consider how much they consume. We can focus attention on the relation between saving and investment (rather than on the total of consumption plus investment). Saving is a "leakage" from the stream of spending and income; it may or may not be matched by an "injection" of investment spending.

Private saving and investment are not the only types of leakage and injection. We can conveniently regard government tax collections in excess of government spending as a leakage from the spending stream and thus as a kind of saving; government spending in excess of tax collections is an injection into the spending stream and in that sense is a kind of investment. (Government spending covered by taxes is neither leakage nor injection but a part of the main spending stream, a kind of government consumption on behalf of the taxpayers.) This simplifying dodge yields the following definitions, which will be understood in what follows:

---

out of which absorption may be undertaken. In this view, any effective adjustment process or policy works by correcting prices that initially convey incorrect information. The exposition in the text can hardly help reflecting the misunderstandings and lack of consensus that still prevail among economists.

Saving = amount of private after-tax income not spent on consumption

+ the government budget surplus (if any);

Investment = expenditure to build private capital goods, inventories, etc.,
+ the government budget deficit (if any)

Expenditure generates money income, but income may be less or more than fully re-spent. Saving is a gap between income and consumption that needs to be closed, as by investment in newly produced capital goods. Intended investment (also called *voluntary* or *planned* or *scheduled investment*) may either less or more than fully fill the gap of intended (voluntary, planned, or scheduled) saving, since different groups of people generally make investment and saving decisions. An excess of intended saving over intended investment depresses production and employment. An excess of investment over saving expands production and employment if idle resources provide scope for this expansion (and also inflates prices, especially if "full employment" has already been reached). When intended saving and intended investment are equal, money income is in equilibrium.

Given the existing level of prices and wages, some level of money national income is just high enough but not too high to support full employment and full-capacity production. There is no automatic tendency, however, for saving and investment to be equal at just this right level of money income. Adjustments in interest rates, for instance, do not automatically keep saving and investment equal at the ideal level of income. (Even if interest rates did keep the amounts of loans supplied and demanded equal, this would not be the same as keeping saving and investment equal. Saving is not necessarily a supply of loans: for instance, savers may hoard some of their savings. Investment is not necessarily a demand to borrow savings; it may be financed, for instance, out of accumulated holdings of money or with newly created money.)

Although there is no automatic tendency for saving and investment to be kept equal at the level of national money income that

is just right for full employment at the existing level of prices and wages,[6] there is *some* tendency for saving and investment to become equal. They are made equal not so much by changes in the level of interest rates as by changes in the level of income itself. The explanation hinges on Keynes's "fundamental psychological law": the marginal propensity to consume is less than 1. In plain English, consumption does not ordinarily change by the full dollar amount of a change in income, i.e., people save more dollars out of a large income than out of a small income. If saving is greater than investment, income falls. In accordance with Keynes's "law," people reduce their saving. Eventually it no longer exceeds investment. Now suppose the reverse: Investment exceeds saving. Income rises. Eventually the rise of income to its equilibrium level raises saving to equality with investment.[7] The equilibrium level is not necessarily ideal. It may be too low to employ all willing workers and buy all potential output at prevailing wages and prices. On the other hand, it may be so high that reaching it involves price inflation.

In the elementary Keynesian theory re-

---

[6] This proviso is crucial to getting the analysis straight (as distinguished from deriving policy recommendations). It is now generally recognized that the so-called Keynesian underemployment equilibrium depends on downward rigidities in prices and wages. Without them, not even the famous "liquidity trap" could cause underemployment equilibrium.

[7] The reader to whom this is not thoroughly familiar may benefit by constructing a numerical example. Prepare a table with columns headed Income, Consumption, Saving, Investment, and Consumption + Investment. (Leave space at the right for adding two more columns later.) In the Income column, write figures of 20, 50, 80, 110, and so on, standing for billions of dollars a year. To represent the Keynesian assumption that consumption depends on income in a fairly definite way and changes by less than the full amount of any change in income, write 50 for consumption out of income of 50 and make consumption larger or smaller by 20 for every increase or decrease of income by 30. Saving, being income minus consumption and thus changing by one-third as much as any change in income, is −10 at income of 20, 40 at income of 170, and so on. Assume that investment is given at 30 and write this figure in each position down the investment column. Finally, fill in the Consumption + Investment column. Observe that saving equals investment and consumption plus investment equals income only at the income level of 140. Discrepancies at any other level tend to drive income toward this equilibrium level.

viewed here, investment, unlike consumption and saving, does not depend on income in any fairly definite way. Technological innovations, businessmen's expectations and moods, interest rates, and other influences affect it. Government deficit spending counts as what Sir Dennis Robertson called "honorary" investment. Suppose investment rises by $40 billion a year above its previous level, while the consumption-income relation is such that consumption changes by $\frac{2}{3}$ and saving by $\frac{1}{3}$ of any change in income. Saving will rise by $40 billion and thus match the increased investment only if income rises by 3 times as much, or by $120 billion.[8] Until income has risen to its new equilibrium level, an excess of investment over saving will keep driving it up. The change in investment thus has a multiple effect on income. Soon we shall extend this principle of the *multiplier* to cover the effects of changes in imports and exports.

Meanwhile, a more intuitive grasp of what the multiplier means will be helpful. Suppose that investment rises to a sustained level of $1000 per time period more than before; perhaps the government is deficit-spending on new defense programs. Suppose, also, that people in general save $\frac{1}{10}$ and consume $\frac{9}{10}$ of any increase in their incomes. Now, a first round of people—construction workers, owners of companies supplying construction materials or ordnance, etc.—have $1000 of extra income in all. These first-round people spend an extra $900 on consumption, providing extra income for a second round of people—grocers, tailors, etc. These second-round people spend an extra $810 on consumption, providing extra income for a third round of people, and so on. Each figure in the series of extra incomes is $\frac{9}{10}$ of the figure before it. Ultimately the total of extra incomes would be $10,000. (Carrying this

arithmetic into a great many rounds will bring the total as close as one pleases to $10,000, without ever exceeding it.) Since an initial addition of $1000 to the rate of spending per time period ultimately gives rise to $10,000 of additional income, the multiplier is said to be 10.[9]

These examples show that the greater the respending on consumption and the smaller the leakage into saving at each round of income, the greater the ultimate effect of an initial increase in spending will be. The multiplier works in the downward direction, too. Suppose there is an initial drop in investment. To arrive at a new equilibrium, saving will have to fall by the same amount; and since changes in saving are only a fraction of any changes in income, income must fall by several times as much as the fall in saving and investment.

Our examples have supposed that investment (including government deficit spending) is what initially changes to touch off the multiplier process. Keynesian theory does often suppose that investment is the type of spending most subject to independent change, while consumption depends passively on income. However, if independent changes in consumption did occur—if the consumption-income relation changed in such a way that consumption would be $10 billion more or less than before, for instance, at any given level of income—then these changes would have multiplier effects of the sort already described.[10]

---

[8] To complete the example of the last footnote, add an Increased Investment column with figures of 70 all the way down. In a Consumption + Increased Investment column, add this 70 to whatever consumption still would be at each level of income. Note that saving equals increased investment and consumption + increased investment equals income only at income of 260. At any other level, discrepancies drive income towards this new equilibrium. The rise of income by 120 (from its old level of 140) is 3 times as large as the increase of investment by 40 (from its old level of 30).

[9] This example assumes that the initial increase in spending is an increase in the *flow:* spending is a certain amount higher than before in *each* of the time periods to which the figures relate. As a result, the total increase in the flow of income equals the initial increase in the flow of spending multiplied by the Multiplier. On the other hand, if the initial increase in spending is a one-shot dose, not repeated in later time periods, income at first spurts up by the amount of this dose and then gradually drops back to the original level. In the meanwhile, income is larger than it otherwise would have been; and over time these dwindling increments to what income would otherwise have been add up to the initial shot of extra spending multiplied by the Multiplier. This standard Keynesian conclusion depends, incidentally, on slurring over what is happening to the quantity and circulation of money.

[10] Recall that for the sake of simplicity we have been regarding tax-financed government spending as a kind of consumption, a government budget surplus as a kind of saving, and a government budget deficit as a kind of

While it is true that an initial rise or fall in a particular type of spending will typically raise or lower income by more than its own amount, the apparent precision of the multiplier analysis is deceptive. Gardner Ackley offers an analogy concerning the number of students in his national-income course. If the "marginal propensity of men to enroll" is ⅗—if, from one year to the next, the increase in men's enrollment is ⅗ of the increase in total enrollment—then the increase in total enrollment is 2½ times the increase in women's enrollment. The "sex multiplier" is 2½.[11] A less pretentious way of considering what multiplier analysis deals with is to recognize that an initial increase in spending either brings new money into circulation or speeds up the circulation of existing money and will ultimately raise total money income by perhaps several times its own amount. Money is continually spent and respent. Conversely, an initial decline in spending either takes money out of circulation or slows velocity down and will ultimately reduce total money income by perhaps several times its own amount, since the money would otherwise have kept getting spent and respent.

---

investment. From this one might think that an increase in government spending cannot raise income if it is financed entirely by increased tax collections and therefore produces no government deficit to count as a kind of Investment. But this conclusion would be wrong. The part of private incomes that the government taxes away and spends itself is *entirely* spent on what has been defined as a type of consumption, whereas the part of private incomes not taxed away is partly saved and only partly spent on consumption. Therefore, an increase in tax-financed government spending means an increase in the part of incomes that is *entirely* rather than only partly spent on consumption and so means an upward shift in the relation of total consumption to total income. The result is a rise in the equilibrium level of income. This effect could be illustrated by systematically raising the consumption figures and lowering the saving figures in the table referred to in footnotes 7 and 8. Conversely, a drop in government spending exactly matched by a drop in tax collections can lead to a lower equilibrium level of income, even though no government budget surplus appears. An extensive literature on the "balanced-budget multiplier" explores these effects in detail. The reasons why this principle does not necessarily provide an argument for ever larger government budgets (or against cutting the budget if the Russian menace ever somehow vanished) should be too obvious to dwell on.

[11] Gardner Ackley, *Macroeconomic Theory*, New York: Macmillan, 1961, pp. 309-312.

Income Effects and International Trade

Imports and exports now enter the analysis. Spending on imports, like saving, is something "done with" income that does not, by itself, maintain the continued flow of spending and income at home. Spending on imports does provide a demand for goods and services and in turn for labor and other factors of production—but for *foreign*, not domestic, factors (at least not directly). Imports are indeed a leakage from the domestic income stream. Exports, like investment, are an injection: they represent spending on domestic goods and services and so are a source of income for domestic factors of production that does not proceed from domestic income. In what follows, then, leakages include imports as well as saving (including any government budget surplus), and injections include exports as well as investment (including any government budget deficit).

Suppose that Inland's income is in equilibrium: total injections equal total leakages. The balance of payments is also in equilibrium. Now an autonomous increase in exports disturbs this twofold equilibrium; that is, exports per time period rise because of some change occurring independently of income-and-expenditure or other relationships built into the theoretical model. Perhaps Outlanders' tastes shift in favor of Inland goods; perhaps the Outland government cuts tariffs. Even a business boom in Outland would be an autonomous stimulus to exports from Inland's point of view. Anyway, the injections into Inland's home income stream now exceed the leakages from it. Income rises. Producers of exports do more spending out of their increased incomes, including more spending on domestic goods and services, which provides more income for additional "rounds" of Inlanders. The export boom multiplies Inland income.

Inlanders can afford not only to spend more than before on domestic goods and services but also to do more importing and saving. These leakages rise until they reach the increased level of injections. Inland income rises by more than the amount of the new export injections because people spend much or most of all additional income on domestic goods and services; only part of any additional income goes for additional imports and saving. Suppose that an autonomous increase in exports provides $100 per time period of additional injections, which must be matched by additional leakage to restore income equilibrium; and suppose that people will use one-third of any additional income for additional saving plus importing. The necessary $100 of additional leakage is one-third of $300, which is therefore the amount by which income must increase to arrive at its new equilibrium level. An additional $100 of exports brings about 3 times as large a rise in income.

What happens if injections initially come to exceed leakages not because of an increase in exports but because of an autonomous cut in imports (perhaps due to Inland's imposition of a tariff)? Some spending that used to leak out of the home income stream to buy imports now goes toward home goods and services instead. Inlanders producing replacements for imports enjoy increased incomes; and they can afford to spend more for consumption, providing additional income for still further "rounds" of Inlanders. The initial excess of injections over leakages thus makes income rise. Since total leakages must rise until they again equal total injections and since probably only a fraction of additional

income goes into leakages, the rise in income may be several times as large as the initial excess of injections over leakages. Again a foreign-trade multiplier is at work.[12]

The last example has a bothersome complication: the initial *cut* in imports generates a rise in income, which in turn generates a rise in leakages, including imports. Which really occurs—a cut or a rise in imports? The answer is that the autonomous cut in imports is partly offset by an income-induced *tendency* for imports to rise. The rise in income makes imports rise *relative to what they would have been* if the new tariff had been the only influence at work. Figure 5.1 shows a continuing surplus of the unchanged exports over the reduced imports; the effect of increased income on imports goes only part-way toward maintaining balance-of-payments equilibrium. This outcome is based on plausible assumptions. In particular, imports are not the only leakage: saving also rises with income. At the new equilibrium level of

---

[12] The fact that a new tariff or other import controls may lead to a rise in home income is hardly an argument for these controls or hardly a refutation of the traditional analysis of protective tariffs. A rise in *money* income may represent mere price inflation rather than a rise in real production. But even if unemployment and underproduction had been prevailing, the question remains whether import restrictions are the best remedy. There are several reasons for doubt—in particular, the availability of more direct ways of providing enough effective demand for full employment.

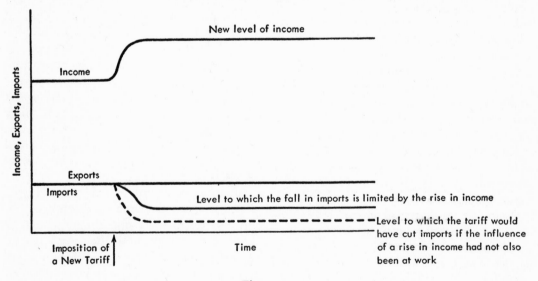

Figure 5.1.

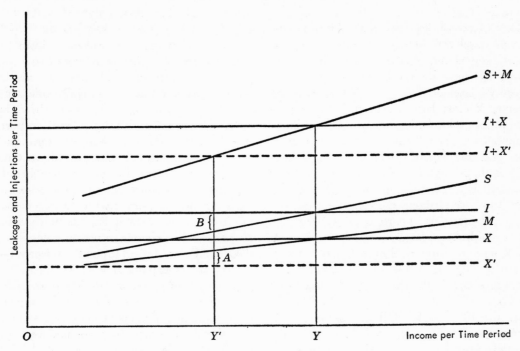

Figure 5.2. An Autonomous Fall in Exports

income, the injection represented by an excess of exports over imports is matched by a leakage in the form of an excess of domestic saving over domestic investment. Because changes in total leakage are made up only partly of changes in imports (changes in saving being another part), income effects considered alone (separate, for instance, from changes in cash balances and prices) are unlikely to do the full job of maintaining balance-of-payments equilibrium. This incompleteness of adjustment will have to be considered more fully later on.

The foreign trade multiplier can lower as well as raise domestic income. An autonomous fall in exports or rise in imports makes injections fall short of leakages. Income falls until it has dragged leakages down to the level of injections. Since only a fraction of income leaks into saving and imports, income will have to fall by more than the amount of the necessary fall in leakages.

Figure 5.2 illustrates all this. It shows Inland's investment, exports, saving, and imports (measured vertically) in relation to the level of home income (measured horizontally). The horizontal lines for investment and exports show the preliminary

assumption that these two quantities are determined by influences outside the model and not by the level of home income. The height of the $I + X$ line, representing total injections, is the combined height of the I and X lines. The lines for saving and imports slope upward from left to right in such a way as to show that of any increase in income, part—but only part—goes for additional saving and additional imports (and the rest, presumably the bulk, goes for additional consumption of domestic goods and services); similarly, when income drops, part but only part of the necessary cutbacks are in saving and imports (and the rest of the economizing is done on domestic consumption). The $S + M$ line is the vertical summation of the saving and import lines.

Originally, income is in equilibrium at the level OY, where the intersection of the $I + X$ and $S + M$ lines shows injections and leakages equal. The balance of payments is also in equilibrium, as shown by the intersection of the X and M lines. Now exports fall autonomously to the level shown by the dotted line X'. Correspondingly, there is a new and lower total-injection line $I + X'$. As long as the level of income has not yet fallen, total injections are now less than total leakages. This excess of leakages makes income fall to the level OY', where, as shown by movement down and leftward along the $S + M$ line, leakages are finally cut down to the reduced level of injections. The drop in income, $Y'Y$, is larger than the autonomous drop in exports, illustrating the multiplier. Imports do not fall fully as much as exports because only part of the reduction in leakage takes the form of a reduction in imports; the rest is a reduction in saving. The bracketed distance A shows the continuing though reduced excess of imports over exports. This excess of leakages from income over injections into income through international trade is matched by an excess of investment over saving domestically, shown by the bracketed distance B. Under the assumptions underlying the diagram, the fall in income and in turn of imports only partially corrects the initial disturbance to balance-of-payments equilibrium.[13]

----

[13] Since an external deficit is an excess of absorption over real income, it may seem odd at first thought that a *fall* in real income should contribute even partially toward shrinking the deficit. Why should absorption fall more than income? The reverse seems more plausible: faced with a drop in income, people typically retrench only in part on consumption (or on consumption plus real investment, if the latter is also recognized as variable) and make the rest of their adjustment, at least in the short run, by retrenching on their saving also (or even by dissaving).

The answer to the paradox is that the initial autonomous fall in exports imposes a drop in income to which absorption has not yet adjusted. People temporarily find themselves absorbing more in relation to income than they intend. Even if income fell no further, they would retrench. But this retrenchment imposes a still further fall in income, and so on and on as Multiplier theory describes. Since each successive drop in income has itself already been imposed by further retrenchment in absorption, it does not exceed the latter; and there remains the deficit-shrinking effect of people's original efforts to pull absorption down into line with what they consider appropriate to their reduced income. The merely partial removal of the trade deficit reflects the fact that the marginal propensity to absorb is less than unity— that retrenchment impinges only partly on absorption and for the rest impinges on saving.

This whole point may be put briefly if less exactly: If absorption is in excess of income and if the two are geared together in a fairly definite way, then simultaneous declines in both can reduce the *absolute* excess of absorption. Income, absorption, and the difference between them all shrink to a smaller scale.

While the paradox raised by the absorption approach can thus be answered, the income-adjustment mechanism

The Foreign Repercussion

The developments just surveyed from Inland's point of view have counterparts in or repercussions on Outland, the rest of the world. May not these help bring trade completely back into balance, after all? The initial autonomous fall in Inland's exports may have been due to a change in tastes and be an autonomous fall in imports from Outland's point of view. This fall in the schedule of leakage out of Outland income causes Outland income to rise, with the result that Outland's imports do not fall as much, after all, as the initial change would otherwise have dictated. From Inland's point of view, the decline in its exports is restrained (the export lines does not shift downward as much, after all, as Fig. 5.2 shows). This restraint on the decline in exports contributes, along with the already considered income-induced fall in Inland imports, to a more nearly complete balancing of trade.

A foreign repercussion may also be at work when the initial autonomous disturbance is internal to one country. Suppose that Inland develops an investment and income boom, causing a rise in imports and an external deficit. This implies a rise in Outland's exports and income and, in turn, in Outland's purchases from Inland. The repercussion tends to hold down the size of Inland's external deficit.

In neither of these examples, however, is the repercussion likely to be strong enough to restore complete balance. The reason is a positive marginal propensity to save in each country: in neither country will upsetting the initial equality between leakages and injections bring about such a change in income that the import leakage undergoes the entire change necessary to restore equality; the domestic saving leakage will make part of the response to the change in income. This may be understood by supposing the contrary for the sake of argument: in Outland, the domestic saving leakage is either zero or does not *change* at all with income; imports are

----

does prove inefficient in requiring *both* absorption and real income to fall to shrink an excess of the one over the other.

the only leakage that responds. If, then, leakages fall below injections because of a downward shift in the relation of imports to income in Outland, as in the first example considered, equality can only be restored by a large enough rise in Outland income to *induce* a full recovery of the import leakage in accordance with the import-income relation. If injections exceed leakages because of a rise in exports to domestically booming Inland, as in the second example, then equality can only be restored by a large enough rise in Outland income to induce a matching rise in imports. A response in the saving leakage has been ruled out by hypothesis. But when we realistically allow saving to respond and to play a part in restoring equality between leakages and injections, we see that a rise in Outland income will not induce a change in imports fully large enough, by itself, to undo the autonomous fall in imports in the first example or to match the rise in exports in the second example. And since balanced trade is not restored for Outland, it is not restored for Inland either.

One practical consideration (if it is not out of place amidst these abstractions) also argues against a complete balancing of trade through the foreign repercussion: foreign governments need not just sit back and allow the influence of trade with Inland to multiply home incomes up or down; domestic policy measures are available.

Induced Investment

Induced investment, that is, the response of domestic investment to changes in income, provides a conceivable if not very realistic exception to the conclusion about incomplete balancing of trade. Consider together now a model that does not and a model that does allow for induced investment. Both models start with trade and income in equilibrium, with total injections equalling total leakages:

$$I + X = S + M$$

Now exports increase autonomously. (Circled algebraic signs attached to the letters indicate autonomous changes; uncircled signs indicate income-induced changes.) Injections thus exceed leakages, and income accordingly rises:

$$I + X\oplus > S + M$$
$$Y\uparrow$$

At a new higher level of income, total injections are again matched by total leakages. But exports and imports may or may not be back in balance, depending on whether or not a rise in investment interacts with a rise in income.

Without Induced Investment
$$I + X\oplus = S^+ + M^+$$
Since $S^+ > I$,
$$X\oplus > M^+$$

Thus there is a continuing (though reduced) export surplus.

With Induced Investment
$$I^+ X\oplus = S^+ + M^+$$
Since I^+ *may* $\gtreqless S^+$,
$$M^+ \ may \gtreqless X\oplus$$

Thus full correction or even overcorrection of the export surplus is possible. The actual outcome depends on how strongly investment responds to the export-initiated rise in income.

As an example of overcorrection, a country in deep depression somehow enjoys an autonomous increase in exports. The increased income and employment in export industries touch off an upward spiral of business recovery. With activity and confidence improved, businessmen step up their investment in buildings, machinery, inventories, and other capital goods. The return of prosperity leads people to buy not only more domestic goods and services but also more imports, and the rise in imports may conceivably outstrip the autonomous increase in exports that started the whole process off.

The key element in full adjustment or overadjustment is that investment responds to a change in income at least as strongly as saving. In our earlier examples, even those recognizing the foreign repercussion, what prevented complete external adjustment was a response of the domestic saving leakage in the same direction as income, investment being unaffected. But in our present example, the investment injection can respond as fully as the saving leakage, or more so; the marginal propensity to *save-net-of-investment,* so to speak, can be zero or negative. An economy with a negative *net* marginal propensity to save would be unstable in isolation from foreign trade: a random disturbance to income equilibrium would make total spending rise or fall cumulatively. It is far-fetched to suppose given "propensities" to consume, invest, and save out of real income that could cause such behavior; instead, cumulative income changes presuppose propensities changing along with the quantity of money.

Money in the Income-adjustment Theory

Even less far-fetched examples of the income-adjustment mechanism tacitly assume that the flow of money income and expenditure in a country can go up and down in passive response to influences arising from foreign trade. This implies a variable domestic money supply. In abstract logic, variations in velocity could conceivably accommodate wide variations in money income and expenditure, even with a constant money supply. To some slight extent, this accommodation is even plausible. When Inland is running an external deficit, foreigners may be willing to accept some of the net payments due them by acquiring balances in Inland currency and simply holding them for a while; or speculators may acquire balances in the belief that the weakness of the Inland currency (within the gold points) is only temporary. These foreign-held or speculator-held balances presumably have a lower velocity than balances held by typical Inlanders, and the average velocity of the Inland money supply falls somewhat.[14] When

Inland develops a balance-of-payments surplus, conversely, the average velocity of money may rise as cash balances return from foreigners' or speculators' ownership into ordinary domestic use. Expectations may also influence velocity in the same direction. When developments in foreign trade are tending to depress income, Inlanders may become more cautious than before and desire larger cash balances relative to income and expenditure, just as the reverse may happen when trade developments are tending to raise income.

Yet these accommodations in demands for cash balances relative to income and spending are but fringe possibilities. Realistically, the multiplier theory must presuppose a variable money supply.[15] Under a gold standard or a system of pegged exchange rates, it is obvious, furthermore, how developments in foreign trade do change a country's domestic money supply in the same direction as income.

Once we recognize all this, we see what limited applicability the theorem about incomplete balance-of-payments adjustment has. As long as an initial export surplus persists, even though shrunken, acquisitions of gold or foreign exchange still are expanding the local money supply. (This is true unless the monetary and banking authorities pursue an "offsetting" policy. *Ad hoc* suppositions about policy or other autonomous developments can of course play havoc with the conclusions of any strand of theory.) Increased cash balances will promote more spending, on imports as well as on other things. As long as foreign transactions are out of equilibrium, home income cannot be in equilibrium either. Theories of incomplete external adjustment that assume fixed "propensities" to import, to consume domestic goods, and to save miss the point that such propensities simply

---

[14] If the foreign creditors or the speculators acquire short-term securities in Inland instead of actual cash balances, they tend to make interest rates lower than they otherwise would have been. With the opportunity cost of holding cash balances correspondingly lower for foreigners and speculators and members of the domestic economy alike, desired cash balances relative to income and expenditure are likely to be larger—velocity is likely to be lower—than otherwise. (On the other hand, the overabsorption that the deficit represents would have tended to raise interest rates in the first place.)

The present discussion does not maintain that these effects are important. Rather, it illustrates what sort of theoretical straws one would have to grasp at to explain how income might vary as described by the foreign-trade-multiplier theory solely through accommodations in velocity rather than in the quantity of money.

[15] For emphasis on the importance of explicit attention to the quantity and velocity of money in income theory, see J. J. Polak, "Monetary Analysis of Income Formation and Payments Problems," IMF *Staff Papers,* **VI,** November 1957, pp. 1-50, J. J. Polak and Lorette Boissonneault, "Monetary Analysis of Income and Imports and Its Statistical Application," IMF *Staff Papers,* **VII,** April 1960, pp. 349-415, and J. Marcus Fleming, "Money Supply and Imports," IMF *Staff Papers,* **VIII,** May 1961, pp. 227-240.

cannot remain fixed indefinitely in the face of persistent change in the money supply. The cash-balance effect may be weak, but its existence and not its strength is the crucial point. (As a practical matter, of course, waiting for this effect to cure a deficit might be disastrous for the money and banking authorities, whose gold reserves might run out in the meanwhile.)

Income or multiplier theory was in a dilemma. Because changes in velocity could not fully account for the income changes it described, it had to recognize the money supply as variable. And once this was recognized, the notion of an external imbalance persisting even after income reached a new equilibrium level would have implied that velocity undergoes passive changes *opposite* to those dismissed as inadequate to support the theorized movement in income. For example, if a persistent export surplus were to keep adding to the money supply, yet income were to level off, velocity would have to keep falling; people would have to be demanding ever larger cash balances in relation to their incomes and expenditures. This is implausible.

The cash-balance effect not only rules out income equilibrium without balance-of-payments equilibrium but also suggests how adjustment to an export spurt may conceivably overshoot the mark and cause an import surplus. This is most easily conceivable if the money and banking system practices "reinforcement," engaging in multiple expansion on the basis of increased gold or exchange reserves, if income responds fully to monetary expansion and imports respond fully to income growth only with substantial lags, and if the development making for the original export spurt was temporary in the first place. In this way, a favorable development could conceivably lead to a balance-of-payments crisis.

Export Responses and Combined Adjustment Effects

In reviewing foreign-trade-multiplier theory, we have so far considered only how imports respond to changes in home income, how exports respond to changes in *foreign* income, and how exports and imports *affect* home income. We have said nothing about how exports respond to home income. Yet at an increased level of income, the home population is likely to bid more vigorously not only for imports but also for exportable goods and for domestic goods producible by diverting labor and resources away from export production. This response contributes to increasing any import surplus due to a domestic boom or to reducing any export surplus originating in the foreign-trade sector.

These export responses seldom receive much attention in the abstract application of income theory to international trade. The reason is apparently related to neglecting or assuming away price and wage changes, so that changes in money income correspond entirely to real changes in production and employment. Nowhere in the range of variation considered does real income come close enough to the maximum level set by limitations of resources and technology for additional spending to push up wages and prices; nowhere in the range considered does real income fall from close enough to this full-employment limit to worsen unemployment so significantly in comparison with what it already was that the additional downward pressure on wages and prices at last breaks their rigidity. All changes in income and employment must be tacitly supposed to leave *changes* in the pool of idle resources small in relation to the great unemployment existing even at both extremes of the range of variation considered. If this is so, a rise in home income and expenditure does not withhold any exportable goods from the foreign market or any resources from export production because plenty of idle resources still remain available to meet both domestic and foreign demands. A fall in income and expenditure does not divert any home-consumed exportables to the foreign market or any resources into export production because only the state of foreign demand, not resource limitations, had been keeping exports no greater than they were. The possibility of a price decline that might stimulate foreign purchases is ignored or assumed away. At a certain level of theoretical abstraction, such simplifications are useful, especially if realistic complications can later be grafted onto the analysis.

In actuality, changes in money income consist partly of changes in real production and employment and partly of changes in prices and wages. Export responses then do play a role both in intensifying an external disequilibrium due to domestic disturbances and in correcting an external disequilibrium due to external disturbances. A boom of domestic origin tends not only to raise imports but also to shrink exports. (Conceivably, of course, exports could rise in money value while shrinking in quantity; foreign demand might be inelastic. In the real world of less-than-perfect competition, though, changes in the tightness of nonprice terms of sale as well as in price affect the quantities and values of goods sold.) A domestic slump, conversely, tends on the export and import sides alike to cause a balance-of-payments surplus. (These remarks refer, of course, to cyclical variations in the degree of utilization of a given total of resources. Secular growth in resources and total output may well tend to expand exports.)

If a rise in foreign demand for Inland exports raises home income, Inland demand strengthens not only for imports but also for exportable goods and for domestic goods using factors otherwise available for export production. Higher prices or reduced availability, or both, tend to keep exports from increasing in full and unhampered response to the initial rise in foreign demand. (This restraint on export growth accompanies the promotion of imports resulting from a rise in Inland's domestic relative to import prices as well as from the rise in income.) Foreign demand may also be discouraged and restrained by a lengthening of export delivery dates.

For another example, suppose that Inland demand shifts autonomously from home to imported goods. The resulting fall in income tends not only to restrain the initial rise in import demand, but also to cut down home purchase of exportable goods and of domestic goods made with factors capable of shifting into export production. Foreigners take

additional exports in response to Inland's more eager sales efforts.

The combined operation of cash-balance, real-income, price, delivery-time, and sales-effort effects, fully effective though it may be in maintaining or restoring balance-of-payments equilibrium if policy does not thwart or counteract some of its aspects, still gives only slight grounds for satisfaction. The variation of real income as one corrective for external disturbances represents a *departure* from a theoretically ideal system frictionlessly maintaining equilibrium on all goods and factor markets through prompt price and wage adjustments.[16] Regrettable though the fact may be, real-income variations do play an important part in adjustment under conditions of international monetary linkage.

Interregional Adjustments

Real-income, cash-balance, and price effects work together to keep transactions in balance among regions of a single country. Regional balance-of-payments crises rarely develop, regional balances of payments are seldom even mentioned, and marked differences in price-level and income-level changes from region to region are seldom conspicuous in the short run; all this testifies to how smoothly palliatives and adjustments can occur under monetary unification. The lesser degree of protectionist interference with interregional than with international trade, as well as the smaller burden of transportation costs, leaves interregional trade especially responsive to price differentials. Equilibrating shifts in relative price and income levels are ordinarily hardly noticeable. Moreover, when the money and capital markets are active and nationally integrated and when liquid and nationally marketable securities are abundant and widely held, compensatory flows of short-term capi-

---

[16] This is not quite the same thing as denying that external disturbances would affect income at all in a theoretically perfect system. Changes in supplies and demands in international trade and thus in the terms of trade would still affect the quantity of goods obtainable for domestic use from a full-employment level of production. What *would* ideally be absent is waste through unemployment, as well as changes in its extent.

tal are likely to cushion the impact of temporary balance-of-payments disturbances and make multiple contractions and expansions of regional money supplies unnecessary. (Compensatory capital flows come especially close to being automatic where all banking is conducted by a few large banks with branch offices throughout the country; close correspondent relationships among unit banks can provide an approximation to this financial integration.) Suppose, for example, that newly recognized opportunities cause an investment boom in one state. Local incomes rise and so do purchases from other states. Balance-of-payments difficulties are avoided, however, when the local banks sell some of their U.S. government securities and other short-term assets in the national money market in order both to finance the local investment spending and to meet the drain on their reserves and avoid a multiple contraction of their credit and deposits. Furthermore, the original improvement in local investment opportunities may well attract long-term capital from other parts of the country. Or suppose that the outside demand drops for the products of a particular state. Money and bank reserves tend to leave the state in payment for its excess imports, but again, banks will cushion the impact by selling some of their security holdings on the national market. Borrowing externally through the intermediary of the district Federal Reserve Bank or in the Federal funds market is another possibility, as is a deliberate transfer of U.S. Treasury deposits into the deficit region to lessen the strain on banks there. In the face of a persistent disequilibrium in interregional trade, of course, this palliation of deficits could not continue indefinitely: sooner or later the banks would run out of salable assets; and sooner or later the adjustment mechanism working through money supplies, incomes, and prices would have to be allowed its full effect. But the palliation may suffice to keep the adjustment from being sharp and conspicuous.

Some effects connected with export of securities from a deficit region go beyond palliating disequilibrium and contribute to restoring equilibrium by tending to restrain absorption. Selling securities at any cut in

their prices represents a rise in interest rates. Closely connected with this is the tendency of interest rates to be bid up in the deficit region because of the excess of investment over saving that the deficit amounts to. If increased interest rates do anything to promote saving or restrict investment, the effect is in the direction of re-equilibrating the balance of payments. Furthermore, selling securities represents running down the total of financial assets held in the deficit region. Just as people are unwilling to run down their cash balances without limit, so are they unwilling to run down their other financial assets without limit; the decline in security holdings, like a decline in cash balances, helps restrain absorption. (Even financial assets not actually sold have their total money value reduced to some extent by any decline in their prices.) Furthermore, flexibility of security prices contrasts with the official pegging of the gold or foreign-exchange value of a country's money under a fractional-reserve system. Securities contrast with money, then, in that no official price-propping constitutes a subsidy making real wealth or income seem larger from the viewpoint of individual economic units than it actually is from the community's point of view. The larger security holdings are relative to money supply, income, and so forth, the smaller is the relative scope for pegging the external value of money to falsify price signals and partially shelter individual economic units from full awareness of aggregate economic circumstances.

The Federal tax and expenditure system may operate helpfully, and even spontaneously through its elements of "built-in flexibility," by transferring funds into deficit regions. A final reason why payments disequilibria and correctives for them are generally inconspicuous within the United States is that labor, capital, and business enterprise are mobile. Differences in legal systems, traditions, and language impede interregional much less than international mobility. When demand shifts away from the traditional products of a region, conspicuous deflation need not occur there. Some of the inhabitants will move to work elsewhere, while others will find jobs in industries attracted by idle facilities and manpower or perhaps aided by favoritism in the award of Federal government contracts.

But interregional adjustments do not always work inconspicuously and smoothly. Several decades ago, before the establishment of the Federal Reserve System and especially before banks held large quantities of government securities readily salable throughout the country, interregional payments problems *were* conspicuous in the United States. Bank credit creation in frontier regions caused local money incomes, prices, and imports from the rest of the country all to rise. Readjustment sometimes occurred harshly through serious strains on bank reserves for which no ready palliative was available.[17] Even today difficulties in adjustment (in which minimum-wage laws may perhaps play a part) are sometimes evident in localized depressions in regions that have suffered a drop in the national demand for their products. (This matter of "depressed areas" will come up again in a comparison of the exchange-rate adjustment mechanism with the combined price-and-income mechanism.) Even the more typical interregional synchronization of business conditions raises some questions about the convenience of the price-and-income mechanism, as well as providing evidence of the mechanism at work.

International Transmission of Business Fluctuations

Examples already considered have illustrated a double relation between domestic business conditions and foreign trade. Domestic prosperity or depression and external surplus or deficit do not go together in any simple way; the relation depends on how the causation runs. On the one hand, the *adjust-*

ment process operates: autonomous developments causing an export (or import) surplus tend to raise (or lower) home income and so to affect imports in such a way as to reduce the imbalance in trade. On the other hand, a *transmission* process operates; impulses of depression or inflation originating within a country cause an external surplus or deficit and communicate themselves abroad.[18] This transmission process now deserves a bit more attention. First, contagion occurs as described by multiplier theory. Depression cuts a country's imports, which are other countries' exports. Their export slump depresses business in these other countries. Conversely, a country undergoing inflation stimulates expenditure in other countries by increasing its imports from them. Countries thus confronted with an export slump or export boom also find their gold or exchange reserves and their money supplies shrinking or expanding in consequence; money-supply changes accommodate the income changes described by the multiplier theory. Deliberate domestic policy may conceivably offset these contractionary or expansionary tendencies transmitted through international trade, though, under fixed exchange rates, at the cost of perpetuating external disequilibrium and, for a deficit country, of risking a crisis. But the *spontaneous* process is clearly one of international contagion.

A study by Oskar Morgenstern documents the international connection of business conditions under the gold standard. His findings, summarized in Table 5.1, indicate that the four countries considered were all undergoing general business expansions or contractions together more often than not. (Yet if months of expansion and months of contraction had been equally likely and if there had been nothing more than a chance association between business conditions in different countries, then one would have expected four

---

[17] On this historical point as well as on the cushioning by interregional transactions in securities and flows of short-term capital, see James C. Ingram, "State and Regional Payments Mechanisms," *Quarterly Journal of Economics,* LXXIII, November 1959, esp. pp. 626-629. In this article, in his *Regional Payments Mechanisms: The Case of Puerto Rico,* Chapel Hill: University of North Carolina Press, 1962, and in his proposals for international monetary reform (reviewed in a later chapter), Ingram has made important contributions to adjustment theory; the above discussion has drawn heavily on them.

[18] Exceptional responses—such as might occur if a country's imports were on the whole "inferior goods" —are hardly worth detailed attention. Less implausible is the possibility that a domestic boom due to improved investment opportunities might attract enough long-term capital from abroad to improve the balance on account of all independently motivated transactions, even while causing a deficit on current account.

countries all to share the same trend of business only one-eighth of the time.) The table shows, furthermore, that the international conformity of business trends was greater before World War I, when the international gold standard was flourishing, than after the war, when the gold standard was restored only in a modified form and for only part of the period considered. As Morgenstern himself says with particular reference to Great Britain, France, and Germany before World War I, the parallelism maintained during both shorter and longer business cycles supports the thesis of not merely a covariation of independent factors but of a "transmission and an interlocking of the cycles."[19]

Economic interdependence under the gold standard is illustrated not only in general business activity but also in interest rates. During the period 1880–1913, and especially the last twenty years of this period, the heyday of the international gold standard, the central-bank discount rates of virtually all of twelve major countries tended to rise and fall together, at least in their larger movements.[20] This parallelism seems mainly due to the inverse correlation of discount rates and central-bank reserve ratios and, in turn, to both the inverse correlation of these ratios with levels of economic activity and to the international parallelism of business fluctuations. In addition, the parallelism of discount rates may have been partly due to "defensive"

Table 5.1. Percentages of Months in Which the Indicated Countries Were Undergoing General Business Expansions or Contractions Together

	Prewar (Sept. 1879–Aug. 1914: 419 months)	Postwar (June 1919–July 1932: 157 months)
Great Britain and France	86.2%	68.8%
Great Britain and Germany	90.2%	60.5%
France and Germany	89.7%	61.1%
All three European countries	83.1%	45.2%
All three European countries and the United States	53.5%	35.6%

SOURCE: Reprinted from Oskar Morgenstern, *International Financial Transactions and Business Cycles*, Princeton, N. J.: Princeton University Press, 1959, pp. 45, 49. By permission of Princeton University Press. Copyright 1959.

changes: when one or more important central banks raised their rates, others may have done the same to guard against outflows of short-term funds and gold; and when some lowered their rates, others may have felt safe in following suit. (A more detailed discussion of the international effects of discount rates appears in a historical context in Chapter 14.)

Conclusion

A brief closing comment on this chapter can only mention, not meaningfully summarize, its main theme. When the monetary systems of different countries are closely linked together through fixed exchange rates, balance-of-payments disturbances tend to be adjusted by movements in money supplies, price levels, the relative prices of domestic and international-trade goods, incomes, and interest rates. The more completely rigidities keep changes in money incomes from taking the form of changes merely in money prices and wages, the larger must changes in real incomes and employment be. The same factors that operate in the balance-of-payments adjustment process under fixed exchange rates also operate in the international transmission of business fluctuations.

---

[19] Oskar Morgenstern, *International Financial Transactions and Business Cycles*, Princeton, N.J.: Princeton University Press for the National Bureau of Economic Research, 1959, p. 52.

It seems plausible, incidentally, that Morgenstern's method of counting the months in which different countries shared the same business trend is more likely to understate than overstate the international conformity of business fluctuations. Lags in this conformity presumably characterize a genuine causal process; yet these lags would introduce a rather spurious element of nonconformity into the counting of months. For brief remarks on differences in phase of business cycles in the late nineteenth century and on what Clark Warburton called a seesaw movement between the United States and Great Britain, see Milton Friedman and Anna Jacobson Schwartz, *A Monetary History of the United States, 1867–1960*, Princeton, N.J.: Princeton University Press for the NBER, 1963, p. 98.

[20] The discount rates are charted and their parallelism noted in Arthur I. Bloomfield, *Monetary Policy Under the International Gold Standard: 1880–1914*, New York: Federal Reserve Bank of New York, 1959, pp. 35-38.

ᔥ Appendix to Chapter 5: The Adjustment of Trade to Capital Movements

Independently Motivated Capital Movements

An independently motivated capital movement has been the traditional theoretical example of balance-of-payments disturbance. For some reason not directly connected with trade in goods and services, Inlanders want to invest funds in Outland: higher interest rates or better profit prospects there, changes in taxation or other government policies in one country or the other, or a rise in saving, of which part seeks placement abroad. Perhaps Outlanders take the initiative, seizing favorable opportunities to float new securities on the Inland market. Or perhaps Inland has lost a war and must pay cash reparations.

Starting with international transactions in balance, the capital movement now means overall disequilibrium in independently motivated transactions. Restoring equilibrium involves cutting the capital-exporting country's goods-and-services imports or expanding its exports, or both, and conversely for the capital-importing country. How can trade so adjust? The answer is trivial if the capital movement occurs by way of a loan "tied" to use of the proceeds in the lending country or by way of credit granted by commodity exporters. The question arises most clearly if the Outland borrowers want to spend the proceeds mostly in their own country rather than especially on Inland goods. All parties, by assumption, are interested only in the transfer of *money* capital and do not know or care about the necessary adjustments in trade. Yet if the loan is to make more resources available in the borrowing country and fewer in the lending country, a "real" counterpart to the merely financial operation must somehow occur.

It makes no important difference whether the bonds are denominated in the currency of the lending or of the borrowing country and whether it is the Outland borrowers or the Inland lenders who must take the initiative in exchanging one currency for the other on the foreign-exchange market. Either way, holdings of domestic money by the ordinary public (the public excluding banks and other dealers or speculators in foreign exchange) initially go down in Inland and up in Outland. The banks or other foreign-exchange dealers, for their part, initially increase their assets (or reduce their liabilities) in lending-country currency and reduce their assets (or increase their liabilities) in borrowing-country currency. If the banks and other dealers are willing simply to accept these changes for a while, without trying to reverse them in the wholesale foreign-exchange market, they are making possible a transfer of cash balances and purchasing power from the lenders to the borrowers. This transfer is still possible even though the banks and dealers do reverse the intial changes in their positions, provided that speculators, in their stead, are willing to increase their balances of Inland currency and reduce their balances of Outland currency.[1] If speculators did so (or, for that matter, if the banks and dealers speculatively refrained from reversing the initial changes in their currency positions), their motive would be confidence that the market weakness of Inland and strength of Outland currency would prove only temporary and that the exchange rate would bounce back from Inland's gold export point. (Even under flexible exchange rates, in fact, accommodating speculation is conceivable.)

Perhaps, however, neither banks and other lenders nor outright speculators will accept these accommodating changes in their currency positions. Gold will then flow, or the foreign reserves

---

[1] Whether done by banks and other dealers or by speculators, this amounts to a transfer of short-term capital from the long-term borrowing country to the long-term lending country. In this way a temporary offsetting of the main capital flow helps accomplish the transfer of cash balances and purchasing power between the ordinary publics of the two countries that in turn helps translate the main financial operation into a net flow of real goods and services from the lending to the borrowing country.

of Inland's exchange-pegging authority will be drawn down. Repercussions on money supplies and price and income levels will then promote the adjustment of trade.

Incomplete Adjustment by Purchasing-power Transfer

Before returning to these other aspects of adjustment, we should look more closely at the transfer of purchasing power. It is true that if the Outland borrowers had not borrowed abroad, they might have borrowed at home, but then other Outlanders would have had less purchasing power at their disposal than in the absence of the international loan. Slightly lower interest rates and easier credit rationing than in its absence may help to bring the more abundant purchasing power to the attention of Outlanders generally. If this goes to buy Inland goods and services, the international real transfer occurs without further ado. To the extent that the borrowers spend the proceeds of the loan at home instead, they are passing on the additional purchasing power to their fellow Outlanders, some of whom may increase their imports. Inland lenders, to be able to grant the foreign loan, may cut down their buying of both home and Outland goods. More probably, they reduce or eliminate loans that they would otherwise have made at home; would-be borrowers and their fellow Inlanders from whom they would have bought goods and services now have less purchasing power than otherwise at their disposal and so buy less of both home and Outland goods.

For several reasons, however, a complete international transfer is unlikely to take place in this way alone. First, Inlanders and Outlanders will probably not reduce and increase their respective total spending—at least not "on the first round"—by the full amount of the loan; changes in domestic leakage will account for the difference. Second, changes in total spending will probably impinge only fractionally on purchases abroad rather than at home. For example, if total expenditure in each country goes down or up by only 80 percent of the purchasing power transferred or received and if expenditures on foreign goods and services change by only 30 percent of the change in total expenditure, then external expenditure goes down by only .80 × .30 = 24 percent of the loan in the lending country and goes up by only the same percentage in the borrowing country. The balance of trade in goods and services moves "in favor" of the lending country by only 24 + 24 = 48 percent of the amount of the loan.[2]

But this "first round" is not the whole story. The cut in domestic spending on output in the lending country has not been fully matched by a rise in export sales, and the rise in domestic spending on output in the borrowing country has not been fully offset by a fall in export sales. Total sales and hence total incomes fall in Inland and rise in Outland. Changes in income affect further "rounds" of spending, and contraction and expansion may proceed in the respective countries as multiplier theory describes. Will not incomes continue to change until Inland has reduced its imports and Outland has increased its imports enough fully to accomplish the real transfer of the loan? If behavior of the money supply and the velocity of circulation permit and if policy does not interfere—and these are important provisos—further rounds of adjustment may indeed result in a more nearly complete real transfer than the first round alone suggests (depending on just how people allocate their incomes or purchasing power among imports, domestic spending, and saving).

Even so, a complete transfer is unlikely. Total leakages out of the stream of spending on each country's products will have responded enough to the change in income to stop any further change in income before trade has fully adjusted to the loan. A fall in saving will help check the fall in Inland income and a rise in saving will help check the rise in Outland income before incomes have changed enough fully to adjust the two countries' imports. This result is comparable to the already explained incomplete adjustment to other balance-of-payments disturbances by way of income effects alone, strictly conceived.[3]

_____

[2] But a full (or more than full) "real" transfer is conceivable. If the marginal fractions of purchasing power spent and of expenditure devoted to imports were 9/10 and 5/9 respectively in each country, the balance of trade in goods and services would move in favor of the lending country "on the first round" by 9/10 × 5/9 + 9/10 × 5/9 = 100 per cent of the loan. Realistically, though, countries do not devote large enough fractions of their total expenditure to buying each other's rather than domestic goods. Furthermore, the repercussions occurring (unless prevented by policy) on subsequent "rounds" of income and expenditure may partially neutralize rather than reinforce the "first-round" international adjustment.

[3] Numerical examples to clarify this point have had to be sacrificed for the sake of brevity. For the general approach, however, see J. E. Meade, *The Balance of Payments,* London: Oxford University Press, 1951, pp. 125-148.

Other Elements of the Adjustment Process

An analysis of narrow purchasing-power-transfer and income effects is incomplete and oversimplified, especially if it assumes definite parameters regarding saving and domestic and import spending. Actually, for example, the lenders or their fellow countrymen might not reduce their own spending; if the foreign loan opportunity had not been available, they might simply have hoarded the money, perhaps because a depression was discouraging home consumption and investment. What happens to the velocity as well as quantity of money is an important question. Another is whether the monetary-fiscal authorities of the two countries resist any cumulative inflationary or deflationary processes for the sake of domestic stability or promote them for the sake of fixed exchange rates or gold parities.

Under a fractional-reserve gold or foreign-exchange standard, magnified money-supply and price-level developments go beyond the purchasing-power-transfer effects mentioned so far and make a distinct contribution to the otherwise incomplete adjustment of trade to the loan, much the same as in our earlier examples of autonomous disturbances in goods-and-services trade. The shrinkage of cash balances and the decline in the prices of domestic factors of production relative to the prices of internationally traded goods make people in the lending country see that fewer real resources are currently available than would have been available in the absence of the loan and that they must cut their absorption of goods and services accordingly. Opposite developments promote absorption in the borrowing country. Corresponding supplements to adjustment by purchasing-power transfer under flexible exchange rates are a matter still to be considered.

Intergovernmental Transfers

Unrequited intergovernmental transfers, such as postwar reparations, introduce no new principle. Yet they deserve special notice because of the famous Keynes-Ohlin controversy of the late 1920s[4] and because of the distinction it introduced between the budgetary and transfer problems. In meeting the Allies' demand for reparations payments, the German government faced the budgetary problem of levying taxes or otherwise raising the necessary amounts of home money. The transfer problem concerned possible difficulties in achieving the German export surplus necessary to provide the required foreign exchange. Keynes did mention how the purchasing-power transfer itself tended to promote German exports, but he assigned it a minor role and focused attention on the price changes disadvantageous to Germany that would be needed to produce a large enough export surplus. The *real* disposable incomes of Germans would thus be lowered not merely by the taxes levied to pay reparations (the budgetary burden) but also by the price changes (the transfer burden). Furthermore, Keynes thought, even this change in relative prices might not achieve the necessary German export surplus. Perhaps physical limitations would prevent any great expansion of German exports. Or perhaps foreign demand for them might prove inelastic, so that price cuts would lower their total gold value.[5] Keynes concluded: "Only those who believe that the foreign demand for German exports is very elastic, so that a trifling reduction in German prices will do what is required, are justified in holding that the Transfer Problem is of no great significance apart from the Budgetary Problem."[6]

Ohlin, on the other hand, apparently envisaged no great depreciation of the German currency or deflation of the German price and wage level. The Germans, having surrendered purchasing power to pay reparations, would be less able to afford imports, while the foreign recipients would have more purchasing power with which to buy German exports. Of course, only fractions of the cutbacks in spending made by German taxpayers and of the additional spending done by the foreign beneficiaries would impinge directly on internationally traded goods. But the changes in spending on domestic goods also—decreases in Germany and increases abroad—would tend to produce secondary contraction

---

[4] See their articles, reprinted from the *Economic Journal*, March and June 1929, in American Economic Association, *Readings in the Theory of International Trade*, Philadelphia: Blakiston, 1949, pp. 161-178, as well as the article immediately following: Lloyd A. Metzler, "The Transfer Problem Reconsidered," reprinted from the *Journal of Political Economy*, June 1942.

[5] Supposed physical limits to amounts of existing German exports were something of a red herring. New goods might have come onto the list of exports. Price changes as well as heavy taxation could have motivated cutbacks in German home consumption and so have increased the quantites of goods available for export even if total production of export-type goods had been physically limited. And even if the foreign demand for German exports had been inelastic, price changes might have played a further role in contributing to an export surplus by cutting *imports*.

[6] *Loc. cit.*, p. 167.

and expansion, giving further reason for labor and capital to concentrate on export production in Germany and to shift from it into home-market production abroad. Important aspects of the adjustment mechanism would operate even if German prices did not decline at all relative to prices in the countries receiving reparations.

To illustrate his optimistic view, Ohlin pointed out that during the few preceding years Germany had borrowed sums abroad considerably outweighing its reparations payments; if any transfer problems existed, it had been one of accomplishing a "real" transfer *into* Germany. Yet no such transfer problem had become conspicuous enough to arouse discussion.

The role of government budgeting deserves more emphasis than Keynes and Ohlin gave it. If the governments of two countries wanted to do all they could to accomplish a "real" transfer between them, the paying government should raise the necessary sum (or more) by increasing taxes (thereby reducing the disposable income of its citizens) or by cutting its own domestic expenditures; and the other government should use the payments received (or more) to cut taxes or to expand its own domestic expenditures. The purchasing-power-transfer effect would be completely absent if, in contrast, the paying government neither increased taxes nor cut its spending but simply inflated the necessary funds into existence and if the receiving government neither cut taxes nor increased its spending but simply held the funds received idle. The paying government might conceivably withdraw some gold coins from circulation, replacing them with newly printed paper money, and then deliver the gold to the receiving government, which might simply hold it against some future contingency without letting it influence the budget or the country's money supply. Such a situation would be uninteresting, for no genuine transfer problem would exist if gold were the ultimate means of settlement and no room was left for further repercussions.

Though unfavorable shifts in the relative prices of import and export goods and home factors of production may indeed lay a transfer burden on a paying country in addition to the budgetary burden, this does not necessarily prevent an adjustment of trade to the payment. Consider postwar reparations imposed in a world of barter. The victors might say in effect to the vanquished: "You must expand your deliveries of goods to us, or reduce your acquisitions of goods from us, or both, so much that your total deliveries of goods to us, valued in terms of our own goods, exceed our total deliveries to you by the amount we specify." The task of complying is greater that it would be if barter exchange ratios did not move against the defeated country, but this is simply an aspect of the kind of reparations demand made. The defeated country will be unable to discharge this obligation only if its people cannot accomplish the necessary production and bear up under the necessary deprivation —only if they are too poor. In other words, the transfer problem is included in the budgetary problem and can be solved if the latter can be solved. Admittedly, though, the defeated country might already be importing so little that little room remained for creating an export surplus by further import cuts, and the victors' demand for its exports might be so inelastic that increased physical amounts would be worth only reduced value amounts on their markets (even though the increased real disposable income of the victors was shifting their demand curves rightward). Two types of unfavorable foreign demands—the insistence on reparations measured in a particular way and the inelastic market demand—would be imposing poverty on the defeated country. This and the transfer problem would be intermingled.

Multilateral Aspects of Capital Movements

Some complications appear when we go beyond the usual two-country model and recognize that many countries exist. How can trade adjust to capital movements if borrowers or their fellow countrymen increase their purchases not in the lending country but elsewhere and if lenders or their fellow countrymen reduce their purchases not in the borrowing country but elsewhere? The purchasing-power transfer and other gold-standard processes then tend to give the lending country an export surplus in trade with third countries. The adjustment process can best be understood by considering it while still incomplete. Perhaps the consolidated balances of payments of the third countries are in overall equilibrium, but their trade deficits with the lending country and their surpluses with the borrowing country still do not fully match the flow of capital to be transferred. There would then still be "too much" lending-country currency and "too little" borrowing-country currency being offered on the foreign-exchange market, promoting further gold flow and further monetary contraction and expansion in the respective countries. They would accordingly tend further to expand their respective net sales to and net purchases from the third countries, if not from each other directly. Another conceivable transitional stage of incomplete adjustment would have the third countries in overall balance-of-payments surplus, with excess exports to the borrowing country outweighing excess imports from the lending country. With their currencies in overall excess demand (not merely bilateral excess demand, thanks to arbitrage), the third countries would then gain gold; but the rises in their money supplies, incomes, and prices relative to those of the contractionary lending country would be in some sense more extreme than the relative declines in their money supplies, incomes, and prices in relation to those of the expansionary borrowing country. As an appropriate result, the discouragement of exports and encouragement of imports in third countries' trade with the lending country would be stronger that the continuing encouragement of exports and discouragement of imports in their trade with the borrowing country.

It would be tedious to explore all conceivable halfway stages in the multilateral accommodation of trade; the possibility of real capital transfer *through* third countries as well as directly is clear in principle. Whether the tendencies just described work swiftly enough to avoid difficulties under a gold standard is a serious question. They are more *understandable,* at least, under flexible exchange rates (or will be, after a study of the next chapter). If the third countries had trade surpluses with the borrowing country outweighing their deficits with the lending country at one stage of the incomplete adjustment, then supply and demand on the foreign-exchange market would tend to strengthen third-country currencies in relation to the borrowing-country currency (or restrain the original tendency toward relative weakening) to a greater extent[7]

---

[7] This extent would be measured not necessarily in percentage movement of rate quotations but rather in the influence of the exchange-rate movements on the flow of trade (which involves various demand and supply elasticities).

than this pattern tended to weaken third-country currencies in relation to the lending-country currency (or restrain the original tendency toward relative strengthening). As a result, third countries would find their surplus in trade with the borrowing country either tending to shrink or else tending to expand less than their trade deficit with the lending country was tending to expand. The balances of payments of third countries would tend back into multilateral equilibrium.

The discussion of international capital movements is not meant to appraise their effects on welfare but merely to consider further the adjustment to balance-of-payments disturbances. Still, it is worth while to mention the parallel between the multilateral possibilities of the "real" transfer process and the fact that the transfer need by no means take the form of whatever capital goods the borrowers may wish to buy with the proceeds of the loan. Instead of exporting the particular goods that the borrowers may want, the lending country may export goods in whose production it has a comparative advantage, even though these may be demanded by persons in the borrowing country other than the actual borrowers or even only by persons in third countries. Similarly, the borrowers need not obtain the particular goods they desire from the lending country or, for that matter, from any foreign country. If they can obtain these goods more cheaply or otherwise more satisfactorily from some third country or even at home, a net transfer of real goods and services into their country still means that they are obtaining more real resources for their own projects without, on the whole, taking resources away from their fellow countrymen. International real transfers can take place "automatically" on a multilateral basis. The direct financial arrangements for an international loan or transfer may take place between persons in two countries only, but this financial bilateralism need not deprive trade of its multilateral character or distort it out of conformity with comparative advantage.

Exchange-rate Adjustment and Other Mechanisms: A Preliminary Comparison

∽ 6

The Exchange-rate Mechanism

How exchange-rate variation can equilibrate the balance of payments should be easy to understand now that other mechanisms have been explained. Some disturbance creates a deficit in Inland's balance of payments. At the old exchange rate, Inland's dollar is in excess supply and Outland's peso in excess demand. Depreciation of the dollar under free-market pressures, or its devaluation if the rate had been officially pegged,[1] raises the price of foreign goods in dollars, restraining imports, and lowers the price of Inland goods in pesos, promoting exports. Adjustment of trade in this way, as through the price-level-adjustment mechanism of the gold standard, might conceivably go awry if demands were extremely inelastic. With the total Outland-peso value of Inland's exports reduced more than that of Inland's imports, the worsened imbalance on the exchange market would make the dollar depreciate further, making Inland's deficit still greater.

Setting aside this theoretical curiosity until Chapter 8, we shall take a closer look at the "normal" adjustment process. In reality, export prices in home currency do not remain constant, and shifts occur in the relative prices of domestic and internationally traded goods. As the dollar depreciates under pressure of a balance-of-payments deficit, the dollar prices of Inland's imports rise. Dollar prices rise even though what appears from the Outland point of view as a drop in Inland demand may somewhat reduce the *peso* prices of the

Outland goods sold to Inland. For trade moving in the opposite direction, the new exchange rate cheapens Inland exports in Outland pesos and so stimulates Outland purchases. From the Inland point of view this appears[2] as an increase in the demand for exports, bidding up their dollar prices. At the new exchange rate, in short, Inland's imports and exportable goods alike tend to rise in price relative to domestic goods. Domestic or nontraded goods include such things as houses and haircuts and, in particular, labor and other factors of production. The price rise of internationally traded goods relative to domestic goods and factors of production leads Inlanders to cut down on importing and on domestic consumption of goods they could export and to concentrate more than before on production for export. The fuzzy dividing line between international and domestic goods shifts so as to make more goods than before profitably exportable. In the theoretical extreme case of infinite price elasticity in all relevant supplies and demands, no *actual* shift in the relative price levels of international and domestic goods would be observed: an infinitesimal exchange depreciation would slash Inland's imports and would spur her offer of exports in response to what, from her point of view, appeared as an increase in the Outland demand for them. The sectional-price-level shift would then be vir-

---

[1] *Depreciation* is the broader term. When a distinction is intended, *devaluation* implies official action to fix the foreign-exchange value of a currency at a lower level than before.

[2] The increase in Outland demand is *apparent* only, since the demand schedule relating Outland's desired purchases of Inland goods to alternative prices *in pesos* is pretty much the same as before. Outlanders will buy more than before at any given dollar price, not because their demand has become more intense but because that price now represents fewer pesos. Inlanders, however, perceive that the schedule of desired Outland purchases in relation to *dollar* prices has shifted to the right.

tual; loosely speaking, Inland's imports and exports would respond to the relative price rise of international goods that would otherwise have occurred. The more sensitively quantities demanded and supplied respond to price changes, the smaller need observed price changes actually be.

A sectional-price-level shift occurs in reverse in Outland, the surplus country. Exchange appreciation of the peso lowers the peso prices of imports from Inland and also causes an apparent decline in Inland demand for Outland exports, lowering their prices as well. Outland domestic goods and factors of production rise in price, relatively. Outlanders shift toward buying international goods and away from producing them. The more sensitively Outlanders respond to prices, the less marked does the actual shift in prices have to be in order to correct the initial surplus in Outland's balance of payments.

The Ideal Similarity of Exchange-rate and Price-level Mechanisms

Ideally, the ultimate real changes that preserve or restore equilibrium in a disturbed balance of payments are essentially the same under the exchange-rate mechanism as under the price-level mechanism of international monetary linkage. The qualification *ideally* means that the adjustments considered are those that would take place if each mechanism operated in a theoretically perfect way. We abstract from frictions and suppose that both mechanisms operate with equal promptness, smoothness, and ease, and with equal absence of unwanted side effects. (Differences in these respects will be explored later.) We also abstract from such complications as debts fixed in the money of one country or another and speculation on exchange-rate or price-level changes. *Ultimate* changes refer to the new equilibrium that either mechanism would attain, considered apart from the processes and timing of getting there and apart from the influence that the path followed would, in reality, have on the final position. *Real* changes refer to physical quantities produced and traded, real incomes, and relative prices (price *ratios*)—all distin-

guished from mere money magnitudes and absolute levels of prices in money.[3]

To see the similarity of adjustment, consider some change in tastes that shifts demand partly away from Inland onto Outland goods. Preventing or curing a deficit in Inland's balance of payments requires bringing to bear on the decisions of Inland's families and firms the fact that the country's real economic position has worsened and that absorption must be restrained. The buying power of Inland's domestic factor incomes over internationally traded goods must be reduced. But keeping the gold parity or exchange rate of the Inland currency fixed without allowing the loss of gold or foreign-exchange reserves to deflate Inland's money supply and prices would mean blocking the change in economic signals needed fully to apprise individual decision-makers of the country's worsened real circumstances. Blocking these signals means subsidizing continued absorption by drafts on the gold or foreign-exchange reserves. Allowing either the gold-standard or the exchange-rate adjustment mechanism to operate, in contrast, does change the signals appropriately and does discontinue the subsidy to overabsorption. Under the gold standard, real cash balances fall as gold losses shrink the nominal money supply. Under the exchange-rate mechanism, depreciation or devaluation of the Inland currency lowers the purchasing power of the existing nominal money supply over import and export goods. Under either system, domestic goods and services fall in price relative to internationally traded goods; and the real buying power of the incomes of Inland factors of production falls. Under the gold standard, the general levels of domestic prices and money incomes fall while the gold prices of internationally traded goods remain more

---

[3] Even on this level of extreme abstraction, at least one dissimilarity between the two mechanisms must be noted. Under a gold standard, some real resources go into providing monetary expansion over the long run, diverting them from other uses; the absolute level of prices affects the profitability and volume of gold mining and so, because of general economic interdependence, in principle affects all prices and quantities in the economic system to some extent. Some other dissimilarities on this same level of detail might be mentioned.

nearly unchanged; with exchange-rate adjustment, the Inland-currency prices of internationally traded goods rise while domestic prices and money income remain nearly unchanged. But *relative* movements are ideally the same. Under either method of allowing the economic signals to change and of avoiding continued subsidy to overabsorption, real incomes fall in Inland (and rise in Outland) because of the hypothesized initial shift in demand from Inland to Outland goods, just as one would expect if all trade were by barter and no money existed.[4]

A comparison of adjustment processes turns out similarly if the initial disturbance is an independently motivated capital flow from Inland to Outland. Insofar as the international transfer of purchasing power and the associated tightening of credit in Inland and loosening of credit in Outland do not by themselves restrain absorption in the one country and promote it in the other strongly enough to accommodate trade fully to the capital movement, further signals are needed. Inlanders must realize that fewer real resources are *currently* available for their absorption than before the loan was made. Either monetary contraction in response to gold flows or exchange depreciation of the Inland currency has the effects already described on real cash balances and on the relation between prices and factor incomes in Inland (and conversely in Outland).

These similarities, it must be repeated, refer to real outcomes in the absence of frictions. General price levels tend to move in opposite directions under the two mechanisms, and so do production and employment levels, in the absence of wage and price flexibility. Under fixed exchange rates, an independently motivated capital outflow tends to *deflate* the domestic money supply, prices, and production and employment. These changes are not the *result* of a goods-and-services export surplus but rather a part of the means of bringing the surplus about. Under fluctuating exchange rates, the capital outflow causes exchange depreciation and an export surplus directly. With the money supply remaining under domestic control, this net withdrawal of goods and services tends to *raise* prices in home currency, as well as production and employment.[5]

For a final comparison, consider a monetary rather than a real disturbance causing a deficit: inflation in Inland at a time of already full employment. The way that new money is put into circulation (government expenditures in excess of tax collections or an easing of credit), the rise in cash balances, the rise in money incomes relative to the less fully inflated prices of internationally traded goods, the drawing down of gold and foreign-exchange reserves—all cause apparent improvements in the economic positions of individuals, even though the country's real economic position has by hypothesis not improved, and all subsidize overabsorption while they last. Ideally, the gold-standard process reverses these monetary and price changes (or prevents them in the first place). Alternatively, depreciation of the Inland currency undoes these distortions by allowing the Inland-currency prices of internationally traded goods to keep pace with domestic cash balances and prices and incomes; it stops the overabsorption promoted by false price signals and financed by drafts on the country's external reserves. Of course, an exchange rate that equilibrates the balance of payments can-

---

[4] An original disturbance in the reverse direction would leave Inland's currency *under*valued at the old exchange rate if the resulting balance-of-payments surplus were kept from expanding the local money supply and so from bidding up the prices of domestic goods and factors of production relative to import and export prices. In maintaining an undervalued currency by accumulating foreign exchange at a higher local-currency price than it would be worth on a purely private market and thus in keeping import and export prices artificially high in local currency, the authorities would in effect be subsidizing what might be called either "underabsorption" or the net "production" of foreign exchange through an export surplus. Either appreciating the Inland currency or allowing the local money supply to expand would rectify the signals given by relative prices and bring the country's improved economic circumstances to bear on the decisions of private families and firms.

[5] Cf. Gottfried von Haberler, *Prosperity and Depression*, new ed., London: Allen & Unwin, 1958, pp. 446-450; Egon Sohmen, *Fluctuating Exchange Rates: Theory and Controversy*, Chicago: University of Chicago Press, 1961, pp. 25-26; and Rudolf R. Rhomberg, "A Model of the Canadian Economy under Fixed and Fluctuating Exchange Rates," *Journal of Political Economy*, **LXXII**, February 1964, p. 21.

not by itself offset *all* consequences of inflation, including the transfer of wealth from creditors to debtors. A gold or foreign-exchange standard, in contrast, does tend to check the domestic inflation.[6]

This is one of the practical differences between the two ideally similar adjustment mechanisms. Another concerns how long drafts on external reserves continue to subsidize overabsorption while adjustment of the price signals is still incomplete. In making prices signal a changed real situation and in avoiding drain on any external reserves, the flexible exchange rate operates more quickly. A closely related difference concerns the frictions that bedevil the ideally similar operation of the two mechanisms. Ideally, fluctuations in employment and in overall real economic activity are neither an integral part of the gold standard or of the exchange-rate mechanisms nor a distinct adjustment mechanism in their own right. They represent frictions in the response of prices and wages to changes in expenditure patterns and money supplies. Ideally, overall production and employment never undergo deflation; only prices and wages do.

Ideally, in short, the adjustment mechanisms operating under monetary linkage and under flexible exchange rates are similar; in practice, they depart from the ideal in different ways and degrees. A realistic comparison must emphasize the frictions that may impede and the production-and-employment variations that may accompany one or both of them. As part of this fuller comparison, we must next examine the problem of maintaining both internal and external balance.

Expenditure and Price Policy for Internal and External Balance

External balance simply means balance-of-payments equilibrium. *Internal balance* might be defined as full employment *plus* price-level stability, except that even purely domestic obstacles may keep these two domestic goals

from being entirely compatible.[7] More realistically, then, internal balance must refer to a high level of employment and production with no more movement of the general price level than is necessary to this primary goal. Yet still another difficulty remains. If monetary inflation somehow occurs and if the price system is not to be thrown out of commission by the general shortages characteristic of suppressed inflation, policy must allow the price level to rise. In short, internal balance represents whatever compromise is considered best on domestic grounds between the goals of full employment, a smoothly working market mechanism, and price-level stability.

Two general types of policy are available for pursing internal and external balance. The first is expenditure policy, which concerns the total flow of money expenditure in a country. The second type is price policy, operating through price adjustments. "Prices" include not only the prices of ordinary goods and services but also wage rates, prices of other factors of production, and exchange rates. Our abstract comparison of the gold-standard and exchange-rate mechanisms gave equal status to the price adjustments working through domestic price levels and those working through exchange rates. With both mechanisms working frictionlessly, flows of *real* expenditure were all that mattered, and these were ideally unaffected by the money expenditures that corresponded to them. But now, realistically allowing for frictions that cause variations in real demand and hence in production and employment, we must recognize price-level and exchange-rate adjustments as *sub*categories of price policy, which contrasts with policy governing flows of money expenditure.

Actually, it is a bit narrow to speak of price and expenditure *policy*. Changes may occur in spontaneous response to market forces, without any deliberate official action. "Policy" to cure a balance-of-payments deficit might simply consist of passively permitting either

---

[6] This does not mean that a gold or foreign-exchange standard is inherently less inflationary than rival systems, but simply that it tends to keep each country in step with monetary conditions in other countries—stability, inflation, or deflation alike.

[7] The main obstacles are those stressed in theories of "wage-push inflation." These and other aspects of the problem of internal and external balance are examined in J. E. Meade, *The Balance of Payments,* London: Oxford University Press, 1951, esp. chaps. VIII-X.

the deflation of the money supply, spending, and prices or the exchange depreciation that the deficit would itself touch off. Even internally, adjustments may occur of their own accord: the price-and-wage cuts appropriate for curing depression and unemployment in the absence of positive expenditure policy would tend to come about, though slowly and painfully, under the pressure of gluts of labor and commodities. For this reason, "policy" will usually mean either passively *permitting* the appropriate adjustments or, if necessary, actively *promoting* them. The word will not always refer to deliberate official action.

Expenditure Policy Alone

The policies required for internal and external balance will sometimes coincide and sometimes clash. Let us first consider expenditure policy alone putting aside any possibility of corrective adjustment through prices, wages, and exchange rates. Table 6.1 considers two alternative types of disturbance tending to inflict an external deficit on Inland: (1) an inflationary impulse originating at home, and (2) any of several kinds of disturbance originating wholly or partly abroad, such as a foreign depression, a cheapening of foreign goods, or some change in tastes or technology or tariffs causing demand to shift from Inland onto Outland goods. Previous discussion should make the items in the table self-explanatory; for example, an export slump would inflict both a trade deficit and income deflation on Inland, requiring expenditure contraction to remedy the former and expenditure expansion to remedy the latter. Not only trade in goods and services but also capital movements may respond to expenditure policy. This is true if expenditure policy works through, or involves, changes in interest rates. The reduction in interest rates (reduction, at least, until the policy had succeeded in restoring domestic prosperity) would tend to worsen a balance-of-payments deficit (or reduce a surplus) not only by affecting trade but also by promoting an outflow (or reducing an inflow) of capital.

If the initial disturbance were the opposite of those shown in the top line of Table 6.1, each of the entries below would also be the opposite of the one shown.

The table suggests that when a disturbance originates at home, the expenditure policies required for internal and external balance coincide. When the disturbance originates abroad, or in the foreign-trade sector, the internal and external requirements clash. In general, when a deflationary or inflationary

Table 6.1. Inland Responses to Domestic and Foreign Disturbances
(Expenditure Policy Alone)

	Initial Domestic Disturbance	Initial Foreign Disturbance
Type of disturbance	Home inflation	Foreign depression, or cheapening of foreign goods, or shift of demand from Inland to Outland goods
Internal tendency in Inland	Inflation	Deflation
Tendency in Inland's trade	Deficit	Deficit
Expenditure policy for internal balance in Inland	Contractionary ⎫	Expansionary ⎫
Expenditure policy for Inland's external balance	Contractionary ⎬ Required policies coincide	Contractionary ⎬ Required policies clash

disturbance originates within one country, the ideal expenditure policy, from its own and foreign viewpoints alike, is correction of the disturbance at the source.

Some disturbances can be at least partially external to *all* countries concerned, as when a change in tastes or technology or tariffs shifts demand from Inland onto Outland goods. Inland develops internal deflation and an external deficit; Outland, internal inflation and an external surplus. If both adopt expenditure policies for internal balance—expansionary in Inland and contractionary in Outland—the imbalance in trade grows all the worse. If both adopt expenditure policies for external balance—contractionary in Inland and expansionary in Outland—the domestic imbalances grow all the worse.

Is there any way to avoid policy clashes by somehow having one country pursue internal balance and the other external balance? Outland, toward whose goods demand has shifted, might concentrate on getting rid of its external surplus by an expansionary expenditure policy, while Inland would concentrate on sustaining domestic income by a similar expansionary policy. If both expand expenditure with appropriate vigor, both could achieve external balance and Inland could achieve internal balance. But Outland's inflation then becomes all the worse; the entire conflict is concentrated into a worsened internal imbalance in Outland. The reverse pairing of objectives—contractionary policies in both countries as Inland sought external and Outland internal balance—produces no better result: again, balanced trade is conceivably attainable, but at the cost of shifting the entire conflict into Inland in the form of intensified deflation.

Even when internal and external policy requirements coincide in *direction,* they may clash in *degree.* More precisely, they may coincide in direction until policy has changed conditions to the extent that the requirements then clash even in direction. Consider a country sharing a world wide depression[8] and

running an export surplus. Both internal and external objectives call for an expansionary policy. But it would be extreme coincidence if the same degree of expansion were needed for both. On the one hand, if the export surplus were relatively slight, it might vanish while internal depression was still only partially remedied. Further expansion to finish curing the depression would shift the balance of payments into deficit. On the other hand, if the internal depression were relatively slight, it might be completely cured while an export surplus still persisted. Further expansion to cure this surplus would cause domestic inflation.

Conflicts of direction and degree arise because only one policy weapon, expenditure policy, has as yet been considered for pursuing two policy goals.[9] The problem is to hit two targets with a single shot. If the two targets just happen to be perfectly in line with each other, the feat is possible, but policy makers cannot always count on this happy coincidence.

---

[8] A clear-cut example requires an at least partially external disturbance. For if the country were suffering from a purely domestic depression that had not yet spread to other countries, policy might conceivably just remedy this depression and therefore also just remedy the export surplus it would cause.

[9] Expenditure policy employs various subweapons—open-market operations, debt management, and adjustments in taxes, government spending, bank reserve requirements, and central-bank discount rates. Whether this fact can make control of the flow of money expenditure count as more than a single policy weapon is considered in the appendix to this chapter. The argument there reaches a generally negative answer. Meanwhile, we continue to regard the choice among various budgetary or central-bank operations for affecting expenditure as an essentially administrative detail unable to split expenditure policy into aspects as distinct from each other as any of them is from price policy (including exchange-rate policy).

A noteworthy discussion of the required relation between the number of policy goals and the number of policy weapons is presented by Jan Tinbergen in *The Theory of Economic Policy,* Amsterdam: North-Holland Publishing Company, 1952, chaps. IV and V and esp. pp. 39-40, and in *Economic Policy: Principles and Design,* Amsterdam: North-Holland Publishing Company, 1956, esp. p. 55 and chap. 4. Tinbergen counts exchange-rate variation as a possible policy weapon, but there is little difference between regarding the adoption of rate flexibility as the addition of a policy weapon and regarding it as abandonment of the policy goal of a particular rate. Either way, any excess of the number of policy goals over the number of policy weapons is reduced by one.

Price Policy Alone

The previous section set price policy aside to consider expenditure policy alone; this section does the reverse. Downard price policy lowers a country's wages and price relative to those of other countries either by actual cuts in terms of local currency (if it is rigidly linked to foreign currencies) or else by exchange devaluation or depreciation. Upward price policy works either through price-and-wage increases in terms of local currency or through a rise in the currency's foreign-exchange value. Again we must emphasize that *policy,* in this context, does not necessarily mean positive action by the authorities. It may simply mean passively *allowing* market pressures to work their normal effects on domestic prices or the exchange rate. Table 6.2 lists some disturbances and the appropriate remedies.

This table requires somewhat more explanation than Table 6.1. Even some of the terminology is different. The inflationary domestic disturbance is here called "boom" rather than "inflation" because the price increases that would tend to occur are considered a policy response, even though passive, and a different word is needed for the condition that would prevail in their absence. Barring price increases, the inflation would be a "suppressed" one, involving general shortages of labor and goods and sabotage of the price mechanism. A cure for inflation in this sense would be inflation in the quite distinct sense of upward price adjustments; an excessive flow of purchasing power can be cut down by a cut in the purchasing power of each unit of money spent.

Even when working through exchange appreciation rather than through price and wage increases in home currency, upward price policy would tend (though more feebly) to restore internal balance: the new price relations would divert some purchases, by both Inlanders and Outlanders, onto Outland and away from Inland goods. This diversion, though appropriate to Inland's domestic situation, would tend to cause inflation in other countries previously enjoying internal balance. A related difficulty is that Inland's upward price policy would worsen the external deficit already associated with her domestic boom.

The table suggests downward price policy, perhaps rather misleadingly, to remedy the balance-of-payments deficit. Forcing down the

	Initial Domestic Disturbance		Initial Foreign Disturbance	
Type of disturbance	Boom at home		Foreign depression, or cheapening of foreign goods, or shift of demand from Inland to Outland goods	
Internal tendency in Inland	Boom		Depression	
Tendency in Inland's trade	Deficit		Deficit	
Price policy for internal balance in inland	Upward	Required policies clash	Downward	Required policies coincide
Price policy for Inland's external balance	Downward		Downward	

Table 6.2. Inland Responses to Domestic and Foreign Disturbances

Inland price level would make the "suppressed" character of the suppressed inflation all the worse, and though it might make Outlanders more *eager* to buy Inland goods, it might not make more such goods actually available to them. After all, however, an extreme enough devaluation of Inland currency might make import and export goods so expensive in Inland currency that Inlanders, despite their generally excessive purchasing power, would cut down their purchases of such goods enough to get rid of the country's deficit.

Let us now consider an initial domestic disturbance opposite to the one shown in the table: a depression that originates at home, causing an export surplus. An active policy to promote money expenditure is ruled out by our consideration of price policy alone. Downward price policy is the next best answer. Wage and price cuts in terms of home currency tend to restore real production and employment because each ordinary money unit of cash balances and of expenditure represents more real purchasing power than before and goes further in buying goods and hiring labor. Expenditure in real terms thus goes up, even though changes in the nominal money supply and in money expenditure are ruled out. Wage and price cuts would also have an expansionary domestic impact through their influence on Inland's foreign trade. They would divert some Inland and Outland purchases alike from Outland to Inland goods, stimulating Inland economic activity (at the cost, though, of tending to "export" unemployment to Outland).

This price-induced shift of purchases from foreign to domestic goods, not any increase in the real purchasing power of the existing expenditure flow and money supply, provides the expansionary impetus to domestic economic activity when downward price policy works through exchange depreciation rather than through wage and price cuts. Since it lacks the internal real-purchasing-power effects of such cuts, downward price policy is a feebler stimulus to domestic activity when it works through exchange depreciation alone. It is true that devaluation to a sufficiently low pegged rate can also help promote internal

balance by creating or expanding an external surplus that brings reserve gains, money-supply growth, and positive operation of the foreign-trade multiplier, as well as an opportunity for expenditure policy to become actively expansionary without causing balance-of-payments difficulties. But this means using price policy and at least passive expenditure policy *in combination,* something we are not yet ready to consider.

In ideal theory, price policy alone is adequate to achieve internal balance eventually. But to show this is not to endorse it for this purpose. Working through the exchange rate, it has only relatively indirect and feeble effects at home. Working in the downward direction through wage and price cuts, it is unattractive and impractical for familiar reasons involving wage and price stickiness, expectations, and the like. But the ultimate effects are as described. Even if price policy did work in ideal frictionless fashion, conflicts between internal and external objectives would sometime bedevil reliance on it alone, and it is important to understand when and how.

Luckily, this conflict is absent—at least in direction, if not in degree—when the initial disturbance is of external origin. As Table 6.2 shows, downward price policy is appropriate for coping with both the external deficit and the domestic depression caused by an export slump of external origin.

There is a curious contrast between the clashes of internal and external objectives that may occur when expenditure policy is used alone and when price policy is used alone. The required *expenditure* policies clash when an initial disturbance is external to a country and coincide when the disturbance is internal. But the required *price* policies clash when the disturbance is internal and coincide when it is external.

Alternative Policy Combinations

Because of this contrast and also because price policies for internal balance are feeble when working through the exchange rate and impractical and unattractive when working through domestic wage and price levels, a presumption arises in favor of combining expenditure policy used mainly for internal balance with price policy used mainly for external balance. Strictly speaking, it is not legitimate to pair particular weapons with particular goals: all weapons and goals intertwine in a single integrated system, and a change in any one aspect of this system in principle affects all the others. Still, pairing weapons and goals according to their *main* interconnections has a certain plausibility.

Expenditure policy for internal and price policy for external balance, while intuitively attractive, is not the only conceivable pairing. The alternative is price policy primarily for internal and expenditure policy primarily for external balance.[10] This comes close to the idealized theory (if perhaps not the actuality) of the traditional gold standard. A country with an externally caused balance-of-payments deficit incurs a deflation of expenditure and money supply through operation of the foreign-trade multiplier and loss of gold, which checks the tendency to overimport. This deflation would also cause unemployment and a slump in production, however, unless wage and price cuts so raised the purchasing power of the money unit that the flow of expenditure, though shrunken in money terms, nevertheless remained adequate in real purchasing power to provide enough demand for a full-employment level of production. Ideally, the necessary wage and price cuts would occur automatically, under the pressure of the oversupplies of labor and goods that would otherwise glut the market.

Further consideration of this expenditure-and-price mechanism demonstrates why it is not possible to identify one aspect of it strictly with external and the other with internal goals. Some cross-association is bound to occur. The drop in wages and prices tends, for example, to sustain domestic economic activity not only in the way previously described but also by shifting purchases from foreign to domestic goods and by permitting, without danger to the balance-of-payments position, an active or passive policy of moderating the

monetary contraction otherwise being imposed by the external deficit. The more promptly wages and prices adjust downward and the more sensitively trade responds to the changed relation between domestic and foreign prices, the less severe the expenditure deflation must be for the sake of the balance of payments.

Now consider this same "gold-standard" policy combination in a country with depression and an external *surplus*. (The cause might have been some spontaneous increase in the thriftiness or liquidity preferences of the public.) The consequences of the external surplus tend to sustain income and expenditure at home, but since this tendency is probably not strong enough by itself, wages and prices fall under the pressure of gluts on the market. These price adjustments help restore full employment both by diverting some additional purchases from foreign to domestic goods and by making each money unit "go further" in providing real demand. The recovery of domestic economic activity and purchasing power encourages imports and restrains exports and so overcomes the external surplus that the price adjustments would otherwise perpetuate. The more readily the domestic economy recovers, the smaller do these downward price adjustments have to be.

The intuitively preferable first pairing of weapons and goals—expenditure policy for internal and price policy for external balance —would accomplish price adjustments most easily through the exchange rate. Expenditure policies to resist internal disturbances would ordinarily also be appropriate to correct the impact of these internal disturbances on the balance of payments; but so far as the expenditure policy required for internal balance does not exactly coincide in degree with the requirement for external balance, the exchange rate can help take care of the latter. As for external disturbances to the balance of payments, the exchange rate can provide the required adjustment. It is true that removing or preventing a deficit through exchange depreciation, for example, tends to expand or at least resist contraction of domestic expenditure, with results that run

---

[10] These two pairings are what Meade calls "principle 1" and "principle 2." See Meade, *op. cit.,* pp. 157-162.

counter to the primary effect of the new exchange rate on trade. But this means not that depreciation must be ineffective but simply that it must go further than would have been necessary if domestic expenditure had been allowed to shrink. Again we see the need for two types of policy for the successful pursuit of two goals. Chapter 8 will argue an important corollary: if each country were to pursue a positive policy of stabilizing domestic expenditure (or its growth trend, in line with "real" economic growth), the income and expenditure responses that may weaken the external effectiveness of exchange-rate variation would be avoided.

Further Practical Differences between the Two Policy Combinations

Both pairings of policies with goals are abstractly logical. The difference is in how practical each is. Price policy for internal balance, or even for external balance when exchange-rate variation is ruled out, sometimes requires adjusting the whole level of wages and prices in local money, which is especially awkward when the adjustment has to be downward. In correcting external imbalance, the relative behavior of sectional price levels is ideally the same under both mechanisms: relative to the prices of internationally traded goods, the prices of domestic goods and factors of production must go down in a deficit country and up in a surplus country. But with flexible exchange rates, this shift takes place mainly by changes in the local-currency prices of international goods, with the prices of domestic goods and factors of production being less directly and sharply affected.[11] Under the gold standard or a similar system, the shift takes place mainly by

changes in the prices of domestic goods and factors of production; and if rigidities limit or retard price and wage cuts necessary to correct a balance-of-payments deficit and to maintain full employment in the face of shrunken expenditure, the outcome is unpleasant. Adjustments to a balance-of-payments deficit must permeate the whole domestic economy, reducing prices and wages and incomes in various degrees. The gold standard requires a crude, "shotgun" process of adjustment; and since it will not work frictionlessly, deflation to remedy the external deficit cuts production, employment, and real incomes as well as prices, wages, and money incomes. "But what a paradox! The country has been buying abroad more than it can afford. Surely the remedy should be to produce *more* rather than *less*."[12]

The gold-standard mechanism changes a wrong exchange rate into a right one not by changing the rate itself but by adjusting everything else. This approach reminds Professor Röpke of a circus clown who, seeing that the chair was too far from the piano, tried, with sweat streaming down his face, to push the piano towards the chair.[13] Exchange-rate adjustment pushes the chair instead; it is a more delicate and selective method, operating directly where changes are really required—in the markets for internationally traded goods and services. Professor Friedman has made a similar comparison. General price and income adjustments resemble arranging for more daylight hours after work on summer evenings by having everyone adjust his daily schedule so that he does everything one hour earlier. Instead of making these myriad detailed changes in our habits, we simply adopt daylight saving time. Changing one price, the exchange rate, rather than a multitude of internal prices, offers similar simplicity.[14]

---

[11] Some adjustment in domestic prices must still occur, as the principle of general economic interdependence teaches. Domestic-goods prices would generally move opposite to international-goods prices under a policy of keeping the home currency stable in overall purchasing power. However, the necessary domestic adjustments are less extreme under flexible exchange rates than under the gold standard. The exchange-rate mechanism operates *primarily* on the prices of international goods, whereas the gold-standard mechanism operates primarily on domestic prices and income.

[12] R. G. Hawtrey, *Bretton Woods for Better or Worse,* London: Longmans, Green, 1946, p. 10.

[13] Wilhelm Röpke, "Le rideau de fer monétaire," *Revue Economique et Sociale,* VIII, January 1950, p. 32. This quip is especially interesting, coming as it does from an economist who favors return to a gold standard.

[14] Milton Friedman, "The Case for Flexible Exchange Rates," *Essays in Positive Economics,* Chicago: University of Chicago Press, 1953, p. 173.

Wage-price Flexibility through Exchange Rates

The greater ease of changing one price than many suggest how fluctuating exchange rates can in effect put flexibility into sticky wages and prices. The importance of flexibility is best grasped by imagining its absence. As wants, resources, or technology change, resources would have to shift not in response to increases in the prices and costs of some products and resources and declines in the prices and costs of others but in response to the more wasteful and unpleasant spurs of shortages of some products and resources and gluts or unemployment of others. Flexible exchange rates could make the prices of each country's labor and products flexible, after all, as translated into the currencies of other countries. If demand for a country's products falls off, exchange depreciation could partly absorb the impact by lowering their foreign-currency prices and so helping to sustain foreign purchases. It would also benefit the country's import-competing industries and ease some transfer of resources out of the damaged export industries.

Consider the United States during a nation-wide slump in the demand for automobiles. In order either to keep up sales and output or to guide resources into other lines of production under the spur of something less stark than actual unemployment, automobile prices would have to fall in terms of the single nationwide currency that in fact exists, and at least an interruption in wage increases for automobile workers would also be necessary. Now suppose, instead, that each state has its own independent fluctuating currency.[15] The slump in demand for Michigan's automobiles depresses the exchange value of Michigan's "edsel." This depreciation cuts automobile prices outside Michigan, helping maintain sales and production despite the reduced demand. It also benefits Michigan's other export industries and import-competing industries, providing some job opportunities there for displaced automobile workers. Depreciation of the edsel raises prices in Michigan of im-

ported and exportable goods (other, presumably, than automobiles); in fact, this is how a necessary cut in real wages is accomplished despite obstacles to a cut in money wages.[16] If the industries burdened with increased costs of imported materials are export industries, higher selling prices in edsels will partly compensate. The burden is heavier for industries importing materials but selling their products at home, but discouragement of these industries is appropriate to the unavoidable real worsening in Michigan's external trade opportunities. So is the price incentive to substitute local for imported materials.

We must not paint too cheerful a picture. Since depreciation of the edsel does nothing by itself to expand the Michigan money supply and thus is not generally inflationary,[17] the rise in import and export prices implies deflationary pressure on other prices and wages inside Michigan. If these are rigid downward, the deflation of demand causes cutbacks in production and employment. Depreciation of the edsel may shift the problem of unemployment partly from the automobile industry to other industries. But under the alternative of fixed exchanges, actual shrinkage of the money supply in Michigan and contractionary operation of the external-trade multiplier would have made the spread of unemployment worse.

Still another consideration suggests that flexible exchanges do provide some net protection against unemployment. An initial drop in the outside demand for Michigan products and so in the derived demand for

---

[15] What follows is a piece of analysis only and is not meant as even a hint at a policy proposal.

[16] This does not mean that a Michigan cost-of-living index constructed by any reasonable method would vary in full proportion to exchange rates. Even in a single state the cost of living is not wholly made up of imported and readily exportable items: consider shelter, services, and the local-labor component of goods at retail. But collective bargains gearing wage rates to a cost-of-living index, together with an acquiescent monetary policy, would seriously impair the exchange-rate substitute for downward money-wage flexibility. To phrase the matter more generally, economic policy faces a dilemma when important interests refuse to adjust to adverse supply-and-demand changes and resist any form of downward adjustment in the relative prices of whatever they sell.

[17] The original real worsening in trade opportunities does tend to raise prices somewhat, on the average, since real income would unavoidably fall even if the flow of money income were kept unchanged.

Michigan factors of production could conceivably exert its effect in either of two extreme forms: unemployment, with Michigan factor prices rigid, or factor price cuts sufficient to maintain purchases and avoid unemployment. A flexible exchange rate makes Michigan factors price-flexible in terms of outside currencies and goods and thus enables the effect of the drop in demand to approach the second extreme form more closely than otherwise. In short, a fluctuating edsel permits Michigan factors to absorb the effects of reduced demand more fully in the form of worsened terms of trade and less in the form of unemployment. If the former coal miners of West Virginia could accept their economic misfortunes in reduced real wage rates rather than in unemployment, they might be better off than they are now. West Virginia coal would be able to hold its market better in the face of competition, or other local industries might expand or new industries be attracted into the area. The existence of depressed areas in the United States even during times of prosperity testifies to the importance of wage-price flexibility or some substitute for it.

Effective price flexibility through exchange rates would have the further though minor advantage of promoting price competition. The producer of each particular product would find that the prices quoted by outside competitors, as translated at fluctuating rates, were undergoing continual (though usually slight) changes relative to his own price. It would be difficult to maintain a rigid price not only in terms of all currencies but perhaps even in terms of the local currency. The more nearly standardized a product, the less feasible would quasi-oligopolistic price inflexibility be. Continual slight fluctuations in the prices of rival producers, as translated at flexible rates, would pose some slight obstacle to collusion or a live-and-let-live policy of rigid prices. Even "pattern" wage bargaining could be impeded somewhat.

But this overstates the case. Exchange-rate flexibility is, after all, only a crude and unselective substitute for flexibility in each individual wage and price. Still, the two types of flexibility are by no means rivals: fixed rates do not promote and flexible rates do not impair detailed wage-and-price flexibility. It is true that the more flexible wages and prices were individually, the less a free exchange rate would have to move when the world market conditions for some particular product changed. This is no reason for rejecting any substitute flexibility, however, when detailed flexibility is in fact inadequate. Substitute flexibility would be most satisfactory if currency areas coincided with economically homogeneous regions. If we could start with a blank slate in designing an ideal world and did not have to consider a historically established pattern of fiscal, monetary, and banking systems, we would not carve out separate currency areas according to today's national boundaries. The smaller the area in which each currency circulated and the less varied the economic activities carried on there, the more nearly would exchange-rate flexibility approximate industry-by-industry or even firm-by-firm wage and price flexibility. The geographic area encompassing each single enterprise might conceivably have its own independent fluctuating currency; someone has even tauntingly said that each individual person might have his own currency. But this would surely be going too far, for money loses its very meaning unless it can be held as a reserve of purchasing power regularly acceptable by most of the other economic units to which the holder may wish to make payments. Beyond some admittedly indefinable point, the proliferation of separate currencies for ever smaller and more narrowly defined territories would begin to negate the very concept of money. Furthermore, having many hundreds or thousands of separate currencies would make the market for each one quite thin. Individual transactions might be large enough relative to the total supply of and demand for an individual currency to cause sharp random exchange-rate fluctuations. Speculation would then be inadequately stabilizing, and groups of speculators might even be able to dominate the market for individual currencies and manipulate rates to their own advantage. Currency areas as small as the states of the United States would probably be unacceptable because of the sheer nuisance of so many foreign exchange transactions and the expense of printing many separate currencies and administering many central banks. (The example of Michigan and its local currency was not a proposal but merely an attempt to dramatize a piece of analysis.) Particularly when interregional monetary unification already exists, undoing it is not an attractive idea. But when countries have not unified their fiscal and monetary systems and when currency exchanges already are necessary for international payments, the quasi-flexibility that free exchange rates can put into wages and prices is worth considering.[18]

Asymmetrical Sharing of Adjustment Burdens

Another important point of comparison between rival mechanisms concerns how deficit and surplus countries share the burdens of adjustment. In the frictionless ideal operation of *all* mechanisms, adjustments of relative prices and real quantities are the same. Each country makes its absorption and production equal (except for independently motivated capital movements), and the question of sharing the burden is meaningless. But in actuality, frictions and delays in adjustment cause additional burdens—unemployment, inflationary distortions, and the like. It is therefore worth inquiring in what countries and in what directions most of the changes in money expenditure and money price levels are likely to occur.

Under the gold (or foreign-exchange) standard, gold flows affect money supplies and spending more strongly in the countries with the greater marginal degrees of pyramiding of ordinary money onto a fractional

gold base, other things being equal. Equal absolute changes are, of course, different percentage changes for countries of different size, but for an external imbalance of a given size *relative* to a country's economy, the country presumably shares the adjustment burden in inverse relation to its gold reserve ratio. Differences in monetary velocities and in the marginal propensities to import and save that determine foreign-trade multipliers blur this presumption. Price changes may not correspond closely with expenditure changes because of countries' different initial degrees of unemployment and slack in production and different degrees of price-and-wage flexibility. But we certainly would not say that a deficit country escapes its share of the adjustment burden to the extent that monetary deflation affects real activity instead of prices and wages; quite the contrary.

Even apart from all this hedging, the question of how burdens are shared is particularly complex when some countries are on a gold-exchange or foreign-exchange standard instead of a gold coin or bullion standard.[19] Consider a drain of reserves between two ordinary members of such a system, each of which holds its monetary reserves in the currency of some center country. The impact on each will be much the same as if each had been on an actual gold standard, and the size of its reserve ratio is relevant. A drain between an ordinary member and the center country will work asymmetrically. The ordinary member will be affected much as if gold had flowed under a gold standard, but in the center country the domestically held money supply (understood to include not only actual money but also near-moneys that other countries might hold as reserves) will change only by the absolute amount of the international reserve flow. When the center country runs an external surplus or deficit, its ordinary bank balances (and near-moneys) move into or out of the possession of its own residents and out of or into the possession of foreigners. It experiences no multiple expansion or contraction of money.[20] There is no such multi-

---

[18] See Bela Balassa, *The Theory of Economic Integration,* Homewood, Ill.: Irwin, 1961, pp. 263-268, and Robert A. Mundell, "A Theory of Optimum Currency Areas," *American Economic Review,* LI, September 1961, pp. 657-665. Mundell's optimum would strike a balance between the advantages and disadvantages of having many small independent currency areas. On the one hand would be an approach to intraregional economic homogeneity; on the other would be thin markets and the nuisance of exchanging currencies. Furthermore, the smaller each area, the more heavily imports would count in the cost of living and the greater would be the pressure to tie wages, in effect, to the price of foreign exchange, destroying the hoped-for flexibility in real wages.

[19] The following relies in part on Meade, *op. cit.,* pp. 183-189.

[20] However, if the foreign banks or monetary authori-

plication, anyway, unless its authorities deliberately engineer it out of concern for the *difference* between the country's gold reserves and the amount of its money and near-moneys held as reserves by foreigners. If its authorities fail to do so, the center country leaves the bulk of the adjustment to the member country. The center country largely avoids the "discipline of the gold flows" that it would experience under a full-fledged international gold standard. This avoidance is particularly significant when the center country is running a deficit, for the member countries with the corresponding surpluses may not cure the imbalance by allowing their reserve gains to have their full impact on their own money supplies, incomes, and price levels. Their authorities may want moderate surpluses to continue as a way of building up their reserves of center-country currency in step with their general growth of income and international trade. The imbalance may then continue indefinitely, with the center country's external liabilities growing ever larger in relation to its gold reserves. The danger heightens that a scramble for actual gold may some day pull down the whole increasingly precarious structure. In essence, the United States is nowadays in some degree a center country of the kind described above. The growth of American external liabilities in settlement (or perhaps one should say *non*-settlement) of chronic deficits since 1950 has convinced many observers that the dangers mentioned above are indeed realistic. Chapter 26 will have more to say about this problem.

The center country is affected even by imbalances between two other countries if one of them belongs to the exchange-standard system and uses its currency as reserves but the other does not. A member country gaining actual gold from a nonmember will presumably exchange it for balances of center-country currency, following whatever motives led its authorities to choose an exchange

standard rather than gold standard in the first place. The center country gains gold reserves, then, even without running a balance-of-payments surplus itself. If the imbalance between the other countries is in the reverse direction, then the authorities of the nonmember country, unwilling to hold their new reserves in the form of foreign exchange, will convert them into gold drawn from the center country.

This possibility may lead the authorities of the center country to subtract member-country holdings of its currency from its total gold reserves to estimate its net or effective gold reserves. So defined, the net gold reserves of the center country will be unaffected by transfers among other countries, regardless of which are or are not members of the exchange-standard system. For example, if a nonmember gains reserves from a member and converts them into gold, the drain on the gross gold reserves of the center country is matched by an equal fall in its foreign liabilities. Even imbalances between the center and a member country will have effects much as under a regular gold standard if it is the *net* gold reserves that govern monetary responses in the center country. A rise or fall in liabilities to a member spells a fall or rise in the center's net gold reserves, to which its domestic money supply is now supposed to be more or less definitely geared.

But if this is how the center country responds to external imbalance, then the gold-exchange standard does not "economize" on gold after all; the multiple pyramiding of domestic money supplies in both center and member countries onto the central gold base is avoided. Either net reserves govern money supplies and the exchange standard does not economize on gold (though in historical fact this was its main purpose) or else the system is a precarious one. (Economizing on gold is precarious both because the center country has to shoulder part of the burden of readjusting to imbalances between member and nonmember countries and also because, for an indefinite period, the center country escapes "the discipline of the gold flows" that imbalances with member countries would otherwise impose on it.) Actual

---

ties insist on holding their external reserves as deposits with the central bank of the center country rather than as ordinary commercial-bank deposits or near-moneys, their losses and gains of such reserves can spell gains or losses of domestic monetary reserves for the commercial banks of the center country. These may then engage in multiple expansion or contraction of credit and deposits.

practice under the exchange standard has usually come closer to landing on the second horn of this dilemma.

Still another asymmetry may occur in the sharing of adjustment burdens under a fractional-reserve gold or exchange standard. It is implied in the question whether or not ratios between gold reserves and domestic money supplies remain fairly stable when gold flows in or out. The marginal gold-reserve ratio may well be larger, and the response of the domestic money supply smaller, for inflows than outflows. An imbalance leading to an inflow of reserves is seldom if ever a serious difficulty requiring prompt correction; the authorities may simply allow the reserves to pile up without promoting all the multiple domestic monetary expansion required to maintain a constant reserve *ratio*.[21] Of course, complete "sterilization" of inflowing reserves is neither easy nor likely; their purchase by the authorities as required to keep exchange rates fixed tends to expand domestic bank reserves and the money supply much as would a central-bank open-market purchase of securities, and actual counterexpansionary action would depend on deliberate policy. But even partial sterilization by surplus countries throws an all the larger share of the adjustment burden onto the deficit countries. Furthermore, deficits call more urgently for action, since reserves losses are a more critical problem than gains. Even if a country had previously built up a comfortable margin of reserves beyond the legal or the supposedly prudent ratio, the limit to what it can stand to lose is much more definite than the almost nonexistent limit to the reserves that a surplus country can absorb. Much more than is true of a surplus country, a deficit country must act to restore balance and protect its reserves; and if it is to abide by the gold-standard rules against exchange depreciation and *ad hoc* controls over trade and payments,

this action can only be to deflate. Because adjustment burdens fall more urgently on deficit than on surplus countries and because adjustment to a deficit means deflation, the gold standard has a deflation bias *if actually adhered to*. (This is not to say that the gold standard cannot be inflationary; it has been, as from about 1896 to 1914. The foregoing refers to whatever bias may be inherent in the relative intensities of pressures to adjust on deficit and surplus countries.)

Asymmetries of the Adjustable Peg

In considering whether the alternative adjustment mechanism may have any asymmetries and biases of its own, we must distinguish between changes in officially fixed rates and fluctuations in continuously free rates. The former system, the "adjustable peg," is an attempted halfway house between the two extremes of full international monetary linkage and full national monetary independence. Insofar as countries are reluctant to adjust their exchange parities and instead make both maintaining them and avoiding controls a leading policy goal, the system approximates the gold or gold-exchange standard and distributes adjustment burdens as already described. But since World War II, at least, countries have been understandably reluctant to deflate for the sake of external balance; "full employment" is the watchword of policy. A country will simply try to "ride out" an external deficit; its authorities will hope that the imbalance will somehow or other vanish of its own accord before too long, and they will meanwhile continue to peg the exchange rate by drawing on reserves or international loans. But it is still true that deficits and reserve losses pose a more pressing problem than surpluses. A country with a persistent deficit will ultimately impose controls as a palliative or, in accordance with the logic of the adjustable-peg system, will devalue. But it will not actively deflate.

Just as under the gold standard, the need to act falls more urgently on deficit than on surplus countries. But the preference for devaluation over deflation makes the adjustable-peg system contrast sharply with a gold

---

[21] France and the United States were accused of such a "sterilization" of gold gains during the 1920s. A more recent and conspicuous example is West Germany's understandable reluctance to let the massive growth of her gold and dollar reserves since 1950 have its full domestic inflationary impact.

standard that is meant to be permanent and whose rules are obeyed. An inflationary bias emerges in several ways. In the sometimes lengthy intervals between exchange-rate adjustments, when some countries are hopefully "riding out" deficits and losing reserves, others are running surpluses and gaining reserves. Without wanting to, a surplus country tends to "import" inflation in three overlapping ways: (1) an export surplus spells withdrawal of real goods and services from the home economy; less than the full value of the country's current production is available for satisfying demands on the home market; (2) the foreign-trade multiplier operates in the expansionary direction; and (3) the authorities create new domestic money as they buy the local residents' surplus earnings of foreign exchange to keep exchange rates pegged. Under a fractional-reserve banking system, official purchases of foreign exchange or gold, as of securities or anything else, expand the volume of bank reserves and set the stage for a multiple expansion of ordinary deposit money. Deliberate monetary or fiscal measures can conceivably counteract or neutralize these spontaneous inflationary pressures, but successful neutralization tends to frustrate balance-of-payments adjustment, perpetuating the troublesome surplus and the need for domestic measures to resist its inflationary impact. For the sake of being able, without inflation, to make the involuntary loans to foreigners that the foreign-exchange accumulations represent, a country must impose higher taxes or tighter credit on the economy than would otherwise be necessary. The dilemma is compounded if anti-inflation policy involves interest rates high enough to attract funds from abroad, increasing the amount of foreign exchange that the central bank must buy to maintain exchange-rate stability. These purchases further tend to expand the domestic money supply, and borrowers of the inflowing foreign funds presumably pay higher interest rates on them than the authorities earn on their involuntary foreign-exchange accumulations. Domestic policies for monetary stability cannot be as consistent, vigorous, and relatively pain-

less as they could if some mechanism were continuously correcting balance-of-payments disequilibria. Despite everything, though, it is possible that surplus countries might succeed at least for a while in "sterilizing" their reserve gains, sometimes completely and often partially. But if they sterilize less completely and less typically than deficit countries avoid deflation—which is probable—the adjustable peg has an inflationary bias.

Sterilization by surplus countries has already been noted as an at least minor problem for deficit countries under the gold standard. From the standpoint of surplus countries, the prospects for successful sterilization are probably dimmer under the adjustable-peg system than under the gold standard. Imbalances are likely to be larger and longer-lasting because authorities in deficit countries, knowing that they can always devalue or impose controls as a last resort, are less willing to deflate as a corrective. Furthermore, a general desire to keep exchange rates fixed except for infrequent adjustments breeds international arrangements to help deficit countries "ride out" their supposedly temporary troubles. The more these devices enable deficit countries to avoid or postpone or mitigate the controls or devaluations otherwise necessary, the slighter is their immediate need to restrain imports and push exports and the stronger, therefore, are price-raising demands relative to supplies in the world markets for their imports and exports. And better-financed deficits for some countries mean larger and more persistent surpluses for other countries, together with problems of imported inflation. The hope that deficits and surpluses will alternate is hardly reassuring, for the alternation will take place at generally higher levels of spending than if special finance for deficits had not been provided.

A surplus, with its inflationary impact, may indeed reverse itself in time. But the deflationary impact of a subsequent deficit is hardly a full and satisfactory offset to what may have happened earlier. Trying belatedly to undo an accomplished inflation courts unemployment and recession. A country will resist deflationary pressures from abroad even when they come against a background of inflation imported earlier. A "ratchet" is at work.

A related aspect of this "ratchet" shows up in a radically simplified example concerning either several industries within a single country or several countries in a world of pegged currencies. Suppose that something such as changed consumer preferences shifts demand away from the products of industry or country A onto the products of industry or country B. Prices and wages are bid up in B but exhibit downward rigidities in A. Demand next shifts from B to industry or country C, again raising some prices and wages without correspondingly reducing others. Now demand may shift back toward A, perhaps still in a depression from the first shift. Wages and prices may or may not go up there; in any case, they have gone up and stayed up in B and C. Mere shifts—perhaps only temporary shifts—in the pattern of demand may thus raise the *average* level of wages and prices.[22] Under the unlikely policy of stabilizing money supplies or total spending, these wage-and-price increases would entail unemployment, but acquiescent monetary expansion would consolidate them. Within a country, this dilemma stems from inadequate two-way flexibility of wages and prices; internationally, it stems from lack of continuous balance-of-payments adjustment through either domestic price-and-wage flexibility or continuous exchange-rate flexibility.

Perhaps it is not yet clear what serves as the growing reserve basis for the expansion of national money supplies. Without monetary expansion the inflationary tendencies already described could not go very far. One answer may be the creation of "international liquidity" under various schemes to shore up the adjustable-peg system. Even apart from this, the devaluation bias of the system provides an answer.

Precisely because deficits and reserve losses are more critical problems than surpluses and reserve gains, countries are more likely to devalue to adjust to internal inflation or to escape other deficit tendencies than they are to revalue upward to escape inflationary pressures from abroad.[23] One important check to upward revaluation is the prospect of strong complaints from the export interests whom it would harm (the greater influence of special producer interests than of the general consumer interest is a well-known fact of practical politics, amply illustrated in tariff policies). Furthermore, since no one knows how to calculate a new equilibrium exchange rate at all precisely, there is always the danger that a revaluation might prove excessive. Or the conditions that had seemed to justify it might blow over of their own accord. The temptation is to sit tight and do nothing. The same temptation also tends to delay action when conditions call for devaluation, especially since the move may seem like a confession of earlier financial mismanagement or may give political opponents an opportunity to charge mismanagement. But conditions can eventually force devaluation in a much truer sense than they can force revaluation. If devaluation must finally come, it is more likely to err on the large side than on the small side. Since they in any case incur the odium of changing the rate, the authorities might as well not make a change so small that they leave themselves open to the question whether it really was necessary. Since they cannot calculate an exactly correct new rate, they might as well play safe and avoid risking the need for a confidence-shaking second devaluation soon afterward. Also, a switch from overvaluation to undervaluation of the currency may give the authorities a chance to rebuild their depleted reserves. Excessive devaluation sets the stage for inflationary influences working through the balance of payments. Over the long run, the devaluation bias means that even a fixed world stock of

---

[22] Charles L. Schultze reports detecting some such ratchet mechanism at work domestically; *Recent Inflation in the United States,* Joint Economic Committee Study Paper No. 1, Washington: U.S. Government Printing Office, 1959.

[23] For historical documentation of the devaluation bias of fixed exchanges, see Henrik Åkerlund, *Guldparistandarden,* Stockholm: Grafiska Konstanstalten Tryckeri, 1959, pp. 85-88. Upward revaluations, when such rarities occur, are likely to err on the small side.

gold (or whatever else serves as basic international reserves) would grow in value expressed in national currencies; and given the modern insistence on a large measure of national freedom to pursue full-employment policies, an abundance of international liquidity is more likely to promote than a scarcity is to restrain the inflation of national currencies.

Even the gold standard, like the adjustable-peg system, suffers from this inflationary devaluation bias. Over the long run, gold goes up in price and thus in the amount effectively available to "support" the growth of national money supplies. Despite the firmest of intentions, gold parities cannot be kept fixed forever; forced devaluations and depreciations are a familiar historical fact. Over the long run, the gold standard *is* an adjustable-peg system, but with the adjustments infrequent. The *deflationary* bias previously attributed to the gold standard operates in the relatively short run, the inflationary bias secularly. There is no incompatibility between these two biases. Both operate because adjustment burdens fall more urgently on deficit than on surplus countries. This means deflation as long as deficit countries can manage to stick to the gold-standard rules, devaluation when the game is up. In practice, forced devaluations are seldom reversed. Sporadic long-run currency erosion is no less real just because short-run deflations interrupt the process. Short-run and long-run troubles do not just compensate for each other. When a streamroller is rolling over you from south to north, it is no consolation to know that later on it will probably roll over you again from north to south.

Fluctuating Exchanges

The system of independent national currencies with freely fluctuating rates stands at the opposite extreme from the gold standard. Whether it has asymmetries and biases of different kinds than those discussed here, whether it suffers from and promotes various kinds of instability, whether it impedes trade and investment and generally disrupts international economic integration, and whether

it has still other disadvantages—all these questions will be explored in later chapters. Meanwhile, it is worth noting that it largely escapes several of the specific asymmetries and biases of the gold standard and the adjustable-peg system.

Most fundamentally, free rates avoid imposing the more urgent need for action and the bulk of the adjustment burden on deficit rather than on surplus countries. This two-sidedness is a distinctive feature which deserves emphasis. No authority need decide about allowing or promoting deflation or inflation; the short-run deflation bias of the gold standard is absent. No authority need decide about adjusting a pegged rate downward or upward. No authority operates with the understandable human tendency to err on the large side when deciding on devaluations and on the small side when deciding on upward revaluations. The rate adjusts itself under impersonal market pressures. It moves upward for a country that would otherwise have had an external surplus just as readily as it moves downward for a country otherwise in external deficit (both movements considered relative to the currencies of countries in approximate external balance). The asymmetry and the inflationary devaluation bias of the adjustable peg are absent.

Since imbalances do not go uncorrected for long periods, countries otherwise in surplus can avoid the inflations—inflations irreversible in practice, because of downward wage and price stickiness—that they might otherwise sometimes import or that they could neutralize only with difficulty. Continuous balance-of-payments adjustment, together with the effective two-way flexibility that fluctuating rates give to each country's wages and prices in terms of foreign currencies, counters the international aspects of the inflationary "ratchet" associated even with nothing worse than mere temporary shifts in patterns of demand. (See pp. 102-103.)

More broadly, free rates permit compartmentalizing inflationary tendencies. Consider an inflation originating in certain countries under a fixed-rate system. Whether it is due to monetary expansion pure and simple or to acquiescent monetary policy in the face of a "wage push" is immaterial. Trade becomes unbalanced. Other countries experience the familiar monetary and "multiplier" effects of balance-of-payments surpluses. Increased costs of importing from the originally inflationary countries hasten these effects by directly pushing costs and prices upward. (All these effects may be imperceptibly slight if the first countries make up only a small fraction of the world economy and develop only mild inflations; the nature rather than strength of international contagion is what is at issue here.) Under free rates, by contrast, other countries escape not only external surpluses and their consequences but also the apparent "cost push" of increased import prices. Wages and prices in the inflationary countries, though increased in local currency, are translated at promptly depreciated exchange rates. This keeps the export prices of inflationary countries and their demands for the exports of other countries from increasing from the viewpoint of the latter. The *pattern* of prices and demands seen by other countries does change somewhat, since wages, prices, and demands in terms of local currency in inflationary countries do not all rise in equal proportion. As translated at the new exchange rates, some individual prices and demands rise and other fall. But the new exchange rates do prevent any unequivocal increases, from the viewpoint of other countries, in the general level of prices charged by and demand emanating from the first.

Depression as well as inflation can be compartmentalized under free rates. Exchange depreciation under free-market pressures can save countries not originally involved in foreign depressions from balance-of-payments deficits and their deflationary consequences. "The free-exchange system eliminates . . . the most important carrier of the boom and depression bacillus—namely, the flow of money across frontiers."[24]

None of the foregoing means that free rates, in and by themselves, can ward off all troubles, ranging from hangnails to unemployment. They are no substitute for appropriate domestic policy. By lessening interference from balance-of-payments difficulties, they simply give a country's monetary and fiscal authorities a better *opportunity* to maintain internal balance in the face of foreign depression, or at least to maintain as good a compromise between full employment and a stable price level as domestic obstacles allow. Still, no conceivable combination of exchange-rate and domestic policies—nothing short of total prohibition of foreign trade—can insulate a country completely from foreign economic developments.[25] Depression

---

[24] Gottfried von Haberler, *op. cit.,* p. 446. No country ever seems to have made a thoroughgoing experiment with free exchanges as a buffer against foreign business fluctuations, but some accidental examples illustrate the possibilities revealed by theory. As price and income levels sank in gold-standard countries after 1929, the Spanish government reluctantly allowed the peseta to depreciate severely against gold currencies. The Spanish price level

sagged only moderately, and the depression was less severe in Spain than in other countries. Walter H. Delaplane, "The Spanish Peseta since 1913" (unpublished dissertation), Durham: Duke University, 1934, pp. 128-129, 135, 138, 158, 207; Anon., "Eine 'systematisch unstabile Währung'. Die spanische Peseta," *Währung und Wirtschaft,* IV, August 1935, p. 130. Spanish national income held up well in the early 1930s; Colin Clark reproduces the figures in *The Conditions of Economic Progress;* 2nd ed., London: Macmillan, 1951, p. 156.

Exchange depreciation of her silver-standard currency spared China internal deflation and the contagion of the world depression for the first two years after its outbreak in 1929. See p. 310 below.

Considerable other evidence suggests that countries with depreciated currencies weathered the 1929 depression better than countries that clung longer to their old gold parities. See James W. Angell, "Exchange Depreciation, Foreign Trade and National Welfare," *Proceedings of the Academy of Political Science,* XV, June 1933, p. 291, and Richard A. Lester, *Monetary Experiments,* Princeton: Princeton University Press, 1939, p. 275.

[25] Besides being much weaker under flexible than under fixed exchange rates, the international contagion of business fluctuations even tends to work in the opposite way. At least, so goes one plausible line of reasoning. (See Svend Laursen and Lloyd A. Metzler, "Flexible Exchange Rates and the Theory of Employment," *Review of Economics and Statistics,* XXXII, November 1950, pp. 281-299. Egon Sohmen gives a lucid and on the whole concurring discussion of this argument in *Flexible Exchange Rates,* ca. p. 95.) Suppose that a depression in Outland lowers the demand for Inland's exports, causing its currency to depreciate on the exchanges. Import prices rise in Inland currency, while the primary effect of the drop in Outland demand keeps the depreciation from raising export prices to the same extent (if at all). Since import prices rise relative to export prices while imports and exports remain equal in value (though at a new level—one key assumption, incidentally, is the absence of any capital movements accommodating a temporary imbalance), import *quantity* falls relative to export *quantity.* Real demand is shunted toward Inland's domestic output and domestic factors of production. Employment tends to rise, unless already

abroad narrows the scope of gains from trade by making foreign countries poorer and less valuable trading partners. Under any set of domestic policies, depression abroad, like any other important changes in world supplies and demands, will affect a country's pattern and terms of trade and require changes in its resource allocation and the composition of its output. Because of the changed pattern of demand and the short-run immobility of labor and other resources, no monetary-fiscal policy whatever can maintain just the right amount of spending on the output of each sector of the home economy, all at the same time. A policy expansionary enough to avoid all pockets of unemployment will cause inflationary pressures in other sectors; a policy restrictive enough to avoid all inflation will leave some pockets of deflation.[26] Some compromise is unavoidable.

The best a country can hope for is what free exchanges permit—freedom for domestic monetary and fiscal policy to ward off the economy-wide inflation or deflation that foreign disturbances might otherwise impose. According to one line of reasoning, the free flexibility of exchange rates actually increases the effectiveness of monetary policy for domestic stability. Expanding the money supply and reducing interest rates to counter a recession—or even just letting interest rates fall spontaneously, as they typically do in a re-

cession—tends to cause a capital outflow. The balance of payments would be in overall deficit—*except* that the home currency depreciates on the exchanges to whatever extent necessary to cause an export surplus of goods and services large enough to match the capital outflow. This export surplus represents a timely addition to the demand for domestic output and domestic factors of production. An anti-inflationary monetary policy, conversely, influences capital movements so as to make the home currency appreciate, bringing a net inflow of goods and services into the country and imposing restraint on the pricing policies of domestic producers. This reinforcement of domestic policy, says Egon Sohmen, no doubt exaggerating, "is perhaps the most persuasive reason for the advocacy of flexible exchanges. . . ."[27]

Even if the free-rate system avoids some asymmetries and biases of rival systems, doesn't it have other and perhaps worse ones of its own? No systematically unequal imposition of adjustment burdens is apparent, particularly if rates are allowed to respond just as freely to potential surpluses as to potential deficits. Nor is any deflation bias apparent.

The absense of deflation bias raises suspicion of an inflation bias; a perfectly neutral system is implausible. Under free rates, concern for its balance of payments never forces a country to deflate nor restrains it from inflating. The problem of downward inflexibility of wages and prices is not necessarily any worse than under other exchange-rate systems; but anyway, accidental inflationary impulses that might otherwise prove temporary and remediable threaten to become con-

---

existing full employment puts the entire demand pressure on prices. (Nothing in the process just outlined would tend spontaneously, apart from policy, to cause an offsetting shrinkage in the Inland money supply.)

A more intuitive way of seeing all this is to note that depressed Outland has become an effectively less eager trading partner, which causes Inland's terms of trade to worsen and real income (at the previously existing level of employment) to fall. The worsening of Inland's opportunities for international trade has the same kind of employment-creating or price-raising impact, loosely speaking, as would a bad harvest or an earthquake.

[26] This dilemma due to a changed pattern of demand is presumably more serious when the disturbance is foreign depression than when it is foreign inflation. Depression means a decline in employment and production and real purchasing power in the foreign countries, not simply a decline in price levels that could be allowed for by translation at new exchange rates. Inflation leaves the real economic condition of foreign countries more nearly unchanged, so that translation of their inflated prices at new exchange rates leaves their supplies and demands more nearly unchanged from the viewpoint of the home country.

---

[27] *Op. cit.*, p. 84. See also pp. 83, 85, 123-124, as well as Sohmen, *International Monetary Problems and the Foreign Exchanges*. Special Papers in International Economics, No. 4, Princeton, N.J.: Princeton University, International Finance Section, 1963, pp. 6, 51-54, 65, 70; and J. Marcus Fleming, "Domestic Financial Policies Under Fixed and Under Floating Exchange Rates," IMF *Staff Papers*, **IX**, November 1962, pp. 369-379.

The contrast with fixed exchange rates is striking. An anti-inflationary policy of tight money and relatively high interest rates tends to attract capital, expand foreign exchange reserves and domestic bank reserves, and so promote unwanted monetary expansion. The German experience with this problem in the 1950s, reviewed in Chapter 23, is instructive.

solidated in wage and price structures. The "ratchet" operates. The exchange depreciation that avoids a balance-of-payments deficit allows import and export prices to rise in local currency and, together with the monetary expansion that may have been the initial disturbance, allows a general rise in prices. Exchange-rate pegging, by contrast, lets the country enjoy the anti-inflationary assistance of an actual deficit: the real goods and services in effect borrowed from abroad help hold down prices, while the sale of foreign exchange drawn from official reserves or borrowed abroad mops up liquidity at home. In broader terms, the gearing of the home economy into a not-yet-inflated world environment provides time to correct the inflationary impulse before it is irreversibly consolidated in wages and prices.[28]

What this really means is that the country not so much prevents all inflation as makes inflation of domestic origin inconspicuous by diluting it into the outside world. It shoves its problem onto other countries in many small inconspicuous bits. It may use this opportunity to gain time while correcting inflationary pressures. Or it may not. Inflation, especially "wage-push" inflation, has aptly been characterized as an attempt by different groups to divide up among themselves more than the total national output. Under fixed exchange rates these excessive claims against national output can partly be met—for a while—by dipping into reserves or borrowing abroad. It is not unprecedented for a regime currently in power to subsidize the temporary delights of living beyond the country's means by dissipating its external reserves, passively hoping that the longer-run necessary adjustment will somehow take care of itself and leaving it to some successor regime to impose "austerity." Monetary insulation under fluctuating exchanges, on the other hand, leaves each country more immediately and fully exposed to the wanted or unwanted consequences of its own policies. This is a disadvantage for the less prudent countries and an advantage for the more prudent ones.

Free rates allow a country to drift carelessly into inflation; at the other extreme, they allow it to pursue monetary stability even in an inflationary world. Monetary independence means freedom for recklessness and prudence alike. This is a relevant comment on the further point that under fixed exchange rates, the "discipline of the balance of payments"—the need to worry about deficits—restrains inflationary domestic policy. Sometimes, by coincidence, the "discipline" will work in a welcome direction; at other times, not. And as for "discipline," a free exchange rate may itself be a useful alarm signal, indicating domestic inflationary tendencies more conspicuously than an external deficit would and rallying public protest more promptly. Conceivably, of course, the opposite is true: dwindling reserves may be a greater impulse to timely action than a falling exchange rate; the impression that the exchange rate alone will take care of the balance of payments may make the public apathetic about fighting inflation.[29] But these indecisive considerations relate to the psychology of central bankers, politicians, and voters and not to biases inherent in institutional arrangements.

Conclusion

The expenditure policies required for both internal and external balance coincide when a disturbance is domestic and clash when it is external; the required price policies clash for a domestic and coincide for an external disturbance. This fact, together with difficulties in using price policy for internal

---

[28] See Robert Triffin, *Gold and the Dollar Crisis*, New Haven, Conn.: Yale University Press, 1960, pp. 82-86.

[29] Lionel Robbins, *The Economist in the Twentieth Century*, London: Macmillan, 1954, pp. 98-101 and esp. p. 100. Robbins worries that some otherwise minor disturbance, perhaps an unfavorable "real" change on the world market, will produce exchange depreciation that spreads irreversibly into the whole wage and price structure. It is noteworthy, however, that he explicitly assumes a passively expanding money supply. With the money supply so completely out of control, flexible prices of *anything*, and not just of foreign exchange, would seem to be unsafe.

Emil Küng, *Zahlungsbilanzpolitik*, Zurich: Polygraphischer Verlag, 1959, p. 582, reviews the opinions of several other writers on which is more effective as an alarm signal for mobilizing opinion against inflationary policies— reserve drains or exchange depreciation.

balance, tells in favor of expenditure policy as the main weapon for internal and price policy for external balance. Adjustment works more simply in practice through exchange rates than through general levels of domestic prices, even though the two mechanisms are *ideally* the same. Exchange-rate flexibility contributes to effective flexibility of wages and prices in accordance with the logic of a price system.

The burden of correcting external imbalances falls unevenly on different countries under the gold standard. The incidence depends in part on their different sizes, reserve ratios, marginal propensities to import, and initial degrees of prosperity. How the burden falls is even more complicated under a gold-exchange or foreign-exchange standard, depending in addition on whether each country involved is a center country, an ordinary member of the system, or a nonmember.

In assessing possible inflation or deflation biases of different exchange-rate systems, two considerations stand out. First, deficit countries feel more urgent pressures to correct disequilibriums than do surplus countries, except under freely fluctuating exchange

rates. Second, countries have stronger incentives to resist deflation than to resist inflation. The first consideration tends to make for a deflation bias under permanently fixed exchange rates but for a devaluation and inflation bias under fixed-but-adjustable exchange rates. Under the latter (adjustable-peg) system, surplus countries have a tendency to import inflation irreversibly, and devaluations are more likely than upward revaluations. The second consideration used to be weakened by acceptance of the gold-standard mystique and the associated willingness to deflate to cure balance-of-payments deficits. Since the best of intentions cannot maintain gold parities forever, however, even the gold standard is a system of (infrequently) adjustable pegs and so has a long-run inflation bias in addition to its shorter-run deflation bias. The system of free exchange rates, whatever its other defects may be, apparently has no deflation bias and has an inflation bias only in the sense of not yoking the financially less prudent countries together with the financially more prudent ones.

ᘓᕲᕙAppendix to Chapter 6: Separate Weapons of Financial Policy

Separation of Fiscal and Monetary Policy

Chapter 6 considered cases in which expenditure or financial policy alone, without price policy, could not achieve both internal and external balance; the trouble lay in having more goals than weapons. One conceivable solution might be to split expenditure policy into two separate weapons, monetary policy (interpreted as interest-rate policy) and fiscal policy.[1] For controlling the overall balance of payments, including the private (or independently motivated) capital account, interest-rate policy has a comparative advantage, so to speak. Fiscal policy has a comparative advantage in controlling aggregate demand. While the interest rate and the government budget both affect aggregate demand and, through it, affect the current account of the balance of payments, the interest rate has an additional effect on capital movements.

Let us consider the four possible combinations of internal and external disequilibrium. In the first one, domestic slump coexists with a balance-of-payments surplus, both associated with too high an interest rate or too large a government budget surplus (or too small a budget deficit). A second case has both disequilibriums and both policy errors in the opposite directions from these. When internal and external considerations alike call for the same easing or tightening of financial policy, no distinction between its monetary and fiscal aspects is crucial.

Goals conflict in the other two cases. The authorities might raise the interest rate to deal with an external deficit. An existing domestic slump would then tend to grow worse, but a cut of a certain size in the government budget surplus (or increase in the budget deficit) could just offset this deflationary tendency, leaving

some external improvement through the response of capital movements to the raised interest rate. The current account would not fully wipe out this improvement even if some further fiscal ease now actually expanded aggregate demand. Part of this expansion could now survive a further rise in the interest rate for balance-of-payments purposes. Policies might conceivably combine so that the high interest rate outweighed the fiscal ease fully enough in affecting the balance of payments to cure the external deficit, while the fiscal ease outweighed the same high interest rate fully enough in affecting demand to cure the domestic slump.

In the opposite case of conflicting disequilibriums, the suggested remedy includes cutting the interest rate to reduce an external surplus. The unwanted inflationary tendency could just be offset by a definite degree of fiscal tightening, leaving the response of international capital movements as desired. The current account would not fully undo this move toward overall external balance even if some further fiscal tightening now actually shrank demand. This desired shrinkage could now partially survive a further cut in the interest rate. Conceivably, a low interest rate could outweigh fiscal tightness fully enough in affecting the balance of payments to cure its surplus, while the fiscal tightness could outweigh the low interest rate fully enough in affecting demand to cure the domestic inflation.

In the sense suggested by these last two examples, monetary (interest-rate) policy corrects the balance of payments while fiscal policy corrects the level of aggregate demand. In accordance with Mundell's Principle of Effective Market Classification,[2] each policy aims at the objective on which it has the relatively greater influence. Since the two policies pull in opposite directions, each one has to be more extreme than would be necessary if the objective it is

---

[1] Robert A. Mundell, "The Appropriate Use of Monetary and Fiscal Policy for Internal and External Stability," IMF *Staff Papers*, **IX**, March 1962, pp. 70-76.

[2] *Ibid.*

paired with were the only objective in view; but since each policy has a comparative advantage in reaching one of the two objectives, an overall reconciliation may be found.

Starting in late 1960 or early 1961, the United States attempted something like this solution (with the further refinement of trying to split interest-rate policy itself into two parts). (See p. 448. Besides this experience, several general afterthoughts temper our enthusiasm for the idea. It assumes away concern about the makeup of the balance of payments; it tacitly regards a current-account deficit matched by capital inflow as just as satisfactory as balance in the two external accounts separately. The suggested policy combination may thus only temporarily palliate a fundamental external imbalance.[3] Furthermore, the government budget, the interest rate, the money supply, and the government debt are unavoidably interrelated. How strongly a budget deficit tends to spur demand, for example, surely depends on how it is financed, which also affects the interest rate. For well-known reasons, trying too hard to keep the interest rate artificially low by monetary expansion or high by monetary tightness tends to be self-defeating. The combinations of interest rate and budget position compatible with adequate but noninflationary aggregate demand are interrelated with rates of capital formation and economic growth. A combination of high interest rate for the balance of payments and government deficit for adequate demand would tend to impair growth. This is just one example of constraint on domestic economic performance as long as the exchange rate cannot serve external balance.

Most fundamentally, the whole analysis reviewed here rests on the question-begging assumption that there does exist some combination of interest rate and budget position capable of achieving both goals at the same time. Yet what assures each policy enough potency to achieve its goal even while the other policy pulls in the opposite direction? Suppose that the United States arbitrarily marked the dollar up to twice its present foreign-exchange value. Could *any* attainable combination of interest rate and budget position cure the resulting external deficit without internal deflation or direct controls?

Forward-rate Policy to Cope with Interest-rate Differentials

Another suggestion for reconciling internal and external balance without altering the exchange parity has a longer history of academic dis-

---

[3] *Ibid.*, p. 71n.

cussion. Official intervention in the forward-exchange market could selectively manipulate the interest rates relevant to international capital movements. In effect, these rates could be kept high enough for external balance without requiring a domestic interest-rate and money-supply policy any tighter than necessary for the health of the home economy.

To understand the idea, we must first expand on our earlier explanation of how capital movements respond to interest rates and spot and forward exchange rates. Funds are presumably the more mobile, the more narrowly spot exchange rates are allowed to fluctuate and the more confidence these limits command. With the range zero and confidence absolute, a country with relatively low interest rates would either have to align its rates with those abroad or else risk seeing its foreign-exchange reserves shrink, perhaps to the point where speculation joined higher earnings, after all, in drawing capital out. The possibility of even moderate exchange-rate fluctuations, however, should restrain enthusiasm for uncovered interest arbitrage. A mere ¼ of 1 percent adverse movement while funds were on loan abroad for three months would cancel the gain from an interest differential of one percentage point a year. Arbitrageurs would therefore seek forward-exchange cover for their return into their home currency. In obtaining this protection they would bid up its cost. The rise would be sharp if other persons showed only a limited and price-inelastic willingness to deal on the other side of the forward market as counterparties to the interest arbitrageurs. The scope for profitable interest arbitrage and the national danger from interest-motivated capital outflow would be limited. Anyway, this was a reassuring view commonly held and apparently supported by experience while postwar exchange restrictions and exchange-rate uncertainty continued until the late 1950s.

To make the idea clear, let us consider an interest-motivated temporary transfer of funds abroad. To avoid risk on moving back into home money (crowns), the interest arbitrageurs would sell foreign money (gold) forward at the very time of buying it spot. Spot gold would tend to strengthen against the crown. A weakening of forward gold would probably be more pronounced, since the arbitrageurs would probably be undertaking a larger fraction of total forward than of total spot transactions (especially with the central bank dealing to limit spot rate fluctuations). The arbitrage would thus, as usual, tend to use up the opportunities motivating it. This limit to profitable arbitrage would be especially narrow if, as the reassuring view supposed, forward gold would have to fall sharply to induce even a limited volume of additional commitments on the *other side* of the arbitrageurs' forward contracts.

William H. White has pointed out why, after all, the volume of funds available for commitment on the other side of arbitrageurs' forward contracts is *not* likely to be so small and so insensitive to price.[4] His crucial assumption is firm confidence that the spot exchange rate will hold within set limits. Exporters and importers will not then *routinely* make forward contracts to cover future receipts and payments of foreign money; their decisions will depend on the forward rate. Suppose the spot rate is fluctuating within firmly trusted limits of 1.98 and 2.02 crowns per gram of gold. Merchants do not know just where within these limits the rate will be in three months (or whatever the relevant period is); they can only guess in comparing spot rates then and now. An importer due to pay gold in three months can, however, compare the current forward rate with the two spot limits. The closer the forward rate on gold is to the trusted upper spot limit of Cr2.02, the less he risks losing and the more he stands to gain by simply waiting to buy gold spot in three months instead of arranging for it now at such a high forward rate. With the current forward rate exactly *at* Cr2.02, the importer has every reason to shun a forward contract. But when a current forward rate at the opposite spot limit of Cr1.98 presented no chance at all of getting gold more cheaply spot and great risk of its costing more, he would have every reason to make a forward purchase.

The same argument, properly modified, applies to an exporter due to receive gold in three months. A comparison of possible gains and losses counts the more strongly for making a forward sale, the closer the current forward rate lies to Cr2.02; it counts the more strongly for simply awaiting a better spot rate, the closer the forward rate lies to Cr1.98.[5]

Considering the responses of importers and exporters together, we see that the closer the

current forward rate is to Cr2.02, the larger the net quantity of forward gold supplied; the closer to Cr1.98, the larger the net quantity demanded. This responsiveness of traders' supply and demand puts flexibility into the volume of commitments available to match the desires of arbitrageurs. When arbitrageurs are heavily supplying forward gold to cover the return of funds temporarily moved abroad, their supply need not run up against so limited and nearly rigid a demand as to require a sharp fall in the forward rate to clear the market. On the contrary, a sag in the forward rate would tend to cushion itself—and so preserve the scope for profitable interest arbitrage—by inducing ordinary traders to demand a larger net quantity of forward gold.

A key assumption warrants emphasis again: the forward-rate-sensitive behavior of traders that accommodates interest-arbitrage transactions depends on confidence in the spot-rate limits. Without it, traders would seek forward cover against their exchange risks more completely as a matter of routine and with less regard to the level of the forward rate. Their transactions accommodating those desired by interest-arbitrageurs would be less flexible in volume, the forward-rate movement caused by any given change in the volume of interest arbitrage would be larger, and the self-limiting character of this arbitrage would be all the more pronounced.

This reasoning raises doubt whether observations about the interest-sensitivity of capital movements in times of low confidence in spot rates are relevant to times of high confidence. Experience in one situation may have little bearing on another and quite different one. The reasoning also suggests that widening the spot-rate limits might impede troublesome interest-motivated capital movements. The forward rate would then have to rise or fall over a wider range to create a given state of opinion among traders about the chances of the future spot rate's being higher or lower; a given change in the forward rate would elicit a smaller change in traders' net use of forward contracts. There would be less cushioning of the forward-rate movements whereby interest arbitrage destroys its own profitability. A given international interest-rate differential would motivate a smaller transfer of funds. The closer the system came to complete lack of any spot rate limits, the slighter the problem such transfers would pose.

Recognizing all this does not mean condemning all aspects of interest arbitrage and forward ex-

---

[4] "Interest Rate Differences, Forward Exchange Mechanism, and Scope for Short-Term Capital Movements," IMF *Staff Papers*, **X**, November 1963, pp. 485-501.

[5] The convenience of supposing that the imports and exports of Ruritania (the home country) are all priced in gold does not affect the conclusions. If some are priced in crowns, it is the foreign merchant rather than the Ruritanian who must decide whether or not to make a forward contract; but the influence of the forward rate on these decisions remains as described in the text.

change. On the contrary, the theory of interest arbitrage provides the main reason for expecting reasonably priced protection against traders' exchange risks. Is it inconsistent to welcome this aspect, yet regret that rate-sensitive, non-routine forward covering by traders accommodates interest arbitrage? Is it contradictory to suppose that interest arbitrage *will* accommodate commercial covering but that, under flexible spot rates, variations in commercial covering will *not* greatly accommodate interest arbitrage? Mere consistency does not prove an argument correct, of course, but it is a necessary condition.

To consider these questions, we should distinguish between two types of sources of opportunity for profit from interest arbitrage. If the source is an actual interest differential between countries, the authorities would presumably like to see only a small capital outflow suffice to establish the spread between spot and forward rates that would make any larger volume of outward arbitrage unprofitable; they would regret an arbitrage-accommodating response by ordinary traders. Admittedly, a large forward-spot spread would burden commercial covering. Actually, though, the thing to regret would be the interest differential occasioning that spread; and either of the alternatives—a heavy capital outflow or alignment of domestic with foreign interest rates—might be still more regrettable. A prompt, uncushioned adjustment of the forward rate to the interest differential might really be the best attainable outcome.

A contrasting source of opportunity for arbitrage would be an initially *wider* forward-spot spread than any interest differential called for. Besides motivating capital flows, this discrepancy would spell an abnormally high cost of risk protection for some traders. (Others, covering opposite positions, would enjoy a negative cost; but their gain would hardly console the first group.) The authorities would then be glad if only a small flow of arbitrage funds sufficed to shrink the forward-spot spread and hold it at interest parity. Again, they would like to see variations in commercial covering cushion the self-destroying tendency of interest arbitrage as little as possible.

In the first example, arbitrage *expanded* an initially inadequate forward-spot spread into line with a supposedly troublesome interest differential; in the second, arbitrage *shrank* an initially excessive spread into line with the interest differential (which could be zero). In both cases, the authorities would like to see the interest-parity forward premium or discount reached with a minimum actual flow of arbitrage funds; they would regret variations in commercial covering that accommodated interest arbitrage and kept a large volume of it profitable. Such unwanted accommodation would be slight when traders always routinely sought forward coverage against exchange risk. Variations in commercial covering would also be absent, of course, when

rigidly fixed exchange rates commanded complete confidence; but then, unfortunately, interest-arbitrageurs would no more need forward cover than traders would.

When spot exchange rates dependably kept within narrow limits do accommodate interest arbitrage, some palliative for the problem of capital flows may seem all the more necessary. Now we are ready to consider official operations in forward exchange, as suggested by Keynes in the early 1920s and often by others since then.[6] Suppose the Ruritanian authorities want to check an outflow or even promote an inflow of private funds, but without letting interest rates rise at home. They could support the forward crown by selling forward gold as cheaply, relative to the spot price, as would correspond to interest parity, or even more cheaply. The artificially high price of a covered return into crowns would check an interest-motivated outflow of funds in the first place. A foreigner wanting to return eventually into his own gold currency could move into crowns at the spot rate (say Cr2.01 per gram) and at the same time arrange to buy gold back later at the supported forward rate on the crown (say Cr1.99 per gram). By thus selling gold and contracting for its cheaper repurchase, he would in effect collect a subsidy on the interest received on a loan of the crowns in the meanwhile. Foreigners with funds already on loan in Ruritania would have a similar inducement not to take them home.

Might the Ruritanian authorities risk not having the gold to honor their forward contracts with? Apparently not; there would be no danger beyond any possible problem of having scanty reserves anyway. In part, the authorities merely commit gold forward that they would otherwise have lost sooner because of capital outflows through the spot market. Any actual capi-

---

[6] See Paul Einzig, *A Dynamic Theory of Forward Exchange,* chapter 32. As Einzig notes in chapter 34, the idea had been anticipated in practice by the Austro-Hungarian Bank.

The following paragraphs have benefited from John H. Auten's examination of the idea in "Monetary Policy and the Forward Exchange Market," *Journal of Finance,* **XVI,** December 1961, pp. 546-558. (Auten, pp. 556-557, interprets Keynes as advocating the separation of external and internal interest rates by means of forward-rate policy to make possible attracting an actual capital inflow to match a current-account balance-of-payments deficit. Auten himself would use forward-rate policy merely to avoid an unwanted capital outflow. He thus does not reject forward intervention but merely cautions against too ambitious a use of it.)

tal inflows currently bring in the gold that the authorities sell forward (or else reduce the country's existing external liabilities). The authorities pay the *de facto* interest subsidy in home, not foreign, currency. The only additional problem directly involved is that foreigners might want to convert into gold the crowns they receive as interest and the crowns they save in buying back their original gold at its officially cheapened forward price. But continued official forward operations might keep reattracting or retaining these and other foreign-owned funds.

Can Ruritanians as well as foreigners collect the interest subsidy? Apparently not: the way it is offered makes it available only to persons who start and *finish* in gold, with protection against exchange risk in the meanwhile. (Strictly speaking, of course, citizenship does not matter; what does matter is the currency begun and ended with.) However, the range of fluctuation permitted in spot exchange rates does bear on the question. Suppose the authorities peg the forward crown at 520 milligrams of gold (only Cr1.92 per gram), considerably stronger than its upper spot limit of 505 milligrams (Cr1.98 per gram). Now even a Ruritanian can profit at his own government's expense. He buys a gram of gold forward at Cr1.92 and counts on selling it spot at maturity of his contract for not less than Cr1.98. In effect the government sells for Cr1.92 the gold it will buy back if necessary to keep its price no lower than Cr1.98. People would seize this opportunity on a vast scale. The cost to the government would be in home rather than foreign money, true enough, but it could be a heavy cost.

The opportunity for profit at government expense is no longer limited to persons starting with and wanting to end with gold because everyone is (by assumption) confident that the crown will *not strengthen* above its existing upper spot limit. This disbelief in any upward revaluation would be especially firm and prevalent when the occasion for the official forward support was some fundamental *weakness* in the crown's general position. To keep some distinctions clear, let us repeat: General weakness further constrains forward-rate policy when the spot rate limits are so narrow that, whatever the exact current spot rate may be, a wide enough forward premium on the crown to make short-term investments in Ruritania attractive to foreigners would require a forward rate above the crown's upper spot limit, for then Ruritanians could profit at their own government's

expense by means of *un*covered arbitrage. On the other hand, *strength* of the crown in the sense of a currently high spot rate would complicate the authorities' dilemma in a slightly different way by narrowing the scope for pushing the forward rate on the crown to an adequate premium while still keeping it within the upper spot limit. (If a high current spot rate does happen to be a symptom of a strong general position, however, official support operations of any kind are less likely than otherwise to be needed. Ironically, the constraints just described are likely to matter least when forward policy is least needed.)

Adequate scope for differentiating interest rates from the home and foreign points of view therefore requires not too narrow a range of spot-rate fluctuation (as Keynes and other advocates of the policy have realized). The crown's spot rate needs room to be low currently so that its current forward rate can be high in comparison without being above the upper spot limit. Ruritanians would then shy away from what would otherwise seem bargains in forward gold for fear that when they took delivery at the maturity of their contracts, they could resell the gold spot only for still fewer crowns. Once again, the more exchange flexibility is allowed, the more freedom domestic policy can have from problems of international interest differentials. Barring that flexibility, authorities might understandably and desperately wish that interest differentials did not have much influence on capital movements, after all, and so did not pose much of a problem to be somehow palliated (but then the alternative idea of using actual interest-rate policy for external balance while fiscal policy served internal balance would not have much relevance, either).

Even if the interest subsidy offered by official forward pegging could be confined to foreigners, a questionable feature would remain. Effectively paying foreigners higher interest rates than correspond to the marginal productivity of capital at home spells a waste of national resources. True, the waste would doubtless be less than that of unemployment due to too tight a domestic financial policy pursued for the sake of the balance of payments. This means only that successful forward intervention would at best reduce the cost of facing the conflict between internal and external policy considerations under fixed exchange rates; it does not banish that conflict.

Balance-of-payments Adjustment by Direct Controls

✑ 7

Barring adjustment through prices, incomes, or exchange rates, direct controls are necessary to force an equilibrium in the balance of payments. But putting the matter this way is not quite exact. A deficit can persist only so long as it can be financed. If no more resources are available for exchange-rate pegging, yet both exchange depreciation and formal controls over expenditures abroad are ruled out, the rate can be maintained only in some such manner as by strictly enforced prohibition of transactions in foreign exchange at other than the official rate. Unofficial rationing would then develop and would favor persons most friendly with exporters earning foreign exchange or persons who (figuratively) stood in line earliest at the offices of the exchange dealers. Or, more probably, persons earning foreign exchange would not sell it for home currency at all but would spend it abroad on goods to be imported and sold at prices reflecting a *de facto* devaluation of the home currency. If the authorities were still unwilling to tolerate market methods of adjustment, they would probably introduce official controls, after all, to force equilibrium in a tidier manner.

Types of control available include quantitative restrictions (quotas) and *ad hoc* duties on imports, as well as exchange control (including systems of multiple exchange rates). Special measures to increase earnings of foreign exchange, such as export subsidies, are akin to these controls in being *ad hoc* remedies for a deficit. (Reverse types of control, incidentally, might be used to banish a balance-of-payments surplus, but since a surplus is a less pressing problem and anxiety to find remedies less familiar, the entire discussion that follows will assume a deficit.)

Quotas and Import Licensing

Restricting imports by quantity seems like a straightforward remedy. The authorities allow only so many automobiles, cameras, tons of wheat, or gallons of wine into the country each month or year. But setting a quota is a complicated job, even for one single product. A *global quota* simply limits the total amount of the product allowed into the country during each year or other time period but does not specify where the product may come from or who is entitled to import it. The difficulties are obvious: home importers and foreign exporters will stampede to get their shipments into the country before the limit has been reached. Stockpiles build up at the beginning of the quota period, leaving no more imports allowable until the beginning of the next period. Merchants whose goods arrive too late to win entry suffer extra expense, and all bear some risk. Wasteful haste pays better than judicious market research and shopping for the best terms. The profits of trade in the quotaed commodities go largely by luck to the particular importers and foreign suppliers able to get their goods into the country first, though the expenses of abnormal haste eat into these profits. Furthermore, the global quota tends to discriminate against the most distant foreign suppliers because of the expenses of shipping back goods denied entry.

For all these reasons, governments in practice reject global quotas in favor of licensing administered to keep imports within some intended limit. But then an allocation problem arises. How, for example, are the scarce privileges of marketing the commodity to be parceled out among the various exporting countries without unfair discrimination? It is no answer to say that each foreign country may supply the same percentage of the total allowable imports, for some countries are naturally more and others less important as suppliers; equal allocations would in fact discriminate. One answer is to allocate trading rights among foreign suppliers in proportion to the amounts supplied in some "previous representative period." But this tends to freeze the pattern of trade according to historical accident and the more or less arbitrary choice of a base period. It discriminates against countries whose comparative advantages as a supplier of the commodity in question have increased since then and in favor of those whose competitive position would have weakened in a free market. It hampers importers of the home country in shopping around for the best bargains.

When controls wielded by other governments keep surplus earnings in transactions with one foreign country from being freely usable to cover excess expenditures in transactions with another, the home authorities are likely to feel compelled to discriminate among foreign sources. But when this problem is absent, the simplest approach is to allocate import licenses only among home importers, leaving each free to buy from whatever foreign source seems best to him. But how should this allocation take place? To grant or refuse licenses simply on the merits of each individual application is open to obvious abuses. Permitting each importer an equal volume of imports would be nonsensical because of the different sizes and fields of specialization of the various firms and because of the difficulties of deciding who qualifies as an importer of each commodity. Granting licenses in proportion to the shares of importing done in some "previous representative period" tends to assure relatively inefficient firms their historic shares of the market, while restraining firms that

could have expanded by virtue of greater efficiency or smaller profit margins. Any base period that might be chosen is likely to have involved some untypical circumstances that result in unfair treatment of particular importers, and no provision for adjustment in such "hardship cases" can be fully satisfactory. The question of admitting new firms to the trade is particularly thorny. The restriction of total imports to a smaller quantity than what the home population would want to buy at a price just covering the foreign supply price plus transportation and marketing expenses and normal profit gives the imports a special scarcity value, and the chance to cut themselves in on the corresponding abnormal profit spurs newcomers to seek admission to the field. Reserving part of the total import quota to newcomers tends to encourage this socially functionless entry into a field probably already overfilled with facilities and personnel, yet barring entry tends to suppress new and protect stagnant methods of service.[1]

Artificially restricting imports gives the licenses a scarcity value. Who receives the quota profit depends on just how the licenses are allocated. The importers favored by history and the choice of a base period may receive the profit if the licenses are allocated in this way. If some system of domestic price control tries to keep the importers from charging higher prices than would have prevailed if imports had been unrestricted, then the benefit may go to the fortunate consumers who happen to get the scarce but price-controlled imports. Foreign suppliers may cut themselves in on the quota profit, raising their prices to correspond to the imposed scarcity of their wares in the importing country, if the restricted trading privileges are allocated to them rather than to the importers.[2] The foreigners may also gain if the licenses, though issued to domestic importers,

---

[1] On this and several points developed later, cf. Emil Küng, *Zahlungsbilanzpolitik,* Zürich: Polygraphischer Verlag AG., 1959, Part 5, esp. pp. 640-643.

[2] Some such arrangement is not unknown: the United States and other countries have occasionally pressured Japanese and Hong Kong industries into "voluntarily" limiting their exports of particular products.

carry restrictions about the amounts to be bought in designated countries. This arrangement reserves a definite share of the market to each foreign source, provided that the overall degree of import restriction and the resulting scarcity value of the commodity in question are great enough to make it worth the importers' while to import the full amounts permitted to them despite the need to pay more for imports from some countries than from others.

A system that leaves some of the quota profit to the foreigners spells higher prices for the restricted imports and worsened terms of trade. Carelessness with controls might even worsen instead of improve the restricting country's balance of payments. Suppose, for example, that the country had been importing ten automobiles per week at a price of $2,000 each. Now a quota of five cars per week is imposed. Demand for imported cars is so inelastic that no price below $5,000 will cut the number demanded down to five. Also assuming circumstances enabling the foreigners to collect the entire scarcity premium, the country's total expenditure on imported cars is $25,000, as against the $20,000 previously spent, the balance of payments deteriorates by $5,000.[3] Anomalies of this sort could be avoided by more careful licensing or by limiting imports not in physical quantity but in total value. This would be on the borderline between quotas and exchange control. Even then, the scarcity premium might fall to persons considered undeserving.

Ad Hoc Import Duties

Perhaps the simplest solution is for the restricting government to collect the quota profit itself by charging fees for import licenses. It might decide the total amount of each particular commodity to be admitted into the country per month or year and then auction off the corresponding licenses.[4] This arrangement amounts to levying import duties designed to restrict imports of each commodity to the desired quantity. The only real difference is an administrative one: under the licensing system, the government fixes the total import quantity and lets the license fee set itself at auction at whatever level makes the quantity demanded conform; under the tariff system, the government can only in principle but not in practice know the precise rate of duty necessary for the desired restriction.

Charging duties or license fees has several advantages over limiting quantity alone. Reserving the scarcity premium to the government is not only probably fairer than arbitrarily giving it to private traders but also avoids promoting overcapacity in the importing business. By operating through the price system instead of trying to override it, duties or the equivalent are less likely to require bolstering by additional interventions (such as domestic price control or rationing of the restricted imports). By raising revenue, duties or fees have some effect against any domestic inflation that may be playing a part in the balance-of-payments difficulties. Levying or increasing a duty makes the domestic but not the foreign price of the imported commodity higher than it would be in the absence of restrictions and therefore, unless demand is completely inelastic, reduces the quantity demanded in terms of physical volume and foreign-currency value both.

Not only import duties but also export duties and subsidies might be used to help correct a balance-of-payments deficit. An export tax might be levied on commodities known to be in inelastic foreign demand, so that the foreigners would spend a larger total amount of their own money on reduced physical quantities. The terms of trade of the taxing country would also improve. For products known to have a highly elastic foreign demand, an export subsidy could be granted

[3] Cf. J. E. Meade, *The Balance of Payments,* London: Oxford University Press, 1951, pp. 276-280.

[4] How such an auction might operate is described in *ibid.,* p. 286n. A similar system for auctioning off foreign exchange to be made available for other than "essential" purposes had already been proposed by Robert Triffin in "National Central Banking and the International Economy," in Lloyd A. Metzler and others, *International Monetary Policies,* Washington: Board of Governors of the Federal Reserve System, 1947, pp. 69-70; and such systems have been used in Brazil and some other Latin American countries.

to cheapen them and increase their total foreign-currency proceeds. The balance of payments would then improve at the expense of worsened terms of trade.

As a balance-of-payments corrective, import duties and export duties and subsidies are less suitable than exchange-rate adjustments in affecting invisible transactions. (If it were possible to collect a uniform rate of duty on foreign exchange bought for all purposes and to pay a subsidy at the same uniform rate on sales of foreign exchange acquired in all ways, this would be equivalent to exchange depreciation of the home currency.)

Advance Deposit Requirements

Just as tariffs discourage imports by raising their cost, so do advance deposit requirements for imports.[5] Under this system, when an importer applies for permission to import particular goods or to buy the necessary foreign exchange, he must deposit funds amounting to some specified percentage of the value of the goods. In some countries and for goods judged particularly nonessential, this figure may range up to several hundred or even a few thousand percent. The funds, deposited in a commercial bank, must usually be transferred to a special account at the central bank. The authorities will not return the deposit to the importer until a period has elapsed that ranges, under the systems of different countries, from a few days to many months. The importer bears the cost of tying up his own funds during this period, suffering a possibly sizable loss in their purchasing power in countries with rapid inflation, or else he must borrow funds at a corresponding interest rate. In extreme cases, the unavailability of a loan frustrates the import transaction, though such loans are usually rather easy to get (one reason being that the required deposit serves as a guarantee of the loan).

Import duties can have an anti-inflationary effect through the government budget; advance deposits can serve as a tool of anti-

inflationary monetary policy by temporarily reducing the liquidity of claims on the banking system and by sequestering commercial bank reserves at the central bank. These effects go into reverse when the deposits are released, and the timing may prove awkward.

Advance deposit systems are most common in Latin America but have also been tried elsewhere. Several reasons have prompted resort to this bizarre type of control. It may be comparatively easy to adopt, especially if international agreements hamper manipulation of tariffs or other controls. It may be convenient for domestic monetary policy in countries where using other weapons requires legislative approval obtainable only with delay, or where a more obvious tightening of credit would meet public resistance. It may, in effect, compel importers to lend funds wanted to cover a government budget deficit. The system is usually regarded as temporary, but the larger an accumulation of required deposits has been allowed to grow, the more awkward dismantling it becomes. Another disadvantage is that it tends to harm competition by discriminating against new and small importing firms and in favor of those with stronger finances and better connections.

Exchange Control

The desire to regulate capital transfers and invisible as well as commodity trade leads to exchange control. This may be defined as a system of regulations designed to assure both that foreign exchange coming into the possession of residents of the controlling country is sold in official channels and that this exchange is used only for approved payments abroad. The regulations usually try to plug up the evasion of conducting international business in ways that keep foreign exchange out of the possession of citizens of the controlling country in the first place. Exporters may be required to insist on payment in prescribed foreign currencies; or if the foreign buyers are allowed to make payment in the currency of the exporting country, they must have acquired this currency only in approved ways. Ex-

---

[5] See Eugene A. Birnbaum and Moeen A. Qureshi, "Advance Deposit Requirements for Imports," IMF *Staff Papers*, VIII, November 1960, pp. 115-125.

change control is almost always associated with fixed exchange rates, since there would otherwise be little need to requisition and ration foreign exchange. Conceivably, though, the rate could be left unpegged, with the controls modifying private supply and demand to make the home currency stronger than it otherwise would be.

Thorough control requires an extensive apparatus to block many ways of obtaining foreign exchange outside official channels. Residents of the controlling country who want to buy some unauthorized import or spend money abroad for some other unauthorized purpose might, for instance, simply mail domestic paper money abroad. This smuggled currency would sell in the foreign market at a discount from the official rate, since foreigners buying it to pay for imports from the controlling country would have to use it illegally. To fully prevent the *de facto* depreciation of the domestic currency involved in such transactions, the exchange-control authorities would have to examine or spot-check mail leaving and entering the country and also search departing and entering travelers for illegal amounts of currency.

Another way to acquire unauthorized foreign exchange, or, rather, to accomplish the result for which it was wanted, would be private compensation. Merchants in Inland and Outland might agree that each would buy specified goods in his own country for shipment to the other. Since it is the Inlander, we suppose, whom government controls are making especially eager to carry out the deal, he would have to offer goods worth more than the Outland goods received for them as valued at the domestic prices prevailing on the two markets and at the official exchange rate. The deal would thus imply a *de facto* devaluation of the Inland currency. Furthermore, the Inland authorities would lose the foreign exchange that they might have acquired for disposal through official channels if their country's exports had been sold in the normal way instead. To stamp out private barter, the authorities would need, at least in principle, to supervise all import and export transactions.

Tourists might make similar compensa-

tion arrangements. Suppose that some Inlanders want to spend more than their foreign-exchange allotment while traveling in Outland. They might have friends or relatives pay their expenses there in return for a promise to reciprocate when the Outlanders later visited Inland. The matching of expenses to be paid by the Outlanders and by the Inlanders would presumably imply a rate of exchange discounting the Inland currency below its official parity. This example suggests how difficult it would be to plug all loopholes. The Inland authorities could hardly investigate each occasion when an Inlander bought a restaurant meal or paid a hotel bill for a visiting foreigner on suspicion that this hospitality might be part of a private compensation arrangement.

Another complication is the need to check whether each foreign-exchange allotment really is used for the specified purpose—to see, for instance, that exchange allotted for imports of "essential" food or raw materials is not in fact diverted to some unauthorized "luxury." It would even be necessary to supervise import prices. Otherwise, an Inland importer who wanted foreign exchange for unauthorized purposes might arrange for his Outland supplier of some authorized import to bill him at too high a price but pay him a secret rebate. Supervision of export pricing would also be necessary. Otherwise an Inland exporter might underbill his foreign customer and deliver only the corresponding amount of foreign exchange to the control authorities, while receiving a prearranged secret extra payment from the foreign customer. These last examples illustrate the difficulty of confining controls to capital movements alone (even though such limited control is envisaged, for instance, in the Articles of Agreement of the International Monetary Fund). Capital transfers could be accomplished by way of ordinary and apparently legitimate import and export transactions unless detailed supervision were undertaken to uncover irregularities.

Similarly, so-called leads and lags in commercial payments could be a vehicle for capital transfers. Suppose people want to get funds out of Inland, perhaps fearing devaluation. Inlanders exporting goods priced in foreign currency will be anxious to delay receiving payment in order to hold claims in foreign currency as long as possible. The foreign purchasers will probably cooperate in this delay, especially if they receive credit from their Inland suppliers on advantageous terms. Inlanders importing goods to be paid for in foreign currency have an incentive to hasten their payments for fear of a rise in the local-currency price of foreign exchange, and the resulting reduction in the debt owed to foreigners amounts to a capital export. It is a complicated matter to control business in such detail as to specify how fast Inlanders must collect their claims on foreigners and how slowly they must pay their foreign debts. The complexities are similar if goods are priced and are to be paid for in Inland currency. The foreign buyers of Inland exports will have an incentive to delay their payments in hopes of devaluation, and the resulting growth of Inland claims on foreigners amounts to a capital export. Foreigners who have sold goods to Inland will press for especially prompt payment of the amounts due them in Inland currency, thus reducing Inland's outstanding foreign debt. Changes in timing may affect not only payments but also the placement of orders: Inland's imports will tend to be hastened and exports delayed. It is probably true that the capital movements and similar effects on Inland's balance of payments accomplished by changes in timing are inherently both temporary and limited in potential amount: a return to more normal payments practices implies a reversal of the capital outflow. But the original capital outflow can be very unwelcome to the Inland authorities while it goes on, and they may be hard put to control it. It may even help force a devaluation.

Another method of capital export akin to leads and lags involves credit obtained by companies doing business both in Inland and abroad. Such a company might reduce its borrowing from Outland banks and increase its borrowing from Inland banks, accomplishing what would amount to an outward transfer of capital. So many devices are available for evading control confined to capital movements alone that really tight control would involve supervising all foreign transactions, all imports and exports of goods and services, all commercial credit granted in international trade, and all borrowing and lending by companies doing business at home and abroad. If the motives for international capital transfers were very strong, strict control would require reading the mail and searching the clothing and baggage of travelers.

An exchange-control system requires precautions to minimize interference with legitimate international banking. If Inland is a country of leading importance in international trade, its currency is widely used in normal times for quoting prices and stipulating payments. Traders in many countries ordinarily hold working balances of its currency, and banks and other firms providing financial services to foreigners might account for a good part of Inland's international earnings. Exchange control might make foreigners reluctant to hold bank accounts in Inland unnecessarily or to invest funds in its market. A trend might develop away from pricing commodities and stipulating payments in Inland currency. Foreigners would dislike having the convertibility of their funds into other currencies subject to the whim of the Inland controllers. To assuage foreign fears on this score, the Inland authorities could establish a system of nonresident accounts. Bank accounts owned by nonresidents could remain freely convertible into foreign exchange at the official rate of exchange at any time and for any purpose. Except for possible fears of devaluation or of changes in the regulations, then, Inland currency might be just about as suitable for holding by foreigners as it had ever been.[6] Under this system, payments by residents into nonresident accounts would have to be just as strictly controlled as residents' purchases of foreign exchange, for funds once transferred to a nonresident become freely convertible into foreign exchange.

---

[6] This paragraph implicitly refers to the system of nonresident accounts since December 1958 and of American accounts before then in the exchange controls of the United Kingdom.

Multiple Exchange Rates

In exchange-control systems of the type considered so far, foreign exchange is allocated for various types of import or payment abroad according to *ad hoc* decisions or rules of thumb. Instead, exchange might be allocated by selling it at different prices to importers of different products or to persons making payments abroad for different purposes. It might be sold relatively cheap, for example, to pay for imports officially considered "essential" or for goods being imported by agencies of the government itself. For other transactions considered less worthy of encouragement—"luxury" imports, perhaps, or travel, donations, or investment abroad—exchange might be sold at a relatively high price. Charging an especially high price for foreign exchange to pay for imports of certain goods resembles levying import duties on such goods under a unitary exchange-rate system, except that the duties can be levied not only on commodities but also on invisible transactions. Sale of foreign exchange cheap for other purposes amounts to an import subsidy.

On the export side, the authorities may pay a comparatively high local-currency price for the foreign-exchange proceeds of certain exports so as in effect to subsidize them, perhaps on the supposition that the foreign demand for them is highly elastic. A relatively low price might be paid for the foreign-exchange proceeds of other exports, including staple exports for which foreign demand was thought to be inelastic. The system of multiple exchange rates can operate as a selective system of import and export duties and subsidies, with the rate calculated for each particular type of transaction according to supposed essentiality, demand elasticity, or other considerations.

Multiple rates also resemble duties in providing revenue. By buying foreign exchange more cheaply on the average than it sells, the government can profit from its monopoly of exchange transactions. Such a system would tend to mop funds off of the domestic market and so have a deflationary or anti-inflationary effect. If the domestic-currency prices of for-

eign exchange were higher on the average for import transactions than for export transactions, the country might conceivably even have an export surplus with trade valued in foreign currency but an import surplus with trade valued in domestic currency. Even though trade in goods and services produced larger earnings than expenditures of foreign exchange, an import balance as measured in domestic currency might be exerting an anti-inflationary influence on the domestic economy.[7]

Many variations on the multiple-rate system are possible. One would combine fixed official rates and fluctuating rates. Importers of favored commodities could buy foreign exchange at the fixed rate, while importers of less-favored commodities would be shunted to the "free" market, where foreign exchange would command a higher price. Purchases of foreign exchange for travel, capital transfer, and other invisible transactions might also be confined to the free market. A gamut of different effective rates of exchange might be established by defining several categories of transactions, for each of which the buyers of foreign exchange would be allowed a specified percentage at the favorable official rate and required to buy the remainder in the less favorable free market. A multiplicity of exchange rates would appear on the export side of the market, also, if the regulations permitted different percentages of the foreign-exchange proceeds of various commodities to be sold at the advantageous free-market rate according to the degree of encouragement officially intended for each category of exports.

Multiple exchange rates have been employed in many countries and have been quite common in Latin America, though considerable simplification has taken place in recent years. The Brazilian system in effect at the end of 1960 is an example.[8] (It represented a

---

[7] On this last point, see Shu-Chin Yang, *A Multiple Exchange Rate System, An Appraisal of Thailand's Experience, 1946–1955,* Madison, Wis.: The University of Wisconsin Press, 1957, pp. 77-78.

[8] International Monetary Fund, *Twelfth Annual Report on Exchange Restrictions,* Washington: 1961, pp. 52-59, *International Financial Statistics,* August 1961, pp. 60-63.

radical simplification of systems previously in effect and gave way to still further simplification in 1961.) The official and parity rates of 18.36, 18.50, and 18.92 cruzeiros per dollar had very limited applicability. The Bank of Brazil requisitioned the foreign-exchange proceeds of "first-category" exports (cocoa beans and green and roasted coffee) at a rate of 90 cruzeiros per dollar and the proceeds of "second-category" exports (cocoa derivatives, castor beans, and crude mineral oil and derivatives) at 100 cruzeiros per dollar. Proceeds of all other exports, of most invisible transactions, and of capital imports had to be surrendered at a so-called free-market rate. This rate was fluctuating in the vicinity of 190 cruzeiros per dollar at the end of 1960, but immediate cash payment of only 130 cruzeiros was made, with the balance paid in six-month notes of the Bank of Brazil. On the import side, foreign exchange to pay for newsprint bought by printers whose publications weighed 80 grams or less was available at 67.57 cruzeiros per dollar. For imports of newsprint by printers whose publications weighed more than 80 grams, as well as for government payments, specified government imports, wheat, petroleum and petroleum derivatives, imports for the petroleum and printing industries, and certain other preferential imports, and also for amortization and interest on registered loans, credits, and financing, exchange was available at 100 cruzeiros per dollar. A "free-market" rate fluctuating in the vicinity of 195 cruzeiros per dollar applied to most invisible imports and all capital transactions not carried out at preferential rates. Exchange for imports of most commodities had to be bought in auctions held separately for two categories of goods. For "general-category" imports (raw materials, equipment, and other production goods, as well as consumer goods deemed to be in short domestic supply), the auction rate was about 229 cruzeiros per dollar at the end of 1960. For "special-category" imports (other goods, comprising only about 5 percent of all auction imports), the rate was about 640 cruzeiros per dollar. The auctioned foreign exchange was generally not made available until after the lapse of 150 days,

though successful bidders had to pay for it within a very few days. Special exchange auctions were held from time to time for separately listed goods used in agriculture and for fruits from Uruguay. Special regulations were in effect for trade with countries with which Brazil had bilateral payments agreements. In addition to being subject to the various foreign-exchange regulations just described (and described in an oversimplified way, at that), exports and some imports were subject to licensing.

Multiple-rate systems permit selective adjustments to equilibrate a country's balance of payments. In effect, the home currency can be devalued only for those types of import and export transactions in which the response to price is thought to be most sensitive. The only important advantage over duties and subsidies is that the multiple-exchange-rate system can more easily cover a broader range of transactions, invisible as well as visible.[9] Extensive supervision of exchange transactions is necessary, however, to prevent unauthorized arbitrage—for example, to keep people from buying foreign exchange relatively cheap, supposedly for one of the favored purposes, and then reselling it to other persons who want foreign exchange for less favored purposes and who would otherwise have to buy it at a less favorable rate.

An Appraisal of Possible Advantages

Complexities in enforcing particular types of control do not necessarily condemn the whole approach. A judicious combination of controls might be the answer. An appraisal involves value judgments as well as facts and analysis. It also implies a *comparison* with the more nearly "automatic" mechanisms of adjustment; and since some of their possible defects still remain to be examined, the present appraisal can be tentative only.[10]

---

[9] For an appraisal of the possibilities of using multiple exchange rates to manipulate trade in the interest of economic development programs, see Eugene R. Schlesinger, *Multiple Exchange Rates and Economic Development*, Princeton, N.J.: Princeton University Press, 1952.

[10] There is always the danger, in appraising some line of policy, of setting up and blowing down straw men or of reporting arguments in weak versions only. The best an admitted skeptic can do is to keep this danger in mind

In the next few pages, some comments immediately follow each statement of an advantage claimed for controls. This arrangement merely serves convenience and is not meant to dismiss each advantage as completely illusory.

1. Controls can keep balances of payments in order when other methods of adjustment would work painfully, if at all. Controls make less deflation of expenditure necessary to improve the balance of payments by any given amount (or they increase the scope for an expansionary policy to combat depression at home). Deflation of aggregate expenditure is an inefficient way of improving the balance of payments, especially if consumption of imports and exportable goods responds downward only slightly, if resources have little mobility from home-market into export production, and if foreign demand for additional exports is absent. Furthermore, expenditure deflation impinges more heavily in the aggregate on home-market goods than on imports and so causes unemployment (unless goods and factor prices are more completely flexible than is likely). Controls, on the contrary, tend to create employment by switching demand away from imports onto home-mar-

ket goods. They offset some of the damage to employment done by expenditure deflation and make a given balance-of-payments improvement possible with less unemployment than if deflation had been the only weapon used.[11] This gain presumably outweighs any unemployment that carelessly designed and administered controls might inflict on factors of production employed together with imported materials. As for sparing a country from deflation for the sake of the balance of payments, however, controls are not the only method of adjustment capable of doing that. The case for controls depends on defects in other mechanisms.

A related argument is that direct controls could work more rapidly and effectively than any alternative in coping with sudden severe disturbances such as war, foreign depression, or domestic harvest failure. Market mechanisms might not be absolutely unworkable—the home currency might be allowed to depreciate sharply to a level that, barring speculation or extremely low demand elasticities, would be bound to equilibrate the balance of payments—; but adopting direct controls as an emergency measure might prove less burdensome than severe, even if temporary, exchange-rate movements. (Why and how may be seen from arguments still to follow.) On the other hand, the tightening and loosening of controls in response to changes in supply and demand, or even the knowledge that the authorities stood ready to wield controls when they saw fit, could also hamper trade. Adjustable controls could require wasteful temporary shifts of factors of production into and out of import-competing and out of foreign export industries.[12] In-industries in the controlling country and into

and *try* to present the case for controls fairly. With one exception, the discussion that follows covers what seem to be the real arguments. The exception concerns a psychological basis for shifting the burden of proof onto the opponents of controls. So many kinds are available that if some are demonstrably inappropriate, others almost certainly must be appropriate. A loose analogy with the general economic principle of marginalism suggests that neither complete reliance on nor complete rejection of controls is sensible; the best position must be somewhere in between. Not to control the balance of payments directly in any way or to any extent seems like a highly exceptional policy. Rejection of controls can be imputed to some sort of superstitious trust in the magic of the price system, to a callously comfortable belief that things will work themselves out for the best if left alone, to a doctrinaire insistence on laissez-faire. Advocacy of controls—if not of one particular kind, then of some other kind—can, by contrast, be represented as a more pragmatic, practical, realistic position. The clash of opinions can be represented as a dispute between ivory-tower dogma and practical awareness. In my judgment, this way of thinking provides the most deep-seated basis for advocating direct controls. The anticontrols position, as well, admittedly has a basis in psychology and political philosophy. But whatever the psychological underpinnings of the different points of view may be, it should be possible to discuss rationally how well rival policies harmonize with the value judgments that anyone would avow openly.

[11] See M. F. W. Hemming and W. M. Corden, "Import Restriction as an Instrument of Balance-of-Payments Policy," *Economic Journal*, LXVIII, September 1958, pp. 483-510. The authors devote only incidental attention to exchange-rate adjustment but do recognize it as an alternative to controls and even mention (esp. pp. 509-510) that whereas import restriction tends to increase employment only by diverting expenditure from imports onto home-produced goods, the shift in relative prices resulting from devaluation does so both by discouraging imports and by increasing the efficiency with which expenditure deflation tends to shift goods and resources into meeting a stimulated export demand.

[12] Cf. Küng, *op. cit.*, pp. 586-587.

cidentally, the argument for controls in exceptional emergencies implies reliance on other adjustment mechanisms in normal times.

2. Just as controls over trade might be warranted in emergencies, so exchange control might be useful to check speculative "hot money" movements or other unwanted capital transfers. As already emphasized, though, close supervision of all international transactions would be needed to block many ways of transferring capital indirectly. (Extensive supervision might not be necessary if the authorities were content to restrain only certain major long-term capital outflows—those accomplished by floating foreign security issues in the home market, for example. But such capital outflows presumably pose a less sudden and critical problem than the others that are so difficult to control.) Furthermore, control confined to capital movements, with current-account transactions supervised but permitted if judged bona fide, would be no complete adjustment mechanism and no substitute for one affecting current-account as well as capital transactions.

3. When something happens that would otherwise cause a balance-of-payments deficit, resort to controls may perhaps prevent or lessen the rise in the home price level and the worsening of the terms of trade that would have accompanied exchange depreciation instead. Later chapters examine these two worries about depreciation in greater detail; here we can only mention the main points of comparison. In tending to make imported goods more expensive, import controls are similar to depreciation, not different from it. (Strictly speaking, it is neither depreciation nor controls that tend to raise prices, but the unfavorable occurrences requiring some response or other.) Controls also tend to raise prices in the way a reversal of technical progress would, since they interfere with the gains from international specialization. As for the terms of trade, the use of import restrictions or duties can avoid cheapening exports in favor of foreigners the way devaluation would.[13] Foreign suppliers of imports

may shave their prices somewhat to help hold their market. In principle if not very accurately in practice, the authorities could judiciously apply different rates of duty or degrees of restriction to different goods so as to achieve the best possible combination of effects on the terms and balance of trade in the light of different supply and demand elasticities. A vast literature relevant to appraising this possibility covers such matters as the sacrifice in trade volume to obtain better terms, the attendant concept of an "optimum" degree of trade restriction, questions of the amount and permanence of improvement obtainable in the light of long-run demand and supply elasticities, practical difficulties of actually estimating the relevant elasticities for the purpose of adopting suitable restrictions and continually modifying them, attempts by other countries to counter-manipulate the terms of trade, alternatives to terms-of-trade manipulation as a vehicle for agreed international redistribution of wealth or income, and fundamental ambiguities in the very concept of terms of trade.

Furthermore, if controls really can ward off the bad effects of some occurrence tending to worsen both the balance of payments and the terms of trade, then, it would seem, controls to improve the terms of trade would already have been advisable in the first place. The terms-of-trade argument for controls or duties does not make a case against relying at the same time on one of the "automatic" mechanisms as the primary method of balance-of-payments adjustment. The key presumption to be examined is that some new development tending to cause a deficit and otherwise to require deflation or exchange depreciation increases at the same time the

---

[13] When Hemming and Corden finally face the issue squarely in their article on import restriction (*op. cit.,* esp. p. 510), the only clear-cut advantage over devalu-

ation they claim for controls concerns the terms of trade. (They also barely mention speed of operation, political and administrative considerations that might cut either way, and the opportunity to discriminate according to how restricting imports from various sources might affect the supply of credit and export sales as well as the terms of trade.) Hemming and Corden conceive of an optimum policy combination determined by balancing three effects at the margin: of controls in distorting resource allocation (but improving the terms of trade), of expenditure deflation in causing unemployment, and of devaluation in worsening the terms of trade. Ideally, they say, marginal damages should be equal for a marginal degree of balance-of-payments improvement in each of the three ways.

stringency of control that is "optimal" on terms-of-trade grounds.[14]

4. The question of how countries share the gains from trade brings to mind a broad range of issues that will also turn out to involve the distribution of income or wealth, but now the *domestic* distribution. Though often only dimly seen, these considerations probably have great importance in actual policy making.

Direct controls can restrict imports more selectively than "the blind forces of the market" would. Controls can keep foreign exchange from being wasted on "nonessential" or "luxury" imports and can conserve it for "essentials." At least, selective import duties or multiple exchange rates can penalize its nonessential use. In this way, the relatively poor consumers of imported essentials can escape and can shift to the relatively rich consumers of imported luxuries some of the burden of abstinence that a market method of adjustment would otherwise indiscriminately impose. If wealthy playboys were allowed to take lengthy pleasure trips abroad, they would bid up the price of foreign exchange and so raise the prices of imported food consumed by the poor and the prices of imported capital goods needed for industrial reconstruction or development. It was no doubt considerations of this sort that led European countries at the end of World War II to fix their currencies at overvalued levels in relation to the dollar, to cope with the attendant balance-of-payments difficulties by direct controls, and, in general, to impose austerity" in a deliberate and overt manner.

These arguments, like those for consumer rationing in wartime, do have considerable force. But they need some qualification. For one thing, it is hard to distinguish clearly and consistently between luxuries and essentials. Suppose, for example, that the British authorities tightly ration foreign exchange for Mediterranean cruises but classify oil as an essential import. Some of the oil may go for heating at English vacation resorts that operate on a larger scale than they would have done if the cruises had not been restricted. The restrictions may in effect divert English labor and other factors of production from other activities into providing recreation services in which other countries have a comparative advantage. In view of the English climate, it may well be that the marginal units of foreign exchange spent on imported oil and so forth go to satisfy wants no more urgent—while satisfying them less effectively —than the wants otherwise satisfied by marginal units of exchange spent on foreign travel.

Such examples suggest at least two lessons. First, restricting imports of supposed nonessentials is likely to promote imports of their substitutes and also divert domestic and imported resources or materials into home production of substitutes. The diversion may hamper exports as well.[15] Secondly, it is idle to try to decide on some abstract, philosophical basis which wants and commodities are frivolous and which essential. The controllers cannot know except in a very rough-and-ready way how relatively important various imports and foreign expenditures are. They

---

[14] Sidney S. Alexander, "Devaluation versus Import Restriction as an Instrument for Improving Foreign Trade Balance," IMF *Staff Papers,* I, April 1951, pp. 379-396, esp. pp. 388-389, seems to assert such a presumption. The appropriate tightening of import restriction accompanies devaluation automatically if the restriction is imposed in the form of an ad valorem tariff.

More precisely, Alexander appears to envisage a devaluation undertaken, independently of any change in supplies and demands in foreign trade, in order to shrink a previously existing trade deficit. The real issue, however, is the presumption that a tightening of previously optimal import restrictions is the best response to a *change* in supplies and demands that would otherwise *cause* a trade deficit. Egon Sohmen, *Fluctuating Exchange Rates: Theory and Controversy;* Chicago: University of Chicago Press, 1961, pp. 14-15, further questions whether Alexander's argument tells in favor of tighter controls when nobody knows whether or not those already existing are or are not above the "optimum" level.

[15] Licenses to import materials might be made contingent on using the materials in export production, but enforcement would be difficult. What could the authorities do, for example, if producers claimed that they *had* produced their goods for export but had not been able to sell them abroad because of the overvalued exchange rate and so had had to sell them on the home market after all? And anyway, earmarking imported materials for export production would tend to release similar domestic materials for home-market production. On some of these and other awkward repercussions, see Küng, *op. cit.,* pp. 644-645, 654-655, 666, and *passim.*

must rely in part on expert advice from persons engaged in the affected lines of business. The allocation of foreign exchange is influenced by a "competition in lamentation"; there is a tendency to consider needs the greatest in the sectors that howl the loudest.[16] The controllers may even consider how foreign governments might react to their decisions. A more fundamental part of the problem hinges on one of the major teachings of economics: things are not useful because of their physical characteristics alone. Usefulness is a relation between things and human wants; and the marginal usefulness or utility is the smaller the more abundant the particular thing considered. Ideally, decisions about restricting the supply of various things ought to consider their essentiality or usefulness *at the margin*. It is easy to imagine circumstances in which an additional dollar's worth or an additional ounce of penicillin or polio vaccine would contribute less to human satisfaction than an additional dollar's worth or an additional ounce of orchids.

Official attempts to lay down distinctions between luxuries and necessities sometimes become ridiculous. At one time the Norwegian government restricted purchases of bathtubs to persons whose doctors had certified their need for one. Sir Stafford Cripps, during his tenure at the British Exchequer, was once questioned in the House of Commons about the possibility of allowing imports of French cheese; he replied that only "serious cheese" could be permitted.[17]

It is particularly dubious to try to distinguish between essential and frivolous imports according to whether they contribute to production or merely to "unnecessary" consumption. All production supposedly aims at satisfying human wants, immediately or ultimately. Producing machinery or constructing factories is not inherently more worthy than producing restaurant meals or nightclub entertainment, for the machinery or factories are pointless unless they can sooner or later give rise to goods or services (including, perhaps, national defense) that do satisfy human

wants. Similarly, it would be odd to administer import controls so as to discriminate against some goods and in favor of others merely because these others were raw materials to be embodied in exports. For the export trade is not carried on as an end in its own right; exports are in effect the price paid for the imports whose ultimate services consumers desire. To favor production-oriented or export-oriented imports over consumption-oriented imports is to prefer a roundabout achievement of ultimate consumer satisfactions to a more direct achievement merely because of its greater roundaboutness; it is to confuse ends and means.

One possible answer to this point is that certain distortions in the economic system cause businessmen and consumers to choose the immediate satisfaction of wants, even though indirect methods of satisfaction have a yield sufficiently greater to more than justify postponing the ultimate satisfactions. In comparison with some sort of social point of view, private decision-makers might be taking too much thought for the present and not enough for the future. Controls could then conceivably compensate or correct for existing distortions. But if so, a convincing case would have to specify what these other distortions were and why direct controls over international transactions were the best way of dealing with them; slogans are not enough. Incidentally, if controls over trade really were desirable to offset other distortions in the economy, the case for them would seem to be a general one, not especially related to balance-of-payments difficulties.

Barring specific known distortions for which controls might be a corrective, the idea naturally arises of letting ultimate consumers appraise "essentiality." Give up trying to make sweeping philosophical comparisons; instead, let people act on their own comparisons of the satisfactions expected from another dollar's worth of this and another dollar's worth of that. Let consumers and businessmen judge and act on the intensities of the wants that various domestic and imported goods can satisfy, either directly or by contributing to further processes of production. Let them bid for the imports they want

---

[16] *Ibid.*, p. 690.

[17] Wilhelm Röpke, *Internationale Ordnung—heute*, Erlenbach-Zürich: Rentsch, 1954, p. 286.

and for the foreign exchange with which to pay for them.

This advice can be challenged. In effect, it calls for "rationing by the purse." How meaningful is it to judge the essentialities or utilities of various goods by what people are prepared to pay for them? The wealthy man's $5000 vacation abroad may have less social importance than the imported food or machinery that the same amount of foreign exchange would have bought. The price system cannot take account of facts like this.

This argument, if sound, applies at home as well as in foreign trade. So applied, the argument is familiar: the unhampered price system perversely provides cream for the dowager's pampered cat while the poor widow's baby lacks milk. The choice of policies lies between direct remedies for the problems of poverty, including direct taxes and transfer payments, and redistribution attempted through rationing and excise taxes and subsidies to keep real incomes from corresponding to money incomes. While the latter approach cannot be condemned completely, it does have familiar disadvantages, especially those connected with its making things have different price ratios and different marginal rates of substitution for different persons.

If applying direct controls and selective excise taxes and subsidies to domestic transactions is a clumsy and indirect way of redistributing real income, how much more so it is to try pinching and squeezing international transactions in particular for the same purpose. If luxury imports are restricted to maintain a favorable exchange rate for imports of essential goods used by relatively poor persons, the redistributionary purpose of the import controls calls for corresponding controls over domestic production and trade as well. Otherwise, resources would be diverted into the relatively inefficient local production of substitutes for the restricted luxury imports. It would be ironic if the controls permitted imports of machinery for domestic luxury industries. Anomalous results might occur in all sorts of indirect ways; for example, even though the local luxury industries fostered by the import controls

used locally built machinery, the resulting total demand for machinery might be great enough to stimulate imports by other industries that might otherwise have bought their machinery at home. Restricting the use of foreign exchange for frivolous purposes might intensify the use of foreign exchange for apparently serious purposes, all without blocking the satisfaction of supposedly frivolous desires but simply causing them to be satisfied in a less efficient way. Restrictions on imports of flowers, for example, might stimulate growing flowers locally in greenhouses heated by coal, and a consequent reduction in coal exports might mean that the foreign exchange saved in one direction was lost in another.

Curing a balance-of-payments deficit involves cutting the country's total of private and public consumption and investment. Income-distribution considerations may perhaps argue for cutting back on luxury consumption in particular. Even so, as long as some goods in each category will still be consumed in the new situation, it is not clear why the cut in luxury consumption should be especially concentrated on imports. Perhaps the pattern of comparative advantage even calls for cutting imports mainly of essential rather than luxury goods; an import-replacing expansion of domestic production of essentials could be aided by cutbacks on the domestic production of luxuries.[18]

If, despite everything, possibilities of influencing the domestic distribution of real income are thought to justify selective controls over trade, the question arises why their use should hinge on balance-of-payments difficulties. Should redistributionary controls be relaxed whenever the balance-of-payments situation happens to turn favorable? If redistribution is the purpose, why shouldn't the

---

[18] If the foreign supply is elastic for the imported luxuries and inelastic for the imported necessities, and if domestic industry could rather easily convert from luxury to essential production, terms-of-trade considerations would call for concentrating import restrictions on the essentials rather than on the luxuries. On all this, see Meade, *op. cit.,* p. 318n. Incidentally, this point is not meant to recognize a clear distinction between "luxuries" and "essentials"; it merely mentions some problems to consider *even if* the distinction could meaningfully be made.

controls be administered accordingly, with balance-of-payments equilibrium being taken care of in some further way? One more possible argument for controlling luxury imports may be mentioned for the sake of completeness, even though saying much about it would arouse suspicion of blowing down straw men. It involves the international demonstration effect.[19] If people in a poor country become acquainted with the high standards of living prevalent abroad and with the attractive goods available there, their propensity to consume may be higher and their propensity to accumulate capital lower than if they had remained more nearly in ignorance of foreign consumption standards. Restrictions on luxury imports may be a way of protecting this salutory ignorance. (One further argument for controls is considered in the appendix to this chapter.)

Further Problems with Controls

Some general remarks about controls still need to be pulled together.

1. Controls are open to the same sorts of objections on "efficiency" grounds as are developed in the traditional analysis of protective tariffs versus free trade, and whatever qualifications apply to that analysis apply here also. Even though intended solely for balance-of-payments purposes, furthermore, controls give at least incidental protection against foreign competition to domestic producers of items in which the country had a comparative disadvantage. Vested interests develop and press for continuance of the controls even after the original need for them has passed. Vested interests also develop in the "quota profits" created by certain types of restriction. And speaking of vested interests, one might mention trade experts and controllers who like to think that their services are too important for their country to dispense with.[20]

Somtimes the inefficiency caused by controls is obvious even to noneconomists. When the Mexican government was trying to stave off the devaluation of 1948, it banned imports of trucks but not of spare parts. Mexicans found it worthwhile to import parts and assemble trucks locally at a greater cost, even in foreign exchange, than the cost of ready-built trucks. Under a system adopted in Brazil in 1953, petroleum could be imported at a preferred exchange rate of 33.82 cruzeiros per dollar, while repair parts for trucks and buses had to be imported at a rate fluctuating up towards 150 cruzeiros per dollar. This made maintaining and repairing trucks and buses artificially expensive relative to the cost of gasoline. It did not pay truck operators to spend one dollar for repairs that would improve engine efficiency enough to save three dollars worth of gasoline, since the differential exchange rates meant that three dollars for gasoline cost fewer cruzeiros than one dollar for repair parts. This was one reason why the average truck consumed 4.3 tons of gasoline a year in Brazil compared with 2.7 tons in the United States. Other inefficiencies of this type were also apparent, such as the use of limestone to make cement instead of fertilizer while fertilizer was being imported at preferred exchange rates. Because newsprint was imported at a preferential rate of 18.82 cruzeiros per dollar, Brazilian producers could not compete and began switching their output into other kinds of paper. More and more foreign exchange was used to import newsprint, leaving less available for the import of machinery and parts.[21]

2. One fundamental difficulty with relying on controls for equilibrium is that a deficit on current account corresponds to attempts by the country's residents to "absorb" goods and services in excess of aggregate production. At full employment, no room remains for a remedy through greater production; in fact, the inefficiencies caused by controls would, if anything, interfere. People's attempted overspending accompanies an excess of liquid purchasing power in their hands: given the prevailing level of prices (includ-

[19] Cf. Ragnar Nurkse, *Problems of Capital Formation in Underdeveloped Countries*, Oxford: Basil Blackwell, 1953, esp. pp. 58-75.

[20] Cf. Küng, *op. cit.*, pp. 671-672.

[21] Yale Brozen, "Solutions for the Brazilian Dollar Shortage," *Current Economic Comment*, May 1955, pp. 22-23.

ing the prices of internationally traded goods and services at prevailing exchange rates), the purchasing power of the total money supply is larger than the aggregate of real cash balances that persons and institutions desire to hold. Barring a disinflationary policy, the market method of adjustment is for the real money supply to be cut down to what people are willing to hold by a rise in prices, notably including the home-currency prices of internationally traded goods as translated at increased quotations on foreign currencies. In addition to this, the cheapening of domestic goods and factors of production *relative* to internationally traded goods brings substitution and real-income effects into play.[22] If these market adjustments are prevented, merely introducing import controls will not remedy the generally overblown demand. If people are restricted from spending their money on certain imports, they are likely to spend part of it on other imports. If controls apply broadly and tightly enough to cut *total* spending on imports, people will divert their expenditure to goods produced at home, including exportable goods and home-market goods employing resources diverted from export production. Damming up purchasing power in one place lets it seep through in another. Import restrictions cannot eliminate a balance-of-payments deficit unless they can somehow restrict total—including domestic—consumption and investment and make people more acquiescent than before in saving and holding cash balances. Temporarily, controls may do this: when people are blocked in spending their money in some ways, they may need some time to decide how else to spend it. Some disinvestment, including disinvestment in inventories of imported materials, may occur. But continued success would require not merely maintaining but repeatedly tightening the controls.[23]

Professors Röpke and Brozen have described the problem picturesquely. When the government forbids people to import gourmet cheeses or bathtubs or automobiles or to take other than strictly limited vacations abroad, it leaves money "burning holes in their pockets" and possibly itching to be spent on other imports or on exportable goods or on goods and services using resources that might otherwise have gone into import-competing or exportable goods. To keep a wealthy Brazilian from spending his money on an imported automobile or on foreign travel may accomplish little saving of foreign exchange. Instead, he may use it for a luxurious home or for other domestically produced luxuries. If import restrictions keep an Englishman from giving his wife a Swiss watch for Christmas, "it is scarcely to be assumed that he will give her a savings-account passbook instead; rather, he will try to hunt up some other luxury good."[24]

Some writers have concluded that import restrictions at full employment can in themselves do substantially nothing at all to shrink absorption and so shrink a balance-of-payments deficit.[25] But this conclusion goes too far. The undoubted possibility of curing a deficit by completely prohibiting *all* imports suggests that less sweeping restrictions should be able to reduce imports directly by somewhat more than they reduce exports indirectly. The case against controls is not that they are totally ineffective but that they are inefficient. While they leave in operation the subsidy that an artificially low price of foreign exchange gives to absorption, they do narrow the range and restrict the quantities of goods on which people can in fact collect this subsidy. Controls shrink the effective real purchasing power of the existing money supply not by allowing the prices of

---

[22] None of this means, of course, that a deficit can result only from actual monetary inflation. A deterioration of trade opportunities can reduce a country's real income, leaving the previously appropriate money supply and money income level excessive, until prices adjust.

[23] Cf. J. J. Polak, "Monetary Analysis of Income Formation and Payments Problems," IMF *Staff Papers*, **VI**, November 1957, p. 30.

[24] Brozen, *op. cit.*, p. 23; Röpke, *op. cit.*, pp. 287-288. The translated quotation is from Röpke. His pages 282ff., which have largely inspired the present treatment, examine "austerity" in foreign-trade policy as an aspect of suppressed inflation in general.

[25] For example, Hemming and Corden, *op. cit.*, esp. pp. 495 and 509.

foreign exchange and internationally traded goods to rise in free markets but by creating shortages that make prices rise anyway and also by directly keeping people from spending their money as they wish. Prices alone do not measure the entire loss in the purchasing power of money.

The absorption approach suggests one further problem when an external deficit is associated with a policy of suppressed inflation and extreme "austerity." Having a country live within its means may involve not only restraining consumption but also stimulating production, yet enforced austerity tends to hamper it. The state may try to limit luxury spending, but there is one luxury that, without going totalitarian, it can hardly deprive people of—leisure. Although people may still care about earning money to spend later on, after austerity will have been relaxed, their incentives to work harder or longer for more mere money become relatively weak if their present incomes already cover their ration of artificially cheap "necessities" permitted by the controls, if social services take care of other necessities such as medical care, and especially if purchases of additional "luxuries" are restricted or forbidden. Perhaps the best example is Germany before the reforms of mid-1948. The contrasting policy of allowing the price mechanism to operate offers people the incentive of using any additional money earnings for whatever goods and services they themselves desire.

3. For the reasons already reviewed, and others, direct controls tend to be self-necessitating: the existence of certain controls not conforming to the logic of a price system tends to create conditions that appear to call for more such controls. One illustration concerns exchange control in particular. If foreign countries keep their currencies from being freely convertible into others, the residents of a country still lacking such controls would find that their surplus earnings in transactions with some countries could not be freely sold to meet excess expenditures in other countries. Their authorities would now worry not merely about a multilateral balance of transactions with the rest of the world as a whole but also about balance with other countries separately. Unless they were to allow a free exchange market in which the controlled foreign currencies would very probably be quoted at broken cross-rates of exchange, the authorities would find themselves driven to institute controls of their own to increase the degree of bilateral balance. Of course, countries might collaborate to lessen the necessities for bilateralism by establishing some arrangement such as the European Payments Union to improve the external convertibility of their currencies. The possibility that cooperative relaxation of some controls can facilitate relaxation of others illustrates in reverse their self-necessitating nature.

A more sweeping way in which controls breed controls is in tending to reduce the price-responsiveness of flows of trade, creating the very inelasticities of demand that seem to make reliance on automatic market adjustments risky. When the very purpose of direct controls is to override price incentives in international trade, it is hardly surprising when they do just that and, consequently, discredit reliance on the price mechanism. This pessimistic propostion has an optimistic corollary: removal of direct controls over world trade should be a cumulative process, each stage helping to restore the price-responsiveness of trade and so facilitating still further decontrol.

4. The consequences of using direct controls are at least potentially unfair. For one thing, controls almost inevitably discriminate not only among the purposes for which foreign exchange may be used but also among persons and firms and perhaps among foreign countries. *Discrimination* is admittedly a pejorative term here, and controls might instead be called wholesomely *selective*. But whatever word is used, controls do involve numerous arbitrary decisions by the authorities. It is difficult to be precise, for example, about what might constitute administering import quotas and exchange controls so as not to give especially unfavorable or favorable treatment to the exports of particular countries. And reliance on direct controls

may create opportunities for playing favorites among local importers or other users of foreign exchange, opportunities that in some countries may put a strain on the moral standards of the officials.[26]

Exchange control, bluntly characterized, deprives some persons of their property at less than its market value for the actual or supposed benefit of others. A man who sells goods or delivers lectures or writes for publication abroad and thus earns foreign exchange in an honest and proper way may not use it as he wishes but must surrender it for home currency at a price that is almost certain to be artificially low (since there is little reason for exchange control except in connection with a policy of officially setting or influencing exchange rates). George Winder mentions the allocation of hundreds of thousands of dollars to a well-known British retailer for opening a shop in New York. At the rate of $4.03 per pound sterling prevailing at the time, a rate at which "every importer in England was begging for dollars," this allocation virtually gave away many thousands of pounds to the fortunate retailer. And who in effect paid for this gift? Other British businessmen from whom honestly earned dollars were compulsorily requisitioned. The government was taking dollars from one and giving them to another at a price below what the parties would have freely agreed upon.[27]

To worries over requisitioning some persons' property for the benefit of other persons, the reply may be made: "So what? Taxes do that, too, but only anarchists condemn all taxation. Furthermore, all property rights are creations of the law, and none are absolute." In turn one may ask how well the kind of requisitioning associated with exchange control accords with acceptable canons of taxation and with conceptions of property rights worthy of being fostered by law. Can the particular redistributions of income and wealth that result from exchange control be defended in their own right, or are they haphazard and capricious?

The courts, the legislature, public opinion, the press, and the academic community all are handicapped in resisting unfairness in the administration of controls. The issues are too technical. The courts, for example, must depend largely on the determinations of the experts—that is, the controllers themselves —as to matters of fact, and independent scholars can concern themselves with basic principles but hardly with details of administration.[28]

5. A list of arguments pro and con must mention some still broader and less "economic" consequences of having controls extensive and strict enough to suppress extreme disequilibrium. Many kinds of opportunities for evading controls or for avoiding their intended results need to be suppressed. In allocating foreign exchange, the difficulty of distinguishing between business trips and pleasure trips abroad suggests just one of many respects in which controls do the opposite of putting the burden on the big operator for the sake of the little man. On the contrary, a system of controls puts a premium on having "contacts" and on engaging in far-flung and diversified activities.

Exchange control is a kind of regulation that has built-in incentives for violation. The more generally the regulations are obeyed, the more profitable does violation become for a law-breaking minority. For by staying out of the black market and shunning questionable deals, the law-abiding citizens are refraining from bidding up the black-market or *de facto* price of foreign exchange. This makes its illegal acquisition more attractive for the law-breakers than it would be if they had more competition. The law-breakers reap something in the nature of a scarcity rent from the scarcity of their willingness to break the law. Law-abiding citizens may feel with some justification that they are being dupes and that their own very obedience is providing illegal profit for less conscientious persons. This point becomes clearer when one contrasts a law against capital export with a

---

[26] Applicants for import licenses may find it worth while to invest money "to help the official to decide to whom he shall hand out the valuable permit." (Meade, *op. cit.*, p. 277.)

[27] George Winder, *The Free Convertibility of Sterling*, London: The Batchworth Press, 1955, pp. 58-59.

[28] Cf. Küng, *op. cit.*, pp. 674-675.

law against murder. By refraining from murder, law-abiding persons do nothing to make murder significantly easier or more profitable for others.

The gift of a scarcity rent to violators is only one reason why direct controls are sometimes said to breed cynicism and disrespect for law. Enforcement requires declaring illegal many things that are not in themselves morally wrong and so tends to blur the distinction between right and wrong. Furthermore, if the prohibitions are to be strictly enforced—if borders are to be closely patrolled, if travelers are to be thoroughly searched, if suspects are to be shadowed—many policemen and much of the time of the courts must be diverted from dealing with crimes that are morally wrong as well as illegal.

All this raises questions about the effect of controls on freedom. Some persons are inclined to classify restrictions on spending as interferences with mere "economic freedom," supposed to be less worthy than other types. But they may be less complacent about controls extending to purchases of foreign books and periodicals, contributions to causes or organizations headquartered abroad, and foreign travel for scholarly or other serious nonbusiness purposes. Restrictions on the transfer of capital by a person wishing to emigrate from his home country perhaps belong in the same category, as does requisitioning foreign exchange earned on lecture tours abroad or from books sold abroad. Intentionally or not, such controls interfere not merely with material pursuits but even with the expression and propagation of knowledge and opinion. Different aspects of life do not fall neatly into separate compartments.

To point this out is not to erect freedom into an absolute and condemn all interferences with it. Different aspects or segments of freedom—freedom for particular actions and of particular persons—necessarily clash. The liberal ideal is to devise social institutions that minimize such conflicts. According to this ideal, the key economic fact of scarcity should be brought to bear on consumption and investment decisions in a more impersonal and less arbitrary way than by government control. Each person would decide for himself how to restrict his activities to correspond with his limited resources and his own circumstances and preferences. If he wishes to stint himself on material goods in order to spend money on intellectual or ideological activities, he is free to do so.

Conclusion

The presumption in favor of market processes depends on whether they can work satisfactorily, and our investigation of this question is far from completed. We cannot condemn all alternatives regardless of circumstances and purposes. Perhaps a respectable if not conclusive case can be made for direct controls—or more probably for tariffs instead—to improve the terms of trade of certain countries; and the familiar arguments are not downright fallacious for using import controls to foster infant and defense industries, to promote economic development, and to promote the diversification of economies judged to be precariously specialized in and dependent on the export of one or a few primary commodities. To restate and appraise all of these possibilities would take us into the traditional discussion of free trade versus protection and would range too far afield from an examination of alternative methods of balance-of-payments adjustment.

✑ Appendix to Chapter 7: A Case for Discriminatory Direct Controls

Discrimination to Minimize the Destruction of Trade

Ragnar Frisch has developed a case for making direct controls *discriminatory,* if they are to be used at all, when the balance-of-payments deficits of a number of countries correspond to the surplus of one particular country or of only a few countries.[1] The argument is that if each deficit country nondiscriminatorily restricted its imports from all sources, from surplus countries and fellow deficit countries alike, the total cut in world trade would be greater than under discrimination.

A numerical example will prove helpful. Table 7A.1 supposes a world of two deficit countries and one surplus country. The figures shown for exports and imports per time period are supposed to include all credit and debit items on current account and independently motivated capital account, so that the deficits and surpluses refer to the needed accommodating movements of international reserves and short-term capital.

[1] Ragnar Frisch, "On the Need for Forecasting a Multilateral Balance of Payments," *American Economic Review,* **XXXVII,** September 1947, pp. 535-551.

The figures outside the parentheses describe the initial situation. Ruritania's and Graustark's deficits of 15 and 4, respectively, match the US surplus of 19. Ruritania's exports equal only one half of her imports, and Graustark's export/import ratio is 9/10. Now the authorities in each deficit country try to correct their imbalance by restricting imports to the level of existing exports. Thus, Ruritania and Graustark cut back imports to 50 and 90 percent, respectively, of their earlier levels. Each country's restriction is nondiscriminatory: its same percentage cutback applies to imports from all sources.[2]

The new situation is shown by the figures in

[2] This way of interpreting "nondiscrimination" is open to some question. If the same cuts were to be accomplished by *ad valorem* import duties rather than by direct controls, the pattern of supply and demand elasticities might well require each deficit country to apply different rates of duty to imports from different sources. Nondiscrimination in the sense of uniform import cuts does not, in general, coincide with nondiscrimination in the sense of restrictions equivalent to uniform *ad valorem* duties. Defining nondiscrimination in the former sense simplifies the discussion, however, without affecting the principle being illustrated. See Meade, *op. cit.,* p. 406n. in particular, as well as his chapters XXVIII through XXXI in general.

Table 7A.1. An Example of Imbalance and Its Removal

Exporting Country	Importing Country			Total Exports	Deficit (−) or Surplus (+)
	Ruritania	Graustark	US		
Ruritania		7 (6.3)	8	15 (14.3)	−15 (−0.7)
Graustark	13 (6.5)		23	36 (29.5)	− 4 (−6.5)
U.S.	17 (8.5)	33 (29.7)		50 (38.2)	+19 (+7.2)
Total Imports	30 (15.0)	40 (36.0)	31	101 (82.0)	

parentheses in each cell and by such of the original figures as remain unchanged. (US imports do not change; perhaps the US has a full-employment policy that neutralizes any deflationary influence stemming from the decline in its exports.) Although each country has restricted its imports by a percentage calculated to cut them down into line with its previous exports, the deficits have not been eliminated; more than one-third of the original total imbalance remains (and Graustark's deficit has actually increased). The reason is that the nondiscriminatory import restrictions of each deficit country have also shrunk the export market of the other. To this extent, the restrictions have merely shuffled the burden of the deficits around between the deficit countries instead of concentrating the restrictions on the exports of the surplus country. Even the merely partial removal of the imbalances has cut total world trade (total exports = total imports) from 101 to 82. If nondiscriminatory restrictions are to eliminate the imbalance completely, they will have to be tighter and the shrinkage in world trade even greater.

The advantage of discriminatory controls can be shown by going back to the original unbalanced position and supposing that each deficit country leaves imports from the other unaffected while discriminatorily cutting imports from the US by the amount of its own previous overall deficit. The new situation is as in Table 7A.1, except that Ruritania's imports are 2 from the US and 15 in total, Graustark's imports are 29 from the US and 36 in total, total US exports are 31, all deficits and surpluses are 0, and world exports (= world imports) are 82. This shrinkage of total world trade is the same as had been necessary for only *partial* elimination of imbalances and smaller than would be necessary for *complete* elimination of imbalances by tighter nondiscriminatory controls. Total world trade has had to shrink by only the amount of the previous total deficits (= total surpluses). In fact, the discriminatory method would probably shrink total trade even less than this, since the restrictions on imports from the US might induce residents of Ruritania and Graustark to import more from each other. In part, that is, the restrictions could cause a mere diversion rather than destruction of trade.

This happy outcome could fail if the US retaliated. While perhaps politically understandable, retaliation would have little economic rationale. The US might consider it "unfair" that only her exports should be cut. But even

if the deficit countries restricted their imports from all sources in equal proportion, the US would suffer the same total reduction in its export trade. Balancing trade without any change in US imports means cutting US exports by a definite amount—down to the level of these imports—no matter *how* this cut is made. The only advantage the US could gain by insisting on nondiscrimination would be the *Schadenfreude* of seeing other countries suffering cuts in their exports also.

The US of our examples is a hypothetical country, but it may not be amiss here to introduce a well-phrased comment on policy of the real U.S. The former editor of the London *Economist* noted that official American opinion had recovered from its immediate postwar resentment of anything smacking of discrimination against American exports.

After all, Europeans cannot be expected to spend more dollars than they have and, having exhausted their dollars, it is really not reasonable to object to their using the pounds and francs and lire they do have. Why should I be prevented from spending my vacation at Monte Carlo simply because I do not have the dollars to go to Miami?[3]

The example of imbalance considered so far was easy to remedy (on paper) because each deficit country's overall deficit was smaller than its imports from the surplus country. A more challenging pattern of imbalance would have one country's overall deficit larger than its imports from the surplus country. Restricting imports from the surplus country alone would not suffice; one deficit country would have to restrict imports from the other deficit country as well.

In an example of many countries and with still more complicated imbalances, direct restrictions might cut a deficit country's imports from another country, either in deficit or in balance, which would in turn cut its imports from still another deficit or balanced country, which would finally in turn cut its imports from a surplus country. The indirect nature of the adjustments would require total world trade to shrink by more, perhaps much more, than the amount of imbalances being eliminated. Where the cuts are made is crucial. No one country should concentrate its import cuts on a second country if some third country has still greater need, in some sense, to concentrate its own cuts on that second country. The general

[3] Geoffrey Crowther, *Balances and Imbalances of Payments*, Boston: Harvard University, Graduate School of Business Administration, 1957, pp. 60-61.

objective is "the quickest ultimate concentration of the cuts upon the surplus countries."[4] A carefully planned program would damage trade less than a spiral of indiscriminate import restrictions, with countries successively intensifying their own restrictions to match the drop in exports caused by earlier rounds in the process of restriction by other countries.

These considerations reveal an inadequacy of the "scarce-currency clause" of the Articles of Agreement of the International Monetary Fund. (See Chapter 19). This clause authorizes discriminatory exchange restrictions in special circumstances against transactions with a country whose overall payments surplus is so large that its currency becomes generally "scarce." The inadequacy is that the best program of direct controls may go beyond requiring discriminatory restrictions on expenditures by deficit countries in the scarce-currency country: it may also require discrimination against other surplus countries and even against balanced or deficit countries.

The merits of an internationally coordinated program are perhaps easier to appreciate if we think of it as an initially nondiscriminatory control system modified by the partial *removal* of controls, namely, of certain controls on trade *among* the countries that would be in deficit or in balance in the absence of any remedial measures. Yet despite the superiority of planned discriminatory controls over haphazard nondiscriminatory controls, the method, even at its best, does have shortcomings.[5] First, trade restrictions do little toward reaching adjustment by stimulating the exports as well as restraining the imports of deficit countries. (In this one respect, discriminatory controls may compare unfavorably with nondiscriminatory controls; for the latter, by hampering trade even among deficit countries, may prod their exporters into greater sales efforts in the surplus countries.) Second, establishing an optimum pattern of controls runs into practical difficulties: in obtaining relevant, accurate, and timely data about trade patterns, about substitutabilities in production and consumption, and about elasticities of supply and demand; in factually comprehending the immensely complex interrelations involved; in obtaining loyal cooperation among countries in adopting and enforcing precisely the controls and only the controls recommended by the international experts in charge of the program; and in making prompt modifications as circumstances change. Third, difficult though it is to contrive restrictions that shrink total world trade by the least possible amount, even this is not the real goal. The mere volume of trade is surely but a very crude indicator of welfare obtained by international specialization. Nothing ensures that the particular flows of trade designated for elimination or shrinkage would be the relatively most dispensable ones.[6] An internationally planned program of controls would ideally try to take account of how essential trade in particular commodities from particular sources to particular destinations was, but international agreement on this would be elusive. Finally and most generally, discriminatory trade controls merely palliate the balance-of-payments symptoms of underlying maladjustments in prices, costs, incomes, and production patterns at existing exchange rates. They do not fully allow trade to develop in accordance with comparative advantage.

Though open to these strictures, the case for discriminatory controls is instructive. It serves as a reminder of how complex the adjustments are that a changing world continually calls for. It shows the advantage of selectivity over indiscriminate restriction. Finally, it prompts the question whether some alternative might not be a more practical means of selectivity.

Selectivity without Discrimination

To approach this question, we may note the parallelism between the idea of imposing discriminatory controls or duties on imports from surplus countries and the idea of discriminatorily subsidizing (or taxing, if demand is inelastic) exports to the surplus countries. If a deficit country has import restrictions effectively equivalent to a 10 percent *ad valorem* duty on imports from a surplus country and also has a 10 percent *ad valorem* subsidy on exports to that country, this combination corresponds, ignoring nontrade transactions, to a 9.1

[4] J. E. Meade, *op. cit.,* p. 414.

[5] A number of criticisms of Frisch's approach are summarized in Charles P. Kindleberger, *The Dollar Shortage,* New York: The Technology Press of MIT and John Wiley & Sons, Inc., 1950, pp. 228-229; William R. Allen and Clark Lee Allen (eds.), *Foreign Trade and Finance,* New York: Macmillan, 1959, pp. 491-495; and Meade, *op. cit.,* pp. 414-417.

[6] In ideal competitive equilibrium, all flows of trade are in some sense of equal importance at the margin; but this does not mean that *intra-marginal* chunks of equal money value also represent equal chunks of welfare.

percent depreciation of its own currency in terms of the surplus country's currency.[7] The selectivity desired in a system of controls and subsidies to balance trade might as well be achieved by a multilateral pattern of exchange-rate adjustments.

Appreciation of surplus-country currencies and depreciation of deficit-country currencies (relative to the currencies of countries roughly in balance) would selectively influence trade patterns in several distinguishable ways. Exports from deficit to surplus countries would be spurred by: (1) the cheapening in surplus countries of imports from deficit countries relative both to home-produced goods and to imports from other surplus countries and from balanced countries; and (2) the increased profitability, for producers in deficit countries, of export sales to surplus countries relative both to sales at home and to sales in other deficit countries and in balanced countries. Imports of deficit from surplus countries would decline because of: (3) the increased prices in deficit countries of imports from surplus countries relative both to home-produced goods and to imports from other deficit countries and from balanced countries; and (4) the decreased profitability, for producers in surplus countries, of export sales to deficit countries relative both to sales at home and to sales in other surplus countries and in balanced countries.

This repatterning of trade would share a selective feature with a scheme of discriminatory controls: deficit countries would reduce their imports from surplus countries while reducing trade among themselves little if at all. Trade among deficit countries might even increase in substitution for their reduced imports from surplus countries; but, on the other hand, the increased exports of deficit to surplus countries might displace some trade among deficit countries. This adjustment by way of exchange rates would presumably shrink total world trade either not at all or less than even judiciously discriminatory restrictions would.

Flexible exchange rates could correct complicated imbalances (or, rather, avoid them in the first place). Suppose that Ruritania has no room to correct her overall deficit solely by cutting her imports from the US, the surplus country, and so (if relying on import restric-

tions alone) must also cut her imports from another deficit country, Graustark, with the latter in turn cutting her imports from the US by more than the amount of her original overall deficit. Exchange-rate flexibility might work by expanding exports to the surplus country, but we rule out this possibility for the sake of closer comparability with reliance on import controls alone. Suppose the Ruritanian crown and Graustark florin initially depreciate by equal percentages against the US dollar. Since the original trade pattern left little scope for cuts in Ruritanian imports from the US, since export expansion has been ruled out by assumption, and since no change in the crown-florin rate has yet affected trade between the two deficit countries, Ruritania's overall deficit is not yet fully corrected. Since Graustark had ample room for cutting imports from the US, however, depreciation of the florin against the dollar brings Graustark all or part of the way toward balance while Ruritania remains in overall deficit. The crown now depreciates further against the dollar and at last also against the florin. (Actually, of course, these changes would occur concurrently.) The new pattern of rates restrains Ruritanian imports from Graustark. Despite her appreciation relative to Ruritania, Graustark can have depreciated enough relative to the US so that the cut in her imports from the US exceeds her original overall deficit by enough also to match the drop in her exports to Ruritania. In final effect, then, Ruritania makes up for limited room to cut imports from the US directly by cutting them indirectly through the intermediary of Graustark.

This example gives an unrealistically *un*favorable account of the market process of multilateral adjustment, since we have ruled out export stimulation for the sake of comparability with the controls scheme.

Market adjustments take place without the need for any centralized gathering of data and formulation of plans and without anyone's crudely regarding all flows of trade between particular countries and in particular products as comparable for welfare purposes in terms of money value alone. They also avoid the alternative of crude official judgments about the relative dispensabilities of the various flows of trade. Such judgments can be made marginally rather than globally and can be made in a decentralized way by the persons most closely concerned and possessing the relevant detailed knowledge.

---

[7] On the similarities among selective trade controls, duties and subsidies, and exchange-rate adjustments, see Meade, *op. cit.*, pp. 418-419.

The Stability Conditions

 8

Stable and Unstable Markets

So far, other methods of balance-of-payments adjustment seem less attractive than exchange-rate variation. But this conclusion cannot stand without further attention to some possible defects of that method.

The present chapter returns to the danger that the exchange-rate mechanism, like the price-level mechanism of the gold standard, might work perversely because demand was not price-sensitive enough. The chapter seeks to formulate more precisely the so-called stability conditions for normal operation. The analysis refers to exchange rates but could readily be modified to refer to the price-level mechanism also.

Consider the supplies and demands for foreign exchange diagrammed in the three parts of Fig. 8.1. (Why only the parts of the curves in the immediate vicinity of the intersection have been drawn will become apparent later.) In parts (*a*) and (*b*) of the diagram, random deviations from the unpegged equilibrium exchange rate are self-correcting. The directions of the arrows show this. At "too high" a price of foreign exchange in home currency, an excess quantity of exchange supplied would drive the rate down. At "too low" a rate, an excess quantity demanded would bid it up. In part (*c*), however, deviations from equilibrium are self-aggravating. At too high a rate, excess demand bids the rate still higher; and a rate too low would sink still lower. The trouble stems from a backward-sloping supply curve of foreign exchange, although, as (*b*) shows, even this cannot cause instability if the normally-sloping demand curve is elastic

enough. A backward-sloping supply curve would reflect an inelastic foreign demand for home exports (as explained in Chapter 2).

None of the diagrams (*a*), (*b*), and (*c*) has an upward-sloping demand curve for foreign exchange, for that would show an exception to the ordinary law of demand, and such a theoretical curiosity is out of the question here. A rise in the price of foreign exchange and thus in the home-currency prices of foreign goods would hardly make home buyers want to buy increased quantities of foreign goods and of the foreign exchange with which to pay for them. Thus the question of stability boils down to whether the supply curve of foreign exchange is backward-sloping and, if so, whether this peculiarity is offset by sufficient elasticity of the downward-sloping demand curve.

The Stability Formula

The elasticities of supply and demand for foreign exchange trace back to the elasticities of supply and demand for import and export goods and services with respect to their prices in the currencies of the sellers and buyers. (For simplicity, the following analysis supposes that imports and exports of goods and services make up the only items in the balance of payments. Suitable interpretation, however, could take other items into account.) A lively dispute has raged over these elasticities. They supposedly express the responsiveness of quantities to price. But what things besides price are tacitly allowed to vary, and what other things really are considered constant? How meaningful, legitimate and useful are these elasticity concepts?

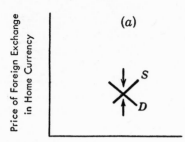
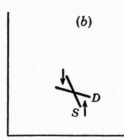
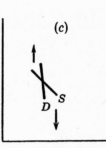

Quantities of Foreign Exchange Demanded and Supplied per Time Period

Figure 8-1. Stable and Unstable Exchange Markets

The whole issue will be clearer if, before facing it, we first ponder the formulas in which the elasticities appear.

In the formulas that follow, the e's stand for supply elasticities and the η's for demand elasticities; the subscripts m and x refer to the imports and exports of Inland, the home country. Thus:

e_m = elasticity with respect to price in Outland currency of Outland's supply of Inland's imports.

e_x = elasticity with respect to price in Inland currency of Inland's supply of exports to Outland.

η_m = elasticity with respect to price in Inland currency of Inland's demand for imports from Outland.

η_x = elasticity with respect to price in Outland currency of Outland's demand for Inland's exports.

The elasticities of supply are positive for normal upward-sloping supply curves. The elasticities of demand are positive, too, on the definition whereby normal downward-sloping demand curves are said to have positive elasticity.

In terms of these elasticities, the criterion of normal rather than perverse influence of exchange-rate changes on the balance of payments is

$$\frac{e_x (\eta_x - 1)}{e_x + \eta_x} + \frac{\eta_m (e_m + 1)}{e_m + \eta_m}$$

If this expression is positive, the market is stable; if negative, unstable. The derivation of this expression is left to the appendix of this chapter; the chapter itself tries only to draw the implications of the expression and make them seem intuitively reasonable. The criterion applies precisely, with the elasticities in it interpreted as nearly ordinary price elasticities, only if domestic income levels remain stable—only if domestic money supplies and incomes do not somehow get out of control as a direct or indirect consequence of exchange-rate variation. Keeping various possible influences separate in this way seems necessary to a manageable analysis; we can consider complications later.

The test expression can be negative, indicating a perverse exchange-rate mechanism, only if η_x, the elasticity of Outland's demand for Inland's exports, is less than 1, making $\eta_x - 1$ negative.[1] Even if η_x were actually as small as zero, however, the entire test expression could be kept positive by the other elasticities in it. Earlier chapters have made it clear, without algebra, that high demand elasticities are favorable to normal responsiveness of the balance of payments. The role of the supply elasticities may be investigated by rewriting the algebraic criterion as

$$\frac{\eta_x - 1}{1 + \dfrac{\eta_x}{e_x}} + \frac{\eta_m + \dfrac{\eta_m}{e_m}}{1 + \dfrac{\eta_m}{e_m}}$$

When $\eta_x > 1$ and the left-hand term is positive, it is "desirable" (for the sake of stability)

---

[1] The two supply elasticities (like the demand elasticities) must almost certainly be positive (or at worst zero); the conditions necessary for a backward-sloping supply curve are especially unrealistic when applied to the exports in general of a whole country.

that this term be large, thus that the denominator $1 + \eta_x/e_x$ be small, and thus in turn that e_x be large. When $\eta_x < 1$ and the left-hand term is negative, however, it is "desirable" that the absolute value of this negative term be small and thus that e_x be small.

In the right-hand term, when $\eta_m > 1$, a given absolute decrease in η_m/e_m represents a larger percentage decrease in the denominator $1 + \eta_m/e_m$ than in the numerator $\eta_m + \eta_m/e_m$ and thus increases the value of the ratio. It follows that when $\eta_m > 1$, a low value of η_m/e_m, and so a high value of e_m, is favorable to stability. On the other hand, when $\eta_m < 1$, a given absolute increase in η_m/e_m represents a larger percentage increase in the numerator $\eta_m + \eta_m/e_m$ than in the denominator $1 + \eta_m/e_m$ and thus increases the value of the ratio. It follows that when $\eta_m < 1$, a high value of η_m/e_m, and so a low value of e_m, is favorable to exchange stability.

Each of these conclusions about supply elasticities will now be restated, together with a verbal attempt to make it seem intuitively reasonable:

When the Outland demand for Inland exports is elastic, it is "desirable" (for the sake of stability) that Inland's supply of exports be elastic also. Reason: if depreciation of Inland's currency and the consequent cut in the Outland-currency price of Inland's exports is effective enough in stimulating Outland's purchases to increase their total Outland-currency value, then it is "desirable" that there be as little interference as possible with this price cut. In particular, the depreciation should raise the Inland-currency price of exports as little as possible: slight price increases should suffice to call forth the necessary increases in the quantity of exports supplied.

When the Outland demand for Inland exports is inelastic, it is "desirable" that Inland's supply of exports be inelastic also. Reason: if depreciation and the consequent cut in the Outland-currency price of Inland's exports is so ineffective in stimulating Outland's purchases that their total Outland-currency value falls, then it is desirable that there be as much interference with this price cut as possible. In particular, the depreciation should greatly raise the Inland-currency price of exports:

large price increases should be required to call forth the necessary increases in the quantity of exports supplied.

When Inland's demand for imports is elastic, it is "desirable" that the Outland supply be elastic also. Reason: if depreciation and the consequent rise in the Inland-currency price of imports is very effective in restraining imports, it is desirable that there be as little interference as possible with this price rise. In particular, the Outland-currency price should fall as little as possible: slight price drops should suffice to curtail the quantity of imports supplied from Outland to Inland.

When Inland's demand for imports is inelastic, it is "desirable" that the Outland supply be inelastic also. Reason: if depreciation and the consequent rise in the Inland-currency price of imports is rather ineffective in restraining imports, interference with this price rise does little damage. On the contrary, a better chance of reducing the total Outland-currency value of Inland imports hinges on a drop in their Outland price. Thus Outlanders should be relatively dependent on the Inland market: sharp price reductions should be necessary to curtail the quantities supplied even slightly.

Returning to the original algebraic criterion

$$\frac{e_x(\eta_x - 1)}{e_x + \eta_x} + \frac{\eta_m(e_m + 1)}{e_m + \eta_m}$$

we readily see that, regardless of demand elasticities, if both supply elasticities are zero, a normally-working exchange market is assured, for the expression reduces to $\dfrac{\eta_m}{\eta_m}$, or 1, which is positive.

The zero import supply elasticity means that when depreciation of Inland's currency causes what from Outland's point of view appears as a drop in Inland's demand, Outlanders are so dependent on the Inland market that they act to keep their sales unchanged by absorbing the entire effect of the depreciation through price cuts in terms of their own currency. Inland's zero export supply elasticity means that despite depreciation, the quantity of Inland's exports and hence their Outland-currency price and total

Outland-currency value all remain unchanged. The net result for Inland is a reduction in the Outland-currency value of its imports, no change in the Outland-currency value of its exports, and thus an improvement in its balance of payments.

In fact, if either one alone of the supply elasticities is zero, stability is still assured. As just shown, a zero export supply elasticity keeps the total Outland-currency value of exports unchanged when Inland's currency depreciates, thus ruling out the shrinkage of export proceeds that would have to characterize a perversely-working mechanism. When the import supply elasticity is zero, the stability criterion reduces to

$$\frac{e_x (\eta_x - 1)}{e_x + \eta_x} + \frac{\eta_m}{\eta_m} \quad \text{or} \quad \frac{\eta_x - 1}{1 + \frac{\eta_x}{e_x}} + 1$$

Now, no matter how near zero η_x is, the left-hand term cannot be larger negatively than 1, so that the entire expression cannot be negative. At worst, with $\eta_x = 0$, the expression reduces to $-1 + 1$, or 0, indicating the borderline between normal and perverse response of the balance of payments to the exchange rate.

The well-known case of both supplies being infinitely elastic can best be approached by rewriting the test expression as

$$\frac{\eta_x - 1}{1 + \frac{\eta_x}{e_x}} + \frac{\eta_m \left(1 + \frac{1}{e_m}\right)}{1 + \frac{\eta_m}{e_m}}$$

Making all the e's infinite reduces to zero all the little fractions of which they are denominators, so that the test expression becomes simply $\eta_x + \eta_m - 1$. Thus the stability condition is satisfied if either demand elasticity, or even if merely the sum of the two of them, exceeds 1. This simple condition for the case of infinitely elastic supplies has long been familiar[2] and is sometimes mistaken for the *general* stability condition. Actually, even lower demand elasticities will suffice when the supply elasticities are less than infinite.

When each of the supply and demand elasticities is *between* zero and infinity, as in reality, the stability condition can usefully be rewritten[3]

$$\frac{e_m e_x (\eta_m + \eta_x - 1) + \eta_m \eta_x (e_m + e_x + 1)}{(e_m + \eta_m)(e_x + \eta_x)}$$

Now, since each of the individual elasticities is positive, the denominator of this expression is assuredly positive and may be ignored. In the numerator, the only negative element is the -1 in the first parentheses. Again we see that stability is assured if the two demand elasticities add up to 1 or more and is still easily possible even of their total is less than 1. Substituting numbers into $e_m e_x (\eta_m + \eta_x - 1) + \eta_m \eta_x (e_m + e_x + 1)$ shows that when each supply elasticity is 10, it suffices for stability that each demand elasticity be only a shade over 10/21 (or one can be lower with the other enough higher). When each supply elasticity is 5, demand elasticities of just over 5/11 each suffice; when each supply elasticity is 2, demand elasticities of just over 2/5 each suffice; when each supply elasticity is 1, demand elasticities of just over 1/3 each suffice; when each supply elasticity is 1/2, demand elasticities of just over 1/4 each suffice, and so on.

Empirical Clues about Elasticities

All this makes the elasticity requirements for a normally working exchange-rate mechanism hardly appear very exacting. Familiar facts suggest that they are likely to be satisfied in the real world. First, the world demand for a single country's exports is likely to be elastic because of competition with similar exports from other countries; buyers in the world market may have plenty of opportunity to shift toward or away from a particular country's exports according to price comparisons. The principle is the same as that which explains why the demand for wheat grown on a particular farm is extremely elastic even

---

[2] Abba P. Lerner, *The Economics of Control*, New York: Macmillan, 1947, p. 378.

[3] By straightforward though tedious manipulation. Incidentally, this is the form in which the stability condition seems most commonly to appear in print. It is essentially the same, for instance, as appears in Lloyd A. Metzler, "The Theory of International Trade," in Howard S. Ellis, ed., *A Survey of Contemporary Economics*, Philadelphia: Blakiston, 1948, p. 226.

though the overall demand for wheat may be extremely inelastic. (The chief exception would be for a country the great bulk of whose exports consisted of one or more products in highly inelastic overall demand and facing no great competition on the world market.) The principle can be expressed by the formula

$$\eta_x = \frac{1}{a}\eta_w + \frac{b}{a}e_c$$

in which η_x = the elasticity of world-market demand for a particular export commodity supplied specifically by Inland, η_w = the elasticity of world-market demand for that commodity from all exporting countries in general, e_c = the elasticity of export supply from countries competing with Inland, a = Inland's share of the world export market, and b = the competitors' share of the market.[4] If Inland has half the world market for exports of the commodity and all its competitors together have the other half, if the elasticity of world-market demand is ½, and if the elasticity of competitors' supply is actually as unfavorable as zero, the elasticity of demand for

Inland's export is still $\frac{1}{\frac{1}{2}} \cdot \frac{1}{2} + \frac{\frac{1}{2}}{\frac{1}{2}} \cdot 0$, or 1. If

Inland has ⅓ and its competitors ⅔ of the world market and if the elasticities of world

demand and competitors' supply are each only ½, Inland faces an export demand elasticity of 2½.

A second consideration is that the existence of some domestic production of an import-type commodity makes the elasticity of demand specifically for the import higher than the elasticity of demand for the commodity in general. This is expressed by a formula whose derivation parallels the one given in the last footnote:

$$\eta_m = \frac{1}{f}\eta_D + \frac{h}{f}e_s$$

where η_m = the elasticity of import demand, η_D = the elasticity of demand for the commodity in general, e_s = the elasticity of supply from domestic production, f = the share of foreign goods in the total home market for the commodity, and h = the share of home goods in the market. For example, if the elasticity of general demand and the elasticity of supply from home production were each only ½ and if imports and the home-produced commodity were sharing the market half-and-half, the elasticity of import demand would be 1½. Even if supply from home production were completely inelastic, the elasticity of import demand would still be greater than the elasticity of general demand. This may be seen by substituting 0 for e_s in the above formula, which then

becomes $\eta_m = \frac{1}{f}\eta_D$. Now, since f is a fraction smaller than 1 and $\frac{1}{f}$ a number greater than 1, $\eta_m > \eta_D$. Furthermore, even if general demand for the commodity had zero elasticity, the existence of some domestic supply with some elasticity would give some elasticity to the import demand. Substituting 0 for η_D makes the formula become

$\eta_m = \frac{h}{f}e_s$. If the general demand had zero elasticity, if home supply had an elasticity of 1, and if imports were furnishing half of total consumption, the import demand would have an elasticity of 1. Algebraic pre-

---

[4] Except for some change in symbols and in the sign convention for demand elasticities (here the definition is used whereby demand elasticity is positive), this formula is taken from Fred C. Shorter, "Jute Production Policies of India and Pakistan," *Indian Economic Journal*, III, July 1955, p. 44 and footnote.

Derivation: Let W = world-market quantity demanded, C = quantity supplied from competing countries, $W - C$ = quantity demanded of Inland's export, and P = price. By the definition of elasticity,

$$\eta_x = \frac{-P}{W - C} \cdot \frac{d(W - C)}{dP}$$

$$= \frac{\dfrac{-P}{W}\dfrac{dW}{dP}W}{W - C} + \frac{\dfrac{P}{C}\dfrac{dC}{dP}C}{W - C}$$

$$= \frac{W}{W - C}\eta_w + \frac{C}{W - C}e_c$$

Now $a = \dfrac{W - C}{W}$, $b = \dfrac{C}{W}$, and $\dfrac{b}{a} = \dfrac{C}{W - C}$

cision vanishes when domestically produced commodities are not substantially identical to the competing import goods. Still, the broad conclusion holds that domestic production of import-competing goods contributes to elasticity in the specific demand for imports and that this contribution is the greater, the greater is the substitutability between domestic and imported goods and the greater the volume of domestic production relative to imports.

By close analogy with the formula for import demand elasticity, a formula can readily be derived for export supply elasticity (the task is left to the reader as an exercise). This shows that the existence of some domestic consumption of export goods makes the export supply elasticity greater than the total supply elasticity. This is true even if the domestic consumption demand is completely inelastic. Furthermore, even if the country's total production of the export commodity were completely unresponsive to price, the supply for export would still have some price elasticity as long as there were some domestic demand having some elasticity. These principles of export supply elasticity are relevant because when import and export demand elasticities are greater than 1, large values of the corresponding supply elasticities strengthen the normal operation of the exchange-rate mechanism.

A third general consideration about elasticities is that price changes can affect not only the quantities imported and exported of goods already traded but also affect the composition of the list. Depreciation of Inland's currency not only will increase sales of goods already being exported but also may make possible the export of some new goods. At the level of the exchange rate at which the export of some new Inland good just becomes possible, the elasticity of export demand for it is infinite. Similarly, depreciation not only will restrict Inland's imports of particular goods but also may cause some goods to drop off the import list entirely. For this reason, among others, a statistical study of demand elasticities for the particular goods already entering into a country's trade will tend to understate the overall elasticities of

demand for the broad range of actual and potential imports and exports; yet these are the elasticities relevant to the question of exchange stability.

Elasticity Measurements

For several years after World War II, attempts to measure import and export demand elasticities kept being reported for many individual countries. Almost invariably the elasticities were surprisingly low, occasionally low enough to suggest taking the perverse-elasticities case seriously. Soon, however, critics explained a number of statistical pitfalls causing such a bias toward zero in the measured elasticities as to make them practically meaningless. (Furthermore, some of the apparent inelasticity of demand in international trade had been due to quotas, tariffs, and other government controls precisely intended to keep trade from responding sensitively to price. That the price mechanism shows signs of being affected by deliberate interferences with its responsiveness is no evidence against its workability under more favorable policies.) A start was also made on developing refined methods yielding elasticities more nearly like those to be expected on general grounds. For several reasons it now seems sufficient simply to give citations to this literature rather than review it here.[5] First, the apparent outcome of this

[5] J. Hans Adler, "United States Import Demand during the Interwar Period," *American Economic Review*, XXXV, June 1945, pp. 418-430; Tse Chun Chang, "The British Balance of Payments, 1924-1938," *Economic Journal*, LVII, December 1947, pp. 475-503; Chang, "The British Demand for Imports in the Inter-War Period," *Economic Journal*, LVI, June 1946, pp. 188-207; Chang, "International Comparison of Demand for Imports," *Review of Economic Studies*, XIII (2), 1945–1946, pp. 53-67; Chang, "A Statistical Note on World Demand for Exports," *Review of Economics and Statistics*, XXX, May 1948, pp. 106-116; J. Tinbergen, "Some Measurements of Elasticities of Substitution," *Review of Economic Statistics*, XXVIII, August 1946, pp. 109-116; Randall Hinshaw, "American Prosperity and the British Balance-of-Payments Problem," *Review of Economic Statistics*, XXVII, February 1945, pp. 1-9; A. J. Brown, "The Rate of Exchange," pp. 75-106 in T. Wilson and P. W. S. Andrews (eds.), *Oxford Studies in the Price Mechanism*, Oxford: Clarendon Press, 1951; Fritz Machlup, "Elasticity Pessimism in International Trade," *Economia Internazionale*, III, February 1950, pp. 118-137; Guy H. Orcutt, "Measurement of Price

discussion itself suggests that the danger of critically low elasticities has received attention entirely out of proportion to its importance for the real world. Second, the purchasing-power-parity doctrine (explained in Chapter 10) permits side-stepping some statistical difficulties and empirically judging whether demand elasticities in the real world are above or below the value critical to exchange stability. Third, an analysis to be reviewed below shows that stable equilibrium levels of exchange rates must necessarily exist. Even if demand elasticities were perversely low at prices corresponding to some levels of exchange rates, other rates would necessarily exist at which these elasticities simply could not remain perversely low.

Secondary Effects: Income Changes

Before showing this, we should mention two or three effects that could modify the stability criterion already developed. First are various "income effects." For example, a country may have been maintaining the exchange value of its currency only by tolerating persistent depression at home. If the government now decides to resolve this conflict between the goals of external balance and domestic prosperity by devaluing the currency, it may be able to pursue an expansionary monetary and fiscal policy. As business improves, spending on imports increases along with spending on domestic goods and services. This income effect could conceivably swamp the influence of changed relative prices resulting from devaluation. Two distinct influences are at work. (Though devaluation and an expansionary financial policy would no doubt be linked in the minds of the policy makers, they are two distinct changes in the situation: devaluation does not automatically and inevitably

impose the change in domestic policy.) For the sake of manageable analysis, the effects of separate causes must be considered separately; different strands of analysis may be combined later. No one strand is disproved by showing that other influences join in determining the complex outcome in the real world.

A more relevant challenge to the price-elasticity analysis might show that interfering income effects result spontaneously from the change in the exchange rate. Suppose that currency depreciation or devaluation shrinks the country's import surplus or expands its export surplus. The associated multiplier effect tends to raise national income (assuming unemployment before). With increased incomes people import more than otherwise. Currency depreciation improves the country's balance of payments less than if its effect had not been diluted by the income effect.

Can we go further and conclude that the income effect could turn an otherwise stable foreign-exchange market into an unstable one? Probably not. If the income effect did make the exchange-rate mechanism work perversely, then currency depreciation would cause the balance of payments to *deteriorate*. But then, contradictorily, the foreign-trade multiplier would reduce rather than increase national income; and imports in turn would be restrained rather than stimulated. At worst the income effect would deprive exchange depreciation of all effect on the balance of payments, but it would not turn an otherwise stable mechanism into a perverse one. As long as an import-stimulating rise in home income depends on a depreciation-induced improvement in the balance of payments, the income effect merely weakens but does not reverse the net response of the balance of payments to a change in the exchange rate.

Another thought bolsters this tentative conclusion. Suppose that the country starts with a deficit in its balance of payments. As shown in the second footnote to the Appendix to this chapter, the deficit makes the elasticity requirements for a normal mechanism less exacting than they would be with initial

Elasticities in International Trade," *Review of Economics and Statistics,* **XXXII,** May 1950, pp. 117-132; Arnold C. Harberger, "Some Evidence on the International Price Mechanism," *Journal of Political Economy,* **LXV,** December 1957, pp. 506-521. Hang Sheng Cheng has surveyed these and other published studies in "Statistical Estimates of Elasticities and Propensities in International Trade," IMF *Staff Papers,* **VII,** April 1959, pp. 107-158. He provides greater detail in a lengthy mimeographed supplement to his paper.

equilibrium. If, despite this, the elasticities are only barely favorable enough for normality, then depreciation will reduce the deficit as measured in *foreign* money but will increase it as measured in *home* money. (A decreased amount of foreign money can equal an increased amount of home money if the home-money price of foreign money has risen.) As to whether the foreign-exchange market works normally and whether the country has balance-of-payments trouble or not, the deficit measured in foreign money is the one that counts. But the deficit measured in home money is the one relevant to the multiplier effect on home income.[6] If the deficit measured in home money increases (though the foreign-exchange deficit decreases), then the foreign-trade multiplier tends to reduce home income. This, in turn, tends to restrain imports. In short, the secondary income effect due to currency depreciation tends, in the borderline case, to reinforce the normal primary effect of depreciation. Now let us consider a case in which the country originally enjoys balance-of-payments equilibrium, or perhaps even a surplus. Assuming for the sake of argument, contrary to the conclusion so far, that income effects made the otherwise stable exchange market work perversely, then currency depreciation would create a balance-of-payments deficit. Now, since by hypothesis the import and export supply and demand elasticities would have been favorable enough for a normally working exchange market had it not been for the income effects and since the existence of a balance-of-payments deficit relaxes the elasticity requirements for normality, it seems that the new deficit could cause the market to work normally (at least if the import and export supply and demand elasticities are no less favorable at the new than at the old points on the respective curves). Even if the market is only barely normal in the new situation, further depreciation would, as already explained, reduce the foreign-exchange deficit while increasing

the deficit measured in home currency. If so, the secondary income effects would reinforce the new-found stability of the exchange market.

The income effects so far canvassed, other than the one resulting from policy, have all involved changes in income stemming from the initial change in the balance of payments. But if currency depreciation somehow affects the level of home income directly, rather than only through the balance of payments, the conclusions reached so far become less definite. For example, since depreciation changes the pattern of relative prices, some residents of the home country are better off and some worse off than before, and if the persons benefited have a higher propensity to consume than the persons harmed, the country's overall propensity to consume may rise. Thus both home income and imports tend to rise. Another possibility for a rise in the propensity to consume and thus in income and imports lies in the fact that depreciation tends to lower the prices of home factors of production *relative* to the prices of internationally traded goods, thus lowering the real income corresponding to any given level of money income from the viewpoints of income-receivers. If the fraction of real income saved falls as real income falls, as is conceivable in some situations, this means that the schedule of consumption expenditure in relation to money income rises, with the consequences already mentioned.[7] Still another conceivable "direct" income effect hinges on the inducement provided by the depreciation for people to switch some demand toward the relatively cheapened products of the depreciating country and away from the relatively more expensive products of the rest of the world. This increased demand would tend to have a

[6] Albert O. Hirschman, "Devaluation and the Trade Balance: A Note," *Review of Economics and Statistics*, **XXXI**, February 1949, p. 53.

[7] Cf. Lloyd A. Metzler, "Exchange-rate Stability Considered," *Econometrica* Supplement, **XVII**, July 1949, pp. 109-110; and Svend Laursen and Lloyd A. Metzler, "Flexible Exchange Rates and the Theory of Employment," *Review of Economics and Statistics*, **XXXII**, November 1950, esp. pp. 286-291, 297. A further discussion in the same *Review* clarifies this argument: William H. White, "The Employment-Insulating Advantages of Flexible Exchanges: A Comment on Professors Laursen and Metzler," **XXXVI**, May 1954, pp. 225-228, and Laursen and Metzler, "Reply,'" pp. 228-229 in the same issue. Also see footnote 25 on pp. 105-106 above.

multiplier effect on home income, stimulating imports in turn.[8] The rise in income and imports occurring by way of any of these three effects could mean a perverse net response of the balance of payments to depreciation even when the price elasticities of import and export supply and demand, considered by themselves, indicated a neutral or weakly normal response. The stability condition would then be more stringent than our formulas indicate.

The analysis becomes hopelessly untidy when one tries to allow for all the income effects already described and others readily invented. Effects are even conceivable that tend to make depreciation more effective; the change in relative prices might redistribute incomes, for example, in such a way as to lower the national propensity to consume. It does seem that such roundabout effects of depreciation directly on income and, in turn, of income on imports are likely to be weak in comparison with the primary influence of depreciation on imports and exports, so that the stability condition already derived in terms of price elasticities does not need to be modified much—but this statement admittedly defies quantification. It must be emphasized that these income effects presuppose instability in national incomes. For changes in *real* rather than money income, in particular, to interfere seriously with the normal results of currency depreciation, unemployment and subcapacity production must have previously prevailed. The effects are incompatible, then, with a successful policy of maintaining stable and prosperous domestic business conditions. Yet part of the rationale of exchange-rate flexibility is that it would permit independent national stabilization policies. Successful domestic stabilization would help preserve the effectiveness of exchange-rate variations in equilibrating the balance of payments. Though the stability condition expressed in terms of price elasticities might have to be modified for analyzing the effectiveness of deliberate adjustments in pegged exchange rates in a world of passively unstable national incomes, the condition seems roughly correct for appraising the workability of freely fluctuating rates for a country pursuing a successful domestic policy.

Secondary Effects: Price Levels

Besides income changes, price-level changes might also be thought to threaten making an otherwise normal exchange-rate mechanism work perversely. Could this happen if currency depreciation somehow pushed up the internal prices of goods and services in full or partial sympathy with the price of foreign exchange? Probably not. Currency depreciation corrects a balance-of-payments deficit by making internationally traded goods more expensive in relation to domestic goods and factors of production in the depreciating country and cheaper in relation to domestic goods and factors elsewhere.[9] In the worst realistically conceivable situation—which would presuppose expansion of the home money supply—all prices would rise in the depreciating country in proportion to the price of foreign exchange. Foreign-currency prices of exports would remain the same as before, and so, presumably, would the quantities and total foreign-currency proceeds of exports. Quantities and total foreign-currency values of imports would also remain unchanged, since imports would not have become more expensive in relation to labor and other domestic goods. The balance of payments in terms of foreign currency would be unchanged.

Depreciation could hardly make prices of domestic goods rise *faster* than prices of internationally traded goods, so encouraging

---

[8] The increased demand operates directly and not just through the balance of payments. Even though the relation between the total money values of imports and exports remained unchanged or even worsened (because of a decline in the total foreign-currency value—though not quantity—of exports), depreciation would still tend to stimulate home-currency expenditure on home-produced goods. Cf. Arnold C. Harberger, "Currency Depreciation, Income, and the Balance of Trade," *Journal of Political Economy*, **LVIII**, February 1950, p. 51.

[9] There is no conflict between the stability-condition and sectional-price-level analysis. The stability condition concerns *how strongly* import and export quantities must respond to price changes for depreciation to succeed. The sectional-price-level analysis investigates *why* and *how* imports and exports respond to exchange-rate variations.

imports and discouraging exports; on the contrary, it is precisely the internationally traded goods whose prices are most directly pulled upward along with the price of foreign exchange. Thus, while responses of the internal price level to the exchange rate might possibly lessen the sensitivity of the balance-of-payments to exchange-rate changes, they would not make an otherwise normal mechanism perverse. At worst, sympathetic movement of the internal price level would render exchange-rate variations ineffective in equilibrating the balance of payments. This issue of induced instability in the domestic price level provides a familiar objection to flexible exchange rates (and is explored in Chapter 10), but it is distinct from the question of elasticity requirements for a normal adjustment mechanism.

Secondary Effects: Imported Materials

Another complication has to do with imported raw materials embodied in exports.[10] Even if depreciation did increase the foreign-exchange proceeds of exports, part of these would have to go to pay for the necessary additional imports of raw materials. Furthermore, the use of imported raw materials lessens the degree to which depreciation enables a country's exporters to attract customers by quoting lower prices in foreign currency, since depreciation raises costs in home currency.

In doing so, depreciation raises the schedule of home-money prices necessary to call forth various quantities of exports. In effect, using imported materials makes a country's export supply less elastic than otherwise. How export supply elasticity enters into the stability conditions has already been shown: when foreign demand is elastic, a low supply elasticity lessens the effectiveness of exchange-rate variations, but when foreign demand is in-

elastic, a low supply elasticity contributes to a normal effect. It seems to follow that a high import content in exports lessens the sensitivity of the balance of payments to exchange-rate variations when foreign demand is elastic but might contribute to a normal reaction when foreign demand is highly inelastic.

Imports of materials need not necessarily increase in proportion to any increase in exports. The volume of materials imported depends not on exports alone but on the country's overall production. At any given level of production, an increase in exports might simply divert imported materials from making goods for domestic consumption into making the additional export goods. Furthermore, to assume that the proportion of imported materials in export products stays constant whatever the exchange rate is illegitimate to assume away any substitution between home and foreign materials, as well as any shift from high-import-content toward low-import-content exports.

All this further suggests that while the use of imported materials in exports may conceivably make the balance of payments less sensitive to exchange-rate variations than otherwise, it does not make the elasticity requirements for normality any more stringent. In any case, the imported-materials effect is hardly decisive. Even for countries with very "open" economies, like those of Western Europe, imported raw materials account for only a small fraction of the value of the exports embodying them. For a country like the United States, the fraction is almost negligible.[11]

Secondary Effects: Summary

Canvassing secondary income, price-level, and imported-materials effects yields no conclusive indication that the stability requirements already derived are either too stringent or not stringent enough. (The likeliest exception has to do with income changes produced directly by an exchange-rate variation.) There is some reason, however, for thinking

---

[10] Cf. Lloyd A. Metzler, "Exchange-rate Stability Considered," *Econometrica* Supplement, **XVII**, July 1949, p. 109, Metzler, "The Theory of International Trade," in Howard S. Ellis (ed.), *A Survey of Contemporary Economics,* Philadelphia: Blakiston, °1948, p. 230 n., A. J. Brown, *op. cit.,* p. 78, and G. Stuvel, *The Exchange Stability Problem,* Leiden: Stenfert Kroese, 1950, pp. 172-174.

[11] J. J. Polak and T. C. Chang, "Effect of Exchange Depreciation on a Country's Export Price Level," IMF *Staff Papers,* **I,** February 1950, p. 51.

that secondary effects may lessen the sensitivity of the balance of payments to exchange-rate variations, damping normal and perverse reactions alike. But the dividing line between normality and perversity remains at least approximately specified by the algebraic sign of the previously-stated expression

$$e_m\, e_x\, (\eta_m + \eta_x - 1) + \eta_m\, \eta_x\, (e_m + e_x + 1)$$

The discussion of secondary effects has been tedious and unrealistic but was necessary in order to not simply ignore matters considered important by competent students. In the real world it is unlikely—as later pages try to show—that an exchange market would be in that dubious borderline where secondary effects might be decisive.

Short-run Instability

One might suppose that since a country's demand for imports and the foreign demand for its exports are both very inelastic in the very short run, the foreign-exchange market might work perversely in the short run. And since time is just a succession of short runs, a free exchange market might be unstable in the long run also. The quantity of something demanded at a newly established price depends, among other things, on how long a time buyers have had to react to the new price (as well as on what the previous price was). The shorter this time, the less responsive buyers are. Strictly speaking, one ought not to speak of *the* demand curve; there is a whole sheaf of demand curves, one for each of the infinitely many conceivable lengths of adjustment period. Similar comments apply to supply curves also.

If demands for internationally traded goods are inelastic in the short run, so too—and presumably even more so—are supplies, and their inelasticity is then a stabilizing element. It would be odd indeed if short-run demands were too inelastic yet short-run supplies too elastic for normality. But if this peculiar short-run situation did prevail, shrewd speculators might well realize that perverse movements in a free exchange rate were only temporary. They would not think in the economists' jargon of stability conditions, but that would not matter. If they succeeded in profiting from short-run rate fluctuations, they would be tending to iron them out and would be providing unofficial financing for "riding out" temporary disequilibriums.

Granted that the supply of and demand for foreign exchange arising from actual exports and imports are inelastic in the very short run, so are the production-supply of and consumption-demand for any ordinary commodity. Though the analogy is not perfect, since a short-run commodity supply curve could hardly slope negatively, it is still instructive. Why don't the continual shifts in the short-run inelastic supply and demand curves for any competitively marketed commodity make price fluctuate violently? Because absorption and release of the commodity into and from stocks—in a sense, speculative stocks—prevent this. Similar absorption and release of foreign exchange into and from stocks held by private dealers and others would tend to keep short-run supply and demand inelasticities from causing extreme fluctuations in a free market. (A full appraisal of how likely this is must await a separate chapter on speculation.)

One might fear perverse exchange markets in a war-devastated world where urgent relief and reconstruction needs made import demands inelastic. Apart from the possibility that inelastic demands might be accompanied by the stabilizing inelasticity of the corresponding supplies, there is the fundamental point that urgency of need is not the same thing as inelasticity of demand. The only demand that counts on a market is demand backed up by willingness and ability to pay. Despite urgent needs, impoverishment itself may force people to behave on the market with great price-sensitivity. (Arguments for helping war-impoverished people, if persuasive, need not be adorned with references to inelastic demands and perverse markets.)

Instability due to Fixed Obligations

The existence of fixed obligations to foreign countries, such as interest and amortization payments or indemnities, might conceivably keep the exchange-stability conditions from being satisfied, provided the foreign demand for exports were very inelastic at the same time. If the obligations to foreigners were fixed in domestic currency, they would affect the foreign-exchange market as imports of demand elasticity equal to 1 and so could not cause perversity. Obligations fixed in foreign currency, however, would have the same effect on the exchange market as imports in absolutely inelastic demand.

Recognizing this does not contradict what is said a few pages later on about the elasticity conditions for exchange stability necessarily having to be satisfied at *some* level of the exchange rate. Some price of foreign exchange is so high in terms of home currency that the debtors obliged to make the fixed payments to foreigners would have to default. Despite the rigidity of the obligations fixed in foreign currency, the effective demand for foreign exchange with which to actually meet these obligations would come to have some elasticity.

Perverse Elasticities under Free and under Fixed Exchanges

In the unlikely case of perversely low demand elasticities, not only free exchange rates but any other system allowing unrestrained private international dealings in currencies and commodities would be unworkable. Government controls would have to maintain an artificial equilibrium. Currency depreciation and deflation of the home price level, currency appreciation and inflation of the home price level, are alternative methods of correcting a balance-of-payments deficit or surplus. If the relevant elasticities were too low for normal operation of the exchange rate, then (as mentioned in Chapter 5) the price-level mechanism of the gold standard would also work perversely.[12] Correcting a

deficit would then call for either currency appreciation or price level inflation. Inflation would raise export (as well as domestic) prices, but foreigners, having an inelastic demand, would spend a greater total amount on the inflating country's exports. Since the country's import demand is also inelastic, the cheapening of imports relative to inflated domestic prices would expand imports only slightly.

The parallelism between the price-level and exchange-rate processes provides a further chance to test the theory of perverse elasticities against experience. Why do we not observe balance-of-payments troubles among the regions of a single country? Their absence from interregional trade, free from government controls, is perhaps not quite conclusive evidence, however. Deflation of real income and employment and cash balances as well as of prices and money income in the region that would otherwise have a deficit might account for balance-of-payments equilibrium even in the perverse-elasticities case. On the other hand, the explanation might be that the reduction in real income restores equilibrium not in spite of perverse elasticities but rather by making the people of the deficit country unable to afford an inelastic effective demand for imports. Whatever the explanation, it is worth pondering how, if the perverse-elasticities case is anything more than a theoretical toy, trade *within* countries stays in balance nowadays and how international trade stayed in balance under the historical gold standard.

A Paradox and the Solution

By now the reader surely has sensed a paradox. Chapter 3 suggested that balance-of-payments problems (as distinguished from problems of sheer poverty) are impossible if the government does not concern itself with trade, exchange rates, reserves of gold or foreign exchange, and so forth. After the people of a deficit country have used up their holdings of foreign exchange and exhausted their credit with foreigners, the country's cur-

[12] Joan Robinson, "The Pure Theory of International Trade," *Review of Economic Studies,* **XIV** (2), 1946-1947, No. 36, pp. 102-103, carries on her analysis in terms of varying money wage rates with rigid exchanges, although, as she emphasizes, her argument could readily be transposed into terms of variable exchange rates. Similarly, Abba P. Lerner, *op. cit.,* pp. 377-378, discusses the elasticity requirements for balance-of-payments stability in terms of gold flows and variable price levels rather than exchange rates.

rent international accounts are bound to come into balance, regardless of "essential needs" for imports "or any other of the obfuscating phenomena with which the matter has been, and continues to be, surrounded."[13] Yet the theory of perverse elasticities still implies otherwise.

How can common sense be reconciled with this theory? Are the stability conditions wrong, or is common sense superficial? Neither. Demand elasticities must necessarily become high enough to satisfy the conditions. If all else fails to assure a normal adjustment process, then the country's demand for imports must turn elastic. The reason becomes clear when we think what the contrary would mean. The people of the deficit country would spend larger and larger total amounts per time period of their own money on imports as import prices, tied to the price of foreign exchange, rose higher and higher. But they could not keep doing this on and on because they do not have infinitely large incomes and accumulations of assets from which to spend. Eventually, as import prices rise, total home-currency expenditure on imports could no longer rise. Some price of foreign exchange must be so high that the country's import demand would become elastic, itself satisfying the condition for a normally reacting balance of payments. At worst, the borderline case would be reached.

Admittedly, though, it is just abstractly conceivable that even this conclusion might fail: no matter how high-priced imports might become in local currency, total spending on them might always rise just a bit further, asymptotically approaching but never quite reaching the complete exhaustion of income. But this picture of people devoting 99 percent and 99.99 percent and ever closer to a full 100 percent of their entire incomes to imports, no matter how high their prices and thus no matter how low the import-purchasing-power of the country's exports, presupposes downright negligible possibilities of switching consumption away from imports toward home-market or export-type goods and of switching production away from exportables into home-market goods or import substitutes. No elaborate statistical investigation is necessary to rule out this truly weird picture; even empirical knowledge of the kind pervasive enough to force itself on the most resolutely abstract of theorists is enough.

It is still conceivable that people might have no faith in the future value of the home currency and refuse to hold cash balances larger than they considered absolutely necessary for transactions purposes. In trying to get rid of money almost as soon as received, they would be bidding up the prices of foreign exchange and other things. Surely, one might say, there can then be no stable equilibrium in the exchange market. A more defensible interpretation, however, is that the equilibrium exchange rate keeps rising because of continuous shifts in supply and demand in an inflationary environment. As long as the money supply keeps rising or the demand for real cash balances keeps falling, domestic prices and money incomes would be rising, and with them the demand for and the price of foreign exchange. If this monetary inflation did not keep on swelling domestic money incomes, people could not keep on spending more and more money on imports. Genuinely perverse elasticities would not be the correct interpretation. Incidentally, if the perverse-elasticities case really did prevail, then domestic price inflation would reduce the deficit or increase the surplus in the balance of payments of the inflating country. The very fact that inflation did *not* contribute to stability on the exchange market would disprove the perverse-elasticities hypothesis.

Multiple Equilibriums

Beyond some degree of exchange depreciation of Inland currency, import demand would be elastic and the reaction of the balance of payments normal. A symmetrical argument demonstrates a degree of appreciation of Inland currency beyond which the foreign demand for Inland exports would be

[13] Frank D. Graham, *The Theory of International Values,* Princeton, N.J.: Princeton University Press, 1948, p. 275. Cf. Graham, *Exchange, Prices, and Production in Hyper-inflation: Germany. 1920–1923,* Princeton, N.J.: Princeton University Press, 1930, pp. 26-27.

elastic and the reaction of the balance of payments again normal: if the Outland-currency price of Inland currency rose still higher, Outlanders could no longer afford to go on spending ever larger amounts per time period of their own money to buy Inland goods. Any unstable equilibrium exchange rate and its range of balance-of-payments perversity would thus be flanked above and below by ranges of normal reaction.[14] These considerations do not provide absolutely airtight theoretical proof, however, that an unstable equilibrium would be flanked by upper and lower equilibrium rates. For reasons already mentioned (but dismissed on inescapable empirical grounds), it is abstractly conceivable that the relevant elasticity might approach but never reach or exceed unity as the exchange rate moved extremely high or low. Or it is just barely conceivable that even though the two ranges of normal reaction did exist, the respective rise or fall of the exchange rate within them would promote balance-of-payments equilibrium so feebly as never quite to achieve it. (For one thing, as

[14] Cf. Alfred Marshall, *Money Credit & Commerce*, London: Macmillan, 1923, p. 352; Heinrich Freiherr von Stackelberg, "Die Theorie des Wechselkurses bei vollständiger Konkurrenz," *Jahrbücher für National-ökonomie und Statistik*, CLXI, September 1949, pp. 40-41, and the graph on p. 60; Milton Friedman, *Essays in Positive Economics*, Chicago: University of Chicago Press, 1953, p. 160n.; Egon Sohmen, "Demand Elasticities and the Foreign-Exchange Market," *Journal of Political Economy*, LXV, October 1957, pp. 431-436. The present discussion tries to take account, as well, of an attack on Sohmen's reasoning by Jagdish Bhagwati and Harry G. Johnson in "Notes on Some Controversies in the Theory of International Trade," *Economic Journal*, LXX, March 1960, esp. p. 93n., and also of Sohmen's "Comment" and the two authors' "Rejoinder" in *Economic Journal*, LXXI, June 1961, pp. 423-430.

Experimentation with Marshallian offer curves of the kind that Bhagwati and Johnson present in their 1960 article, p. 91, suggests that what they call "terminability" of each country's import demand suffices for Sohmen's conclusion. As the two authors state in their 1961 rejoinder, "the proposition that an unstable equilibrium is always bounded by stable rates . . . does not hold in strict theory but requires an empirical assumption of insatiability *or* terminability to support it. . . ." (p. 427; emphasis on *or* supplied). Now "terminability" simply means that there is *some* limit beyond which people would rather discontinue trade than accept still more unfavorable terms of trade. Everyday observation amply justifies an inference that in no country would people give their entire annual national output for one single milligram per year of imported goods.

the exchange rate raises the price of imports in one country toward infinity, it lowers the price toward zero in the other, and while the budget restraint implies that the import demand elasticity must at the very least become almost unitary in the country with rising import prices, the corresponding elasticity may approach zero in the other country as imports become almost free.) Nevertheless, it is overwhelmingly likely that the two stable equilibriums *would* exist on either side of the unstable one. Inland's demand curve for foreign exchange touches the price axis at some very high price—if at none lower, then when the smallest unit of foreign goods worth having costs Inland's entire national income. This demand curve would have a normal intersection with the supply curve, which could not be more backward-sloping than a rectangular hyperbola. At the other extreme, there must almost surely be some price of foreign exchange so low that the supply curve, after intersecting the demand curve normally, touches the price axis; some Outland price of Inland currency must be so high that Outlanders would buy no Inland goods whatever. This same conclusion about the supply curve also follows from looking at the matter from the standpoint of the suppliers of foreign exchange, that is, Inland's export producers. These exporters might be so dependent on the Outland market that, to hold it, they fully or partially offset the effect of the Inland-currency appreciation on the Outland-currency price of their goods by marking down their Inland-currency price. But there must be some degree of appreciation so extreme and therefore some Inland-currency price of exports so low that exporters would be unwilling to go further in trying doggedly to hang on to any remnant of their Outland market. This might happen because the opportunities either to sell all former export goods on the home market instead or to switch from export goods into other lines of production had finally become less unattractive than such unrewarding export business.

Figure 8.2 illustrates multiple intersection of the foreign-exchange supply and demand curves. (The reader now knows why the

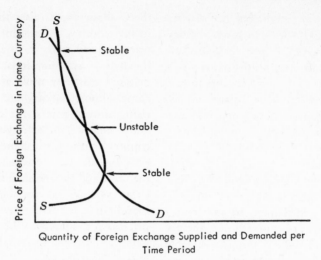

Figure 8.2.

graph of unstable equilibrium at the beginning of the chapter showed only the parts of the curves in the immediate vicinity of the intersection.) A freely fluctuating exchange rate would tend to shoot away from the unstable equilibrium toward one or the other of the stable levels, which one being pretty much a matter of chance. The lower of the stable equilibrium levels provides the more favorable terms of trade for Inland. Furthermore, the Inland authorities could nudge the exchange rate towards this level, around which it would then gravitate under the influence of private market forces. Official sales of foreign exchange (borrowed if necessary) would do the trick. After the rate had moved toward the self-maintaining favorable equilibrium, the authorities could profitably buy back the foreign exchange at a lower home-currency price than that at which they had sold it.[15]

Perverse Elasticities: Summary

The perverse-elasticities case would not be unfavorable for a deficit country and would not make a free exchange market unwork-able. It would depend upon peculiar local bulges or dents in the relevant supply and demand curves, so to speak, and could easily be escaped from into a position of improved terms of trade and a normally working exchange-rate mechanism. In the real world, though, each exchange rate very probably has only one equilibrium, a normal one. The stability condition is not at all exacting and ought to be easily met. Many internationally traded products are supplied competitively by producers in several countries, and many imports and exports constitute only a fraction of the consumption and production of similar goods in the importing and exporting countries. These facts imply that demands in international trade are amply elastic. So does the purchasing-power-parity doctrine (explained in Chapter 10), which shows why currencies tend to exchange, on free markets, at rates that approximately translate their respective purchasing powers. If this doctrine is true, the picture of rates perversely shooting away from these equilibrium levels is quite implausible.

Referring to the theory that equilibrium in international trade might be unstable, Alfred Marshall said, ". . . it is not inconceivable, but it is absolutely impossible." Frank Graham called it "solemn nonsense." Wilhelm Röpke mocked "hypothetical-curiosity" theories exhibiting that "characteristic combination of a maximum of ingenuity more

---

[15] By abstrating from shifts in the curves—that is, from dynamic developments such as inflation, deflation, speculation, and changes in tastes—the discussion here remains in the context of the perverse-elasticities controversy, which is concerned with possible absence of a stable static equilibrium. It continues to follow Sohmen's 1957 article.

geometrico and a minimum of 'judgment.'. . ." Gottfried Haberler found is "difficult to understand why anyone should find it necessary to fall back on such implausible and farfetched hypotheses as the sudden appearance in the fourth decade of the 20th century of stubborn real inelasticities of international demand (of whole continents and a great variety of countries). . . ."[16]

Alternatives to the Elasticities Analysis: The Absorption Approach

The elasticities approach to the analysis of exchange-rate variation has drawn much criticism, notably from S. S. Alexander.[17] According to him, to say that the response of the balance of payments depends on certain elasticities is mere implicit theorizing unless the elasticities are independently specified. The stability formula derives purely from the manipulation of definitions and has no operational content unless the nature is specified of the functions whose elasticities are involved. The functions might be specified so that the elasticities are "partial" elasticities, indicating how sensitively import and export quantities respond to their own prices when other prices and national incomes all remain unchanged. In fact, however, exchange-rate adjustment cannot leave other things unchanged, and repercussions through them will probably work against the primary effects. The stability formula is thus not necessarily correct if the elasticities in it are interpreted as "partial." On an alternative interpretation, the elasticities are "total," measuring the price-responsiveness of import and export quantities when not only their own prices but also incomes and other prices change as they will change in direct or in-

direct response to the exchange-rate adjustment. The usual stability formula is then tautologically correct—and empty. If the elasticities are defined as referring to price-quantity relations when all things change as in fact they would in response to an exchange-rate adjustment, then no one could know how large these elasticities were without *already* having a complete analysis of the whole response of domestic and foreign economies to the rate adjustment. To say that the effect on the balance of payments depends on the (total) elasticities boils down to saying that it all depends on how the economic system behaves.

Finding this not very helpful, Alexander suggests his "absorption" approach instead. As earlier chapters have repeatedly recognized, an import surplus is identical to an excess of absorption (consumption plus investment) over national output or income, and an export surplus is identical to underabsorption. If exchange depreciation is to improve a country's balance of payments, it must somehow increase national income or output relative to absorption or—the same thing—decrease absorption relative to income or output.

Next Alexander lists and discusses various "effects," or ways in which devaluation might either increase output or restrict absorption. First is the "idle-resources effect": somehow or other, unemployed resources, if there were any, might be put back into productive use. No reason suggests itself why devaluation would have a powerful effect of this sort. Furthermore, for any such effect to improve the balance of payments, the "marginal propensity to absorb" would have to be less than 1: additional consumption and investment would have to absorb less than the full amount of any increase in income or output, and this is uncertain. Second is the "terms-of-trade effect": devaluation presumably makes foreign goods and services more expensive relative to home goods and services and factors of production, thereby reducing the real buying power of and real absorption by the home population. This effect tends to be outweighed, says Alexander, by an adverse primary impact on the foreign balance,

[16] Marshall, *op. cit.*, p. 354, Graham, *The Theory of International Values*, p. 297; Röpke, "Devisenzwangswirtschaft: das Kardinalproblem der internationalen Wirtschaft," *Aussenwirtschaft*, V, March 1950, p. 29n.; Haberler, "Monetary and Real Factors Affecting Economic Stability," *Banca Nazionale del Lavoro Quarterly Review*, IX, September 1956, p. 97.

[17] See "Effects of a Devaluation on a Trade Balance," IMF *Staff Papers*, II, April 1952, pp. 263-278, and "Effects of a Devaluation: A Simplified Synthesis of Elasticities and Absorption Approaches," *American Economic Review*, XLIX, March 1959, pp. 22-42.

since the worsening of the terms of trade tends to cheapen the money value of exports relative to that of imports. Third is a set of possible "absolute-price-level effects." Among these might be the effect of devaluation in reducing the total real value of cash balances; and in their efforts to rebuild their real cash balances into an appropriate relation with levels of real income and transactions, individuals and businesses might reduce their consumption and investment relative to income. Or aggregate absorption might be reduced by a shift in the distribution of income, perhaps toward taxes and profits at the expense of wages (i.e., toward low-absorption from high-absorption economic units). A particularly dubious possibility hinges on what Alexander calls "money illusion": an increased price level might (or might not) dissuade people from some purchases, even though their money incomes had risen in proportion. Finally, there may be various miscellaneous minor price-level effects. Some of these may even influence the balance of payments unfavorably; for example, a rise in prices resulting from devaluation may unleash inflationary expectations that actually increase absorption.

None of these "effects" appears powerful and dependable. Some are likely to prove fleeting. For example, the domestic money supply may respond to the needs of trade at the increased price level, thereby both undoing the shrinkage in real cash balances that would otherwise tend to restrict absorption and also supporting a general price inflation that impedes any equilibrating shifts in relative prices. (Alexander finds such a passive response of the money supply quite realistic.) The impression emerges that devaluation can do little to correct a deficit.

This analysis is illuminating but calls for some comment. For one thing, the use of a parameter labeled "propensity to absorb" plays down the question whether price changes accompanying devaluation might not helpfully alter this propensity.[18] The opinion that

devaluation may worsen the terms of trade so as to increase import value relative to export value despite a slight favorable change in physical quantities invites two comments. First, devaluation does not *necessarily* worsen the ratio of export to import prices (see Chapter 9). More important, the question whether adverse price movements will outweigh favorable quantity movements touches the essence of the "elasticities" approach, and the answer is far from immediately obvious. The absorption approach does not actually deny that the changes in relative prices brought about by devaluation are effective in encouraging substitution, both at home and abroad, between domestic and internationally traded goods, but it buries these responses to price rather obscurely among the apparently feeble "effects" that it does consider. The opinion that effects working through changes in the total real value of cash balances would probably be washed out by a passive monetary expansion in the devaluing country concerns responses that are, after all, a matter of policy and deserve forthright emphasis as such. Lax management of the money supply abetting a spiral of domestic inflation and repeated devaluation would prevent reaching any equilibrium. The persistence of balance-of-payments trouble would then imply nothing about how effective devaluation would be under different domestic policies.

A Reconciliation of the Absorption and Elasticity Approaches

J. Black has restated the absorption approach and its pessimistic implications with a clarity that points the way toward reconciliation with the elasticities approach.[19] An excess of absorption (consumption plus investment) over income produced becomes, in Black's equivalent terminology, an excess of domestic investment over domestic saving. Devaluation or any other measure to correct a balance-of-payments deficit must somehow reduce investment or increase saving or both. Black thinks a cut in investment unlikely and pro-

[18] Fritz Machlup, "Relative Prices and Aggregate Spending in the Analysis of Devaluation," *American Economic Review*, XLV, June 1955, pp. 255-278, esp. p. 275. This article has suggested some of the comments that follow.

[19] J. Black "A Savings and Investment Approach to Devaluation," *Economic Journal*, LXIX, June 1959, pp. 267-274.

ceeds to search for possible additions to saving. Devaluation might raise saving by raising real income, but only in an economy with unemployment and slack productive capacity. At full employment, the repercussions of devaluation might conceivably redistribute real income toward high-saving classes. The opposite is equally conceivable. The effect is either weak or perverse. By itself, devaluation at full employment can do little to remedy a deficit.

Paradoxically, a different view makes the deficit itself, rather than its cure, seem implausible and in need of explanation. (Recall Chapter 3.) Since a country's balance of payments is an aggregate of the balances of the individuals and institutions composing the country, it as a whole could not have a deficit unless some individuals or institutions in it were living beyond their incomes or dissipating their resources. The central bank or other official exchange-rate-pegging agency may be doing so by drawing down its reserve of gold and foreign exchange and receiving in return domestic currency whose lesser equilibrium value would be evidenced by the very fact that the agency was being called upon to sell more foreign exchange than was being offered to it at its pegged price. Only in terms of the price imposed by its own unbalanced transactions does the agency appear to be maintaining rather than dissipating the value of its assets.

For an instructive parable, suppose that Ruritania's balance of payments has been in equilibrium at a freely fluctuating exchange rate hovering around 1 Ruritanian crown per U.S. dollar. Now an eccentric wealthy Ruritanian with ample bank deposits in New York, acting on some strange whim, offers dollars for sale at only 1/2 crown each. This rate prevails for all transactions; no one will pay more for dollars earned by Ruritanian exporters. The exchange appreciation of the crown cheapens import-and-export-type goods relative to domestic goods, including Ruritanian labor and other factors of production. Laborers and other factor-owners gain buying power over international-trade goods and scarcely lose buying power over others. The wealthy eccentric is in effect subsidizing his fellow countrymen's purchases. Because of the effective increase in their real incomes, Ruritanians buy more goods and services, especially the cheapened imports and export-type goods. Ruritania develops a balance-of-payments deficit. In the outside world, the depreciation of currencies relative to the Ruritanian crown lowers factor incomes in terms of goods imported from and exported to Ruritania. (By enabling his fellow countrymen to spend the balances that he had previously been holding idle in the outside world, the Ruritanian eccentric is reducing the real resources currently available to the foreigners.) Because of the great size of the outside world in comparison with Ruritania, however, this income effect would discourage purchases from and encourage sales to Ruritania only rather feebly in comparison with the pattern of relative prices caused by exchange-rate pegging.

If some worried official were now to ask what might remedy the deficit in Ruritania's balance of payments, an "elasticities" economist might suggest depreciation of the crown, that is, an end to exchange-rate pegging by the wealthy eccentric. An "absorption" economist would be doubtful, pointing out that removal of a deficit implies an increase in saving or an even less likely reduction in investment and that exchange depreciation can do little to promote either.

Ruritania's deficit admittedly does imply "overabsorption" or "undersaving" on the part of the country as a whole, *including* the eccentric. *Other* Ruritanians as a group may nevertheless be living within their real incomes as they see them. The country's deficit stems from a dissipation of the eccentric's resources and a related distortion of the prices that give meaning to money incomes and that guide consumption and investment decisions. An end to exchange pegging would remove the price distortions that had been making real income seem larger from the viewpoint of ordinary persons than it was from the national viewpoint.

Black's skeptical question is a crucial one: "How . . . does devaluation tend to bring about an increase in savings?"[20] How, in

---

[20] *Ibid.*, p. 269.

other words, does it raise the propensity to save (or reduce the propensity to absorb) out of a given income? An answer must emphasize the fundamental ambiguities in the very concepts of total production, total income, and total absorption and especially in the concepts of the difference between absorption and production or income, of saving, and of an import or export surplus. These concepts are particularly tricky when the magnitudes are supposedly measured in real terms. In an open economy, for instance, real income and real output are not necessarily identical: some home production is sold abroad, and some foreign goods are imported for use at home, and the real income corresponding to a given pattern of physical production depends on prices.[21] Any sum or difference of heterogeneous goods and services requires measurement in money terms; prices are necessarily involved. A change in prices will change the relation between income and absorption (between saving and investment) both as a matter of sheer arithmetic and also by confronting buyers and sellers with new price incentives. A rectification of distorted price signals is what, from one point of view, reduces the propensity to absorb or increases the propensity to save, even out of a given real income, in a devaluing country.[22] From the point of view of individuals themselves, however, the change in absorption reflects not so much a reduced *propensity* to absorb as a cut in the real size of the incomes out of which their absorption must take place. A further but possibly minor aspect of adjustment through devaluation is the "real-balance effect" already mentioned. Domestic currency loses some of its purchasing power over international-trade goods, impoverishing individuals and businesses to some slight extent, disrupting the desired composition of asset-holdings, and tending to promote frugality in buying goods and services.

This last effect presupposes that domestic goods and services do not fall in price enough to compensate for the rise in international-trade goods and so maintain the overall purchasing power of cash balances. To justify this presupposition, let us *try* to conceive of such exactly compensating price movements. No fall in real cash balances would then be at work to restrain total absorption, while the reinforced shift in relative prices would switch expenditure away from international-trade goods and toward domestic goods. Domestic prices would again be bid up, some rise in the general price level would occur after all, and the shrinkage of real balances would come into play. In fact, any expenditure-switching policy (such as devaluation or the tightening of import restrictions) tends to raise the price level unless accompanied by a separate expenditure-reducing policy (such as monetary or fiscal measures).[23] For an expenditure-switching policy to produce a helpful real-balance effect, it need not necessarily be accompanied by an *active* expenditure-reducing policy, though the monetary expansion that would neutralize the effect must be avoided.

Even when the money supply is not actually expanding, "balance-of-payments deficits and difficulties are essentially monetary phenomena";[24] and it is a merit of the absorption

---

[21] Machlup, *American Economic Review*, June 1955, pp. 268-270. Machlup especially criticizes Alexander's concept of a " 'real' trade balance."

[22] *Ibid.*, pp. 265-266, suggests that the liberalization of trade made possible by abandoning an unrealistic exchange rate may improve the allocation of resources and so raise real income. This is a further, though probably minor, way in which an excess of real absorption over real income might be reduced.

[23] Cf. Harry G. Johnson, *International Trade and Economic Growth,* Cambridge, Mass.: Harvard University Press, 1958, pp. 153-168 and esp. pp. 165-167. Johnson's terms "expenditure-switching" and "expenditure-reducing" refer to *real* expenditure rather than its nominal money value.

The rise in the price level upon which the real-balance effect depends (unless, of course, devaluation is accompanied by measures to shrink even the nominal money supply) does not mean that devaluation is inflationary *tout court*. First, without continuing monetary expansion, the rise in prices is a one-time adjustment and not a continuing process. Second, whether avoiding a devaluation prevents even this rise in prices depends on what the alternative is. Import restrictions are equally an expenditure-switching policy (cf. Johnson, p. 167) and are likely to affect the price level much as devaluation would. For further explanation, see chapter 10.

The role of the real-balance effect in balance-of-payments adjustment is recognized in Michael Michaely, "Relative-Prices and Income-Absorption Approaches to Devaluation: A Partial Reconciliation," *American Economic Review*, L, March 1960, pp. 144-147.

[24] Johnson, *op. cit.*, p. 157.

approach to illuminate this fact. For an excess of expenditure over income implies that individuals and businesses are running down their cash balances. Domestic money disappears from circulation when it is paid into the official exchange-rate-pegging agency to buy foreign exchange. People's willingness to content themselves with reduced cash balances in real terms and relative to income and expenditure spells a rise in velocity. A continuing balance-of-payments deficit depends on a continuing rise in velocity of this sort. This is true, that is, unless the monetary authority continually creates new domestic money to replace what it absorbs from circulation through its sales of foreign exchange. Whichever corresponds to the balance-of-payments deficit—the implausible continuing rise in velocity or a continuing re-creation of domestic money—deserves emphasis as a monetary phenomenon.

Absorption economists are uneasy about the switch from a saving-and-investment analysis to the elasticities analysis of how "imports and exports are determined as the result of the interplay of supply and demand in particular markets, with no reference at all to savings and investment."[25] But we have good reason to focus attention on particular markets and especially on the foreign-exchange market. It is natural to inquire how effectively an increase in the home-currency price of foreign exchange would reduce the quantity of it demanded from an official agency offering it at a pegged price. Furthermore, it is natural to focus attention on the size and consequences of the subsidy that currency overvaluation gives to absorption. The higher the relevant elasticities, the more scope and meaning this subsidy has. The higher the income-elasticity of demand for import-and-export-type goods and the closer their substitutability with domestic goods, the more the home population as a whole currently gains from the artificial cheapening of the former goods. The greater, accordingly, is the exaggeration of real national income from private points of view relative to the national point of view.

Finally, we are particularly concerned with

the foreign-exchange market in order to appraise the workability of free price determination in it. The elasticities approach is useful in organizing this appraisal. It helps bring commonplace empirical facts to bear on the question, such as that competition occurs between imported and domestic goods at home and between the exports of various countries on the world market, that not all resources are irrevocably specialized in the production of particular goods, and that incomes are of finite size.

In summary, each of the two approaches to devaluation analysis deals only implicitly with the aspects of adjustment that hold the center of the stage in the other. As usually presented, the absorption approach is preoccupied with propensities to consume, save, and invest and seems to have little room for the incentives created by changes in relative prices. The elasticities approach is preoccupied with relative prices and seems to ignore the question of total absorption out of total income. The two approaches can be reconciled by recognizing how exchange rates and prices affect the sizes of real incomes and real cash balances from the point of view of the persons who make decisions about absorption and how the conditions underlying the elasticities affect the scope and size of the subsidy that overvaluation affords and the size of the discrepancy between private and national views of real income. Reconciliation dispels the "devaluation pessimism" spawned by the pure absorption approach.

Another Criticism of the Elasticities Approach

Like Alexander, E. Victor Morgan calls the whole elasticities approach into question, but in a different spirit and on different grounds.[26] The concept of demand or supply elasticity strictly applies only to a physically homogeneous commodity and only when all relevant variables other than its own price (including incomes and the prices of all other goods) stay unchanged. Yet imports and exports are far from homogeneous, and the

---

[25] Black, *op. cit.*, p. 268.

[26] "The Theory of Flexible Exchange Rates," *American Economic Review*, XLV, June 1955, pp. 279-295.

response to a change in exchange rates involves changes not merely in import and export quantities but also in the "mix" of goods traded. The fundamental impact effect of a depreciation is to cheapen home factors of production relative to foreign factors. The depreciating country's goods, in turn, become relatively cheaper, but the response is by no means simple. It may become profitable to export some goods not previously exported and to discontinue some imports entirely. Changes will occur in the relative importance of various goods in both the import and export lists. Export- and import-competing industries will exert strengthened demands for factors of production. Home-currency prices will rise sharply for some factors and only slightly for others, depending for each on whether its supply elasticity is low or high and on how intensely other industries bid to retain it. Industries using large proportions of factors still remaining relatively cheap will tend to expand; industries using large proportions of factors becoming relatively expensive will expand little or will shrink. Similar but opposite changes occur in nondepreciating countries.

The language of supply and demand elasticities for imports and exports as a whole masks this thoroughgoing reallocation of resources and repatterning of production. Any such elasticity must involve the relation between price and quantity indexes of some sort; yet no index number can take account of the changes in import and export mixes that are the very essence of adjustment. "When we use the words elasticity of demand (or supply) for imports (or exports) we quite literally do not know what we are talking about."[27]

But is it necessary to throw out elasticities entirely? Perhaps they need only be reinterpreted a bit, in a way that the elasticity approach has presumably taken for granted all along. What matters for the stability of the foreign-exchange market is how *total money values* of imports and exports respond to price changes. If a 1 percent reduction (through exchange depreciation) in the foreign price

of a country's exports would cause foreigners to spend a 1 percent smaller total amount of their own money on the export goods, the elasticity of foreign demand may be said to be zero. If a 1 percent price reduction causes a 3 percent rise in total foreign expenditure, the demand elasticity is 4. Price elasticity of demand is approximately 1 + the elasticity of total expenditure with respect to price (the sign convention is understood whereby demand elasticity is normally positive). Supply elasticity may be similarly interpreted. If a 1 percent rise in the home-currency price of a country's exports would cause only a 1 percent rise in the total home-currency value of exports supplied, the supply elasticity may be said to be zero. If a 1 percent price rise would cause a 3 percent rise in value supplied, the elasticity of supply is 2. The elasticity of supply is less by 1 than the elasticity of total value supplied with respect to price. Since this way is available for translating the usual elasticities approach into terms of meaningful elasticities of total expenditure or value, it is no serious defect of the usual approach that it analyzes total money values of imports and exports into prices multiplied by rather fictitious homogeneous physical quantities. This fiction allows the convenience of the familiar terminology used in discussing ordinary commodity markets. The criticism best applies not so much to the standard elasticity criterion of exchange-market normality itself as to econometric attempts to estimate elasticities by observing how price and quantity indexes vary together over time. These attempts presumably underestimate the effectiveness of the exchange-rate mechanism by failing to allow for the *changing* nonhomogeneity of imports and exports.

Morgan also criticizes the usual elasticity approach as unable to take adequate account of the changes in income necessarily associated with changes in exchange rates. In particular, he criticizes the use of marginal propensities to import as parameters. Goods entering into or disappearing from trade or increasing or diminishing in relative importance do not all have the same income elasticity of demand, and the supposed parameters will themselves change with devaluation. Supply and demand

---

[27] *Ibid.*, pp. 282-284.

curves are likely, furthermore, to shift independently of devaluation-linked changes in income. All this is true. Yet however complex the process of response of import and export values to exchange-rate changes may be, it is meaningful to discuss its sensitivity. Far from impugning the conclusions of the traditional elasticity approach, an emphasis on changing import and export mixes and on other kinds of response to changed relative prices only reinforces them.[28]

---

[28] In fact, reinforcing these conclusions is Morgan's purpose. Besides criticizing the elasticity approach, he makes a positive contribution. If devaluation and the consequent cheapening of Inland relative to Outland factors of production is to *worsen* Inland's balance of payments, a necessary (but not sufficient) condition is that Outlanders spend a smaller amount of their own money on Inland goods than before. This implies an increase in Outlanders' expenditure on their own goods, provided that the total flow of their expenditure does not change. (Given a successful stabilization policy, the total flow of Outland money expenditure would not fall. In the face of a cheapening of Inland goods in terms of Outland factors of production, analogous to an improvement in productivity, a policy of price-level-stabilization would even call for some slight monetary expansion in Outland.) This increase in Outland expenditure on Outland goods would be diffused over numerous goods, with complicated substitutions perhaps taking place. Still, there would have to be at least one good for which the increase in Outland demand was greater than the reduction in Inland demand. For this one good, at least, an increase in relative price would have to tend to increase the excess quantity demanded. Only if the market for at least one good were unstable, therefore, could Inland's depreciation have a perverse effect on the balance of payments. This would be an odd situation indeed. (*Op. cit.,* p. 281; cf. pp. 285-286, 289-293.)

For somewhat similar remarks about exchange instability implying instability in the market for at least one individual commodity, see Harry Johnson, *op. cit.,* p. 164.

✑ Appendix to Chapter 8: Derivation of the Exchange-Stability Conditions[1]

Symbols

e_f = elasticity of supply of foreign exchange with respect to its price in terms of home currency. (If e_f is 2, for example, this means that a 1 percent rise in the home-currency price of foreign exchange so stimulates exports that their total foreign-currency value becomes 2 percent more than before.)

η_f = elasticity of demand for foreign exchange with respect to its home currency price. (An η_f of 3 means that a 1 percent rise in the home-currency price of foreign exchange would lead to a 3 percent reduction in imports valued in foreign currency. An algebraic sign is built into this definition of demand elasticity so that a normally sloping demand curve is said to have a positive elasticity.)

e_m, e_x, η_m, and η_x are as defined on p. 137 above. In these symbols, the e's stand for supply elasticities and the η's for demand elasticities; the subscripts m and x refer to the imports and exports of the home country. The elasticities of supply are algebraically positive for normal upward-sloping demand curves are said to have demand are positive, too, for the definition is understood according to which normal downward-sloping demand curves are said to have positive elasticity.

A 1 percent devaluation of the home currency —a 1 percent cut in its foreign-currency value— is the same thing as a 1 percent rise in the home currency price of foreign exchange. Of course, it is not strictly and precisely the same: consider that a 50 percent devaluation of the home currency would mean a 100 percent increase in the home-currency price of foreign exchange. But the smaller the devaluation is, the more nearly

are the two percentages identical: .001 percent devaluation is very nearly identical to .001 percent rise in the price of foreign exchange. Throughout the present derivation, it is convenient to take 1 percent as representing an extremely small change in the rate; though the resulting formula is strictly true only for an infinitesimally small change. The same infinitesimality assumption made explicit here is, of course, implicit in the derivation of the formula by calculus.

Assuming initial balance-of-payments equilibrium, with the quantities of foreign exchange supplied and demanded equal, an autonomous devaluation by 1 percent will raise the quantity of foreign exchange supplied by e_f percent and decrease the quantity demanded by η_f percent and so make the quantity supplied exceed the quantity demanded by $(e_f + \eta_f)$ percent of the quantity initially supplied-and-demanded.[2] This expression is positive except in the perverse-elasticities case.

---

[1] This method of derivation, though tedious, uses only the simplest algebra. It follows up some hints given in A. C. L. Day, *Outline of Monetary Economics,* Oxford: Clarendon Press, 1957, chaps. 30 and 31.

[2] If the country originally had a balance-of-payments deficit, with the quantity of foreign exchange demanded for imports exceeding the quantity supplied by exports, an η_f percent reduction in the quantity of foreign exchange demanded would amount to *more than* η_f percent when expressed as a percentage of the quantity of foreign exchange *supplied*. Consequently, a 1 percent devaluation would reduce the *excess* quantity of foreign exchange demanded by somewhat more than $(e_f + \eta_f)$ percent of the original quantity of foreign exchange supplied. Even if $e_f + \eta_f$ totalled only zero, the excess quantity of foreign exchange demanded would still be reduced somewhat. The point of this is that when we consider a country with an already-existing balance-of-payments deficit, the elasticity requirements for devaluation to improve the balance of payments as measured in foreign currency (which is the relevant measurement) are somewhat less exacting—somewhat *easier* to satisfy—than the requirements stated in a formula derived on the assumption of initial equilibrium in the balance of payments. The worse the balance-of-payments deficit, the more likely it is that depreciation would be effective in reducing it. Albert O. Hirschman makes this point in *op. cit.,* pp. 50-53.

The Expression for e_f

To translate this criterion into terms of the import and export supply and demand elasticities used in the text of this chapter, we must first develop expressions for e_f and η_f separately. A 1 percent exchange depreciation of the home currency leads to the following percentage increase in the quantity of foreign exchange supplied:

1. The percentage increase in the total home-currency value of exports − 1.

   [The subtraction of 1 takes account of the fact that the depreciation has reduced by 1 percent the foreign-currency equivalent of amounts expressed in home currency.]

2. This = the percentage increase in the home-currency price of exports + the percentage increase in the quantity of exports − 1.

3. = the percentage increase in the home-currency price of exports + η_x (1 − the percentage increase in the home-currency price of exports) − 1.

   [The expression in parentheses is the percentage reduction in the foreign-currency price of exports, which is the 1 percent depreciation less the—almost certainly smaller —percentage increase in the home-currency price of exports. This expression multiplied by the elasticity of foreign demand for the exports yields the percentage increase in the quantity of exports.]

This, by straightforward rearrangement, becomes

4. The percentage increase in the home-currency price of exports $\times$ (1 − η_x) + η_x − 1.

5. Now, the percentage increase in the home-currency price of exports = the percentage increase in the quantity of exports $\div e_x$

   [Recall that e_x is defined as the percentage increase in the quantity of exports $\div$ the percentage increase in the home-currency price of exports.]

Recalling steps 2 and 3 above, we see that

6. The percentage increase in the home-currency price of exports = η_x (1 − the percentage increase in the home-currency price of exports) $\div e_x$

Straightforward solution of this equation yields

7. The percentage increase in the home-cur-

rency price of exports $= \dfrac{\eta_x}{e_x + \eta_x}$

Substituting this into step 4 shows that the initially assumed 1-percent depreciation makes the quantity of foreign exchange supplied increase by the following percentage:

8. $\dfrac{\eta_x}{e_x + \eta_x} (1 - \eta_x) + \eta_x - 1,$

   which can be rearranged into

9. $\dfrac{\eta_x - \eta_x{}^2 + e_x\eta_x + \eta_x{}^2 - e_x - \eta_x}{e_x + \eta_x}$

   and into

10. $\dfrac{e_x (\eta_x - 1)}{e_x + \eta_x}$

This is e_f.

The Expression for η_f

The assumed 1 percent depreciation of the home currency brings about a percentage decline in the total foreign-currency value of imports and of foreign exchange demanded equalling:

11. The percentage decrease in the quantity of imports + whatever percentage decrease there may be in the foreign-currency price of imports.

The home-currency price of imports rises by 1 percent because of the devaluation, mitigated by whatever percentage decrease there may be in the foreign-currency price of imports. This net percentage multiplied by the elasticity of home demand for imports yields the percentage decrease in the quantity of imports. Thus the expression in step 11 becomes:

12. η_m (1 − the percentage decrease in the foreign-currency price of imports) + the percentage decrease in the foreign-currency price of imports.

13. = η_m + (1 − η_m) the percentage decrease in the foreign-currency price of imports.

We now recall that the elasticity of foreign supply of imports is defined as percentage decrease in quantity of imports supplied $\div$ percentage decrease in foreign-currency price of imports

Thus:

14. The percentage decrease in the foreign-currency price of imports = the percentage decrease in the quantity of imports $\div e_m$

By the reasoning used in going from step 11 to step 12, we now have:

15. The percentage decrease in the foreign-currency price of imports $= \eta_m(1 -$ the percentage decrease in the foreign-currency price of imports$) \div e_m$

Straightforward solution of this equation yields:

16. The percentage decrease in the foreign-currency price of imports $= \dfrac{\eta_m}{e_m + \eta_m}$

Substituting this into 13 makes the expression for the percentage decrease in the quantity of foreign exchange demanded become:

17. $\eta_m + (1 - \eta_m) \cdot \dfrac{\eta_m}{e_m + \eta_m}$ which simplifies via

18. $\dfrac{\eta_m e_m + \eta_m{}^2 + \eta_m - \eta_m{}^2}{e_m + \eta_m}$ into

19. $\dfrac{\eta_m (e_m + 1)}{e_m + \eta_m}$

This is η_f.

Combination of the Two Preliminary Expressions

With expressions now derived for e_f and η_f, their sum, whose algebraic sign provides the desired stability criterion, becomes

$$\frac{e_x (\eta_x - 1)}{e_x + \eta_x} + \frac{\eta_m (e_m + 1)}{e_m + \eta_m}$$

This is the expression already introduced in the text of this chapter. By straightforward though tedious addition, expansion, and simplification, it reduces to the form more commonly met with in the literature:

$$\frac{e_m e_x (\eta_m + \eta_x - 1) + \eta_m \eta_x (e_m + e_x + 1)}{(e_x + \eta_x)(e_m + \eta_m)}$$

The Terms of Trade

 9

This chapter tries to organize and extend the scattered remarks already made about the relation between a country's exchange rate and terms of trade. This relation is of theoretical interest and also bears on policy issues, since a familiar worry about either devaluing or freeing the rate to cure a balance-of-payments deficit is that the terms of trade would worsen.

Some Necessary Distinctions

In considering how a change in the exchange rate affects the terms of trade, we have to distinguish among: (1) an "autonomous" change in the rate, considered apart from changes in supplies and demands in international trade and apart from changes in controls, (2) the underlying supply-and-demand changes themselves, which would make a free rate change or would put trade out of balance and eventually lead the authorities to alter a pegged rate, and (3) the changes in controls that the authorities may make in response to supply-and-demand changes or in association with an exchange-rate adjustment. We shall first inquire how an autonomous rate change, with other things equal, affects the terms of trade. In fact, of course, the authorities presumably do not make an autonomous rate change out of sheer whim but in response to conditions produced by some earlier underlying change. Here, though, we are interested in how the terms of trade move from their level of just before the exchange-rate adjustment, and the earlier change in underlying conditions is ancient history.

If a devaluation shrinks or removes a balance-of-payments deficit that was actually somehow being financed (rather than being suppressed by controls), it necessarily worsens the country's so-called gross barter terms of trade.[1] This decline in the ratio of the country's total import quantity to total export quantity is trivially obvious: the country retrenches toward living within its means.

Another familiar consequence of devaluation is that it reduces the real purchasing power of domestic factor incomes over internationally traded goods; it does so by discontinuing or reducing the subsidy that was, in effect, being paid out of the country's dwindling external reserves. This is not a change in any generally recognized terms-of-trade concept, but it is akin to a kind of terms-of-trade change and deserves mention again because it may be what people vaguely have in mind if they suppose that devaluation necessarily worsens the terms of trade.

The most usual concept is the so-called net barter or commodity terms of trade—the quantity of imports obtainable for a given quantity of exports, i.e., the ratio of an export price index to an import price index. A loose impression sometimes prevails that devaluation must necessarily worsen the terms of trade even in this sense, since it can succeed in improving the balance of payments only by making exports cheaper and imports more expensive. Devaluation lowers export prices in *foreign* currency but raises import prices in *domestic* currency. The relevant comparison, however, is between export and import prices expressed in the same currency. Which

[1] For definitions of this and other terms-of-trade concepts, see Jacob Viner, *Studies in the Theory of International Trade,* New York: Harper & Row, 1937, pp. 319, 558ff.

one does not matter; the relative price change is the same either way. Considering prices in the home currency is perhaps a bit more convenient.

Devaluation and the Net Barter Terms

As the analysis of balance-of-payments adjustment showed, devaluation raises the home-currency prices of exports and imports alike. There is no conclusive presumption which prices rise by a larger percentage. If the Outland demand for Inland exports is highly elastic, the demand increase apparent from the Inland viewpoint is substantial; and if the Inland supply is inelastic, the upward impact is more strongly on price than quantity. On the import side, if Inland demand is highly elastic and Outland supply highly inelastic (that is, if Inlanders would cut their imports severely rather than pay substantially increased prices and if Outlanders are dependent on the Inland market and would absorb substantial price cuts in their own currency rather than suffer substantial loss of sales), then the Inland prices of imports rise only slightly. Inland's terms of trade, the ratio of export to import prices, thus improve. In the opposite circumstances, with export prices rising but little because of inelastic foreign demand and elastic home supply and import prices rising much because of inelastic home demand and elastic foreign supply, devaluation worsens Inland's terms of trade.

The effect of devaluation on these "commodity" or "net barter" terms can be described more precisely with the elasticity symbols already defined in the last chapter. Devaluation will *improve* (and appreciation worsen) a country's terms of trade if the demand elasticities are high relative to the supply elasticities, that is, if

$$\eta_m \eta_x > e_m e_x$$

$$\text{or} \quad \frac{\eta_x}{e_x} > \frac{e_m}{\eta_m}$$

$$\text{or} \quad \frac{\eta_x}{e_m} > \frac{e_x}{\eta_m}$$

With these inequalities reversed, devaluation worsens the terms of trade.[2]

Joan Robinson finds it reasonable to suppose that η_x/e_m, the ratio of export demand elasticity to import supply elasticity, is typically less than one. In general, each country is more specialized in production than in consumption and thus tends to be a more important factor in the world market for its exports than in the world market for its imports. For this reason, the world demand for a country's exports is likely to be less elastic than the supply to it of its imports. The ratio e_x/η_m, on the other hand, is likely to exceed one, particularly since dependence on imports for products not produced at home tends to make for a low import demand elasticity. But these observations are very casual, and the inference Mrs. Robinson draws from them that an "independent" devaluation is likely to worsen the terms of trade is no more than a weak presumption. The reverse is readily conceivable.

The relation between the effects of devaluation on the balance of payments and on the net barter terms of trade can be summarized as follows:

	IMPROVES BALANCE OF PAYMENTS	WORSENS BALANCE OF PAYMENTS
Improves terms of trade	Possible	Impossible
Worsens terms of trade	Possible	Possible

When the balance-of-payments reacts normally, devaluation can either improve or worsen the terms of trade; in the perverse-elasticities case, devaluation can only worsen the terms of trade. This relation may occasionally be of use in factual studies. If (but not only if) devaluation improves a country's terms of trade, the relevant demand elasticities are shown to be high enough for the balance of payments to respond normally —assuming, of course, that it is the devalua-

[2] These expressions coincide with the criteria stated by Joan Robinson, "Begger-My-Neighbor Remedies for Unemployment," *Readings in the Theory of International Trade*, Philadelphia: Blakiston, 1949, pp. 399-400. For a derivation, see the appendix to this chapter.

tion which has changed the terms of trade and not other changes in the total situation. After the French and Finnish devaluations in the late summer of 1957, for example, each country's commodity terms of trade appeared to *improve* slightly. (See the export and import price indexes published in monthly issues of *International Financial Statistics*.)

The relation just stated is intuitively reasonable. For depreciation to affect the balance of payments normally, supply elasticities may be either high or low absolutely or in comparison with demand elasticities, except that when demand elasticities are extremely low, the corresponding supply elasticities must also be low. (The words *high* and *low* are to be understood in the light of the formulas already presented.) In general, then, demand elasticities may be either high or low in relation to supply elasticities, and this relation is, loosely expressed, the test of how devaluation affects the terms of trade. For devaluation to affect the balance of payments perversely, demand elasticities must be low both absolutely and in relation to supply elasticities. This relation between elasticities indicates that devaluation then worsens the terms of trade.[3]

The Effect of Underlying Real Changes

Next we shall consider the second type of change listed on the first page of this chapter —not devaluation itself, but an underlying

[3] Mere numerical examples of elasticities suffice to show that the terms of trade may move either way when the balance of payments reacts normally to devaluation. A proof that perverse response of the balance of payments to devaluation necessarily entails worsened terms of trade is slightly more complicated. In symbols, the proposition is that if

$$e_m e_x (\eta_m + \eta_x - 1) + \eta_m \eta_x (e_m + e_x + 1) < 0,$$

then

$$\frac{\eta_m \eta_x}{e_m e_x} < 1$$

The first expression may be rearranged into

$$\frac{\eta_m \eta_x}{e_m e_x} < \frac{1 - \eta_m - \eta_x}{e_m + e_x + 1}$$

Now, the fraction on the right side must be smaller than 1 (though not negative, since the sum of the two demand elasticities is less than 1 in the perverse case under consideration). The required conclusion follows:

$$\frac{\eta_m \eta_x}{e_m e_x}$$

is smaller than an expression itself smaller than 1.

supply-and-demand change that would create a balance-of-payments deficit and sooner or later lead the authorities to devalue or that would cause a free exchange rate to depreciate spontaneously. The changes to be considered are real ones—the kind represented by shifts in Marshallian reciprocal-demand curves— rather than purely monetary changes such as Inland inflation, which currency depreciation could ideally just take account of so as to leave the real situation unchanged. One standard example of a real development unfavorable to Inland and her terms of trade is a decline in the Outland demand for her exports.[4] The price of these exports would fall in both currencies, but with nothing directly happening to import prices, so long as the exchange rate remained unchanged. If Inland tastes spontaneously shifted toward imports from Outland, import prices would rise in both currencies with nothing directly happening to export prices, given an unchanged rate. Again the original change, by itself and even apart from the appropriate exchange-rate adjustment, worsens the terms of trade. The same is true of the original change *accompanied* by the rate adjustment necessary to maintain balance-of-payment equilibrium (as can be understood by imagining the terms-of-trade changes necessary to maintain continuous supply-and-demand balance in a world of barter).

Do we have a paradox? We have seen that an unfavorable demand shift, whether or not accompanied by devaluation to avoid an external deficit, worsens the terms of trade. Yet the devaluation considered by itself (apart from whatever made it necessary) may either improve or worsen the terms. It follows that the unfavorable demand shift, by itself, may worsen the terms of trade either more or less than is appropriate for full adjustment with a new exchange rate. This is understandable. With Inland's export supply inelastic, exchange rate unchanged, and import prices

[4] Not much will be said about real developments tending to worsen the terms of trade yet *favorable* to Inland, though examples readily come to mind, such as technological progress in Inland's export industries. Of course, this progress could be an unfavorable development if Inland's exporters were competing among each other in the face of an inelastic world demand.

not directly or immediately affected, a drop in Outland demand causes Inland's export prices and terms of trade to fall substantially. Devaluation, when it finally comes, raises export prices in Inland currency part way back to their initial level, especially if Outland demand is elastic; and while Inland's import prices now tend to rise, their rise is proportionately less than that of export prices if Inland's import demand were highly elastic and the Outland supply inelastic. All in all, devaluation partly—but only partly—reverses the worsening of the terms of trade caused by the initial demand shift. But if the elasticities are such that devaluation by itself worsens the terms of trade, then the initial demand shift, by itself, brings only part of the ultimate worsening. It should not be necessary explicitly to write out all conceivable cases in order to justify the conclusion that an unfavorable real change accompanied by an appropriate or free-market exchange-rate change necessarily worsens the terms of trade, that the rate change by itself may move the terms either way, and that, accordingly, the unfavorable real change by itself, may either underworsen or overworsen the terms as compared with full adjustment to a new balance-of-payments equilibrium.

The reader may think he sees an exception, after all, to the proposition that the unfavorable real change, together with the appropriate or free-market exchange-rate adjustment, necessarily worsens the terms. With demand elasticities perversely low, *upward* revaluation of the Inland currency would seem to be appropriate to remedy the balance-of-payments deficit otherwise emerging; and (since devaluation in the perverse-elasticities case necessarily worsens the terms of trade) upward revaluation would improve the terms. However, the Inland currency would not appreciate under free-market pressures, so the proposition remains unimpaired for a *free-market* movement of the rate. As for an upward revaluation, it would have to be an officially contrived rather than a free-market adjustment; and, as such, it need not have awaited any unfavorable demand shift in trade. As long as the perverse-elasticities case prevails in a country's balance of payments,

its authorities are not fully taking advantage of its monopoly-monopsony position in international trade (just as a monopolist in an ordinary market is not taking full advantage of his position if he is charging a price for his product so low as to leave the demand still inelastic). With adequate information and nationalistic motivation, the authorities would have avoided the perverse-elasticities case and had the country's balance of payments in stable equilibrium in the first place, so that the appropriate contrived exchange-rate adjustment would be in the same direction as the free-market adjustment. Thus the statement above is correct: the commodity or net barter terms of trade move in the same direction as a free-market or appropriate exchange-rate adjustment accompanying some initial real disturbance.

None of the conclusions reached so far establishes a case for or against flexible exchange rates as compared with the alternative price-level mechanism of equilibrating the balance of payments, since, apart from sticky prices, outstanding debts and other long-term contracts, and other frictions, both accomplish the same real adjustments—in the terms of trade as well as in other relative prices and in quantities. As far as the terms of trade are concerned, the issue is between either of these "market" mechanisms, on the one hand, and the use of controls (including *ad hoc* duties) on the other. For two reasons, exchange-rate pegging cannot maintain favorable terms of trade by itself in the face of an unfavorable event causing a balance-of-payments deficit: first, even by itself, the event worsens the terms; second, a deficit cannot be financed indefinitely.

Artificial Improvement of the Terms of Trade

Even tariffs and other controls cannot keep the terms of trade unchanged, though they may keep them more favorable than otherwise. How they can is a familiar story. They and the currency overvaluation they support are ways for the country to exploit the less-than-perfect price elasticity of the foreign demand for its exports and of the foreign supply of its imports. In effect, they establish a selling cartel in the sale of home currency and goods and a buying cartel in the purchase of foreign currency and goods. Controls and overvaluation restrain competition among the country's individual importers and individual exporters, enable the country to act more nearly as a unit on the world market, and make it appear from the foreign point of view less eager to trade than it would be under free-market conditions. This reduced eagerness enables it to exact a better deal from foreigners.

Also familiar are the reminders that improvement in the terms of trade comes at the expense of the volume of trade, that there is therefore such a thing as going too far in improving the terms of trade and reducing the country's gains from trade, defined in any plausible way, that high long-run supply-and-demand elasticities in international trade limit opportunities for much lasting success in manipulating the terms;[5] that optimum manipulation of the terms of trade would require overcoming administrative and other practical difficulties and exercising detailed and adaptable control over individual import and export goods in the light of detailed and constantly revised knowledge of the changing and interdependent supply and demand elasticities for each, that one country's gain in this way would be other countries' loss, and that rounds of manipulation and counter-manipulation might very well result in a net loss for all concerned.

Ideally devised and administered tariffs or other controls could indeed change a country's supplies and demands in international trade so that the equilibrium exchange value of its currency would be higher than otherwise. The rate would then not even have to be pegged; it would fluctuate around the higher level under the influence of supplies and demands modified by the controls.

It is not enough to consider the terms of trade of a country as a whole. We must ask who "the country" is and what actual persons gain from their manipulation. The strengthened exchange value of the home currency as a result of controls keeps down both the quantity and home-currency prices of exports, so that export producers do not gain. Because an import surplus cannot be financed indefinitely, controls or duties (or, in their absence, haphazard rationing of scarce foreign exchange) must eventually keep imports down to what export earnings can pay for. The population thus does not enjoy its "improved" terms of trade in the form of larger quantities of imports than would otherwise be available (except in the unlikely case that the foreign demand for the country's exports is actually inelastic at free-market prices). The restricted imports must be rationed somehow, if not by price. It is little consolation to deprived consumers to know that foreign suppliers may be receiving a lower price than they otherwise would.

If consumers in general do not enjoy more imported goods than would otherwise be available, who *does* benefit from the improved terms of trade? The answer depends on just how imports are restricted to what can be paid for. Chapter 7 considered how import quotas or licensing or foreign-exchange rationing can give a special scarcity profit to favored importers (or even, conceivably, to foreign suppliers)—unless the expense of scrambling for the scarce import privileges dissipates this profit. The government might try to suppress this abnormal profit and divert the benefit to consumers by putting price ceilings on imported goods, but this still would not make any more goods available. The consumers who benefited would be, for instance, those who were lucky enough to arrive at the stores when some cheap but scarce imports happened to be on sale. Other consumers would lose—those who would have bought the imports under free-market conditions but cannot find what they want under the regime of controls. Coupon-book rationing might be used to avoid this haphazard result, as well as to deprive importers of abnormal profits and keep down prices. The consumers who then benefit are those whose ration permits them to buy more imports than they would have bought at prices corresponding to unmanipu-

---

[5] This is one of the main themes of Frank D. Graham, *The Theory of International Values,* Princeton, N.J.: Princeton University Press, 1948, esp. pp. 343-344.

lated terms of trade; others lose. So far as controls really do succeed in restricting imports yet keeping down their cost to consumers, money that cannot be spent on them tends to be diverted onto other goods and to raise their prices. The most plausible bright spot in the picture so far is that manipulation of the terms of trade keeps available at home some goods that would otherwise have been exported.

The government itself is the beneficiary if it maintains improved terms of trade by collecting high enough import duties or import-license fees. The government could use these revenues to reduce domestic taxes or to increase government services. Ideally, the terms-of-trade improvement would accrue in this way to the general population. This is presumably preferable to letting the improvement fall to not-particularly-deserving private traders in restricted imports or to particular consumers who happen to be favored by official rationing or by price control and haphazard rationing.

Actually, favorable terms of trade resulting from unconstrained supply and demand and favorable terms maintained by hampering free choice in the purchase of imports are two different things. The people of a country may gain little from knowing that their imports have been kept artificially cheap in relation to their exports or in relation to their labor and other productive factors, if they are not free to buy all they want on these "improved" terms. It is as if price controls had made shirts attractively cheap but almost unobtainable. There is so vast a difference between the price at which one *can* buy and the price at which one *cannot* buy that the two concepts ought not to bear the same label *price*. And the same could be said about the concept *terms of trade*.

Terms of Trade and Real Income

When official devaluation or free-market depreciation replaces controls as a means of suppressing a balance-of-payments deficit, worsened terms of trade need not bring a cut in real income. To show this, Fritz Machlup

suggests the analogy of a free-lance writer who has been selling fewer magazine articles than he has time to write. Now he cuts the high price that he had previously been asking; he worsens his terms of trade. Quite conceivably the reduced price so effectively promotes the sale of his articles that the writer earns more income than before and cures an actual or threatening deficit in his personal balance of payments. To change the analogy a bit, the writer may have been fully occupied even before cutting his price but spending only part of his working time writing and the rest of the time doing his own housework. Cutting the price enables him to place more articles, take in more money, and hire a housekeeper who will free his time for writing the additional articles. He avoids a personal financial crisis and enjoys a higher standard of living than before. This happy result depends, of course, on an adequate degree of price-sensitivity in the demand for his articles. What was true for the writer may be true for a country: abandoning currency overvaluation and the controls that had been supporting overvaluation may raise real national income in any plausible sense of the term. The freer flow of trade may employ previously idle resources, and a higher degree of international specialization may permit reallocation of resources into relatively more productive lines. Accepting "worse" terms of trade may be necessary to obtain the beneficial reemployment-of-idle-resources and resource-reallocation effects.[6] Of course, none of these possibilities discredits the theoretically sound (if actually impractical) concept of controls that provide the optimal compromise between trade shrinkage and terms-of-trade improvement. But experience suggests that controls are likely to err on the tighter-than-optimal side (especially in view of high long-run supply-and-demand elasticities), and it is worth realizing why devaluation that brings worsened terms of trade is by no means necessarily harmful on balance.

---

[6] Fritz Machlup, "The Terms-of-Trade Effects of Devaluation upon Real Income and the Balance of Trade," *Kyklos,* **IX,** 1956, pp. 417-449, esp. 429-436.

The Foreign Debt Burden

Just as controls and currency overvaluation may improve a country's terms of trade, so they may conceivably lighten its burden of foreign debt. If businessmen or the government must pay interest and repay capital sums fixed in foreign currency, keeping up the exchange value of the home currency will keep down the home-currency cost of these payments. But this will not necessarily make it easier for the country as a whole to pay its foreign obligations; overvaluation hampers exports and, unless foreign demand is actually inelastic, makes foreign-exchange earnings smaller than otherwise. The real debt burden depends more on the purchasing power of the money in which the debt is fixed than on anything that might be accomplished by manipulating the exchange rate with controls. Actually, the debt burden for a country as a whole is a vague concept. Private or governmental organizations with foreign debts to pay may indeed benefit from being able to buy foreign exchange cheap; but they benefit at the expense of others, such as exporters and some consumers of imports, who are harmed by currency overvaluation or the controls necessary to maintain it. Overvaluation does not so much lighten the debt burden as shift some of it onto other persons.

Conclusion

This chapter does not dismiss the terms of trade or foreign debt burdens as unimportant. If the foreign demand for a country's exports falls off, if foreign supply prices of imports rise, if intensified buying competition from other countries raises the cost of imports, or if the currencies in which external debts are expressed rise in purchasing power, the country suffers. But it is not so much the changes in exchange rates in response to shifts in international supplies and demands as these shifts themselves that are responsible for changes in the terms of trade. Exchange-rate policy can neither avert the unpleasantness of unfavorable real developments nor create the benefits of favorable developments that have not actually occurred. In so far as terms-of-trade considerations warrant exchange-rate pegging, what they more basically warrant is the duties or other controls that make the rate-pegging feasible. This argument is well known, and subject to well-known limitations. Ideally, it calls for selective duties or controls on individual items entering into trade according to their individual supply and demand elasticities; overall control to keep up the exchange value of the home currency is only a crude substitute.

Appendix to Chapter 9: Derivation of the Formula for the Effect of Exchange-rate Variation on the "Commodity" or "Net Barter" Terms of Trade

Symbols

m = proportionate change in quantity of imports $\left(\dfrac{\Delta M}{M}\right)$

x = proportionate change in quantity of exports $\left(\dfrac{\Delta X}{X}\right)$

p_m = proportionate change in the home-currency price of imports $\left(\dfrac{\Delta P_m}{P_m}\right)$

p_x = proportionate change in the home-currency price of exports $\left(\dfrac{\Delta P_x}{P_x}\right)$

c = proportionate change in the foreign-exchange value of the home currency $\left(\dfrac{\text{new value} - \text{old value}}{\text{old value}}\right)$. (For depreciation of the home currency, c is negative; for appreciation, positive.)

$p_m + c$ = proportionate change in foreign-currency price of home imports.

$p_x + c$ = proportionate change in foreign-currency price of home exports

$t = p_x - p_m$ = proportionate improvement ($+$) or worsening ($-$) in the home country's terms of trade (in the ratio of export prices to import prices). [For example, if a certain exchange-rate change makes export prices rise by 3 percent and import prices rise by 2 percent, then the terms of trade improve by $3-2=1$ percent. This formulation is approximately correct and approaches being exactly correct when the changes involved are extremely small.]

NOTE again that all of the above symbols refer to proportionate changes rather than to absolute magnitudes.

The elasticity symbols are the same as previously defined.

$$t = p_x - p_m$$

The expression for p_x

1. $p_x = \dfrac{x}{e_x}$ $\left[\text{Because } e_x = \dfrac{x}{p_x}\right]$

2. $x = -\eta_x(p_x + c)$ $\left[\text{Because } \eta_x = -\dfrac{x}{p_x+c}\right]$

3. $p_x = -\dfrac{\eta_x(p_x + c)}{e_x}$

4. $p_x = -\dfrac{\eta_x c}{e_x + \eta_x}$

The expression for p_m

5. $p_m = -\dfrac{m}{\eta_m}$ $\left[\text{Because } \eta_m = -\dfrac{m}{p_m}\right]$

6. $m = e_m(p_m + c)$ $\left[\text{Because } e_m = \dfrac{m}{p_m + c}\right]$

7. $p_m = -\dfrac{e_m(p_m + c)}{\eta_m}$

8. $p_m = -\dfrac{e_m c}{e_m + \eta_m}$

The expression for t

9. $t = p_x - p_m = -\dfrac{\eta_x c}{e_x + \eta_x} + \dfrac{e_m c}{e_m + \eta_m}$

$$= c\left(\dfrac{e_m}{e_m + \eta_m} - \dfrac{\eta_x}{e_x + \eta_x}\right)$$

This means that the terms of trade move in the same direction as the foreign-exchange value of the home currency when the expression in parentheses is positive. The two move in opposite directions—depreciation of the home currency would *improve* the terms of trade—when the expression in parentheses is negative.

The expression in parentheses may be rewritten:

10.
$$\frac{e_m e_x + e_m \eta_x - e_m \eta_x - \eta_m \eta_x}{(e_m + \eta_m)(e_x + \eta_x)}$$

$$= \frac{e_m e_x - \eta_m \eta_x}{(e_m + \eta_m)(e_x + \eta_x)}$$

Since the denominator is bound to be positive, it may be neglected. Depreciation improves or worsens the terms of trade according to whether the numerator is negative or positive.

In other words, depreciation *improves* the terms of trade if

$$\eta_m \eta_x > e_m e_x$$

that is, if
$$\frac{\eta_x}{e_x} > \frac{e_m}{\eta_m}$$

or, if
$$\frac{\eta_x}{e_m} > \frac{e_x}{\eta_m}$$

If the inequalities are the other way around, depreciation worsens the terms of trade.

Exchange Rates and Price Levels

❧ 10

Exchange rates interact not only with balances of payments and terms of trade but also with national price levels. How do price levels govern exchange rates? Is an opposite influence—from exchange rates to prices—of any real importance? Might this influence even sabotage balance-of-payments adjustment? Can the relation between exchange rates and price levels offer any evidence on demand elasticities in international trade and thus on prospects for exchange-market stability?

Purchasing-power Parity

The purchasing-power-parity doctrine bears on these questions. It observes that people value currencies for what they will buy.[1] If one Inland dollar buys as much goods and services as three Outland pesos, a free exchange rate would hover in the range of 3 pesos per dollar. An actual rate that unmistakably undervalued the peso ($.25, say, instead of the equilibrium $.33) would make Outland goods and services seem like bargains to Inlanders, whose eagerness to snap them up would flood the market with dollars seeking to buy pesos. From the Outland point of view, the high Inland prices as translated into pesos at the disequilibrium rate would discourage buying. Imbalance on the foreign-

exchange market would bid the rate back toward the purchasing-power-parity level. Corrective pressures would operate not merely through changes in the volume of trade in a given list of goods and services but also through changes in the composition of that list. Currency undervaluation makes the general level of prices of a country's productive factors low relative to foreign levels, enabling the country's businessmen to compete in world markets with an expanded variety of products, while restricting imports in variety as well as in volume.[2] Responses of trade that might be small in relation to a country's total imports and exports could still be large in relation to any deficit or surplus in its balance of payments.

The purchasing-power-parity doctrine in no way denies that supply and demand determine a free-market exchange rate. Rather, it points out certain properties of supply and demand and of the level toward which they tend to push the rate.

If the doctrine is correct, the theory of elasticities so low as to permit cumulative and disequilibrating fluctuations does not apply to reality. Strong pressures tend to keep the actual rate in the vicinity of a determinate equilibrium level at any given time, even though this level does change over time if the price levels of the two countries concerned move out of step with each

---

[1] Rudiments of the purchasing-power-parity doctrine date back at least to British discussions of the depreciation of the paper pound during the Napoleonic Wars. Cf. Jacob Viner, *Studies in the Theory of International Trade,* New York: Harper & Row, 1937, pp. 124–126, 379–380; Gottfried Haberler, *A Survey of International Trade Theory,* rev. ed., Princeton, N.J.: International Finance Section, Princeton University, 1961, pp. 45–47. Gustav Cassel reformulated and vigorously urged the doctrine during and after World War I.

[2] E. Victor Morgan has emphasized these and related points, though without relating them to purchasing-power parity. See "The Theory of Flexible Exchange Rates," *American Economic Review,* **XLV,** June 1955, esp. pp. 282–284; cf. Gustav Cassel, "International Trade, Capital Movements, and Exchanges," *Foreign Investments,* Chicago: University of Chicago Press, 1928, pp. 15–16.

other. The purchasing-power-parity doctrine is not merely or even chiefly a formula for actually calculating precise equilibrium rates. More basically, the doctrine describes stabilizing pressures that keep an exchange rate from oscillating chaotically and instead keep pushing it toward a definite equilibrium level, hard though it may be to specify a precise figure.

Rival Doctrines

Before reviewing standard criticisms of the doctrine, we should note what other theories it was intended to answer. Chief among these was the balance-of-payments theory, which attributed market strength or weakness of a currency to strength or weakness of the country's balance of payments. During the Napoleonic Wars, explanations of the depreciation of the paper pound (or rather, as some insisted, of the appreciation of gold) commonly stressed Britain's heavy flow of outward payments. Early difficulties in pegging the Austrian crown at its newly established gold value in the 1890s were likewise blamed on a passive balance of payments. The rapid fall of the German mark after World War I was widely ascribed to heavy reparations obligations.[3] Now, no one denies that external influences working through the balance of payments can affect a country's internal monetary conditions. But it is misleading to insist on the balance-of-payments explanation of a currency's weakness on the exchange market to the *neglect* of how the domestic money supply and price level are behaving. Balance or imbalance in a country's external transactions, far from one-sidedly determining the exchange rate, is largely a *consequence* of the relation between the exchange rate and relative price levels. When Professor Cassel, after World War I, directed attention to the different degrees of inflation in different countries and to the relative purchasing powers of their currencies, he was certainly making an

advance over the man-in-the-street economics of the balance-of-payments theory.

This theory is in some respects resurrected in the newer and more sophisticated notion of the equilibrium rate of exchange. At a currency's equilibrium foreign-exchange value, a country's reserves of gold and foreign exchange might fluctuate quite a bit from month to month or even from year to year but would remain approximately stable (or approximately on a long-run growth trend) on the average over a period of at least several years. According to the doctrine, this medium-run equilibrium-on-the-average in the balance of payments must not depend on *ad hoc* trade and exchange controls or on toleration of domestic depression or inflation.[4] The International Monetary Fund seems to have been initially predicated on some such notion—that there is some pattern of fixed exchange rates which, unsupported by direct controls and by unwanted depressions and inflations, would keep a country's balance of payments in equilibrium on the average over a period of several years at least. Whenever an unmistakable disequilibrium appeared, the adherents of this doctrine could agree that the equilibrium rate pattern had not in fact been chosen but would presumably argue that some other fixed rate pattern, though hard to specify, *would* have satisfied their criteria. It is difficult to see what kind of observational evidence could bear on such a contention. To try to establish the concept of a durable equilibrium rate by sheer definition is to beg crucial questions. The doctrine vaguely defines the equilibrium rate of exchange as one which, if fixed for at least several years, would make things work out just fine. But it does not tell how to calculate the rate even approximately, nor even set forth the general principles determining it. The purchasing-power-parity doctrine, defective and vague though it may be, comes closer than any of its rivals to having a specific content.

---

[3] See Viner, *op. cit.*, pp. 138–148; Howard S. Ellis, *German Monetary Theory, 1905–1933*, Cambridge, Mass.: Harvard University Press, 1937, esp. chaps. 12 and 14; and Theodor Hertzka, *Wechselcurs und Agio*, Vienna: Manz, 1894, pp. 94, 156.

[4] Cf. Ragnar Nurkse, "Conditions of International Monetary Equilibrium," *Readings in the Theory of International Trade*, Philadelphia, Blakiston, 1949, and W. M. Scammell, *International Monetary Policy*, London: Macmillan, 1957, pp. 49–54.

Numerical Calculations: A Subsidiary Aspect

Two versions of the parity doctrine—the absolute or positive version and the comparative version—have been put forth. Actually, these are not so much two different versions of the doctrine itself as two approaches to implementing its rate-calculation aspect, which, in turn, is less fundamental than the stabilizing-pressures aspect already mentioned. The absolute or positive approach tries to compare the purchasing powers of two money units at a given time. An Outland price level three times as high in pesos as the Inland price level in dollars suggests an exchange rate of roughly 3 pesos per dollar. But such a comparison of price levels presupposes some one assortment of goods and services that can be priced in both countries and that accurately represents the types and relative quantities of various goods and services produced and consumed in each country. In fact, though, no one assortment can typify economic life in both of two countries at the same time; national patterns of production and consumption differ too much.

The impracticality of calculations according to the absolute or positive version of the parity doctrine forces resort to the comparative version. This makeshift relates the current parity exchange rate to changes in the purchasing powers of the two currencies since some past base period when the actual exchange rate was supposedly in equilibrium. If the Inland price level has tripled over a certain period of time while the Outland price level has been multiplied by six—if Outland has suffered twice as much price inflation as Inland—then the Inland dollar should command about twice as many Outland pesos as before.

These ideas may be expressed in formulas. In them, *then* refers to the base period and *now* to the period for which the theoretical parity exchange rate is being computed. The formula for this rate in units of home currency per unit of foreign currency is:

$$\begin{array}{l}\text{Theoretical price} \\ \text{of foreign cur-} \\ \text{rency now}\end{array} = \begin{array}{l}\text{actual price} \\ \text{of foreign cur-} \\ \text{rency then}\end{array} \times$$

$$\left\{\dfrac{\dfrac{\text{home price level now}}{\text{home price level then}}}{\dfrac{\text{foreign price level now}}{\text{foreign price level then}}}\right.$$

Thus, the larger the increase in the home relative to the foreign price level, the more home cents it takes to equal one foreign peso. (Incidentally, the year for which the price index stands at 100 may be different for the two countries; all that matters is how much each country's own price index has changed between *then* and *now*.)

In computing a time series of purchasing-power parities between two currencies, always using the same base period, the following arrangement simplifies the arithmetic:

$$\begin{array}{l}\text{Theoretical price} \\ \text{of foreign cur-} \\ \text{rency now}\end{array} = \begin{array}{l}\text{actual price} \\ \text{of foreign cur-} \\ \text{rency then}\end{array} \times$$

$$\dfrac{\text{foreign price level then}}{\text{home price level then}} \times \dfrac{\text{home price level now}}{\text{foreign price level now}}$$

All of this expression except the last ratio on the right can be worked out once and for all and used repeatedly in calculating the theoretical rate for each successive month or year.

To compute purchasing-power parities for a number of foreign currencies, all for the same current period and all based on the same past period, the most convenient arrangement is:

$$\begin{array}{l}\text{Theoretical price} \\ \text{of foreign cur-} \\ \text{rency now}\end{array} = \begin{array}{l}\text{actual price} \\ \text{of foreign cur-} \\ \text{rency then}\end{array} \times$$

$$\dfrac{\text{foreign price level then}}{\text{foreign price level now}} \times \dfrac{\text{home price level now}}{\text{home price level then}}$$

The last ratio can be computed once and used in all the calculations. Suppose price levels and base-period exchange rates are as shown in Table 10.1.

The ratio of the 1965 price level to the 1937 price level for Inland is 130/65, or 2.

Multiplying this figure by the 1937 exchange rate $\times \dfrac{1937 \text{ price level}}{1965 \text{ price level}}$ for each of the foreign countries yields purchasing-power parities for 1965 of 37.5¢ for Ruritania, 52.9¢ for Graustark, and 2.1¢ for Laputa.

For exchange rates expressed not in cents per foreign unit but in foreign units per Inland dollar, the parity formula becomes:

$$\begin{matrix} \text{Theoretical number} \\ \text{of foreign units} \\ \text{per dollar now} \end{matrix} = \begin{matrix} \text{actual number} \\ \text{of foreign units} \\ \text{per dollar then} \end{matrix} \times$$

$$\left\{ \dfrac{\dfrac{\text{foreign price level now}}{\text{foreign price level then}}}{\dfrac{\text{home price level now}}{\text{home price level then}}} \right.$$

As before, rearrangements will simplify the arithmetic of computing a time series of theoretical exchange rates between two currencies and the theoretical rates of a number of foreign currencies on the home currency at the same time for all. It is instructive to recalculate the previous example in terms of foreign units per dollar, noting the equivalance.

Comparative vs. Absolute Versions

The great convenience of the comparative approach is that it sidesteps direct comparison of the purchasing powers of different currencies at a given time. No standard assortment of goods and services, representative of economic activity at home and abroad,

Table 10.1. Price Indexes and Base Exchange Rates for Illustrative Purchasing-power-parity Calculations

Country	1937 Price Index	1965 Price Index	1937 Actual Exchange Rate in Inland Cents per Foreign Unit
Inland	65	130	
Ruritania	40	160	75¢
Graustark	90	170	50¢
Laputa	30	570	20¢

need be devised and priced in both places. Instead, each country's own price index, constructed in its own way and representative of local economic life, can be used. All that need be compared internationally are the degrees of change in the separate national indexes. Whatever general price indexes are available may be used—wholesale price indexes, cost-of-living indexes, etc.—though the same type of index should presumably be used for both countries whenever possible. If wholesale and cost-of-living indexes are both available for both countries, two purchasing-power parities can be calculated; fairly good agreement between the two would strengthen confidence in them.

The convenience of the comparative version is also the source of its weaknesses. It is only an expedient made necessary because the theoretically more relevant absolute version is so awkward to apply statistically. The purchasing-power-parity doctrine is primarily concerned with the forces at work determining an exchange rate at a given time; what may have happened in the past is, in principle, ancient history. Yet the comparative version deals with price-level changes over a span of time. Any inaccuracies in the price indexes of the two countries concerned affect the calculated parity exchange rate. Long time spans rob price indexes of both accuracy and even clear meaning. The assortment of goods and services whose prices constitute each country's price level has changed. The degree of similarlity or dissimilarity between the two national economies may also have changed, thus further vitiating any international comparison. Moreover, the base-period actual exchange rate necessary to comparative-version calculations may not have been an equilibrium rate at the time, perhaps because of government pegging or other controls, because of anticipations stemming from rapid price changes, because of other temporary or special influences, or because of mere accidental or random deviations from equilibrium. A disequilibrium base-period exchange rate impairs all purchasing-power-parity calculations. Still another complication is that transportation costs and the severity of tariffs and other trade barriers may have changed since the base period. All these difficulties relate to a makeshift way of calculating parities; they do not impugn the logic of the parity doctrine itself. In particular, they do not discredit its more fundamental stabilizing-pressures aspect—the analysis of automatic correctives of overvaluation or undervaluation.

Some objections apply to the comparative and positive versions of the doctrine alike. Either involves the notion of purchasing powers of currencies over things *in general*. How does this square with the analysis of Chapter 6, which shows how exchange-rate changes affect trade by causing shifts *within* general price levels, shifts in the relative prices of internationally traded and domestic goods? If relative price changes are crucial, what becomes of the notion of general price levels and general purchasing powers? One answer is that actual shifts in sectional price levels will not be large when supply and demand elasticities in international trade are high and when small shifts suffice to modify production and consumption patterns. Consider the extreme case of infinite elasticity in Inland's demand for imports and supply of exports. Then, if Inland's currency were somehow to tend to depreciate on the foreign exchange market, the Inland price level of internationally traded goods would not rise at all. The resulting decline in consumption and increase in production by Inlanders of internationally traded goods would be "caused" by the virtual sectional-price-level shift that would *otherwise* have actually occurred. Now, to the extent that the purchasing-power-parity doctrine holds true, the supply and demand elasticities are indeed high; the tendency of exchange rates to hover around their purchasing-power-parities is incompatible with low elasticities requiring large divergent shifts in the prices of domestic and international goods.[5] The fuzziness and shiftability of the line between domestic and international goods

is a further reason why the concept of sectional-price-level shifts does little damage to the logic of the purchasing-power-parity doctrine. Finally, it is a matter of common observation and elementary monetary theory that sizable changes in the monetary determinants of a currency's purchasing power cause a general correspondence in the broad movements of domestic- and international-goods prices—correspondence far overshadowing any divergence associated with exchange-rate changes.

Standard Objections to the Parity Doctrine

Obscurities in the concepts of general price levels and general purchasing powers of currencies provide one set of objections to the parity doctrine in either its positive or its comparative version. Another is that transportation costs, tariffs, quotas, exchange controls, and other obstacles to trade may allow an existing exchange rate to overvalue or undervalue a currency in relation to a calculated purchasing-power parity without corrective tendencies operating through alterations in the flow of trade. For an extreme example, consider a country whose very restrictive tariffs and import quotas limit imports (and indirectly exports) to an insignificant percentage of total domestic production and consumption. At prevailing exchange rates, foreign goods might seem great bargains to the citizens of this country, yet these people might be unable to bring these bargain goods in over the wall of trade barriers, and so they could not undo the overvaluation of their home currency by eagerly demanding foreign exchange.

As for transportation costs, these merely keep the actual exchange rate from adhering closely to purchasing-power parity but do not discredit the concept of parity itself. Similarly, because of costs related to shipping gold, an exchange rate under the international gold standard need not stay exactly at mint par—it can fluctuate within the gold points—without discrediting the concept of mint par. In permitting deviations from exact parity, transportation costs under the international gold standard and under independent paper cur-

---

[5] This is not a circular argument. It does not pretend to furnish independent support for the parity doctrine but only seeks to clear up an apparent logical inconsistency between the sectional-price-level and purchasing-power-parity analyses.

rencies have differences in degree but not in kind. How great this difference is is an empirical question about which more must be said later.

Tariffs, quotas, exchange controls, and other man-made trade barriers, if restrictive enough, could admittedly ruin the responsiveness of trade to prices and so make the parity doctrine irrelevant.[6] The doctrine is meant to deal with relatively free markets and, in fact, to help appraise their workability. Rigorous controls may make the doctrine, like many other propositions of economic theory, incomplete descriptions of reality.

A further line of objection, which critics generally (but mistakenly) regard as decisive against the purchasing-power-parity doctrine, stresses how many transactions besides those in goods and services can give rise to supply and demand on the foreign-exchange market. Loans, loan repayments, unilateral transfers of gifts, royalties, and indemnities—all can affect exchange rates without necessarily involving relative price levels. Quite true. Yet there are limits to how far out of line with relative price levels such nontrade transactions can push exchange rates. These limits (imprecise though they may be) are essentially what the parity doctrine is all about. A marked rise of a currency above purchasing-power-parity, perhaps as a result of borrowing abroad, would create price incentives tending to spur imports and check exports. This, together with a direct reduction of current spending power in the lending country and an increase in the borrowing country, is how the financial aspects of a capital movement are translated into a real net inflow of goods and services into the borrowing country (or a reduction in a previous net outflow). Such responses in the flow of trade may add to the quantity of foreign exchange demanded for imports and subtract from the quantity supplied by exports so as largely to match the increased quantity supplied by the loan without calling for any great change in the exchange rate. If this translation of financial into real capital movement met temporary obstacles or delays, speculators might well realize the situation and buy and thus support the temporarily depressed currency of the lending country.

Nontrade transactions could similarly be cited, and not much less properly, as an objection to the theory of mint par under the gold standard. Many types of transactions besides gold transactions give rise to supply of and demand for gold-standard currencies without discrediting an emphasis on their relative gold contents. Gold arbitrage limits deviations of gold-standard exchange rates from their mint pars; under free exchanges, analogously, shifts in goods-and-services trade can limit deviations from purchasing-power parity. Both mint par and purchasing-power parity are theories of *par*. Neither theory insists that exchange rates stay precisely at their par values; neither stands or falls according to whether or not they do.

The analysis of nontrade transactions applies also to the further argument that not only prices but also income levels influence trade and exchange rates. This is true; yet price-induced trade readjustments can restrain large deviations from purchasing-power parity. Besides, cyclical developments affecting incomes are likely to affect prices in the same direction, so that there need be no conflict between price and income influences on exchange rates. As for long-run growth or decay of real economic activity, an economy's import demands and export supplies are likely to be affected in the same direction.

The purchasing-power-parity doctrine does not deny that "structural" changes—changes in technology and tastes apart from monetary changes—can affect both exchange rates and the terms of trade (particularly of interests heavily specialized in producing or consuming the individual commodities most directly

---

[6] Interferences severely distorting an exchange rate away from the purchasing-power ratio of the two currencies might, however, still leave the rate powerfully related to the relative purchasing powers. Suppose, as an extreme example, that uniform ad valorem import duties and export subsidies create such a spread between the home and foreign prices of a country's imports and exports that the foreign-exchange value of its currency is double what it would otherwise be. Even so, a change in relative price levels could still bring about a roughly proportionate change in the distorted exchange rate, and random rate fluctuations could still be self-correcting.

involved).[7] However, the doctrine does describe price-induced adjustments in trade flows that will limit nonmonetary exchange-rate movements. Although structural changes can indeed, within limits, modify the systematic distortion of an exchange rate from some calculated purchasing-power parity, the rate can still be highly stable in the sense that price incentives will limit or reverse, rather than intensify, random departures.

Commodity Points and Commodity Arbitrage

At about the time that Gustav Cassel began resurrecting purchasing-power parity, his fellow countryman, Eli Heckscher, introduced a concept that should have tempered the enthusiasm of attacks on the doctrine. Just as gold-standard exchanges fluctuate within the gold points, so paper exchanges fluctuate within "commodity points." Just as the spread of upper and lower gold points from mint par depends on the costs of shipping gold, so the spread of upper and lower commodity points from "price parity" (as Heckscher called it) depends on the costs of and other obstacles to shipping commodities.[8] There are, of course, differences: the spread between commodity points is usually larger than the spread between gold points, and commodities are not, like gold under an international gold standard, supplied and demanded at government-guaranteed prices. Commodity points are more nebulous than gold points (though even gold points are

not absolutely precise), and, as considered later, price parities are partly resultants rather than purely determinants of exchange rates.

Heckscher's analysis can be improved by explicitly noting that an exchange rate has not just a single pair of upper and lower commodity points but many—one pair for each good or service that actually or potentially enters into international trade.[9] Strictly speaking, an exchange rate also has a great many purchasing-power pars: for each commodity or service marketed in both of two countries, there is some potential level of the exchange rate that equates the two local-currency prices. The purchasing-power parity may be conceived of as some sort of central tendency among these individual parities.

Commodity points and price parity suggest the concept of commodity arbitrage (in analogy to the gold arbitrage under an international standard). If, under freely fluctuating exchange rates, the price of foreign exchange sinks below the import point for a particular commodity, traders will import the commodity at a profit. This arbitrage demand for foreign exchange will tend to buoy up the rate. If the price of foreign exchange rises above a commodity export point, traders will profitably export the commodity and help to hold down the exchange rate. Though such arbitrage is hardly distinguishable from ordinary international trade, the arbitrage concept is useful: it fits in well with the worldwide character of supply and demand for the staples of commerce when intermeshing of national markets is not deliberately restricted. L. B. Zapoleon, writing about 1930 of factors tending to narrow interregional differences among prices as translated at going exchange rates, stressed such things as organized commodity exchanges; the alertness of traders and speculators in raw materials and of manufacturing consumers of raw materials; improvements in transportation; methods of preserving "perishable" foods; transmission of price quotations and conclusion of arbitrage operations by cable,

---

[7] A change in the terms of trade does not necessarily even require a change in purchasing-power parity. A country's export and import prices might change in opposite directions, leaving a general price level unchanged in some average sense. C. Haberler, *op. cit.,* p. 50.

[8] Eli F. Heckscher, "Växelkursens grundval vid pappersmynfot," *Ekonomisk Tidskrift,* **XVIII,** 1916, pp. 309–312; see also Heckscher, "Price Levels and Rates of Exchange: The Theory," in Heckscher et al., *Sweden, Norway, Denmark, and Iceland in the World War,* New Haven, Conn.: Yale University Press, 1930; Heckscher is here more concerned with the fallacy of the purchasing-power-parity doctrine interpreted as a precise formula than with its broad truth, but his intentions do not impair the usefulness of his concepts. Cf. L. B. Zapoleon, "International and Domestic Commodities and the Theory of Prices," *Quarterly Journal of Economics,* **XLV,** May 1931, pp. 422–423.

[9] See Gottfried von Haberler, *The Theory of International Trade,* 3d impression, London: Hodge, 1950, pp. 32, 34; and J. B. Condliffe, *The Commerce of Nations,* New York: W. W. Norton & Co., 1950, p. 307.

telegraph, and radio; establishment of commercial information services, definite commodity standards, facilities for settling commercial disputes, and modern banking and credit systems; the "interindustry competition" arising in part from development of synthetic materials and working to tie together the prices of seemingly unrelated commodities; and the reduction in differences in consumer demand arising from local custom as education and international contacts develop. While government policies have sometimes made the worldwide interconnection of markets less tight than when Zapoleon wrote, other factors he stressed—in particular, those related to technological progress—have continued to gain in relevance. For all these reasons, neither the actual volume of international trade nor the presence or absence of trade in particular commodities indicates the full interconnection among prices on domestic and world markets. Even mere potential shipments help maintain international price alignment.[10]

Some Evidence on Purchasing-power Parity

These considerations are qualitative only. In trying to give more definite meaning to such terms as *narrow* spread between commodity points and *close* price interconnections, we must consider whatever purchasing-power-parity calculations can be made, imperfect though they are. Of course, not even a close correspondence between actual and calculated rates would mean much if the actual rates determined the prices entering into the parity calculations much more strongly than the prices determined the rates. This question of which way the causation mainly runs will require a section to itself later on. In view of the reassurance to be offered there, the considerable correspondence found between actual and calculated rates testifies in favor of the more basic stabilizing-pressures aspect of the parity doctrine. Correspond-

ences are all the more impressive in view of the statistical and logical difficulties, already discussed, of specifying parities precisely. Actual exchange rates of, say, half or twice parities calculated in any plausible manner are highly unusual, yet if there were nothing at all to the parity doctrine, actual exchange rates of only a few percent or of several hundred percent of calculated rates would not uncommonly appear by change. Haberler remarks on the "great theoretical interest" attaching to the "considerable degree of correlation" observed in the movements in different countries even of retail prices, as made comparable at prevailing exchange rates. When trade is not drastically controlled and when no wars or other great structural upheavals separate the periods compared, "it would hardly be possible to find . . . a case where an equilibrium rate is, say, 15–20 percent off purchasing power par."[11] Some examples will bring to mind the kind of evidence readily available.

During the American Civil War, when the West Coast kept the gold standard while the rest of the Union used paper greenbacks, the commodity price level in the East rose by roughly the same percentage as the greenback price of gold. The price level in the East roughly doubled from 1860 to 1864, while prices stayed about the same on the West Coast. A Federal employee earning 100 greenback dollars a month could buy roughly the same amount of goods, whether he spent his greenbacks in the East or exchanged them for 50 gold dollars and spent them in the West.[12] Over the whole period 1861–1879, the ratio of the actual to the purchasing-power-parity exchange rate of gold in greenbacks (these rates being practically equivalent to greenback rates on the pound sterling) fluctuated between a maximum of about 121 percent and a minimum of about 88 percent on an annual basis. The first major discrepancy, the wartime rise of the price of gold to at most about 20 percent

---

[10] Zapoleon, *op. cit.*, pp. 409–459. See also Condliffe, *op. cit.*, pp. 301–311, for a description of how closely world markets were integrated in the late nineteenth century when the general extent of governmental trade restrictions was relatively slight.

[11] Haberler, *The Theory of International Trade*, p. 39, and *A Survey of International Trade Theory* (1961 edition), p. 51.

[12] Richard A. Lester, *Monetary Experiments*, Princeton, N.J.: Princeton University Press, 1939, pp. 169–170.

above its calculated parity, seems remarkably small in view of its important cause, namely, the interruption of cotton exports as a source of foreign exchange. The second major (but smaller) discrepancy, the low price of gold in relation to purchasing-power parity from the end of the war through 1871, seems due to heavy foreign purchases of U.S. government bonds and railroad securities.[13]

The currency upheavals after World War I furnish some more recent experience. In his study of the fluctuating pound-dollar rate from 1919 to 1925, W. F. Stolper found that speculation apparently played little part in determining the actual rate; most of its rather moderate deviations from purchasing-power parity could be satisfactorily explained in terms of levels of business activity in Britain and the United States. Although cost-of-living indexes are generally supposed to reflect prices of internationally traded goods less strongly than do wholesale indexes, Stolper found that purchasing-power parities corresponded with actual exchange rates even better when calculated with cost-of-living indexes than when calculated with wholesale or raw-materials price indexes.[14]

Frank D. Graham calculated comparative-version purchasing-power parities in United States cents (based on wholesale price indexes and 1913 mint pars) for twelve fluctuating

European currencies during the period 1919–1923. He then expressed each parity as a percentage of the actual exchange rate for that month. Discrepancies were large only for Germany, whose exchange rate during the hyperinflation doubtless reflected anticipation of a continued fall of the mark. For the eleven other countries (Sweden, Switzerland, Spain, Norway, Netherlands, Czechoslovakia, Great Britain, Denmark, Belgium, France, and Italy), Graham gives 492 monthly "observations" in all (not a full 660 because data are missing for some countries in some months). His results may be summarized by saying that purchasing-power parity fell above or below the actual exchange rate by not more than 35 percent in 97.2 percent of the country-months; by not more than 25 percent in 91.5 percent of the country-months; by not more than 15 percent in 72.2 percent of the country-months; and by not more than 5 percent in 27.2 percent of the country-months. In conclusion, Graham pointed out "in most cases a rather close correspondence between actual exchange rates and the theoretical pars based on relative prices. . . . If we exclude Germany, the clustering around the 100% figure is marked and aberrations were apparently self corrective."[15]

J. M. Keynes made similar calculations of the purchasing-power-parity dollar rates of the pound, franc, and lira from August, 1919, to June, 1923. Comparing the calculated and actual rates, he reached conclusions similar to Graham's: ". . . the influences, which detract from the precision of the purchasing power parity theory have been in

[13] Milton Friedman and Anna Jacobson Schwartz, *A Monetary History of the United States 1867–1960*, Princeton, N.J.: Princeton University Press for the National Bureau of Economic Research, 1963, pp. 61–80, 85–86. The figures of 121 and 88 percent were read off charts on pp. 65 and 74.

[14] W. F. Stolper, "Purchasing Power Parity and the Pound Sterling from 1919–1925," *Kyklos*, II, 1948, esp. pp. 244, 247–249, 251. Calculating comparative-version parities on the basis of the prewar exchange rate and changes from prewar price levels in Britain and the United States, Stolper presents a chart of actual and theoretical exchange rates, but not the actual numbers. My calculations yield actual dollars-per-pound exchange rates for July as the following percentages of the corresponding purchasing-power-parity rates derived from United States and British cost-of-living indexes based on 1914: 113.8 in 1919, 98.8 in 1920, 101.7 in 1921, 106.0 in 1922, 99.4 in 1923, 94.8 in 1924, and 102.2 in 1925 (after the return to the gold standard). The underlying data are from League of Nations, *International Statistical Year-Book, 1929*, Geneva, 1930, pp. 241, 243, and from Board of Governors of the Federal Reserve System, *Banking and Monetary Statistics*, Washington, 1943, p. 681.

[15] The term "100% figure" refers to the purchasing-power parity as a percentage of the corresponding actual exchange rate. Frank D. Graham, *Exchange, Prices, and Production in Hyper-inflation: Germany, 1920–1923*, Princeton, N.J.: Princeton University Press, 1930, quotations from pp. 117, 121, underlying figures from pp. 118–120. Lester (*op. cit.*, pp. 200, 212) carried purchasing-power-parity calculations for the Danish and Norwegian kroner forward by quarter-years to 1927 and 1928 and found deviations of actual from calculated rates to be almost always within a few percent. In his study of trade and exchange rates after World War I, Jean Weiller encountered, among other difficulties, the fact that deviations from purchasing-power parity were seldom large enough to show clearly the effects of over- or undervaluation of currency. *L'influence du change sur le commerce extérieur*, Paris: Rivière, 1929, pp. 132–133, 192).

these cases small, on the whole, as compared with those which function in accord with it. ... The Purchasing Power Parity Theory, even in its crude form, has worked passably well."[16]

Since the Spanish peseta fluctuated all through the 1920s (and for several decades before), it provides particularly interesting evidence. A frequency distribution of actual monthly-average dollar rates on the peseta expressed as percentages of the corresponding purchasing-power parities for 1920 through 1929 shows that in only two months of this period did this percentage fall as low as the 77.5 to 82.5 range; in only three months did it rise as high as the 117.5 to 122.5 range. The actual rate kept within the range of 12.5 percent below to 12.5 percent above purchasing-power parity in 82.5 percent of the months.[17]

The period since World War II provides additional evidence. In the 81 months from October 1950, the actual monthly average of the fluctuating rate between the U.S. and Canadian dollars kept close to a calculated purchasing-power parity. With wholesale price indexes used in the calculations, the actual rate was within 3.5 percent of parity in 96 percent of the months; with cost-of-living indexes used, the actual rate stayed this close to the calculated parity in 83 percent of the months. Even *changes* from one quarter-year to the next in actual and in parity rates were generally correlated, feebly for calculations using cost-of-living indexes but to a statistically significant degree for calculations using wholesale price indexes.[18] Any such detectable short-run correspondence at all between exchange-rate and price movements is noteworthy, especially considering the narrow range of fluctuation of the rele-

vant variables in the Canadian experience. Consider a correlation of short-term changes in body weight and in food intake for a person whose weight and eating habits were both quite stable; given the narrowness of fluctuations actually experienced, statistical methods could hardly be expected to detect the *a priori* obvious association.

Peru, Mexico, and Thailand all experienced longer or shorter periods of exchange-rate variation beginning in the late 1940s; and they too exhibit an unmistakable correspondence between price levels and exchange rates, a correspondence that seemed to improve upon adjustment or abandonment of exchange-rate pegging or upon simplification of systems of fluctuating rates.

The Peruvian and Mexican experiences cover periods when exchange rates were sometimes pegged rather than continuously free to fluctuate, and pegging has been all but universal for other countries since the war. Comparison of fixed rates with purchasing-power parities, though a rather unfairly hard test of the doctrine, is not entirely irrelevant. Respectable correspondence would suggest either that relative price levels influenced what exchange rates could successfully be fixed or else that the domestic money supply in each country had to be regulated actively or passively so as to keep the home price level in line with foreign prices at prevailing exchange rates. Cassel himself noted that the rate of exchange between two gold-standard currencies must correspond to the ratio of their purchasing powers. "The purchasing power of each currency has to be regulated so as to correspond to that of gold"; only then will it be possible to keep exchange rates near their mint pars.[19]

Such considerations suggested working out purchasing-power parities for all countries whose relevant figures appeared in *International Financial Statistics*. Their actual exchange rates against the dollar in July 1957 were expressed as percentages of the computed rates. (For countries with multiple exchange rates clustering fairly close together, the average rate was used; countries

---

[16] J. M. Keynes, *A Tract on Monetary Reform*, London: Macmillan, 1923, pp. 99, 105.

[17] Derived from the actual and purchasing-power-parity rates in United States cents (computed with wholesale price indexes on a 1913 base) given in Walter H. Delaplane, "The Spanish Peseta since 1913" (unpublished dissertation), Durham, N.C.: Duke University, 1934, pp. 251–55.

[18] For details on this and other postwar evidence mentioned in the next few pages, see my "A Rehabilitation of Purchasing-Power Parity," *Journal of Political Economy*, Chicago: The University of Chicago Press, LXVI, December 1958, pp. 524–528. Copyright 1958 by The University of Chicago.

[19] Gustav Cassel, *Post-War Monetary Stabilization*, New York: Columbia University Press, 1928, p. 31.

with widely divergent multiple rates had to be omitted.) For countries publishing two or more wholesale indexes, the one *least* inclusive of internationally traded goods was chosen; for countries publishing both wholesale and cost-of-living indexes, an average of the two purchasing-power parities was compared with the actual exchange rate. A prewar base period was used (1937 for most countries), making the results reflect price and exchange-rate changes over an eventful span of about 20 years. For no one of the 30 countries that could be considered was the actual exchange rate in U.S. cents as low as 80 percent or as high as 200 percent of purchasing-power parity (the Philippine figure of 197 percent appeared quite exceptional). The actual-to-parity ratio fell inside the range of 75 to 125 percent for three-fourths of the countries; two-thirds of the countries had ratios between 80 and 120 percent.

Implications for Exchange Stability

Room hardly remains to doubt a broad correspondence between actual and purchasing-power-parity exchange rates, especially in comparison with the huge discrepancies to be expected if the doctrine were quite wrong. But "how close is close"? How rough can this correspondence be and still tend to discredit the worry about exchange-market instability due to low demand elasticities? An instance of poor correspondence between an actual and a calculated rate might be due to one or both of two conditions—low and perhaps perversely low elasticities, or the familiar statistical inaccuracies and ambiguities and "ancient-history" element in comparative-version parity calculations.

In considering the first of these possibilities, we must remember that if an unstable-equilibrium exchange rate did exist, stable equilibriums would necessarily flank it above and below. Now suppose that an actual and a purchasing-power-parity exchange rate diverge widely: each is half or double the other. The new actual rate would be half or double the base-period rate as adjusted into a parity in accordance with any change in price levels over the span of time involved

in the calculations. If the new exchange rate and the price-adjusted old exchange rate would both be workable and if we exclude the second (statistical-difficulties and "ancient-history") explanation of the discrepancy between them, then each must approximate one of three multiple-equilibrium levels explained in Chapter 8. Over the vast range of values in which the three multiple equilibriums (one unstable and two stable) might lie, they are in fact so close together that each is no less than half or no more than twice the other. Within this narrow range positions exist in which demands in international trade are inelastic enough to cause perverse operation of the exchange market. Yet the price level of imports would only have to rise from these positions by under 100 percent in order to press buyers so sharply against their budget restraints as to convert seriously inelastic import demands into elastic demands. It seems implausible that imports (from both the home and the foreign viewpoints) would be in such extremely inelastic demand as to cause exchange-market instability and yet would bulk so large in budgets that a less than doubling of their prices would bring the budget restraint into play enough to render the demand elastic. In view of these implications, even such large discrepancies as actual exchange rates of half or double the corresponding purchasing-power parities would hardly demonstrate the existence of multiple equilibriums and perverse elasticities. In fact, discrepancies so large are not at all common. If the perverse-elasticities case is advanced to explain such discrepancies as have actually been found, the multiple equilibriums implied by the argument would have to be implausibly close together.

It follows that observed discrepancies must be explained largely in terms of the second group of difficulties: inappropriate base periods; disequilibrium exchange rates (including base-period rates), often imposed by official pegging; tariffs, quotas, and other interferences with trade, payments, and exchange rates and changes in the stringency of these interferences; the attenuated meaningfulness of price-level comparisons over long spans of time; the crudity of some price indexes; distortion by price controls and rationing of some prices entering into indexes; distortions of relative prices by not yet digested inflations; and changes in the structure of national economies.

Most fundamentally, the comparative version of the purchasing-power-parity doctrine, used in all the calculations mentioned, is not the doctrine itself—and, in particular, is not its basic stabilizing-pressures aspect—but is, rather, a mere makeshift method of statistical application. The reasons for bothering with makeshift calculations of this sort are, first, that alternative approaches seem even worse and, second, that even the observed approximate validity of the rate-calculation aspect of the parity doctrine, despite all the statistical difficulties that might interfere, speaks well for its stabilizing-pressures aspect. Even crude calculations can indirectly provide some further "bits and pieces of evidence" on whether demand elasticities are high enough for proper operation of the international price mechanism.

The Influence of Exchange Rates on Prices

As already noted, the statistical evidence in apparent support of purchasing-power parity loses its force if exchange rates *determine* rather than reflect the price levels used in the calculations. But meaningless statistics would be among the least of the troubles from causality running in this direction. Exchange-rate variations might be ineffective or even self-aggravating. Either spontaneous depreciation of a free-market exchange rate or deliberate devaluation of a pegged rate might push up the country's general price level.[20] Any such inflationary impetus would

be objectionable both in its own right and also for tending to frustrate improvement in the balance of payments. Depreciation or devaluation does not become ineffective, however, merely because the home-currency prices of internationally traded goods go up; the sectional-price-levels analysis reveals this to be a key part of the adjustment mechanism. The worry is that not only internationally traded goods but goods in general might rise in price, frustrating the necessary change in price relations.

How might this happen? As the price of foreign exchange in home currency rose, so would the prices of imports and exports. These price increases might communicate themselves to domestic goods for which internationally traded goods were direct or indirect substitutes or into which they entered as raw materials. The cost of living would rise, unleashing pressures for higher wages, which in turn would push up costs of production and further feed the price spiral. The problem would be especially serious if contracts linked wages and other payments to price indexes. This is the general line of argument, anyway, and it is not to be dismissed summarily. Later pages of this chapter will mention historical episodes in which exchange depreciation did seem to spur inflationary spirals.

Much depends on whether domestic monetary conditions permit such a spiral. Given "monetary stability"—whose meaning will become more definite as the discussion proceeds—not even the prices of import and export goods and services would rise fully in proportion to the price of foreign exchange (unless home import demand and export supply were totally inelastic, which monetary stability itself seems to preclude, and unless the corresponding foreign supply and demand were infinitely elastic). In fact, some domestic prices would tend to go down. This can be shown in a preliminary way by adapting Fisher's equation of exchange so as to split up PT into prices of and transactions in domestic and internationally traded goods and services. Thus,

$$MV = P_d T_d + P_i T_i$$

---

[20] See Lionel Robbins, *Economic Planning and International Order*, London: Macmillan, 1937, pp. 288–289; Lionel Robbins, *The Economist in the Twentieth Century*, London: Macmillan, 1954, pp. 98-101; Paul A. Samuelson, "Disparity in Postwar Exchange Rates," in Seymour E. Harris (ed.), *Foreign Economic Policy for the United States*, Cambridge, Mass.: Harvard University Press, 1948, p. 404; Hubert Henderson, "The Function of Exchange Rates," *Oxford Economic Paper*, n.s. I, January 1949, esp. pp. 6–9; Sidney S. Alexander, "Effects of a Devaluation on a Trade Balance," IMF *Staff Papers*, II, April 1952; pp. 270–272, 274; and Scammell, *op. cit.*, pp. 91–92.

Suppose that MV, the total flow of expenditure of domestic money, does not rise. Then any rise in P_i, the price index of internationally traded goods, must be accompanied by a fall in one or more among T_i, T_d, and P_d. There is no strong reason to expect a fall in T_i, the total physical volume of transactions in internationally traded goods occurring on the home market and settled in home currency. Devaluation presumably increases exports and thus the total of home-market transactions in goods destined for export. On the other hand, devaluation *tends* to reduce imports. There is no need, however, for transactions in imports to fall by more than transactions in exports rise, particularly if expanded export earnings permit import purchases that had formerly been choked off by foreign-exchange rationing or import controls. T_d, the total physical volume of transactions in home-market goods, would hardly fall, either, unless as one result of a deflation of effective demand that would also tend to lower the prices of these goods. Hence increased prices of internationally traded goods will make P_d, the price index of domestic goods, tend to fall. Incidentally, "goods" is understood to include "services"; and the domestic price level whose fall is likely is a very inclusive one, taking into account, among other things, the prices of domestic factors of production.

Our reassuring conclusion rests so far on little more than an algebraic tautology. We may have to make some qualifications that hinge on what causes and what accompanies the exchange depreciation of the home currency, a question faced in the next section of this chapter. Meanwhile, it may be helpful to recast our reasoning with closer attention to the quantity of money and to velocity or the demand for cash balances. Suppose that depreciation does raise the home-currency prices of internationally traded goods. With no compensating declines in other prices, people would begin to find their cash balances too small in relation to their transactions, incomes, and wealth at the new higher average price level. They would therefore try to enlarge their cash balances by becoming less ready to buy

goods and securities and more ready to sell. As a result, prices would eventually fall until people again were satisfied with their cash balances (which add up to the existing money supply, assumed to be unchanged in nominal size). Though these downward price adjustments might encounter frictions and delays, causing recession and unemployment, the conclusion stands that any initial price rise provoked by exchange depreciation would be accompanied, on balance, not by further inflation but by some compensatory deflation. If the initial price rises are not reversed, then prices of other goods must fall—still assuming, of course, no inflation of the money supply. Conversely, if exchange appreciation depressed some prices, others would rise in compensation.

Even with a stable money supply, however, it is abstractly conceivable that depreciation could increase total spending and the general price level. It and the accompanying rise in the prices of international goods might undermine confidence in the future purchasing power of money and so lead people to economize more than before in demanding cash balances.[21] During rapid monetary inflation, velocity does indeed rise in this way. But with a stable money supply, any effect of depreciation on velocity should prove temporary. A continuing inflation of expenditure and prices would presuppose a continuing rise in velocity and not merely a shift to a higher level (not merely, that is, a once-and-for-all shift to greater economizing on real cash balances). Yet a single upward shift in velocity is the normal response to expectations of steadily continuing price inflation: a continuing rise in velocity would presuppose expectations of continually *accelerating* inflation, which, to be well justified, would in turn presuppose a continuous acceleration of velocity. Attempts to conceive of inflation proceeding by its own bootstraps, with the money supply stable, thus lead to contradictions. Actually, when people saw

---

[21] Completeness requires mentioning one additional but probably minor reason: the lessened buying power of the earnings of home factors of production over internationally traded goods may make people feel too poor to afford holding as much purchasing power as before in the form of cash.

that the dreaded inflation was not continuing, they would seek to replenish their temporarily and inconveniently small holdings of real cash balances. This drop-back in velocity would stop or reverse any initial rise in the general price level. (No one argues that velocity always returns to one definite level. Innumerable factors influence it. The present argument merely denies that movements in velocity are *self*-perpetuating.) Inflationary anticipations would be especially unlikely if domestic policy were known to be aiming resolutely at domestic monetary stability.

The most plausible worry is that the domestic money supply might passively *respond* to changes in exchange rates and prices. The monetary and banking system might adjust the money supply to the "needs of trade" in the sense of the real-bills doctrine; increased money values of goods might, for instance, be thought to justify bigger bank loans to finance their production and marketing. If escalator clauses or labor-union pressure geared domestic prices or wages to import and export prices, the authorities might permit accommodating increases in the money supply to avoid unemployment. This problem would tie in with the broader one of institutional arrangements to make full employment compatible with monetary stability. A government budget deficit might enter the picture. Whenever money-supply variations do permit a causal chain running from exchange rates to prices, the situation is due not to inexorable linkages but to policy, active or passive.

Aside from the matter of which way causation ran, such situations, if observed, would support rather than refute the purchasing-power-parity relation between price levels and exchange rates. They would further suggest that if the money supply had been autonomously controlled, the exchange rate would not have dominated the price level. Skepticism about observed correlations between exchange rates and ratios of price levels might perhaps be saved by contending that the price indexes used in purchasing-power-parity calculations are made up chiefly of those prices that are governed by exchange rates, with the prices that undergo compensating opposite changes largely left out. Indeed, we should be willing to calculate purchasing-power parities with very inclusive price indexes, when available, and not solely with price indexes for internationally traded staples or even solely with wholesale price indexes. In addition, we should consider whether the structure of a country's relative prices is so subject to the alleged distortion as to rob purchasing-power-parity calculations of significance. Actually, various domestic and international goods and services are related in price, though not rigidly, by the fact that some are ingredients of others, by the use of common factors of production, and by direct or indirect substitutability in consumption.[22] Furthermore, the monetary factors which primarily determine a country's general price level cause a parallelism in major price movements of domestic and international goods that overshadows any divergence associated with exchange-rate changes.

For many commodities, changes in the quantity shipped internationally amount to only a small fraction of the quantities appearing on markets at home and abroad, so that changes in trade flows may affect domestic prices only slightly. Besides, though arbitrage in one particular commodity would hardly suffice to check an exchange-rate deviation, the rate would need to move only a little further to affect trade in another commodity and then perhaps another and another. The rate could hardly dominate all the many individual price parities and pairs of commodity points. Rather, these would provide a "defense in depth" against random exchange-rate fluctuations.

A crude analogy illustrates the stronger influence of prices on exchanges than of exchanges on prices. Suppose we put a large magnet and a needle close together on a slippery table. Each will attract the other, but the final position of the two depends more on the magnet's than on the needle's initial position. Similarly, in free markets prices domi-

---

[22] The close price interdependence among supposedly "domestic" and supposedly "international" commodities is the main theme of Zapoleon's article, already cited; see also Condliffe, *op. cit.*, pp. 306–310.

nate exchanges rather than the reverse. An uncontrolled exchange rate is a sensitive and mobile price. Many goods and services have "sticky" prices. Price levels will sooner or later respond to the pressure of changed monetary conditions, but, barring monetary instability and barring an accompanying widespread use of escalator clauses, it is farfetched to suppose that flexible exchange rates will dominate even the relatively sticky prices of a great many goods and services.

Devaluation, Controls, and Prices

How devaluation or free-market depreciation of a currency affects a country's price level depends very much on the previous state of the balance of payments. If a realistic new exchange rate *replaces* trade-throttling import and exchange controls that had been maintaining an artificial equilibrium in the face of currency overvaluation, the result may be the opposite of inflationary. If controls had previously been concentrating inflationary pressures entirely on the home economy, a devaluation that permits exports and so also imports to expand need have no net inflationary effect. Devaluation may help undo previous distortions in the relations between prices and incomes at home and abroad. "Indeed, devaluation may be an essential part of the process of change from inflation to stability."[23] Trade flows more freely. A more efficient pattern of specialization results and tends to raise what is loosely but traditionally called the total real income of the devaluating country. If the flow of expenditure and *money* income remains unchanged, the rise in *real* income implies a fall in the general price level.

The argument in this simple version assumes not only constant money expenditure[24] but also competitive conditions and full employment both before and after the devaluation. (If noncompetitive distortions and underutilitization of resources had previously prevailed, it would be trivial to show that remedies involving devaluation might not necessarily raise the general price level.) The argument further assumes price and wage flexibility, so that shifts of demand away from particular goods and services will cause price reductions rather than just reduced purchases and output. (Even if prices and wages are "sticky," however, their downward *tendencies* mean that devaluation is not unequivocally inflationary.)

Perhaps the chief qualification has to do with the possibility that the trade controls associated with the earlier currency overvaluation might have been improving the country's terms of trade; sacrifice of this improvement may cost the country more in welfare or real income than it gains from an improved allocation of resources. In other words, the country's trade restrictions and currency overvaluation might have been approximately "optimal" (in the sense of the terms-of-trade argument) before devaluation and might become definitely suboptimal afterwards. It is unnecessary to repeat here the questions of Chapter 9 about how individuals benefit from "the country's" artificially favorable terms of trade, about how relevant to actual policy the concept of optimum terms is when conditions are always changing and detailed knowledge is unavailable, and about whether retaliation might not obstruct a country's efforts to benefit at the expense of its neighbors. Conceivably, anyway, devaluation and trade liberalization might reduce real national income, implying a rise in the general price level.[25]

---

[23] Edward M. Bernstein, "Strategic Factors in Balance of Payments Adjustment," IMF *Staff Papers,* **V,** August 1956, pp. 166–168. Egon Sohmen formalizes this general line of argument in "The Effect of Devaluation on the Price Level," *Quarterly Journal of Economics,* **LXXII,** May 1958, pp. 273–283.

[24] Bernstein even sees one case in which devaluation would cut expenditure relative to available output. In a country with full employment and a trade deficit financed by foreign aid or a capital inflow, devaluation

means that importers pay more than before for foreign exchange and exporters receive more for their foreign-exchange earnings. Real income is transferred from importers to exporters. Also, the government receives more from importers for whatever foreign exchange is provided by foreign aid. This may help cut expenditure and bring it into balance with output plus aid. *Op. cit.,* pp. 166–167.

[25] Sohmen (*loc. cit.*) explicitly recognized this possibility but judged that trade is typically restricted to far more than the optimal extent in the world of today, so that devaluation and relaxation of controls would mean moving towards rather than away from the optimum.

In brief, any price-*lowering* tendency of devaluation presupposes the conditions in which trade liberalization would be beneficial in the traditional sense. But the full benefits depend on a time-consuming adjustment toward a new pattern of production more nearly in accordance with comparative advantage. In the short run, however, there is no conclusive presumption that devaluation will lower rather than raise the general price level. Whatever happens to other prices, the home-currency prices of exports will rise.[26] The possibility of a short-run upward average price movement despite the downward long-run tendency points to the moral "that there is all the more reason to take those measures early whose fruits are known to take some time to mature."[27]

Further doubt concerns just what type of price level it is that sooner or later tends downward. Declines in the prices of domestic goods and services, including labor and other factors of production, may indeed offset rises in the prices of international goods in a very comprehensive price index. But this gives no assurance that a more ordinary wholesale or retail price index will go down or even hold steady. Neither the equation-of-exchange nor the cash-balance analysis ensures that devaluation will not raise the money cost of living to consumers. A partial answer is that devaluation will necessarily tend to raise import prices only if imports had previously been free of restrictions. But if restrictions had existed to force balance-of-payments equilibrium despite an overvalued currency and are now simply replaced by an equilibrium exchange rate, imports need not become any scarcer and more expensive within the devaluing country than before. Expanded export earnings may even permit more abundant and therefore cheaper imports.

The argument, to summarize, is that removal of exchange-rate disequilibrium tends to make the use of resources more efficient and the price level lower, given stable monetary conditions. A technical characteristic of index numbers tends to obscure this result, however, in historical examples of actual devaluations. For practical reasons, most available price indexes are of the Laspeyres type, in which prices are weighted by the quantities of goods and services bought in some base period. Such an index has the bias of not being able to do justice to the "qualitative" improvements in real income, including an increase in the variety of foreign goods and services possibly made available by relaxation of trade controls. For goods and services that become available only with devaluation and trade liberalization, the pre-devaluation prices are in effect infinite; yet their cheapening cannot show up in the usual price index. For other goods, the bias still exists, though to a slighter extent. In the assortment of goods bought after devaluation, those whose prices have fallen will have gained ground relative to those whose prices have risen; yet this shift in buying patterns is not reflected in price indexes of the usual kind.[28]

The worry that depreciation tends to be inflationary implies that overvaluation of a currency on the exchanges can be anti-inflationary. This idea must rest on some implicit contrast between overvaluation accompanied by a current-account deficit and a devaluation which restores balance-of-payments equilibrium. Actually, the emphasis belongs on whether or not a current-account deficit exists rather than merely on the exchange rate. An excess of imports over exports can indeed have an anti-inflationary influence while it lasts. Excess imports are a net addition to the goods and services available on home markets and do tend to hold down prices. Furthermore, the sale from official reserves or from the proceeds of foreign loans or gifts of foreign exchange to pay for the excess imports can act like an open-market sale of securities, enabling the authorities to mop up some of the domestic supply of bank reserves and money. When a current-account deficit actually exists in the balance of payments, the price level is being kept down by a subsidy in

[26] Randall Hinshaw, "Further Comment," *Quarterly Journal of Economics,* **LXXII,** November 1958, pp. 624–625.

[27] Egon Sohmen, "Reply," *Quarterly Journal of Economics,* **LXXII,** November 1958, p. 629.

[28] Cf. *Ibid.,* pp. 628–629.

effect being granted to domestic purchasers either by their own government, which is selling its accumulated external reserves at an artificially low price, or else by foreigners who may be making loans or grants. These anti-inflationary effects can last only so long as finance is available for an actual deficit.

When a country devalues to remove an actual deficit—rather than to get rid of controls that had previously been forcing an equilibrium—the resulting price increases, particularly of international-trade goods, are appropriate. They tend to discourage consumption in general by lowering the real purchasing power of the current incomes of domestic factors of production.[29] This reduction in current real incomes from the point of view of individual recipients is not necessarily a matter for regret, since continued subsidization of current consumption by drafts on foreign reserves or loans or grants would mean risking a sudden forced return to reality in some future crisis. An end to this subsidization out of the reserves does, however, mean an end to the temporary net inflow of goods and services into the country that had corresponded to the deficit. In this respect, the impact is undoubtedly inflationary.

The anti-inflationary possibilities of currency overvaluation as long as an actual balance-of-payments deficit can be financed are symmetrical with the already familiar ways in which undervaluation and a surplus can be inflationary. The latter is a more realistically important possibility because the limits to a surplus in size and duration are looser than the limits to a deficit. Recognizing the inflationary impact of undervaluation does not discredit the purchasing-power-parity doctrine. For one thing, the process does involve expansion of the money supply and could not go far without it. Furthermore, the doctrine is particularly relevant to a system of free exchange rates; yet undervaluation of a currency, together with inflationary official accumulation of growing foreign-exchange reserves, is characteristic of pegged rates.

---

[29] For a parable illustrating why this is appropriate when a deficit is to be remedied, see Hinshaw, *op. cit.,* esp. pp. 620–623.

Depreciation and Domestic Inflation
Historical Examples of Exchange

Historical experience, by itself, cannot settle the question whether devaluation is inflationary. Devaluation or free-market depreciation has often registered inflation due to other causes. Yet striking instances are well known, as in Europe after World War I, in which exchange depreciation appeared to push up internal prices. In Austria after late 1920, and especially in the second half of 1921 and in the summer of 1922, the price of foreign exchange appeared to lead the rise of the price level and of the bank-note circulation. Rising prices of imported materials boosted domestic production costs. Producers began estimating costs in foreign currency, adding a profit margin, and translating the result into Austrian crowns at the latest exchange rate. Retailers adopted similar practices. Escalator clauses in labor contracts reinforced the influence of exchange rates. The spiral of exchange rates dramatized the folly of holding savings in the form of rapidly melting crowns. The printing presses rolled to cover government budget deficits, which, from 1919 through 1922, amounted to half or two-thirds of government expenditures. The more the crown sank, the harder financial reform looked. Government spending, including costly food subsidies until their belated abolition in 1922, rose roughly in step with the price level. Specific taxes and the prices of goods sold by the state (such as tobacco and rail transportation) lagged, and much of the real value of income taxes vanished in the lag between assessment and collection. Superficially, at least, exchange depreciation *caused* the price increases, the deficits, and the swelling issues of paper money. This interpretation gains apparent support from the fact that exchange-rate stabilization in August 1922 preceded price-level stabilization in September. Exchange stabilization was started artificially: when supply and demand were not equal at the desired rate, an official agency made up the difference. Foreign loans and government pledges of financial probity helped restore confidence and make stabilization possible.

With confidence returning, the demand to hold purchasing power in the form of crown balances revived; and to prevent this slump in velocity from causing a disastrous deflation, the Austrian National Bank issued much additional money, paying out crowns to acquire foreign exchange.[30]

The German hyperinflation that climaxed in 1923 is an even more striking example of the apparent sequence of exchange depreciation, price increases, swollen government deficits, and fresh issues of paper money. It is hardly surprising that depreciation of the mark on the foreign exchanges often ran ahead of price increases inside Germany, since the government's chief method of getting foreign exchange for reparations payments to the Allies was to have the Reichsbank print new mark notes and sell them on the exchange market.[31] Frenchmen, in the mid-1920s, could not be sure that their franc would not suffer the same virtual annihilation as the crown and mark. From 1922 (and especially from 1924) through the middle of 1926, fears of mounting inflation centered on the government's financial difficulties and showed themselves most promptly on the foreign-exchange market.

In Austria, Germany, and France alike, the stage of inflation in which exchange-rate movements loomed as a causal element came only after several years of wartime and postwar government deficits financed by the printing press. Even in the advanced stage of the German inflation, according to Bresciani-Turroni, continuing exchange depreciation and price increases were dependent on continuing currency issues. Whenever monetary expansion slackened, German merchants and industrialists had to dishoard some of their foreign exchange onto the market, and the exchange rate improved. If the government and the Reichsbank could have held the line against fresh issues of money, confidence in the mark would have returned, the ab-

normally low demand for real cash balances would have proved temporary, and the mark would have strengthened. This is suggested by developments in November 1923, when the government finally mustered the energy for monetary and budget reforms.[32]

A lag of monetary expansion behind price spurts and exchange depreciation in the process of rapid inflation proves little or nothing about true causation. The sequence typically reflects anticipations. When a government has pumped out new money month after month, people may reasonably expect the money to keep on deteriorating. A lag of prices behind exchange rates proves similarly little. A currency does not lose value at one stroke or at a uniform pace with respect to all goods and services. Some prices are "stickier" than others. An unpegged exchange rate is among the least sticky of prices. It is especially prompt to reflect actual and anticipated changes in price levels and monetary conditions.[33] But this is not at all the same thing as *determining* price levels and monetary conditions.

China after 1870 provides a plausible example of the exchange rate appearing to determine the prices not only of internationally traded goods but also of services and immovable goods. China was on a silver standard. After about 1870, when the major trading countries began to demonetize silver, the gold price of silver dropped year by year. After an intermediate rise during World War I, the price of silver resumed its downward trend in 1920. As China's silver currency depreciated in relation to gold currencies, wholesale commodity prices rose in port cities. The prices increases spread inland, affecting retail markets, the cost of living, and wage rates. Even rents, leases, and land values were gradually reappraised.[34] Yet this experience does *not* show that exchange deprecia-

[30] J. van Walré de Bordes, *The Austrian Crown*, London: P. S. King & Son, Ltd., 1924, *passim*.

[31] Benjamin M. Anderson, *Economics and the Public Welfare*, New York: Van Nostrand, 1949, p. 94; Graham, *op. cit.*, pp. 135–136.

[32] Costanino Bresciani-Turroni, *The Economics of Inflation*, London: Allen & Unwin, 1937, pp. 398-402.

[33] For supporting examples from the history of the greenbacks during the American Civil War, see two works by Wesley C. Mitchell: *A History of the Greenbacks*, Chicago: University of Chicago Press, 1903, esp. pp. 187-238, 209-210, 276-279; and *Gold, Prices, and Wages under the Greenback Standard*, Berkeley: University of California Press, 1908, esp. pp. 40-41, 251, 282.

[34] Condliffe, *op. cit.*, pp. 307-309, 396-397.

tion, in itself, can push up the general domestic price level. Not only did China's currency depreciate on the exchanges; the money supply also rose. The decline in the world commodity value of silver made silver flow into China, where, if the inflow had not occurred, silver would have retained a higher purchasing power than elsewhere. Growth of the money supply is the true explanation of rising prices. Instead of showing anything about how exchange fluctuations would affect internal prices under a system of independently managed national paper currencies, the Chinese experience illustrates the repercussions on trade, money, and prices of exchange undervaluation of a currency on a commodity standard.

Summary

The purchasing-power-parity doctrine is more concretely meaningful than rival theories of exchange-rate determination. The usual *a priori* objections to the doctrine, whatever they may imply about prospects for its accurate statistical application, do not discredit its relevance to appraising the probable stability of free exchange markets. Comparisons of actual exchange rates with calculated purchasing-power parities generally show a correspondence which is particularly impressive in view of all the statistical difficulties (as distinguished from errors of principle) that might blur it.

The possibility of causation running from exchange rates to prices hardly discredits the parity doctrine. Regarding whether devaluation or depreciation is generally infla-

tionary, certain distinctions are crucial. First, a devaluation that cures a previous actual balance-of-payments deficit and thus ends the temporary pleasures of living beyond current national resources does tend to raise prices. Devaluation to replace controls that had previously been forcing an equilibrium is quite another matter. Second is the question whether devaluation carries the foreign-exchange value of the home currency toward an equilibrium level or away from and below it. Equilibrium exchange rates and the avoidance of trade-balancing controls tend to promote resource allocation in accordance with comparative advantage and thus tend to be anti-inflationary, at least in the long run. It is pegged undervaluation of a currency, together with the resulting export surplus, that tends, in contrast, to be inflationary. Third is whether or not the domestic money supply is being kept stable (that is, either fixed or growing only in line with real economic growth). Only if monetary inflation is occurring at home or is being precariously suppressed in a psychologically inflationary atmosphere is exchange depreciation likely to feed an inflationary spiral. A policy of internal balance would leave little reason to fear domestic inflation resulting either from devaluation to an equilibrium level or from free exchange-rate fluctuations in lieu of controls to maintain balance-of-payments equilibrium. But if a country cannot or will not maintain internal balance independently and if it needs the anti-inflationary discipline of potential balance-of-payments crises at fixed exchange rates, then, by assumption, exchange flexibility is inflationary in a permissive sense.

Speculation

◈ II

This chapter reviews the grounds for perhaps the most common worry about free exchange rates—that disruptive speculation might dominate the market. The chapter tries to clarify distinctions between self-aggravating and stabilizing speculation and show what conditions are conducive to one kind or the other. In reviewing theories of speculative behavior, it considers equilibrium positions from the viewpoints of speculators themselves, the supposed natural selection of speculators, and analogies between speculation in currencies and in commodities and securities. It compares and contrasts speculation under free and under pegged exchange rates.

When a currency shows signs of depreciating or appreciating, speculators may hasten to sell or buy it and so intensify the movement. Even commodity trade might react perversely: the rise of import and export prices expressed in a currency depreciating under speculative pressure, instead of checking the country's imports and spurring its exports in the normal way, might breed expectations of further price movements and so hasten imports and retard exports. With exchange speculation and perverse responses of trade reinforcing each other, even the country's internal economic conditions might be disrupted. At least, so goes a familiar line of argument.[1]

Speculators' Equilibrium

How generally applicable is that argument? To begin an appraisal, let us consider the decision-making of an individual speculator. Equilibrium in his holdings of foreign exchange may be described by the equation[2]

$$e = (I - i) + (r - c),$$

where

e = the expected percentage rise in the home-currency price of foreign exchange (e is negative if foreign exchange is expected to decline on the market; the following discussion refers to speculative purchases of foreign exchange, but it could easily be modified to deal with transactions in the opposite direction)

I = the interest rate in the home country

i = the interest rate abroad

r = the subjective allowance for risk involved in holding foreign exchange and, in particular, for uncertainty about the expected movement in the exchange rate

c = the marginal yield of intangible convenience provided by foreign-exchange assets. (For many speculators, c may be substantially zero, or, if the marginal convenience yield

---

[1] See Ragnar Nurkse, *International Currency Experience,* League of Nations, 1944, esp. pp. 210-211.

One must be careful in worrying about speculation on capital account and current account both. As Milton Friedman has pointed out (*Essays in Positive Economics,* Chicago: University of Chicago Press, 1953, p. 176n.), Nurkse seems to be asserting an arithmetical impossibility —that destabilizing transactions may occur on both ac-

counts simultaneously in a context in which the two exhaust the balance of payments.

For lurid textbook visions of speculation under fluctuating exchange rates, see Leland J. Pritchard, *Money and Banking,* Boston: Houghton Mifflin, 1958, pp. 541-544, and Theodore Morgan, *Introduction to Economics,* 2d ed., Englewood Cliffs, N.J.: Prentice-Hall, 1956, pp. 667-668.

[2] The analysis centered around this equation leans primarily on S. C. Tsiang, "A Theory of Foreign-Exchange Speculation under a Floating Exchange System," *Journal of Political Economy,* LXVI, October 1958, pp. 399-418, which in turn develops ideas of J. M. Keynes and Nicholas Kaldor. Several modifications here require absolving Tsiang for possible errors while crediting him with the general approach.

of domestic assets is also taken into account and *c* interpreted as the excess of the marginal convenience yield of foreign assets over that of domestic assets, it may even be negative.)

These symbols all refer to percentages over time spans of the same length, perhaps one month.

The equation describes the situation in which a speculator would wish neither to increase nor decrease his holdings of foreign exchange: the marginal revenue he expects on them equals the marginal cost, adjusted to allow for uncertainty. At the margin, his expected gain on foreign exchange equals the net interest cost of borrowing (or not lending) funds at home and placing them abroad (a negative cost if the interest rate were higher abroad than at home) plus risk allowance net of convenience-yield.

As a speculator's holdings of foreign exchange grow, other things being equal, the total of the terms on the right side of the equation rises. His subjective risk allowance rises as he puts more and more of his eggs in one basket. Any partially offsetting convenience-yield on foreign assets declines in accordance with the principle of diminishing returns or diminishing marginal utility. The interest rate the speculator must pay on domestic money borrowed to finance his operations may rise as lenders grow wary of his increasing debt at home and increasing long position in foreign exchange. More realistically, we may regard *I* as indicating not only a rising domestic interest rate in the strict sense of the term but also a tighter rationing of credit to the speculator as his debt grows.

For speculators as a class, the risk premium, convenience-yield, and home and foreign interest rates must be taken as averages, in some sense, of the ones pertaining to individual speculators. Still, as speculative holdings of foreign exchange grow, *r-c* moves in the same direction as for an individual speculator, and so do interest rates. Increased borrowing at home and lending abroad would tend to raise interest rates or tighten credit rationing at home and depress interest rates abroad.[3]

The behavior of *e,* the expected increase in the price of foreign exchange, is more uncertain. Although purchases by a single atomistic speculator would hardly influence present and expected future exchange rates, the aggregate purchases of all speculators might well do so. At the worst, speculative purchases might cause or intensify an uptrend in the rate, raising *e* and perhaps even raising it faster than the terms on the right side of the equation. Expectations might become self-justifying. This argument cuts two ways: if the fundamental determinants of exchange rates are stable and if speculators happen to operate in accordance with them, the idea of a normal range of rates arises and, barring sharp changes in fundamentals, becomes self-reinforcing. Random break-outs from the normal range would seem like fleeting opportunities for profit, and seizing them would tend to reverse them.[4]

Even if speculators kept adding to their *stocks* of foreign exchange for some time, this would not necessarily imply continued growth in their demand for a *flow* into these stocks per day, week, or month. Even while still adding to their stocks, they might no

---

[3] The home interest rate rises under two influences:

(1) the primary effect of the increased demand for loans (or reduced supply of loans) by the foreign-exchange speculators, and (2) the secondary effect of the reduced supply of loans (or increased demand for loans) by people in general, who may desire to hold increased transactions cash balances because of the increased flow of income and expenditure (perhaps at a slightly increased price level) that may have been caused by the country's export surplus corresponding to the net speculative purchases of foreign exchange.

The more flexibly the interest rate responds to these two pressures, the less induced change will occur in money income and in the price level. In the extreme case where the money supply is kept constant and where the level of the interest rate has no effect whatever on desired cash holdings, the rise of the interest rate in response to the pressure of the speculators' demands for funds will suffice to choke off an equal amount of demand for funds for investment and consumption, so that the inflationary effect on total expenditure will be absent. The overall "cost-push" effect of the rise in the prices of foreign exchange and of imports and exports would then presumably be negligible, since it would be unsupported by an increase in the total flow of spending. See *ibid.,* pp. 406-407.

[4] See Guillermo Subercaseaux, *Le Papier-Monnaie,* (trans. from Spanish), Paris: M. Giard and E. Brière, 1920, pp. 201-204. According to Subercaseaux, the idea of normality had a stabilizing influence in the markets for the Russian and Austrian paper currencies in the nineteenth century.

longer be contributing to bidding up the exchange rate (as distinguished from keeping it up). While the total on the right side of the equation continued to rise, the basis for self-justifying upward revisions in *e* would disappear. Unless nonspeculative fundamentals were tending to push the rate up, the flow of speculative demand would hold steady, slow down, stop, or reverse itself.

Speculative trends lacking an objective basis meet still other built-in checks. At any hour and at any price prevailing in a free, unpegged market, effective bullish and bearish sentiments are pretty evenly matched. Otherwise, the free-market price would already be different from what it in fact is. The mere fact that it has been rising for some time does not mean that people quite generally expect it to be still higher an hour or a month later. A speculator can switch sides. While some new bulls may appear as a price climbs, some bulls turn into bears, and conversely as a price falls. In one respect, the rate movements caused by speculation themselves tend to weaken the incentives for more such trading. Suppose speculators expect the peso to weaken to 60 to the dollar from the current rate of 50. Their initial sales depress the peso to, say, 52 per dollar, and the knowledge that profit-taking will later add to the demand for pesos tends to support the expected future rate at, say, 58. The expected profit margin shrinks from 10 pesos per dollar to 6; some speculation tends to reduce the expected profit from further speculation.[5] Even when operating on the basis of wrong forecasts, speculators tend to move the current and expected future rates against themselves, thus limiting their expected profit and the volume of their operations.

This mention of selling pesos in hopes of buying them back cheaper reminds us obliquely about forward exchange. Does our earlier approach based on the equation $e = (I - i) + (r - c)$ remain valid when speculators operate in forward and not just spot exchange? Consider speculators buying some foreign currency forward. The dealers making contracts with them will buy spot exchange to keep their positions covered, temporarily withdrawing funds from the domestic loan market and supplying them to the foreign market. If these dealers for some reason failed to cover by buying spot exchange, the bid-up forward rate and the not yet affected spot rate would give others an opportunity for profitable arbitrage in buying spot and selling forward exchange, temporarily transferring loanable funds abroad. Interest rates would tend, though perhaps only weakly, to rise at home and fall abroad. In accordance with the principle of interest parities, this would mean a larger premium (or smaller discount) on forward exchange in relation to spot than in the absence of the speculation and the resulting arbitrage. The relation between spot and forward rates would move in a way unfavorable to further speculation. (In oversimplified terms, the speculators would bid the forward rate against themselves.) These movements correspond, loosely, to the rise in $I - i$ in the earlier analysis. As for *c*, the marginal convenience-yield, it does not accrue to the speculators themselves when they are not holding spot exchange; but it does accrue either to the dealers who acquire spot exchange to cover their positions as counterparties in forward contracts with speculators or to others who acquire it in arbitrage. Their *c* presumably does go down as their holdings go up, affecting their willingness to make contracts and thus affecting the spread between forward and spot exchange rates much as a rise in home and fall in foreign interest rates. The risk premium *r* rises on the more-eggs-in-one-basket principle as speculators go longer in foreign exchange, regardless of whether they do so by forward or spot transactions.

On the left side of the equation, the expected rise in the price of foreign exchange likewise presumably behaves in pretty much the same way, regardless of whether speculators operate spot or forward. Current rate movements still affect and respond to expectations. The currently prevailing spot and forward rates move closely together, any small spread conforming to the interest-parities relation, in turn affected by changes

[5] Cf. J. E. Meade, *The Balance of Payments,* London: Oxford University Press, 1951, pp. 219-220.

equally taken into account in the analysis of pure spot speculation (changes, that is, in I, i, and c).

The self-limiting aspect of speculators' bidding rates against themselves also still holds good when speculators operate by buying forward and later, after taking delivery of foreign exchange under their maturing contracts, selling spot. (Typically, the speculators will not take actual delivery and then resell the exchange in a separate transaction; they will simply receive or pay the net amount of their gain or loss. The effect, though, is the same.) Whether we suppose speculation to take place only in the spot market or in the forward market also thus leaves the analysis the same in its essentials. Assuming spot operations helps keep the discussion from being cumbersome.

Self-aggravating Speculation

Having justified glossing over the distinction between spot and forward speculation, we return to search for further ways in which exchange speculation might conceivably be self-aggravating rather than self-limiting. Bear speculation on the home currency (bull speculation on foreign exchange) could conceivably contribute to continuing inflation of domestic prices and money incomes. Far from restraining itself as it ran counter to the fundamental conditions governing the relative values of currencies, speculation might determine these fundamentals. Conceivably the rise in the price of foreign exchange might discourage any *actual* capital outflow in the aggregate; speculators on the two sides of the market might just be dealing with each other. Any actual net purchases of foreign exchange by speculators as a group must be matched by sales by nonspeculators; any actual net outflow of capital must be matched by an export surplus in goods and services; sheer arithmetic demands this. Under free exchange rates, as Chapter 6 has shown, the combination of capital outflow, exchange depreciation, and current-account surplus has an expansionary tendency in the home economy.

The process has two interrelated aspects.

First, the rise in the price of foreign exchange may exert an upward "cost push" on domestic prices and wages by way of increased home-currency prices of import and export goods (perhaps including both raw materials and cost-of-living items). The export surplus means that real goods and services in the aggregate have become scarcer than before at home. Second, the rise in exports or fall in imports may have an expansionary "multiplier" effect on home incomes. The velocity of money rises. The persons who reduce their demands for domestic cash balances relative to income and expenditure are the speculators themselves or the persons induced to cut down their cash balances by a rise in interest rates or by expectations of inflation. So far as the factors considered here are concerned, the process will not level off until speculators become content with their holdings of domestic and foreign money. The inflationary process is essentially the same as one due to a widespread desire to shift from cash into real goods. In fact, we might well think of speculators as shifting into the real goods corresponding to the country's export surplus and then selling these goods to the foreigners for foreign money. This fiction illuminates the principles involved.

Merely describing these effects raises doubts about their strength. Desired shifts from domestic cash balances into foreign exchange must ordinarily be small in relation to the total domestic money supply and the flow of domestic income and expenditure. Except in a time of rapid inflation, the foreign-exchange speculators would be only a minority of the population. Even the speculators cannot reduce their domestic cash balances below zero, and there is also a fuzzy limit, at least, to how much they might borrow from the cash balances of others. Not only their ability but also their desire to keep on exchanging domestic for foreign money weakens as their speculative positions grow, as our earlier analysis suggests. Conceivably, self-justifying bear speculation on the home currency might hinge on expectations that kept an inflationary rise in velocity going— it is often easy to obscure economic principles by an *ad hoc* appeal to expectations—but whether the expectations can persist in the absence of any basis more objective than their own consequences is open to the doubts mentioned in Chapter 10.

The only really plausible ways that speculation might remain cumulatively self-reinforcing all involve monetary expansion. The central bank might create fresh domestic monetary reserves to rescue commercial banks beset by unexpectedly large adverse clearing balances in the unstable economic climate or beset by a run of depositors anxious to have actual currency immediately available for buying foreign exchange or other assets. The initial upward push on the price level and spending stream might cause monetary expansion through a government budget deficit or a banking policy compliant with the supposed "needs of trade." An economy whose money supply thus responded passively, continually "ratifying" or "supporting" otherwise limited upward pushes on prices, would be unstable even without international contacts. Foreign exchange is just one more asset persons may fly into when they fear for the value of the home currency; it is just one among many potential triggers of disturbance. The lack of positive control over the money supply, rather than speculation in particular, is what calls for a remedy.

Even in this most unfavorable case of continuing monetary inflation, speculation need not drive exchange rates cumulatively out of contact with the purchasing-power ratio of home and foreign money. In a severe and continuing inflation, interest rates include a "price premium": lenders insist on and borrowers will pay enough to cover the expected rise in the price level. The high money cost of borrowing to finance speculative purchases of foreign exchange and the alternative opportunity to preserve the real value of one's capital by making loans at interest rates high enough to more than compensate for the expected rise in prices tend to restrain the speculative demand for foreign exchange. (This is another implication of the equation $e = I - i + r - c$.) If people should come to expect an accelerated rise in the prices of domestic goods and foreign exchange alike, then the domestic interest rate is likely to

incorporate a still larger price premium, and what would otherwise be a stimulus to intensified demands for foreign exchange again is counterbalanced.[6]

Speculation and Welfare

More will be said later about speculation that is less violent but still destabilizing. Meanwhile, the foregoing discussion should not suggest that speculation is characteristically harmful and that the only apology for it concerns possible limits to its extent. On the contrary, speculation at its best can contribute to welfare, understood in any common-sense way. Suppose that the market rate on the Ruritanian crown, free from official intervention, keeps Ruritania's external transactions on current account always in balance in the absence of private borrowing, lending, and speculation. Now the foreign demand for Ruritanian products slumps. The crown weakens from an old rate of 5 to a new rate of 6 per dollar, restricting imports and supporting exports. At home, imports become scarcer and more expensive in relation to wages and other factor earnings. Assuming omniscience, we further suppose that the slump in foreign demand, the worsened trading opportunities, the crown's depreciation, and the corresponding scarcity of foreign-trade goods inside Ruritania all are temporary: the situation is fated to right itself again in six months. If so, it would be a particular hardship for the Ruritanians to concentrate their necessary frugality with foreign-trade goods solely during these six months. They would benefit if they could somehow transfer some foreign-trade goods from the future, when they will be relatively abundant again and of correspondingly low marginal utility, to the present time of scarcity and high marginal utility. Speculators might in effect give Ruritania a loan of foreign exchange to cover a temporary excess of imports over exports by seizing the opportunity to buy crowns during their temporary depreciation and holding them for resale after their recovery. The crown would weaken less than

---

[6] Tsiang considers this point to be quite important. (*Op. cit.*, p. 412.)

otherwise. (The subsequent recovery would also be slightly weaker, for if speculation were to restrain the dip and leave everything else unaffected, it would amount to a never-withdrawn capital inflow into Ruritania. The deterioration of Ruritania's fundamental trading opportunities, even though temporary, requires the exchange value of the crown, averaged over the fullness of time, to be very slightly below what it otherwise would have been.)

To vary the example, consider a permanent deterioration of Ruritania's international trading opportunities. In time, the Ruritanians might be able to readjust without undue pain by directly and indirectly shifting factors of production out of the most harmed export industries into other export industries and into import-competing industries. In the short run, however, factors are less mobile and supplies and demands less elastic, and continuous balance in Ruritania's international current account might require massive price changes. Without a cushion of speculation, the crown might sink to 8 per dollar from the initial rate of 5. Later, as time eased readjustments in production and consumption, the rate might recover to 6. Though trading opportunities have worsened permanently, there is, as in the first example, an interval of particular scarcity of foreign-trade goods, corresponding to the temporary depreciation of the peso even below its new long-run-equilibrium value. As before, speculators who profitably bought crowns during their deepest dip and sold them after their recovery would be not only smoothing out rate fluctuations but also, in effect, granting Ruritania a short-term loan to cover a temporary import surplus. They would be transferring foreign-trade goods from the future to the immediate period of relative scarcity and high marginal utility.

In stabilizing the crown against the later-to-be-reversed part of its depreciation, the speculators are helping to cushion adjustment to the underlying deterioration of opportunities. Two extremes are conceivable. One is no cushioning at all: Ruritania's exports must pay for its imports at all times; and at first, a painful curtailment of imports and

drive to export is necessary under the prod of a particularly severe depreciation of the crown. The opposite extreme is complete cushioning: the prolonged financing of a Ruritanian import surplus either by (mistakenly excessive) speculation or, until its international reserves ran out, by an official agency. Eventually, a crisis and sharp depreciation would probably occur after all. The best degree of cushioning and best pace of adjustment is somewhere in between. Difficult to define though this optimum admittedly is, it is a standard in comparison with which official exchange-rate management tends to make adjustment sometimes too slow and sometimes too fast: sometimes the bulk of the reserves goes to prop up an uneconomic rate; at other times, a sharp devaluation occurs.[7]

In a third example, emerging conditions will eventually cut the foreign demand for Ruritanian exports or worsen Ruritania's export-supply capacity. Because these trends are gradual and because of long-term contracts and other elements of inertia, however, the pattern of international trade would not change much for a while. If there were no speculation and if current-account transactions alone held sway on the foreign-exchange market, the rate would remain at about its old level. Only later, as the changing fundamental conditions took effect, would the crown depreciate. But if speculators foresaw these developments, they would sell crowns at once (perhaps by forward contracts), hoping to buy them back later more cheaply. The hastened depreciation would begin stimulating exports and retarding imports at once, and a commodity export surplus would match the speculative capital outflow. Later, as speculators moved capital back to collect their profits, the country could have an import surplus. In effect, the speculators would lead Ruritanians to postpone some consumption from a time when foreign-trade goods were still relatively abundant and of low marginal utility to the later period of relative scarcity and high marginal utility.

---

[7] On the question of the optimum pace of adjustment and optimum cushioning, see Milton Friedman, *op. cit.*, pp. 184-186.

Price incentives for reallocating resources would also come earlier. Speculation would smooth the adjustment to worsened trading opportunities by causing it to begin sooner. The process is roughly similar to what happens when speculators foresee a poor grain harvest and, by bidding up the price in the present, induce consumers to stint their present consumption of relatively low-marginal-utility grain so that it will be available as high-marginal-utility grain in the future. As this comparison shows, speculation need not always *resist* price or exchange-rate movements in order to be appropriate (in the light of plausible value judgments); sometimes it is appropriate for future developments to cast their shadows before them as hastened price signals.

A fourth example supposes a domestic price inflation not significantly related to international transactions or foreign-exchange speculation and not generally expected to keep getting worse. Without speculation, elements of inertia in the supply of and demand for foreign exchange (such as existing contracts for import and export transactions) might delay a full depreciation of the crown in line with its diminished purchasing power. Meanwhile, there would be a resulting distortion, unrelated to real changes in supplies and demands, in the relative prices of import and export goods, on the one hand, and domestic goods and factors of production on the other hand. Speculators would be helping prevent this temporary distortion if they foresaw the ultimate effects of the inflation on the exchange rate and sold crowns.[8]

Speculation has benefited Ruritania in all four examples. From the viewpoint of the rest of the world, the first two examples involve temporary cheapness of Ruritanian goods. Speculative stabilization of the exchange rate would stretch out over time not only the Ruritanians' necessary economies in the consumption of foreign-trade goods but also the foreigners' enjoyment of the temporarily improved terms of trade with Ruritania. In the third example, from the foreign viewpoint, also, speculation both advances the adjust-

ment in time and stretches it out. Even when the adjustment is to improved conditions, this stretching-out might be an advantage: a benefit presumably means more if it can be accepted at an orderly pace than if it must be accepted suddenly. In the fourth example, speculation would overcome temporary distortions of relative prices from both the Ruritanian and foreign points of view. In all four examples, then, the gains do not go to Ruritanians only at the expense of foreigners.

These examples suggest an analogy between speculation and arbitrage. Arbitrage moves something from a submarket or place where it is less valuable to a submarket or place where it is more valuable. Speculation based on a correct diagnosis of fundamental supplies and demands is arbitrage in time. Speculators "move" foreign exchange (and, ultimately, the foreign-trade goods corresponding to it) from a point in time of lesser value to a point in time of greater value. The source of speculators' profits is akin to that of arbitrageurs' profits, or, for that matter, of truck drivers' wages: speculators, arbitrageurs, and truck drivers alike share in the values that they almost literally create by transforming lower-valued into higher-valued goods through a relocation in time or space.[9] The difference between arbitrage and speculation is the uncertainty connected with dealing at different points in time. The arbitrageur *knows* the prices ruling in the markets both where he buys and where he sells; the speculator must guess the future. Furthermore, the time sequence of the speculator's markets gives rise to notions of trends, which may sometimes help and sometimes hinder forming sound judgments about future prices. This difference relates to how generally speculators succeed in buying cheap and selling dear but does not detract from the similarity between the values created by arbitrage and by speculation when speculators *do* succeed.

---

[8] Cf. Tsiang, *op. cit.*, p. 414.

[9] This statement refers to the aggregate of all speculative profits and losses. Qualifications will be made later about profits that some speculators make at the expense of less competent speculators. Incidentally, nothing said here implies a judgment about how ethically entitled to their incomes speculators, arbitrageurs, or truck drivers may be.

Mistaken and Excessive Speculation

Since speculators sometimes fail, we should modify our earlier examples to consider speculation in the wrong direction. In the first two, speculators were supporting the Ruritanian crown during what would otherwise have been temporary or temporarily excessive weakness. Mistaken speculation, by contrast, would mean interpreting the early depreciation as a sign of still more to come and selling the crown and depressing it further. Later, when the speculators finally realized their mistake and bought back crowns (sold foreign exchange) to cut their losses, they would make the crown recover, temporarily, still further than it would otherwise have done. By moving some of the foreign exchange available to nonspeculative traders from the earlier period of its greater to the later period of its lesser value, the speculators would in effect have been moving the foreign-trade goods available to the Ruritanian economy from a time of relative scarcity to a time of relative abundance. Such speculation, based on a wrong forecast even of the *direction* in which nonspeculative supply and demand would move the rate, has aptly been named "perverse."[10] Transforming high-marginal-utility goods into low marginal-utility goods impairs total welfare, on any plausible interpretation of welfare.

Even so, it is not certain that nonspeculators in general are harmed. If speculators have no monopsonistic or monopolistic influence over the prices at which they buy and sell, the losses of mistaken speculators may well exceed the aggregate loss. If the speculators bear their own losses and do not impose them on other persons by bankruptcy or default, a net gain may conceivably remain for nonspeculators as a group.[11] When the speculators buy, they raise the price against themselves, benefiting the nonspeculative sellers, and when they sell, they lower the price against themselves, benefiting the nonspeculative buyers. It is true that nonspeculative buyers are harmed the first time and nonspeculative sellers the second. On the whole, however, nonspeculators' gains presumably exceed nonspeculators' losses each time. When the speculators buy and raise the price, the nonspeculative sellers enjoy their gain on a correspondingly increased volume of sales, while the nonspeculative buyers suffer their loss on a reduced volume of purchases; when the speculators sell and lower the price, the nonspeculative buyers enjoy their gain on an increased volume of purchases, while the nonspeculative sellers suffer their losses on a reduced volume of sales. In other words, when speculators are buying, the losses imposed on nonspeculative buyers are matched by the gains of the nonspeculators who sell to them, and there remains the net gain on the nonspeculators' sales to the speculators. When speculators are selling, the losses imposed on nonspeculative sellers are matched by the gains of the nonspeculators who buy from them, and there remains the net gain on the nonspeculators' purchases from the speculators.

It hardly seems worthwhile to press this point by a fuller analysis, complete with diagrams. The argument would still suffer from interpersonal comparisons and the other familiar defects of the crudest (but most usable) version of the concepts of consumers' and suppliers' surplus. The argument does not distinguish between Ruritanians and foreigners, and there is no obvious ground for ruling out the possibility that all or more than all of the aggregate gain of nonspeculators might go to the foreigners. Furthermore, any manageably simple version of the argument assumes that the nonspeculative supply and demand schedules are definitely given at any particular time. In fact, however, any price change shifts at least one of the schedules. Even for any ordinary competitively traded commodity, the supply and demand schedules and the price all are interdependent; this is notably true of foreign exchange. Finally, the worsened instability of exchange rates caused by perverse speculation may cause damage offsetting any benefit of the kind just de-

---

[10] On "perverse" speculation and "grossly excessive" speculation, see Meade, *op. cit.,* pp. 220-224.

[11] See A. P. Lerner, *The Economics of Control,* New York: Macmillan, 1944, pp. 88-95, and J. E. Meade, "Degrees of Competitive Speculation," *Review of Economic Studies,* XVII (3), no. 44, 1949–1950, esp. pp. 160-161.

scribed. Thus we do not have an actual proof that even perverse speculation benefits non-speculators. But we do have reason to question any contrary idea that perverse speculation necessarily harms nonspeculators on the whole. A net benefit is easily conceivable on the basis of an interpersonal comparison of gains and losses that, while crude, at least has no special bias contrived to yield this result.

Besides correct speculation and perverse speculation, "grossly excessive" speculation should be mentioned. Instead of perversely intensifying a merely temporary depreciation and instead of appropriately hastening a depreciation called for by changing fundamentals, speculation might, for a while, stabilize exchange rates too much. The price incentives for necessary readjustments of production and consumption would be delayed. Eventually speculators would see their error and rush to undo their positions, temporarily driving the rate to the other side of its new equilibrium level. Too much stability in the short run would have been bought at the cost of too much instability later on. In effect, speculators would have transported foreign-trade goods in time, keeping them unduly abundant in the present at the cost of undue scarcity for a while later on. (Even so, the foregoing considerations still apply: the speculators might conceivably bear all of more than all of the aggregate loss themselves.)

Speculative exchange-rate stabilization might be considered excessive for still another reason. Exchange-rate flexibility is a form of price flexibility, which has a role to play in continually adjusting production and consumption to changing circumstances. Even seasonal fluctuations may have their value. For a clear-cut example, suppose that all of Ruritania's imports and exports consist of nonstorable services—tourism, perhaps. The factors of production used in producing tourist services are typified by resort hotels, specially trained personnel having little opportunity for slack-season employment at acceptable wages, and the like. When tourist services are not bought, the factors specialized in producing them go to waste. From De-

cember to March, demand is weak for tourism in wintry Ruritania but strong for tourism in summery Graustark, in the opposite hemisphere. Nevertheless, for institutional reasons (cartel or government regulations, the awkwardness of frequent changes, or the like), the local-currency prices of tourist services are not flexible enough to equate supply and demand at all times. From December to March, tourist facilities are largely idle in Ruritania, while in Graustark they are in excess demand and are crudely rationed by the necessity of making reservations far in advance. A flexible exchange rate between the Ruritanian crown and the Graustark florin would partially overcome this difficulty. A depreciation of the crown between December and March would, in effect, cut the prices charged Graustarkians for tourism in Ruritania and raise the prices charged Ruritanians for tourism in Graustark, and so give residents of both countries alike a price incentive to substitute tourism in Ruritania for tourism in Graustark in these months. The seasonal underutilization of Ruritanian facilities and the excess demand for Graustark facilities would both find a partial remedy. Of course, exchange-rate flexibility is a crude and unselective substitute for the flexibility of individual prices and wages, and industries other than those in a position comparable to that of tourism might be adversely affected, but the example is pertinent in showing that ironing out fluctuations is not always and necessarily an unqualified good even when the fluctuations are fated to reverse themselves. When exchange-rate flexibility is supplementing inadequate flexibility of individual prices and wages and, in particular, when *nonstorable* goods and services are involved and a temporary slump in buying them would mean a waste of factors of production, then speculative stabilization of exchange rates might plausibly be judged inappropriate.[12] This point is probably

---

[12] The earlier analysis of how the loss from incorrect speculation might be more than fully borne by the speculators themselves, leaving a gain for nonspeculators, does not seem applicable here. That analysis presupposed flexible prices always equilibrating speculative plus nonspeculative supplies and demands. Here, by contrast, the difficulty stems from excessively rigid prices and exchange

not very important in reality. It is worth making, however, as a counter to any idea that stabilization is necessarily a good thing and that speculation is to be praised or condemned according to how much or how little stability it produces. If exchange-rate fluctuations were quite clearly temporary or seasonal, private speculation would probably iron them out; but even if it did not, this failure would not necessarily be a matter for regret.

The Analogy Between Foreign Exchange and Commodities

For ordinary commodities, the role of flexible prices in balancing supply and demand is generally recognized, even though official price-pegging might supposedly eliminate harmful speculation and relieve producers, traders, and users of some risk. Continually changing conditions call for continual adjustments in resource allocation; keeping prices from fulfilling their rationing and production-motivating functions might be more disruptive than price fluctuations and the speculation that may feed on them. Why, then, do not these same considerations tell against pegging exchange rates?[13] Well, some writers reject the analogy between exchange rates and ordinary prices. It allegedly ignores the fundamental fact about money—that it is important primarily as a unit of account and that everything priced in one money is affected by its value in terms of other moneys.[14] Such arguments do not distinguish sharply enough between the foreign-exchange value and the purchasing power of a currency. To Americans, the price of French francs *is* like the price of any ordinary commodity; it is the price of an "ingredient" used in "producing" imports from France, just as the price of cotton cloth is the price of an ingre-

dient used in producing shirts. To Frenchmen, likewise, the price of dollars is similar to an ordinary commodity price. As for the interdependence between exchange rates and other prices, there is no evident difference of principle between this and the general interdependence of commodity prices in a closed economy. Any argument about an especially disruptive interdependence involving exchange rates must be explicitly developed to be meaningful; interdependence in itself does not destroy the commodity analogy. Emphasis on the distinctive functions of money—its use as a unit of account and debt-paying medium—would seem a better argument for stabilizing the domestic purchasing power of money than for stabilizing exchange rates.

Jacob Viner develops a more sophisticated objection to the commodity analogy. As in the market for short-term loans and the short-term interest rate and in the price of gold under a gold standard, he finds something peculiarly crucial in the foreign-exchange market and exchange rates. Its zero storage cost and low financial carrying cost make foreign exchange especially subject to speculation. He distrusts routine application of standard speculation theory to "a commodity whose supply and whose demand have no upward or downward limitations arising out of cost limitations on output or out of want limitations on 'marketability.'"[15] By this, Viner means that the price of one country's fiat money in terms of another's has no ceiling or floor derived from real costs affecting supply or from direct or indirect utility either as a consumer good or as an ingredient in production. Fiat money can be produced in unlimited amounts at negligible cost. Similarly, sellers of commodities or of other currencies will accept it in unlimited amounts, though at a correspondingly low value. The implication is that the limits within which speculation can push exchange rates around are much less close and definite than those ruling in commodity markets. Commodity

rates and the consequent imbalances between quantities demanded and supplied.

[13] See Charles R. Whittlesey, *International Monetary Issues,* New York: McGraw-Hill, 1937, p. 32.

[14] Michael Lindsay Hoffman, "The Economics of Fluctuating Exchanges" (unpublished dissertation), Chicago: University of Chicago, 1942, p. 352. Hoffman is elaborating on F. A. von Hayek, *Monetary Nationalism and International Stability,* London: Longmans, Green, 1937, pp. 5-6.

[15] Jacob Viner, "Some International Aspects of Economic Stabilization," in Leonard D. White (ed.), *The State of the Social Sciences,* Chicago: University of Chicago Press, 1956, p. 291.

prices are dominated by supply and demand factors reflecting costs of production and utilities, but the domestic or international value of a currency can be practically anything, since cost and utility play practically no role.

To individual persons and firms, however, a foreign currency does indeed have a cost of production and a utility, quite as an ordinary commodity does. To the businessmen who "produce" foreign exchange for the home economy, it has a real cost of "production" in the export goods that are "transformed" into it on the international market and, more basically, in the domestic factors of production used in making these exports. Similarly, the businessmen who demand foreign exchange as an "ingredient" in "producing" import goods find that it does have a utility or productivity, much as any other ingredient or intermediate good. The exchange rate between two currencies does have an objective basis, after all, in their respective purchasing powers over goods and services. Even if only loosely controlling, this basis contradicts any notion that no cost or utility factors limit the play of speculation.

Money is essentially costless to the authorities or institutions that create it, though not to ordinary persons and firms. Exchange depreciation of a currency may put pressure on the issuing authorities "to increase its output, to speed up the printing presses, or to make larger entries in the books which in the monetary field represent, in relation to the stock of money, what farms and factories represent in relation to stocks of other commodities."[16] Our whole earlier analysis of mutual influences among exchange rates, price levels, and money supplies bears on this worry. The trouble would be with policies and institutional arrangements and not with speculation as such. Viner himself recognizes that his distinction between speculation in commodities and in foreign exchange would not be valid if countries were successfully stabilizing their price levels.[17]

Firm control over the domestic money supply provides little reassurance about speculation feeding on the domestic instability of

foreign currencies. Still, the damage that domestically stable countries would suffer, with rate fluctuations intensified by speculation, might well be less than the damage from linkage to the unstable foreign currencies at fixed rates.

In comparison with most staple commodities traded on organized markets, foreign exchange presumably has a high elasticity of demand and supply and a correspondingly low susceptibility to price fluctuations caused by random shifts in supply and demand. Foreign exchange is like a commodity with many uses; it is an "ingredient" of a wide variety of goods and services imported from many places. Similarly, it has many sources of supply, obtainable by producing a wide variety of goods for a wide range of foreign customers. Ordinarily, then, there is reason to doubt whether foreign exchange is a commodity subject to the wide price fluctuations and the kind of speculation often characteristic, for instance, of wool, sugar, rubber, tin, cocoa, and other staples.[18]

The Natural Selection of Speculators

One line of reasoning emphasizes a *natural selection* of successful speculators whose activities generally tend to be stabilizing. Other speculators, it is true, may be unable to assess the fundamental supply and demand conditions governing prices; they may be unduly inclined to expect short-run price fluctuations to continue in the same direction; they may buy and sell according to whim or emotion or mass mood. Precisely because they are so often wrong, however—so goes the argument—they will lose money and be forced to curtail or cease their operations. More competent and better-informed speculators will make profits and be able to expand their operations. Their very profits show that they have, on

---

[16] *Ibid.*, p. 292.
[17] *Ibid.*, p. 294.

[18] Further objections could be raised regarding foreign exchange as the output of the home country's export firms and the chief input of its import firms: for example, movements in its price tend to drag prices of certain other goods along with it; its supply curve could conceivably bend backwards; and price changes (even merely speculative price changes) tend to affect the *schedule* of its cost of "production." But such things are equally conceivable for commodities in the literal sense of the word. The commodity analogy remains suggestive.

balance, been buying at low prices and selling at high prices. The natural selection of profit and loss rewards and promotes stabilizing speculation and penalizes and eliminates destabilizing speculation.[19]

Two closely related objections challenge this reasoning. First, it is not certain that profitability necessarily implies a stabilizing effect. Second, the shrewder speculators may make profits not so much by assessing fundamental supplies and demands as by predicting price swings caused by the moods of amateur speculators; speculation as a whole still may be destabilizing. Let us examine these two doubts in turn.

Speculators clearly both make profits and exert a stabilizing influence if they buy at the troughs and sell at the peaks of swings in prices. But they seldom can time their actions so accurately. They may not recognize a price trough or peak until it has passed and given way to an uptrend or downtrend. Instead of trying to call the turns in prices exactly, they may choose a better chance of a smaller profit by waiting to see which way the wind is blowing before taking action. Speculative purchases at low but rising prices and sales at high but falling prices will sharpen the price movements and, in this narrow sense, may be considered destabilizing.[20]

In another and probably more meaningful sense, even tardy speculative purchases and sales can still be stabilizing. Since the sole purpose of the next page or two is to show

a possibility rather than prove a necessity, it is legitimate and convenient to postulate nonspeculative supply and demand functions and nonspeculative shifts in supply and movements in price of very simple kinds. For further simplicity, the speculators are assumed to buy in only one period and sell in only one period of each price cycle. In Fig. 11.1, the solid line of Chart A shows how the price of some commodity would move through time in the absence of speculation. The dashed line, where it deviates from the solid one, shows how speculative buying in the second period after the price trough and speculative selling in the second period after the price peak modify the time series of prices. The two parts of Chart B relate to the two periods in which speculators operate. They show the nonspeculative supply and demand and the price they would determine in each period in the absence of speculation, the quantity bought by speculators in the one period and sold in the other, and the prices as modified by speculation. These prices correspond to the dashed line on Chart A. As is clear from Chart B, nonspeculative demand and supply are assumed to depend only on current price and not at all on past price. Furthermore, the nonspeculative demand schedule is assumed to be always the same; the price fluctuations are due to shifts in the supply schedule (perhaps because of seasonal weather changes). Speculative demand or supply presumably depends on further price as predicted in the light of past and present prices, but it is unnecessary here to explore just how the speculators make their decisions; it is enough that they buy and sell in the amounts and at the times shown.

The new series of prices, shown by the dashed lines, is less regular or tidy than the nonspeculative one. Nevertheless, it represents greater stability in the sense that the average deviation (ignoring sign) of the price in each period from the average price over the entire cycle is smaller: the total of these deviations is 58 for the speculation-distorted price pattern and 62 for the nonspeculative pattern. (This result is obvious at once: the nonspeculative and speculative prices are always the same except in periods 6 and 14,

---

[19] "People who argue that speculation is generally destabilizing seldom realize that this is largely equivalent to saying that speculators lose money. . . ." (Friedman, *op. cit.*, p. 175). While recognizing the possibility, Friedman argues against any presumption that a changing body of money-losing amateur speculators would in fact dominate the market.

[20] See William J. Baumol, "Speculation, Profitability, and Stability," *Review of Economics and Statistics,* **XXXIX**, August 1957, pp. 263-271.

The text above appears to make the unrealistic suggestion that prices move in regular cycles. For the sake of mere convenience in providing periods of relatively high and relatively low prices for consideration, such a model is legitimate. However, arguments (such as Baumol's) that depend in an essential way on unchanging (though complicated) supply and demand functions with fixed parameters are considerably more suspect. This point deserves more repetition and emphasis than, for fear of boring the reader, it receives in the following pages.

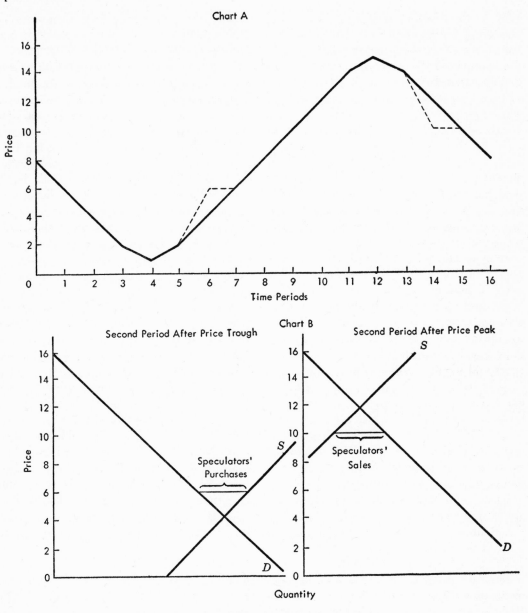

Figure 11.1.

when the nonspeculative price deviates by $4.00 and the speculative price by only $2.00 from the $8.00 average price over the cycle.) Speculators make profits because they buy at a price of $6.00 and sell at $10.00. Furthermore, the speculation is appropriate in the sense that it transfers some of the commodity from a period when its nonspeculative value would have been only $4.00 to a period when its nonspeculative value would have been $12.00. It is true that the speculators would

have been acting even more appropriately if they had concentrated their buying and selling at and around the troughs and peaks of prices, instead of waiting to see uptrends and downtrends already under way. But the example shows that imperfect speculation can, though need not, be better than none at all; it can be "stabilizing" and "appropriate," in quite reasonable senses of these words, even when intensifying parts of upswings and downswings in prices.

By delaying the bulk of their purchases and sales until later than they do in our example, out of anxiety to see price trends still more firmly established before acting, speculators might perversely be buying at above-average and selling at below-average prices. They would be intensifying the instability of prices and transferring the commodity or the foreign exchange they dealt in from times of greater to times of lesser value. But then the speculators would be losing money. The presumption that profitable speculation is stabilizing speculation still seems intact. Apparently the only way to upset this presumption is to postulate that speculation affects price trends and price expectations in such a way as to modify nonspeculative supplies and demands. But when nonspeculators take account of price trends and act according to the resulting expectations, they are no longer "pure" nonspeculators. The problem of drawing a clear distinction between speculators and nonspeculators will require further examination.

By including a speculative element even in the decisions of nonspeculators, it is possible to construct examples in which even profitable speculation by the professionals both sharpens and widens price fluctuations. W. J. Baumol[21] has constructed a model of this sort to serve as a counterexample to and refutation of the reassuring notion that profitable (nonmonopolistic) speculation is necessarily stabilizing. Baumol has prices fluctuating in a sine wave in the absence of speculation. The nonspeculative supply and demand functions generating this pattern are assumed to include recent as well as current prices: high prices tend to create excess supply but *rising* prices tend to create excess demand. The functions describing the behavior of speculators involve their buying shortly after upturns and selling shortly after downturns in prices. Baumol's functions further imply, as a critic has pointed out,[22] that speculators raise their predicted price when the actual price trend is concave upward even though falling and lower their predicted price when the actual price trend is concave downward even though rising. With suitably chosen parameters in the model, speculation can increase the amplitude of price fluctuations. The professional or pure or conscious speculators can destabilize the market while profiting at the expense of others.

We must remember that the supposed nonspeculators are not free from speculative behavior; their transactions are assumed to depend on price trends as well as on prices.[23] Everyone in the model behaves partly in accordance with overt or tacit predictions of future prices and thus is to some extent a speculator. But it is an old story that some speculators might profit and others lose more, with speculation being destabilizing on the whole. While this deserves to be taken seriously (and will later be considered at length), it does not mean that speculators can make profits *in the aggregate* and yet destabilize the market. This is the point at issue.

Anticipating these objections, Baumol constructed another counterexample. In it, nonspeculative purchases depend solely on the current price and not at all on past prices. Nonspeculative sine-wave fluctuations in price stem from shifts in supply, which in turn might be due to seasonal changes in weather. Grafting speculative demand and supply onto this "real cycle" could change the constant-amplitude pattern of price fluctuation into an unstable explosive movement: the price increases produced by speculative purchases would incite still further speculative purchases, and so on, indefinitely. Though destabilizing, this speculation could be profitable in the sense that the speculators' holdings became more and more valuable. But it is premature to describe the speculators' operations as profitable while they are still in midstream, before the paper profits have been cashed. Actually, if the speculators tried to sell and cash their profits, prices would collapse. Baumol concedes, in fact, that his is not actually "an example of destabilizing *profitable* speculation."[24] An autonomous desire to unload speculative holdings is not the

---

[21] *Ibid.*

[22] Lester G. Telser, "A Theory of Speculation Relating Profitability and Stability," *Review of Economics and Statistics,* XLI, August 1959, p. 300.

[23] Baumol himself has recognized and Telser has emphasized this point.

[24] W. J. Baumol, "Reply," *Review of Economics and Statistics,* XLI, August 1959, p. 301.

only thing that might break the speculative spiral. The rising interest cost of financing speculative holdings might dampen the enthusiasm for further purchases, stop the price rise, and prick the bubble.[25] Interest rates would in fact be likely to rise as progressively more funds were demanded (or withheld from supply) on the loan market to finance the growing speculative positions.

The models just reviewed sought to undermine the proposition that profitability for the aggregate of all speculators (including incidental and partial speculators) implies a stabilizing influence. In fact, the *ad hoc* peculiarities of those counterexamples tend to support the proposition as a useful generalization if not airtight theorem.[26] To further rehabilitate it, Lester Telser constructed a model of great generality in which nonspeculative excess demand is inversely related to current price and is unaffected by past prices, while speculative excess demand or supply is proportional to the expected rise or fall in price. The better the speculators predict future prices, the larger are their profits. Mathematics grinds out the conclusion that positive speculators' profits do indeed imply a price-stabilizing influence, on the plausible definition that the variance of actual prices from the mean price measures the degree of instability.[27] In fact, as Telser remarks, speculators may conceivably stabilize prices to some extent even when suffering losses. A radically simple example (not given by him) illustrates this possibility. Suppose that the speculators buy when the price would otherwise be $.75 below average and in so doing bid up the price by $1.00 to $.25 above average; they sell when the price would otherwise be $.75 above average and thus bid the price down to $.25 below average. The speculators lose money, since they buy more dearly than they sell, but they make prices deviate less from the average than they otherwise would have.

The issue is still not completely decided. Perhaps Telser's proof that profitable speculation is stabilizing is not a general one but rather is just one more example of the undisputed facts that it *can* be stabilizing. Baumol still insisted that the relation between profitability and stability is in part an empirical question, not to be settled by *a priori* arguments.[28] Yet the question whether aggregate profitability necessarily implies a stabilizing effect is *not* an "empirical" question; it is a question of logical implication. It is the job of logical analysis to explore under what conditions the suggested proposition would not hold. No number of historical examples in which profitable speculation has been stabilizing can prove that it logically *must* be. And no number of historical examples in which speculation seems to have been destabilizing yet profitable will settle the issue unless the profit-and-loss figures refer to fully cashed rather than mere paper profits and unless they refer to all speculators—amateur as well as professional, inadvertent as well as conscious.

The practical issue apparently resolves into whether *professional* speculation is generally stabilizing. When even predominantly nonspeculative trading is partly based on attempts to predict future prices, when no satisfactory distinction can be drawn between speculative and nonspeculative trading, or when amateur speculators are active, then profitable professional speculation is not necessarily stabilizing. This is a second objection to the natural-selection argument; it must be emphasized and closely examined.

The natural-selection argument expects incompetent speculators to be weeded out, leaving profit-making speculators dominant with their stabilizing influence. The argument is persuasive only when speculative supply and demand are small in relation to total trading. Otherwise, though a speculator still needs superior foresight to succeed, his superiority may lie in sensing the opinions and moods of other speculators rather than in predicting fundamentals. Especially if speculative transactions are a large part of the total, this may be the profitable way to operate. Speculators

[25] Telser, *op. cit.*, p. 301. This point is, of course, part of Tsiang's analysis of speculators' equilibrium.

[26] A newly suggested example of destabilizing profitable speculation involves multiple equilibriums of the exchange rate in the absence of speculation! Murray C. Kemp, *The Pure Theory of International Trade*, Englewood Cliffs, N.J.: Prentice-Hall, 1964, pp. 259-260.

[27] *Op. cit.*, pp. 298-299.

[28] Baumol, *Review of Economics and Statistics*, August 1959, p. 302.

as a group may suffer losses, but with a successful minority winning from the losses of an unsuccessful and changing mass. Keynes likened professional speculation to a contest to pick out the six prettiest faces from a hundred pictures, the prize going to the contestant whose selection most nearly corresponds to the average selection of all contestants. Each has to pick the faces not that he finds prettiest, but that the other contestants, who are looking at the problem in the same way, seem likeliest to pick.[29] Why, then, bother with fundamentals? Why not join in and profit from any ignorant speculative stampede while it lasts?

The distinction between professional and amateur speculation suggests a related distinction between calm and excited times. Unusual excitement grows from prospects of winning large gains (as on the stock market during a boom) or of avoiding large losses of purchasing power (as on the foreign-exchange market during rapid inflation at home). A population seized with speculative mania is looking for big profits in a hurry. Exchange rates between domestically stable currencies, however, would hardly vary sharply or rapidly enough to have strong get-rich-quick appeal to amateur speculators. Fluctuations about a gradually changing equilibrium are the sort of thing that only professionals might hope to profit from.

While ironing out clear deviations from equilibrium, even professional speculators could not be sure of the precise rate called for by commercial supply and demand. Small short-run oscillations, more so than large movements, may be unrelated to nonspeculative fundamentals. If speculation is oriented around the fundamentals, there is thus more reason to expect it to resist oscillations outside of a certain range than within that range. The size of this range differs among markets according to the influence of some idea of a "normal price."[30] As shown a few pages later, this stabilizing idea of a normal price is likely to be more powerful in foreign-exchange markets than in security markets. Another reassuring consideration about speculation on small short-run wobbles in exchange rates is that it is undertaken by banks—though perhaps not deliberately—insofar as they may sometimes be willing to let unbalanced positions developed in transactions with their commercial customers ride for a few minutes or hours. For this reason, very-short-run imbalances between commercial supplies of and demands for particular currencies need not cause correspondingly frequent and violent rate movements. Nevertheless, the question of how wide the range is within which speculation is likely to dominate exchange rates is an empirical one, to be illuminated by historical experience.

The Stock-market Analogy

Worry over the activities of inexpert speculators feeds on a supposed analogy between speculation in currencies and in stocks. Experience with speculation in freely fluctuating exchanges is much less common than acquaintance with the lore of the stock market. It is easy to become impressed by similarities between the two markets,[31] but the differences are at least as noteworthy.

One of the most important differences is the greater strength of the idea of normal price in foreign exchange than in stocks. There is hardly such a thing as a normal price for a share of stock. Presumably it would equal the stream of expected future dividends discounted by the going rate of interest on loans of comparable risk. Except for the very near future, no one knows what future dividends will be. The proper discount factor is also unknown. The price of a stock is a kind of crude average judgment sometimes liable to sharp change, which intrigues amateur speculators. The normal rate of exchange between two currencies is definite by contrast. One can ordinarily be confident that a purchasing-power-parity calculation approximates the equilibrium exchange rate within, say, 20 or 30 percent. If there is a marked discrepancy

---

[29] J. M. Keynes, *The General Theory of Employment, Interest and Money,* New York: Harcourt, Brace, 1936, esp. p. 156. Keynes was referring to the stock market in particular.

[30] Nicholas Kaldor, "Speculation and Economic Stability," *Review of Economic Studies,* VII, October 1939, p. 10.

[31] See Hoffman, *op. cit.,* pp. 220-221, 223n.

between the rates of inflation or deflation in the two countries, one can also judge in which direction purchasing-power parity is tending to change. Judging the nonspeculative value of one currency in terms of another requires less expert knowledge than judging the nonspeculative value of a stock.

Under free international trade, commodity arbitrage would keep exchange rates from deviating far from purchasing-power parity. But there could be no comparable arbitrage in stocks, even if each stock did have a normal value. Even if one could know that speculation was undervaluing a stock, an individual arbitrageur would have no ready way to buy the stock and then sell the physical plant, inventories, goodwill, and other underlying assets. And if a stock were known to be overvalued, there would be even less chance of buying assets for conversion into the stock.

Speculative supplies of and demands for foreign exchange are merely added onto supplies and demands arising out of international trade. But in the stock market, speculative supplies and demands more nearly dominate. Except perhaps for the flotation of new issues, it is hard to imagine what stock-market transactions correspond to nonspeculative sales and purchases of foreign exchange. It is doubtful whether many people buy stocks as a long-run investment, paying sole attention to income prospects and no attention at all to possibilities of capital gain. Where speculators can gauge nonspeculative supplies and demands, as in the foreign exchange market, prices are less subject to emotional influences than where speculators must rely on sensing the moods of other speculators, as in the stock market.

The large volume of commercial transactions tends in another way to make functionless price fluctuations less violent in foreign-exchange markets than in stock markets (particularly than in the stock markets of some decades ago). Large commercial supplies of and demands for a currency, together with arbitrage that keeps various exchange rates mutually consistent, make it difficult for a pool of speculators to dominate the market in some currency and engineer profitable price fluctuations. Monopolistic manipu

lation of exchange rates would require greater boldness and larger resources than any pool of private speculators is ordinarily likely to have.

Another reassuring fact is the greater two-sidedness of the exchange market than the stock market. Bullish and bearish sentiments have more nearly equal opportunities to express themselves. Suppose, for example, that speculators think the dollar price of sterling is higher than fundamental conditions warrant. Bearishness on pounds can easily express itself as bullishness on dollars: Englishmen and other owners of pounds can buy the undervalued dollars. It is more difficult for bearishness on the dollar price of some stock to find full expression, for no country uses that stock as money. Furthermore, well-organized forward markets furnish good vehicles for bearishness on currencies but not on stocks. Admittedly, bears can sell a stock short after first borrowing it, but this method is rather inadequate. (Members of the uninitiated public are plausibly alleged to feel uncomfortable in the unfamiliar position of being in debt for shares of stock. Active bearishness on stocks is discriminated against by rules such as that short sales can be made only after upward price movements and that profits from short positions, no matter how long outstanding, cannot have the benefit of the lower tax rate on capital gains.) Even if stocks were actively bought and sold for forward delivery, as formerly done on some European markets, there still would not exist the same systematic relation between spot and forward prices as in the exchange market. A decline in the forward rate on a currency affects the spot rate through interest arbitrage, but if the forward price of a stock were to sink, arbitrage communicating the effect to the spot price would have to depend on the inadequate expedient of borrowing stock. Inadequate outlets for bear sentiment probably enter into an explanation of the exaggerated and precarious Wall Street bull market of 1927–1929. With bears acting mainly by withdrawing from or staying out of the market rather than by taking positive action, bull sentiment seemed even more dominant than it actually was. This impression encouraged still further bull speculation. Finally, when the rise in prices could no longer be maintained, the crash had to be sharp. It would have been less sharp if many speculators had had short positions to cover. Things would be different on free foreign-exchange markets. Bear speculation on a currency would be just as easy as bull speculation. Short selling would tend to check any unbalanced speculative rise in a currency, and covering of short positions would cushion any subsequent decline.

The reasons why impressions of the stock market cannot be carried over into considering speculation in currencies apply even more strongly to impressions about speculation in land, tulip bulbs, or Old Masters. Something like the boom and collapse of Florida land values in the 1920s, for example, is quite unlikely in the foreign-exchange market. The vitally relevant difference is the practical impossibility of active bear speculation in land. (How can one actively speculate on a fall in land values except by selling whatever holdings one already has, thereby withdrawing from speculation?) Of all speculative markets, the market in foreign exchange seems least vulnerable to booms and crashes resulting from inadequate means of continuous expression for bearish and bullish sentiments alike.

Speculation under Pegged Exchange Rates

The reassurances of the last section apply only to markets in which exchange rates fluctuate freely. Things are different when rates are fixed. It is true that speculation is unlikely to cause trouble under a *full-fledged* international gold standard, for exchange rates are then understood to be fixed permanently, and defense of the gold parity of its currency is the overriding aim of each country's financial policies. Speculation then works in support of gold parities and helps provide accommodating finance for temporary balance-of-payments disequilibriums. A gold standard commanding this degree of confidence existed, however, for at most a few decades in the world's history. Nowadays, exchange-rate adjustments are acceptable, at

least as last resorts, in dealing with "fundamental disequilibrium." Even when rate adjustments are not in fact made, their very possibility can unleash troublesome speculation.[32] If exchange-rate adjustments were to be discussed at international conferences, the result would be general uncertainty between conferences and chaos during them. If exchange-rate adjustments were to be made according to some formula (even a supposedly secret one), speculators still would have a great advantage. In practice, exchange rates are adjusted at the discretion of individual governments. Rumors keep springing up about possible impending adjustments, and these rumors flag speculation on. The historical chapters to follow offer a number of examples.

Those who speculate on adjustments in pegged exchange rates have practically a *sure thing,* a so-called one-way option. When a currency is under suspicion, everyone knows whether it is overvalued or undervalued. There may be some doubt about whether the government will make a rate adjustment, and to what extent, but there is practically no doubt about the direction of any change. If rumors have the government contemplating devaluation of a clearly overvalued currency, its holders have an incentive to sell it quickly before the devaluation takes place. They can profitably buy their balances back afterwards. People committed to make future payments in the suspected currency can speculate against it simply by failing to buy it forward. Considering its obvious overvaluation, there is almost no chance that the suspected currency will be revalued upward rather than devalued. The possibilities are simply devaluation or no change. Devaluation gives the bear speculators an easy profit; no change lets them break even. (The only possible losses are the commissions and other minor expenses of selling a currency and later repurchasing it and a small interest loss if short-term interest rates are lower in the

---

[32] Contrasts in the character of speculation under different exchange-rate systems are emphasized in John Burr Williams, *International Trade under Flexible Exchange Rates,* Amsterdam: North-Holland Publishing Company, 1954, pp. 243-244.

country where the speculative funds are temporarily transferred than in the country whose currency is suspected.)

This assurance that any loss will be slight ordinarily applies fully only to speculation in the spot market, whether by outright currency transactions or by the "leads and lags" to be mentioned presently. If devaluation is strongly and generally expected, the forward quotation on the currency will tend to be below the pegged spot rate. If the expected devaluation does not occur after all, bearish speculators who have operated by selling the distrusted currency forward at its depressed forward rate will have to fulfill their forward contracts and close out their positions by buying the currency at its successfully defended higher spot rate. It should be emphasized *why* speculation in forward exchange is not a sure thing: there is some risk because forward rates are allowed to fluctuate and get out of alignment with spot rates. Even so, the extreme unlikelihood of appreciation of the spot rate enables speculators to calculate their maximum possible losses, and the interest-parity linkage of forward and spot rates, though weakened in a time of extreme distrust and bearish speculation, still has an influence. For this reason, even speculation by way of the unpegged forward market is less risky and approximates a "one-way option" more closely than it would if the spot rate were unpegged also. Speculators enjoy a one-way option just as much when an upward revaluation is expected as when a devaluation is expected. By buying the currency in question, they seize an opportunity for easy profit with practically no danger of loss.

The one-way option is not the only incitement that a system of fixed-but-adjustable exchange rates offers to speculators. Another is the fact that speculators do not, as under a system of fluctuating rates, bid the rate up against themselves as they bullishly buy a currency or bid the rate down against themselves as they bearishly sell. Nor do they again bid the rate against themselves as they later undertake the reverse transactions, closing out their positions (and collecting their profits, if the expected rate adjustment has been made). Under a system of pegged rates, the authorities in effect subsidize speculation by keeping the rate steady except at the very moment of the expected adjustment. Furthermore, the profit from speculation on an official rate adjustment promises to be large. Adjustments in fixed exchange rates are momentous and well-publicized events. They must be substantial to justify the publicity and sometimes odium involved. A devaluing government is likely to make the step large not only to convince the public that it really was necessary but also to leave a margin of safety; devaluing too far seems better than devaluing too little and perhaps soon being forced to devalue again. Besides, the official reserves of gold and foreign exchange may have sunk very low during the period of currency overvaluation; the government may even be in debt for borrowed foreign exchange. Consequently, devaluation, when it comes, may go further than just enough to restore equilibrium in the country's balance of payments; it may aim at a surplus so that the government can rebuild its reserves and repay its borrowings.

Another advantage of fixed-but-adjustable rates over free rates—from the speculators' point of view—is that bear speculation against a weak currency may actually force the hoped-for devaluation. The bears win if they can exhaust the official reserves or the willingness of the authorities to use the reserves in continued pegging. The costs and risks of speculation are small in relation to the possible profit. The lower the reserves fall, the more imminent the collapse of the pegged rate becomes, and the stronger the motives for continued bear speculation. Even if the original rumors were quite untrue, they might force devaluation and so make themselves true.[33] This could happen even if the speculation were not justified by underlying long-run commercial supplies and demands in the exchange market, so that the exchange rate could otherwise be maintained. When the government is about to run out of exchange reserves, mere lectures about the silliness of speculation against underlying supply and

[33] Cf. J. Kymmell, *De Ontwikkeling van het Internationale Betalingsverkeer,* Leiden: Stenfert Kroese, 1950, p. 109.

demand conditions will not discourage speculators who see a good opportunity.

Speculation on adjustably pegged rates offers few if any compensating advantages. Perhaps its only useful function is to dramatize the unsoundness of existing conditions and force the hand of a government that has procrastinated too long. Speculation is rewarded at the expense of the authorities, meaning at the expense of the taxpayers. In defending an untenably overvalued currency, the authorities sell foreign exchange to speculators cheap, only to buy it back at a higher price after the defense collapses. This loss seems particularly regrettable if some of the foreign exchange sold in the futile pegging of the home currency was borrowed abroad; it later must be bought at an increased home-currency price to repay the foreign lenders. The authorities (and general public) also lose, to the benefit of speculators, in the rarer operation of trying to maintain an untenable exchange undervaluation of the home currency. At first the authorities are buying foreign exchange from speculators at an unduly high price in terms of home currency; later, after resistance to appreciation of the home currency has collapsed, the authorities sell foreign exchange to speculators at a lower price. In either type of futile pegging, the losses of the authorities are, from the speculators' point of view, a subsidy and an incitement to their operations. It is no coincidence that pegging breeds an apparent need for controls over capital movements. Unfortunately, the controls may be circumvented unless the authorities extend comprehensive supervision even to ostensibly nonspeculative current-account transactions.

Speculation by way of so-called leads and lags in commercial payments is almost impossible to stamp out. If the Ruritanian crown comes under suspicion, foreigners with crown debts may delay payment as long as possible, awaiting devaluation. Ruritanians owing debts in foreign exchange will hasten to settle them before the foreign-exchange value of their money is reduced. Foreign purchasers of Ruritanian goods and services who would ordinarily cover their future needs for crowns in the forward market will now refrain from doing so, thereby speculating, and Ruritanians who would ordinarily cover future receipts of foreign exchange by selling them forward will now wait, hoping to sell the exchange at an increased crown price. Speculation may even take the form of postponing foreign purchases of Ruritanian goods and hastening Ruritanian purchases of foreign goods. Even when operating in these passive or indirect ways, speculators enjoy an only slightly impaired one-way option. Like overt speculation, this indirect speculation eats into the reserves of the exchange-pegging authorities.

Some students see these dangers less as an argument against pegging spot rates than as one in favor of supporting forward exchange rates as well. The prospects of finding a solution along these lines will be one of the two main topics covered in Chapter 13.

Summary

Theoretical considerations suggest that the standard worries about speculation in foreign exchange are most fully justified in cases of internal financial disorder. (Later chapters consider historical experience.) Yet even in the most unfavorable case of rapid and continuous inflation of the domestic money supply and prices, speculation would not make exchange rates cumulatively lose contact with the purchasing-power ratios of currencies as long as domestic interest rates were allowed to rise apace with inflationary expectations. Several considerations about calmer times are rather reassuring, such as purchasing-power parities as guides to "normal" exchange rates, the closer resemblance of foreign exchange to a commodity than to stock, and the natural selection of speculators by profit and loss. Fixed-but-adjustable rates are more likely than free rates to incite speculation on one-way options through leads and lags. Proposals for palliating this problem are examined later.

Exchange Risk as an Obstacle to International Trade and Investment

ᔐ 12

The Risk and Nuisance of Fluctuations

Even if not intensified by speculation, exchange-rate fluctuations might still be harmful. In selling or buying goods on credit at a price specified in foreign currency, a businessman runs the risk that the exchange rate may have moved to his disadvantage by the time he receives or makes payment. A less obvious risk confronts a businessman who imports goods for resale at home, either after or without further fabrication. A subsequent decline in the price of foreign exchange will reduce the home-currency value of his inventories by cheapening new imports of such goods. Exchange fluctuations may also cause the nuisance of requiring frequent changes in markets and sources of supply or even in inputs and products. They may complicate accounting and price-setting. (These are the unpleasant factors of competitively flexible prices in general, however; and it is not certain that the price rigidities of imperfect competition are on balance preferable.) The various risks and nuisances of exchange fluctuations might make businessmen refrain from some otherwise profitable international transactions. Businessmen would try to compensate themselves by adding larger mark-ups to their selling prices than under stable exchanges. The volume of international trade would be smaller; some potential benefit from the international division of labor would be lost. Or so goes the argument. (Increased prices to compensate for exchange risk would not affect the volume of trade much, however, unless demands had considerable price elasticity; it is inconsistent to worry about fluctuating exchanges on the grounds of possibly perverse elasticities and serious shrinkage from exchange risk both.)

It is *a priori* practically certain that exchange risk tends to hamper trade to some extent. But there are some partial offsets. One minor point is that the risk of loss also involves the chance of gain. Sometimes, furthermore, the risk is more nominal than real. It might then be less risky for a trader to deal in terms of a foreign currency of stable purchasing power than to deal in terms of his own, if it is subject to rapid inflation. Elimination of the nominal exchange risk would mean assumption of a greater risk of loss of purchasing power.

Importers of competitively traded staple commodities may find some compensation for uncovered exchange risk. An importer who must pay later in a foreign currency suffers by any rise in its rate in the meanwhile, but his loss may be partially offset by the corresponding rise in the home-currency price of his imported inventories.

Historical Clues about Exchange Instability and Trade Volume

Such minor compensations, however, hardly alter the fact that exchange-rate instability must, in itself, deter trade. It is of interest, therefore, to see whether this effect is strong enough to show up in actual experience. One possible approach is to compute a correlation between the volume of a country's international trade during individual years and a measure of how widely the country's exchange rate fluctuated during the same years. A clear inverse association would presumably appear if exchange risk had been an important influence. The failure of this test would not, however, actually disprove the thesis of trade deterrence.[1] The burden on trade consists not so much in the fact or the size of fluctuations during particular years as in *uncertainty* about possible changes between the time of making a commitment and the time of making or receiving payment in foreign money. In accepting this point, however, one must also recognize that a system of temporarily fixed exchanges subject to official adjustment at any time does not fully remove this risk.

The objection to correlating rate instability with trade volume does not apply to comparisons of trade in a period of fairly reliable exchange stability with trade in a period of fluctuating exchanges. The United States slid onto an irredeemable greenback currency during the Civil War and did not restore stable exchanges with gold-standard countries until January 1879. The Civil War greatly interfered with American trade, of course, and prolonged postwar deflation in preparation for resumption of gold payments also presumably restrained economic activity. Nevertheless, there seems to be no upward break after 1878 in the trend of postwar trade growth to suggest that exchange instability had in itself previously been an important deterrent. Such evidence fails to appear whether imports plus exports are measured in current dollars or in dollars deflated by a wholesale price index.[2] Evidence of damage done by exchange-rate fluctuations before 1879 still is absent when one compares trade with gross national product, as in Table 12.1, remembering that the entire decade 1869–1878 and the first half of the overlapping decade 1874–1883 were a period of unstable exchanges.

A number of European countries experienced fluctuating exchange rates after World War I before struggling back onto the gold

Table 12.1. Total of American Imports and Exports as a Percentage of Gross National Product, Overlapping Decades, 1869–1908

Decade	Percentage
1869–1878	14.4
1874–1883	14.1
1879–1888	13.2
1884–1893	12.9
1889–1898	13.2
1894–1903	12.5
1899–1908	11.9

SOURCE: Import and export values and Kuznets's estimates of gross national product from *Historical Statistics of the U.S.*, pp. 244–245 and 15. (Relating trade to gross national product is simply a rough way of taking account of secular economic growth and price changes and does not imply that total trade is a component of gross national product.)

standard during the 1920s. The years of fluctuating and then of fixed rates until the Great Depression were so few, however, that computed trends of growth in their international trade in each period would be practically meaningless. Even the yearly figures mean little, for reasons that will be mentioned, but they are presented here because they inevitably come to mind as *possible* sources of meaningful evidence. A clear and unmistakable jump in the trend of each country's trade volume at the time of its exchange-rate stabilization, or the clear and unmistakable absence of such a jump, might have suggested whether or not rate fluctuations had seriously been hampering trade until then. In considering the figures of Table 12.2, the reader should bear in mind the period of immediate postwar reconstruction, the depression after 1929, and the dates of each country's currency stabilization. The United Kingdom returned to the gold standard in April 1925. France stabilized the franc-dollar rate *de facto* in December 1926 and returned to gold *de jure* at about one-fifth of the prewar parity in June 1928. Denmark reestablished the gold standard in January 1927. Italy stabilized the lira *de jure* in December 1927, after approximate *de facto* stabilization several months earlier. The Norwegian krone fluctuated at values only slightly below its prewar dollar parity throughout 1927 and became redeemable in gold again in May 1928. The trade figures for

---

[1] Michael L. Hoffman, who disapproves of fluctuating exchanges, has insisted on this point. "The Economics of Fluctuating Exchanges" (unpublished dissertation), University of Chicago, 1942, pp. 305–306. The test did fail, incidentally, in the two lengthy historical experiences to which I was able to apply it.

[2] For trade values and the price index, see U.S. Bureau of the Census, *Historical Statistics of the United States, 1789–1945,* Washington: Government Printing Office, 1949, pp. 233–234, 244–245.

Table 12.2. Quantum of Exports Plus Imports of Five European Countries, 1919–1931[a]

	United Kingdom	France	Denmark	Italy	Norway
1919	100		100	100	100
1920	109	100	127	106	99
1921	87	79	138	102	65
1922	106	83	164	93	82
1923	114	81	199	105	86
1924	123	91	203	125	88
1925	(126)	92	195	144	90
1926	123	(101)	201	137	92
1927	131	104	(232)	(138)	98
1928	129	108	242	152	(103)
1929	134	115	242	158	114
1930		114	272	148	118
1931		106	278	138	102

[a] Indexes: 1919 = 100, except 1920 = 100 for France. The circled figures are those of the year in which each country's stabilization occurred; see text.

SOURCES: Total quantum indexes of merchandise exports plus merchandise imports (not including invisible trade) were pieced together from separate quantum indexes and from figures of trade at constant prices found in three League of Nations publications: *Memorandum on Balance of Payments and Foreign Trade Balances, 1911–1925,* vol. I, Geneva: 1926; *Memorandum on International Trade and Balances of Payments, 1927–1929,* vol. I, Geneva: 1930; and *Review of World Trade, 1931 and 1932 (First Half),* Geneva: 1932. The figures for the United Kingdom were adjusted to preserve comparability despite separation of the Irish Free State in April 1923. The Italian figure for 1921 had to be estimated on the basis of the first six months only.

each country's year of stabilization are circled in the table.

No reason is apparent why the figures in Table 12.2 might be systematically biased either toward exaggerating or toward concealing any damage inflicted on trade by exchange-rate fluctuations in the periods before stabilization. Nevertheless, skepticism is in order. One reason hinges on the conceptual problems of index numbers generally and, in particular, on the frankly makeshift nature of the trade-quantum indexes shown in the table. Other reasons concern the shortness of the time periods covered, particularly after stabilization, and the unrepresentativeness of the periods, particularly before stabilization. Toleration of fluctuating rates as an expedient, despite the weight of opinion condemning them, is itself evidence of this. Fluctuating rates were not accepted as a permanent system; little incentives existed for full de-

velopment of appropriate institutions, such as forward-exchange facilities. Instead, countries were consciously struggling back toward exchange stability, at prewar parities if possible, meanwhile undergoing postwar readjustments, the depression of 1920–1922, and price-level instability. Furthermore, the dating of periods "before" and "after" stabilization is difficult. Even when it can be pinned down, the date of a particular country's stabilization against the dollar is not necessarily the date when its trade came to be conducted essentially at fixed rates, since some of its trading partners may have stabilized later. Finally, should the figures showing stagnation of trade after 1929 or 1930 be ignored? *A priori* considerations suggest excluding depression periods, but if the artificial fixity of exchange rates actually had anything to do with the origin or severity of the depression (as can plausibly be argued), then it would be these *a priori* considerations rather than pure empiricism that saved the fixed-rate system from showing poor performance.

Since World War II, Thailand, Peru, and Canada have experienced several years of fluctuating exchange rates. Comparisons of their trade with total world trade, as well as comparisons between periods of fixed and fluctuating rates, seem worth trying. Of course, innumerable reasons justify skepticism about the apparent results. In considering the tables that follow, one should remember certain dates. The bulk of Thailand's trade since the war had been conducted at fluctuating exchange rates, and the reform of September 1955 marked neither the abandonment nor the introduction of an effectively fixed rate but rather the unification of a multiple-rate system in which fluctuating rates had long predominated. Thailand finally adopted a fixed par value in October 1963, after holding the exchange rate rigid for about a year and a half. Late in 1948, Peru introduced a fluctuating rate and broadened its use for specified purposes. In November 1949 the fixed rate was abolished completely in favor of two fluctuating rates that diverged only narrowly from each other. From about October 1950 to August 1951 and again from about October 1954 on, however, the central bank intervened so actively on the exchange market (sometimes holding the rate rigid for more than a year at a time) that the system defies definite classification. This ambiguity weakens whatever lessons the Peruvian experience might seem to provide. Canada unpegged its exchange rate at the beginning of October 1950 and abandoned all remnants of its exchange controls in December 1951. It began manipulating the exchange rate in June 1961 and returned to a fixed rate in May 1962. (Chapter 24 discusses the Canadian experience more fully, which explains the dearth of Canadian statistics here.)

For a first comparison, the dollar value of the exports plus imports of each of the three countries has been expressed as a percentage of the dollar value of the exports plus imports of the entire world (excluding Mainland China, the Soviet Union, and Soviet satellites). Table 12.3 shows that the three coun-

Table 12.3. Dollar Values of Exports Plus Imports of Thailand, Peru, and Canada Expressed as Percentages of the Total Dollar Values of World Exports Plus Imports

Year	Thailand's Percentage	Peru's Percentage	Canada's Percentage
1928	0.29	0.30	4.26
1938	0.30	0.31	3.72
1947	0.24	0.31	5.66
1948	0.37	0.28	5.36
1949	0.44	0.28	5.22
1950	0.44	0.31	5.38
1951	0.40	0.32	5.17
1952	0.41	0.34	5.96
1953	0.43	0.34	6.19
1954	0.38	0.31	5.68
1955	0.38	0.33	5.70
1956	0.36	0.35	5.99
1957	0.37	0.34	5.64
1958	0.36	0.34	5.62
1959	0.38	0.30	5.74
1960	0.37	0.35	5.16
1961	0.40	0.40	5.07
1962	0.39	0.42	4.91
1963	0.38	0.39	4.80

SOURCE: Computed from December 1964 and earlier issues of *International Financial Statistics*. The "world" excludes Mainland China, the Soviet Union, and some Eastern European countries. Canada includes Newfoundland from 1949 on (i.e., Newfoundland's foreign trade becomes included in the Canadian figure, but trade between Newfoundland and the rest of Canada becomes domestic rather than international trade); this complication is of small importance.

tries have generally had at least as large a share of world trade since World War II as before. This fact by itself proves nothing, of course, though really serious interference from fluctuating rates might have been expected to reveal itself.

Another comparison employs postwar rates of growth of rough indexes of the physical volume of trade of the world and of the three countries. Growth rates in the subperiods of first fixed and then fluctuating rates are also shown for Canada and Peru (though the qualification about informal pegging of the Peruvian sol at times since 1950 must be remembered). It should be clear, incidentally, that a growth rate for the whole postwar period is in no sense an average of the rates for subperiods. The figure for Thailand is included for completeness, but, for reasons explained in the note to Table 12.4, the apparent faster growth of Thailand's trade than of world trade deserves little attention. Peruvian apparently grew somewhat faster than world trade, especially since the reform of the exchange system in November 1949. Canadian trade apparently grew somewhat more slowly than world trade, surprisingly enough, though the disparity became less marked after Canada adopted the fluctuating rate in October 1950. The slightly slower growth of Canadian than of world trade seems to clash with the earlier finding that Canada's *share* of world trade did, if anything, grow slightly after 1950. The apparent discrepancy must be attributed to a difference in concepts: one approach deals with growth of quantum indexes, the other with percentages of a total expressed in current U.S. dollars.

For Peru,[3] it may be of interest to see how well trade kept pace with national income before and after abandonment of the fixed rate in 1948-1949 and return to a *de facto* pegged rate around 1960. This is shown in Table 12.5.

Unfortunately for providing evidence, Mexico had a fluctuating exchange rate for less than a year, from July 22, 1948 until June 17, 1949. (Official intervention kept the rate from fluctuating *freely;* but since the peso was not

[3] Thailand made no clear transition from fixed to fluctuating rates in the postwar period, and the figures for Canada appear in Chapter 24.

Table 12.4. Rates of Growth of the Physical Volume of Trade: the World, Thailand, Peru, and Canada, 1946–1958

Inclusive Period	World	Thailand	Peru	Canada
	Yearly Average Percentages			
1946–1958	6.8	14.6	7.8	4.5
1946–1949	8.2		0.6	
1946–1950	8.9			1.0
1950–1958	5.7		7.6	
1951–1958	5.5			4.3

SOURCES AND METHODS: Each of the yearly average percentages of growth was obtained by fitting an exponential trend to the annual trade-quantum figures for the period indicated (i.e., by fitting a linear trend to the logarithms of the trade figures). A quantum index of world exports was spliced together from various issues of the United Nations *Yearbook of International Trade Statistics* and the United Nations *Monthly Bulletin of Statistics,* January 1960. For Thailand, separate export and import quantum indexes through 1949 are given in the UN *Yearbook of International Trade Statistics,* vol. I, 1956, p. 557. Various issues of *International Financial Statistics* give current baht values of exports and imports, as well as a wholesale price index with which to deflate these current values roughly, making it possible to piece together a crude total quantum index for the entire period. (It is thus clear that the quantum index for Thailand is especially a makeshift. An additional reason for this is that Thai trade statistics were complicated by the multiple-exchange-rate system in effect until September 1955. Furthermore, the very sharp growth of Thai trade in the earliest postwar years, as shown in the footnote, takes much of the meaning away from the growth trend for the entire postwar period, which includes these years.) For Peru and Canada, all underlying data come from *International Financial Statistics*. Peruvian export and import values in current soles were deflated by separate export and import price indexes and then added together. Canadian export and import quantum indexes were averaged into a total trade index by use of base-year Canadian-dollar values as weights.

The quantum indexes thus derived and to which the trends were fitted are shown below. They have been shifted to a common base year for easier comparison.

Quantum Indexes of Exports Plus Imports
1953 = 100

Year	World	Thailand	Peru	Canada
1946	58	13	64	72
1947	69	34	58	80
1948	70	57	47	77
1949	75	59	70	75
1950	85	96	70	78
1951	95	112	78	86
1952	94	93	87	96
1953	100	100	100	100
1954	105	109	98	95
1955	114	115	104	106
1956	124	118	118	120
1957	131	129	127	118
1958	129	114	123	113

firmly repegged until it had lost 44 percent of its earlier value, any exchange risk was presumably at least as great as it would have been under a system of completely free rates.) One slight compensation, however, was that the brief period of fluctuating rates was flanked on either side by a period of fixed rates. A 15 percent *ad valorem* tax was imposed on most exports when the fixed rate was abandoned, and the American recession beginning in the fall of 1948 might also have

Table 12.5. Ratio of Peruvian Exports Plus Imports to National Income

Year	Percentage
1946	41.0
1947	37.6
1948	29.6
1949	50.5
1950	45.9
1951	53.1
1952	50.1
1953	50.4
1954	51.7
1955	52.2
1956	58.0
1957	57.9
1958	52.7
1959	50.2
1960	52.9
1961	56.8
1962	58.2
1963	53.7

SOURCE: *International Financial Statistics,* March 1955, January 1960, and December 1964.

been expected to hamper Mexican trade. Nevertheless, the total of imports and exports for the year from mid-1948 to mid-1949, 6,446 million Mexican pesos, does not compare badly with the totals of 5,344, 5,718, 7,192, and 9,313 million pesos for the calendar years 1947 through 1950. Furthermore, the postwar uptrend in the ratio of exports plus imports to national income continued during the period of fluctuating rates. This ratio averaged 19.3 percent in 1946 through 1948, 21.3 percent from mid-1948 to mid-1949, and 25.6 percent from 1949 through 1958. It is interesting to note that Mexican trade increased in relation to national income not only during and after the prolonged depreciation of

July 1948 to June 1949 but also after the devaluation of April 1954. The ratio rose to 26.8 percent in 1951, fell to 24.0 percent in 1953, rose after the 1954 devaluation to a peak of 29.0 percent in 1956, and by 1958 had fallen to 22.9 percent.[4] One plausible interpretation is that trade had become hampered as the fixed exchange rate became progressively more unrealistic and then spurted up again for a while after each devaluation approximately readjusted the rate to the degree of inflation thus far experienced in Mexico.

The preceding pages offer apparent examples both of trade damaged by fluctuating exchange rates and of trade flourishing under fluctuating exchange rates. The exchange-rate system is only one of numerous changing conditions that may affect the level of trade at different times. In general, the evidence is inconclusive. Still, exchange-rate instability has not hampered trade severely enough to make the effect unmistakably clear.

Some scraps of evidence gathered by other writers point to this same negative conclusion. The United States Tariff Commission investigated American trade during the period from October 1931 to about March 1932 to see whether the depression had harmed trade with countries that had left the gold standard more or less severely than trade with countries still clinging to gold. The Commission found no clear difference between changes in American trade with the two groups of countries.[5] James W. Angell classified a number of countries according to the stability or instability of their currencies in 1932 and compared the value and weight of the imports and exports of each group in 1932 with the corresponding averages of the figures for 1929 and 1931. He found that the trade of the unstable-currency group had declined distinctly less than the trade of the stable-currency group.[6] Seymour Harris also collected statistics suggesting that in the early 1930s, the trade of paper-currency countries generally declined less than the trade of gold-standard and exchange- control countries.[7]

Some broader and more impressionistic observations are also available. According to Bertil Ohlin, the volume of world trade grew about as fast during the period 1850–1870, before the full international gold standard came into existence, as in the early twentieth century, and faster than during the period of falling prices from the mid-1870s to the mid-1890s. Besides, trade between gold-standard and silver-standard countries grew even when the gold quotations of silver currencies were changing considerably.[8] According to Whittlesey, the years from 1846 to 1880 were not only a period of very active foreign lending but also probably the era of greatest freedom in world trade; an incipient decline of economic internationalism accompanied the emergence of the international gold standard toward the end of this period.[9] Frank Graham goes so far as to maintain that between the two world wars, the "volume, variety, and general beneficence" of international trade tended to be greater when exchange rates were flexible than when they were fixed.[10]

---

[4] All figures are derived from *International Financial Statistics*. The national income figure used for mid-1948 to mid-1949 is the average of the incomes for the two calendar years; the trade figure is the sum of the monthly figures.

[5] United States Tariff Commission, *Depreciated Exchange* (Report No. 44, second series), Washington: U.S. Government Printing Office, 1932–1933, esp. Part I, pp. 2, 4, 5, and Part III, pp. 352, 357, 366, 370 376. Also see the Commission's *Sixteenth Annual Report, 1932*, Washington: U.S. Government Printing Office, 1933, pp. 59-61.

[6] James W. Angell, "Exchange Depreciation, Foreign Trade and National Welfare," *Proceedings of the Academy of Political Science*, **XV**, June 1933, pp. 290-291. In considering this result and the one mentioned in the next sentence of the text, it should be remembered that gold-standard countries did not conduct all their trade at stable exchange rates, since they were trading with some unstable currency countries. Nevertheless, gold-standard countries presumably did a smaller fraction of their trade at fluctuating exchange rates than unstable-currency countries, so that comparison of the two groups is not meaningless.

[7] Seymour Harris, *Exchange Depreciation*, Cambridge: Harvard University Press, 1936, pp. xxiii, 98-107, and *passim*.

[8] Bertil Ohlin, "International Economic Reconstruction," in Joint Committee, Carnegie Endowment—International Chamber of Commerce, *International Economic Reconstruction*, Paris: International Chamber of Commerce, 1936, p. 36.

[9] Charles R. Whittlesey, *International Monetary Issues*, New York: McGraw-Hill, 1937, pp. 89-91, 237.

[10] Frank Graham, *The Cause and Cure of "Dollar Shortage,"* Essays in International Finance, No. 10, Princeton, N.J., Princeton University, 1949, p. 12.

Exchange Rates and Trade Barriers

Innumerable assertions that fluctuating exchanges cut down the volume of international trade have been published without the support of clear historical evidence. The fragmentary evidence reviewed in this chapter leaves such assertions still unsupported. Yet, as *a priori* considerations insist, the risk of exchange fluctuations must almost certainly eliminate some trade that would otherwise occur. Perhaps it is unreasonable to expect historical or statistical support for this proposition since, as Michael Lindsay Hoffman points out, there is no way of measuring the trade "that would exist under otherwise similar circumstances."[11]

This is a key phrase. Granted that, *ceteris paribus,* exchange instability hampers trade, governments cannot stabilize exchange rates while keeping circumstances "otherwise similar." The very policies necessary to maintain fixed exchange rates, and their fixity at disequilibrium levels, may impede trade more severely than the mere risk of fluctuations.[12] Consideration of these matters, as well as of the ways merchants can guard against exchange risks, may help explain the inconclusiveness of the relevant statistics.

If policy keeps both the exchange-rate and price-and-income mechanisms of balance-of-payments adjustment from operating, tariffs or other controls may arise as a substitute. Alternatively, accepting deflation in the interest of external balance hampers trade. According to several interpreters, the rebirth of protectionism even before the collapse of the historical gold standard is not attributable solely to the self-seeking of producer interests. The unpleasantness of the domestic monetary adjustments required by the gold standard led to evasion of its "rules" by devices not generally recognized as evasions. Especially in the depression of the early 1930s, events dramatized the strongest motives for tariffs, quotas, export subsidies, and exchange controls—to conserve gold and defend the national currency.[13] Even when imposed for these reasons, however, import restrictions tend, for political reasons, to outlast the balance-of-payments crisis that may have occasioned them.

Fixed exchanges have a political tendency to promote import barriers by hiding their adverse effects. The benefit to protected home industries is evident; the burden on other industries is not. Under fixed exchanges, adjustments to balance-of-payments disturbances must take place through a pervasive process of wage and price level changes understood only by special students. Under free exchanges, by contrast, one needs little special knowledge to see that a tariff increase would lower the price of foreign exchange and that while the new tariff would benefit the industries given tighter protection, its repercussions would injure other producers of import-competing goods, as well as exporters. These interests could voice definite objections to proposed tariff increases.[14]

Under fixed exchanges, a country may use commercial policy as a tool for creating or enlarging a balance-of-payments surplus to promote home employment. Examples are found in the 1930s. Under free exchanges (as distinguished from variable but manipulated exchanges) such a "beggar-my-neighbor" policy works less well. If one country does reduce the exports of another by tariffs against its goods, the other country's currency depreciates, tending to counteract the aggressive country's tariff and restore trade equilibrium. Under free exchanges, with trade enabled to jump tariff walls, governments might see the futility of tariffs as "beggar-my-neighbor" weapons.

---

[11] Hoffman, *op. cit.,* p. 306.

[12] In his *"Ceteris Paribus:* Some Notes on Methodology," *Southern Economic Journal,* **XXIV,** January 1958, pp. 259-270, James M. Buchanan has incisively dissected the errors in a number of economic theories purporting to keep constant some relevant magnitudes that simply *cannot* remain constant in the face of changes in the magnitudes considered. A similar criticism should apply to analyses that purport to study the effects of certain policy changes while keeping constant other relevant circumstances that *cannot* remain constant.

[13] See Arthur D. Gayer, *Monetary Policy and Economic Stabilisation,* 2nd ed., New York: Macmillan, 1937, pp. 44-47; and Jørgen Pedersen, *Pengeteori og Pengepolitik,* Copenhagen: Busck, 1944, p. 195.

[14] Henry C. Simons, "Currency Systems and Commercial Policy," in Commission of Inquiry into National Policy in International Economic Relations, *International Economic Relations,* Minneapolis: University of Minnesota Press, 1934, pp. 346-347.

Trade barriers and exchange depreciation are different in regard to retaliation. Retaliatory trade barriers can cancel out whatever benefit a single country might have got from its commercial policy, harming all countries involved by interference with the international division of labor. But retaliatory exchange depreciation does not leave any comparable interference with trade: two countries cannot impose and maintain a depreciation of their own currencies in terms of each other's. And *free* exchanges, by definition, leave no opportunity for beggar-my-neighbor or retaliatory depreciation.

Some economists have worried that trade barriers are more likely to result from fluctuating than from fixed exchanges. The reason seems to be that if some countries allow their currencies to depreciate, other countries, finding themselves in balance-of-payments trouble, will adopt protectionist measures in self-defense. These measures may in turn make the fluctuating currencies depreciate further, calling forth additional protectionism by the other countries, and so forth. Besides, exchange instability may make governments cautious in drawing up commercial treaties. When the danger of sudden and substantial exchange-rate changes exists, governments may hesitate to commit themselves to cuts in trade barriers. They may keep the machinery of emergency import control in readiness. Commercial treaties may be subject to denunciation on short notice or may include reservations regarding exchange-rate changes.[15]

This reasoning tacitly recognizes that protectionism is more likely to flourish in countries trying to maintain fixed exchange rates than in free-exchange countries. The erection of trade barriers against alleged exchange dumping is an effect not so much of fluctuating exchanges in particular as of general horror at all opportunities to obtain foreign goods on particularly favorable terms. While

fluctuating foreign currencies may give protectionists a superficially plausible argument for stricter import barriers, the same necessary connection does not exist between fluctuating currencies and trade barriers as exists between overvalued currencies and trade barriers.

Furthermore, when free currencies depreciate on the exchange market, they must do so in response to conditions that would otherwise have caused balance-of-payments trouble for the countries concerned. If these countries did not allow their currencies to depreciate, they might have had to meet the situation with extra import barriers or export subsidies or internal deflation or disinflation. These measures, like depreciation, would cut down on imports from other countries. A country with an overvalued currency cannot avoid trade barriers simply by not depreciating unless it has such ample reserves of foreign exchange that the authorities can use them freely without fear of their possible exhaustion.

The argument about how depreciation may impel *other* countries to erect trade barriers usually seems to contemplate a sudden overcorrection of a previous overvaluation, so that the depreciating country's new undervaluation puts other countries under strain. But this is less a characteristic of *freely* fluctuating exchanges than of flexibly pegged or managed exchanges. When a free currency depreciates, it does not necessarily put pressure on foreign countries. Suppose that as a country reflates at home in order to promote recovery from a depression, its currency depreciates passively on the exchanges. This does not steal markets from foreign countries, for the income effect of the reflation tends to offset the price effect of the depreciation. Adjustment of exchange rates to equilibrium levels promotes trade; depreciation puts pressure on the outside world only if it carries the exchange value of a currency below equilibrium.

As for the danger that fluctuating exchanges would obstruct international commercial agreements, this much seems true: fluctuating exchanges do complicate appraisals of the worth of proposed "concessions" in commercial policy and do complicate intergovernmental planning as to precisely what degree

[15] T. E. Gregory, "The Reports of the Experts to the Joint Committee: A Personal Survey," *International Economic Reconstruction*, Paris: International Chamber of Commerce, 1936, pp. 171, 189-190. Also see "Report of the Expert Committee" in *ibid.*, p. 222, and Margaret Gordon, *Barriers to World Trade*, New York: Macmillan, 1941, pp. 12-13.

of protectionism each contracting government shall retain. But free exchanges facilitate rather than obstruct *voluntary* steps toward freer trade, as contrasted to unenthusiastic participation in a game which, to judge from reference to tariff cuts as "concessions" or sacrifices, is seen as a game of "You cut your throat and I'll cut mine."

Disequilibrium Exchange Rates

It is superficial to blame interference with trade on trade barriers when clinging to wrong exchange rates is what makes these barriers seem necessary. In the 1930s, for example, exchange controls and quotas were probably less responsible for the contraction in trade than the maintenance of overvalued parities. Professor Nurkse has put the point well:

That the mere rate at which one currency is exchanged for other currencies can [affect the volume of trade] is not an easy or familiar notion to the general public, whereas the instruments used to support an overvalued currency —exchange control and quotas, among others— are immediately evident and so are apt to be regarded as the real cause of the fall in trade. But it should be clear that a country with an overvalued currency necessarily suffers a decline in its competitive capacity to export and that consequently its imports, in so far as they must be paid for by exports, have to be cut down accordingly; the means by which the cut is effected are of secondary interest; they may be exchange restrictions, import licenses, quotas, prohibitions or even tariffs. In the conceivable extreme case where a currency's external value is so high that exports decline to zero, the result would be complete national autarky.[16]

If a government decrees and rigidly enforces too high an exchange value for its currency, it makes exports unprofitable and foreign exchange for imports correspondingly scarce. In the absence of official import controls or exchange rationing, unofficial and haphazard equivalents would inevitably develop. Undervaluation of the currency, on the other hand, will discourage imports by making them unduly expensive. Exports seem very profitable,

---

[16] Ragnar Nurkse, *International Currency Experience,* League of Nations, 1944, p. 184. Also see p. 169.

but unless private parties or the authorities are willing to go on and on accumulating foreign exchange without using it (thus making interest-free or low-interest loans or ultimately even gifts to foreigners), or unless foreigners have inexhaustible reserves of the undervalued currency, export as well as import trade will decline. (Imports and, in turn, exports would revive, however, if a decline in the purchasing power of the domestic currency were to end the undervaluation. This might occur if the authorities created additional domestic money to finance their accumulations of foreign exchange at the fixed rate.)

This reasoning suggests that the volume of trade is larger at equilibrium than at disequilibrium exchange rates, just as the amount of a commodity changing hands per time period in any ordinary competitive market is greater at the price than equates supply and demand than at some different floor or ceiling price. This conclusion may not apply, however, when the overvalued-currency countries have ample enough reserves to satisfy all demands for foreign exchange at the official rates. The increase in their imports over what the volume would be at equilibrium rates might then be as large as or larger than the reduction in their exports. But this exception depends on truly ample foreign-exchange reserves. Maintaining exchange stability by import barriers is not at all the same thing as maintaining it by the lavish use of inexhaustible reserves.

Since underlying supplies and demands are continually changing, a fixed exchange rate is usually a disequilibrium rate, just as an officially fixed commodity price would usually be a disequilibrium price. If an exchange rate or a price is fixed by the government—and can be counted on to stay fixed—trade is no longer hampered by the risk of fluctuation. But does removing this risk tend to promote trade more than the disequilibrium price tends to hamper it? Merchants may indeed *worry* less about risk under fixed exchanges than under free exchanges, but part of the reason may simply be that fixed disequilibrium rates rule some potential trade so completely out of consideration that there is no point in worrying about risk connected with it.

Something can even be said in favor or clearly temporary or seasonal exchange-rate fluctuations. If shifting supplies and demands cause the equilibrium rate to change seasonally, stabilization at some average level would cause a discrepancy between actual and equilibrium rates throughout most of the year and so might hamper trade. (Think of the regrettable consequences that would flow from officially stabilizing Florida hotel rates at some average level throughout the year.) Generally speaking, seasonal fluctuations seem particularly useful in the prices of nonstorable goods and services. Now, many services enter into international trade—shipping services, harbor and dock use, the labor of stevedores and of employees of trading firms, and so forth. Also, not all internationally traded commodities are storable. Seasonal rate fluctuations may be useful in tending to even out the quantities of these nonstorable goods and services demanded throughout the year.

The case for pegging still would not be conclusive even if fluctuations were clearly a *net* deterrent to trade. This might not be too high a price to pay for greater freedom in domestic monetary and fiscal policy. Furthermore any trade that exchange risk might destroy would probably be trade in articles whose international cost differences would be the smallest—trade in articles in which the exporting countries had the smallest comparative advantages over the importing countries.[17] More precisely, the *segments* of trade destroyed would be those for which the *marginal* comparative advantages would rise most slowly as trade shrank. Even though welfare cannot actually be measured, a presumption emerges that exchange risk shrinks welfare less than in proportion to the total volume of trade. The same cannot be said of controls adopted to support disequilibrium exchange rates, since they are often imposed in notorious disregard of comparative advantage.

Finally, exchange risk is not peculiar to a system of freely fluctuating rates. It also characterizes any other system under which rate changes are possible. When countries pursue independent and uncoordinated monetary and fiscal policies, the choice cannot lie between fluctuating exchange rates and permanently fixed rates. It lies, rather, between more or less even fluctuation and temporary stability interrupted by occasional sharp changes.[18] Changes need not actually occur frequently in order to cause apprehension.

Protection Against Exchange Risk

A full comparison of rival systems on this score must consider the possibilities of shedding risk. In one respect, as the following discussion will show, the possibilities are sometimes less satisfactory under pegged-but-adjustable rates than under free rates.

A merchant can largely avoid the risk of an unfavorable change in the fluctuating price of foreign exchange by creating an offsetting liability or asset in the foreign currency as soon as he becomes committed to receive or pay it in the future. An American exporter due to receive payment in sterling in 90 days might immediately borrow the sterling in London and sell it for dollars. The cost of this precaution would be any excess of interest paid to the British lender over interest obtainable on the dollars. A foreign electric system ordering heavy machinery in England might borrow *all* the necessary money at home at once, buy pounds at once, and place the money on loan in England until the sterling payments to the English engineering firms fell due. Difficulties, delays, and expenses in borrowing are, of course, obstacles to this approach.

A merchant might find it convenient to have a bank account in foreign money, either abroad or with his bank at home. When he incurred an obligation to pay foreign currency in the future, he could immediately buy it and add it to his account, from which he could make payment at the proper time. When he became entitled to

---

[17] L. L. B. Angas, *The Problems of the Foreign Exchanges,* London: Macmillan, 1935, pp. 176, 180.

[18] Frank D. Graham, "Achilles' Heels in Monetary Standards," *American Economic Review,* XXX, March 1940, p. 28.

receive foreign currency in the future, he could immediately sell the corresponding amount from his account, replenishing it upon receipt of the expected payment. Unfortunately, this requires the merchant to tie up capital; any interest received on foreign-currency accounts might not be an adequate compensation. Furthermore, a merchant doing business with several countries would have to hold several foreign-currency accounts. Such arrangements would be satisfactory only for companies regularly both receiving and making payments in foreign countries. An English insurance company, for example, might guard rather well against fluctuations in the pound-dollar rate by leaving a large part of its premiums collected in the United States invested or on deposit there as a fund from which to make indemnity payments to American customers.

Forward Exchange and Some Minor Inadequacies

The foregoing methods are unimportant compared with forward exchange. An American importer or exporter due to pay or receive sterling in 90 days can protect himself against appreciation or depreciation of the pound in the meanwhile by buying or selling sterling forward. That is, he makes a contract with his bank to buy or sell a given number of pounds in 90 days at a price agreed on in advance. An importer does not have to lay out dollars to buy pounds until he needs them, yet he can be sure of the price at which he will get them. An exporter can grant credit to his foreign customer without running the risk of exchange loss.

All this was explained in Chapter 2, and details need not be repeated here except in considering some inadequacies of forward exchange. One is that forward-exchange contracts do not actually eliminate risk; rather, they offset one risk by another in the opposite direction. For example, an American exporter who is to receive future payment in British pounds stands to lose by depreciation of sterling in terms of dollars and stands to gain by an appreciation. By selling the same number of pounds forward, the exporter takes a

position in which he stands to gain by depreciation of sterling and to lose by appreciation. Now, if the export transaction that is the reason for the forward contract somehow falls through or if the foreign customer is delinquent in paying his debt, the exporter has an uncovered position in foreign exchange and stands to lose if he has to buy sterling at an appreciated price to deliver it to the bank under his forward contract. This is hardly a serious problem, however. At least those firms that import or export in large volume can learn from experience how to make allowance, in buying or selling forward exchange, for the fraction of their commercial transactions that will not be completed as originally planned.

Forward exchange cannot simultaneously protect the importer of a competitively traded staple commodity against both of the risks mentioned earlier—the exchange risk and the price risk. If the importer buys foreign currency forward to guard against its appreciation between the time he orders the goods and the time he is to pay, he still stands a risk of the second kind: if the currency of the supplying country depreciates against the home currency before the importer has disposed of the goods, the value of his inventory falls, since his competitors can now import more of the same goods at a lower home-money price than he paid. By neglecting to make any forward-exchange contract at all, the importer would let the two kinds of exchange risk partially offset each other. If the foreign currency appreciated, he would lose in buying foreign exchange to pay his supplier but would gain on the home-money value of his inventory. If the foreign depreciated, he would gain in buying foreign exchange to pay his supplier but would lose on the home-money value of his inventory. Unfortunately, the two risks do not exactly offset each other and the importer must estimate how and to what extent, on balance, he stands to gain or lose by a change in the exchange rate. Having made this estimate, the importer can judge, though not very accurately, how much foreign exchange to buy.

An importer's dilemma may be particularly

troublesome if he is importing some staple commodity from a country that accounts for a major fraction of the total world supply and whose currency is threatened with devaluation. (Essentially the same dilemma exists if upward revaluation of the home currency is a strong possibility, except that it is not necessary for a large fraction of total imports to be bought in some particular foreign country.) If he does cover his foreign-exchange needs by a forward purchase, he risks the inventory loss just explained. If he hedges against this risk by *not* buying exchange forward and if the expected foreign devaluation is somehow avoided, he may find that his competitors have obtained a price advantage by grasping the opportunity to buy the foreign currency forward at the heavy forward discount reflecting the general distrust of its spot rate. It should be noted, however, that the large forward discount causing the special problem in this example is unlikely to occur except when spot exchange rates are (adjustably) pegged; in the absence of pegging, spot and forward rates would fluctuate fairly closely together, in accordance with the principle of interest parities.

The foregoing examples no doubt exaggerate an importer's problems. Inventory risk is ordinarily likely to be small relative to exchange risk, and an importer would ordinarily do well to obtain forward cover for the bulk of his foreign-exchange needs. (The terms *covering* and *hedging* are often used loosely as complete synonyms. When a distinction is intended, *covering* means arranging for protection against the exchange risk involved in a definitely scheduled commercial or financial transaction. *Hedging* then means arranging for protection against an indefinite and indirect risk linked with a possible rate change.)[19]

The Cost of Forward-exchange Coverage

Even if forward-exchange contracts do offer adequate protection against exchange risk, the possible objection remains that the cost of this protection would appreciably deter trade under free exchanges.[20] The cost to an individual trader is the difference between spot and forward rates of exchange. A forward premium would represent the price of protection to importers. While a burden on importers, such a premium would be an advantage to exporters due to receive subsequent payment in foreign currency: they would realize more home currency by selling exchange forward than by selling it spot. For this reason and also because a forward discount rather than premium may prevail, the cost of using forward-exchange facilities may just as well be negative as positive. There is, of course, no presumption that the positive or negative cost will fall entirely on only one of the parties to an international transaction; it may well be split between them through its effect on the pricing of the goods traded.

In fully free exchange markets, the cost of risk avoidance are ordinarily large neither negatively or positively, since forward and spot rates are closely related. One reason is that commercial demands and supplies of forward exchange partly match each other. While importers want to buy exchange forward, exporters want to sell. Banks and brokers make a business of enabling traders to satisfy each other's requirements, and competition tends to keep margins small enough just to compensate the middlemen for their work. Under normal conditions, furthermore, the spread between the spot and forward rates is aligned with the international difference in short-term interest rates. The explanation, already given in Chapter 2, involves interest arbitrage and the principle of interest parities. Even if London and New York interest rates differed by the improbably large amount of four percentage points a year, for example, the premium or discount from spot on 90-day forward exchange would be only about 1 percent.

Forward Rates under Fixed Spot Rates

Perhaps the idea that forward premiums or discounts would be harmfully large under free exchanges stems from the figures

[19] See Paul Einzig, *A Dynamic Theory of Forward Exchange;* London: Macmillan, 1961, esp. pp. 3-4, 34, 82-85, 89-92, 234-236.

[20] Cf. Nurkse, *op. cit.,* p. 210.

recorded under abnormal conditions, as at times in the 1930s. During 1935 the discounts on three-month forward French francs, Dutch guilders, and Swiss francs reached 27, 22, and 29 percent per annum respectively.[21] The forward French franc was even weaker in 1936. At times before the devaluation in September, the discount on three-month francs went to 37 or 38 percent per annum.[22] Under these conditions, protection against exchange risk was expensive indeed. If an American owner had hedged an asset valued in a fixed number of French francs by a three-month forward sale on January 2, 1935 and by six successive renewals, the cost would have amounted to more than half of the loss that the owner would otherwise have suffered from the devaluation in September 1936. The high cost of hedging induced many businessmen to leave their long positions in francs unprotected.[23]

These large forward discounts betrayed general distrust of the currencies of the European "gold bloc." Demand and supply of forward exchange were very one-sided. At forward rates in line with spot rates, few traders with future obligations in francs would have wanted to buy francs forward to guard against such an unlikely event as appreciation. But those with claims to future francs, or Frenchmen with future obligations in foreign currencies, were eager to sell francs forward, at least if the discount did not seem too large. Outright bear speculation also took place in the forward market.

Why didn't interest arbitrage compensate for the one-sidedness of other supply and demand? It was indeed profitable for holders of francs to sell them spot and repurchase them forward. As these operations involved the sale of spot francs, they increased the gold outflows from France and also tended to reduce the supply of loanable funds, increasing French interest rates.[24] Though arbitrage *was* tending to equate the forward franc discount to the difference between French and foreign interest rates in two ways—by supporting the forward franc and by raising French interest rates—it could not do the job completely. For one thing, arbitrage could not pull the spot franc appreciably down toward the forward franc as long as France still clung to the gold parity. Furthermore, some Frenchmen, once having got their money out of France, were presumably reluctant to bring it back again by buying forward francs. Perhaps even more important was the fact that the French government tried to discourage interest arbitrage. Also, Great Britain and other countries tried to help the gold-bloc governments in their fight against what they considered speculation.[25]

Since commercial demand for and supply of forward exchange are seldom equally strong and are especially unlikely to be so when the spot rate is inappropriate, "legitimate" traders can be sure of finding cover at moderate discounts or premiums only in an active market broadened by speculation and interest arbitrage. Exchange restrictions, even if confined to capital transfers, interfere with interest arbitrage. To the extent that "legitimate" traders can find cover only with their fellows dealing in the opposite direction, forward rates may have to deviate far from spot rates in order to equate "legitimate" supplies and demands.

One side or the other of the forward market is especially likely to languish when a pegged spot rate is generally distrusted. When a currency is expected to fall, holders of claims to future payment in it will be able to cover them only at unattractive forward rates. Even if outright speculators are prevented from selling the distrusted currency forward, selling pressure on the forward rate still exceeds buying pressure, for people committed to make future payments in the cur-

---

[21] A. A. van Sandick, "Memorandum on the Technique of the Forward Exchange Market and the Elimination of Uncertainty," *The Improvement of Commercial Relations between Nations and the Problems of Monetary Stabilization,* Paris: International Chamber of Commerce, 1936, p. 306.

[22] Paul Einzig, *The Theory of Forward Exchange,* London: Macmillan, 1937, pp. 480-481; Martin Wolfe, *The French Franc Between the Wars,* New York: Columbia University Press, 1951, p. 164. The figures refer to pound-franc rates.

[23] Charles P. Kindleberger, "Speculation and Forward Exchange," *Journal of Political Economy,* XLVII, April 1939, p. 176.

[24] Einzig, *The Theory of Forward Exchange,* pp. 192–193.

[25] *Ibid.,* pp. 377–378; Kindleberger, *op. cit.,* p. 172.

rency have ample reason not to buy it forward.

Large forward discounts on currencies with precariously pegged exchange values prove nothing about the probable costs of hedging under free exchanges. This point is important. Indeed, because of large and unstable discrepancies between spot and forward rates, exchange risk can at times be a bigger deterrent to international trade under pegged-but-adjustable exchanges than under fluctuating exchanges. How often precariously pegged rates actually do change is not decisive. The point is that traders bear in mind the risk of changes and that protection against this risk becomes expensive under pegged exchanges precisely when traders most feel the need for it. Under free rates, by contrast, there is no general opinion that the spot rate will move only in one particular direction, since the current spot rate *already* reflects the balance of opinion. Consequently, neither buying nor selling pressure predominates in the forward market. Furthermore, freedom for capital movements allows interest arbitrage to keep forward rates near their interest parities in relation to spot rates. Since speculators realize this, speculation helps keep discrepancies between spot and forward rates small and transitory.

Miscellaneous Costs of Forward Cover

This optimistic conclusion perhaps needs to be slightly qualified. Pledging collateral, if it were required, would be an additional cost of risk protection. When a bank finds itself with a net long or short position in some currency as a result of forward contracts with its customers, it offsets this position by selling or buying the currency. If one of its customers defaults on his forward contract, the bank has an uncovered position in the currency and may suffer an exchange loss. To protect itself, the bank may require a customer to put up some collateral or margin to guarantee performance of his forward contract. The collateral required would be worth only a fraction of the amount of the contract, since default by a customer costs the bank not the whole amount, but only the possible loss

on that amount because of an unfavorable exchange-rate movement. Still, putting up even a relatively small capital in collateral or margin might increase the true cost of protection. In practice, however, banks seldom ask traders to guarantee their forward contracts with collateral. The reason is that a bank ordinarily makes forward contracts only with its regular customers, whom it has learned to trust and who probably have deposits in the bank anyway.

In appraising the total cost of forward-exchange protection, one should remember several facts. First, while provision of forward-exchange facilities does use up some labor and resources, so does the operation of spot markets. Even if forward exchange vanished, much of the cost would probably still have to be incurred in maintaining ordinary exchange facilities. Secondly, the many kinds of governmental and intergovernmental activities involved in trying to keep exchange rates pegged have costs of their own. Actually, these various costs come in addition to rather than instead of the costs of forward-exchange facilities, since when exchange rates are pegged but insecure, traders still feel the need of forward-exchange cover. Furthermore, cost-cutting competition among banks prevails in supplying forward-exchange facilities, whereas there can be no similar competition in the supply of governmental and intergovernmental measures. One final point rests on a value judgment that costs should ordinarily be borne by the people in whose interest they are incurred: the cost, such as it is, of protection against free-market exchange fluctuations falls on the producers and consumers of internationally traded goods, whereas the expense of governmental measures falls largely on taxpayers in general.

Long-term Exchange Risk

Forward exchange does not provide perfect protection against long-term exchange risk. If a construction company is doing work in a foreign country and is to receive payment in the foreign currency only after the lapse of well over a year, how can it protect itself against exchange risk? Special arrangements can sometimes be made, and long-term forward contracts might become regularly available if sufficient demand arose and exchange restrictions did not interfere; the recent trend of forward-exchange practice is encouraging in this respect.[26] But the construction company in our example has no really good answer to its problem if banks do not make forward contracts of maturities as long as it requires. Still, it can eliminate most of its exchange risk by selling the currency it expects to receive by a three-month forward contract and then renewing the contract every three months.

For the sake of as simple an explanation as possible, let us consider what an American exporter might do to avoid exchange loss on £1 to be received six months in the future, even though three-month contracts were the longest obtainable. First, he sells £1 to his bank three months forward at a price of about $3.00. (We assume that the spot rate at the time is exactly $3.00; *about* means plus the forward premium or minus the forward discount, which, in accordance with the principle of interest parities, will ordinarily be only a fraction of 1 percent.) If the spot rate is unchanged when the forward contract comes due, our exporter buys £1 in the spot market for $3.00, delivers it to the bank to fulfill the contract, and receives the agreed price of "about $3.00." Then he again sells one pound three months forward at a price of about $3.00 (but probably not precisely the same forward price as before). (Actual practice, of course, telescopes these separate steps

together.) By the time this second contract comes due, the exporter has received from his English customer the £1 that is the occasion for these procedures. He delivers it to the bank and receives the agreed price of about $3.00, no matter what may have happened to the exchange rate during the second three months.

Now let us suppose the same situation, except that by the end of the first three months the spot pound has depreciated to $2.00. To fulfill his forward contract, the exporter buys £1 in the spot market for $2.00 and delivers it to the bank for the agreed price of about $3.00. Then, to guard against further depreciation, he again sells £1 forward for three months, this time at a forward rate of about $2.00. This he receives when he finally delivers £1 at the end of the second three months. This price, together with the profit of about $1.00 taken in closing out the first contract, amounts to approximately the rate of "about $3.00" that the exporter had originally counted on. If the pound, instead of depreciating, had appreciated to $4.00 during the first three months, the exporter would have lost about $1.00 in closing out his first contract, but this loss would be approximately offset by his receipt of about $4.00 under the second forward contract.

If an American importer is committed to pay £1 six months in the future, he can protect himself by buying £1 three months forward and then renewing. The original forward rate is approximately equal to the $3.00 spot rate. At the end of three months, the importer takes delivery, paying the agreed price of about $3.00. If by then the spot pound had appreciated to $4.00, the importer would collect a profit of about $1.00. Because of this, he would in effect pay only the approximate net price for the pound that he had originally counted on, even though he took delivery at the end of the second forward contract at the new rate of about $4.00 specified in it.

These examples show that a series of short-term forward contracts can remove most of a long-term exchange risk. Most, but not all. For one thing, a merchant risks not being able to get a new forward contract when an old one expires. Barring the outbreak of war

[26] One-year forward contracts are now fairly common in New York, and even a number of three-year contracts have been made. Alan R. Holmes, *The New York Foreign Exchange Market*, Federal Reserve Bank of New York, 1959, p. 38. In Sweden, forward contracts may be made for one year, with a half-year extension possible. Bent Hansen, "Interest Policy, Foreign Exchange Policy and Foreign Exchange Control," *Skandinaviska Banken Quarterly Review*, **XL**, January 1959, p. 16. In an article dealing with British and Continental practices (*Economic Journal*, September 1960, pp. 486, 493), Paul Einzig mentions that forward exchange up to 12 months is now a matter of routine, that contracts in some currencies are becoming available for maturities of up to 4 years, and that long-term forward exchange will become a matter of routine before many years. Einzig also mentions four-year contracts in his *A Dynamic Theory of Forward Exchange*, pp. 58, 548.

or the imposition of crippling exchange controls, however, the forward market will not suddenly vanish. More substantial is the risk of being able to renew a forward contract only on unfavorable terms. The forward seller risks the emergence of a large forward discount from the spot rate, and the forward buyer risks the emergence of a large premium. The risk consists not in the possibility of large fluctuations in spot or forward rates, which in themselves are relatively harmless, but in the possibility of *divergent* spot and forward rate movements. Interest arbitrage ordinarily prevents large divergences.

Here we begin to see another difference between exchange risk under freely fluctuating and under pegged-but-adjustable rates. The forward rate can deviate considerably from a *pegged* spot rate because of one-sided selling or buying pressure in the forward market when the spot rate is generally considered untenably high or low. Also, precisely because the spot rate is pegged, it cannot move to help close the gap between itself and the forward rate. Finally, controls sometimes used in maintaining a fixed spot rate may interfere with the interest arbitrage that would otherwise keep the gap between spot and forward rates narrow. Under pegged rates, changing rumors about the imminence and size of an exchange-rate adjustment are sometimes likely to make the forward premium or discount not only large but also highly unstable. Behavior of forward discounts on the European gold-bloc currencies before the devaluations of 1936 illustrates these points. Similar if less spectacular examples of large and unstable forward discounts on supposedly stable currencies are found since World War II. The large forward premium on the German mark in terms of sterling that emerged in the late summer of 1957 is particularly instructive because it stemmed from rumors of exchange-rate adjustments that in fact were not made.

A businessman may feel almost as much risk in a long-term position in a foreign currency under pegged exchanges as under free exchanges. No one can be certain that a pegged rate will not be altered within the next few months or years. Yet because the forward premium or discount may vary widely, a trader cannot count on hedging his risk economically by successive renewals of short-term contracts. Under free exchanges, possible variations in the forward premium or discount are a less serious threat to advantageous renewal of forward contracts. Therefore, irremovable long-term exchange risk may even be a less serious problem under free exchanges than under pegged exchanges. This point deserves thoughtful consideration. And in reality, the makeshift of renewals is unnecessary when long-term contracts are available.

There is still less risk, of course, when a country will sacrifice full employment and price-level stability, if need be, to the supreme goal of preserving the parity of its currency under a full-fledged international gold standard. But a *hybrid* system may well pose a worse problem of exchange risk than either extreme of monetary nationalism or monetary internationalism.

Types of Forward-exchange Contract

After considering whether forward exchange contracts provide a hedge against long-term risk, we should ask whether or not forward contracts are available only in standard maturities—30, 60, and 90 days. What recourse is open to a trader who wants to buy or sell a currency in 45 or 75 days or who does not know the exact date when he will need to buy or sell it? For one thing, a combination of spot and forward transactions should be able to meet the problem at no great expense. Odd-length contracts are also possible. Already, in fact, banks will tailor the lengths of contracts to the needs of their customers. Banks also offer contracts permitting the customer to make or take deliver whenever he chooses during a specified week or half-month or month.

Similarly, banks will tailor the denominations of contracts as customers wish; it is quite possible to sell, say £716 15s. 2d. forward. Large importing and exporting firms might be content to make contracts in round numbers. However, forward-exchange facilities are not just for big traders; even small businesses can use them.

Availability of Forward-exchange Facilities

A common worry about forward exchange as protection against exchange risk is that its facilities are available only to the traders of a few leading countries. However, even if a small trader in some remote country were ignorant of forward exchange, his trading partner in an important foreign market might be willing to quote prices in the small trader's own currency in order to get his business. According to Einzig, German exporters, who had access to forward exchange facilities, made striking headway before World War I in such outlying districts as the interiors of Brazil and China.[27]

A similar worry is that exchange markets could not be expected to quote minor currencies in terms of one another. A Finnish importer of goods from Honduras could hardly hope to buy forward lempiras in terms of markkas. However, if there were a forward market between the markka and sterling and a forward market between the lempira and sterling, then the markka and lempira would be linked indirectly by forward-exchange facilities. If it were to their advantage, importers and exporters in little countries could, as they largely do now, agree on prices in terms of sterling or some other important currency and then avoid exchange risk by forward dealings in the local currency and sterling. Little countries would need to have a forward market in only the one or two most important foreign currencies. Alternatively, the custom might arise of pricing exports and imports of small countries in grams of gold, so that a market in gold futures in each country would suffice to protect local exporters and importers against exchange risk.

History gives encouragement about the likelihood that adequate forward markets

would develop under free exchanges, if given a chance. Throughout the 1880s the Vienna bourse dealt actively in German mark notes for forward delivery, and forward dealings had probably begun several decades earlier. There were also occasional forward dealings in Vienna and Trieste in sterling and French francs against fluctuating Austrian crowns. Berlin had an irregular market in forward rubles after the Russian paper money became inconvertible during the Crimean War. This market gained importance in the late 1870s, when a large and steady export of grain from Russia developed and when the Russian government printed paper money to finance its war with Turkey. St. Petersburg had a less important forward market. The United States had active forward-exchange markets several decades before World War I; these markets probably originated during the period of the Civil War greenbacks. At that time New York definitely had a well-organized market in gold futures, which was practically equivalent to a market in forward sterling. Long before World War I, fluctuations in the exchange rate between silver and gold gave rise to a forward sterling market in Shanghai. Japan had forward exchange facilities in sterling, dollars, and francs. Argentina, Brazil, Chile, Egypt, Spain, Portugal, and most other civilized countries, according to Einzig, had active forward markets before World War I. Forward exchange markets were especially active in the period of exchange fluctuations after World War I. During the 1930s, merchants could buy and sell forward sterling, dollars, French and Swiss francs, guilders, belgas, escudos, Canadian dollars, Scandinavian currencies, and the major Latin American and Oriental currencies. Before interference from exchange restrictions or internal troubles, good forward markets had also existed in other currencies, such as reichsmarks, lire, and pesetas.[28]

An account of the forward-exchange market in as small as country as Chile before

---

[27] Einzig, *The Theory of Forward Exchange*, pp. 50-51.

[28] *Ibid.*, pp. 37-39, 42-46, 379-380; Van Sandick, *op. cit.*, p. 297; Gerhart v. Schulze-Gävernitz, *Volkswirtschaftliche Studien aus Russland*, Leipzig: Duncker & Humblot, 1899, *passim* between pp. 499-536.

World War I is relevant to judging whether adequate hedging facilities might arise under free exchanges. The Chilean peso was so unstable that all purchases and sales of foreign exchange were forward transactions, unless otherwise specifically agreed. Spot transactions were for small amounts only. Since mailboats sailed from Valparaiso for Liverpool every other Tuesday morning, most forward-exchange contracts were arranged to fall due on the Monday before each departure. Forward contracts were made for the nearest mail-day and for each of the 25 following, so that traders could cover foreign-exchange commitments for as long as a year in the future. Most contracts were for multiples of £500. Traders dealt in forward exchange, free from government control, on a bourse, in the banks, and even on the streets. There was also a well-developed renewal market, giving speculators the opportunity to continue their forward-exchange positions.[29]

Exchange Risk and International Lending

A twin to the worry that exchange fluctuations would hamper international trade is the worry that they would discourage international borrowing and lending. If a lender makes a loan in the currency of a foreign borrower, whether for 30 days or for 30 years, he runs the risk that the foreign currency will be worth less in his own currency at the time of repayment than when he made the loan. If the loan is in the lender's currency, the borrower risks having to repay at a time when that currency has appreciated against his own. Of course, the chance of gain from a favorable rate movement stands against the chance of loss from an unfavorable one. This obvious point should be remembered throughout the present discussion.

If forward-exchange facilities can overcome the exchange risks associated with trade, why can't they do the same for the risks associated with international lending? In fact, individuals *can* protect themselves from ex-

change risk on short-term international loans. Interest arbitrage is a prime example: an arbitrageur who is temporarily transferring funds abroad sells the foreign currency forward at the same time he buys it spot. However, borrowers and lenders can all get rid of their exchange risks only when the flows of capital into and out of a country match each other. Forward exchange cannot get rid of the exchange risk on a *net* outflow or inflow. Lenders placing funds abroad will not only buy the foreign currency spot to pay for the securities bought but will also want to sell the currency forward to cover bringing their funds home again. If the capital movement is supposed to be a *net* outflow from the lending country, the safety-minded lenders will predominate as sellers of the foreign currency in the *forward* market. Now, who are the corresponding buyers of forward foreign exchange, i.e., forward sellers of the currency of the *lending* country? They must largely be arbitrageurs who, in order to be able to sell the lending country's currency forward without risk, have bought it spot. (These arbitrageurs may, of course, be nationals of the lending country who are buying their own currency spot with funds borrowed abroad.) In buying and holding the currency of the lending country, the arbitrageurs are transferring capital *into* that country. The ordinary capital export in the form of foreign security purchases is matched by a capital import through arbitrage in the spot and forward markets. Thus, if capital exporters insist on covering all of their exchange risk, they will fail to accomplish any net capital export at all.[30]

The same is true of an international loan expressed in the lenders' currency. The borrowers will want to cover their repayment by buying that currency forward. But the arbitrageurs who sell it forward will cover themselves by buying it spot. As before, this

[29] Rudolf Dunker, "Kursspekulation und Kurssicherung in südamerikanische Valuten, speziell in chilenischer Währung," *Bank-Archiv,* 15 Oct. and 1 Nov. 1909, esp. pp. 40-41.

[30] This reasoning expands on Harold Barger, "Speculation and the Risk-Preference," *Journal of Political Economy,* XLVI, June 1938, p. 402. Also see *Bretton Woods for Better or Worse,* London: Longmans, Green, 1946, pp. 100-104, where R. G. Hawtrey reaches the same conclusion: if no one were willing to bear the risk of exchange-rate instability, net lending would cease to be international.

amounts to an offsetting flow of capital into the country that superficially appears to be exporting capital.

This analysis requires some qualification. Not all those who serve as counterparties in forward contracts with risk-avoiding lenders or borrowers need be risk-avoiding arbitrageurs; some may be speculators who deliberately assume exchange risk by leaving their forward sales of the lending country's currency uncovered by spot purchases. A net international capital movement can then take place with nonspeculative borrowers and lenders protected against exchange risk.

Still, it remains true under unstable exchanges that international lending inevitably involves exchange risk to be borne by *somebody*. There are no obvious grounds for assuming that speculators would operate in the right direction and shoulder enough of the risk to leave international lending just as active under unstable exchanges as, other things being equal, it would be under stable exchanges. Exchange instability apparently is a genuine deterrent to international capital movements.[31]

This disadvantage is not peculiar to *freely fluctuating* exchange rates, however; rather, it characterizes all systems of changeable exchange rates, including pegged-but-adjustable rates. If the exchange rate changes in the harmful direction during the life of an international loan, it makes no difference to the losers whether the change occurred through free-market fluctuations or through one or more adjustments in official pegging. It is not enough that governments try to avoid frequent rate adjustments. To eliminate exchange risk over the life of medium and long-term international loans, countries must sacrifice enough of their national monetary and fiscal independence to make exchange-rate adjustments unnecessary. For encouragement of international lending, artificial stabilization of exchange rates cannot take the place of a thoroughly international monetary system. Exchange control might interfere with the initial transfer of whatever international loans people were willing to make. Existing or possible future exchange controls would make lenders worry about difficulties in getting their capital and interest earnings, as well as dividends or profits on equity investments, out of the borrowing country when the time came. Such potential difficulties discourage international lending just as exchange risk does—and without really eliminating the risk. It is an oversimplification to argue that freely fluctuating exchange rates discourage and fixed exchange rates encourage international investment. Rather, the distinction is between fluctuating or pegged rates under independent national monetary systems, on the one hand, and permanently fixed rates under an international monetary system such as the full-fledged gold standard, on the other.

Exchange Rates and Purchasing Powers

The purchasing-power-parity doctrine suggests that large real exchange losses or profits on an international loan under the flexible exchange rates are improbable unless financial and price-level conditions in the two countries have diverged substantially during the life of the loan. When the relative purchasing powers of the two currencies have changed, the exchange profit or loss may come as an approximate offset to what would otherwise be a loss or gain in real purchasing power. To illustrate, let us suppose that an international loan is in terms of the lending country's currency, that the lending country avoids deflation and inflation, and that the exchange rate is free to fluctuate. If inflation has occurred in the borrowing country by the time that the loan must be repaid, the borrower must pay more of his local money for the necessary amount of lending-country currency than he originally expected. However, because of the inflation in his country, the average borrower may find it no more difficult to earn the increased amount of local money than it would have been to earn the amount originally expected if the local money had not depreciated in purchasing power and exchange value. If everything is as just de-

---

[31] For historical examples, see Guillermo Subercaseaux, *Le Papier-Monnaie,* Paris: Giard & Brière, 1920, pp. 228-234.

scribed except that deflation rather than inflation occurs in the borrowing country, the
borrower enjoys an exchange profit: repayment of the loan in the currency of the lending country requires less of his appreciated
local currency than he originally expected to
need. However, the average borrower suffers
an offset to this exchange profit in the fact
that deflation increases the difficulty of earning local money.

The outcome differs according to whether
the loan is expressed in the currency of the
lending or the borrowing country. The various possibilities involving price-level stability
in one country and inflation or deflation in
the other are summarized in Table 12.6. In
the table, B and L stand for *borrower* and
lender, respectively. *Exch gain* and *exch loss*
mean, respectively, that the rate at which one
buys or sells foreign exchange in connection
with debt repayment is more favorable or
more unfavorable than originally expected.
PP gain means that the borrower repays in
(or buys the needed foreign exchange with)
domestic money units of lower purchasing
power than originally expected, or that the
lender receives repayment in (or sells the foreign exchange received for) domestic money

units of higher purchasing power than originally expected. *PP loss* means that the borrower repays in (or buys the needed foreign
exchange with) domestic money units of
higher purchasing power than originally expected, or that the lender receives repayment
in (or sells the foreign exchange received for)
domestic money units of lower purchasing
power than originally expected. *Neutral*
means that debt repayment is made or received in domestic currency which has remained stable in purchasing power.

The table shows a capricious redistribution
of wealth between lender and borrower when
the loan is expressed in a currency of unstable
purchasing power. When it is expressed in a
currency of stable purchasing power, one of
the parties experiences a "neutral" effect,
while the other experiences exchange-rate and
purchasing-power effects that run in opposite
directions (if they occur) and tend roughly
to compensate for each other. The advantage
of expressing loans in a currency of stable
rather than unstable purchasing power holds
true of domestic and international loans alike.
For countries where domestic borrowing and
lending are greater than international borrowing and lending, purchasing-power sta-

Table 12.6.   Gains and Losses on International Loans

		Loan in Lender's Currency	Loan in Borrower's Currency
Stability in Lending Country	Inflation in Borrowing Country	B: Exch loss offset by PP gain L: Neutral	B: PP gain, not offset L: Exch loss, not offset
	Deflation in Borrowing Country	B: Exch gain offset by PP loss L: Neutral	B: PP loss, not offset L: Exch gain, not offset pro- vided B does not default
Stability in Borrowing Country	Inflation in Lending Country	B: Exch gain, not offset L: PP loss, not offset	B: Neutral L: Exch gain offset by PP loss
	Deflation in Lending Country	B: Exch loss, not offset L: PP gain, not offset provided B does not default	B: Neutral L: Exch loss offset by PP gain

bility seems correspondingly more important than exchange-rate stability, if a choice between the two policies must and can be made. A domestically stable currency would also provide a good standard of deferred international payments.

Exchange Loss on Capital Transfers

Professor Nurkse has noted another characteristic of fluctuating exchanges that tends to impede capital movements. Suppose that Americans borrow £10 million in England, the debt being expressed in pounds. Selling these borrowed pounds for dollars drives down the pound from an initial rate of $5.00 to, say, $4.00. After the capital transfer is completed, the exchange rate reverts to the normal $5.00 per pound. When the time comes to pay back the loan, the American debtors must buy £10 million. The extra demand for pounds drives the pound rate to, say, $6.00, and the Americans have to spend $60 million to repay the sterling for which they had earlier realized only $40 million. If the loan had been expressed in dollars rather than in pounds, the English lenders rather than the American borrowers would have suffered the exchange loss. The loan agreement might arrange some shifting or sharing of the loss, but it could not contrive to avoid it entirely.[32]

The initial depreciation of the pound is part of the process that translates the financial capital movement into a real net flow of goods and services into the United States by way of increased imports or reduced exports or both, and the later appreciation of the pound is part of the process that translates the financial repayment into a real repayment. We must consider whether a comparable effect does not occur under fixed exchanges. Real transfer of a large international loan by means of the price-specie-flow mechanism of the gold standard theoretically causes price-level movements analogous to the exchange-rate movements just described. As a result of an international flow of gold, American borrowers find the purchasing power of the loan lower in America than they had expected,

while Englishmen find that they have lent money of higher purchasing power than they had expected. Repayment of the loan involves another flow of gold, lowering prices in America and raising them in England. Thus the borrowers repay the loan in money whose purchasing power in America is higher than at the time of borrowing, and the lenders receive repayment in money whose purchasing power in England is lower. It is not obvious which are more harmful: these purchasing-power losses or the corresponding losses under fluctuating exchange rates.[33] Neither type of loss is apparent under a system in which countries pursue monetary and fiscal independence and yet try to keep exchange rates fixed. Under this hybrid system, "automatic" price effects play no fundamental part in transferring capital internationally or in equilibrating balances of payments, which is one reason why such a system is fragile.

Under fluctuating exchanges, the loss described by Nurkse falls largely on the borrowers or lenders in the unmistakable form of a money loss. Under an international money standard, the corresponding purchasing-power loss is less evident and is more fully diffused onto third parties. There is something to be said for keeping any such loss clearly apparent to the persons responsible for it, especially when the capital movements involved would be of the hot-money rather than the investment variety.

Nurkse's example admittedly exaggerates the loss for the sake of clarity in exposition. In normal times, net capital movements are small enough in relation to the value of trade in goods and services that changes in them produce only moderate changes in the total demands for or supplies of currencies, and the resulting exchange-rate movements should not be disruptive. Furthermore, the purchasing-power-transfer mechanism—that is, decreased spending by lenders (or by fellow citizens to whom they would otherwise have

---

[32] Ragnar Nurkse, *Internationale Kapitalbewegungen*, Vienna: Springer, 1935, pp. 70-73.

[33] Cf. Whittlesey, *op. cit.*, pp. 171-175. The above discussion of loan losses under the gold standard considers only price effects and abstracts from purchasing-power-transfer and income effects; it is on the same level of abstraction as Nurkse's discussion of the loss under free exchanges.

lent) and increased spending by borrowers (or by fellow citizens from whom they would otherwise have drawn funds)—supplements the exchange rate mechanism in translating the financial transfer into a net international flow of goods and services. When the borrowers spend the entire loan on goods of the lending country, transfer of the loan has no direct effect on the exchange rate, and the same is true, *mutatis mutandis,* of the eventual repayment.

Still, it does seem probable that the purchasing-power-transfer mechanism would ordinarily work less well under free exchanges than under the gold standard. Under an international standard, gold movements or the equivalent can facilitate the appropriate contraction of spending in the lending country and expansion of spending in the borrowing country. But under independent national standards, no money flows between countries. Instead, the exchange rate moves, tending to shift purchases of internationally traded goods toward the lending country, causing expansion there, and away from the borrowing country, causing contraction there. The respective upward and downward price-level tendencies are intensified by the fact that the real transfer of the loan, so far as it begins to succeed, makes fewer goods available to be bought within the lending country and more available in the borrowing country. These tendencies, which run counter to the primary and appropriate cut in spending by the lenders and rise in spending by the borrowers, might conceivably be resisted by continued adherence to policies of internal monetary stabilization.[34]

To say that the purchasing-power-transfer mechanism may work with difficulty under free exchanges is not to say that it will not work at all. The long-term American borrowers of Nurkse's example can spend their borrowed English funds in America only by selling them for dollars. Potential purchasers include not only importers of English goods

but also holders of idle dollars who might be induced to switch temporarily into sterling assets. Speculators, in particular, might do so in the justifiable belief that any impact effect of the original loan in depressing sterling exchange would be only temporary. Speculative purchases of sterling amount to a short-term loan to England. Thus, a short-term loan *to* the long-term lending country by persons dishoarding funds held in the long-term borrowing country facilitates the transfer of purchasing power appropriate to the primary loan.[35] This lessens the exchange-rate change necessary to effect a real transfer of capital.

Fixed Exchanges as Window-Dressing

Encouragement of international lending is not much of a point in favor of fixed exchanges if the fixity is only temporary. Anyone lending to a foreign borrower should realize that he is taking a risk not only on the individual borrower himself and on the exchange rate (if the loan is expressed in the foreign currency) but also on the ability of the foreign country as a whole to achieve an export surplus (or an inflow of new capital) by which interest payments and capital repayment can eventually be made. Far from eliminating such risk, precarious exchange stability increases it if currency overvaluation impairs the debtor country's ability to export. If exchange stability *is* assured by keeping internal monetary and business conditions in step with external developments, the deflation and recession (and to a lesser extent, the inflation) that may accordingly have to be imported from time to time may hamper the debtor enterprises or governmental units in earning enough money or collecting enough taxes to service their external debts. Exchange stability imitated by such expedients as exchange control and moratoria on foreign debt payments clearly does not benefit foreign creditors. Under freely fluctuating exchanges, some countries, no longer able to conceal unfavorable conditions or policies behind a facade of exchange stability, might indeed have more

---

[34] Cf. P. B. Whale, "The Theory of International Trade in the Absence of an International Standard," *Economica,* n.s. III, February 1936, pp. 29-32; and Gottfried von Haberler, *Prosperity and Depression* (4th ed.), London: Allen & Unwin, 1958, pp. 446-447.

[35] Cf. Carl Iversen, *Aspects of the Theory of International Capital Movements,* Copenhagen: Levin & Munksgaard, 1935, pp. 312-324, esp. pp. 316-317.

trouble than otherwise in obtaining foreign loans.

Equity Investment

Fluctuating exchanges might discourage some international borrowing and lending but would not rule it all out. (Canada's reassuring experience under fluctuating exchange rates is discussed in Chapter 24.) Exchange risk certainly would not rule out all international investment, though it presumably would induce some investors to buy shares of stock rather than bonds of foreign enterprises. There is little reason to suppose that fluctuating exchanges would thwart international direct investment. Equity investment provides some protection against depreciation of the currency of the capital-importing country, for if inflation occurs, the money profits of enterprises should rise accordingly. Exchange risk poses a particularly small obstacle to international investment when a parent enterprise intends to bring home income from its foreign properties in kind rather than in money, as in the form of oil or iron ore. Besides providing investors with some hedge against depreciation of the foreign currency, equity investments should ease the problem of transferring earnings out of the "debtor" country. Unlike bonds, shares of stock do not entail a fixed amount of service charges that are supposed to be transferred abroad every year despite the condition of the balance of payments. A country can transfer large volumes of dividends to foreign investors when it is prosperous, making only small transfers during difficult times. A further advantage of foreign equity investment, and particularly of direct rather than portfolio investment, is that when the exchange value of the "debtor" country's currency is unusually weak, foreign investors have an incentive to plough current earnings back into their properties, waiting until the balance-of-payments situation is more favorable to repatriation of profits.[36] Capital inflow by way of direct rather than portfolio investment also tends to be accompanied by entrepreneurial

and technical ability, which underdeveloped countries typically need fully as much as foreign capital.

Risk, Trade, and Investment: Summary

On *a priori* grounds it seems practically certain that, other things being equal, the risk of exchange fluctuations tends to reduce the volume of international trade. However, the resulting loss of welfare would, if measurable, probably turn out to be less than proportionate to the loss of trade volume. Besides, fixing exchange rates itself violates the condition of other things being equal. Any shrinkage in trade because of risk may well be outweighed by the trade-promoting effect of rates allowed to adjust toward changing equilibrium levels. Even rate-pegging, incidentally, does not remove risk as long as danger remains that pegged rates will have to be changed. Free exchange rates are conducive to trade so far as they enable countries to dispense with controls for balance-of-payments purposes and provide the opportunity for independent domestic stabilization policies. Finally, both theory and history suggest that forward-exchange facilities would offer merchants adequate and inexpensive protection against the risk of rate changes in free and unrestricted markets. This protection might even be more satisfactory under freely fluctuating than under pegged-but-adjustable exchanges, since forward premiums or discounts are apt to become comparatively large and unstable when pegged spot rates come under suspicion.

Exchange risk probably would deter international borrowing and lending to some extent. However, the fault is not peculiar to free exchanges. A system of fixed-but-adjustable exchanges, or even an insecure gold standard, presents similar, though less constantly conspicuous, risk. The relevant distinction is not so much between free rates and pegged rates as between either fluctuating or pegged rates under independent national monetary systems on the one hand and permanently fixed rates under an international monetary system on the other. The purchasing-power-parity doctrine teaches that borrowers and lenders would be unlikely to experience large

---

[36] Whittlesey, *op. cit.*, pp. 167-170.

gains or losses of real wealth from changes in free exchange rates except when the currency in which the loan was expressed suffered a change in purchasing power. The monetary problem involved in credit operations, domestic as well as foreign, is not just the narrow one of exchange-rate instability but rather the broader one of purchasing-power instability.[37] To try to peg exchange rates when this problem remains unsolved is to palliate symptoms. Finally, risk under fluctuating exchanges does not strangle all international investment; in particular, it is probably not an important deterrent to direct and other equity investments, types of investment that have much to recommend them relatively.

---

[37] To split hairs, the problem is not one of instability but of unpredictability; for if the purchasing power of a currency were going to change in a way fully known in advance, free-market interest rates would allow for the change and avoid unwanted redistributions between debtors and creditors.

Stabilizing Official Intervention

 13

The first two sections of this chapter, together with the summary immediately following them, review proposals for solving a problem described toward the end of Chapter 11—the problem of one-way-option speculation under the present-day system of pegged exchange rates. The proposed policy weapon is official intervention in the forward-exchange market. The remaining sections of the chapter review the compromise idea of giving up on fixed exchange rates but still retaining official market intervention to smooth out the movements of floating rates.

Speculation and Arbitrage

Some students see the dangers of self-justifying speculation against a pegged currency less as an argument against pegging spot rates than as one in favor of supporting forward rates also.[1] They interpret the immediate cause of a drain on the official reserves as arbitrage rather than as speculation as such. Suppose that bearishness on the Ruritanian crown (expressed in speculative demands for forward foreign exchange, more universal forward covering of commercial commitments to pay foreign currency, and lesser prevalence of forward covering of commercial commitments to receive foreign currency) drives the crown's forward rate to an abnormally large discount from spot. Arbitrageurs can now profit by selling crowns spot and buying them back forward. In defending the spot rate against the arbitrageurs' spot sales, the authorities lose reserves. Covered interest arbitrage, not speculation, is the immediate cause of the drain; it transmits to the spot market the speculative pressure in the forward market. The covering part of the arbitrage operations, considered by itself, amounts to taking a position opposite to that taken by speculators; it tends to hold down the speculative forward premium on foreign exchange (i.e., forward discount on the crown). The more powerfully even a small volume of arbitrage can shrink this premium to the point of making any larger volume of arbitrage unprofitable, the slighter the danger to the official spot reserves. On the other hand, the less powerfully arbitrage tends to destroy its own profitability, the stronger seems the case for official intervention to destroy it.[2]

[1] A. E. Jasay, "Bank Rate or Forward Exchange Policy," *Banca Nazionale del Lavoro Quarterly Review*, No. 44, March 1958, pp. 56-73; A. E. Jasay, "Forward Exchange: The Case for Intervention," *Lloyds Bank Review*, October 1958, pp. 35-45; John Spraos, "Speculation, Arbitrage and Sterling," *Economic Journal*, LXIX, March 1959, pp. 1-21. Bent Hansen discusses the proposal sympathetically but without complete agreement in "Interest Policy and Foreign Exchange Policy" and "Interest Policy, Foreign Exchange Policy and Foreign Exchange Control," *Skandinaviska Banken Quarterly Review*, vol. 39, October 1958, pp. 114-121, and vol. 40, January 1959, pp. 15-27. Further discussion appears in J. H. Auten, "Counter-speculation and the Forward Exchange Market," *Journal of Political Economy*, LXIX, February 1961, pp. 49-55; R. Z. Aliber, "Counterspeculation in the Forward Exchange Market: A Comment," *Journal of Political Economy*, LXX, December 1962, pp. 609-613; Henry Goldstein, "Counter-speculation in the Forward Exchange Market: Some Further Comments," *Journal of Political Economy*, LXXI, October 1963, pp. 494-500; R. Z. Aliber, "More About Counterspeculation in the Forward Exchange Market," *Journal*

of Political Economy, LXXI, December, 1963, pp. 589-590; and Paul Einzig, *A Dynamic Theory of Forward Exchange*, London: Macmillan; New York: St. Martin's Press, 1961, chapters 44-48, esp. 44 and 45.

[2] Unfortunately, variations in commercial covering might accommodate the arbitrage: shrinkage of the forward premium on foreign exchange might be resisted by increased buying of forward foreign exchange

Another example of arbitrage seen as the immediate cause of pressure in the spot market concerns a foreign buyer of Ruritanian goods. He can speculate against the crown by getting his trade financed in Ruritania, contriving to owe crowns. Alternatively, he may finance his trade at home, at the same time taking a bear position in crowns on the side by selling them forward. If he chooses the former course (which tends to delay an inflow of foreign exchange into the Ruritanian reserves), it must be because the relations among spot and forward exchange rates and different countries' interest rates make this a cheaper form of speculation than the latter course; and these are arbitrage considerations. A foreign company with funds on deposit in Ruritania, fearful of devaluation, could either sell its crowns spot, thus tending to drain the Ruritanian reserves, or else keep holding its crowns while covering them with a forward sale. If the company expected not only a devaluation of the crown but also an upward revaluation of the Graustark florin, it could buy florins with crowns either spot or forward. In each example, the choice could be described as an arbitrage decision. The same may even be said of speculation by way of leads and lags. Suppose that a foreign buyer of Ruritanian goods priced in crowns lags his remittance or even his purchases, awaiting a devaluation. Why should he do this unless he can speculate against the crown more cheaply this way than by leaving his schedule of payments and purchases undisturbed and selling crowns forward? Suppose that a Ruritanian importer, afraid of being caught with a foreign-exchange obligation if the crown is devalued, hastens his remittance or his purchases. What, if not a cost advantage, could be a sound reason for doing this instead of buying foreign exchange for-

ward? The leads and lags that harm the Ruritanian reserves are due not to speculation as such but to the particular form of speculation that arbitrage considerations recommend. More generally, whenever people shun forward transactions in favor of transactions that immediately strain official reserves, their decision must involve the very interest-rate and spot-and-forward-rate relationships that govern ordinary interest arbitrage. In this sense, even outright speculation in the spot rather than forward market could be described as arbitrage.

Counterspeculative Support of Forward Exchange

This interpretation seems like a sterile attempt to lay down substantive propositions by changing the accepted meanings of words. Its advocates say, however, that their terminology has the advantage of emphasizing the remediable aspects of speculative situations. It suggests how official manipulation of arbitrage incentives could make all bear speculation against the crown take the form of forward sales, "thereby rendering it harmless to the . . . reserves."[3]

If the authorities bought crowns (sold foreign exchange) forward on a large enough scale to keep the forward crown from sinking to any abnormal discount, they could deprive arbitrageurs of any chance to profit from selling crowns spot and repurchasing them forward. The intervention would likewise eliminate speculators' incentive to go bearish on crowns by reserve-depleting spot rather than forward sales. Importers and exporters who would otherwise speculate by leads and lags would find that they could take equivalent short positions more advantageously in the forward market.[4] Not even "one-way option" speculation could eat into the reserves

---

by importers (whose speculative motive for being especially sure to cover is reinforced by improvement of the price at which they can do so) and by reduced sales of forward foreign exchange by exporters (whose speculative motive for not covering and instead waiting to sell foreign exchange spot later on is reinforced by the less attractive forward rate). As explained in the appendix to Chapter 6, however, commercial covering is more likely to vary in response to the forward rate when the support limits of spot exchange rates are trusted than when they are distrusted or nonexistent.

---

[3] John Spraos, *op. cit.,* p. 8.

[4] However, traders might not behave so "rationally." They might consider outright forward-market speculation unpatriotic or otherwise undesirable, yet consider shrewd timing of their trade and payments only a matter of sound business judgment. Even worse, some might continue leading and lagging while speculatively selling crowns forward besides. Cf. Goldstein, *op. cit.,* p. 497 and footnote.

as long as official intervention lured it all into the forward market.

Several objections to the proposal have been made, and answers have been offered. First, keeping the forward discount on a suspected currency small not only affects the form of bear speculation but also tends to increase its total amount by in effect subsidizing it. This effect may only be slight if speculators do not operate on fine margins and if their general distrust of the pegged currency swamps alertness to the forward-spot spread, seen as the cost of taking a bear position.[5] On the other hand, the forward rate itself is not the only influence: the accompanying publicity designed to persuade speculators of the "rationality" of operating forward instead of spot might well induce some speculation that would not otherwise have occurred at all. A more cheerful thought is that avoiding a conspicuous forward discount might promote confidence in the crown and so deter speculation against it—but such arguments appealing to psychological influences are notoriously unsure.[6] Besides possibly affecting the total volume of speculation, forward support may also attract additional *net* forward sales of crowns to the authorities by parties other than outright speculators. Importers committed to future payments in foreign exchange will be especially sure to cover their commitments by buying these currencies forward if their forward quotations are held down. Exporters committed to future receipts of foreign exchange will be especially reluctant to sell it forward and especially content to maintain an uncovered long position if its forward price is held down. (On the other hand, the whole speculative atmosphere may so dominate traders' decisions that the level of the forward rate is only a comparatively slight influence on covering practices.) Net forward sales of crowns to the authorities might also increase in connection with an increase in imports relative to exports, as explained a few pages later on.

Advocates of the forward-support policy would not be alarmed by even a vast growth of the authorities' forward contracts to buy crowns and deliver foreign exchange, provided that these contracts matched pure speculation only. There is no limit to official support of a currency in the forward market comparable to the limit to spot support posed by exhaustible reserves. The authorities need only keep their nerve (whereas nervously discontinuing intervention as pressure mounted would probably intensify the speculation). Speculative short-sellers of crowns will have to buy them spot with foreign exchange when the time comes to deliver crowns under their forward contracts; foreign exchange will thus flow into the official reserves at the same time that the authorities have to deliver it under their maturing contracts. Meanwhile, speculation cannot force a devaluation and saddle the authorities with the costs of carrying out their contracts, for its successful diversion into the forward market means that it depletes no reserves, and, as just mentioned, the official forward operations could be as large as necessary for this diversion. As for forward sellers of crowns who need buy none to make delivery because they had been holding crowns (or assets readily salable for crowns) all along, they could have sold the crowns spot in the first place anyway; hence the proposed policy does no harm and even has the merit of delaying such drains as the reserves could in any case have suffered.

This view is too optimistic. Surely the authorities cannot be indifferent to how much of their forward activity matches pure speculation by short-sellers who will have to buy crowns spot to make delivery and how much matches forward sales by persons already holding crowns—perhaps foreign companies operating in Ruritania and hedging to protect the value of their crown assets. Some holders who would simply have stood pat and taken their chances in the absence of an

---

[5] R. Z. Aliber, "Counterspeculation in the Foreign Exchange Market: A Comment," pp. 609, 612.

[6] Paul Einzig quotes a European central banker to the effect that forward support of a currency at an obviously artificial rate "attracts an amazing volume of selling from the most unexpected quarters." Einzig also notes that the British authorities stopped supporting forward sterling during the 1957 crisis when they found that the artificial forward rate, far from relieving the pressure, stimulated speculative and quasi-speculative pressure. "Some Recent Developments in Official Forward Exchange Operations," *Economic Journal*, **LXXIII**, June 1963, pp. 252, 241.

attractive opportunity to hedge might move out of crowns by delivering them when their forward contracts matured in the event of devaluation in the meanwhile. If devaluation had not then yet occurred, hedgers might make delivery of crowns they already held but could spare only temporarily (or, for example, might obtain crowns to deliver by temporarily running down inventories held in Ruritania), hoping to buy their crown assets back again profitably after the still momentarily expected devaluation. Since the authorities cannot know who will eventually take delivery of the foreign exchange they are selling forward and what the unknown ultimate recipients will do with it, they remain in the dark about the nature and extent of the pressure against the crown. By not intervening forward and by suffering spot reserve losses instead, the authorities would at least know where they stood and would be less inclined wishfully to postpone fundamental corrective measures.[7]

Honoring a massive volume of contracts made under the forward support policy would prove costly to the authorities if they did lose their nerve and finally devalue. In effect, then, they lose their freedom to devalue; but, on an optimistic view, this nearly ironclad guarantee against devaluation itself further deters speculation.[8] A worry harder to dispel concerns the possible upward revaluation of one or more of the foreign currencies in which the Ruritanian authorities had been operating; that decision would be out of their hands. And anyway, even the best of intentions and strongest of nerves might not be able to prevent devaluation of the crown. Just as going deeper and deeper actually into debt to foreigners to obtain foreign exchange for ordinary spot support of a currency would leave the currency's existing parity increasingly suspect, so suspicion would grow as official forward commitments grew bigger and bigger in relation to actual reserves. The size of

these commitments might not be published, but it would be the subject of rumor—rumor perhaps even more disturbing than actual figures. Speculators might begin to wonder where in the world, even with the most honorable of intentions, the authorities were going to get the foreign exchange to meet their mounting commitments in case their heroism somehow failed. (Sales of foreign exchange by short-sellers buying crowns for delivery at the maturity of their contracts would then not provide the full answer, since each crown would be worth less foreign exchange, after devaluation, than at the rate specified in the maturing contracts.) Speculators and others might reasonably fear the imposition of controls to their disadvantage. Official publicity about the cost advantages of confining speculation to the forward market would seem less relevant and convincing. Transfers through the spot market could grow. Knowing that a forced devaluation *could* be the outcome, speculators might expect the authorities to give up before they had taken on disastrously heavy forward commitments.

Mention of heavy forward commitments brings to mind an oversight in the reassuring argument that these commitments can hardly become much heavier than spot reserve losses would have been anyway in the absence of forward support. Perhaps the argument is right that forward support only changes the form of speculation and does little to increase its total volume. But this is true, if at all, only of the volume per time period. The longer a speculative situation lasts before coming to a climax—the more time that distrust of the crown has to grow and to motivate new speculators and embolden old ones—the greater the cumulative volume of speculation can be. The time that can elapse until speculation in the spot market comes to its climax is limited by the size of the reserves; the duration of speculation diverted to the forward market is not so limited. A denial that this consideration is relevant would have to rest, again, on the assumption that devaluation simply *will not* occur.

On a highly abstract level, there is much to the argument that pure speculation, com-

---

[7] This point, particularly concerning the dangers of unavoidable ignorance about the counterpart of official forward transactions, has been much stressed by Paul Einzig, *A Dynamic Theory of Forward Exchange*, p. 510, and *Economic Journal*, June 1963, pp. 248-249.

[8] Auten, *op. cit.*, p. 55n., attributes this argument to A.E. Jasay's evidence before the Radcliffe Committee.

pletely unjustified by any adverse fundamentals in trade and normal capital movements, could not defeat a bold, resolute, and if necessary unlimited forward support policy. But the distinction between pure speculation and speculation related to fundamentals can be made confidently only with hindsight.[9] Fundamental disequilibrium, absent at first, might develop later, forcing a devaluation that would be costly in proportion to the counter-speculation meanwhile undertaken. One reason why forward support is only a short-term palliative is that it affects only transactions that can have forward cover, and these do not ordinarily include long-term capital transfers. A domestic interest-rate level too low in view of foreign levels and of the exchange rate is likely to promote an outflow of long-term capital, despite forward intervention to manipulate short-term flows.[10] Even the current account of the balance of payments could worsen because of forward support of the currency. The prevailing forward rate affects the profitability of an import or export transaction involving a future payment or receipt to be covered against exchange risk. Imports are more attractive to Ruritanians and Ruritanian exports less attractive to foreigners if the forward crown is kept strong than if it is allowed to weaken.[11] Overvaluation of a currency in both the spot and forward markets is more of an overvaluation than overvaluation in the spot market alone (strictly speaking, the distinction is between forward overvaluation due to direct support and lesser forward overvaluation merely paralleling the spot overvaluation). In the face of continuing unmistakable overvaluation, an import surplus will eventually drain the reserves and put an end to spot support. This will happen, anyway, unless forward operations can go beyond merely deterring capital outflow and can promote an actual continuing capital inflow matching the current-account deficit. This would imply keeping the forward quotation on the home currency stronger than its interest parity. It would imply that the home government kept subsidizing the build-up of a heavier and heavier debt to foreigners. If declining credit-worthiness would limit straightforward borrowing to finance ordinary support of the spot rate, it is not clear how equivalent indirect efforts could succeed without limit.

Summary

The foregoing survey does not necessarily condemn all sorts of official forward operations under all circumstances; the case against diehard rigid pegging is not in itself a case against all intervention.[12] It does cast doubt, though, on whether forward intervention can effectively banish trouble from speculative capital movements under pegged spot rates. Paradoxically, troublesome capital movements are likely to arise both from speculation when

[9] Cf. Paul Einzig, *A Dynamic Theory of Forward Exchange*, p. 506. ". . . I came to realise in the light of experience the difficulty of drawing the line between speculative pressure unwarranted by deep-lying disequilibrium, and speculative pressure that is but a manifestation of such disequilibrium."
J. Marcus Fleming and Robert A. Mundell explain why the forward-support technique is appropriate only for meeting a deficit whose cause is not merely temporary but inherently self-reversing. Something like a harvest failure would not be an appropriate occasion, since no reversal would necessarily occur to allow the authorities to undo their forward-exchange position. A more appropriate occasion would be a nervous flight of funds, based on some misunderstanding, from a basically sound currency. "Official Intervention on the Forward Exchange Market: A Simplified Analysis," IMF *Staff Papers*, XI, March 1964, pp. 15-17.
[10] Hansen, *Skandinaviska Banken Quarterly Review*, vol. 39, October 1958, p. 121.
[11] *Ibid.*, p. 120. Paul Einzig, *The Theory of Forward Exchange*, London: Macmillan, 1937, chapter 23; Einzig, *A Dynamic Theory of Forward Exchange*, pp. 212-213, 272; and S. C. Tsiang, "The Theory of Forward Exchange and Effects of Government Intervention on the Forward Exchange Market," IMF *Staff Papers*, VII, April 1959, pp. 104-105. Subject only to the obvious

qualification that the balance of payments must be normally rather than perversely responsive to the spot rate as well, Tsiang's reasoning is recognized as valid amidst otherwise critical comments by Auten, *op. cit.*, pp. 53-54. Also see Fleming and Mundell, *op. cit.*, pp. 11-12, 15.
[12] Resisting a speculative and quasi-speculative *inflow* of funds by pegging down the forward premium on the home currency can have awkward consequences but, unlike resistance to an outflow, cannot lead to calamity. How long in foreign exchange the authorities can afford to go has no limit comparable to that on going short.
Note, incidentally, that the bulk of the academic discussion about the pros and cons of various forward support strategies takes for granted a pegged spot rate that may require some sort of defense or other.

fixed parities are distrusted and, as already shown in the appendix to Chapter 6, from interest differentials when the parities are trusted.

The Dual Purpose of Exchange Equalization Accounts

Policy-makers disillusioned with fixed exchange rates yet worried about speculative disorders and burdensome risk under freely fluctuating exchanges might seek an answer in operating an exchange equalization account, also called an exchange stabilization fund. The idea represents a compromise between fixed and free rates, but a different compromise than the adjustable-peg system. The exchange-rate mechanism would be allowed to keep balances of payments in equilibrium over the long run, but routine official trading in the market would iron out speculative, accidental, and otherwise purely temporary fluctuations.

A stabilization fund might strive, as its second purpose, to cushion the domestic monetary and credit impact of disturbances arising from international trade or capital movements. Strictly speaking, the fund would neutralize not so much the foreign disturbances themselves as what would otherwise be the consequences of moderating their influence on exchange rates. Buying or selling foreign exchange to resist appreciation or depreciation of the home currency has an expansionary or contractionary domestic monetary impact much the same as that of central-bank open-market operations in domestic securities. The fund could neutralize this impact by selling or buying securities whenever it bought or sold foreign exchange.

Problems of Domestic Monetary Insulation

The best known of the funds operating in this way is the British Exchange Equalisation Account, managed by the Bank of England as agent for the Treasury. At its beginning in 1932, it held only British Treasury bills and so could operate in only one direction, buying gold or foreign exchange with sterling. In its early years, the Account did, in fact,

operate most (but not all) of the time to resist tendencies toward an unwanted appreciation of the pound. Its foreign assets kept growing, and the government repeatedly had to give it fresh sterling assets. Despite the original idea that the Account should merely smooth out erratic exchange-rate fluctuations due to "hot-money" transfers or other temporary influences, it came increasingly to resist trends and actually to determine the rate. Even now that the Account has the explicit task of not merely smoothing the rate but of fixing it within definite narrow limits, its function of insulating domestic monetary and credit conditions remains pretty much the same as before.[13]

The Account holds sterling almost entirely in "tap" Treasury bills.[14] It finances purchases of gold or foreign exchange by cashing some of its tap bills, obliging the Treasury to sell that many more tender bills to private investing institutions. When it sells gold or foreign exchange, the Account puts the sterling received into tap bills; and the Treasury reduces by that much its issue of tender bills to the private money market. The Account and the Treasury, taken together, in effect pay for foreign exchange bought and dispose of the sterling proceeds of foreign-exchange sold by increasing and reducing their borrowing from the public; the open-market operations in foreign exchange and in Treasury bills run in offsetting directions.[15]

Numerous complications prevent perfect insulation of the home economy. As an example, let us consider a flight by foreigners from their own money into British bank deposits.[16] The Exchange Equalisation Account absorbs

---

[13] Cf. R. S. Sayers, *Modern Banking*, 4th ed., Oxford: Clarendon Press, 1958, p. 159.

[14] "Tap" bills are short-term securities issued and redeemed by the Treasury at any time for the convenience of government departments and certain overseas monetary authorities having funds for temporary investment. They are distinguished from "tender bills," which the Treasury auctions off to the general investing public every week in predetermined amounts.

[15] Committee on the Working of the Monetary System, *Report* ("The Radcliffe Report"), *Cmnd.* 827, London: Her Majesty's Stationery Office, August 1959, pp. 34, 268.

[16] See W. Manning Dacey, *The British Banking Mechanism,* 2nd rev. ed., London: Hutchinson & Co., 1958, pp. 104-107.

the inflowing foreign exchange or gold to resist an unwanted appreciation of the pound; but since it acquires the necessary sterling by selling Treasury bills from its own portfolio (through the intermediary of the Treasury), it avoids the net creation of additional domestic bank reserves. If the commercial banks buy these bills, they have more of them as assets, more foreign-owned deposits as liabilities, and unchanged reserves. But on the one hand, the rise in deposits reduces their reserve ratios, while on the other hand, their increased bill holdings raise their ratios of total liquid assets (cash, bills, and call loans) to deposits. Since British banks traditionally strive for both cash reserves and total liquidity amounting to rather definite percentages of deposits, the operation just described presupposes that the banks had previously had some excess cash reserves and probably, as a reason for buying the Treasury bills, some deficiency of noncash liquid assets. If the Exchange Equalisation Account had had to absorb the speculative inflow of foreign funds when the banks had had no slack in their cash ratios, it could have avoided actual deflationary pressure only by selling some of the Treasury bills to the Bank of England for sterling it needed, instead of selling all the bills to the commercial banks. One may wonder why the Account and the Treasury could not have mopped up the bank reserves that purchase of the inflowing foreign funds would otherwise have produced by selling bills to the British public generally instead of to the banks. One complication in either approach is uncertainty about who would be the ultimate new holders of the bills. Even if the authorities could somehow sell bills to the public alone, simply releasing bank deposits from domestic to foreign ownership with no change in their total or in bank reserves, the effect of the total operation might still be slightly deflationary, since deposits would presumably be less active under foreign than domestic ownership (as in fact is implied by the foreigners' assumed motive in acquiring the deposits). To offset the domestic monetary effects of speculative capital movements completely, then, the authorities cannot aim at anything so relatively simple

as stabilizing total bank reserves, or the total of domestically owned deposits, or the total of deposits under domestic and foreign ownership alike; they would have to know and take account of the different velocities of deposits under different ownership. Incidentally, if the foreigners fleeing from their home currency wished to hold their new sterling assets entirely in the form of Treasury bills, and if the British authorities knew this, then their task would be simpler. At the other extreme, complete insulation would not be even theoretically possible if the foreigners wished to acquire assets whose total supply the authorities could not manipulate (shares of corporation stock, for example).

It makes some difference to the task of the authorities whether the disturbance to be offset is a "hot-money" transfer or is something more nearly "normal," such as a supposedly temporary imbalance on goods-and-services account. When a speculative capital inflow occurs, it may be appropriate to allow almost as large an increase in the total volume of bank-account money if the foreigners are going to treat their new accounts pretty much as idle hoards. But when the authorities acquire foreign exchange corresponding to a balance-of-payments surplus on current account, allowing an equivalent increase in bank-account money would be inflationary, since it would be held by residents and would presumably be about as active as the bank accounts already in existence. If official purchases of foreign exchange were financed by selling bills to the commercial banks, the banks' reserves, at least, could be kept unchanged. As in the preceding example of the capital inflow, however, this operation would presuppose that the banks had had above-normal cash reserves (and probably below-normal total liquidity) in the first place; otherwise, the Bank of England would have to create some additional reserve cash for the banks by buying some of the Treasury bills sold by the Account—which implies allowing the country's international current surplus to retain some net expansionary domestic effect. The task of approaching complete neutralization would be easiest for the authorities if they could persuade the British nonbank public to hold fully as much in additional Treasury bills as the country's surplus earnings of foreign exchange; in the final position, ignoring intermediate stages, the public would then be holding additional bills equivalent to the net excess exports of goods and services, the Exchange Equalisation Account would be holding fewer bills and more foreign exchange, and the commercial banks would find their reserves, deposits, and ratios unchanged. (Yet even this outcome would not spell complete neutralization. The public's additional holdings of highly liquid Treasury bills, together with the increased interest rate necessary to attract into the bills funds fully equal to the external surplus, would presumably promote a slight increase in the velocity of circulation of actual demand deposits and currency.)

Given a British current-account deficit, the Exchange Equalisation Account must release gold and foreign exchange to support sterling. Its task is simplest if the British public wishes to pay for its net surplus purchases of foreign goods and services with Treasury bills previously held. If the public wishes to draw down its bank accounts instead, the banks will lose reserves and have to sell Treasury bills or other assets to replenish them. If the banks were the sole sellers of the bills bought by the Exchange Equalisation Account, their reserves would remain unchanged, their cash reserve *ratio* would rise (because of the fall in deposits), and their liquidity ratio would fall (because bill holdings and deposits fell by equal absolute amounts). If the banks could not respond this way because they had not held superabundant total liquidity in the first place, and if, as assumed, the public did not sell all the bills sought by the Account, then the Bank of England would have to sell some bills to the Account and absorb some cash from it, partially tolerating the original deflationary tendency. The alternative would be to cut the yields on government securities enough to make the public, as a whole, part only with securities and not with demand deposits in paying for the foreign exchange needed for the surplus imports. Again, the question remains whether an unchanged volume of bank reserves and bank deposits spells

complete neutralization if a change in interest rates is necessary in the process.[17]

In summary, exact neutralization of the effect of external transactions on a country's domestic monetary and credit situation is usually impossible, not only in practice but even in theory. Any pronounced expansionary or contractionary influence, however, can at least in principle always be restrained. The techniques of an exchange equalization account are not the only weapons available; there is also the whole armory of monetary and fiscal policy. Detailed attention to the domestic operations of an exchange account is thus rather uninteresting. The separation between exchange account, central bank, and treasury is chiefly legalistic. If their actions are coordinated—and in practice, no one of them can overlook the consequences of the others' actions—the three can be considered together under the collective name of the "monetary authorities." Not the exchange account but rather these "authorities" decide whether, when, and how to try to insulate the domestic structure of money and credit from the effects of external disturbances or exchange-stabilization operations.[18]

Official Exchange-market Operations

Official measures to insulate the domestic economy interfere with balance-of-payments equilibration through price-and-income effects. The question arises of how far domestic stabilization is compatible with official operations in foreign exchange.

The answer implied by the distinctive purpose of exchange-stabilization funds is—indefinitely. For the idea of stabilization, as distinguished from rigid pegging, is that rate

---

[17] The foregoing examples concern transactions between Britain and countries outside the Sterling Area. Given the practices actually followed, a British surplus or deficit in trade with the rest of the Area produces effects on bank deposits and reserves in Britain not much different from those that would occur in a region of a monetarily unified country. On this and on the consequences of imbalances in trade between the outer Sterling Area and the outside world, see Sayers, *op. cit.*, esp. pp. 163-164.

[18] Cf. W. A. Brown, Jr. in chapter VI of Ragnar Nurkse, *International Currency Experience*, League of Nations, 1944, p. 154.

variations should indeed serve as the chief method of achieving external balance. A fund should do no more than smooth out functionless erratic wobbles (perhaps due to random mismatching-in-time of commercial supply and demand or due to speculation). Functional exchange-rate movements—those in response to the changing fundamentals of tastes, technology, weather, harvests, price levels, monetary and fiscal policies, and reasonable expectations about all of these—would have full scope to maintain balance-of-payments equilibrium at all times except perhaps in the very short run. The fund would not resist fundamental rate trends. Its intervention would not involve exchange control in the specific sense of requisitioning and rationing foreign exchange. Since the fund would buy and sell gold and foreign exchange in the open market rather than directly control private transactions, its activity would be fully as compatible with a free-market economy as are open-market operations for domestic monetary policy.

This prospectus is attractive. The chief question about implementing it concerns how the managers of the fund are to distinguish promptly between fundamental and temporary rate movements. Hindsight is not enough. If the managers were as able to foretell the future or to diagnose the present as they ideally should be, they could speculate as private parties, iron out temporary fluctuations without risking public money, and earn handsome profits. But then, according to one point of view, no *official* fund would be necessary. If the authorities possessed information not generally available to private speculators, they might best simply make this information public (unless it had to be kept secret for security reasons).

Spokesmen for this point of view have indeed argued that for private competitive speculators and official stabilization funds alike, profit and loss indicate whether or not their operations have had a stabilizing effect.[19] The profit-and-loss test is meant to apply to a market in which oscillations occur around an unchanging average rate; an uptrend or downtrend over the period considered would raise the problem of revaluing the fund's foreign assets and would blur the profitability criterion. Ideally, the profitability criterion also presupposes that the fund, like each individual speculator, carries out only a very small fraction of the total transactions in the market. For if the fund's own purchases and sales had an appreciable effect by themselves on the prices paid and received, then the most profitable volume of operations would fall short of the most stabilizing volume. Extreme examples show why. If the fund were to stabilize the rate completely, it would always buy and sell at the same stabilized price and would make zero profits. At the other extreme, a very small volume of operations would narrow the range of fluctuation hardly at all; properly timed purchases and sales could yield a maximum profit per unit, but on such a small volume of transactions that the total profit would be negligible. The most profitable volume of operations is somewhere in between. The fact that profitable operations are stabilizing does not imply that stabilizing operations are necessarily profitable; least of all does it imply a simple correspondence between degree of profitability and degree of stabilizing effect.

This consideration seems to discredit the profitability test in appraising the success or failure of an official fund. It is hard to imagine a fund that acted as a perfect competitor: its very purpose implies operations large enough to influence the rate.[20] But if a fund did operate on so small a scale as not to affect the rate appreciably, it would be idle to use the profitability criterion (or any other criterion) to judge whether its influence had been stabilizing or not; by hypothesis, the influence would be negligible.[21] Continued

[19] Milton Friedman, *Essays in Positive Economics*, Chicago: University of Chicago Press, 1953, p. 188; Harry C. Eastman and Stefan Stykolt, "Exchange Stabilization in Canada, 1950–4," *Canadian Journal of Economics and Political Science*, XXII, May 1956, pp. 221-233.

[20] Charles P. Kindleberger, "Exchange Stabilization Further Considered: A Comment," *Canadian Journal of Economics and Political Science*, XXIII, August 1957, p. 408.

[21] Paul Wonnacott, "Exchange Stabilization in Canada, 1950–4: A Comment," *Canadian Journal of Economics and Political Science*, XXIV, May 1958, pp. 262-265.

insistence on the profitability criterion of success reflects a policy opinion that a fund *ought* to keep its operations on a very small scale; profit or loss might then indicate whether its intentionally slight influence had been slightly stabilizing or slightly destabilizing.[22] (Whether the fund "ought to" exercise such self-restraint is a topic for discussion a few pages later on.)

Resistance to all rate movements would presumably have a stabilizing influence if the fluctuations were around a steady average rather than around an uptrend or downtrend.[23] Figure 13.1 will help show this. The "free rate" is the exchange rate that would have prevailed in the absence of official inter-

vention; the solid line shows its time path. The "modified" or "observed" rate is the one actually prevailing under the influence of the fund's transactions; the dashed line shows its path. Under the assumed policy of resisting all observed movements, the fund begins buying foreign exchange as its price sinks. The observed or modified rate continues to sink, since the fund does not aim at complete stabilization. Nevertheless, its purchases of foreign exchange keep the falling observed rate above the free rate. When the downtrend of the observed rate finally gives way to an uptrend, the fund's policy of resistance calls for a switch from buying to selling. But from then on, with the fund selling foreign exchange, the observed or modified rate lies below the free rate. To the left of its own trough, the observed rate is above the free rate; to the right of its trough, the observed rate is below the free rate.[24] The trough of the

---

[22] Harry C. Eastman and Stefan Stykolt, "Exchange Stabilization Once Again," *Canadian Journal of Economics and Political Science*, **XXIV**, May 1958, pp. 266-272.

[23] The conclusion about a stabilizing influence would still hold true even if the rate fluctuated up and down around a longer-run trend; but such behavior is of little interest because it would imply that the fund, in resisting all movements, was developing a cumulatively and untenably unbalanced position over the longer run.

The analysis that follows was introduced by Wonnacott and extended by Eastman and Stykolt in the articles cited in the two preceding footnotes.

[24] The conclusion that the observed rate is falling and above the free rate whenever the fund is buying and is rising and below the free rate whenever the fund is selling apparently depends on a tacit assumption that the free rate at each point of time is affected neither by the fund's earlier interventions nor by expectations about its later interventions.

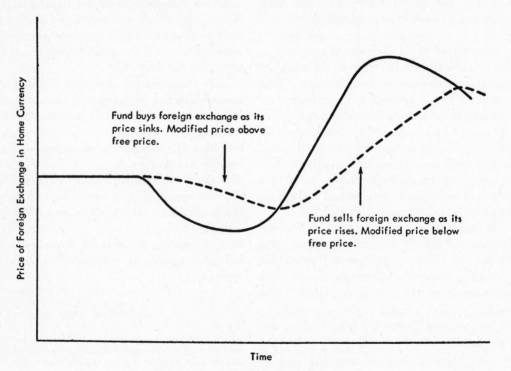

Figure 13.1. Exchange Fund Operations

observed rate must, therefore, lie on the path of the free rate. Furthermore, this point must lie to the right of and higher than the free-rate trough. (A coincidence of the observed and free troughs is a barely conceivable limiting case. As a little experimenting with the diagram will show, it is impossible for the observed trough to lie on the free-rate path to the left of the latter's trough and yet for the observed rate to the left of its own trough to be above the free rate and to the right of its own trough to be below.) The same reasoning, *mutatis mutandis,* shows that the peak of the observed rate lies on the path of the free rate to the right of and below the latter's peak. In short, the extremes of the observed rate occur after the corresponding extremes of the free rate and deviate less from the longer-run average rate. Operations that counter all fluctuations around a trendless average rate are indeed stabilizing. It is not obvious that such operations must be profitable, but if they are, there must be some most profitable volume of them, in between a negligibly small volume and a volume large enough to produce absolute rate stability and zero profits.

Tactics and Problems of Intervention

Even though the profit criterion turns out to have a very limited applicability and even though something may be said, under certain hypothetical circumstances, for a policy of countering all rate movements, the practical case for official intervention gains little from this discussion. For one thing, even if it could be known that particular rate movements will prove purely temporary, it is far from clear that they are functionless. (See p. 197 above.) More importantly, no fund *can* be sure that the rate movements it observes are mere oscillations around a steady longer-run average. In practice, any fund faces the formidable problem of distinguishing promptly between rate movements that do and those that do not represent the beginnings of fundamental shifts in trend. Even speculation-induced movements in exchange rates cannot be presumed independent of the main trend, since informed speculators may be taking account

of basic supply and demand conditions in international trade and of expected changes in them. Even if a stabilization fund attempts only to offset supposed speculative influences, buying when speculators are thought to be selling and selling when speculators are thought to be buying, it may find itself working against anticipations of the basic trend. Instructing the account to offset speculative movements presupposes that it can know what the nonspeculative equilibrium exchange rate is going to be. A policy supposedly confined to ironing out unwarranted fluctuations can drift into a policy of pegging exchange rates at levels that ultimately prove inappropriate. This danger was illustrated by various funds during the 1930s, including the British.[25] Several Latin American experiences with supposedly fluctuating exchanges in the 1950s and early 1960s also illustrate the drift from smoothing into pegging.

If a fund holds a currency close to a definite level for months at a stretch, changing to a new level only occasionally, it is likely to affect speculation much as would a policy of fixed-but-adjustable rates. When speculators come to realize that the account is temporarily maintaining an undervaluation or overvaluation of the currency, they can be fairly confident of which way the exchange rate will move if it does. Like explicit pegging, exchange-fund operations can actually encourage functionless capital movements by giving speculators plenty of time to get into the market at attractive prices. An overvalued currency is probably more of an invitation to bear speculation than an undervalued one is to bull speculation: if the bears can exhaust the fund's exchange reserves or its willingness to continue selling foreign exchange cheaply, they force the depreciation they had been betting on.

Even if a fund manages to steer clear of actual rate pegging, it still may worsen the very speculation that it is supposed to neu-

---

[25] Cf. W. A. Brown's chapter in Nurkse, *op. cit.,* p. 143; Leonard Waight, *The History and Mechanism of the Exchange Equalisation Account,* Cambridge: Cambridge University Press, 1939, pp. 138-140; Walter A. Morton, *British Finance, 1930–1940,* Madison, Wis.: The University of Wisconsin Press, 1943, pp. 126, 128.

tralize. To avoid giving speculators tips on a sure thing, it must keep at least some of its activities and intentions secret. But then speculators will guess. The idea of a "normal" exchange rate is less likely to prevail and to exert its stabilizing influence when speculators must guess at the whims of an official agency not limited to profit seeking than when they need consider only "fundamentals" such as price levels and supplies and demands in international trade. Destabilizing speculation feeds on mysteries, gossip, and rumor.

These generalizations about exchange-fund operations and speculation have a striking parallel in the officially stated reasons why the Federal Reserve System, from 1953 until late 1960, usually avoided intervention in the market for long-term government securities and confined its domestic open-market operations to "bills only." Because of their short maturity and the relatively great activity of their market, Treasury bills fluctuate much less in price than do long-term bonds when the Federal Reserve undertakes a given volume of purchases or sales. Yet operations in bills and in bonds have substantially the same power to affect the quantity of bank reserves and bank deposits, which is the main channel through which open-market policy works. The Federal Reserve could therefore regard the following disadvantage of operating in the thinner and more price-volatile bond market as ordinarily decisive: Professional dealers, realizing that the Federal Reserve was in a position to dominate the market, would necessarily attach great importance to clues about its current intentions. They would be anxious to avoid bucking any price trend that they suspected the Federal Reserve of setting; on the contrary, they would try to increase or reduce their bond inventories according to whether they thought the Federal Reserve had embarked on a program of buying or of selling. With the Federal Reserve potentially dominating the market, dealers would almost unavoidably try to divine the deeper or longer-run significance of each bit of trading that it was known or thought to be undertaking; they would try to get on its side. Unfortunately, the traders

might sometimes read undue significance into minor shifts in Federal Reserve operations; they might sometimes jump onto a bandwagon that in fact was going nowhere. They might bid bond prices up or down to a level that proved untenable, and the original sharp fluctuations would give way to another in the reverse direction. Price instability of this sort would result, to repeat, from speculation based on anticipations about the operations and intentions of a powerful official trader.[26] Freely fluctuating foreign-exchange rates are presumably supposed to resemble long-term bond prices in their potential unsteadiness (otherwise there would be little grounds for official stabilization in the first place), but if the supposition is true, the difficulties of official intervention in the one market seem relevant to the other market as well.

Sometimes the suggestion is made that an exchange fund could do more to combat disruptive speculation than to incite it. In particular, the fund could manipulate the exchange rate aggressively to punish unwarranted bear speculation against the home currency.[27] The fund would first suck the bears into a trap, letting the home currency show signs of weakness to attract plenty of short selling. Then, after the speculators had acquired a large short position, the fund would pursue a strong counteroffensive, driving the exchange value of the currency above where it stood when the bear attacks began. Forced to cover their short sales at high prices, the speculators would suffer big losses, to the

---

[26] An official rationale of the bills-only policy, largely along this line, appears in Winfield W. Riefler, "Open Market Operations in Long-Term Securities," *Federal Reserve Bulletin*, **XLIV**, November 1958, pp. 1260-1274. The answers of government securities dealers to a questionnaire distributed by the Joint Economic Committee, Eighty-Sixth Congress, generally endorsed the official theory; see Part 6C, especially pp. 1861-1874, of the Committee's *Hearings on the Government's Management of its Monetary, Fiscal, and Debt Operations*, Washington: U.S. Government Printing Office, 1959.

[27] Cf. Lowell M. Pumphrey, "The Exchange Equalization Account of Great Britain, 1932–1939: Exchange Operations," *American Economic Review*, **XXXII**, December 1942, p. 815; Frank D. Graham, "Achilles' Heels in Monetary Standards," *American Economic Review*, **XXX**, March 1940, p. 23; Charles R. Whittlesey, *International Monetary Issues*, New York: McGraw-Hill, 1937, pp. 121-122.

profit of the fund. They would soon learn their lesson, and the problem of speculation would be alleviated—or so the proposal goes.

There *are* a few historical examples of official manipulation of this sort. Throughout the 1880s the Russian press had been campaigning against speculation in rubles on the Berlin market; and after making improvements in government finances, the Russian Finance Minister, Count Witte, finally moved to squelch it. In 1892 he forbade Russian subjects to deal in forward exchange. In 1893 he imposed a tax, mostly for statistical purposes, 0.01 percent on exports of ruble notes. When considerable speculative short selling of rubles developed in 1894, agents of the Russian government in Berlin bought large amounts of ruble notes for forward delivery. Then Witte suddenly forbade the export of ruble notes from Russia. Since the forward contracts called for delivery in actual notes and since the Russian government's agents insisted on actual delivery and refused mere payment of an exchange difference, the short sellers were at Witte's mercy. He finally authorized export of the necessary ruble notes at a penalty price. Because of the discouragement that these losses gave to further speculation and also because of official exchange stabilization during the process of putting the ruble onto the gold standard, dealings in forward rubles were on a very moderate scale thereafter.[28] A better-known example is the punishment of bear speculators against the French franc in March 1924. Armed with a loan of dollars from the House of Morgan and supported by an abatement of inflationary anticipations following a tax increase, the French government was temporarily able to drive up the exchange value of the franc to a level that meant heavy losses for the bears.

A government agency may create a bear squeeze by exercising the monopoly power that individual private speculators do not have in an active market. Armed with official

power and prestige, a fund's managers may feel little moral restraint against playful or vindicative treatment of speculators. Even so, it is hard to see how the bear-squeeze technique could discourage supposedly undesirable speculation without also risking discouragement of the useful sorts of speculation. Sometimes underlying supply and demand conditions do warrant a decline in a currency, and bear speculation may be useful in hastening a smooth transition. But if speculators knew that an exchange fund was watching them and that it had a sadistic propensity to play cat and mouse with them, they might decide to quit the market. Or speculation might tend to become one-sided, with speculators willing to take long positions but unwilling to take short positions in currencies managed by exchange funds. This one-sidedness might tend to permit exaggerated bullishness in the managed currencies, making the reactions all the more sharp when they finally came. Such one-sidedness would not necessarily and always develop, however. Speculators against clearly overvalued currency might count on outlasting the fund's ability to prolong a bear squeeze.

Historical examples illustrate how official intervention may sometimes be more disruptive than equilibrating. Agents of the Russian government tried to support the ruble in 1861, 1862–1863, and 1875–1876. After the stock of foreign exchange had run out and the government had suffered losses, the ruble depreciated—probably more sharply than it would otherwise have done. Made wiser by these experiences, the Russian government refrained until the 1890s from further attempts to control the exchange rate.[29] In 1906 the Spanish Treasury, apparently seeing a chance to restore the long-depreciated peseta to par, began selling French francs on the exchange market to intensify an appreciation of the peseta that was already under way. At first, this intervention incited short sales of francs and panicky selling by holders of foreign exchange. Later, realizing

---

[28] Paul Einzig, *The Theory of Forward Exchange*, London: Macmillan, 1937, pp. 40-41; G. W. M. Huysmans, *Termijnhandel in Valuta*, Roermond: J. J. Romen & Zonen, 1926, p. 81; Gerhart v. Schulze-Gävernitz *Volkswirtschaftliche Studien aus Russland*, Leipzig: Duncker & Humblot, 1899, pp. 524-526.

[29] Gerhart v. Schulze-Gävernitz, *op. cit.,* pp. 528-530. According to Arthur Raffalovich, futile support of the ruble around 1863 left the Treasury burdened with a new debt of 15 million pounds and cost it a loss of 70 million rubles. "Histoire du Rouble-crédit," *Journal de la Société de Statistique de Paris,* **XXXVII,** October 1896, p. 365.

that the peseta's support was at the cost of Spain's foreign-exchange reserves, Spaniards took advantage of the temporary bargain price of francs in terms of pesetas. A contemporary Spanish economist judged that speculators' efforts to infer the intentions of the Finance Ministry from each development on the market were aggravating the instability of the rate and that a market free from official intervention would have been more stable.[30] In June 1928 the Spanish government created the Exchange Intervention Committee, which fought exchange fluctuations with funds borrowed abroad. The Committee apparently did narrow the range between weekly highs and lows of the peseta but could delay the downward trend only for short periods. Support of the peseta exhausted the Committee's foreign funds and caused it to suspend operations between February and June 1929. After a few months of resumed activity, the Committee again ceased functioning in October, when foreign banks refused fresh credits. Again, the peseta sank. With commodity prices in Spain holding steady in the face of an incipient worldwide deflation, the government was unable to peg the exchanges. Its efforts, though, left the government in debt to London and New York banks. Raising an internal gold loan to repay the external debt increased the demand for foreign exchange and drove the peseta to still lower levels from December 1929 to January 1930. In April 1930 the Exchange Intervention Committee was finally abolished. Later in 1930 and in 1931 the government imposed strict exchange controls, yet the peseta kept sinking still lower as depression deepened in the outside world.[31]

A few months after its establishment, the British Exchange Equalisation Account saw sterling weakening in the second half of 1932. The pressure stemmed in part from tension about the war debt payment to the United States coming due in December. Though for a time the Account tried to defend the pound, it declined in the step-wise manner characteristic of a currency with a weak underlying trend but with artificial support. Finally, not having had time to acquire enough gold and foreign exchange, the Account had to stop supporting the pound and let it sink to a low of $3.17 in November. Early in 1933 the situation was reversed. The Exchange Equalisation Account kept the pound from rising above $3.45, although many observers thought that it would have gone to $3.80 or more in a free market. The Account was supplying cheap pounds for speculative buyers and thus enabling them to win profits later. After the depreciation and devaluation of the American dollar in 1933–1934, the British Account kept the exchange rate close to $5.00 until mid-1938. Then, at last, Britain's increasingly adverse trade balance drew tardy recognition that the pound was overvalued. The Account met growing demands for gold and dollars, letting the pound depreciate only in small steps. The delay in letting the pound find its free-market level naturally incited purchases of gold and dollars while they were still being kept relatively cheap. In August, the developing crisis over Czechoslovakia intensified this speculation. By February 1939 the Account had retreated to a rate of $4.68 per pound. There the Account held until just before the outbreak of World War II, although that rate—generally recognized as indefensible in the long run—was a standing invitation to bear speculation.[32]

In contrast to all the foregoing, there is at least one prominent example of an official exchange fund that seems neither to have engaged in unduly persistent pegging nor to have disrupted the market by breeding speculation about its own intentions. This is the Canadian fund, operating from October 1950 until June 1961 under circumstances described in Chapter 24. The fact that the Canadian

[30] Francisco Gil y Pablos, *Estudios sobre la Moneda y los Cambios*, Madrid: Hijos de Reus, Editores, 1906, Appendix, esp. pp. 334, 347-351.

[31] Walter H. Delaplane, "The Spanish Peseta since 1913" (unpublished dissertation), Duke University, 1934, pp. 118-123, 150-156, 213-214.

[32] Waight, *op. cit.*, pp. 21, 111-114, 119-120; Morton, *op. cit.*, pp. 128-129; William Adams Brown, Jr., *The International Gold Standard Reinterpreted*, New York: National Bureau of Economic Research, 1940, II, 1137-1138, 1146-1147; Pumphrey, *op. cit.*, p. 811. The floating French franc of 1937–1938 provides still another example of speculation against an exchange stabilization fund; see pages 319-321 below.

fund operated with rare and notable self-restraint tends, if anything, to support, by contrast, the lessons apparently taught by experience with more ambitious funds.

Concluding Comments

When official accounts are at work, exchange-rate determination becomes, at least potentially, a political matter. Though the managers of a fund may sincerely intend only to iron out undue fluctuations, they necessarily must use their own judgment about what fluctuations are "undue." Rates thus become a matter of official decision. Though exchange funds may be used as instruments of international cooperation, they may also be used as instruments of currency warfare. At least, their very existence makes accusations of competitive exchange depreciation (or appreciation) plausible. The same is true if the national authorities are known to be operating in the exchange markets even without estab-

lishing separate funds for this specific purpose; unequivocal renunciation of all official intervention would presumably be necessary to allay suspicion. The internationally owned and operated exchange stabilization fund proposed by Lerner and Meade[33] as a substitute for national funds would presumably avoid nationalistic manipulation of exchange rates; but even if the various diplomatic and administrative difficulties could be overcome, it would still face some of the problems characteristic of national funds: a drift from rate smoothing to actual rate pegging and incitement of destabilizing speculation based on interpretations and anticipations of its own activities and intentions. It is an open question whether a fund operating modestly enough to avoid these dangers would really be missed if abolished.

---

[33] Abba P. Lerner, *The Economics of Employment*, New York: McGraw-Hill, 1951, pp. 360-362; J. E. Meade, *The Balance of Payments*, London: Oxford University Press, 1951, pp. 225-226.

Part II

HISTORY AND POLICY

A series of historical chapters begins here. They survey the policies pursued as circumstances unfolded, and they close by surveying present-day proposals for the reform of international monetary policies. An attention to history is worthwhile because historical references abound in the traditional lore of international monetary economics and because the supposed "lessons" of historical experience have played a great role in the formation of policy. For the interwar period, whose "lessons" have been so influential, and for the period since World War II, a rather detailed chronicle of events seems appropriate. For the period before World War I, a broader survey will suffice.

The Gold Standard before World War I

∽ 14

Rise of the International Gold Standard

An international gold standard exists when most major countries maintain two-way convertibility between gold and their national monetary units at substantially fixed ratios and leave inward and outward shipments of gold substantially free from interference. This system is a normal state of grace, hallowed by centuries of practice, from which the world has fallen away only in very recent decades— or so goes a widely believed myth. In fact, a full-fledged international gold standard held wide sway for at most about 40 years just before World War I. True enough, the use of gold (and silver) coin dates back to antiquity, but a fixed and supposedly permanent value relation among various types of money is a development of the past two centuries. Before then, even within single countries, various kinds of money had circulated in chaos. The idea of fixing the value of all moneys in relation to standard gold coin became common only in the nineteenth century.

The full-fledged gold standard arose in Great Britain. The background of its evolution from a loose bimetallism goes back to the seventeenth and eighteenth centuries. Sir Isaac Newton, as Master of the Mint, played a part by calculating the value of the gold guinea in terms of silver shillings. We may conveniently take up the story at the time of the Napoleonic wars. England was then experiencing wartime inflation and an irredeemable paper currency. The Bank Restriction Act, in force from 1797 to 1821, forbade the Bank of England (at its own wish, of course) to redeem its notes in gold. An act of 1798 forshadowed further development away from bimetallism and toward

the full gold standard by suspending the free coinage of silver and reaffirming a £25 limit on the legal-tender power of silver coin. The Coinage Act of 1816 authorized the gold sovereign, a 20s. or £1 gold piece first coined the following year. Its gold content confirmed the mint price of a standard ounce of gold (11/12 pure) that had been recognized since the middle of the eighteenth century: £3.17s. 10½d. Silver money was subordinated to gold and further limited in its legal tender power only to payments up to £2. The continued irredeemability of the paper pound and the market quotation of gold at a premium above its theoretical value deprived the 1816 coinage law of its full significance for a while. Finally, a law of 1819 required the Bank of England to make its notes redeemable in gold bars at the coinage price of gold by May 1821 and in coin by May 1823. Actually, full redeemability in coin was achieved in 1821, but at the cost of rapid credit contraction, further price deflation, industrial distress, and widespread unemployment. The law of 1819 had already repealed restrictions on the melting of coin and the export of coin and bullion. The paper pound was equivalent to the gold sovereign, and England was on a full gold standard.[1]

The United States at this time was legally on a bimetallic standard: the Coinage Act of 1792 had defined a gold dollar and a silver dollar 15 times as heavy. (Gold dollars were not actually minted until 1849, but the gold

---

[1] R. G. Hawtrey, *The Gold Standard in Theory and Practice* (5th ed.), London: Longmans, Green, 1947, Chapter III; Albert Feavearyear, *The Pound Sterling* (2nd ed., revised by E. Victor Morgan), Oxford: Clarendon Press, 1963, esp. pp. 152-155, 172, 188, 212-213, 221, 223.

content of the dollar was implied by the weight of gold coins of larger denominations.) The American mint ratio of 15 to 1 clashed with a ratio of about 15½ to 1 prevailing on world markets. Since the U.S. Mint was accepting gold at less than its market value, little gold came to it for coinage, and the United States was in effect on a silver standard.

The Coinage Acts of 1834 and 1837 reversed this disparity by slightly cutting the gold content of the dollar and setting a new mint ratio of very nearly 16 to 1. Since the United States was now valuing silver less highly relative to gold than was the world market, little silver was offered for coinage, and the United States was in effect on a gold standard. Considering this development, should we say that the international gold standard arose in the 1830s? Probably not. For one thing, the United States was on gold only acidentally; bimetallism was still the legally prescribed standard. Second, the United States was still too small a country for its practice to carry much weight in an assessment of world monetary arrangements. Third, the United States was not permanently on gold; the Civil War was to interrupt its metallic standard. The international gold standard as a system consciously adhered to by the major trading countries still had not arisen.

The ratio of 15½ to 1 ruled on world gold and silver markets because of the dominance of France's bimetallic system, dating from the period of the French Revolution and embodying this ratio. Being in effect on both the gold and silver standards at the same time, France was standing ready to deal in the two metals in unlimited quantities and at fixed prices. France was prepared to hold a large enough stock of each in relation to world demand and supply to govern the price ratio.

French bimetallism incidentally tended to stabilize exchange rates between gold-standard and silver-standard currencies. The British pound and French franc, for instance, were linked by their relative gold contents, while the French franc and Indian rupee were linked by their relative silver contents. The exchange rates between gold and silver currencies, such as the pound and the rupee,

could fluctuate more widely than within the range of gold points of two gold currencies, of course, since silver was more expensive to ship than a quantity of gold of the same value and since a kind of combination of gold points and silver points was operative, with the spread reflecting the costs of shipping, melting and recoining both metals.

Around 1850, gold from newly discovered fields in California and Australia began pouring onto world markets and revolutionizing the relative values of gold and silver. Yearly world gold production had averaged under £2 million in the period 1821–1830 and about £7½ million in 1841–1850 but reached about £31 million in 1853.[2] With increased supplies thus tending to depress the value of gold, the French bimetallic ratio of 15½ to 1 came to overvalue gold, making the franc in effect a gold currency. The same was all the more true of the dollar at the U.S. mint ratio of 16 to 1.

In hopes of promoting an international standardization of currencies on a bimetallic basis, the Latin Monetary Union was formed in 1865 by countries whose standard monetary units were equal to the French franc: France, Belgium, Switzerland, and Italy. Greece joined in 1868. Each member was to issue standard coins in denominations of 100, 50, 20, 10, and 5 francs in gold and 5 francs in silver,[3] and these coins were to circulate freely throughout the union. In addition, each member country could mint subsidiary coins in amounts up to 6 francs per inhabitant, and public offices of all member countries were to accept these coins in payments of up to 100 francs.

The situation around 1870 was, in short, still far from an international gold standard. England was fully on gold. Several legally bimetallic countries were in effect on gold. Germany, Holland, Scandinavia, and the Orient still had silver standards. Various wars and revolutions in the period 1848–1871 had inflated several important countries, including Russia, Austria-Hungary, Italy, and the United States, onto irredeemable paper. Even the French franc suffered a slight and brief

---

[2] Hawtrey, *op. cit.*, pp. 47, 81.

[3] Troubles with irredeemable paper money kept Italy and Greece from fully joining this system.

depreciation as a result of the Franco-Prussian War.

Then, in the early 1870s, movement toward an international gold standard picked up momentum. The German Empire, newly established and due to receive a sizable war indemnity from France, led the way. Germany's earlier silver standard had been credited with some advantages, such as stability of exchange rates in trade with Russia and Austria, but this advantage had been lost for some time because of inflation off silver onto inconvertible paper in the latter two countries. The German government now adopted the gold mark as its new monetary unit, discontinued the free coinage and unlimited legal tender of silver, and began selling silver on a large scale in order to buy gold. The glut of silver on world markets was swollen by new discoveries in Nevada and elsewhere, by the eventual effects of the discontinuance of the free coinage of silver in the United States in 1873, and by the subsequent demonetization of silver in various other countries. The overabundant silver at first began flowing into the monetary systems of countries whose silver or bimetallic standards still guaranteed a market for it. These countries faced the threat of monetary inflation and a correspondingly severe drop in the buying power of their money units. Suspending the free coinage of silver seemed to offer the only protection. France and her associates in the Latin Monetary Union limited the coinage of standard silver pieces in 1874 and entirely discontinued it in 1878, thus transforming their bimetallism into a "limping gold standard." Holland and the Scandinavian countries acted similarly. Gold replaced silver as the standard money in all European countries except the few still on irredeemable paper. The collapse in the monetary demand for it of course made silver depreciate all the more sharply in relation to gold.

The United States was also gradually moving toward the international gold standard. In 1873, when Congress omitted the silver dollar from the list of coins to be minted, the country was still using the inconvertible greenbacks dating from the Civil War inflation. For this reason and also because the world-wide depreciation of silver had not yet become pronounced, this end to the government's unlimited market for silver brought forth no strong protest at the time. Only later did mining interests label it the "Crime of '73." The act of 1873 did, however, mark the end of bimetallism as the legal standard from which the inconvertible paper was regarded as a temporary departure. (In a sense, though, the limited legal tender of the silver "trade dollar" between 1873 and 1876 was still providing a latent bimetallism at the ratio of 16⅓ to 1.) A return to convertibility would now mean gold monometallism. By 1879 the economy had "grown up" enough to the money supply and price deflation had gone far enough to permit resuming convertibility at the prewar gold content of the dollar.

The role of silver under bimetallism died harder in the United States than in Europe. Silver-mine interests wanting price support for their product formed a political alliance with farmers burdened by debt and hopeful of relief through inflation. (Actually, the long-term trend in prices had been downward since the end of the Civil War, and some extra expansion of the money supply would have been appropriate.) The miner-farmer alliance found its most conspicuous expression in the Populist movement of the 1890s, which campaigned, among other things, for the free and unlimited coinage of silver at the ratio of 16 to 1. Though the alliance never succeeded in reestablishing full bimetallism, it did secure passage of the Bland-Allison Act of 1878 and the Sherman Silver Purchase Act of 1890. These compromises required the Treasury to buy specified amounts of silver each month and issue corresponding amounts of silver dollars or silver certificates. With the money so issued contributing to a threatened exhaustion of the country's gold reserve and a forced abandonment of the gold standard, President Cleveland persuaded a special session of Congress in 1893 to repeal the Silver Purchase Act. McKinley's defeat of Bryan, who campaigned in 1896 for the free coinage of silver, helped seal the fate of bimetallism. The Gold Standard Act of 1900 consolidated the monetary standard that had existed in the United States since 1879.

The events preceding adoption of the gold standard in Austria-Hungary and in Russia are of particular theoretical interest. After a long record of paper-money inflation interrupted by periods of stabilization on silver, both countries were again driven off their traditional silver standards around the middle of the nineteenth century by issues of paper money to meet the expenses of revolutions and wars. Then, as silver depreciated on world markets in the 1870s and afterwards, the value of the silver "contained" in the standard gulden and ruble threatened to sink down to the purchasing power of the paper units. Once the value of silver began sinking still lower, owners of silver bullion would have taken advantage of the guaranteed market provided by the free coinage of silver into guldens and rubles. Silver would have poured into Austria-Hungary and Russia, inflating their money supplies and pulling down the purchasing powers and foreign exchange values of their currency units in step with its sinking value. To forestall this unwelcome development, both countries suspended the free coinage of silver, Austria-Hungary in 1879 and Russia in 1893. Thus Austria-Hungary began thirteen years and Russia four years during which the national currency unit was "hanging in mid-air," with a value exceeding that of its traditional metallic content. This phenomenon, a puzzle to some economists of the time, illustrates the quantity theory of money; suspension of free coinage helped maintain the scarcities and so the purchasing powers of the two moneys. In 1892 Austria-Hungary began adopting a gold-exchange standard, replacing the paper gulden with a gold crown worth half as much. Russia, after building up a gold reserve, moved rapidly into a gold standard in 1897. The story of the Spanish peseta, another former silver currency inflated into inconvertibility, partially parallels that of the gulden and ruble. Spain also aimed at a gold standard, but unsuccessfully.

India traditionally had a silver standard, and during the years when French bimetallism at 15½ to 1 was dominant, the exchange rate between the rupee and the British pound was fairly stable. But with the decline of silver in the 1870s and afterward, the rupee-pound rate underwent widening fluctuations. In 1893 the Indian government suspended the free coinage of silver to check further depreciation, but the rupee continued sinking for a while in partial sympathy with silver until it briefly reached a low point of barely more than half its earlier gold value. Until 1898 the rupee resembled the gulden and ruble in having a scarcity value greater than the bullion value of its silver content. Then it was pegged against the pound sterling at two-thirds of its earlier value by adoption of the gold-exchange standard, that is, by official buying and selling on the foreign-exchange market to maintain the chosen rate.

Similar measures put other Far Eastern currencies onto gold. The Philippine peso, for example, was tied to the dollar under a gold exchange standard after the United States took over the Philippines. Japan adopted a gold standard in 1897. By World War I China was almost alone among major countries still clinging to a silver standard. In Latin America, it is true, several countries still had inconvertible paper money. But the gold standard was the target and the prevailing idea of normal; going back to silver was no longer a live issue.

Beginning in the 1890s, growing supplies of gold eased the worldwide transition to the gold standard. Gold was found in the Klondike-Yukon area and in South Africa. The cyanide process of refining gold was introduced. The more abundant supply of gold helped countries such as Austria-Hungary and Russia to acquire reserves for their new gold currencies. Along with growing use of checking-account money, it also helped to stop and reverse the downtrend in prices that had been going on for two or three decades. Pro-silver agitation in the United States slackened. From 1896 to 1910, wholesale prices in the United States rose on the average by some 50 percent—all while the dollar was firmly tied to gold.

It may seem paradoxical that increased output of gold after 1849 and 1896 and the resulting depreciation of gold and increased output of silver in the 1870s and the resulting depreciation of silver both contributed to the spread of the gold standard. Yet there is no real contradiction. The two depreciations of gold were comparatively mild: the earlier one tended to ease legally bimetallic countries onto a *de facto* gold standard, and the later one worked to avoid deflationary pressure as countries newly adopting the international standard built up their gold reserves. The later depreciation also helped quiet the fears of bimetallists that two monetary metals were necessary to avoid a deflationary scarcity of reserves. By contrast, the depreciation of silver that began in the 1870s was sharp, supposedly threatening price inflation in countries clinging to silver or bimetallism (which would in effect have become a silver standard). This threat brought action to downgrade silver.

The international gold standard was a comparatively brief episode in world history. We cannot specify a precise date when it began. It did not exist in 1870 and did exist in 1900. World War I marked its end, for the postwar attempts at restoration can hardly be considered successful. The international gold standard was in full sway only from perhaps 1897 to 1914, less than twenty years.[4]

London as the Center

Before World War I the pound sterling was by far the currency most commonly used in pricing goods and services and making international payments. Ordinary British merchants dealt only in pounds, shillings, and pence, letting the foreigners struggle with the mystery of the foreign exchanges.[5] Even much trade that never touched British shores was priced in sterling and financed with sterling drafts and acceptances. For example,

an American importer of Japanese silk might arrange for his own bank to honor sterling drafts drawn by his supplier. The Japanese exporter would sell these drafts to his bank for yen. The American importer would pay dollars to his own bank, which would either deal through a correspondent bank in New York to buy the necessary sterling or else would use balances of its own already held in London. The Japanese bank would collect the sterling due on the draft at its maturity and so in effect take over a sterling balance previously owned by an American bank.[6]

What had made sterling such an international currency and London such a dominant financial center? Britain's leading position as importer, exporter, and source of long- and short-term capital made it convenient for foreign suppliers, customers, and debtors to hold working balances in sterling: funds temporarily to spare could be lent at interest in London with great safety. The unrivaled facilities of the London money market assured that any bill endorsed by one of the British acceptance houses could be discounted at the world's most favorable rates. Britain's commercial and financial leadership stemmed in turn from a combination of historical factors, including: the policy of free trade, which was firmly established by the middle of the nineteenth century, a head start in industrialization, generating wealth and savings available for loan and investment abroad, and early reestablishment of a firm gold standard in 1821. Actually, it hardly occurred to people in those days to speak of sterling as convertible: there was nothing better to convert it into. The identity of gold and sterling seemed almost a law of nature. Even more than the link with gold, sterling's general acceptability and unrestricted transferability promoted confidence. The Bank of England operated before World War I with a gold reserve often below and only very rarely above the range of £30 to 40 million, in contrast with reserves in the neighborhood of £50, £100, and £120 million held by central banks with lesser responsibilities, those of Austria-Hungary, Russia, and France. (Since World

---

[4] J. B. Condliffe, *The Commerce of Nations*, New York: Norton, 1950, p. 362, singles out 1897 as the starting date. Perhaps he had it in mind as the year when Russia and Japan went on gold, when Austria-Hungary enjoyed its first full year of uninterrupted success in operating a gold-exchange standard, when McKinley became President of the United States after campaigning in defense of the gold standard, and when price indexes registered a rise after decades of deflation.

Arthur I. Bloomfield dates the international gold standard as indicated in the title of his monograph, *Monetary Policy Under the International Gold Standard: 1880–1914*, Federal Reserve Bank of New York, 1959.

[5] William Adams Brown, Jr., *The International Gold Standard Reinterpreted*, New York: National Bureau of Economic Research, 1940, I, 638.

[6] Condliffe, *op. cit.*, pp. 383-384.

War II, in further contrast, British reserves have been regarded as dangerously low even when over £600 million.) ". . . contemporaries were torn between criticism . . . and admiration" of how "such vast transactions, both domestic and external, [were] handled with so small a reserve."[7]

Rough equality between payments to and from Britain kept the world well supplied with sterling: no "sterling shortage" developed at all comparable to the "dollar shortage" sometimes experienced after World War II. Britain generally ran a surplus on current account in the balance of payments, with earnings from exports and on foreign investments exceeding expenditures on imports. Rather than accumulate it in barren gold, Britons constructively made this surplus available for additional overseas loans and investments. Furthermore, there was some tendency for the British balances of trade and of long-term lending to move in offsetting directions over the business cycle, which contributed to overall external equilibrium of the rest of the world as well as of Britain itself. London investment banking houses were highly specialized according to types of securities, types of enterprises, and overseas geographical areas, just as stock-market operators and commodity experts were similarly specialized. By World War I an estimated one-third of all accumulated British wealth had taken the form of private foreign investment. Adjusted to the size of the American economy in 1955, this could mean something like $300 or $400 billion, as against an actual figure of about $25 billion. In the four decades preceding World War I, about 40 percent of British savings was invested overseas. Corresponding figures for America in the 1950s would have

amounted to a capital outflow upwards of $20 billion a year, as contrasted with an actual net private outflow of some $1 to $3 billion. In the few years just before World War I, one-tenth of British national income consisted of returns on overseas investment; the comparable American figure in the 1950s was well under 1 percent. British foreign investments shortly before World War I amounted to roughly twice the French, more than three times the German, and many times as large as the foreign investments of any other country. Probably something over half of the British foreign investment was outside the British Empire, largely in the United States and Latin America.[8] Figures such as these highlight the contrast between Britain's financial leadership in the days of the international gold standard and America's much less dominant position nowadays; they show the special nature of the historical circumstances in which the international gold standard worked as well as it apparently did.

Britain's role in international economic affairs before World War I took the form of *private* trade and investment, not of government grants and loans. Much of the British foreign investment and lending, though privately supplied, went to foreign government units or to government-guaranteed enterprises. The bulk of British capital export in the period 1870–1913 took the form of purchases of fixed-interest securities. Overseas government bonds and railway securities together accounted for about two-thirds of the total international investment in this period, and further British investment went into other public-utility undertakings. No major proportion of investment went for "colonial"-type ventures—that is, mines, plantations, and similar undertakings producing for the investing countries.[9]

The British money market played an even

---

[7] Paul Bareau, "The Position of Sterling in International Trade," *Banking and Foreign Trade*, London: Europa Publications Limited for the Institute of Bankers, 1952, pp. 152-53; Brian Tew, *International Monetary Cooperation*, London: Hutchinson's University Library, 1952, pp. 121-122; Feavearyear (Morgan), *op. cit.*, p. 314 (from where the quotation is taken).

The continuing stability and convertibility of sterling and other leading gold currencies were never seriously questioned, and major or sustained 'runs' on them virtually never occurred. Confidence held firm despite continuing public concern in England and some other countries regarding the adequacy of the gold reserves. Bloomfield, *op. cit.*, p. 21.

[8] Most of these estimates are from the statement of John H. Adler, citing A. K. Cairncross, in *Foreign Economic Policy*, Hearings before the Subcommittee on Foreign Economic Policy of the Joint Committee on the Economic Report, Washington: U.S. Government Printing Office, 1955, pp. 453, 463, and from Condliffe, *op. cit.*, pp. 325-327.

[9] Ragnar Nurkse, *Problems of Capital Formation in Underdeveloped Countries*, Oxford: Blackwell, 1953, pp. 28-29.

more direct role than the long-term-capital market in the working of the international gold standard. When England returned to gold after the Napoleonic Wars, banking was carried on almost entirely by private partnerships. Several hundred operated outside London, free from any significant special regulation, keeping reserves in whatever form and amount they themselves saw fit, and making loans and issuing paper money. Deposits and checks were still little used in the provinces. Inside London, about 60 banks were operating, including the country's largest and soundest. Except for the Bank of England, they did not issue their own banknotes. Instead, they granted loans by crediting the borrower with a deposit or by paying out Bank of England notes. London businessmen were already well accustomed to checking accounts.[10]

As the British money market evolved further, businessmen increasingly made payments to each other by transferring claims on London banks. The use of checks spread from London throughout the country and was well established by the 1880s. Joint stock banks, better able to amass large capitals, grew at the expense of banking partnerships. Through mergers and otherwise, the number of banks fell from around 600 in 1824 and 250 in 1865 to 55 in 1914 and even fewer after that. Most of the banking business eventually came into the hands of the "big five"—the Midland, Westminster, Lloyd's, Barclay's, and National Provincial. (This is true of England and Wales; Scotland and Northern Ireland have banking systems of their own, and commercial banks there even today have limited banknote-issue privileges.) England, like Canada but in contrast with the United States, developed a branch banking system, with a few giant banks operating many offices throughout the country.

Certain functions now performed by banks in the United States gravitated in England into the hands of special *acceptance houses,*

which evolved from leading London mercantile firms. They profited by knowing the credit-worthiness of a great many merchants and manufacturers in Britain and throughout the world. The typical client of an acceptance house was a merchant buying goods or otherwise becoming obligated to make a payment in the near future. Foreign trade gave rise to the bulk of the acceptance business. The client would arrange to pay the house, and his supplier or creditor would be authorized to draw a draft ("bill") on the house instead of on the merchant himself. The house would "accept" the draft when properly drawn and presented, thus guaranteeing payment when due. Bills accepted by one of the specialized houses had a much higher credit standing than bills drawn directly on their clients would have been. As high-quality obligations, they could be sold on the London money market at the most favorable rates of discount available. For a commission, little-known but reliable firms could thus take advantage of the credit standing of acceptance houses, which were in effect guaranteeing the soundness of paper rather than actually providing loans. The lending was done by discount houses and others who bought paper and held it until maturity.

The *discount houses* were (and still are today) a small number of firms that profited by judicious investment in short-term paper. They operated with their own capital and with funds borrowed from the banks and deposited by the public. They had evolved from bill brokers (middlemen between short-term investors and merchants wishing to discount bills) and from bill dealers, who combined the brokerage function with the holding of bill portfolios of their own.

The institutions of the late-nineteenth-century London money market illustrate remarkable specialization. According to Walter Bagehot, "a very great many of the strongest heads in England spend their minds on little else than on thinking whether other people will pay their debts." The typical bill-broker or banker

. . . is a kind of "solvency-meter," and lives by estimating rightly the "responsibility of parties," as he would call it. . . . The moment any set of

---

[10] This and the next few paragraphs draw in part on P. T. Ellsworth, *The International Economy,* New York: Macmillan, 1950, pp. 243-257; Condliffe, *op. cit.,* chap. XI, and Committee on Finance & Industry, *Report* (The "Macmillan Report"), London: His Majesty's Stationery Office, 1931, pp. 25-45.

traders want capital, the best of them, those whose promises are well known to be good, get it in a minute, because it is lying ready in the hands of those who know, and who live by knowing, that they are fit to have it.[11]

Bank Rate and the Gold Standard

Responsibility for administering the country's gold reserve gradually fell upon the Bank of England. The Bank had originally been established in 1694, largely to make loans to the government, act as its banker, and issue paper money. Private stockholders owned it until 1945. Gradually the ordinary commercial banks in London and many in the rest of the country grew accustomed to keeping reserves against their own demand liabilities partly in the form of Bank of England notes and partly in deposits at the Bank. The ordinary banks held shrinking fractions of their reserves in gold coin. Even before the gold standard had become internationally established, the Bank of England had come to hold Britain's only important gold reserve. It had acquired special responsibilities, in fact, though the directors of the Bank shrank from admitting them explicitly and preferred to insist that theirs was just one, though the largest, among profit-seeking banks. Only tacitly did the Bank admit special responsibility by keeping a reserve larger in proportion to liabilities than ordinary banks did. Even so, the Bank's gold reserve was precariously small in relation to the total volume of claims directly and indirectly pyramided upon it; in the late nineteenth century it amounted to only 2 or 3 percent of the country's total money supply.[12]

Furthermore, the Bank came to function as a "lender of last resort" in time of stringency. Occasionally, when exceptionally large demands for credit or drains of currency into circulation or of gold abroad menaced the liquidity of ordinary financial institutions, the Bank would come to the rescue, providing funds by heavy rediscounts of bills and advances. The Bank could hardly have shoul-

dered this responsibility unless the British government had been willing in emergencies to waive the requirements of the Bank Act of 1844. This act had split the Bank of England into a banking department and a note-issuing department and had required pound-for-pound gold backing (or, to a limited extent, silver backing) for all bank ntoes beyond a specified fiduciary issue (originally £14 million, later increased from time to time as the note-issue privileges of other banks lapsed). Parliament had intended to give Britain an "automatic" or unmanaged money supply in accordance with the classical theory of the gold standard: the country's currency stock would supposedly vary by the absolute amount of inward and outward flows of gold. The emergency waivers of this Bank Act took the form of so-called "Chancellor's letters" or "crisis letters." The Chancellor of the Exchequer issued them in 1847, 1857, 1866, and at the start of the war in 1914. Such a letter was a message urging the Bank to rediscount abundantly to make available the funds necessary for relieving the panic on the money market. The Bank was not to worry if such action led it to issue banknotes in excess of the provisions of the Bank Act; the Chancellor promised that, in such an event, the government would have Parliament pass a special law making the action legal retroactively.

This willingness to waive the principles of the 1844 law spelled abandonment of the ideal of a self-regulating, unmanaged monetary system. Another development relieving the British money supply of a rigid tie to the gold stock was the increasing growth of checking-account money relative to currency and coin. Actually, it is questionable whether a money supply rigidly geared to the gold stock would have proved acceptable even in the unlikely event that such a system could have been maintained. The remarkable growth of the British economy in the nineteenth century required an adaptable money supply. According to Barrett Whale, "the Act of 1844 has worked satisfactorily because it did not work in the way designed."[13]

---

[11] Walter Bagehot, *Economic Studies*, London: Longmans, Green, 1880, pp. 45-46.

[12] Jacob Viner, *International Economics: Studies*, New York: Free Press, 1951, p. 124.

[13] P. Barrett Whale, "A Retrospective View of the Bank Charter Act of 1844," in T. S. Ashton and R. S.

Ever since publication of Walter Bagehot's highly influential *Lombard Street* in 1873, the Bank of England's special duty was generally recognized. "Bagehot's rule" called for the Bank to lend copiously in times of critical credit stringency, but at a high rate of interest. By custom, commercial banks needing funds did not go directly to the Bank of England. Instead, they would press the discount houses to repay loans and would let their own holdings of bills mature without replacement. In this way the pressure was transmitted to the discount houses, which were "forced into the bank"—forced, that is, to rediscount some of their paper at the Bank of England.

The rate charged on such rediscounts, known as "Bank rate," was analogous to the discount (or rediscount) rate of the Federal Reserve banks in the United States nowadays, but far more important. The dominance of the Bank of England among British financial institutions and a conventional linkage of commercial-bank deposit and loan rates to Bank rate meant that the whole structure of rates in the money market, and to some extent even long-term interest rates, moved in sympathy with Bank rate. Its manipulation was a vital weapon for the custodian of remarkably slender gold reserves. Drains of currency into circulation or of gold abroad, perhaps in response to temporary deficits in the British balance of payments, fell on the reserves of the Bank. To counter such losses Bank rate would go up. Conversely, the Bank would lower its rate when gold reserves were unusually plentiful. It had learned to heed Bagehot's advice: keep a margin of safety in the reserves, and adjust Bank rate before the reserves fall too close to a safe minimum.

Just how did Bank rate influence inflows and outflows of gold? A rise in the rate, together with the sympathetic rise in other money-market rates, would make London a relatively more attractive place to lend and a relatively less attractive place to borrow. The resulting shift in international capital movements would support or strengthen sterling on the foreign exchanges, changing the incentives for gold arbitrage so as to discourage

an outflow of gold or even promote an inflow. A cut in Bank rate tended to work in the opposite way. London's undisputed position as world financial center avoided any problem of two or more centers of the same rank acting at cross-purposes. London was dominant both as international borrower and as international lender: it borrowed heavily in the form of foreigners' holdings of bank deposits and money-market paper and lent heavily through the long-term securities market and by discounting the bills that financed trade throughout the world. New loans in each direction were always being made afresh and old loans always coming due and subject to renewal or repayment. Even if there were no increase in British borrowing abroad, a restraint on lending would make gold flow in as foreigners paid off maturing old debts. Bank rate could control flows of capital and gold effectively because it had so much material to work on.

According to the traditional interpretation, which may or may not suit historical reality, Bank rate worked through a second channel also in correcting the balance of payments. Besides palliating temporary disequilibriums by guiding flows of capital, it provided a more fundamental cure. An increase in the rate tended to tighten credit generally, thereby retarding investment in inventories and fixed capital goods, slowing the general pace of business, and depressing prices and perhaps employment also. These price and income effects would tend to check imports and promote exports. A cut in Bank rate would unleash opposite tendencies. This traditional interpretation is well summarized in the report of the Cunliffe Committee, which was set up in Britain towards the end of World War I to make recommendations about postwar monetary policy:

4. When the exchanges were favourable, gold flowed freely into this country and an increase of legal tender money accompanied the development of trade. When the balance of trade was unfavourable and the exchanges were adverse, it became profitable to export gold. . . . [If the gold drain reduced the Bank of England's ratio of reserves to liabilities] in a degree considered dangerous, the Bank raised its rate of discount.

Sayers (eds.), *Papers in English Monetary History,* Oxford: Clarendon Press, 1953, p. 130.

The raising of the discount rate had the immediate effect of retaining money here which would otherwise have been remitted abroad and of attracting remittances from abroad to take advantage of the higher rate, thus checking the outflow of gold and even reversing the stream.

5. If the adverse condition of the exchanges was due not merely to seasonal fluctuations, but to circumstances tending to create a permanently adverse trade balance, it is obvious that the procedure above described would not have been sufficient. It would have resulted in the creation of a volume of short-dated indebtedness to foreign countries which would have been in the end disastrous to our credit and the position of London as the financial centre of the world. But the raising of the Bank's discount rate and the steps taken to make it effective in the market necessarily led to a general rise of interest rates and a restriction of credit. New enterprises were therefore postponed and the demand for constructional materials and other capital goods was lessened. The consequent slackening of employment also diminished the demand for consumable goods, while holders of stocks of commodities carried largely with borrowed money, being confronted with an increase of interest charges, if not with actual difficulty in renewing loans, and with the prospect of falling prices, tended to press their goods on a weak market. The result was a decline in general prices in the home market which, by checking imports and stimulating exports, corrected the adverse trade balance which was the primary cause of the difficulty.

6. When, apart from a foreign drain of gold, credit at home threatened to become unduly expanded, the gold currency system tended to restrain the expansion and to prevent the consequent rise in domestic prices which ultimately causes such a drain. The expansion of credit, by forcing up prices, involves an increased demand for legal tender currency both from the banks in order to maintain their normal proportion of cash to liabilities and from the general public for the payment of wages and for retail transactions. In this case also the demand for such currency fell upon the reserve of the Bank of England, and the Bank was thereupon obliged to raise its rate of discount in order to prevent the fall in the proportion of that reserve to its liabilities. The same chain of consequences as we have just described followed and speculative trade activity was similarly restrained. There was therefore an automatic machinery by which the volume of purchasing power in this country was continuously adjusted to world prices of commodities in general. Domestic prices were automatically regulated so as to prevent excessive imports; and the creation of banking credit was so controlled that banking could be safely permitted a freedom from State interference which would not have been possible under a less rigid currency system.[14]

One striking thing about this quotation is how complacently the Committee, entranced with supposedly automatic correctives, viewed adjustments working through deflation of money, prices, production, consumption, and employment.

Various parts of the traditional view have been challenged. Robert Triffin, for one, believes that the adjustment mechanism operated in Britain itself in the opposite way, in important respects. Increases in London interest rates readjusted the balance of payments not so much through their effects on the British economy as through their effects elsewhere, especially in primary-producing countries.[15] Triffin's argument is that a rise in Bank rate attracted capital and gold from abroad so effectively that it tended to relieve rather than accentuate deflationary pressures in Britain; deflation would be more likely to fall upon the countries from which the capital was drawn. A cut in Bank rate, conversely, would promote an outflow of capital, tending to reduce expansionary impacts upon the British economy. International capital movements thus thwarted or delayed the fundamental price readjustments that changes in the rate were designed to stimulate.[16]

---

[14] Committee on Currency and Foreign Exchanges after the War, *First Interim Report* (Cd. 9182), London: His Majesty's Stationery Office, 1918, pp. 3-4.

[15] Robert Triffin, "National Central Banking and the International Economy," in Lloyd A. Metzler, Robert Triffin, and Gottfried Haberler, *International Monetary Policies*, Washington: Board of Governors of the Federal Reserve System, 1947, p. 59. Compare P. Barrett Whale, "The Working of the Pre-war Gold Standard," in Ashton and Sayers, *Papers in English Monetary History*, pp. 151-164.

[16] Triffin, *op. cit.*, p. 60. This argument tacitly presupposes a mechanical adjustment of market interest rates in step with Bank rate—"mechanical" in the sense that interest rates rise or fall apart from any domestic restriction or expansion of the money supply. This presumption may or may not be historically justified—quite possibly things did work that way in the short run—,

British experience did not conform to the classical picture, which really portrayed price relations among a large number of equally important countries. Because of Britain's dominance in the world economy before 1914, however, expansionary and contradictionary tendencies in Britain tended to engulf most other nations at the same time. Since the bulk of foreign exports was financed through London and since foreign bills far outweighed inland bills in the London discount market, a tightening or loosening of credit in Britain could be expected to affect the prices of foreign goods more drastically and directly than domestic prices. These movements might be further magnified by induced contraction or expansion in the foreign banking systems, especially as tightened credit there would not, as in London, attract compensatory capital movements from abroad. Another point in Triffin's skepticism about the classical view of relative price movements is that Britain's imports, consisting mainly of foodstuffs and raw materials, presumably responded more sensitively in price to changes in credit and business conditions than did Britain's largely industrial exports. If Britain's Bank-rate policy failed to accomplish the price-level readjustments of classical theory, as Triffin argues, the main reason is the thoroughly *international* character of the London money market. The system approximated the automatic gold standard of the classical model less than it did a centralized sterling exchange standard managed by the Bank of England.[17] ". . . the automatic operation of the gold standard . . . was more or less limited to the sphere of the Bank of England and was satisfactory in its results only because London was then by far the most powerful financial centre in the world . . . and could thus by the operation of her bank rate almost immediately adjust her reserve position. Other countries had, therefore, in the main to adjust their conditions to her."[18]

The Bank had charge of the reserves not only of the London money market but of the worldwide trade and investment cleared through London. Yet the myth of an automatic, self-regulating system was so strong that even when the directors of the Bank took positive action in raising or lowering Bank rate in response to depletion or growth of the gold reserve, they thought of themselves not as active managers but as middlemen giving effect to impersonal market forces.[19] Actually, there was some scope for discre-

---

but the argument would hardly apply if the rise or fall of interest rates was associated with domestic restriction or expansion of the money supply. Restrictions on growth of the money supply of which higher interest rates were simply one aspect, or acceleration of monetary growth of which lower interest rates were simply one aspect, should affect the balance of payments in the classical way.

[17] *Ibid.*, pp. 58-63.

[18] Committee on Finance & Industry, *op. cit.*, p. 125.

The view of the pre-1914 system as a managed sterling standard has been challenged. There is no evidence to show that the Bank of England regarded itself as money manager for the world or as acting otherwise then to protect its reserves. It did not accumulate excess reserves in good times and release them in times of strain in order to counteract inflationary and deflationary tendencies. Its reserves were inadequate for the global task of stabilization, and it sometimes had to impose otherwise unwanted deflationary pressure on the British economy in order to protect both its slender reserves and the gold convertibility of sterling.—For this interpretation, see John M. Letiche, *Balance of Payments and Economic Growth*, New York: Harper & Row, 1959, p. 23, and Lloyd Mints, *Monetary Policy for a Competitive Society*, New York: McGraw-Hill, 1950, p. 107.

If "management" means "a conscious attempt to influence the trend of commodity prices, there was certainly no management; at that time the Bank of England never sought to prevent the variations in the output of gold from producing their normal effect on the currency and credit structure and consequently on prices. Neither can it be said that the Bank of England or other central banks regarded it as their task to control the business cycle, except that, in accordance with their customary practice, they would react against speculative excesses by increasing interest rates and, conversely, lower their rates when, in times of depression, the demand for credit became less acute." Bank for International Settlements, 13th *Annual Report* (1942–1943), p. 126.

The fact that the Bank of England raised and lowered Bank rate almost solely out of concern for its own reserves hardly settles the issue of management, however. The Bank *did* manage the nineteenth-century gold standard in the sense of dominating it—which is not to say that the Bank's actions were in accordance with modern ideas of contracyclical policy and not to deny that they appeared to be dictated by circumstances instead of being freely chosen.

[19] Condliffe, *op. cit.*, p. 359. In a more general context, Albert O. Hirschman writes: ". . . in the minds of many economists, the central banker became a sort of honorary member of the market forces." *The Strategy of Economic Development* (paperbound ed.), New Haven: Yale University Press, 1961, p. 64n.

tionary management, even though in England as in other gold-standard countries, maintaining the gold parity of the currency was the overriding objective of policy and the reserve ratio its major guide. Central bankers did not operate by rigid, mechanical rules. They constantly had to use judgment on such matters as whether or not to act in a given situation, on how and how vigorously and when to act, and on the policy instruments to be used (for the discount rate was not their sole weapon).[20]

Critics of the traditional view may be right in maintaining that the English Bank rate policy operated less to keep domestic money, credit and price conditions passively in step with world conditions than actively to dominate and determine those conditions. They may be right in questioning the price-income-and-employment channel through which Bank rate supposedly operated. They do seem right in questioning the supposed automaticity of the pre-1914 gold standard. But, in any event, there seems little doubt that countries outside Great Britain had to keep fairly well in step, forgoing any major degree of monetary independence, if they meant to keep their currencies on the gold or sterling standard. And there seems little reason to doubt the effectiveness of Bank rate in influencing international flows of capital, whatever may be said about the further consequences of the rate and of these flows. Belief in its effectiveness was epitomized in the old City saying that 7 percent would bring gold from the North Pole. Funds would not have moved so sensitively from country to country, of course, if the confines of the gold points had not kept exchange-rate fluctuations so small that potential losses on this score were overshadowed by the profits offered by the international differentials in interest rates.

Supplements to Bank Rate

Bank rate was not the only means of influencing international gold flows. In addition, there were the so-called "gold devices" —expedients enabling the Bank of England to vary somewhat the prices at which it bought gold and at which it redeemed banknotes in gold.[21] The Bank was legally required to redeem its notes on demand in gold sovereigns. The gold content of a full-weight sovereign implied an official selling price for coined gold of £3.17s. 10½d. per standard ounce (11/12 pure). The Bank was also required to issue banknotes in exchange for bar gold at the price of £3. 17s. 9d. per standard ounce. But nothing prevented the Bank from paying more than the specified buying price for gold when anxious to attract additional gold into its reserves. Of course, the Bank could not offer so much more that arbitrageurs would find it profitable to redeem banknotes in sovereigns, melt the sovereigns into bars, sell the bars to the Bank at the especially favorable price, redeem the banknotes so obtained, and so on. Another way of in effect slightly raising the buying price for gold was to accept foreign coins instead of standard bars, sparing gold importers the expense of melting and refining. Occasionally the Bank offered gold importers interest-free loans equal to the value of gold in transit. Conversely, when unnecessarily abundant reserves made the Bank willing to facilitate gold exports, it might redeem its notes in bars or in foreign coin for exporters who found gold in this form more suitable than sovereigns. As the Bank became less willing to see gold go abroad, it might offer bars and foreign coins to exporters on increasingly less favorable terms. It might even insist on its legal right to redeem banknotes in sovereigns alone, thereby saddling gold exporters with the possible expenses of melting and reminting into coins of the coun-

---

[20] Bloomfield, op. cit., esp. pp. 23, 25-26.

Bloomfield (pp. 43-44, 61) also expresses skepticism about the importance of the "second channel," involving prices, incomes, and employment, through which discount-rate policy was supposed to affect the balance of payments. Clinging to the gold standard sometimes was a hardship for individual countries, especially the less developed ones; but there is not much evidence that discount-rate increases were harshly deflationary and caused severe unemployment. Restrictive credit policies apparently served more to slow down or temporarily halt secular economic expansion than to impose an absolute deflation of incomes and prices.

[21] See R. S. Sayers, "The Bank in the Gold Market, 1890-1914," Papers in English Monetary History, pp. 132-150, and Feavearyear (Morgan), op. cit., p. 330.

try of destination. The ultimate in protecting the Bank's gold reserve this way was to redeem notes in worn sovereigns of barely the minimum legal weight. Such expedients were not unusual, at least after 1890, and may occasionally have made it possible to keep Bank rate lower than otherwise would have been necessary.

Various "gold devices" were also often used by American and continental authorities. All central banks, according to Oskar Morgenstern,[22] sometimes tried to attract or hold gold by means other than the discount rate, no matter how often they denied it. In Germany, interest-free loans were given to importers of specie, and exports of specie were impeded. Similar devices worked rather successfully in France. These devices put some slight variability into the gold values of monetary units and slightly increased the range of possible exchange-rate fluctuations. So doing, they nibbled at the fringes of the very idea of an international gold standard.

Fostering noncurrency methods of payment and the issue of small-denomination notes in efforts to economize further on the use of gold[23] amounted to further nibbling; for measures that deliberately modify and loosen the linkage between the quantity of gold and the quantity of money run counter to the idea of an impersonally regulated money supply. These measures foreshadowed the massive attempts to economize on gold under the gold-bullion and gold-exchange standards of the late 1920s.

Still other features of later systems, including some aspects of present-day arrangements, also were occasionally, though not typically, evident before World War I: destabilizing speculation and hot-money movements, bear attacks that threatened to force departure from the gold standard and that required resort to extraordinary remedies, concern about the volume of short-term foreign indebtedness, concern about inadequacy of the reserves of individual countries and of international liquidity in the aggregate, and warnings about the need for institutionalized cooperation among the authorities of different countries.[24]

The Myth of the Gold Standard

Understandably enough, these less attractive and less typical facts tend to be forgotten more readily than the sound features of the international monetary system destroyed by World War I. That system even today exerts a peculiar fascination. Gold itself, and hence a currency tied to it, is material for fond legends. Christopher Columbus said, "Gold constitutes treasure, and he who possesses it has all he needs in this world, as also the means of rescuing souls from Purgatory and restoring them to the enjoyment of Paradise."[25] The administrator of the gold system, the Bank of England, was also a symbol: "The old lady of Threadneedle Street, very much like the contemporaneous old lady on the throne, had become a symbol of the solidity, the glory, the far-flung interests, and the incorruptible and beneficent omnipotence of the British Empire."[26] It is natural, though perhaps not logical, to associate the international gold standard with the serene economic progress that prevailed at the same time throughout the world, or at least in Europe and in countries settled by peoples of European descent. The age of the gold standard was an age of relative peace: though limited

[22] *International Financial Transactions and Business Cycles*, Princeton, N.J.: Princeton University Press for National Bureau of Economic Research, 1959, p. 441. Also see Bloomfield, *op. cit.*, pp. 52-55.

For a contemporary Continental description of gold devices and a defense of them as giving the central bank some freedom to manage monetary and credit conditions as seemed appropriate for domestic business, see Julius Landesberger, *Ueber die Goldprämien-Politik der Zettelbanken*, Vienna: Manz'sche k.u.k. Hof-Verlags- und Universitäts-Buchhandlung, 1892.

[23] Bloomfield, *op. cit.*, p. 22.

On the eve of World War I, gold accounted for scarcely more than one-tenth of the world's estimated total monetary circulation and silver for perhaps only one-half or one-third as much as gold. Paper currency and bank deposits already accounted for nearly nine-tenths of the total. Robert Triffin, *The Evolution of the International Monetary System: Historical Reappraisal and Future Perspectives,* Princeton Studies in International Finance No. 12, Princeton, N.J.: Princeton University, 1964, p. 15.

[24] Arthur I. Bloomfield, *Short-Term Capital Movements under the Pre-1914 Gold Standard*, Princeton, N.J.: Princeton University, 1963, pp. 2, 28-29, 44-45, 83-92.

[25] Quoted in R. H. Tawney, *Religion and the Rise of Capitalism*, New York: Harcourt, Brace, 1926, p. 89.

[26] Viner, *op. cit.*, p. 129.

wars were numerous enough between 1815 and 1914, conflagrations involving many countries were unknown. By and large, people were freer from government regulation—freer to transact any honorable business as they saw fit, to make investments, to transfer funds, to travel without formality—than in any age of history before or since. There is a certain charm in the reminiscences of an old German banker of how, during his student days at Heidelberg, he and some friends, one of whom had just inherited some money, left on the impulse of a moment for a tour of Italy, where the Italian banker in the first town they stopped in considered it an honor to cash in gold coin the large check written by the young stranger. There is a similar charm in Jules Verne's story of Phineas Fogg, who left on short notice for his 80-day tour of the world, paying his expenses from a carpetbag full of Bank of England notes, accepted everywhere. The civility and internationality prevalent during the age of the gold standard have such charm for us nowadays that it seems almost sacrilege to ask whether these benefits resulted from the gold standard or, instead, coexisted with it by mere coincidence.

The gold standard, in short, evokes the "good old days." This association is well illustrated by two quotations, the first from Benjamin M. Anderson, a lifelong champion of the gold standard, and the second from John Maynard Keynes, his generation's leading critic of the gold standard:

Those who have an adult's recollection and an adult's understanding of the world which preceded the first World War look back upon it with a great nostalgia. There was a sense of security then which has never since existed. Progress was generally taken for granted. . . . We had had a prolonged period in which decade after decade had seen increasing political freedom, the progressive spread of democratic institutions, the steady lifting of the standard of life for the masses of men. . . .

In financial matters the good faith of governments and central banks was taken for granted. . . . No country took pride in debasing its currency as a clever financial expedient.

London was the financial center, but there were independent gold standard centers in New York, Berlin, Vienna, Paris, Amsterdam, Switzerland, Japan, and the Scandinavian countries. There were many other countries on the gold standard, with some tendency for the weaker countries to substitute holdings of sterling or other means of getting increased earnings. For their purpose the sterling bill was quite as good as gold. . . . But, in general, the great countries held their own gold. They relied upon themselves to meet their international obligations in gold. At times of great crisis a country under very heavy pressure would seek international cooperation and international assistance, and would get it—at a steep rate of interest.[27]

What an extraordinary episode in the economic progress of man that age was which came to an end in August, 1914! The greater part of the population, it is true, worked hard and lived at a low standard of comfort, yet were, to all appearances, reasonably contented with this lot. But escape was possible, for any man of capacity or character at all exceeding the average, into the middle and upper classes, for whom life offered, at a low cost and with the least trouble, conveniences, comforts and amenities beyond the compass of the richest and most powerful monarchs of other ages. The inhabitant of London could order by telephone, sipping his morning tea in bed, the various products of the whole earth, in such quantity as he might see fit, and reasonably expect their early delivery upon his doorstep; he could at the same moment and by the same means adventure his wealth in the natural resources and new enterprises of any quarter of the world, and share, without exertion or even trouble, in their prospective fruits and advantages; or he could decide to couple the security of his fortunes with the good faith of the townspeople of any substantial municipality in any continent that fancy or information might recommend. He could secure forthwith, if he wished it, cheap and comfortable means of transit to any country or climate without passport or other formality, could despatch his servant to the neighboring office of a bank for such supply of the precious metals as might seem convenient, and could then proceed abroad to foreign quarters, without knowledge of their religion, language, or customs, bearing coined wealth upon his person, and would consider himself greatly aggrieved and much surprised at the least interference. But, most important

[27] B. M. Anderson, *Economics and the Public Welfare*, New York: Van Nostrand, 1949, excerpts from pp. 3-4, 6.

of all, he regarded this state of affairs as normal, certain, and permanent, except in the direction of further improvement, and any deviation from it as aberrant, scandalous, and avoidable. The projects and politics of militarism and imperialism, of racial and cultural rivalries, of monopolies, restrictions, and exclusion, which were to play the serpent to this paradise, were little more than the amusements of his daily newspaper, and appeared to exercise almost no influence at all on the ordinary course of social and economic life, the internationalization of which was nearly complete in practice.[28]

---

[28] John Maynard Keynes, *The Economic Consequences of the Peace,* New York: Harcourt, Brace & World, Inc., 1920, pp. 10-12.

Suspension and Attempted Restoration
of the International Gold Standard

∽ 15

The End of an Era[1]

War ended the brief reign of the full international gold standard late in July 1914. A foreign-exchange deadlock resulted at first. As usual, the whole world had debts coming due in London. British financial houses, anxious to play safe by bringing their short-term funds home from abroad, swelled the demand for sterling. London banks sought to bolster their reserves against possible panic by shrinking their loans to the discount houses. On July 27, when London acceptance houses stopped granting new acceptance credits, foreigners lost their most important single current source of sterling. They could still get it by selling their British securities in London. Dumping of securities caused the stock exchange to close on July 31 and stay closed several months. Other European security exchanges closed under similar pressure.

In New York, nervous foreigners hastened to sell their American securities and take home the proceeds. Preparations to export gold strained bank reserves, restricted credit for carrying securities, and worsened the threat of a market collapse. The New York Stock Exchange closed the same day as the London exchange. The United States had already been losing gold because of a passive trade balance and German, French, and Russian accumulations of gold in readiness for war. Further gold shipments would ordinarily have filled the gap between the intensified demand for sterling and the shrunken supply. But hostile cruisers were on the seas, and insurance against wartime risks was unavailable for a few days. Despite a mint par of $4.8665, the pound sterling rose to $6.35 in New York in the last week of July and to $7.00 at the beginning of August for a few transactions in a very thin market. On August 12 the Bank of England agreed to accept gold in Ottawa, and sterling dropped to a more normal rate. Large gold shipments proved unnecessary.

The unusual rise of sterling would have been only temporary, anyway, for wartime demands for American goods soon mounted. By December 1914 the dollar rate on sterling sank to and below par. The franc, the mark, and other belligerent currencies were also weakening.

The international gold standard did not break down completely or all at once. Most countries clung to its legal fictions for some time. "The date when England 'returned to gold' after the war is a landmark in world history, but it is very difficult to determine the date when England left the gold standard to which she returned in 1925."[2] The gold content of the sovereign remained unchanged. Until 1925, private persons still had the legal right to bring gold to the mint for coinage. The Bank's obligation to buy all gold offered at the official price remained in force until 1939. Throughout World War I, private persons still had the legal right to import gold. In fact, though, the Bank of England arranged to buy all incoming gold,

---

[1] General references for this section include W. A. Brown, Jr., *The International Gold Standard Reinterpreted*, New York: National Bureau of Economic Research, 1940, I, Book One, and Benjamin M. Anderson, *Economics and the Public Welfare*, New York: Van Nostrand, 1949, Part I.

[2] Brown, *op. cit.*, p. 28n.

leaving none for private parties. Private gold exports also remained legal, though only theoretically so. Redemption of banknotes in gold, still legally possible, was all but prevented by appeals to patriotism, inquisition into motives, regulations against the melting of gold coin, a ban on buying or selling gold at a premium, and pegging of the exchange value of sterling (from January 1916 on) at only about 2 percent below mint par. The most important departure from the gold standard was quite unofficial: bullion dealers, like the general public, felt that gold exports would be unpatriotic and simply did not undertake any.

The gold standard evaporated piecemeal on the Continent also. Germany, Austria-Hungary, Russia, and France suspended redemption in coin and embargoed gold exports. Yet official obligations to buy gold at fixed prices still stood and gold imports remained legal. The neutral Dutch government at first embargoed gold exports and authorized the Netherlands Bank to suspend specie payments. More typically, however, neutrals interfered with gold imports. Holland did so in 1915, when commodity imports began to lag behind exports and capital and gold flowed heavily inward; and under its "gold repulsion policy," the Netherlands Bank sometimes refused to buy gold. In February 1916, Sweden suspended both the free coinage of gold and the Riksbank's obligation to buy gold at fixed prices, thus restricting the entry of gold imports into the monetary system. Denmark and Norway agreed to pass similar measures when necessary. Spain also became reluctant to accept gold. Such measures sought—not very successfully, as events turned out—to limit the contagion of the belligerents' inflation through balances of payments.

The United States kept most of the legal forms of the gold standard. After American entry into the war, however, persons trying to redeem their paper money in gold ran into unofficial difficulties; and in September 1917, gold exports became subject to official license. The two chief requirements of the gold standard, interconvertibility between paper money and gold and the free inter-national movement of gold, lapsed in one way or another.

Paradoxically, violating the substance of the gold standard enabled many governments to preserve its reassuring symbols—comfortable reserves and familiar exchange rates. Governments badgered their citizens in various ways and degrees to get gold coins out of circulation into official hands. Several countries supplemented these "gold-concentration" campaigns with steps to mobilize foreign exchange. In 1915 the British government began encouraging and in January 1917 began requiring private holders to sell it their foreign securities, which it could then sell for foreign exchange. The French government persuaded but did not compel its citizens to sell it their foreign securities. Germany, too, used persuasion and did not resort to compulsion until March 1917; and even then, the German government promised to replace the commandeered securities three years after making peace with England.

Belligerents used resources so obtained in efforts to support the prewar pattern of exchange rates. Late in 1915 some neutral currencies were tending to rise against sterling and dollars, while the currencies of Italy, Austria, Germany, and Russia were tending to fall. Even the sterling-franc-dollar relation was growing shaky. Control of the sterling-dollar rate began in August 1915, and in January 1916 the rate was definitely pegged at $4.76 7/16, about 2.1 percent below mint par. In April 1916 the British and French governments arranged to stabilize franc exchange. The resources available for allied exchange-rate pegging began running out by the fall of 1916 but were replenished by advances from the U.S. Treasury after the United States joined the war the following spring. Lacking such support, the German and Austrian exchanges continued to sink, and efforts to restrain the fall of the mark definitely failed early in 1918.

Towards the end of the war speculation centered on belief that exchange rates would soon return to "normal." At the time of the armistice, the rates of the Netherlands, Spain, the United States, Great Britain and the Empire, Japan, France, Sweden, Argentina,

Brazil, and Italy diverged remarkably little from the prewar pattern, considering the circumstances.[3]

Postwar Financial Conditions

Faith in a prompt return to "normal" overlooked the profound changes that war had brought. Physical changes included casualties, property destruction and deterioration, and subtler types of erosion of productive capacity. Political changes included the dismemberment of Austria-Hungary, the communization of Russia, and widespread acceptance of extensive government intervention in economic life. Financial changes included the consequences of government borrowing in ways that inflated money supplies. Even the United States government covered roughly 72 percent of its wartime expenditures by borrowing instead of taxation. The French Finance Minister expressed a typical attitude. When questioned in Parliament about the financing of military expenditures, he referred to future indemnities: "The Boche will pay."

War financing more than tripled the French public debt between the end of 1914 and the end of 1918, and between March 1914 and March 1919 the public debt was multiplied more than thirty-fold in Germany and almost nine-fold in the United Kingdom.[4] Table 15.1 shows what happened to currency supplies and price levels in Europe. Inflation was less severe in the United States. Currency outside banks multiplied by about 2⅓ from mid-1914 to mid-1919, and total deposits and currency multiplied by about 1.8. Wholesale prices in 1919 averaged about twice and in 1920 about 2¼ times the level of 1914. (This was a slightly greater degree of price inflation, incidentally, than had been experienced under the Civil War "greenbacks.") Price-level figures for the immediate postwar years must be taken with great reservations because of such distortions as price control and rationing.

Price inflation reached a peak in most coun-

[3] *Ibid.*, p. 70.
[4] Paul Alpert, *Twentieth Century Economic History of Europe*, New York: Henry Schuman, 1951, pp. 34-35.

Table 15.1. Currency Supplies and Price Levels in Europe after World War I as Percentages of Their Prewar Figures (End-of-year Data)

	1918	1919	1920
United Kingdom			
Currency circulation	248	274	294
Wholesale prices	246	297	264
Cost of living	230	236	278
France			
Currency circulation	433[a]	533[a]	541[a]
Wholesale prices	355	432	444
Cost of living	248	285	424
Germany			
Currency circulation	503	760	1230
Wholesale prices	260[b]	803[b]	1440[b]
Cost of living			1158
Italy			
Currency circulation	486	649	769
Wholesale prices	296	416	596
Cost of living	260[c]	323[c]	455[c]
Switzerland			
Currency circulation	248	263	268
Cost of living	211	245	243
Spain			
Currency circulation	173	200	224
Wholesale prices	213	204	214
Sweden			
Currency circulation	348	323	330
Wholesale prices	335	317	267
Cost of living	238	263	271
Norway			
Currency circulation	348	323	386
Wholesale prices	345	322	377
Cost of living	264	291	335

NOTE: The base for the wholesale indexes is the average for 1913; the cost-of-living figures are mostly based on July 1914.

[a] The base figure for 1913 excludes gold coins, most of which were not in active circulation.

[b] End-of-year price indexes for 1918, 1919, and 1920 were 289, 1508, and 2023 for imported goods and 250, 633, and 1323 for domestic products alone.

[c] Average of two indexes for retail prices in Rome and Milan.

SOURCE: League of Nations, Secretariat, Economic, Financial, and Transit Department, *The Course and Control of Inflation*, League of Nations, 1946, p. 88.

tries in 1920 and then gave way to a couple of years of business depression. The United States, with its comparatively mild inflation, was able to discontinue controls over gold exports and so return to a full gold standard in June 1919. Particularly in Germany,

France, and central and eastern Europe, however, inflation went on for several years. The old money units of Austria, Hungary, Poland, Germany, and Russia were practically wiped out. By the end of their respective inflations, prewar price levels had been multiplied by roughly 14,000 in Austria, 23,000 in Hungary, 2½ million in Poland, and 4 billion in Russia.

The German Inflation

The German experience was worse.[5] As one of the classic hyperinflations of history, this episode deserves special notice. The prewar mint par had been 4.2 marks per dollar. In 1918 the quotation averaged 6 marks per dollar. It was 14 in June 1919, 39 in June 1920, 69 in June 1921, 317 in June 1922, nearly 18,000 in January 1923, and around 100,000 in June 1923. From then on the mark sank faster and faster until the climax in November 1923. Wholesale prices averaged about 35 times their prewar level by December 1921. A year later, prices were 1475 times the prewar level. Already, even before the final phase of astronomical figures, inflation was dislocating economic activity.

One source of dislocation was the fact that people were reluctant to hold melting marks and snapped at the chance to buy commodities. Bidding inventories and goods-in-process away from their normal uses tended to impair the smooth flow of production and distribution. Relative prices became distorted as some prices responded more promptly than others. It was often cheaper to travel from one town to another by railroad than from one block to another by streetcar. Wages moved slowly at first and later were tied to prices. Salaries and pensions lagged.

At times the exchange depreciation of the mark ran ahead of the rise in internal prices. The iconoclastic view that this timing shows cause and effect finds some support in the association of a particularly sharp fall in mark exchange in September 1921 with a heavy reparations payment from Germany to the Allies.[6] This payment increased the demand for foreign exchange to be bought with marks. Prices of German imports and exports rose in sympathy with foreign-exchange rates; domestic prices followed. Government expenditures rose with prices. Revenues lagged because specific taxes and nontax revenues (such as railroad fares) were adjusted slowly to the inflation and because income taxes collected in a given year were based on incomes of the year before, when nominal prices and incomes had been much lower. Since the government met its growing deficit by borrowing freshly printed money from the Reichsbank, one might contend that the mark's depreciation was more directly a cause than a consequence of money-supply inflation. Private as well as government demands for credit rose with prices.[7]

This process, at least in its early stages, drew remarkably little effective protest. Inflation creates its own vested interests. For the government, inflationary financing meant following the (temporarily) easiest course. Budgetary laxness possibly fed on the thought that financial chaos could serve as an argument or excuse for scaling down reparations to the Allies. Industrialists and merchants learned to live with inflation and to profit —at least apparently, in terms of nominal marks—from price increases between the time of buying materials, labor, or inventories and the time of selling the product. Exaggerated profitability stimulated capital formation and the capital-goods industries. Labor enjoyed full employment, and arrangements were made for more frequent paydays and for wages scaled to keep pace with prices. Of course, not all persons were able to protect themselves. Creditors lost real wealth to debtors. Great hardship fell on pensioners, holders of insurance, endowed institutions,

---

[5] See W. Arthur Lewis, *Economic Survey 1919–1939*, London: Allen & Unwin, 1949, pp. 23-29; Frank D. Graham, *Exchange, Prices, and Production in Hyperinflation: Germany, 1920–1923*, Princeton, N.J.: Princeton University Press, 1930; and Costantino Bresciani-Turroni, *The Economics of Inflation*, London: Allen & Unwin, 1937.

[6] See John H. Williams, "German Foreign Trade and the Reparations Payments," *Quarterly Journal of Economics*, XXXVI, May 1922, pp. 502-503.

[7] For an analysis of similar experiences during the Austrian inflation that reached its climax in 1922, see J. van Walré de Bordes, *The Austrian Crown*, London: King, 1924.

and small savers inexperienced in putting their liquid wealth into satisfactorily hedged forms.

In January 1923 French troops occupied the industrial Ruhr valley to prod the Germans into fuller and more prompt reparations payments. The Germans responded with "passive resistance," including deliberate absenteeism from industrial jobs. Support of the resisting workers further burdened the German government budget. By the end of October 1923 the government's ordinary receipts were covering only about 0.8 percent of expenditures; the government was raising money almost exclusively by borrowing at the Reichsbank, which in turn simply rolled the printing presses. New money also poured out on loan to private businessmen, who eagerly borrowed with the prospect of repaying some weeks or months later in marks that would have depreciated much further in the meanwhile.

Businessmen took to figuring costs and quoting prices in gold or foreign currency (and some bonds were denominated in dollars, wheat, rye, or other things of relatively stable value). Prices were translated into marks at the moment of sale at the latest exchange-rate quotations. This practice hastened depreciation by increasing the demand for foreign exchange: a merchant, having assumed the obligation to pay a sum in paper marks depending on the exchange rate on the day of payment, would hedge by buying foreign exchange in advance.

This practice is only one reason why the mark should have lost foreign-exchange value more rapidly than internal purchasing power. Another is that persons flying from marks found foreign exchange a convenient asset, stable yet liquid. A more general reason is that a sensitive and competitive market where prices are the very opposite of "administered" is bound to be one of the promptest of all markets in responding to both objective and psychological influences. Moreover, the German government's chief method of raising foreign exchange for reparations payments was to dump newly printed marks on the exchange market. With fresh banknotes having their first impact there, it is no wonder

that exchange depreciation outpaced the mark's loss of internal purchasing power. This phenomenon would probably have been even more striking had not gullible foreigners, until the last stages of inflation, continued buying up mark notes in the belief that the mark must have reached bottom and was due to recover.

In view of all these facts, the role of exchange depreciation in the German inflationary process provides no valid evidence against the quantity theory of money.[8] The inflation first began with monetary expansion to pay for the war and could not have gone on without continued expansion. As for reparations in particular, the depreciation of the mark must be blamed not so much on these payments themselves as on how the government raised money for them. If the government had bought foreign exchange only with marks raised by taxation or by genuine noninflationary loans, so that the wealth transferred to the Allies had been wrested from the German population in these orthodox ways, the depreciation would have been limited. Whether such a Spartan budget policy would have been practical politics is another question, but a *policy* question of this sort upsets no propositions in economic *analysis*.

Ideological influences must not be ignored. A League of Nations report has made pertinent comments:

> . . . the "ideological" soil of German economic thought was favourable to inflation. The quantity theory of money had never gained much ground in Germany. The majority even among the trained economists refused to believe in a chain of causation running from the issue of money to the rise in prices. Most economists attributed the rise in prices to the unfavourable balance of payments and to the consequent fall in the external value of the mark. Helfferich, Minister of

---

[8] In a study of a number of hyperinflations, including the German, Phillip Cagan has shown that velocity depended on expectations about the future rate of increase in prices, as inferred from the observed rate of increase in prices in the recent past, which in turn was related to the rate of expansion of the money supply. See "The Monetary Dynamics of Hyperinflation," in Milton Friedman (ed.), *Studies in the Quantity Theory of Money*, Chicago: University of Chicago Press, 1956, pp. 25-117.

Finance in 1923, was a leading proponent of the balance-of-payments theory. Havenstein, President of the Reichsbank, in so far as he had any theoretical notions at all, adhered to a form of the "banking principle" which told him that the rise in prices created a need for money on the part of business men as well as the government, a need which it was the Reichsbank's duty to meet, and which it could meet without any harmful effects. . . . German economic thought failed to apprehend that the expansion in the money supply was at least an essential *condition* without which the general rise in prices could not have gone far. And this intellectual failure accounts in great part for the weakness of the defences which the spring tide of inflation encountered in Germany.

The management of the Reichsbank . . . followed the old Banking Principle and refused to believe that printing money in favour of business men against genuine commercial bills could have any inflationary effect. The Reichsbank had kept its discount rate unchanged at 5% up to the summer of 1922. Thereafter, it raised the rate by several stages to 90% in September 1923. But even at that rate it was practically giving money away. The fall in the value of the currency was more closely reflected in the market rate on short-term loans, which rose as high as 20% *per diem* or approximately 7300% *per annum*. At the rates maintained by the Reichsbank, the rediscounting of bills made it possible for the commercial banks to extend credits on very favourable terms to business men. For business men, indeed, it became one of the rules of good management to contract as many debts as possible, debts which were later repaid in depreciated money.[9]

Undervaluation of the mark on the exchanges in relation to its purchasing power made it abnormally cheap for foreigners to live or buy goods and services in Germany. This much-deplored *Ausverkauf*, or clearance-sale, of the German economy ended when businessmen started adjusting their prices in step with exchange rates and finally, toward the end of the inflation in 1923, in step not just with current but with expected *future* exchange rates. Internal prices again, as in the early mild stages, rose faster than foreign exchange rates.

By this time prices were not simply rising at a faster rate than the money supply—a phenomenon easy to understand. They came to rise faster even than money supply times velocity. In terms of Fisher's equation of exchange $MV = PT$, T, the physical volume of transactions carried out with money, fell: inflation had caused such disruption that real business activity and employment actually slumped in the last few weeks of inflation in 1923.

Prices had risen so much faster than the money supply that complaints became common of an acute *shortage* of money, despite eventual issue of denominations as high as 100 trillion marks. At one point, Havenstein, the President of the Reichsbank, seriously expressed hope that new high-speed currency printing presses soon to be installed would help overcome the shortage.[10] Of course, the terrific shrinkage of the German money supply in terms of real purchasing power or gold merely reflects how fully people had come to understand the fantastic real cost of holding money.

The currency "shortage" just mentioned explains how Dr. Hjalmar Schacht could succeed in launching a new "Rentenmark" currency (which, as a kind of public-relations device, was supposedly backed by land). The public had been so inconvenienced by lack of stable currency that it was eager to believe in the reform. The demand for Rentenmarks to rebuild depleted real cash balances gave the government a breathing space in which to cover its expenditures with new issues of money while taking steps to balance its budget through spending cuts and tax increases. A drop in velocity offset further monetary expansion. Timely receipt of an international loan under the Dawes Plan of 1924 also helped.

As the inflation of the old Reichsmark reached its climax late in November 1923, a newspaper cost 200 billion marks. Wholesale prices averaged about 1.4 trillion times as high as before the war. The currency reform set one new mark equal to 1,000,000,-

---

[9] Pp. 16-17 and 31 respectively (in the section written by Ragnar Nurkse) of League of Nations, *The Course and Control of Inflation* (1946).

[10] Frank D. Graham later observed that Havenstein's death at the time of currency reform and introduction of the new mark was "a demise which cannot be thought of as other than opportune." *Op. cit.*, p. 12.

000,000 old ones. Germany had experienced the most severe inflation in history up to that time. (The Hungarian inflation of 1946 produced statistics even more astronomical.)

Reparations and War Debts[11]

The financial problems of Germany intertwined with a problem that conditioned international monetary relations throughout the 1920s and early 1930s. In the Versailles Treaty of 1919, Germany acknowledged war guilt and undertook to compensate her victims. Pending final determination of compensable damage, Germany was to begin an interim payment of roughly $5 billion, largely in commodities, mainly coal. Meanwhile, the Reparation Commission produced successive tentative estimates of the total amount due, which was scaled down in April 1921, partly in view of Germany's supposed capacity to pay, to 132 billion gold marks (about $31½ billion). Bonds were to be delivered for this amount and payments on them to be made in yearly installments of 2 billion gold marks plus the proceeds of a 26 percent tax on German exports. More than half of the money was to go to France. An Allied ultimatum prodded Germany into accepting these terms.

Not only Germany's ability but also her willingness to pay was a key question. Another was whether other countries would forego excessive tariffs and let Germany achieve the export surplus necessary for transferring large sums of money. Great Britain generally favored reasonableness and compromise. The French government, engaged in deficit spending to finance reconstruction work, wanted large reparations. In July 1922, with reparations transfers contributing to the downward slide of the mark, Germany asked for a two-year delay in payments, but France refused. In January 1923 the French and Belgians occupied the Ruhr to put pressure on the defaulting Germans. After more than half a year of passive resistance in the Ruhr

—absenteeism, sabotage, neglect of French orders—the Germans gave in and began cooperating with the technicians of the occupation forces.

The final collapse of the mark in 1923 brought a new study of the issue. A special committee of the Reparation Commission, headed by an American banker, produced the Dawes Plan in 1924. It sought to improve Germany's paying capacity by rehabilitating her economy and finances. To support transition from the temporary Rentenmark currency to a gold standard, Germany received an international loan of almost $200 million, mainly subscribed in the United States. This amount equalled four-fifths of the reparations installment payable during the first year of the Dawes Plan. The annual installments were to rise gradually over five years to a standard amount of 2½ billion gold marks (about $600 million). They were to vary thereafter according to changes in the value of gold and were to rise with an index of German prosperity. An Allied agent in Berlin was to supervise German finances related to obligations under the plan. A transfer committee was to see that the transfer of reparations payments abroad took place in such amounts and at such times as not to endanger the new mark.

The Dawes Plan worked well for five years, but it had been conceived as a merely temporary solution and had not set a total reparations figure. In 1929 another international committee drew up the Young Plan. For agreeing to supposedly definite and firm obligations, Germany got a further scaling-down of payments, an end to international control of her finances, and withdrawal of remaining Allied troops. Annual payments under the plan would run for 59 years, until 1988, when 121 billion marks (about $29 billion) would have been paid. The discounted present value of this stream of payments was estimated at 37 billion marks, or under $9 billion. This burden was far below the 132 billion marks set by the Reparation Commission in 1921 (since that was a principal sum, with interest to be extra) and even somewhat below the Germans' own proposal of 1921. Annual Young-Plan payments were

[11] This section draws in part on Alpert, *op. cit.*, pp. 53-61; William Ashworth, *A Short History of the International Economy, 1850–1950*, London: Longmans, Green, 1952, pp. 189 ff.; and James W. Angell, "Reparations," in the *Encyclopedia of the Social Sciences*, New York: Macmillan, 1930, vol. 13, pp. 300-308.

set on a slowly rising scale beginning at only two-thirds of the standard annual payment under the Dawes Plan and averaging only four-fifths of that amount. Payments could be postponed under various circumstances. If the United States should reduce its war-debt claims on its allies, part of the benefit would pass on to Germany in a still further scaling-down of her payments. Part of the German obligation could be commercialized by the issue of interest-bearing bonds, which claimant countries might sell at once for cash. Conditions on the international capital market were so unfavorable at the time, however, that only about $200 million worth of the bonds were actually floated. The Bank for International Settlements was established in Basel, Switzerland, with the task of handling German reparations transfers. To this very day the Bank still carries some of the Young-Plan bonds on its balance sheet, together with a reservation by the public accountants as to their actual value.

Linked with the problem of reparations was that of interallied war debts. Wartime and early postwar loans left the United States government a net creditor for over $10 billion. Great Britain had both borrowed and lent and emerged a net creditor for about $4½ billion. France owed over $3½ billion net. These amounts do not include interest. Other countries owed smaller sums. France, a net debtor, argued that the wartime loans should be regarded as contributions made among allies in a common cause. Britain, though a net creditor, took a realistic view of its chances of collecting on its claims and pressed at the peace conference of 1919 for cancellation of all war debts. In August 1922 Britain announced that it would expect no more from its debtors than it itself had to pay to the United States. The United States denied any legal connection between the interallied debts and reparations from Germany, though France in particular insisted on the economic connection. The United States—"Uncle Shylock" in some circles—saw its loans as binding business transactions, though interest rates might properly be scaled down. With its high-tariff policy during the 1920s clashing with insistence on debt repayment, the United States was able to collect some money from its debtors chiefly because private American loans to Germany and other European borrowers made possible some reparations payments and in turn some interallied debt repayments.

With minor exceptions, war-debt payments came to an end, together with German reparations, less than two years after the Young Plan took effect. (Some details are given in the next chapter.) The United States finally recovered about $2.7 billion, or a little over one-fourth of its claims. How much the Allies received from Germany is not clear, partly because so much was transferred in goods. According to some guesses, Germany paid about 25 billion gold marks from Versailles until the Dawes Plan and about 11 billion under the Dawes and Young Plans, totaling roughly $8½ billion. Payments in 1928–1929 amounted to 12.4 percent of the total cost of government in Germany and to 3.4 percent of the estimated national income. All in all, Germany paid a little under $5 billion, according to estimates of the Reparation Commission, and more than three times that much, according to padded German claims. In comparison, Germany received some $8 or $9 billion from abroad during this period, mostly as loans after 1924 but nearly one-fourth of it earlier by way of losses by foreigners on their holdings of depreciating marks.[12] After 1924, German borrowings abroad ran roughly double German reparations payments; thus the problem of achieving a current-account surplus in the German balance of payments large enough to effect the reparations transfers—and foreign reluctance to accept German goods might have contributed to this problem—was actually sidestepped.

History seldom teaches clear lessons; so much depends on the selection and interpretation of the facts. There seems to be a consensus, however, that the futile effort to collect sizable reparations kept Europe in a turmoil for a dozen years or more. Given the financial policies then prevailing in Germany,

---

[12] Cf. Alpert, *op. cit.*, p. 60; Angell, *op. cit.*, p. 307; and Étienne Mantoux, *The Carthaginian Peace*, New York: Scribner's, 1952, pp. 152-155.

reparations transfers contributed to the hyperinflation; and international wrangling fed German grievances. With regard to intergovernmental debts as well as reparations, the prospect of large international payments unrelated to current production and trade presumably hampered a return to economic and financial tranquility. The outcome probably would have been better if Germany's victims had contented themselves with a definite indemnity collectable within a few years[13] and if the United States had taken a less legalistic attitude toward war debts.

Britain Off Gold

A background has now been set for reviewing two experiences during the 1920s that are widely thought to teach lastingly relevant lessons. These are the contrasting experiences of Britain and France.

World War I destroyed Britain's unchallenged financial dominance.[14] Her already noticeable lag behind newly industrialized countries in production and export growth grew worse. Wartime trade interruptions spurred industrialization in several of Britain's traditional markets. Britain lost ground in shipping and, partly because of wartime sales of assets, as a foreign investor. Reduced current-account surpluses and new demands for capital to reequip industries at home shrank Britain's capital exports and weakened her position as international banker. Even her traditional free-trade policy was dented by import duties imposed during the war to raise revenue and conserve foreign exchange and shipping space and by duties imposed in 1921 to protect strategic industries. These duties applied only to selected goods and were not far-reaching enough to warrant dating the real end of British free trade before 1931, but they were straws in the wind.

The American dollar destroyed the preeminence of sterling without itself taking over sterling's old role. The United States became an international financier during the war, lending abroad to finance an export surplus during its neutrality and later to aid its Allies. Sterling acceptances lost ground to telegraphic transfers because of specific wartime developments, trends in the British banking structure, and gradual changes in trade-financing methods. American cotton exporters, for instance, instead of receiving payment by drawing sterling bills, began using revolving credits granted by American banks while awaiting telegraphic transfers from their British customers. A market for dollar acceptances had already been developing in New York under the encouragement of the Federal Reserve Act, passed in 1913. Foreign-owned bank balances began building up in New York early in the war as belligerent governments prepared for war purchases and as capital took refuge from Europe. After April 1915, when an emergency system of security price floors was abolished, New York had the world's only stock exchange not restricting trading in foreign securities. Belligerents, neutral borrowers whose usual accommodations had been cut off, and even some private British borrowers floated securities in New York.

Meanwhile, the London market saw further changes: (1) the rise of the Treasury bill, (2) reduced power to "compel" and more need to "attract" foreign deposits, and (3) rise of the tied-loan principle.[15] To conserve the resources of the money market for its own Treasury bills, the British government restricted the use of trade bills. The acceptance and discount houses saw their distinctive functions gradually undermined. Secondly, the strength of sterling on the exchanges depended on London's holding the foreign deposits abnormally built up during the war. Yet with the erosion of prewar practices, international traders no longer felt "compelled" to hold London balances. They would require attractive yields from now on. Third, criticism was growing of loans to foreign countries whose industries were encroaching on former British markets. Departing from the traditional British indifference to where the proceeds of loan flotations

---

[13] Nothing is implied here about any supposed *economic* impossibility of Germany's paying and transferring reparations in the amounts originally demanded.

[14] Facts in the following paragraphs come from a number of sources, including, in particular, parts of chapters 7-12 of Brown, *op. cit.*

[15] *Ibid.*, pp. 154 ff.

were spent, the feeling grew that borrowers ought to spend the loans in the lending country.

The report of the government-appointed Cunliffe Committee, issued in August 1918,[16] recognized that sterling had suffered a still-concealed depreciation against gold in some moderate degree then impossible to measure. It worried about the danger of gold losses, once obstacles to gold shipments were removed. The report recommended an early end to government borrowing, a start on repayment of government securities held by the banks, resumption of traditional credit control through Bank rate, and shrinkage of the currency circulation. Without even analyzing whether prewar exchange rates were still appropriate, the report took a return to prewar gold parity for granted. According to some tacit ethical code, apparently, the British paper pound was a binding promise to pay

---

[16] Committee on Currency and Foreign Exchanges after the War, *First Interim Report* (Cd. 9182), London: His Majesty's Stationery Office, 1918.

a certain quantity of gold. Continuing inflation abroad could be hoped for to ease domestic deflation and the return to normalcy.

Wartime artificialities had to be cleared away first, including extensive price control and government domination of food marketing. The most notable decontrol step came early: the wartime peg of the pound-dollar rate lapsed in March 1919. A temporarily fluctuating rate would measure progress in deflating British prices enough more than American prices to make prewar parity workable again. Paradoxically, the month of unpegging also saw gold exports for the first time legally forbidden (until then, they had been restricted by wartime shipping risks, by appeals to the patriotism of the bullion dealers, and by exchange-rate pegging that made them unprofitable). The exchange rate was freed from the influence of import and capital-export controls only by degrees, and its freedom was not complete until late 1919 or early 1920. Administrative arrangements

Figure 15.1 Sterling-Dollar Exchange Rate, Monthly Averages, 1919–1925.
SOURCE: Banking and Monetary Statistics, Board of Governors of the Federal Reserve System, 1943, p. 681.

made in September 1919 and a law passed in 1920 permitted the reexport from Britain of newly mined South African gold. Its price in London paralleled the sterling-dollar exchange rate. From 1920 through 1924, the rate fluctuated almost completely free from official intervention.[17]

The pound reached a monthly average low of $3.38 in February 1920. The lowest single quotation was $3.18, or 35 percent below prewar par. A year and a half of indecisive swings followed. The monthly average rate next rose almost without interruption from a low of $3.63 in July 1921 to a high of almost $4.70 in March 1923. After that it gradually sank to a low of $4.26 for January 1924 and then, with minor interruptions, rose again to near parity in April 1925.[18]

The movement of the exchange rate in relation to purchasing-power parity provides some clues about exchange-rate speculation.[19] The three most significant fluctuations occurred in 1919–1921, the immediate postwar years of abnormal scarcity and inflation followed by sharp recession. Since the major depreciation of the pound that started in June 1920 was apparently in step with the greater fall of American than British prices, only two episodes remain as possible examples of destabilizing speculation. The first began late in 1919. The initial depreciation of the pound against the dollar, which had thus far corresponded to the movement in relative purchasing powers, now speeded up and carried further. The similar behavior of other European currencies at the same time suggests that destabilizing speculation was not the only influence at work. A tightening of monetary policy in the United States suddenly choked off a stabilizing flow of export credits to Europe. The European exchange depreciations were apparently less due to a self-aggravating flight of capital than to a policy-induced cessation of a previous stabilizing flow. Furthermore, the depreciation reversed itself as soon as February 1920; and by April the pound was stronger than it had been in December. The second apparent example of destabilizing speculation was the pound's rapid climb from December 1920 to May 1921, considerably outrunning purchasing-power parity. Steps to establish U.S. government export credits for farm products and negotiations for refunding the British debt to the United States had apparently stimulated bullishness on the pound.

The tide turned in June 1921, but the ensuing depreciation seems merely to have reduced the pound's premium above purchasing-power parity. No significant bearish speculation was apparent. Abatement of the earlier overoptimism might have been partly due to strikes in Britain's two chief export industries, coal and textiles, in the spring of 1921. In addition, the dollar was strengthened by heavy German buying in late May and early June in order to pay reparations. In August 1921, when the exchange rate had come more into line with purchasing-power parity, the pound began to appreciate gradually as it gained in purchasing power relative to the dollar.

From this time on, the exchange rate moved broadly in line with purchasing-power parity. From March to October 1922, however, the exchange rate was sticky despite a rise in the relative purchasing power of the pound. The failure of the pound to appreciate was probably connected with British labor disputes and a deadlock over German reparations. From then on until the return to the gold standard, movements in both the exchange rate and purchasing-power parity were fairly mild and were closely associated.

In summary, the fluctuations of sterling

---

[17] It is true, however, that the Bank of England might have influenced the rate through the timing of its purchases, as agent for the Treasury, of dollars to service the U.S. and Canadian debts. The Bank's gold reserve was practically unchanged from the end of 1920 until April 1925, and its great increase during 1920 was due to transfers from the commercial banks rather than to official intervention on the market. S. C. Tsiang, "Fluctuating Exchange Rates in Countries with Relatively Stable Economies: Some European Experiences After World War I," IMF *Staff Papers*, VII, October 1959, p. 245.

[18] Most of the monthly average exchange rates in this chapter are taken from Board of Governors of the Federal Reserve System, *Banking and Monetary Statistics*, Washington, 1943, p. 681 for the United Kingdom and p. 670 for France.

[19] Tsiang, *op. cit.*, pp. 249-256. Tsiang computed purchasing-power parities on a 1913 base, using the Federal Reserve Board's indexes of wholesale prices in the United Kingdom and the United States.

exchange after the immediate postwar years of inflation and recession were in accordance with purchasing-power parity and, on the whole, were not even as wide as those of either purchasing-power parity or the United Kingdom price level. This relative stickiness suggests that exchange speculation was mainly in a stabilizing direction.[20]

Britain on the Gold-bullion Standard

British motives for finally returning to par strengthened in 1924 when the new German mark was stabilized on gold and when sterling improved following the success of Germany's Dawes Plan loan. The Gold and Silver (Export Control) Act of 1920, which had been protecting the gold reserves of the Bank of England, was due to lapse at the end of 1925. The government would soon—probably in the Budget Speech of April 1925—have to declare whether or not it would extend the act, giving reasons. Considerations of international prestige were working against further postponement of the return to gold.

The Committee on the Currency and Bank of England Note Issues had been appointed in June 1924. Its report in February 1925 found Britain financially strong enough for reestablishment of a free gold market, provided that the internal purchasing power of the pound were raised somewhat further and provided that foreign investments were restricted to the country's normal current-account surplus. The return to the gold standard should be announced immediately, said the report, and control over gold and silver exports allowed to lapse. Foreign credits, though not necessary, would help promote confidence in the restored parity. The circulation of gold coins was considered a non-essential and undesirable luxury.[21]

During this period the Bank of England continued holding total bank reserves, de-

posits, and earning assets stable. In November 1924, restrictions were imposed on placement of new foreign loans in London; and during the year these restrictions were in effect, British loans to foreign governments were nil and to other foreign borrowers negligible. Early in 1925 American credits were obtained to help defend sterling after the return to gold. In April 1925 Bank rate was raised to 5 percent to keep British interest rates above the rising rates in New York.

The stage was now set for the Budget Speech of April 28. The Chancellor of the Exchequer, Winston Churchill, announced that the restrictions on gold and silver exports would lapse and that the Bank of England would redeem legal tender in gold for export. The Gold Standard Act of 1925, passed on May 13, required the Bank to sell gold in ingots of not less than 400 fine ounces for legal tender at the traditional price of £3. 17s. 10½d. per ounce 11/12 fine. Sterling could thus be redeemed in gold in amounts worth no less than almost $8300. Redemption in coin was not required. Only the Bank was to have the right to bring gold bullion to the mint for coinage. The Bank remained obliged, as it had been without interruption ever since 1844, to buy all gold offered to it at £3. 17s. 9d. per ounce 11/12 fine.

Omitting coins from actual circulation aroused little comment; attitudes had changed. During the war the fiction prevailed that money was still redeemable in gold coin, even though gold for export was not actually available. Now the gold standard was proclaimed in effect again because gold exports were again permissible, even though the redemption of money in gold was restricted to this purpose.[22] Other European countries apparently shared this new view.

---

[20] *Ibid.*, esp. p. 256. E. Victor Morgan, *Studies in British Financial Policy, 1914–25,* London: Macmillan, 1952, pp. 364-366, also found "a very close correlation between movements of the exchange and relative prices," apart from the short-lived drop of the pound in mid-1921.

[21] Brown, *op. cit.,* pp. 375-377.

[22] The Currency and Bank Notes Act of July 1928 provided, among other things, that any person in the United Kingdom owning more than £10,000 worth of gold coin or bullion could be made to sell it to the Bank of England at the legal price, unless the gold were being held for immediate export or for industrial use. Thus, if necessary, the Bank could keep private gold hoarding from seriously interfering with its own policies. *Ibid.,* pp. 682-683.

For example, when the Netherlands followed England back onto the gold standard, the Netherlands Bank would sell gold only if exchange rates justified its export. While Americans saw domestic redeemability as the essence of the gold standard, Europeans apparently welcomed the bullion standard as a way to economize on gold and yet have the benefits of the full gold standard.[23]

Britain did not regain parity without trouble. Considerations of legislative timing and of international prestige had forced action before the British and American price levels had been fully aligned at exchange parity. Although nothing better than a very rough measurement is possible, the figure of 10 percent has become the traditional informed guess of how far the restored parity was above the pound's equilibrium value.[24] It is true that the discount on the fluctuating pound had shrunk below 10 percent in July 1924 and below 2 percent early in 1925, but by then exchange-rate quotations were reflecting speculation on the imminent official restoration of parity.

Most prominent among British economists warning against overvaluation was John Maynard Keynes. Keynes was already famous as the author of *The Economic Consequences of the Peace,* which dissected the economic provisions of the Versailles Treaty. He published a pamphlet in 1925 entitled *The Economic Consequences of Mr. Churchill,*[25] warning that the old parity would throttle exports and necessitate further painful deflation in Britain. Similar warnings had been made regarding a return to parity after the Napoleonic Wars, and on both occasions the warnings seem to have been borne out by experience. The deflation in the United States from 1865 to 1879 in preparation for restoring

the greenbacks to the parity in effect before the Civil War is another example.

The further downward adjustment of British prices and wages required to make parity an equilibrium rate might not have been too difficult for a flexible economy (which is not to say that this would have been the best policy even then), but the British economy was not flexible enough. B. M. Anderson cites as typical the example of four companies that had agreed on fixed prices and sales quotas. Three of them could profitably have cut prices to attract new business, but the fourth was burdened by a poor location and outmoded equipment and could have been ruined by price competition. Precisely because the cartel agreement was not legally enforceable (though not itself illegal), the three strong companies felt all the more honor-bound to abide by it.[26] Furthermore, a widespread tendency among British businesses to cling to old production methods and obsolete plant and equipment made cost-and-price cutting all the more difficult. Britain seemed to be in the middle of the theoretical gold-standard adjustment process, stuck there, with unemployment having no marked tendency to depress wages and prices. Union wage scales, unemployment insurance, and unemployment relief tended to hold wages up. Recurrent labor disputes, including a general strike and a lengthy coal strike in 1926, dramatized how hard it was to reduce costs and prices. In time the hope became clearly futile that domestic deflation would restore equilibrium. Foreign countries, either by internal deflation to restore their own parities with the dollar or by stabilizing their currencies at undervalued levels, killed Britain's alternative hope that price inflation abroad would make adjustment easy.

Industrial production generally stagnated. British industry had traditionally specialized in meeting basic rather than readily expansible wants. Depression in the old basic industries (including iron and steel, coal, and cotton textiles, now faced with competition from rayon) was not fully offset by prosperity in newer ones, such as electrical apparatus

---

[23] *Ibid.,* p. 382.

[24] According to W. M. Scammell, for example, "It is generally agreed that . . . the pound was approximately 10 percent over-valued" between 1925 and 1931. *International Monetary Policy,* London: Macmillan, 1957, p. 52n. The view that sterling was overvalued after 1925 is unconvincingly challenged, however, in John T. Walter, *Foreign Exchange Equilibrium,* Pittsburgh: University of Pittsburgh Press, 1951, pp. 14-16.

[25] London: L. and V. Woolf, 1925. The American edition, published by Harcourt, Brace, was entitled *The Economic Consequences of Sterling Parity.*

[26] Anderson, *op. cit.,* pp. 164-165.

and appliances, chemicals, and automobiles. Coal production never regained the prewar level during the entire interwar period. Reasons included increased efficiency in using coal to produce electricity, increased competition from foreign mines and from other fuels, and the inefficiency and high labor costs of the British coal industry. The decline in exports of coal compounded the troubles of British shipping. The total volume of world trade regained the 1913 level only in 1929, then promptly fell off again. Shipbuilding, like shipping, was hard hit: over half of British shipyard workers were unemployed during the 1920s. Even while most other countries were enjoying prosperity, well over 10 percent of the total British labor force was usually unemployed. The "dole," given to families proving their need for relief after exhaustion of unemployment benefits, supported an actual majority of the population in some particularly depressed areas. The deflation, depression, and chronic unemployment of the 1920s and their worsening after 1929, created durable memories and presumably contributed to the growth of anticapitalist sentiment in Britain, to the increasing strength of the Labor Party and its election victory in 1945, and to the lasting importance of "full employment" as a political slogan.[27]

Signs of trouble appeared in the balance of payments and the foreign-exchange market. Small current-account surpluses, seldom reaching one-third or one-half of the prewar real size (after adjustment for the higher prices), did not cover the long-term foreign security issues floated in the highly developed London capital market, and the necessary funds came as short-term inflows from abroad. By 1928 the London market had run up short-term external liabilities of about £500 million gross and £200 million net, in contrast with its net short-term creditor position before the war. Sterling was generally weak from 1925 on. The market price of gold in London persistently tended to stay at or near the selling price of the Bank of England, which was almost continually resisting a

tendency to lose gold. Exchange rates in the late 'twenties contrasted with those of 1888–1914, when the annual average rate on sterling in New York had been below mint par only four times and above par twenty-three. But from 1925 through 1931 the annual rate was above par only once—in 1928, when it averaged $4.8666, as against a mint par of $4.8665.[28]

Did the pains of the 1925 revaluation yield no comparable benefits? Well, no sober weighing of prospective benefits and costs had led to that policy. Instead, the tacit view prevailed that elementary decency required it. Sentiment yearned for the pound once more to "look the dollar in the face." Superficially, though, it might seem a benefit that the "City" of London, while never regaining its unchallenged prewar supremacy, did regain the prestige of a gold-standard center and did attract short-term foreign funds in heavier volume than before the war. In particular, London attracted deposits from the central banks of countries that had adopted the gold-exchange standard. In linking their currencies to the dollar or pound and holding their monetary reserves largely in dollar or sterling bank balances or short-term securities, these countries could earn at least some interest on their otherwise barren reserve funds. This arrangement seemed satisfactory to London bankers also, for it cheaply provided them with funds for profitable relending. Another source of foreign balances in London was the flight of funds to safety during the French monetary difficulties of 1924–1926; these French funds were not immediately repatriated after the franc was stabilized. The French banks, into whose hands these funds gradually drifted, were inclined to retain them to earn the relatively high interest rates offered in Britain's defense of the gold standard. In fact, an abnormally large volume of international short-term money existed in the late 1920s, ready to flit from one financial center to another as risks and earnings opportunities changed. Before the crisis

---

[27] Alpert, *op. cit.*, chap. 6.

[28] Bank for International Settlements, *The Sterling Area*, Basle: 1953, p. 22; Brown, *op. cit.*, pp. 603, 709. The Federal Reserve's *Banking and Monetary Statistics* quotes an average rate of $4.8662 for 1928.

of 1931, London harbored much of these funds.[29]

The advantage of having foreign balances in London was shaky. If they should be quickly withdrawn, as finally did happen, a house of cards would come tumbling down. Though exchange rates on the pound were still stable within the gold points, the situation bristled with latent instability.

In short, British monetary experience in the 1920s consisted of: several years of deflationary struggle back to prewar parity; temporary success in this questionable effort; and then continued business stagnation and chronic unemployment, the need for relatively high interest rates, and a precarious accumulation of mobile short-term foreign funds—all under the influence of an inappropriate exchange rate.[30]

France before Stabilization

French monetary inflation continued until mid-1926 and went far enough to prevent a return to prewar parity. A new parity was finally adopted that somewhat undervalued the franc and caused a balance-of-payments surplus and gold accumulation during the late 1920s.

The franc, like the pound, had been pegged near par during the war. A decline after the unpegging in March 1919 seemed temporary and hardly disastrous; Frenchmen apparently expected an early return to normal. But inflationary government finance continued. The franc fell in relation to the dollar more rapidly than did the pound, and by April 1920 it stood at slightly under one-third of the prewar rate. Then new taxes and the flotation of loans provided a respite from inflationary

finance. Moreover, the French government obligated itself by a convention with the Bank of France and by a law of December 1920 to repay earlier advances at a rate of 2 billion francs a year. Though these repayments were later made either only partially or by means of subterfuges (such as borrowing from other sources, including private banks to which the Bank of France was compelled to lend the necessary funds),[31] the announced policy did at first promote confidence in the currency. The franc moved on the exchange market in general harmony with sterling. From April 1920 to April 1922 it rose from 6.25 to 9.23 U.S. cents. That was to prove the highest monthly level ever reached since December 1919.

The franc was subject to worse strains than sterling. Expenditures on postwar reconstruction from 1919 to 1926 resulted in government budgets that were as large as or larger than wartime budgets (larger in nominal francs, though smaller in real purchasing power). These expenditures, together with war-related pension and interest costs, produced a "consecrated deficit" in a confusing morass of special government budgets. The national debt rose from 173 billion francs in 1918 to 428 billion in 1924. "Le Boche paiera" was the cry. The franc was vulnerable when the wrangle over reparations came to a head in mid-1922. The adamant Raymond Poincaré had already replaced Aristide Briand as premier, interrupting Briand's relatively conciliatory policy towards Germany. Already in May the franc had begun to fall against the dollar and sterling. Later in the year foreign bear speculation became active, undermining the confidence of the French in their own currency. The franc fell to an average rate of 6.86 cents in November 1922. The Ruhr occupation episode began in January 1923.

Until early 1922 speculation and capital flight clearly had not dominated the exchange market; in fact, capital tended to enter France each time the franc slumped considerably. But then a kind of speculation developed that was later to be authoritatively described as illustrating the general "dangers of . . .

[29] Lionel Robbins, *The Great Depression,* New York: Macmillan, 1936, pp. 89-91.

[30] This interpretation is not fully shared, however, even by all economists who understood what was at issue. As sensitive an observer as Gustav Cassel felt that promoting international confidence and international trade through restoration of sterling to its old position as the principal world currency was worth the small sacrifices of the moderate price deflation still necessary. (Cassel estimated that a 6 percent further reduction of the British price level was necessary at the beginning of 1925.) *The Downfall of the Gold Standard,* Oxford: Clarendon Press, 1936, pp. 37, 40.

[31] Tsiang, *op. cit.,* p. 265.

cumulative and self-aggravating movements under a regime of freely fluctuating exchanges. . . ."[32]

For this reason the entire experience deserves detailed reexamination. The decline of the franc in 1922 cannot plausibly be explained by trouble with the balance of payments, which actually improved. Neither does the still moderate expansion of the money supply provide the full explanation. Some French economists (notably Albert Aftalion) later propounded a so-called "psychological theory" to explain the exchange rates of the franc in the period then beginning. The public's willingness to hold francs and, in turn, the supplies and demands on the foreign-exchange market reacted to growing uneasiness about the government budget. Yet the French government persisted in unrealistically counting on reparations to cover its outlays for reconstruction and pensions. The deficit was being reduced year by year, but not eliminated, and the national debt kept rising. Furthermore, when the government had trouble selling its securities to the public, it borrowed directly or indirectly from the Bank of France, which in effect ran a printing press on its behalf. Psychological influences on the foreign-exchange market thus centered on real factors.

In 1923 the government was again unable to comply with the law of December 1920 regarding repayments to the Bank of France. January 1924 saw the failure of a loan floated by the Crédit National, an association of the principal French banks that had been set up in October 1919 to sell its own government-guaranteed bonds to the public and use the proceeds for term loans to industry and for advances to war-damage victims on the security of their claims for indemnity. The failure of this loan was ominous because the government was dependent on the willingness of the public to buy its obligations if it was to escape outright inflationary finance.

Under the continued pressure of bear speculation that had resumed the previous November, the franc kept falling. The rate hit 3.49 cents on March 8, 1924. Increases in the discount rate of the Bank of France in January had proved unable to stop the decline. On March 22, in an atmosphere of crisis, Parliament authorized several fiscal reforms, including a 20-percent increase in most direct and indirect taxes. This law symbolized Parliament's first official recognition that the "Germany-will-pay" program had been wishful thinking.[33] Largely thanks to this show of fiscal realism, Raymond Poincaré's new coalition government was able to borrow $100 million through J. P. Morgan and Company in New York and £4 million through Lazard Frères in London. These foreign funds were promptly used to support the franc on the exchanges, raising it to 6.71 cents on April 22. This "bear squeeze" succeeded in inflicting heavy losses on speculators who had sold francs short. These operations, together with the new tax law and the Dawes Plan, which was due to go into effect in the autumn and which would improve the basis for estimating future receipts from Germany, reversed speculative sentiment. The swing carried so far that the government was able to buy back all the dollars and pounds previously sold to support the franc.

The violent and rather artificial rise gave way to a reaction late in April. On June 1 the franc was down to just under 5 cents. Nervousness stemming from the recent fluctuations persisted. The large size and short average maturity of the floating government debt remained a threat. At the end of 1924 the floating debt was about 60 billion francs, including about 54½ billion francs of *Bons de la Défense Nationale,* of which about 7 or 8 billions were coming due monthly. In addition, about 27½ billion francs worth of longer-term bonds were to mature from July 1925 to May 1926. If the public for any reason became unwilling to renew the maturing debt, the government would have to resort to inflationary borrowing at the Bank of France. Distrust in government economic policies was in fact heightened by the victory in the May 1924 elections of a union of Socialists and Radical-Socialists and replacement

[32] Ragnar Nurkse, *International Currency Experience,* League of Nations, 1944, p. 118.

[33] Robert Murray Haig, *The Public Finances of Post-War France,* New York: Columbia University Press, 1929, pp. 97-98.

of Poincaré in June by the fiscally less conservative Edouard Herriot. (Public dismay at the tax increases enacted in March had probably contributed to the election result.) Towards the end of 1924 and early in 1925 public holdings of *Bons de la Défense Nationale* fell by several billion francs. Current government deficits had now become a less crucial inflationary element than past deficits in the form of a large volume of short-maturity government debt. The government was borrowing from Peter to pay Paul with increasing difficulty.

In April 1925, just when England, by contrast, was returning to the gold standard, the Herriot government had to confess a subterfuge whereby State borrowing at the Bank of France had exceeded the legal limit, with the excess concealed in the Bank's balance sheet under the heading *portfolio*. Herriot's defense was that earlier cabinets had been guilty of similar irregularities. Another disclosure was that the Bank's end-of-1924 balance sheet (and possibly others) had been falsified by concealment of note issues beyond the legal limit under the heading "miscellaneous liabilities." Worry over the fate of the franc was so general that not only merchants and financiers but also working people well understood and avidly scrutinized the figures for "advances to the State" on the asset side and "note issue" on the liability side of the weekly balance sheets of the Bank of France. Repeated increases in the legal limits to these two amounts were taken as ominous signs. Hence the disclosure of actual subterfuges was a particular blow to confidence.

These disclosures, together with the unpopularity of proposals for a 10-percent capital levy or a forced loan, forced the Herriot ministry to resign in April 1925. Caillaux, Finance Minister in the successor cabinet, then tried to meet the financial difficulties by an internal loan to consolidate the floating debt and by further borrowings in America. The internal loan was poorly received and the American loan negotiations fell through in October. Caillaux resigned.

Wholesale prices and the cost of living had continued rising moderately throughout 1925.

The franc was sinking gradually under the pressure of a persistent outward transfer of capital, often through purchases of foreign securities payable in gold. Official support helped keep the New York rate on the franc at about 5.18 cents during March, April, and May and at about 4.70 cents during July, August, and September. Though further restrictions were placed on capital export in October, the temporary pegging of the franc gave way to a rapid decline. The monthly average rate sank to 3.74 cents in December. Emergency taxes calculated to raise about 3 billion francs in a hurry failed to restore confidence. "By the end of 1925 the seemingly uncontrollable wave of exchange depreciation had brought a hysterical note" into financial discussions. The ordinary citizen became panicky, and a general flight from the franc and from monetary securities into commodities and foreign assets got under way, presaging the virtual hysteria of mid-1926.[34]

Here is a good point to summarize the stages of crisis up to the final climax. Though actual government budget deficits and increases in the national debt remained moderate, they were large enough and had persisted long enough to sap confidence. This in turn hampered the sale of new government securities as fast as old ones came due. With the government having to borrow at the Bank of France, increases became necessary in the legal limits of the Bank's advances to the state and its note issue—either forthright increases or devious subterfuges. These inflationary omens still further discouraged public subscriptions to government securities. By July 1926 the Bank's advances to the state had increased 77 percent, notes in circulation had increased 38 percent, and notes in circulation plus demand deposits with four leading commercial banks had increased 43 percent over the levels of only 18 months before.[35]

Business as well as government borrowing fed the inflation. The French banking sys-

---

[34] Martin Wolfe, *The French Franc between the Wars, 1919–1939*, New York: Columbia University Press, 1951, pp. 38-39.

[35] Computed from a table in Tsiang, *op. cit.*, p. 269.

tem was dangerously responsive to the "needs of trade"; as rising prices swelled the monetary volume of business, bank credit expanded correspondingly. Banks could get funds to meet their customers' demand for loans by drawing on their deposits previously made with the Treasury, by cashing government securities as they matured without buying new ones, or by discounting at the Bank of France. Their doing so caused the government all the more financial embarrassment.

Finance minister replaced finance minister in a "waltz of the portfolios." From October 1925 to July 1926 a new minister took office every 37 days, on the average. The climax came in July 1926 when Caillaux, again Finance Minister, spurred by the urgent tone of a report just released by a nonpolitical committee of financial experts, demanded—and was refused—decree-making powers. The Briand-Caillaux government was overthrown and replaced—for two days only—by another Left coalition under Herriot.

The old Finance Ministry had previously asked the Bank of France to buy from the Treasury the $31 million still left from the Morgan loan of 1924. On July 19 the Bank agreed on condition of a corresponding increase in its legal note issue. The Treasury was facing a serious drain from redemption of the short-term *Bons de la Défense Nationale,* yet the new ministry was unwilling either to force their holders to take longer-term securities in exchange (which would have amounted to partial default) or to take the openly inflationary step of increasing the Bank's legal note issue. The Bank remained firm in refusing to buy the Morgan dollars without a legal increase in its note circulation. On July 21, 1926, in order to forestall illegal subterfuges, the governor of the Bank sent a letter to Herriot's finance minister warning, in effect, that the Treasury's small remaining balance at the Bank of France would probably run out by the end of that very day. The balance sheet to be made up that night and published the next day would probably show advances by the Bank to the State in excess of the legal limit, obliging the Bank to cease making payments for the ac-

count of the Treasury. Only one means was available, concluded the letter, to prevent this disaster: immediate parliamentary approval of the proposed transaction on the Bank's terms.

The Treasury's balance at the Bank did not, in fact, quite run out on July 21. That evening the government was overthrown after submitting a bill to sell the Morgan dollars to the Bank *without* raising the note-circulation limit. Immediately after the overthrow, a special session of both chambers of Parliament enacted a bill embodying the Bank's terms.

On this same eventful day, the franc fell on the foreign exchange market to 2.05 U.S. cents. People had the fate of the German mark in 1923 freshly in mind. The cost of living was rising day by day. The Paris mob was protesting against inflation by rioting and by threatening the deputies. On the morning of July 22, Raymond Poincaré agreed to form a cabinet; and the next day Parliament installed the conservative old lawyer, a former premier and a prewar President of the Republic, as premier and finance minister with special powers. Poincaré promised to save the franc by cutting expenditures, cutting pensions, dismissing unnecessary government employees, and raising taxes. His reputation for fiscal conservatism was so great that the mere news of his nomination for office pulled the franc up from its low point of practically 2 cents. Its quotation rose to 3.42 cents in November and 3.95 cents in December.

Poincaré's task was not unduly difficult. Speculation had brought the franc lower than fundamentals justified. Unlike Germany during its inflation, France relied primarily on indirect taxation and on the revenue of fiscal monopolies instead of on taxes on incomes of the year before, and government revenues thus rose with the price level. Government expenditures rose more slowly: approximately 53 percent of them in 1926 went for service on the internal debt and for pensions and so were fixed in terms of francs. Poincaré balanced the budget and even achieved a surplus. To clinch his success, he had some of his basic fiscal reforms enacted into constitutional law.

Toward the end of 1926, after recovering from its panic level to about one-fifth of prewar parity, the franc was stabilized *de facto* by official dealings on the foreign-exchange market. To restrain its further recovery, the Bank of France bought foreign exchange heavily. Before the end of December its net purchases had totaled £5.3 million. They were over £20 million by February 1927 and reached £100 million by May 1927. Most of the purchases were of sterling, giving the Bank of France great power to influence the London money market.

By now it was apparent that the exchange value of the franc was hardly likely to fall in the near future, and rumors persisted that the official pegging which was keeping it down might be relaxed. A speculative flight *to* the franc got underway. The Bank of France did not want to let the franc appreciate, fearing damage to the competitive position of French industry. Neither did it relish the inflationary creation of more francs with which to keep on buying foreign exchange. The Bank believed that the troublesome speculative purchases of francs were being financed by borrowings in foreign money markets at interest rates lower than those prevailing in France. Accordingly, it urged tighter credit abroad, especially in London and Berlin. It began drawing gold from London in May 1927 and threatening further withdrawals unless the Bank of England raised its discount rate. The Bank of England was unwilling to yield, since tighter credit would have been burdensome to the British economy at the time and since it doubted that the problem of one-way-option bullish speculation on the franc could be so easily solved.[36] It is ironic that the problem of speculation on a pegged franc should so soon have replaced the problem of speculation on a fluctuating franc.

Now that a historical survey has prepared the ground, it is appropriate to ponder and appraise the lessons of the French prestabilization experience. The interpretation presented in the League of Nations publication *International Currency Experience* is often cited as the "basis" or "proof" that speculation is destabilizing under freely fluctuating exchange rates.[37] "The post-war history of the French franc up to the end of 1926 affords an instructive example of completely free and uncontrolled exchange variations. . . ." "The dangers of . . . cumulative and self-aggravating movements under a regime of freely fluctuating exchanges are clearly demonstrated by the French experience of 1922–26." "Self-aggravating movements [of exchange rates and trade], instead of promoting adjustment in the balance of payments, are apt to intensify any initial disequilibrium and to produce what may be termed 'explosive' conditions of instability. . . . we may recall in particular the example of the French franc during the years 1924–26."[38]

Actually, the historical details already reviewed undermine these conclusions. Up to early 1922, there was no question of speculation and capital flight dominating the market. For about eight years after the start of inflationary wartime and postwar government finance and about three years after the breakdown of fixed exchange rates, no foreign exchange crisis developed. Actual panic did not ensue until 1926, after about 12 years of inflation and seven years of fluctuating exchanges. The panic came only after protracted budgetary and debt difficulties, price inflation, exchange depreciation, and the recurrent political crises stemming from these troubles, and only after the spread of fear that the franc was about to suffer the fate of the German mark. In view of these circumstances, the French episode hardly supports any general proposition about exchange speculation. If anything, it demonstrates the consequences of irresolution and ineptitude in debt management and in dealing with inflation, especially when the officials in charge suffer from "simple ignorance of monetary economics."[39] With the supply of money and credit as ex-

[36] Lester V. Chandler, *Benjamin Strong, Central Banker,* Washington: Brookings Institution, 1958, pp. 371-374.

[37] On the great influence that this book has had, see Milton Friedman, *Essays in Positive Economics,* Chicago: University of Chicago Press, 1953, p. 176n., and Tsiang, *op. cit.,* p. 244.

[38] Nurkse, *International Currency Experience,* pp. 117, 118, 211.

[39] Wolfe, *op. cit.,* p. 70.

tremely expansible as it in fact was, pegged exchange rates would have worked at least as badly as the fluctuating rates.[40] In fact, although firm exchange fixing had broken down in 1919, there were some official interventions and some unsuccessful attempts at supporting franc exchange during the period 1924–1926. It is ironic that after an end to the internal financial crisis again made exchange pegging feasible, fixed exchange rates came on the scene to take credit for the improved situation.

As for exchange speculation during the French episode, one can plausibly argue that it was equilibrating rather than disequilibrating, apparently being based on a correct diagnosis of underlying financial trends. And it was stabilizing rather than destabilizing in that by dramatizing a bad financial situation with which politicians had temporized too long, it turned attention toward the political improvements necessary to reverse the trends and save the franc.[41]

The Undervalued Franc

The inflation, serious and potentially disastrous though it had been, paradoxically left some elements of strength in the French situation. First, the outward transfer of capital during the years of distrust had built up an accumulation of foreign assets. Depreciation of the franc had stimulated exports and so translated the financial outflow into real terms. Repatriation of funds as profitable investment opportunities appeared at home would tend to strengthen the franc on the exchanges. Second, the chronic monetary crisis had forced necessary tax increases in 1920, 1924, and 1925, and in 1926 had forced fiscal probity under Poincaré's leadership. Finally, the franc had fallen far enough to frustrate attempts to "return to normal" and

to spare France England's costly deflationary struggle. Since the franc had already fallen further in foreign-exchange value than in domestic purchasing power, its stabilization was possible without the preliminary step of a confidence-shaking further depreciation.

The *de facto* exchange stabilization achieved in 1926 was eventually ratified *de jure*. After the parliamentary elections of May 1928, the Bank of France again had to buy large amounts of foreign money to hold down the franc on the exchange market. Hopes revived that temporary pegging would give way to upward revaluation. Even Premier Poincaré continued to harbor the quixotic feeling that national honor called for a return to prewar par, the same feeling that had been so decisive in Britain. Governor Moreau of the Bank of France threatened to resign, however, unless *de jure* stabilization were enacted at once. Advocates of revalorization were championing a hopeless cause; undoing an 80-percent depreciation was out of the question. The French public had already become accustomed to the four-cent franc. A law of June 25, 1928 redefined the gold content of the franc in line with the prevailing exchange rate and required the Bank of France to buy and sell gold at corresponding fixed prices under a gold bullion standard. The law obscured the Bank's authority to buy foreign exchange, and it felt obliged to convert further gains of foreign exchange into gold. It was even reluctant to keep holding all the foreign exchange it already had. Governor Norman of the Bank of England thought it only reasonable for France to cooperate by continuing to hold rather than converting its London balances; but Governor Moreau, who wanted a "real" gold standard, thought he was being generous in holding any London balances at all. He thought London was trying to have the advantages of an international banking center without the obligations.[42]

The new parity slightly undervalued the franc; and, to the particular discomfort of Britain, a balance-of-payments surplus continued bringing gold into France through the rest of the 1920s and in fact through 1932.

---

[40] The extreme elasticity of the money supply, the close statistical correlation between the money supply and the exchange rate, and the difficulties that would have beset a fixed rate system under the circumstances all are emphasized by Tsiang, *op. cit.*, pp. 245, 261, 264, 267-273.

[41] Cf. Friedman, *op. cit.*, p. 176n., and Harry C. Eastman, "French and Canadian Exchange Rate Policy," *The Journal of Economic History*, **XV**, December 1955, p. 408.

[42] Chandler, *op. cit.*, pp. 378-379.

(The effect of current-account deficits on gold movements in 1931 and 1932 was more than counterbalanced by continued inflows of capital.)[43]

Stabilization by Other Countries

Little needs to be added about American postwar monetary experience. The dollar returned with ease to the full gold standard as early as 1919 and thereafter was the guidepost for realignment of other currencies. Rebuilding the gold standard was a gradual worldwide process. Some countries sooner or later regained their prewar gold parities; besides Great Britain, these included the Dominions, Switzerland, the Netherlands and her colonies, Argentina, the three Scandinavian countries, and Japan (which did not drop her wartime gold export embargo until January 1930). The revaluation of some currencies was hastened by bullish anticipation of it. In 1925 and 1926, for example, speculation restored the Danish crown to an overvalued level at which the internal economy suffered deflationary pains.[44] Other countries stabilized after devaluation; besides France, these included Belgium, Italy, Finland, Chile, Czechoslovakia, Yugoslavia, Greece, Bulgaria, Rumania, Estonia, Latvia, and Portugal (which, after three years of approximate stability and two years of de facto stabilization, did not return to gold de jure until June of the fateful year 1931). Austria, Hungary, Poland, Germany, and Russia adopted new currency units (some with the old names) after hyperinflation had destroyed their old currencies. By the end of 1925 some 35 currencies in addition to the U.S. dollar had either been stabilized on gold or had displayed exchange-rate stability for a full year. Three years later the apparent reconstruction of the international gold standard was substantially complete.[45]

The most prominent currency left unstabilized was the Spanish peseta, which had been fluctuating for several decades even before World War I. In 1920 its wartime premium above its theoretical parity disappeared. During the next five years wars in Morocco damaged Spanish finances, and the peseta sank to about three-fourths of its theoretical parity. In 1926 victory in Morocco and establishment of a firm if dictatorial government seemed to promise financial improvement, but the repegging of other European currencies and uncertain expectations of official Spanish pegging at par influenced speculation on the peseta. Official efforts to support the peseta in 1928–1931 kept breaking down, at considerable cost in foreign resources spent and foreign debt incurred. Elaborate exchange controls introduced after the overthrow of the monarchy in the spring of 1931 did not succeed in preventing further depreciation.[46]

The successive stabilizations of the 1920s were separate acts of national sovereignty. Each country mistakenly thought it was tying its currency to gold. Actually, countries were tying their currencies to each other in a piecemeal, uncoordinated fashion. Some parities were chosen under the influence of abnormal short-term capital movements, some for considerations of sheer prestige. The new pattern of rates did not adequately reflect the different degrees of inflation in different countries. "The piecemeal and haphazard manner of international monetary reconstruction sowed the seeds of subsequent disintegration," according to one widely accepted interpretation; it would have been better to set up the network of exchange rates "by simultaneous and coordinated international action. . . ."[47] It was partly in hopes of profiting from this lesson that the International Monetary Fund was established after World War II.

---

[43] Wolfe, op. cit., pp. 128-129.

[44] Bertil Ohlin, La Politique du Commerce Extérieur, Paris: Dunod, 1955, pp. 90-91, cites the Danish episode as an example of disequilibrating speculation under fluctuating exchange rates. This is a less apt example of that system itself than of eagerness to find fault with it, since the speculation was anticipating an official policy of raising the crown and then stopping its fluctuations.

[45] Brown, op. cit., pp. 394, 402, and League of Nations, The Course and Control of Inflation, pp. 92-93.

[46] Brown, op. cit., II, 1031-1034.

[47] Nurkse, International Currency Experience, p. 117.

Troubles with the New System

Before examining this lesson later in its historical sequence, we should note other difficulties plaguing the restored exchange stability of the 1920s. Before World War I, international payments had typically been made in a relatively simple way, by transfer of ownership of bank balances in London. The postwar system had more than this one focus. New York, and to a lesser extent Paris, competed with London. Dollar deposits and drafts rivaled sterling in international clearings and payments. Having more than one major financial center made international clearing more complex and less efficient. The various centers now had to arrange for offsetting claims among themselves and to hold balances with one another for this purpose. Cash and liquid assets had come under foreign ownership in much greater volume than before the war. Funds were liable to move erratically from one financial center to another in response to changing interest rates, changes in confidence or distrust in currencies, and other developments besides deep-seated disequilibriums. This "hot-money" danger had been far less serious before 1914, when no center rivaled London as a place where short-term funds might move and profitably be held.

Not only ordinary traders and banks but also many central banks had grown into the habit, since the war, of holding balances in the financial centers. Their shift to holding their legal monetary reserves largely as bank accounts or liquid securities in the gold-standard countries[48] was a key aspect of the widespread adoption of the gold-exchange standard. This had been recommended by the

Financial Committee of the Genoa Conference in 1922. (Another Genoa recommendation had been stabilization of the purchasing powers of currencies and gold through domestic anti-inflation policies and cooperation among central banks.) The objective of the Genoa system was to make the world's supposedly inadequate gold supply do double duty, "backing" full-gold-standard currencies directly and gold-exchange-standard currencies at one remove. Critics would regard this as a paradoxical attempt both to have and to escape from the link between gold stocks and money supplies that forms the essence of a real gold standard.

Another difficulty was that the arrangement could not be relied on as permanent. The actions of Germany and France were examples. After stabilization of the mark in 1924, the Reichsbank held more foreign exchange than any other European central bank, but it drew down its holdings rapidly in 1925 and again in 1927. In December 1924 foreign exchange made up 63.2 percent of its total of foreign exchange plus monetary gold; in December 1928 this figure was down to 17.5 percent. In 1926 and 1927 the Bank of France acquired the largest stock of foreign exchange of any central bank in the world. Its motive was to prevent an unwanted appreciation of the franc rather than to adopt the gold exchange standard, yet it dominated the whole new system.[49] Late in 1928 and early in 1929 the Bank of France did convert about 4½ billion francs' worth of its foreign exchange into gold. According to its Annual Report for 1932, the Bank had wished to liquidate its foreign exchange ever since 1928; one presumed reason for its delaying was its concern for international repercussions. Other signs of impermanence in the gold-exchange standard were the activities of the "undisclosed buyer"[50] in the London gold market and Italian legislation permitting the central bank

---

[48] *Ibid.*, p. 30, lists the following countries as allowing their central banks, during all or part of the period 1922–1931, to hold their legally required reserves wholly or partly in the form of foreign exchange: Albania, Austria, Belgium, Bolivia, Bulgaria, Chile, Colombia, Czechoslovakia, Denmark, Ecuador, Egypt, Estonia, Finland, Germany, Greece, Hungary, Italy, Latvia, Peru, Poland, Portugal, Rumania, Spain, Uruguay, the USSR, and Yugoslavia. India, New Zealand, Argentina, and Venezuela lacked central banks but were on an exchange standard.

[49] Brown, *op. cit.*, II, 742, 747, 765, 767, 770.

[50] The "undisclosed" or "unknown" buyer was the collective name on the London bullion market for the central banks of Belgium, Switzerland, Poland, and Italy. Their activities from 1925 to 1928 formed part of a so-called "scramble for gold." *Ibid.*, pp. 633-634.

to convert its foreign-exchange holdings into gold. Attempts to liquidate foreign-exchange holdings played a key part in the collapse of 1931.

"Offsetting" versus an Adjustment Mechanism

The postwar system differed in operation as well as in structure from the gold standard as traditionally conceived. In a dimly held and perhaps historically inaccurate conception of the supposed "rules of the game," a central bank had more than the passive duty of interconverting domestic and international currency. With an eye on its reserve *ratio*, it was supposed to make the domestic money supply rise or fall not merely by the same *amount* but roughly by the same *percentage* as the country's gain or loss of gold or other international liquidity. It was supposed to *reinforce* the monetary impact by adjusting its discount rate or its use of other policy weapons to make its domestic assets move in the same direction as its international assets. Gold-gaining and gold-losing countries were supposed to meet each other half way in adjusting domestic money supplies, incomes, and prices to the requirements of international equilibrium. But things did not work this way in the middle and late 1920s. The evidence appears in Ragnar Nurkse's tabulation of changes in the international and domestic assets of the central banks of 26 countries.[51] During the period 1925 through 1929, the international and domestic assets of central banks changed from year to year in the same direction only 26 out of 106 times; they changed in opposite directions 73 times, and changes in one type of asset or the other were negligible 7 times. Over the longer period 1922 through 1938, changes were in the same direction in 32 percent of the instances and in opposite directions in 60 percent. Thus the traditional reinforcement of gold flows was the exception rather than the rule; by and large, central banks appeared to be "offsetting" or "neutralizing" the internal monetary effects of gold inflows and outflows. Surprisingly enough, a similar conclusion appears to hold true for the pre-1914 gold standard as well: year-to-year changes in the international and domestic assets of central banks were in opposite directions more often than in the same direction.[52]

Neither for the period before nor the period after World War I, however, is this conclusion certain. Conceivably the traditional reinforcement of gold flows did generally occur, but with such a lag as to be concealed in the figures of year-to-year changes. Furthermore, and especially before World War I, the apparent neutralization may often have been "automatic" rather than the result of deliberate policy, with international and domestic assets of central banks tending to move in opposite directions under the influence of the business cycle. Also, an inflow of gold, by increasing the liquidity of the money market, may sometimes have caused repayments of debts to the central bank; conversely, an outflow of gold may have tightened the market and increased borrowing from the central bank. Mere passive response to credit demands, even quite apart from any active neutralization, could have made a central bank's domestic and international assets move in opposite directions. (One might argue in reply that keeping the central-bank discount rate unchanged or changing it insufficiently

---

[51] The years of 1922 through 1938 were covered so far as figures were available. On all this, see Nurkse, *International Currency Experience,* chap. IV and especially pp. 69, 237-240, and Committee on Finance & Industry, *Report,* pp. 83-84.

[52] Arthur I. Bloomfield applied Nurkse's test to eleven central banks for the period 1880–1913, or such parts of that period as seemed relevant and for which statistics were available. International assets (gold, foreign exchange, and silver) and domestic income-earning assets (discounts, advances, and securities) moved in opposite directions 60 percent of the time and in the same direction 34 percent of the time (and in the remaining instances, one or the other of the two asset categories underwent virtually no change). *Monetary Policy Under the International Gold Standard: 1880–1914,* Federal Reserve Bank of New York, 1959, pp. 48-50.

Insofar, however, as variation in a central bank's domestic portfolio offset *only a fraction* of any opposite variation in its international assets, the latter might still have a multiple impact on the domestic money supply. Robert Triffin, *The Evolution of the International Monetary System: Historical Reappraisal and Future Perspectives,* Princeton, N.J.: Princeton University, 1964, p. 5.

in the face of changes in the supply of or demand for credit is in itself a policy and that the money supply is more appropriate than the discount rate as an indicator of policy.) Another type of automatic neutralization sometimes working during the years 1925–1928 rested on mobility of private short-term credit in response to interest-rate differentials between various money markets. The traditional interest-rate increase in reaction to a balance-of-payments deficit might attract funds from abroad, and foreign assets would replace part of the central bank's domestic assets. Such "equilibrating" capital flows tend to cushion, or delay the need for, the domestic monetary responses of traditional gold-standard theory.

Allowing for possible lags and for mere passivity in central-bank policy still hardly upsets the conclusion that traditional correctives did *not* occur promptly and actively under the restored gold standard of the 1920s. At times neutralization was clearly deliberate and so was a departure not only from traditional ideas but also from prewar historical reality. From 1920 to 1924 the United States, then the only major country back on the gold standard, received heavy gold shipments in payment for her large postwar surplus of exports, especially to Europe. Rather than let this inflowing gold feed inflation, the Federal Reserve authorities offset its effects, sometimes reducing their holdings of bills and securities on their own initiative and keeping some of the gold outside the credit base by circulating it as gold certificates.[53] In the five years after 1924 the U.S. gold stock changed little on balance, but its year-to-year changes were offset by changes in the domestic assets of the Federal Reserve banks. The Federal Reserve's ratio of gold to demand liabilities remained at nearly twice the legal requirement, further suggesting that the United States did "sterilize" gold during the 1920s.

When reproached for this interference with the traditional adjustment mechanism, the Federal Reserve authorities were inclined to give the obvious answer that they were in effect holding much of the gold merely in trust for gold-exchange-standard countries, who might withdraw it whenever they saw fit.[54] The policy followed was no doubt justified from the domestic point of view, but it did interfere with international equilibration. That this interference did not put an immediate and unbearable strain on world payments is probably due in part to heavy American capital exports at the time. During the four years 1925–1928 the net total amount of foreign long-term securities floated in the United States was twice the amount floated in London. In addition, American businesses were making heavy direct investments abroad.[55]

Not until the second half of 1927 did the Federal Reserve reverse its gold sterilization. Both a slight recession in the United States and willingness to help ease the British gold position then prompted the Federal Reserve to cut its discount rates and buy securities vigorously. Gold flowed out. But, according to a widely accepted interpretation, this brief episode of cheap money fed a stock-market boom that grew highly speculative in 1928 and 1929. The profitability of bull speculation in Wall Street and the high yields obtainable on call loans to speculators shrank American capital exports and attracted funds from overseas. The efforts of the Federal Reserve to check the stock-market boom by renewed tight money, together with the efforts of European countries to check the loss of gold to the United States, led to tight money in many countries almost at the moment when, as hindsight reveals, business activity was turning downward.

The Bank of England apparently followed a systematic policy of neutralization during the six years after the return to gold in 1925,

[53] The Federal Reserve decided to contract credit in the spring of 1923 despite an unprecedentedly large gold reserve. According to R. F. Harrod, this was the first great peacetime step away from the idea that monetary management should be primarily related to the international situation. *The Pound Sterling,* Essays in International Finance No. 13, Princeton University, 1952, p. 4.

[54] Nurkse, *International Currency Experience,* pp. 73-75; John T. Madden and Marcus Nadler, *The International Money Markets,* New York: Prentice-Hall, 1936, pp. 11-13.

[55] Committee on Finance & Industry, *op. cit.,* p. 70.

trying to hold the total volume of credit available to the British economy stable within broad limits and match gains or losses of gold with reductions or increases in domestic earning assets.[56] This hardly meant managing credit with primary regard to the domestic economy; for the credit expansion appropriate to remedy unemployment would have made the gold position even more precarious. In France, the increase in gold and foreign-exchange assets of the central bank following stabilization of the franc at an undervalued level in 1926 was not allowed to have the "rules-of-the-game" influence on domestic money and credit; the country was in no mood for a renewal of inflation.[57]

The general conclusion suggested so far had already appeared in the Macmillan Report, issued in England in June 1931. The report blamed "the instability of post-war international finance" partly on the fact that "Movements of gold have ceased of late to have what used to be considered their 'normal' effect on the domestic credit policy of certain countries, notably France and the United States. In recent years it has been impossible to rely on action being taken by both the country losing gold and the country gaining gold to preserve international

equilibrium, the one meeting the other half way. . . ."[58]

The Façade of a Restored Gold Standard

In summary, the gold standard of the late 1920s was hardly more than a façade. It involved extreme measures to economize on gold through withdrawing gold coins and adopting gold-bullion or gold-exchange arrangements. It involved the neutralization or offsetting of international influences on domestic money supplies, incomes, and prices. Gold-standard methods of balance-of-payments equilibration were largely destroyed and were not replaced by any alternative. The new system has aptly been described as "a temporary exchange pegging device"; it consisted of "pegging operations on a vast scale."[59] Some of the pegs were at clearly wrong levels. With both the price-and-income and the exchange-rate mechanisms of balance-of-payments adjustment out of operation, disequilibriums were accumulated or merely palliated, not continuously corrected. Too much depended on *ad hoc* policies and switches in policy. Mistakes in diagnosis and lags in the effectiveness of policies threatened perverse results.

---

[56] Nurkse, *International Currency Experience*, pp. 75-76.

[57] *Ibid.*, p. 77.

[58] Committee on Finance & Industry, *op. cit.*, pp. 68-69.

[59] Brown, *op. cit.*, II, 805. The epithet "façade" is also Brown's.

The Great Depression and the End of the Gold Standard

✒ 16

The Background of Depression

A continuation of the historical survey is worthwhile for revealing in what degree and in what ways the international monetary system was precarious. The conditions menacing international arrangements and general business activity were thoroughly intermingled. Precarious positions were being shored up and adjustments delayed in individual lines of production, in currency parities, and in international payments. Agriculture is a notable example of the first kind. The quick postwar recovery in European agriculture brought no corresponding cutbacks in North America and other areas of great wartime expansion in farm output. The prices of the staple foodstuffs and fibers of international commerce came under severe downward pressure in the middle and late 1920s. Governments or government-encouraged cartels were trying to support the prices of wheat, sugar, coffee, rubber, tin, copper, nitrates, and other primary products by such devices as holding supplies off the market. These interferences with the price signals that would otherwise have promoted gradual cutbacks in excessive production threatened, together with growing stockpiles, to make a crash in price all the more severe when it finally came and all the more damaging to the balance-of-payments positions and the currency parities of the primary-producing export-oriented countries. The farm depression in the United States accounted for most of the bank suspensions, numbering an average of 700 a year in the last four years of the 1920s.

International imbalances, such as reflected in the American current-account surplus, were to a large extent being temporarily palliated by international lending. In this way, the strong suction of gold into the United States from 1921 through 1924 was on the whole stopped and even very slightly reversed from 1925 to the beginning of 1929. American loans in the immediate postwar years had been mainly for relief and rehabilitation in Europe. In the early and middle 1920s a number of loans were arranged through intergovernmental cooperation to help such countries as Austria, Hungary, Germany, Belgium, Poland, and Italy put their finances in order and stabilize their currencies. Then German borrowing offset and more than offset German reparations payments. American private lending to Central Europe, especially Germany, expanded vastly in the late 1920s. Many of the loans were for commercially unprofitable projects that contributed little to the ability of the debtors to pay interest and repay the principal when due. National and municipal governments floated bonds in the American capital market to pay for public works. In some areas, such as Latin America, much of the international investment did contribute to production, but of coffee and other commodities already in oversupply. Toward the end of the decade an increasing proportion of international lending, British as well as American, was at short term, and many short-term loans were being used to finance long-term capital projects.

The gold-exchange standard, with many central banks holding substantial parts of their legal reserves in the form of the bank deposits or securities of London and a few other financial centers rather than in actual gold, spelled a precarious direct and indirect pyramiding of claims on a narrow ultimate gold base. Any serious strain on a full-gold-standard center would cause difficulties for its satellites, and conversely, heavy withdrawals by the satellites would cause difficulties for the center.

The system of the 1920s was not merely precarious; it contained seeds of monetary deflation in particular. Whether or not there was an overall shortage of gold—a question much discussed at the time—the existing supply was unevenly distributed. The United States in the early 1920s and France in the late 1920s acquired and kept unduly large shares of the world's gold. Other countries, including England, were in much the same position as if there had been an overall shortage. Their external positions required restrictive policies at home, while countries with relative surpluses of gold were reluctant, for fear of inflation, to pursue the expansionary policies that would have eased the strain on the others. For the world economy as a whole, monetary policies were thus bedeviled by a clash, manifesting itself differently in different countries, between domestic and balance-of-payments considerations. Policy could not aim at a single consistent set of objectives.[1]

The worldwide downward drift in commodity prices even several years before the depression struck may well be evidence that the international monetary system had a deflationary bias. Between 1923 (after recovery from the postwar depression) and 1929, sensitive commodity price indexes compiled on the same basis for different countries showed declines ranging from 10 percent in the United States to 20 percent in Great Britain. Between 1925 and 1929 the average prices of commodities moving in international trade fell by over 10 percent.[2] In the United States, the annual average index of wholesale prices had recovered by 1925 to only 7 percent above its 1922 depression trough. From 1925 to 1929 the index fell 8 percent. By 1928, in fact, it was already down to its previous trough on an annual average basis. The U.S. consumer price index recovered by 6 percent between 1922 and 1926 and then fell to 3

---

[1] Three of the six conditions listed by Edward M. Bernstein as causing "centers of deflation in the world economy in the 1920's" are the overvaluation of sterling, the undervaluation of the French franc, and "a lack of sufficient gold and foreign exchange reserves to avoid the spread and intensification of depression and deflation." (Bernstein's other three causes are reparations and other German economic problems, agricultural depression in the United States, and highly protective American tariffs.) *International Effects of U.S. Economic Policy,* study paper no. 16 for the Joint Economic Committee; Washington: U.S. Government Printing Office, 1960, p. 8n.

Per Jacobsson, late Managing Director of the International Monetary Fund, suggests that the decline in agricultural prices in the latter half of the decade and the general deflation from 1929 on were partly connected with excessive gold contents of currencies. ". . . if the parities had been fixed at a lower level the individual countries would not have had to worry too much about whether they possessed sufficient cover, particularly in gold, in relation to their notes and sight liabilities." As early as 1917 Jacobsson had insisted that efforts to maintain prewar reserve ratios would threaten a deflationary bias, and in 1931 the Gold Delegation of the League of Nations recommended a reduction in reserve ratios. *Some Monetary Problems International and National,* London: Oxford University Press, 1958, pp. 18-19.

In the judgment of J. R. Hicks, the world "was trying to manage with a gold supply, which was . . . extremely inadequate" in relation to the price and wage inflation that had occurred during and after World War I. Inadequate adjustment of exchange rates contributed to the weakness of the Bank of England and the German Reichsbank, interfering with their responsibilities as lenders of last resort. *A Contribution to the Theory of the Trade Cycle,* Oxford: Clarendon Press, 1950, p. 163n.

According to the Macmillan Report, issued in England in 1931, debtor countries were usually unable "to adjust their balance of payments so rapidly and completely as to permit a complete cessation of borrowing; yet, in so far as they export gold, their credit as borrowers suffers. Thus, having lost their gold and not being able to borrow, they are forced off the gold standard. And creditor countries, on the other hand, when they have accumulated more than their fair share of gold, far beyond their legal requirements, fearing to provoke an inflation by letting the new gold produce a rise in prices, try, in effect, to make themselves insensitive to further imports. Thus, when equilibrium is profoundly upset between creditor and debtor nations, the whole world suffers. The adjustments to be made are greater than can be accomplished by a movement of short-money funds or by a small alteration in prices. The debtor countries suffer a serious deflationary crisis and some of them, probably failing to meet their problems by drastic measures, may be forced off the gold standard; the creditor countries will be affected both by the depression in the debtor countries and by the influx of large quantities of gold. Here is, perhaps, the major part of the immediate explanation of the collapse of international prices. . . ." Committee on Finance & Industry, *Report,* London: His Majesty's Stationery Office, 1931, pp.83-84.

[2] H. V. Hodson, *Slump and Recovery,* London: Oxford University Press, 1938, p. 34.

percent below the 1926 level in both 1928 and 1929.

Growth of the U.S. money supply during the 1920s was slow in comparison with the annual growth of 4 percent or so that seems appropriate in the light of long-run experience. Defined as total deposits adjusted and currency outside banks, the money supply in mid-1929 was 38.4 percent above the level of mid-1920, 14.2 percent above mid-1925, and 0.9 percent above mid-1928. Defined as demand deposits adjusted and outside currency, the mid-1929 money supply was only 10.4 percent above mid-1920, 4.9 percent above mid-1925, and 1.2 percent above mid-1928. (At a 4 percent annual rate of growth, the mid-1929 money supply would have been 42.3 percent above the 1920 level and 17.0 percent above the 1925 level.)

These figures perhaps suggest incipient tendencies but certainly do not warrant any sweeping conclusions about unmistakable deflation in the late 1920s. One familiar contrary line of interpretation of the subsequent crash emphasizes credit expansion and an unusual inflation without general price inflation. The most conspicuous signs of inflation were localized, notably in Wall Street. By September 1929, Standard and Poor's monthly average index of common stock prices had shot up to twice the level of less than two and a half years before. The Federal Reserve had begun its most notable episode of cheap money in the second half of 1927 with the partial purpose of easing the strain on the gold reserves of the Bank of England. This is an example of the lack of steady, consistent policies during the 1920s and of the use of *ad hoc* expedients based in variable degrees on internal and balance-of-payments considerations. The policy of 1927 appears to have unintentionally fed the Wall Street boom, so attracting speculative money to the United States and frustrating its own international objectives. The later reversion to tight money, as well as the high interest rates on call money used in financing stock-market speculation, also attracted funds from all over the world, under the system of fixed exchange rates, and gave rise to domestically inappropri-

ate tight-money policies in countries tending to lose gold.[3] On Wall Street, stock market activity had evolved into the stage where the typical speculator kept buying not because he thought earnings and dividends justified the prevailing prices but because experience had taught him to expect that he could sell out later at a profit to other speculators still more daring than himself. By this time, a mere leveling off of stock prices would cause speculators to lose interest and would bring on the crash. Widespread holding of stocks on narrow margins made the crash feed on itself, once it began. But neither the stock market crash nor any other specific shock can properly be blamed for the severity of the depression that followed. The main emphasis apparently belongs on a passive monetary policy that permitted the total U.S. money supply to shrink by more than one-fourth in less than three years.

The foregoing paragraphs sketch in an admittedly oversimplified and incomplete background of a complicated process of economic deterioration. The emphasis on matters related to international monetary arrangements should not give the impression that the entire explanation lies in this sphere.

Signs of depression had already appeared at various times between late 1927 and mid-1929 in Australia, the Dutch East Indies, Germany, Finland, Brazil, Poland, Canada, and Argentina; but serious depression did not spread widely until after the industrial downturn in the United States in mid-1929 and the stock crash in October. The first impact was a reversal of the surge of speculative foreign money that had been coming to New York to share in the stock-market boom; sterling strengthened briefly to an average of 1½ cents above par in December, and London gained gold. The more lasting impact, however, was a virtual stop to American lending abroad and a repatriation of American funds. The protectionist Smoot-Hawley Tariff of 1930 reinforced the effects of depression in contracting American imports. All in

---

[3] Cf. Paul Einzig, *A Dynamic Theory of Forward Exchange,* London: Macmillan, 1961, pp. 316-317, 528-529.

all, total American spending and lending abroad shrank by two-thirds between 1927–1929 and 1932–1933.

By mid-1932 world industrial production and the real volume of world trade had both fallen to slightly below 70 percent of their 1929 average levels. Industrial production regained its earlier peak toward the end of 1935. World trade recovered more slowly, almost reaching its earlier peak in 1937, only to fall off again.[4] Table 16.1 gives some indications of the depth and duration of the depression in several major countries. Two countries in particular call for comment. The comparatively good record of the United Kingdom is rather deceptive, reflecting the depressed level of economic activity from which the slide into further depression began; but in part it is genuine, showing the relief provided by the depreciation of sterling in 1931 and the stimulus of a vigorous easy-money policy begun in 1932. Japan's record seems partly due to policies of abundant credit and government deficit spending (largely for military purposes). Furthermore, the yen was allowed to depreciate to whatever

[4] Chart in Bank for International Settlements, 10th *Annual Report* (1939–1940), p. 41.

level necessary to equilibrate the balance of payments without drastic controls. The yen lost almost two-thirds of its earlier gold value, as compared to a loss of about 40 percent by the pound sterling and the dollar. Yet price inflation was moderate; even in 1937, after the jump associated with the invasion of China, the price index had hardly regained its 1929 level.[5]

As the depression deepened after 1929, countries particularly hard pressed by shrinking exports and payments deficits reacted in either of two ways: by leaving the gold standard and letting the currency depreciate or by imposing exchange and import controls. In 1929 and 1930 currency depreciation was the course taken by countries such as Argentina, Brazil, Paraguay, Uruguay, Australia, New Zealand, Venezuela, Spain, and China (whose currency, still on the silver standard, depreciated against gold). Thus far, none of the dominant countries in international trade allowed their currencies to depreciate. Only a few countries, including Spain, Iran, and

[5] On Japan, see W. Arthur Lewis, *Economic Survey 1919–1939*, London: Allen & Unwin, 1949, pp. 118-120, and for the price index, Colin Clark, *Conditions of Economic Progress* (2nd ed.), London: Macmillan, 1951, p. 137.

Table 16.1. Indicators of the Great Depression in Six Countries

	United Kingdom	France	Germany	Canada	United States	Japan
Industrial Production						
Lowest year & production then as percentage of the 1929 level	1931: 86	1932: 74[a]	1932: 58	1932: 68	1932: 55	1931: 92
Year when the 1929 level was regained or passed	1934	1950	1936	1936	1937	1933
Real National Income						
Lowest year and income then as percentage of the 1929 level	1932: 93	1934: 83	1932: 80	1933: 76	1933: 68	[b]
Year when the 1929 level was regained or passed	1934	Postwar?	1934	1938	1937	[b]

[a] After a partial recovery, French industrial production relapsed in 1935 to 78 percent of the 1929 level.

[b] Japanese real income did not decline below the 1929 level, though the 1929 figure was about 1 percent below that of 1928.

Sources: For industrial production, Organization for European Economic Cooperation, *Industrial Statistics, 1900–1957*, Paris, 1958, p. 9. For Germany and Japan, however, the figures are League of Nations data reproduced in Harold G. Moulton, *Controlling Factors in Economic Development*, Washington: Brookings Institution, 1949, p. 374. For real national income, Colin Clark, *The Conditions of Economic Progress*, 2nd ed., London: Macmillan, 1951, pp. 46, 54, 63, 80, facing 101, 136.

Turkey, imposed new exchange controls at that time. Until the late spring of 1931, the depression in many respects followed the course of ordinary business slumps of the past. The gold standard was still intact in Western Europe and the United States. Steadiness or slight increases in seasonally adjusted figures of industrial production in Germany and the United States even offered some hope during the first few months of the year. In Great Britain and most other countries, however, economic activity kept on sinking.

The 1931 Crisis on the Continent

Against this background a worldwide financial and economic relapse occurred. A chain reaction involved one currency after another. Telling the story of one crisis such as this seems worth while because it reveals the shakiness of the gold-standard façade, because it illustrates some general characteristics of speculation against pegged exchange rates, and because it offers sheer morbid fascination. The story may be begun with the Austrian Credit-Anstalt.[6] This firm, founded by the Rothschilds in 1855 and associated with that family ever since, had assets and liabilities amounting to 70 percent of the total for all Austrian Banks. The disintegration of the Austro-Hungarian Empire at the end of World War I had left this bank, like Vienna itself, overextended for the territory remaining to it. Furthermore, the Credit-Anstalt had absorbed another financially weak institution in October 1929. The stock-exchange and business slump of 1929–1930 ate into the value of the bank's portfolio. In the second week of May 1931, a run on the Credit-Anstalt developed, and its insolvency became publicly known. The Rothschilds, the Austrian National Bank, and the Austrian government stepped in with financial support, relieving the situation for a while. Confidence had been shaken, however, and withdrawals from the Credit-Anstalt persisted throughout May.

Political developments then worsened the situation. With tariffs and other trade barriers mounting throughout the world and trenching on her trade, especially with Hungary,

Czechoslovakia, and the Balkans, Austria had sought relief in a customs union with Germany. An agreement had been announced on March 21, before the Credit-Anstalt difficulties became acute. France, however, chose to regard the proposed economic arrangement, sponsored by the peace-minded Brüning government of Germany, as an *Anschluss,* or political connection between Germany and Austria, in violation of the postwar treaties. The French Chamber of Deputies debated the question in May. The idea of reconciliation with Germany came under attack, and its chief advocate, Briand, failed to win the French presidency. France's great financial power at the time—the large gold and foreign-exchange holdings of her banks—made her government's attitude ominous. Rumors circulated that French bankers were pulling funds out of Austria.

Meanwhile, the finances of the Credit-Anstalt and of the Austrian government were becoming more and more intermingled by way of the state of public confidence. By late May, when the Austrian Parliament passed a law authorizing a government guarantee of new liabilities of the Credit-Anstalt, the shakiness of the government's own credit robbed the gesture of real significance. The run on Austrian banks and the public's demand for foreign exchange was temporarily stemmed, however, by a foreign-currency loan to the Credit-Anstalt arranged by the Bank for International Settlements and a number of leading central banks. Negotiations for a second foreign loan fell through because prospective French lenders wanted to attach political conditions, presumably concerning the proposed customs union with Germany. Unwilling to accept these conditions and also facing domestic opposition on the question of guaranteeing the foreign liabilities of the Credit-Anstalt, the Austrian government resigned on June 16. Hours afterwards, the Bank of England advanced to the Austrian National Bank the amount of the abortive international loan, thereby arousing some resentment in France.

Armed with the British loan, the new Austrian government guaranteed the Credit-Anstalt's existing liabilities to foreign creditors.

---

[6] See, *inter alia,* Hodson, *op. cit.,* chap. III.

The chief creditors, for their part, accepted a standstill agreement not to press their claims for two years. The government also guaranteed deposits at the bank, superseded its management, and retrenched on its expenses. Representatives of the foreign creditors took part in this reorganization.

On June 20, President Hoover proposed a one-year moratorium on all governmental war debts and reparations.[7] The French delayed agreement until July 6, depriving the gesture of much of its psychological effect. Together with the standstill agreement with the principal foreign creditors of the Credit-Anstalt, the moratorium moderated but did not step the run on Austria. In following months the Austrian National Bank lost most of its large stock of foreign exchange. Austria imposed exchange controls in October.

As early as May and June, Austria's plight, paralleled in Hungary, Rumania, and elsewhere, was also raising doubts about the financial condition of Germany. German short-term foreign liabilities were almost double German short-term claims on foreigners. Foreigners saw the danger. Conversion of marks into foreign exchange was, if anything, only accelerated when the Reichsbank tried to stem the tide by raising its discount rate from 5 to 7 percent. In June the Bank of International Settlements, the Bank of England, the Bank of France, and the Federal Reserve Bank of New York undertook to rediscount the total equivalent of $100 million in Reichsbank bills. This credit was originally arranged as a purely temporary measure to avoid excessive end-of-the-month strain on the Reichsbank, and it was due to expire in mid-July; but in fact the credit proved inadequate, and repayment was not even started until the following year. Dr. Luther, the President of the Reichsbank, hastened to London, Paris, and the Bank for International Settlements in Basel in search of a new loan. His zeal perturbed foreign financiers and Germans alike. Partly because

the French insisted upon unacceptable political strings, he had to return from his journey with only vague promises. The proposed customs union with Austria was finally abandoned, anyway, on September 3.

On the very day of Dr. Luther's gloomy return, July 13, the Darmstädter und National Bank closed, victim of a run touched off by failure of the largest German textile company, with which it had a close financial association. Failure of this company had converted a run mainly of Germany's foreign creditors into a flight from the mark into foreign exchange by Germans as well. The Danat Bank, as it was called for short, was reopened later in the month under restrictions, including a moratorium on its debts until July 31 and a government guarantee of its deposits thereafter.

On the day after the Danat Bank failure, the German government decreed a temporary bank and stock-exchange holiday. Rudimentary exchange controls were soon introduced and then tightened. The Reichsbank raised its discount rate to 15 percent for August.

In late August a standstill agreement was reached to immobilize for six months the funds owed by Germans to foreign banks. This and earlier events froze about £70 million of British short-term assets in Germany. Already, at the time of the German bank holiday, Britain itself had begun suffering the withdrawal of deposits held by wary foreigners. Thus the runs on the currencies of Austria, Germany, Great Britain, and other countries overlapped in time.

The 1931 Crisis in Great Britain

Against the background of almost chronic weakness in the British balance of payments, the failure of the Danat Bank in Germany shook the London stock market and the foreign-exchange value of the pound, making gold export profitable for arbitrageurs. To check heavy withdrawals, the Bank of England raised its discount rate from 2½ to 3½ percent on July 23. After further gold losses, the Bank raised its rate again to 4½ percent on July 30—still a "very modest

---

[7] As things worked out, reparations never were resumed after the Hoover Moratorium year. Except for a few token payments, the Allies ceased paying installments on their war debts to the United States. Only Finland continued paying in full.

figure," according to pro-gold-standard historians.

At an inopportune time in mid-year, during the Continental crisis, the Committee on Finance and Industry issued its report (the so-called Macmillan Report). It unintentionally emphasized the vulnerability of sterling by revealing that while London's known short-term sterling claims on foreigners had, as of March, amounted to only about £153 million, much of which was now being immobilized on the Continent, deposits and sterling bill holdings held in London by foreigners amounted to about £407 million. Of course, London was a world banking center, and there is nothing at all unusual about a banker's having demand liabilities far in excess of immediately liquid assets. (In fact, the Macmillan Committee even considered its figures more reassuring than alarming.) In time of crisis, though, the fact is inconvenient. Furthermore, it was generally known that foreign holdings of the 5 percent War Loan alone amounted to hundreds of millions of pounds.

On August 1 the Bank of England announced that the Bank of France and the Federal Reserve Banks had agreed to lend it a total of $250 million. An increase of £15 million in the permissible fiduciary banknote issue also expanded the available gold reserve. One conservative observer interpreted the foreign loan as a sign that the British authorities were indisposed to let the outflow of gold tighten the internal money market and so call the classical corrective forces into play.[8] The deflationary effects of the gold losses were largely offset; about two-thirds of the contraction of the credit base that would otherwise have accompanied the loss of gold was replaced by central bank credit.[9] For better or worse, the "rules of the game" of the gold standard were still being violated.

On July 31 the Committee on National Expenditure (the May Committee) published its report, worrying about an impending deficit in the government budget and recommending cuts in unemployment relief, government salaries, and other expenditures, as well as tax increases. Given the pre-Keynesian notions then prevalent in all three political parties about the evil of a government deficit even in time of depression, the revelations of the May Report were alarming. Prime Minister MacDonald and his government resigned on August 24 because of resentment among fellow members of the Labor Party, both inside and outside his cabinet, over some of the proposed economies. At the urging of the King and of Conservative and Liberal leaders,[10] MacDonald then promptly organized a National government, whose Labor members were repudiated by their own party. The new coalition cabinet was expected to save the gold standard. In a radio speech on the evening of August 25, MacDonald warned of hyperinflation, no less, that would follow a collapse of the pound.[11]

On August 28, reassured by the new government's economy program, a group of French and American commercial banks agreed to make available about $400 million through purchases of British Treasury bills. This new aid, together with presentation on September 10 of a revised and balanced government budget, gave only a brief respite. Withdrawal of funds from England resumed, and the proceeds of the foreign loans were soon used up.

On September 15 the Admiralty announced that pay cuts had caused "unrest" among sailors at Invergordon. This incident, exaggerated into a "mutiny" by some foreign newspapers, speeded up the flight of funds from England. On September 18 the Treasury's request for further credits in New York and Paris met with friendly and sympathetic, but negative, replies. Sensing the impending collapse, the Bank of France belatedly gave orders to each of six New York banks on September 19 to sell £1 million of sterling for its account. This £6 million of selling orders, coming to New York near the end of the short Saturday market, broke the sterling quotation by more than two cents.

[8] B. M. Anderson, *Economics and the Public Welfare*, New York: Van Nostrand, 1949, p. 245.

[9] W. A. Brown, Jr., *The International Gold Standard Reinterpreted*, New York: National Bureau of Economic Research, 1940, II, 1022.

[10] See the authorities quoted in Reginald Bassett, *Nineteen Thirty-One Political Crisis*, London: Macmillan, 1958, pp. 149-150, 155-157, 160, 343, 358-375.

[11] Quoted in *ibid.*, pp. 178-179n.

That evening the Bank of England, after consulting with the British government all along, finally stated that its gold reserve had fallen to the point where it could no longer maintain the gold standard. The Cabinet ratified the inevitable decision the following day, Sunday, and released an official statement announcing that it would introduce the appropriate bill in Parliament, that it had already authorized the Bank of England to suspend gold payments, and that the Stock Exchange would remain closed Monday. Appealing to patriotism, the announcement warned British citizens against further straining the exchanges by buying foreign securities. The banks had agreed to cooperate by restricting British purchases of foreign exchange to those required for the actual needs of trade or for meeting existing contracts. The government would take further measures if they seemed advisable. The announcement concluded:

His Majesty's Government are securing a balanced Budget, and the internal position of the country is sound. This position must be maintained. It is one thing to go off the Gold standard with an unbalanced Budget and uncontrolled inflation; it is quite another thing to take this measure, not because of internal financial difficulties, but because of excessive withdrawals of borrowed capital. The ultimate resources of this country are enormous, and there is no doubt that the present exchange difficulties will prove only temporary.[12]

All on the next day, Monday the 21st, the Commons and Lords passed and the King signed the Gold Standard (Amendment) Act, confirming the cabinet's action and thus "amending" the gold standard out of existence[13] One section of the new act authorized such exchange controls as the Treasury might see fit. On Tuesday the Treasury issued the following order, which was not rescinded until March 2, 1932:

. . . until further notice purchases of foreign exchange or transfers of funds with the object of acquiring such exchange directly or indirectly by British subjects or persons resident in the United Kingdom shall be prohibited except for the purpose of financing: (1) Normal trading requirements; (2) contracts existing before September 21, 1931; (3) reasonable travelling or other personal purposes.[14]

Britain left the gold standard with Bank rate still at 4½ percent, a rate which, according to some pro-gold-standard observers, was too low and indicated failure to employ classical weapons in a real battle to defend the pound. On the other hand, a very high Bank rate during the crisis might have been taken as a sign of desperation and so have even intensified the panicky run on the gold reserves. In any event, the Bank of England raised its rate to 6 percent on the very first day off gold, presumably as a gesture of determination to resist inflation and to rally confidence in the unattached pound.

During the first week, the pound fluctuated between about $4.30 and $3.40 (in comparison with the previous mint par of $4.8665). Foreign holders of sterling suffered a corresponding loss. The depreciation cost the Bank of France, for instance, an amount equal to seven times its capital. The loss of the Netherlands Bank, though only approximately equal to its capital, was the more shocking because it directly resulted from trust in the word of the Bank of England. Dr. Vissering, head of the Netherlands Bank, had telephoned the Bank of England on Friday, September 18, asking whether the gold value of his sterling balance was safe. Though the truth was almost certainly already known to be just the opposite,[15] Dr. Vissering received reassurances. The Netherlands Bank thereupon decided to support the Bank of England by refraining from converting its sterling into gold, as it still could have done. For the resulting loss, the Netherlands Bank was severely blamed by its government; and its next annual report was bitter on the matter. The episode cost Dr. Vissering his job.[16]

---

[12] *Ibid.*, pp. 238-239.

[13] J. M. Keynes, exaggerating, said that sterling had not left gold, but that gold had left sterling. (Brown, *op cit.*, II, 1052.) Keynes's witticism presumably meant that gold had been appreciating in purchasing power and that in September 1931 sterling finally ceased appreciating in step with gold.

[14] *The Economist*, 26 September 1931, p. 555.

[15] Cf. Brown, *op. cit.*, II, 1092-1093.

[16] Anderson, *op. cit.*, pp. 246-247, 252-253; Walter A.

Depreciation of sterling had wider repercussions. Most European stock exchanges closed immediately for various periods of time. The markets in New York, Tokyo, and elsewhere declined. Credit tightened and central-bank discount rates went up in a long list of countries, most strikingly in Scandinavia. Within a few days the Swedish Riksbank lost about 100 million kroner of gold and foreign exchange reserves. Despite closing of the stock exchange, increase in the bank rate, official assurances that the country would stay on gold, and attempts to borrow in New York and Paris, Sweden was driven off the gold standard one week after England. Norway left gold the same day, September 27, and on the 28th, Denmark confirmed the departure from gold already represented by its gold export embargo of the 22nd. At least 35 countries left the gold standard from April 1929 to April 1933, as shown in the following list,[17] though some of the dates are uncertain because of the piecemeal and unofficial manner in which some countries acted at first.

1929
April —Uruguay
November —Argentina
December —Brazil

1930
March —Australia
April —New Zealand
September —Venezuela

1931
August —Mexico
September —United Kingdom, Canada, India, Sweden, Denmark, Norway, Egypt, Irish Free State, British Malaya, Palestine
October —Austria, Portugal, Finland, Bolivia, Salvador
December —Japan

1932
January —Colombia, Nicaragua, Costa Rica
April —Greece, Chile
May —Peru
June —Ecuador, Siam
July —Yugoslavia

Morton, *British Finance, 1930–1940*, Madison: University of Wisconsin Press, 1943, p. 46n. Governor Montagu Norman was away from England at the time for a rest. Bassett, *op. cit.*, pp. 62-63n.

[17] Brown, *op. cit.*, II, 1075, citing Bank of Nova Scotia, *Monthly Review*, September 1933.

1933
January —Union of South Africa
April —Honduras, United States

As the gold standard disintegrated, a large number of countries decided either promptly or within a few years to keep their currencies at least approximately stable in terms of sterling, and therefore fluctuating in sympathy with the British pound against the remaining gold currencies. This practice was the informal birth of the Sterling Area, a group of countries whose currencies were pegged to sterling and whose official reserves of foreign exchange consisted largely of sterling balances. This group came to include the British dominions and colonies (except Canada and Hong Kong), the Scandinavian countries, and a number of other countries such as Portugal, Egypt, Latvia, and Estonia. Several additional countries, including Japan and Argentina, kept their official exchange rates stable against sterling for several years without being generally regarded as members of the sterling block. As the Sterling Area acquired a more formal status under the exchange controls of World War II, the non-British member countries dropped away.

Free Sterling in 1931–1932

The first week of wild fluctuations in sterling exchange in September 1931 was followed by a few weeks of relative dullness, with quotations in the neighborhood of $3.90, about 20 percent below the old par. A sharp decline then carried the rate to a low of $3.23 on December 1, 34 percent below par. Thereafter the pound oscillated upwards toward a brief peak of about $3.80 at the beginning of April 1932. In April the impending establishment of the Exchange Equalisation Account was announced. This Account was to be operated by the Bank of England under Treasury control; its dealings in the market were supposed to smooth out excessive short-run rate fluctuations. Bullishness on sterling abated, and the rate fell back to just under $3.70, where it was stabilized during May and early June. In subsequent months sterling drifted gently downward against the dollar. Table 16.2 shows the monthly average quota-

Table 16.2. Sterling Exchange in 1931–1932

	Monthly Average Rate in U.S. Cents	Percentage of Old Parity
1931		
August	485.7725	99.83
September	453.1260	93.11
October	388.9291	79.92
November	371.9934	76.44
December	337.3707	69.33
1932		
January	343.1210	70.51
February	345.6316	71.02
March	363.9304	74.78
April	374.9994	77.06
May	367.5140	75.52
June	364.6648	74.93
July	354.9564	72.94
August	347.5721	71.42
September	347.1062	71.33
October	339.6163	69.79
November	327.5267	67.30
December	327.8679	67.37

SOURCE: Federal Reserve, *Banking and Monetary Statistics*, p. 681.

tions through the end of 1932. The lowest of the immediate postdepreciation months was December 1931 and the lowest of the entire 1930s was November 1932.

Surveying sterling's first year off gold, the London *Economist* felt that "on the whole sterling has thrived better than might have been expected—certainly much better than might have been inferred from the lugubrious prophecies heard immediately before the suspension of the gold standard."[18]

This judgment is contradicted by the League of Nations' authoritative survey of *International Currency Experience*. It cites the period between abandonment of gold in September 1931 and establishment of the Exchange Equalisation Account the following spring as an example of the unsatisfactory operation generally to be expected of freely fluctuating exchanges. It argues that disequilibrating capital movements were at work in the first few months off gold. The outflow of foreign funds largely determined the depreciation of sterling, while prospects of further depreciation largely determined the out-

flow itself. After a return of confidence early in 1932, the movement became cumulative in the reverse direction. "It was the realization of the exchange market's inability to maintain a stable equilibrium, at any rate in the short run, that led to the establishment of the Exchange Equalization Fund and thus to the abandonment of the principle of freely fluctuating exchanges."[19]

The pound fluctuated in 1931–1932 under circumstances very different from those likely to characterize freely fluctuating exchanges adopted as a permanent system. England had been pushed off the gold standard by a flight from the pound that had been gathering momentum for some time. Whatever bearish speculation the free pound inherited from the gold pound might more justly be blamed on the earlier maintenance of currency overvaluation and on its incitement to one-way-option speculation than on the workings of the free market itself. Furthermore, the continued outflow of funds from England for several weeks after September 20 was not due entirely and perhaps not even mainly to private speculation: general abandonment of the gold-exchange standard meant that several foreign central banks were hurriedly selling their previously accumulated sterling reserves. In fact, a number of central banks *had* to withdraw their balances from England because their statutes required them to hold their exchange reserves exclusively in gold or gold-standard currencies.[20] As will be emphasized later, this scramble for gold put pressure on the gold-standard dollar as well as on the fluctuating pound, leading to increases in the Federal Reserve rediscount rate in order to protect the U.S. gold stock. Another difficulty was that confidence in sterling was partially linked to possibilities of extending the credits obtained in France and the United States during the unsuccessful defense of the gold standard. Even before establishment of the Exchange Equalisation Account, the Bank of England was trading on the exchange market, on balance buying more foreign exchange than it was selling in order to repay

---

[18] *The Economist*, 24 September 1932, p. 537.

[19] Ragnar Nurkse, *International Currency Experience*, League of Nations, 1944, p. 118.

[20] *Ibid.*, pp. 39–40.

the French and American loans. Incidentally, complete freedom for private transactions did not prevail during the period of supposedly free fluctuations; the previously quoted regulations about capital movements must have interfered with private arbitrage and speculation. Furthermore, uncertainties over political, legislative, and economic developments at home and abroad influenced the fluctuations of sterling. Several of these developments in turn came partly as responses to the unsatisfactory operation of the earlier system of exchange-rate pegging that was now cracking up. The British Parliament was dissolved on October 7, for example, and the election on October 27 gave an overwhelming victory to MacDonald's coalition, in which Conservatives inclined toward protectionism were heavily represented. The severe decline of sterling in November was due, among other things, not only to seasonally heavy imports but also to a rush to get imports into the country before enactment of a stopgap tariff on November 19. The subsequent rise of sterling was partly due to the drop in imports after the stopgap tariff went into effect. (A more permanent general tariff replaced it on March 1.) Similarly abnormal influences on the sterling-dollar rate included preoccupation with news about the British and American government budgets, uncertainties about whether or not war debts would be reduced or cancelled, fears late in November about an increase in the fiduciary note issue of the Bank of England, uncertainties about the expansionary consequences of the Reconstruction Finance Corporation and the Glass-Steagall Act in the United States, and exports of gold from India as India moved from a gold to a sterling standard. Speculation was by no means centered on the fate of the pound alone.

Some broader observations are relevant to an appraisal of the fluctuating pound of 1931–1932. Instability is to be expected in a currency that has just come unpegged. With the old value inappropriate, no recent history of equilibrium exchange rates exists to guide buyers and sellers in making their bids and offers on the market. Since the currency could hardly rise in value above the level that had just proved untenable, the immediate specula-

tive pressure is overwhelmingly bearish. Quite understandably, this pressure may temporarily carry the rate below the level corresponding to fundamental supply and demand conditions, setting the stage for an upward reaction. After the initial shock of coming loose from an inappropriate peg had worn off and after the reaction from that shock had run its course, the British pound might well have settled down to narrow fluctuations about a gradually changing equilibrium rate. But the pound never had this chance; the Exchange Equalisation Account came onto the scene and took credit, rightly or wrongly, for whatever degree of stability was observed thereafter. In any case, it is wrong to cite the fluctuating pound of 1931–1932 as a horrible example of what is to be expected from free rates generally. To do so is to criticize fluctuating rates in a situation in which fixed exchange rates could not—and did not—work at all.

American Gold and Banking Crises, 1931–1933

After England left gold in September 1931, the international panic centered briefly on the United States. A foreign run on U.S. gold caused a 15-percent drop in the gold stock from mid-September to the end of October. (The gold drain temporarily ceased in November and December but resumed at the end of the year and continued with some interruption until June 1932.) Within the United States, confidence in the gold standard still endured, and there was little new gold hoarding. Hindsight shows that the country was in little danger at the time of exhausting its reserves and being forced off gold.

Nevertheless, the episode interrupted the half-hearted easy money policy that should have been maintained and intensified if overcoming the depression at home had been the dominant consideration. Allegedly because of legal technicalities tying up gold as collateral for its notes, the Federal Reserve considered that during the fall of 1931 it had practically exhausted its power to buy government securities on the open market to relieve the domestic credit stringency. The rediscount rate of the Federal Reserve Bank of New York jumped from 1½ to 2½ percent on October 9 and to 3½ percent on October 16. The owned (nonborrowed) reserves of banks belonging to the Federal Reserve System fell from $2.1 to $1.3 billion between early September and the end of the year. Given the low reserve requirements then governing banks and the smallness of their excess reserves, the further reserve losses provoked a powerful multiple contraction of bank credit. The country suffered "one of the most violent deflations in our banking history."[21] Between September 1931 and February 1932, demand deposits declined by $2.7 billion, or almost 14 percent. Towards the end of 1931, hundreds of banks were closing each month, tying up hundreds of millions of dollars of deposits. In the last three months of 1931 and the first six months of 1932, the volume of commercial bank loans was shrinking by more than half a billion dollars a month.[22] From August 1931 to January 1932 the money stock fell at the unprecedented annual rate of 31 percent.[23] In the words of one sound-money economist not given to undue worry about deflation, the country had "real money pressure." Athough the situation was not so bad in New York, "There were important parts of the country where good merchants had their loans reduced or even cut off because the banks themselves were short of money." Many banks that could have made loans hesitated out of fear of sudden runs by their depositors.[24] According to A. G. Hart, the whole deflationary episode reflects "panic" on the part of America's financial leaders, including the Federal Reserve authorities. The 1931 Annual Report of the Federal Reserve Board lamely explained that "after the middle of September, in view of the outflow of gold from the country and of currency into hoard-

ing, the Federal Reserve Banks increased their rates on discounts and acceptances."[25]

The drain on U.S. gold reserves had a deflationary influence on fiscal as well as monetary policy. Former Vice President Garner, who was speaker of the House of Representatives at the time, recalls leaving the Speaker's chair to beg for passage of a tax bill to stop the gold outflow and guard the dollar. "At the end of my speech, I said: Now every man in this House that believes in levying a tax bill sufficient to sustain the American dollar, I want him to rise. Every one of the members rose. We did pass a tax bill and it saved the situation."[26]

The technicalities which had supposedly tied up an unusually large part of the country's gold stock as collateral against Federal Reserve notes were overcome by passage of the Glass-Steagall Act in February 1932. The Federal Reserve authorities delayed about ten weeks, however, in buying enough securities on the open market to take advantage of the act's provisions. Partly because of the opportunities provided by the Glass-Steagall Act, the United States was able to weather the renewed foreign drain on its gold stock during the first half of 1932 (especially in May and June) without further credit tightening; in fact, the New York rediscount rate was cut to 3 percent in February and to 2½ percent in June (though all other Federal Reserve Banks except Chicago kept their rates at 3½ percent). The Reconstruction Finance Corporation, created by act of Congress in January 1932 and equipped with funds for lending to banks, railroads, and other pivotal institutions in temporary trouble, also was useful in checking the contagion of financial distress.

In the middle of 1932, signs of business revival appeared: mining, manufacturing, payrolls, department-store sales, commodity prices, and stock prices rose. These good omens were soon to evaporate. Events of that summer were already preparing another tight-money crisis. The Central Republic Bank &

---

[21] H. H. Villard, "The Federal Reserve System's Monetary Policy in 1931 and 1932," *Journal of Political Economy*, XLV, December 1937, p. 725.

[22] Albert Gailord Hart, *Money, Debt and Economic Activity* (2nd ed.), Englewood Cliffs, N.J.: Prentice-Hall, 1953, p. 321.

[23] Milton Friedman and Anna J. Schwartz, *A Monetary History of the United States, 1867–1960*, Princeton, N.J.: Princeton University Press, 1963, pp. 317-318.

[24] Anderson, *op. cit.*, pp. 264, 266.

[25] Quoted in Hart, *op. cit.*, pp. 321-322.

[26] "John Garner at 90 Tells an Inside Story," *U.S. News & World Report*, vol. XLV, No. 21, November 21, 1958, pp. 98-105, quotation from p. 100. The tax bill was passed in 1932.

Trust Company of Chicago appeared vulnerable to runs. General Charles G. Dawes, who had headed this bank before becoming Vice President of the United States and afterwards Ambassador to Great Britain, was now the head of the Reconstruction Finance Corporation. When danger threatened his old associates and depositors, Dawes resigned from the RFC and went to Chicago to attempt a rescue. In his efforts, Dawes found it necessary to ask the RFC for help. Its loan, supplemented by others from some New York and Chicago banks, made possible a reorganization of the Central Republic Bank that protected the depositors, including a large number of country correspondent banks, and perhaps even staved off a chain of bank failures. The assistance of the RFC seemed in accord with both the letter and the spirit of the law creating the agency. Nevertheless, an outcry arose that Dawes as a government official was rescuing himself as a private person.[27] Though apparently unjustified, suspicion grew that the RFC was making loans on a political basis, and its lending policy became more timid thereafter. With Democrats in control of the House of Representatives, the RFC was required first, in August, to report new loans to the Clerk of the House, and later, in January 1933, to report loans previously made. These reports were speedily given to the press, subverting the RFC practice of keeping loans confidential for fear that knowledge of a bank's borrowing would arouse worry among its depositors. Some institutions hesitated to borrow from the RFC for fear of bad publicity. Disclosures in congressional hearings were already shaking trust in banks generally.

Meanwhile, President Hoover was defeated for reelection. This blow to confidence among conservatives may have had something to do with a fresh wave of hoarding and bank failures that set in in December. During the interregnum until Franklin D. Roosevelt took office the following March 4, neither man was in a position to frame long-range policy; and efforts to arrange cooperation between them broke down. Rumors circulated that the new president might take the country off the gold standard despite the Democratic platform. Foreigners began to withdraw gold again early in 1933, and domestic depositors withdrew currency from banks for hoarding or conversion into gold. The difficulties of the Union Guardian Trust Company of Detroit grew worse in January when its indebtedness to the RFC became known. Depositors hastened to transfer their funds elsewhere. The bank's difficulties became critical in February, yet its strategic importance argued against allowing it to fail. On February 14 the governor of Michigan decreed an eight-day statewide bank holiday. (Limited bank restrictions had already been adopted in Nevada, Iowa, and Louisiana.)

With their Michigan funds now blocked, businessmen had ample reason to draw on any bank accounts they happened to have in other states. Bank holidays quickly followed in Indiana, Maryland, Arkansas, and Ohio. Some states enacted legislation permitting bank commissioners to restrict withdrawals, and an act of Congress of February 25 authorized the Comptroller of the Currency to give national banks emergency privileges similar to those protecting state-chartered banks. The wave of bank holidays continued into the first few days of March. The governor of Kentucky, lacking any other constitutional means to suspend banking business, declared successive "Days of Thanksgiving."

As member banks sought funds by rediscounting, the reserves of the Federal Reserve banks themselves slid down toward what they considered the bare minimum level. The Federal Reserve Bank of New York came to the end of its own lending power and was being carried by the other Reserve banks. Since the New York bank was chiefly responsible for meeting the general run on the Federal Reserve System, its position impeded any further large extensions of credit.[28] The New York and Chicago Banks responded on March 3 and 4 by raising their discount rates from 2½ percent to the 3½ percent level already in effect at the other ten Reserve banks. The *New York Times* described this

---

[27] Anderson, *op. cit.*, pp. 274-275. Hodson, *op. cit.*, chap. VII, contains a useful general survey of the American crisis.

[28] Brown, *op. cit.*, II, 1240.

increase as "a perfectly normal and customary expedient in a time of large gold withdrawals"—which is a revealing commentary on the state of economic thinking at the time. The whole episode deserves emphasis. For the second time during the depths of severe depression, the Federal Reserve authorities tolerated and even abetted a deflationary tightening of credit. Of course, it is unfair to blame particular men, given the rules under which they were working and the economic ideas then prevalent.

Significantly, both this episode of early 1933 and the previous one in the fall of 1931 had involved preoccupation with gold reserves and with precautions actually or supposedly necessary to maintain the gold standard in the face of foreign drains. Recovery from the depression required a vigorous easy-money policy (and perhaps other measures as well). Yet concern about the gold standard required, in the judgment of the Federal Reserve authorities, keeping the monetary policy only half-heartedly easy, and required punctuating even this, in the fall of 1931 and the early months of 1933, with bouts of outright monetary tightness. One can of course argue that if only the gold reserve requirements had been lower or had been administered more flexibly, the country could have had the necessary monetary expansion at home while meeting the gold demands of foreigners. But this is an admission that a rigid gold standard is unacceptable. Furthermore, there is surely a limit, even though not a precise one, to how far expansionary policy can go without upsetting the balance of payments or exchange rates.

New Deal Currency Policies

On March 3, inauguration eve, it seemed that the Federal Reserve banks themselves could not long carry on business as usual. Warned of imminent collapse of the whole banking system, President Hoover agreed to proclaim a nationwide bank holiday only if the incoming president would share responsibility. Roosevelt refused. On Saturday, March 4, the Federal Reserve banks and all the leading exchanges closed; and, as the Federal Reserve Board later reported, "business in general was practically at a standstill."[29] New York, Illinois, and 23 other states proclaimed bank holidays. Before the end of the day, banks almost everywhere in the country were either closed or under restrictions. The banking crisis was at its very climax as President Roosevelt took office early that afternoon.

One remark in Roosevelt's inaugural address had special significance for international monetary policy: "Our international trade relations, though vastly important, are, in point of time and necessity, secondary to the establishment of sound national economy. I favor as a practical policy the putting of first things first."

President Roosevelt immediately summoned Congress to a special session. At one o'clock Monday morning, the 6th, claiming authority under the Trading with the Enemy Act of 1917, he proclaimed a four-day nationwide bank holiday, a cooling-off period. Except with the permission of the Secretary of the Treasury, no bank was to "pay out, export, earmark, or permit the withdrawal or transfer in any manner or by any device whatsoever, of any gold or silver coin or bullion or currency or take any other action which might facilitate the hoarding thereof. . . ."[30] A further proclamation of March 9 continued the bank holiday, but the ban on banking business was progressively relaxed. The ban on obtaining gold was generally regarded as a temporary technicality of little significance. Secretary of the Treasury Woodin said, "We are definitely on the gold standard. Gold merely cannot be obtained for several days."[31] Doubt whether the mere private holding of gold had been made illegal was not dispelled until an order of April 5 expressly prohibited "the hoarding of gold coin, gold bullion and gold certificates within the continental United States."

When Congress met on March 9, Roosevelt asked for immediate legislation authorizing

---

[29] *Ibid.*, p. 1249.

[30] The proclamation is reprinted in James Daniel Paris, *Monetary Policies of the United States, 1932–1938*, New York: Columbia University Press, 1938, pp. 164-165.

[31] Ray B. Westerfield, *Money, Credit and Banking*, New York: Ronald, 1939, p. 788.

him to exercise control over banks to protect depositors, to reopen banks found in sound condition, and to reorganize unsound banks and reopen them later. He also asked authority for additional currency issues in case of heavy demands. The Emergency Banking Act, overwhelmingly passed on that very day, reaffirmed the President's authority under the Trading with the Enemy Act to regulate or prohibit transactions in foreign exchange and the export, hoarding, melting, or earmarking of gold and silver coin, bullion, or currency. It also authorized the Secretary of the Treasury, at his discretion, to require delivery to the Treasury of any or all gold coin, gold bullion, or gold certificates.

By Wednesday, March 15, most of the country's banks were back in business. The wave of panicky distrust had passed. Hoarded currency poured back into the banks. When the New York Stock Exchange reopened on March 15, prices were buoyant. When dealings in the dollar were resumed in London on March 13, it was slightly higher in relation to sterling than before the banking crisis. The banks' foreign-exchange transactions were still restricted, however, and paying out gold or gold certificates was still forbidden. The United States government allowed exports of gold under earmark for foreign governments or central banks or for the Bank for International Settlements, and a very few other gold-export licenses were issued in mid-April. The exchange value of the dollar against the French franc (still on gold) remained within the gold points.

On April 18, 19, and 20, while British Prime Minister MacDonald was en route to Washington for conferences, the United States unequivocally left the gold standard. The government announced that it would issue no further gold export licenses, except perhaps under very special conditions. The Secretary of the Treasury was also given power to investigate, regulate, or prohibit all foreign-exchange transactions. These surprise announcements made the dollar fall sharply; the pound rose from $3.44⅝ on April 15 to $3.81½ on April 20.

A Congressional Joint Resolution of June 5 abrogated the gold clause in public and private contracts and made all outstanding obligations to pay in gold coin payable dollar for dollar in any legal tender. The gold clause —almost routinely included in bonds—called for repayment in dollars of the original "weight and fineness" or the equivalent in total gold content. Many bondholders brought suit to recover the larger number of depreciated dollars "containing" the original total amount of gold. The Supreme Court decided in February 1935 that the constitutional right of Congress to regulate the value of money included the right to annul the gold clause in contracts of private parties and state and local governments. As for the gold clause in the U.S. government's own bonds, Congress could not rightly repudiate it. Nevertheless, said the Court, the bondholder had not shown that he had been damaged by the Congressional action. To forestall efforts to show such damage and collect more than the face value of outstanding government bonds, Congress then took away the jurisdiction of the Federal courts to hear such suits. The United States government quite specifically repudiated its own promises.

Unlike Great Britain, the United States had not been driven off the gold standard. Though both imports and exports had fallen, the American balance of payments still showed a surplus on current account. By the beginning of 1933, American short-term debts to foreigners had been so largely paid off that the remainder outstanding fell short of American short-term claims on foreigners. The flight of American capital had not assumed menacing proportions after the end of the banking panic in March, and such flight as there was stemmed from expectations of deliberate departure from the gold standard. Nor was the United States forced off gold by a price level already too high relative to foreign price levels, (though vigorous reflation might have created balance-of-payments trouble later on). The departure from gold was deliberate.

The early Roosevelt administration adopted a hodge-podge of deflationary and inflationary measures. The delay in reopening all but unquestionably sound banks was deflationary. So was the economy budget submitted shortly after the banking crisis. The agricultural programs sought to adjust production to a shrunken volume of monetary demand, rather than the other way around. The law establishing the National Recovery Administration called on each industry to draw up a "code of fair competition" to prescribe maximum hours, minimum wages, and other working conditions, to foster collective bargaining, and to limit price competition. Rising prices as a typical *symptom* of recovery from depression were confused with rising prices as a *cause* of recovery. Rising prices as a frequent *consequence* of monetary expansion were apparently confused with the necessary monetary expansion itself.

On the side of potential inflation was Roosevelt's acceptance on April 18 of the Thomas Amendment to the pending farm bill, which was passed in May. The amendment gave the President discretionary power to cut the gold content of the dollar by as much as 50 percent, to open the mints to unlimited coinage of silver and fix the ratio between silver and gold, to accept silver up to specified amounts in settlement of war debts, to sell up to $3 billion worth of government securities to the Federal Reserve banks, and to put up to $3 billion of new paper money into circulation by redeeming Federal debt. Roosevelt did not use this authority for forthright monetary expansion.

General economic conditions improved remarkably from March to around July. The spurt in prices, production, employment, and payrolls apparently rested on expectations of recovery and on spending to beat the rise in costs that NRA was likely to impose. With its basis so weak, the spurt gave way to relapse in the summer of 1933.

The London Economic Conference

Meanwhile, the United States took the lead in getting countries to forswear additional trade barriers at least until after the forthcoming World Economic Conference. The conference duly opened in London on June 12, with 64 countries represented. France and other gold countries wanted to restore an international monetary standard before lowering trade barriers. Britain and other paper-currency countries feared that an international standard would break down unless excessive tariffs, internal deflation, and other unfavorable conditions were dealt with first. The cleavage of opinions was fundamental. "But the London Conference was held under the auspices of that sort of statesmanship which strives to escape awkward problems by elaborating formulas so vague and so noncommittal that everybody may be able to subscribe to them."[32] Domestic antidepression measures also came up for discussion. If we are dismayed that Daladier of France and Dollfuss of Austria should have called for cutting production down into line with consumption, we can console ourselves with the thought that economic understanding has gained some ground since then.

The American position on exchange stabilization was unclear and remained so after dispatch of Professor Raymond Moley, Assistant Secretary of State, to brief the American delegation. Heightened uncertainty following a statement by the American delegation on June 22 seemed to threaten the few remaining gold currencies and touched off a bear movement against the Dutch guilder, pushing the gold countries toward cooperation in a formal gold bloc. Yet President Roosevelt's apparent attitude left room for hope that some sort of reassuring compromise declaration could be worked out to accommodate the gold countries.

Instead, Roosevelt sent a message made public on July 3 warning against "a catastrophe amounting to world tragedy" if economic recovery measures should be sidetracked "by the proposal of a purely artificial and temporary experiment affecting the monetary exchange of a few nations only." A nation's internal economic soundness, he argued, is more important to its well-being than the price of its currency in terms of other currencies. The American objective of stabilizing the purchasing power of the dollar "means more to the good of other nations than a fixed ratio for a month or two in terms

[32] Gustav Cassel, *The Downfall of the Gold Standard*, Oxford: Clarendon Press, 1936, p. 141.

of the pound or franc." Gold or gold and silver can be important as currency reserves, but discussion of a better distribution of them can properly await "concerted policies in the majority of nations to produce balanced budgets and living within their means. . . ." Restoration of world trade is important, but "temporary exchange fixing is not the true answer." The conference must not be diverted from its purpose of seeking cures to fundamental economic ills.[33]

Roosevelt's message is commonly said to have "torpedoed" the conference. Much of its economic substance would probably command wide agreement nowadays (though one may question its preoccupation with gold and silver reserves and with balanced government budgets even during depression). Perhaps the main fault of the message was the bad diplomacy behind it. Roosevelt was thoughtless in not deciding sooner just what his policy was, in blowing hot and cold about American cooperation in what most delegations regarded as the main objectives of the conference, in giving the initial false impression that he would agree to some sort of exchange stabilization, and finally in making a unilateral decision bound to hurt morale and create bad will. As Moley, Roosevelt's special emissary, reminisced many years later, the "delegates wandered around in a fog" after the conference began, "trying to learn by remote control what Mr. Roosevelt was currently thinking. The whole conference fell to pieces."[34] Yet the delegates lingered around for some weeks more, agreeing on minor matters and finally, as a gesture of unwillingness to confess failure, merely "adjourning" the conference but not closing it.

The New Deal Gold Program

By mid-July, the dollar had dropped more than 30 percent against gold-bloc currencies. (Nevertheless, the government continued selling gold bars to the arts and industries at the old price of $20.67 an ounce until late in August.) Yet the spring spurt in production soon gave way to relapse. Farm prices were sagging. On October 22, 1933, Roosevelt made a radio speech stressing the need first to raise prices and then to stabilize the purchasing power of the dollar. His way was to "control the gold value of our own dollar at home," out of range of "the accidents of international trade, . . . the internal policies of other nations and . . . political disturbance in other continents." As part of his plan for manipulating the dollar, the Reconstruction Finance Corporation was authorized to buy gold from American mines and, when necessary, on world markets. The price was to be set from time to time in consultation with the Secretary of the Treasury and the President.[35]

Roosevelt apparently adopted his gold-buying program under the influence of the well-known Warren-Pearson theory concerning a supposed line of causation running from the dollar price of gold to the general price level. Untroubled by the dubiousness of the theory, the RFC went ahead buying gold, first domestic and later foreign also. Short-term funds speculatively leaving the United States drove the dollar down on the foreign-exchange market at a more rapid pace than the actual rise in the price of gold. On November 6, 1933, the pound sterling appreciated against the dollar beyond its former parity of $4.8665. On November 15, the dollar fell to $5.50 to the pound before a reaction set in.

In January 1934, the President asked Congress to give the government title to all monetary gold held by the Federal Reserve banks (which had acquired the gold previously surrendered by the public). Taking the gold over at the former parity would let the Treasury reap any revaluation profit. The President also asked for an upper limit on the new gold content of the dollar at 60 percent of the old one (the Thomas Amendment already authorized devaluing the dollar to a lower limit of 50 percent). The Secretary of the Treasury was to be empowered to deal in

---

[33] Roosevelt's message is reprinted in Paris, *op. cit.*, pp. 166-167.

[34] Quoted in Anderson, *op. cit.*, p. 331 from the Los Angeles *Times*, 7 April 1945. Reading Roosevelt's mind was important because, for one thing, the Thomas Amendment had given him vast discretionary powers to alter the American monetary system.

[35] The relevant part of the speech is reprinted in Paris, *op. cit.*, pp. 168-169.

foreign currencies to promote exchange stability, and a fund of $2 billion for this pur-
pose was to be set up out of the gold
revaluation profit. These proposals became
the Gold Reserve Act of 1934, signed on
January 30. Next day Roosevelt fixed the gold
content of the dollar at 15⁵⁄₂₁ grains of gold,
9/10 fine, corresponding to 59.06 percent of
the pre-1933 gold content and to a price of
$35 an ounce for pure gold. The book profit
on revaluation of the Treasury's gold reserves was $2.8 billion.

The government announced that it would
buy all gold offered to it at $35 per ounce,
less charges for handling and the equivalent
of minting. Gold would also be sold for
export to central banks. Thus the United
States was back on a kind of gold standard.
It was a "limited gold-bullion standard,"
with redemption in gold "limited" to dollars
held by foreign central banks and governments (and licensed users of gold for the industries and arts).

Heavy gold shipments from Europe and
elsewhere began what Graham and Whittlesey called the "golden avalanche."[36] By
January 1935 the dollar value of the American
gold stock was more than double, and by
the end of 1936 almost triple, what it had been
in January 1934. The inflow kept on until
checked by foreign restrictions during World
War II, and it resumed in the early postwar
years. One short-run reason for the golden
avalanche was the return of American capital
that had fled abroad during the protracted
depreciation of the dollar in 1933–1934. Other
reasons included the attractiveness of the
high gold price to foreign producers and the
balance-of-payments consequences of a dollar
that was undervalued in terms of gold and
foreign exchange; the failure of American
prices as a whole to rise as fast as the dollar
depreciated confronted foreign countries with
the competition on world markets of what appeared to be predatory excessive depreciation.
In the later 1930s, the gold inflow was largely
the counterpart of the inflow of foreign
capital taking refuge from political and economic uncertainties abroad.

The Fluctuating Dollar, 1933–1934

The exchange rate of the dollar against
gold currencies was fixed again after January
1934. Exchange rates with sterling-area currencies were also in practice kept fairly stable.
But for a time, from April 1933 to January
1934, the dollar had been fluctuating on the
foreign-exchange market. This episode provides the author of *International Currency
Experience* with yet another supposed example of disequilibrating speculation under
freely fluctuating exchange rates. The dollar
depreciated, mainly in response to an outflow
of short-term funds, but the American export
surplus fell rather than rose. Foreign buyers
postponed purchases in the hope that the
dollar would become still cheaper. Americans
imported heavily in anticipation of a continued rise in foreign-exchange rates.[37]

Speculation in the fluctuating dollar was
based not so much on assessment of free-
market forces as on guesses about the government's exchange-rate policy and internal fiscal
and monetary policy.[38] The definite embargo
on gold exports in April 1933 made known
official intentions of staying off the gold
standard. The President was anxious to have
the dollar depreciate and apparently wanted
to make sure that all speculation against the
dollar would be fully effective and that gold
exports would not ease the pressure of demands for foreign currencies. The very announcement of this policy was bound to
intensify the speculative capital movements
that had already made some dent in American gold stocks. Fear of inflation helped to
depress the dollar. This fear grew stronger
when, at the time of the embargo on gold
exports, the committee considering the farm
bill adopted the Thomas ("Inflation")
Amendment, which became law on May 12.[39]

---

[36] F. D. Graham and C. R. Whittlesey, *Golden Avalanche,* Princeton, N.J.: Princeton University Press, 1939.

[37] Pp. 118, 120, citing U.S. Department of Commerce,
The Balance of Payments of the United States in 1933,
p. 9.

[38] "For several months, exchange rates were left to be
determined . . . by the consensus of speculative opinion
as to what the government might do later." Hart,
op. cit., p. 378.

[39] Cf. Seymour E. Harris, *Exchange Depreciation,*
Cambridge: Harvard University Press, 1936, pp. 249-50;
Anderson, *op. cit.,* p. 317; Milton Gilbert, *Currency De-
preciation and Monetary Policy,* Philadelphia: University

People knew that the government intended to raise commodity prices by such devices as reduction in the gold content of the dollar, silver policy, open market operations, credit expansion, public-works spending, NRA, and AAA. Still other influences on exchange speculation were the ban on gold hoarding, the congressional gold-clause resolution, and rumors about what the World Economic Conference in London would decide on. For example, rumors that the British, French, and American authorities had agreed or shortly would agree on temporary exchange stabilization caused the dollar to advance sharply in the exchange markets on June 15.[40] On July 3, however, President Roosevelt practically broke up the conference by rejecting exchange stabilization.

Renewed rumors of inflation spurred further flight from the dollar in August and September, intensifying depreciation. The dollar showed strength, however, by recovering from a discount of 35.3 percent in terms of the French franc on September 23 to a discount of only 28.8 percent on October 21. The next day Roosevelt made his speech announcing a deliberate depreciation of the dollar in order to restore commodity prices to predepression levels. He practically told speculators to be more bearish against the dollar.[41] As Nurkse says, "the principal effect of the [gold-buying] policy was to encourage private speculation against the dollar."[42]

In November 1933, rumors of impending stabilization reversed speculative attitudes, and the dollar started to rise. Early in 1934 a large return flow of capital actually embarrassed the government in its attempts to depreciate the dollar. The volume of gold imports necessary to depress the dollar at

that time suggests a high elasticity of demand for dollars.[43] Finally, at the end of January, the dollar was tied back onto gold at a fixed price.

This review of history shows that the exchange value of the dollar was *not* free from official influence throughout the months of fluctuation in 1933 and 1934. Speculators and traders had to keep guessing what President Roosevelt and his advisors had in mind. At times the Administration actually incited destabilizing speculation. Clearly, then, the American experience supports no generalizations about speculation in free markets.

U.S. Silver Policy and Its Repercussions[44]

The story of American silver policy from 1933 to around 1936 is well worth reviewing because it further documents the experimental nature of New Deal monetary policies, provides insights about behavior in a market dominated by official transactions, and illustrates how a country (China) may suffer deflation imposed from abroad. The open-market price of silver reached an all-time low of 24¼ cents per fine ounce (1/85 of the price of gold) late in December 1932 and then turned upward early the following year under the influence of rumors about policies to be adopted by the new Administration.

The congressional silver block made its influence felt. In December 1933, under authority of the Thomas Amendment, enacted in May, President Roosevelt proclaimed what amounted to a buying price of 64.64 cents per fine ounce for all newly mined domestic silver. A Silver Purchase Act was enacted in June 1934. One strange argument used in favor of it had been that it would benefit China by raising the value of her monetary standard, increase her national purchasing power, and stimulate Chinese-American trade. Leaving him considerable discretion

---

of Pennsylvania Press, 1939, pp. 108-109. Not only exchange speculators but also reputable economists worried in 1933 about the possibility of inflation in the United States. Eleanor Lansing Dulles wrote *The Dollar, the Franc and Inflation*, New York: Macmillan, 1933, to warn against inflation by drawing parallels between apparent American trends and French experiences during the 1920s. Also see James W. Angell, "Exchange Depreciation, Foreign Trade and National Welfare," *Proceedings of the Academy of Political Science*, XV, June 1933, pp. 295-296.

[40] Anderson, *op. cit.*, p. 330.

[41] Gilbert, *op. cit.*, p. 110.

[42] *Nurkse, op. cit.*, p. 123n.

[43] Harris, *op. cit.*, pp. 13-14.

[44] This section draws facts from L. Y. Shen, *China's Currency Reform: A Historical Survey*, Shanghai: Mercury, 1941; Hudson, *op. cit.*, pp. 257-266; Paris, *op. cit.*, chap. III; and John Parke Young, *The International Economy*, New York: Ronald, 1942, chap. 24. Monthly and annual average exchange rates are from Federal Reserve, *Banking and Monetary Statistics*, p. 667.

as to where and when and at what prices to buy, the Act directed the Secretary of the Treasury to buy silver at home or abroad until either the price had risen to $1.29 an ounce or silver had come to make up one-fourth by value of the government's total gold and silver stock. A 50-percent tax was levied on profits from speculative transactions in silver. Silver exports were made subject to license. In August, privately owned silver bullion in the United States, with certain exceptions in favor of the industries and arts, was "nationalized" at 50.01 cents an ounce.

During 1935, further policy developments and expectations about them caused a series of speculative upheavals on the world silver market. The world price, the U.S. Treasury's buying price, and expectations about that price all interacted upwards. Late in April a slide began after it became apparent that the Treasury would not continue raising its price. When a market crisis developed in July, apparently because of bearish speculation, the Treasury responded with heavier purchases. A slight reduction in the Treasury's buying price in mid-August caused speculative panic and again prodded the Treasury into large remedial purchases. Later the Treasury slackened its buying.

The world price was down to about 45 cents by early 1936 and to about 35 cents in 1939, before recovering during the war. Meanwhile, the high domestic support price had caused the physical volume of American silver production to triple between the ends of 1933 and 1936. The domestic price was cut in December 1937 and then raised again by a law of July 1939. (The Silver Purchase Act of July 1946 raised the price to 90.5 cents an ounce for domestic and foreign silver alike. The open-market price hovered close to this figure until late in 1961. By then, the Treasury had been selling silver for some time to hold the price *down*. Discontinuance of Treasury sales at this fixed price allowed a rise until a silver dollar was worth a full dollar as bullion. Steps begun in 1963 and 1964 very much reduced the monetary role of silver, and silver dollars practically disappeared from circulation into hoards.)

The vicissitudes of American silver policy had particularly sharp repercussions on China. The price of silver had sagged in world markets after 1929, accentuating a decline already under way before. The foreign-exchange value of the Chinese silver yuan had moved in sympathy, depreciating from a yearly average of 56.9 cents in 1925 and 50.0 cents in 1926 to 41.9 cents in 1929 and 21.7 cents in the trough year of 1932. As late as the time of the London Economic Conference in 1933, Chinese representatives considered this severe depreciation upsetting to their country's trade and were eager for measures to prevent its resumption, though they were not looking for the sharp appreciation soon to be engineered by the United States. Actually, the inflow of increasingly cheap silver to the Chinese cities from the provinces and from abroad had been swelling bank reserves and contributing to a mildly inflationary boom from about 1926 on. This boom continued for some two years after the start of the world depression in 1929; the abundance of its depreciating silver-standard currency insulated China from the contagion of worldwide deflation. In the words of the special economic adviser to the Nanking government, "China benefited substantially in 1930 and 1931 from the fact that the depreciation of silver in terms of gold was saving her from currency deflation. . . ."[45] Business activity held up rather well.

China's two years of prosperity in the face of world depression and the reversal that took place in the second half of 1931 both illustrate the essentially monetary nature of boom and depression. Beginning towards the end of 1931, as England, India, Japan, and other countries left the gold standard, including the United States in 1933, China's silver currency appreciated against the currencies of the countries with which she traded. The yuan's monthly average quotation more than doubled from a low of 19.5 U.S. cents in December 1932 to a high of 41.1 cents in May 1935. As the price of silver rose abroad, arbitrageurs demanded redemption

---
[45] Sir Arthur Salter's report to the government, February 1934, quoted in Hodson, *op. cit.*, p. 259. Also see Salter, "China and Silver," *Economic Forum*, II, Spring 1934, Section II (Supplement), esp. pp. 3-8, 48, 108.

of Chinese paper currency to obtain silver for export. Withdrawals depleted Chinese bank reserves. Money became scarce, credit tightened, prices fell, banks and other businesses failed, and trade stagnated.

The American silver purchase program did not originate these trends, but it prolonged and intensified them. Several times during 1934 the Chinese government reminded the United States about the consequences of the program. In September the Chinese Finance Ministry prohibited until further notice "purchases and sales of foreign exchange . . . except for the purpose of financing (1) legitimate and normal business requirements, (2) contracts entered into on or before September 8, 1934, and (3) reasonable traveling or other personal requirements."[46] This order failed to stop the outflow of silver. In October, after the reply to their latest protest had made the Chinese see the uselessness of trying to sway the United States, the government imposed a 10-percent export tax on silver, together with an equalization charge varying with the world price of silver and intended to be prohibitive. The yuan then fell briefly by some 13 or 14 percent in relation to sterling. In effect China had been forced off the silver standard as far as the foreign-exchange value of her currency was concerned. Internally, however, the deflation continued, since the link with the world silver market had not been cut completely. Hoarding went on in expectation that the currency would be devalued or the silver export restrictions relaxed. The continuing rise in the world silver price was still making itself felt. In Shen's picturesque words, "crafty methods of smuggling silver out of China were incessantly employed by unprincipled miscreants."[47] Between November 1934 and May 1935 the monthly average quotation of the yuan in U.S. cents rose by 23 percent. China was beset with "extreme contraction of currency and credit, rising interest rates and falling commodity prices, declining value of real estate and securities, and widespread business failure and unemployment." In

short, the situation became "most critical" in 1935.[48]

The decline in the world price of silver and the exchange value of the yuan after April 1935 gave the Chinese economy some but not enough relief. During the autumn rumors recurred that China would still more completely leave the silver standard. Finally, on November 3, the government announced an irredeemable paper currency. The government banks were to deal on the market to stabilize the foreign-exchange value of the Chinese yuan at the existing level, slightly over 40 percent of its 1929 gold value. Monetary deflation was stopped and reversed; business activity improved. Hong Kong followed the Chinese reform in November and December 1935 by embargoing exports of silver coins and bullion and setting up an exchange fund to regulate the external value of the currency.

Besides China, other countries in several continents were inconvenienced when, by early 1935, the bullion values of their silver coins had either risen above their face values or seemed likely soon to do so. Mexico, Costa Rica, Peru, Colombia, Danzig, Persia, and the Straits Settlements, among others, made preparations to replace their silver coins and save them from the melting pot. Ironically enough from the standpoint of silver producers, these measures, and therefore the American policy that had led to them, tended to reduce the world's monetary use of silver.

In summary, a clumsy U.S. silver policy seriously inconvenienced a number of countries. China particularly suffered—and at a time, incidentally, when the friendly Nanking government was still insecure and was having difficulty with the Japanese and with communists at home. The nature of the turmoil on the world silver market showed once again how important it is to be clear whether notable episodes of speculative instability reflect the play of decentralized private supply and demand or instead reflect the destabilizing dominance of official transactions and of changing rumors about them.

[46] Shen, *op. cit.*, p. 83.
[47] *Ibid.*, p. 89.
[48] *Ibid.*, p. 91.

Further Currency Experience in the 1930s

✐ 17

Early Struggles of the Gold Bloc

After the widespread depreciations of 1931 and especially after the American devaluation of 1933–1934, the currencies of France, Switzerland, Belgium, the Netherlands, Luxembourg, Italy, Poland, and the Free City of Danzig were still on gold but clearly overvalued. Some of these countries, notably France and Belgium, had returned to the gold standard in the later 1920s at new parities that undervalued their currencies. Protected by the resulting lowness of her prices relative to world prices, France in particular enjoyed a "golden glow" of remarkable immunity to the world depression for its first year or two. French industrial production stayed practically as high in 1930 as in 1929 and in 1931 was down by only 13 or 14 percent. (U.S. industrial production, by contrast, dropped 31 percent from 1929 to 1931.) Though the current-account surplus gave way to a deficit in 1931 and afterwards, the inflow of gold continued to mount for a while, reaching levels of 18.5 billion francs (over $700 million) in each of the years 1931 and 1932. French banks were continuing to repatriate their balances held abroad, and flight capital was flowing in from abroad.[1] After foreign devaluations had raised the relative value of the franc, deflationary pressures began operating through the balance of payments.

The "gold bloc" was formalized during the London Economic Conference in July 1933, when the chief European gold-standard countries signed pledges to stay on gold at existing parities. At a conference in Geneva in September 1934, the gold countries declared themselves more determined than ever to defend their parities. To do so, they had to endure depression well after recovery had begun elsewhere. Experiences with inflation and currency depreciation suffered only a few years before bolstered the notion that the gold standard spelled safety. Actually, internal economic difficulties that in themselves stemmed largely from prolonged deflation—stagnant trade, strikes, budget deficits, weak credit reputations—contributed to the menace of speculative flights from their currencies.

The struggles of France will serve as representative for those of the whole group. In response to the falling prices and increasing imports that confronted French industries, quantitative import limitations were imposed in 1931 as emergency measures. At first the quotas were mainly on farm products, but as the franc became more and more overvalued, quota protection was extended. By 1934 over half the items in the French tariff list were subject to quotas; imports of many items were restricted to less than half the predepression quantities. Internal price deflation also seemed necessary. Wholesale prices in mid-1935 averaged barely more than half of their 1929 level. Farmers especially suffered from the low level of prices. Wages fell and unemployment rose moderately.

Reduced incomes and tax yields created a deficit in the French government budget, which was regretted as a sign that deflationary public finance had to press still further if earlier efforts to save the franc were not to prove in vain. None of the French govern-

[1] William H. Wynne, "The French Franc, June, 1928—February, 1937," *Journal of Political Economy*, XLV, August 1937, esp. pp. 489-493.

ments or parties dared question the goal of a balanced budget. "What we now call 'deficit financing' was then known as 'national bankruptcy.' "[2] The Budget Bill of March 1934 authorized the government of the venerable Gaston Doumergue, who had come out of political retirement to form a "Cabinet of National Union," to impose economies by decree. Government jobs and salaries and even veterans' pensions were cut. Yet a continued drop in revenue outstripped the saving in expenditure; new issues of government securities brought in barely enough funds to keep abreast of old issues falling due.

Discontent with the deflation policy and wrangles over a proposed constitutional reform overthrew the Doumergue government in November 1934. The finance minister of the old government remained in the new one, trying as vigorously as ever to defend the existing gold parity. However, the new premier, Pierre Flandin, apparently had some notion that deflation of prices of final goods had gone far enough and that production might now be made profitable by reduction of costs. His government began gradually relaxing state support of wheat prices and at the same time undertook to restrict planting and adopt oher expedients to deal with wheat surpluses. In January 1935 an industrial-cartellization bill was enacted reminiscent of the American NRA: self-regulation in industry was to be reinforced by law. One of the objects of the new law was to spread employment by shortening the work week, cutting out overtime, and raising the age for leaving school. Steps taken toward the end of 1934 and early in 1935 to lower interest rates formed another recovery measure. The government tried to switch from long-term to short-term borrowing to lessen its competition with private business in bidding for long-term capital. A forced change in its governors made the Bank of France somewhat less reluctant than before to absorb Treasury bills. In the Chamber of Deputies, Paul Reynaud, who had previously urged devaluation, again insisted on a choice be-

tween devaluation and deflation and warned that Flandin's interest-rate policy would tend to raise prices and worsen the overvaluation of the franc. Not much came from Flandin's mild attempt at reflation on the gold standard. Even the lowering of long-term interest rates proved only temporary.[3]

First Cracks in the Gold Bloc

What menaced the French gold standard was not so much actual balance-of-payments deficits as the threat of potential capital flight, a threat intensified by the Belgian devaluation of March 1935. The current-account deficit was shrinking steadily from 1932 to 1935,[4] and in 1934 the Bank of France had actually gained gold and foreign exchange reserves. None of this, however, means that the franc was not overvalued after all, since the balance-of-payments and reserve positions were being maintained by internal deflation and import controls.

The smaller gold countries were less fortunate: Switzerland, the Netherlands, and Belgium were losing gold. Though her remaining gold reserves were still well above the minimum legal requirement, Belgium was generally considered the financially weakest member of the group. She was suffering from unemployment and from a collapse of the international trade on which her economy had so heavily depended; between 1929 and 1934 imports had fallen from 35.6 to 14 billion francs and exports from 31.9 to 13.7 billion francs.[5] Public confidence in the banking system was shaky. The belga (a unit worth five Belgian francs, introduced in 1926 for exchange-market purposes to emphasize the independence of the Belgian currency from the then unstable French franc) was subject to bear speculation. Rumors of devaluation and the consequent capital outflow became particularly intense in November 1934, but loans from American, Dutch, and Swiss banks saved the situation for the time being. A slump in the exchange

[2] Martin Wolfe, *The French Franc between the Wars, 1919–1939*, New York Columbia University Press, 1951, p. 105.

[3] H. V. Hodson, *Slump and Recovery,* London: Oxford University Press, 1938, pp. 364-368.

[4] See table in Wolfe, *op. cit.,* p. 218.

[5] Walter A. Morton, *British Finance, 1930–1940*, Madison: University of Wisconsin Press, 1943, p. 157.

value of the British pound late in February and early March 1935 thrust a fresh crisis upon the gold countries. Further rumors touched off a new bear attack, and on March 17 the government centralized control over all foreign-exchange operations and bullion dealings and forbade noncommercial sales of belgas. Next the cabinet resigned, saying it did not have the overwhelming parliamentary support necessary for successful defense of the currency. The belga weakened on the exchanges while a new coalition was being put together. The impact of increased British tariffs on iron and steel products largely imported from Belgium, the perilous state of the banks, and the impracticality of further deflation and wage cuts combined to force a decision. The new premier, Paul van Zeeland, had been in office only a few days at the end of March 1935 before announcing a devaluation, whose extent was soon afterwards specified as 28 percent. The government reaffirmed belief in gold-standard principles and called (in vain) for an international conference to consider general restabilization of currencies. Belgian economic conditions improved over the next two years, but it is difficult to measure the role of the devaluation in this recovery. A royal decree of March 31, 1936 reestablished the gold standard at the new devalued parity.

The fall of the belga renewed bearishness on the currencies of the Netherlands, Switzerland, Italy, and France. Danzig devalued by 42 percent on May 2, 1935. To meet a gold drain, the Dutch authorities introduced legislation to cut state expenditure and raised the discount rate of the Netherlands Bank. The leading commercial banks were asked to prevent speculation against the guilder, to assure customers that the currency was in no danger, and to keep from expressing doubts about Holland's ability to stay on gold. At the expense of continued internal economic stagnation, the guilder weathered attacks against it in April and May and again in July 1935. Even the Swiss franc, which had a metallic backing of over 100 percent at the end of 1934, came under bear attack after the Belgian devaluation. In May 1935 the forward quotation on the Swiss franc in terms

of sterling fell to a discount of 28 percent a year. Swiss authorities raised the discount rate, asked commercial banks to withhold credit from hoarders of goods, gold or foreign exchange, and called for penalties on persons contributing toward depreciation of the currency. By June 1935, the run on the Swiss franc subsided.

In France, Premier Flandin denied any tie between the French and Belgian currencies. Early in April his government announced that it would mint gold coins to insure confidence in the franc (though a delay of perhaps a few years was likely before enough coins would be ready for circulation and though the coinage was bound to trench upon official gold reserves). His compromise policy of trying to combine cheaper credit with budgetary deflation to defend the franc was failing. The Bank of France raised its discount rate three times in close succession toward the end of May 1935. Budget deficits were continuing to undermine confidence. Despite a technically strong banking position and a gold reserve that would ordinarily have been ample, a run on the franc was in full swing in May and June. On one day in May the discount on three months forward francs in London touched 40 percent a year.[6] The "speculators" who were blamed for these troubles were by no means professionals only, but included ordinary French and foreign businessmen trying to get rid of francs out of ordinary prudence. After being refused power to decree further government economies, Flandin resigned on May 31. His successor survived in office less than four days.

Renewed Attempts at Price Deflation in France

On June 8, 1935, Pierre Laval's new government obtained from Parliament the very emergency powers denied to its predecessors. Trying to balance the budget, Laval raised some taxes and decreed a 10-percent reduction in practically all payments made by the government, including subsidies, salaries (not

---

[6] Bank for International Settlements, 6th *Annual Report* (1935–1936), p. 12. Hodson, *op. cit.,* pp. 369-377, provides many of the other facts above.

only in government employment but even in some subsidized private enterprises), pensions, and interest on domestically held government securities, which spelled partial repudiation of a government contract. (Some exceptions were made for hardship cases, such as those involving the pensions of totally disabled veterans and the salaries of the lowest-paid government employees.) Thousands of government employees and unemployed workers rioted in Paris against these cutbacks. Other decrees attempted to deflate prices in the private economy. All rents were cut by 10 percent. Landlords were allowed a 10-percent cut in interest payable on mortgages. Prices of gas, electricity, bread, and fertilizer were reduced. By the time his special powers expired in October, Laval had issued no less than 549 decree-laws, some of them interfering with private contracts to a degree unprecedented outside totalitarian countries. Whatever the reasons may be, the country did enjoy a brief calm; the Bank of France regained some of its lost reserves, and signs of slow economic recovery were noted. Some economic logic actually can be claimed for Laval's program. If defending the exchange rate rules out monetary expansion to promote recovery from depression— if domestic purchasing power must not be expanded by increasing the number of francs in circulation—then the next best approach is to expand total real purchasing power by raising the purchasing power of each existing franc. Given the number of money units in circulation, it is price-and-wage cuts rather than price-and-wage increases that will tend to promote recovery. Laval's program was roughly the opposite of NRA in the United States, and it made better theoretical sense. The mistake was insistence on doing things the hard way.

Actually, France under Laval was inconsistently deflating and reflating both at the same time. While cutting ordinary budget expenditure, his government was incurring heavy extrabudgetary charges for armaments and public works and was borrowing not only from the public but also from the Bank of France. By the end of 1935 the public debt was 338 billion francs, up 64 billions since 1931. Forty percent of all budget expenditure went to service the national debt, and another 20 percent went for military expenses and pensions.[7] By January 1936 Laval was unwilling to push economy any further and was under fire for the Hoare-Laval proposals to appease Italy in Ethiopia. His resignation created another run on the franc. His successor tried to carry on until the election of a new Chamber of Deputies. During this interlude, on March 7, Hitler reoccupied the Rhineland. The expenses that mobilization would have entailed figured among the reasons for French vacillation at this time.

Italy and Poland Off Gold

Italy's currency policy during the mid-1930s contrasted with that of other members of the gold bloc. Step by step Italy left any semblance of a real gold standard. Although decrees had cut prices and wages, deflation by credit restriction had not been used up to 1934. Public-works spending was contributing to a budget deficit. A fall almost to the legal minimum in the gold reserve ratio of the central bank promoted capital flight and prompted action to defend the balance of payments. The Bank of Italy already had a practical monopoly of exchange transactions. In April 1934 imports of copper, coffee, and wool were subjected to licensing, which would be administered to affect trade with particular countries. A rise in the Bank of Italy's discount rate in November was taken as a sign of threatening devaluation and accelerated the gold loss. In December 1934 Italians were required to declare their foreign securities and balances abroad in case the government should later want to requisition them. Export prices were supervised to prevent undervaluation as a device for secretly accumulating funds abroad. Quotas were used to promote bilateral balancing of imports and exports. These devices for maintaining the lira at an artificial parity meant that Italy had in practice left the gold bloc and was to be classified with exchange-control countries such as Germany. Government control over

---

[7] Wynne, *op. cit.*, p. 504; Wolfe, *op. cit.*, p. 116.

the Italian internal economy and over the foreign exchanges (with requisitioning of privately held foreign securities) was further extended in 1935, especially after the invasion of Ethiopia and the voting of sanctions by the League of Nations that fall.

Poland never had been considered a full-fledged member of the gold bloc. In April 1936 she unmistakably left it by abolishing free dealings in gold and instituting exchange control. The old parity of the zloty was kept, but it had become artificial.

France in 1936

In 1936 the spotlight was back on France.[8] A rather detailed survey is necessary as background for appraisal of the supposed lessons of the ensuing currency experiences. Price deflation had run its course by mid-1935 but still had not cured the overvaluation of the franc. It was even worsening: in the six months between September 1935 and March 1936, the wholesale price level rose by nearly 10 percent. Political developments pushed toward a climax. Elections in May gave the Popular Front a majority in the Chamber of Deputies, and at the beginning of June the Socialist Leon Blum formed a Communist-supported ministry. A wave of sitdown strikes by triumphant workers ended with the government-sponsored "Matignon agreement" of June 8, in which employers accepted collective bargaining and granted wage increases, shorter hours, and fringe benefits—all pushing up production costs. Premier Blum's legislative proposals dealt with public works, farm price supports, nationalization of the armaments industry, reorganization of the Bank of France in the direction of ultimate nationalization, a rise in the age for leaving school, vacations with pay, promotion of collective bargaining, a 40-hour work week with no cut in weekly wages, and modification of Laval's salary and pension cuts. (Blum argued that higher wages would mean increased purchasing power and so benefit the whole nation.) Later he intended to enact a scheme of old-age pensions, further measures to deal with unemployment, and tax reform at the expense of inherited wealth.

Given the increased spending and higher costs and prices that this program involved, it was natural to expect an accompanying devaluation of the franc. Paul Reynaud once again warned that delay would make matters all the more difficult. Even some persons who until then had wanted to stay on gold by means of deflation, such as the statesmen Caillaux and Germain Martin and the economist Charles Rist, now called for devaluation in one guise or another. Blum's finance minister, Vincent Auriol, a former advocate of devaluation, had changed his mind in the opposite direction, however, and now argued against the step lest it lead other countries to devalue in retaliation and tend to raise internal prices without guaranteeing an improvement in foreign trade. He attacked persons who called devaluation "inevitable" and castigated "traitors" secretly holding funds abroad.

Premier Blum hoped for some kind of reflation on the gold standard. Despite economic realities emphasized by his critics, he found reasons for still giving assurances against devaluation. His Communist supporters suspected that devaluation would raise the cost of living and rob workers of their recent gains. Besides, they were not particularly concerned about the health of a capitalist economy. Second, his Popular Front had made campaign promises against devaluation. Finally, Blum feared that devaluation would be fruitless and dangerous unless in accord with some sort of international agreement.

Assurances and exhortations apparently had some brief success. During the summer the franc rallied on the exchanges, the capital outflow abated, and in July the Bank of France even regained some gold. More fundamental conditions determined that this improvement in confidence could be only temporary. Measures were either in effect or in preparation to raise wages and grant fringe benefits, to expand public works, to support wheat prices, and to bring the Bank of France (which was not merely the central bank but also a commercial bank with hundreds of offices) more nearly under gov-

[8] Cf. Wolfe, *op. cit.*, pp. 138-145, 156-158; Hodson, *op. cit.*, pp. 403-414; Wynne, *op. cit.*, pp. 504-510.

ernment control. Under a new governor, the Bank repeatedly cut its discount and loan rates in the first few weeks after the Blum government took office. Unaccompanied by devaluation, however, the government's attempts to promote business recovery failed in almost every sector of the economy. By August the industrial production index had sagged as low as in the worst months of 1932 and 1935. Unemployment grew. Yet, paradoxically for a time of stagnant production, wholesale prices soared almost 25 percent from June to October 1936; "reflation" was being absorbed in higher prices rather than in general business revival. International developments in 1936 contributed to nervousness: Germany remilitarized the Rhineland in March; Italy completed its conquest of Ethiopia in May, marking the end of the League of Nations as an instrument for collective security; and the Spanish Civil War started in July.

In the midst of these disturbances, during the summer of 1936, the government was having familiar difficulties in paying its bills. It sought a credit at the Bank of France, intending not to draw on it if an issue of one-year and six-month "baby bonds" sold well. The issue was floated in July, bearing interest rates of 3.5 and 4 percent, which would have been attractive to British and American investors but for the risk of loss on depreciation of the franc. Subscriptions were disappointing.

By late summer, the respite was over. The government vainly tried to check the outward seepage of capital. A law of August 13 supplemented earlier measures for registering the export of securities and declaring capital held abroad. Buying foreign banknotes was restricted, sale of gold coin was virtually forbidden, and travelers had to declare any precious metals being taken out of the country. It is noteworthy, however, that the Blum government never did impose full-fledged exchange control. Punishment was provided for spreading rumors to shake confidence in the currency and for inciting withdrawal of deposits or sales of government securities, though advocacy of devaluation in good faith was not forbidden.

Further blows to confidence came in September: strikes in the textile industry brought wage increases, and a League of Nations report cited the disparity between internal and external currency values as the greatest obstacle in the way of worldwide recovery and hinted in favor of devaluation of the gold-bloc currencies. The spot exchange value of the franc was still pegged (by gold outflows amounting to $320 million worth between August 7 and September 25), but the forward quotation gave a truer picture: the discount on forward three-month francs at times reached 37 or 38 percent a year. A rise from 3 to 5 percent in Bank rate on September 24, reversing Blum's cheap-credit policy, was taken as indicating not strength but desperation in the face of gold losses. On the next day, rumors drove the discount on forward francs to a level said to represent an approximately even bet on devaluation by 25 percent within three months.

French Devaluation and Its Repercussions

Late on September 25, in almost identical statements released in Paris, London, and Washington, the three governments announced a devaluation of the franc. (The three statements are reprinted at the end of the 7th *Annual Report* (1936–1937) of the Bank for International Settlements.) Though intergovernmental negotiations had been going on for several months, the secret had been well kept. The devaluation apparently surprised the many Frenchmen who had come to trust Premier Blum's guarantees against it. Some earlier statements of the Premier and the Finance Minister had, it is true, listed possible international complications among the reasons for not devaluing, and the French government could now claim that intergovernmental agreement to avoid these complications had changed the situation. In fact, this public-relations aspect, rather than any substantive provisions, was probably the chief purpose of the so-called Tripartite Monetary Agreement. In the joint announcement, the British and U.S. governments "welcomed" the "readjustment" of the franc, promised to avoid disturbing responses to it, barred competitive exchange depreciation, called for relaxation of trade and exchange restrictions, and invited other nations to join in similar pledges. By late in November 1936, Belgium, Holland, and Switzerland had adhered to the agreement. Supplements to the original declaration provided for convertibility of the franc, pound, and dollar at fixed prices prevailing from day to day, thus creating a sort of new gold bloc on a 24-hour basis.

Parliament ratified the devaluation by law on October 1. The Bank of France no longer had to redeem its notes in gold bullion, though the franc was still defined as a gold currency. The cabinet was to fix its new gold content at somewhere between 25.2 and 34.4 percent below the old. When the exchange markets reopened, the franc settled at not quite 4.7 U.S. cents, representing a devaluation of about 30 percent. The Exchange Stabilization Fund set up by the new law supported the franc at this level until late in March 1937. Under the law, private holders of gold were not to profit from the devaluation: they could either sell their gold to the Bank of France at the old rate or hold it and pay the government the amount of increase in its franc value. Undeclared gold could be confiscated. In fact, this provision was neither obeyed nor enforced.[9]

The story so far shows how much economic misery and political turmoil over several years stemmed from the inappropriateness of one single pegged price—that of the French franc. This sacred price, so long and painfully defended, finally had to be adjusted anyway. The final step was brought on not by a massive actual deficit in the balance of payments nor by exhaustion of gold reserves but by a flight from the franc. Perhaps the flight might have been weathered for some time, or even temporarily checked again, but the necessary measures no longer seemed worthwhile. The flight was likely to recur from time to time as long as French political and economic disorder undermined confidence and, in particular, as long as the opinion prevailed that the franc was overvalued.

The French franc pulled other currencies down with it. The Swiss Federal Council met in emergency session on Saturday morning, September 26, and announced that the Swiss franc would *not* be devalued; the Councilors apparently felt that Switzerland faced no such special necessity for devaluation as France had faced. But heavy gold losses prompted a reversal that same afternoon, and the following day the Federal Council instructed the National Bank to cut the gold content of the Swiss franc by between 25.9 and 34.6 percent. The final devaluation, like the French, amounted to about 30 percent. The Swiss decision caused the Dutch government to reverse its initial decision the same day, the 26th; for Holland, with the only important currency still on its predepression gold basis, would have faced unbearable pressure. The government embargoed gold exports, saying ironically that it did so "to prevent being forced to abandon the gold standard."[10] No definite margin of devaluation was set, but a newly established equalization fund kept the exchange rate against the dollar in the vicinity of 20 percent below the old parity. The currency of the Dutch East Indies followed that of the mother country. The Italian lira was already so much subject to exchange control as not to be genuinely on the gold standard. Nevertheless, it was devalued on October 5 to 59.06 percent of its former gold content—a degree of devaluation identical, significantly, to that of the United States dollar in 1934. This step must have been embarrassing to Mussolini, who, in a speech at Pesaro in 1926, had sworn to defend the lira to the last drop of blood and had ordered his words graven in stone. The Czechoslovak crown, which had already been devalued by 16⅔ percent in February 1934, was cut again by from 13 to 19 percent, or to between 28 and 32 percent below its pre-1934 gold content. Latvia devalued by about 40 percent, reestablishing its pre-1931 parity with sterling. Some currencies previously linked to the French franc, such as those of Greece and Turkey, now linked themselves to sterling. Despite rumors of devaluation of the Reichsmark, the German authorities decided

---

[9] Wolfe, *op. cit.*, pp. 146-147.

[10] Hodson, *op. cit.*, p. 418.

against passively following in a move on which they had not been consulted. Anyway, Germany already had multiple exchange rates and comprehensive exchange controls. The only country remaining on gold at the pre-depression parity and without exchange controls was now Albania. From the start, the currency adjustments of 1936 involved much more official intervention in exchange markets and much more management of the rates than had been undertaken in the early months of wide fluctuations after the wave of depreciation in 1931.

Further Weakness and the Floating Franc

The new pattern of exchange rates soon came under renewed strain. Not enough refugee capital returned to France to save the franc from occasional weakness, especially in the forward quotations. A moderate and spotty increase in production in France after the devaluation faded in the spring of 1937. A drop in unemployment was due less to the devaluation than to the work-spreading 40-hour law. Retail and wholesale prices continued rising. All through January and February 1937 Finance Minister Auriol repeated assurances against further devaluation and waged a campaign against rumors. The discount rate of the Bank of France, which had been lowered after the devaluation, was raised again on January 28, but without checking speculative pressure. On the 29th the Stabilization Fund revealed that it had kept the franc pegged only by using its entire allotment of gold, and now it had to borrow more gold from the Bank of France. In February, for the sake of businessmen's confidence, Blum announced a "pause" in further social and economic reform. Some fiscal retrenchment was undertaken. Free trade in gold was reestablished, and the earlier law against undeclared gold holdings was reversed. Blum was determined to maintain a free foreign-exchange market.

Around the beginning of April, the Exchange Stabilization Fund, now managed by a committee of monetary experts, relaxed the peg. The franc soon sank to the minimum support level specified in the law of October 1, or to some 6 percent below the preceding support level and about 34 percent below the old gold parity.

Renewed difficulties for the Exchange Stabilization Fund provoked further capital flight in May 1937. By this time, government promises of no further devaluation only made the speculators more suspicious. The balance of payments on current account was also taking a turn for the worse. The export stimulus of the devaluation was being offset by higher labor costs and general distrust. Earnings from tourism, though improved, were still well below the levels of 1925–1931, and other invisible exports also responded poorly. On the import side, quota and tariff restrictions had been liberalized soon after the first devaluation. The current-account deficit, measured in billions of francs of the gold content of the 1928 law, rose from 0.8 in 1935 to 2.9 in 1936 and to 4.0 in 1937.[11]

By mid-June 1937, the discount on forward francs exceeded 35 percent a year. During June the Stabilization Fund and the Bank of France lost about $350 million worth of gold in resisting speculative attacks. The government, in familiar domestic financial difficulties, had to arrange for interest-free and other loans directly from the Bank of France. Blum resigned on June 21 after being refused emergency decree-making powers to deal with the financial panic.

A second Popular Front government was formed on June 24, with the more moderate Radical-Socialists under Camille Chautemps replacing the Socialists in predominance. Chautemps obtained, until the end of August, the decree-making powers denied to Blum. A decree-law of June 30, 1937 cut the franc from any specific support limits, leaving the Exchange Stabilization Fund now committed only to what Finance Minister Bonnet called a "mobile defense of the franc." The Americans and British had approved what they regarded as a forced rather than a competitive depreciation.

Bear attacks on the floating franc grew intense in September 1937. The Stabilization Fund, retreating from a support level that

[11] Wolfe, *op. cit.,* pp. 154-155, 218.

it had held for about six weeks, allowed the franc to slip almost down to half of its pre-1936 gold value. A reassuring official declaration of rather conservative tone, together with an influx of funds into France following the New York Stock Market crash in the fall of 1937, then came to the rescue. The Stabilization Fund was able to keep the franc steady in November and December, and the discount on the forward franc narrowed. But France entered 1938 in renewed political and economic turmoil. The continuing rise in French prices and the worldwide business recession hampered exports. Disagreement over how to handle a wave of sit-down strikes led in January to organization of a third Popular Front government, with Chautemps still premier and with Blum and other Socialists completely out of the cabinet. Government finances and the exchange value of the franc continued deteriorating. Parliament refused Chautemps new decree-making powers. Hitler annexed Austria. The fourth and last Popular Front government, formed by Blum on March 13, 1938, lasted only one month.

Edouard Daladier put together a new government drawn from the moderate Radical-Socialists and parties on the Right. Armed with decree-making powers, Daladier announced on May 4 that the franc would be fixed at about 179 to the pound sterling and further depreciation stopped. This retreat to a level which, as Daladier hoped, could be "defended victoriously" amounted to a devaluation against the dollar of some 37 or 38 percent below the level prevailing just before the franc was unpegged on June 30, 1937. In terms of gold, the franc was now worth only 42 percent of its value of before September 1936 and only 8½ percent of its value before World War I.[12] Thus eroded, the franc was successfully stabilized in relation to sterling until the outbreak of World War II. During the winter of 1938–1939, for the first time in several years, France experienced a sustained homecoming (chiefly from Engflight. Sterling itself declined against the dolland) of funds that had previously taken

lar during the war scares of 1938, however, and the franc went along, sinking from an average of 2.81 U.S. cents in May 1938 to 2.63 cents in November. It held near that level until the war.

The vicissitudes of the French exchange rate occurred against a background of domestic failure on the part of the Blum government and its successors. Even when the brief business recovery of the spring of 1937 had carried practically to full employment, industrial production was well below predepression levels. This anomaly stemmed from near-stagnation in population growth, a back-to-the-farm movement during the depression, and the legally imposed 40-hour work week; between 1929 and 1937, total hours worked in industry had fallen by one-third. On the eve of World War II, France was less of a manufacturing nation and more of a rural nation than it had been during the 1920s. With qualifications about the problems of comparison over a long time span, it even seems that the level of French industrial production just before World War II was not much greater than just before World War I. Other aspects of the Popular Front program also proved disappointing, including the quasi-nationalization of the Bank of France and the nationalization of the railroads and some heavy industry. Lack of confidence hampered business investment.

A Closer Look at the Floating Franc

It is during this period, specifically, between the unpegging of the franc on June 30, 1937 and the repegging on May 4, 1938, that the author of the influential *International Currency Experience* finds his fourth historical example of the speculative disorders supposed generally to characterize fluctuating exchange rates.[13] But the origin and special features of the situation should be remembered. The unpegging of June 1937 had been preceded by heavy bear speculation on the pegged franc during 1936 and earlier and then, in violation of repeated promises, by the devaluation in September. After this, despite

---

[12] *Ibid.*, p. 181.

[13] Ragnar Nurkse, pp. 118, 120, 123.

inducements to repatriate capital and more assurances against another devaluation, the expected large-scale reversal of capital flight did not occur. The growing danger of war, alarm at Popular Front policies, the continual rise in wages and prices, the sluggishness of industrial recovery, the deteriorating balance of payments, and fears of another devaluation all sapped confidence. The Exchange Stabilization Fund had to keep selling gold and foreign exchange to support the franc, and even after its forced retreat to a lower support level in March 1937, the fund kept on losing gold. Finally, on June 30, the franc was completely cut from gold, and discretionary intervention replaced support within specified limits.

This unpegging of the franc came, significantly, as a last resort, after efforts to hold it steady had collapsed the previous September and had collapsed again in March. Even during the period of the floating franc, exchange rates were not left to private supply and demand alone. The French Fund, sometimes helped by the British Exchange Equalisation Account, intervened in the market from time to time, losing gold in costly efforts to sustain the franc.[14] During the fall of 1937, clues to the fund's gains and losses of gold appeared in the weekly balance sheets of the Bank of France. Gold losses, thus publicized, tended to intensify capital flight by showing that the franc would have been still weaker if it had not been for the official support. Bear speculators profitably knew that any change in the support level would very probably be downwards rather than upwards. Yet complete secrecy about the fund's operations might not have helped much; as long as some kind of official intervention was known to be taking place from time to time, guesses about the intentions of the authorities would have furnished material for rumors and speculation.

In short, the experiences of France in 1937-

1938 have little to do with *freely* fluctuating exchange rates. They are probably less relevant as evidence against that system than as evidence against the adjustable peg.

A Review of Four Historical Examples

Now that we have met with this last, in historical order, of Nurkse's horrible examples of speculation (the others were France in 1922–1926, Britain in 1931–1932, and the United States in 1933–1934), it is appropriate to make some summarizing comments on all four of them. The examples suggest, at most, that fluctuating rates do not work well when exchange-rate pegging does not work at all and has in fact broken down. The examples are instructive in showing some of the conditions that do give rise to actually or apparently disruptive speculation: domestic inflation and disordered government finances; the shock of suddenly unpegging a previously overvalued currency under attack by bear speculation, and the reaction from that shock; prospects for unorthodox fiscal and monetary measures, such as deliberate manipulation of the gold value of a currency as a means of influencing prices and business conditions; domestic policies regarded as hostile to business; and clumsy official intervention in the exchange market, particularly when it repeatedly presents speculators with "one-way options."

Professor Edward C. Simmons has made some pertinent comments on why historical episodes provide poor laboratory data in economics. Floating currencies have always appeared after the supposedly temporary collapse of metallic parities. History cannot tell us what would happen if countries abandoned fixed parities once and for all, stopped intervening in foreign-exchange markets, and managed money at home according to an announced rule. Eagerness to seize on history for supposed evidence against foreign-exchange speculation makes one wonder if anything can be learned from history. A "misreading of economic history . . . underlies the mistaken foreign exchange policies of the present day." It is disheartening "to think that men are so firmly set in their minds

---

[14] On official intervention during this period, see Robert Solomon, "The French Exchange Stabilization Fund," *Federal Reserve Bulletin,* January 1950, pp. 36-37, Leonard Waight, *The History and Mechanism of the Exchange Equalisation Account,* Cambridge: Cambridge University Press, 1939, pp. 109, 111, and Wolfe, *op. cit.,* pp. 178-179.

about the necessity of fixed exchange rates that they are willing to believe all sorts of distortions of past events."[15]

German Economic Nationalism[16]

The chief currencies to escape the wave of exchange depreciation in the 1930s were those of some countries in Central and Eastern Europe. Exchange control maintained predepression parities, and such currency depreciation as occurred did so in concealed forms. Germany provides the classic example of this policy. For the first two years after the start of the depression in 1929, drastic internal deflation kept the mark from becoming seriously overvalued at its fixed gold content. Monetary deflation was supplemented, under the Brüning government, by attempts to lower wages, prices, rents, and interest by administrative decree. Germany developed a "favorable" balance of trade, which grew from 36 million marks in 1929 to 1.6 billion in 1930 and 2.9 billion in 1931; in the latter year, exports, though down from predepression levels, were 43 percent in excess of the even more sharply reduced imports. This commodity export surplus reflects the capital outflow that had replaced the heavy predepression inflow.

During the international liquidity crisis of 1931, a panicky flight of capital led the German government to impose exchange control. The controls that the Nazis were later to perfect into tools for the conscious economic exploitation of foreigners thus originated earlier, as emergency expedients. In September, two months after the unilateral German action, a "Standstill Agreement" was reached with creditors in the United States, the United Kingdom, and West European countries ex-

cept Spain. This agreement, which initially applied to slightly more than one-fourth of Germany's total external debt, was continued with modifications every year until 1939. It provided for only gradual withdrawal of mark balances owned by foreigners and for extension of foreign trade credits granted to Germans. Controls and standstill arrangements thus gave rise to blocked marks, balances available only for restricted purposes. These blocked marks, bought and sold at a discount abroad, were the first of the many special types of mark later to characterize the complex German currency system.

As foreign currencies were devalued, the German mark became increasingly out of line. With a theoretically unchanged gold content, it went from a predepression parity of 23.8 U.S. cents to a new parity of just over 40 cents. Reflation and public works begun under Hitler in 1933 to remedy unemployment raised German incomes and prices and contributed to overvaluation. This was a serious handicap to a country as dependent on international trade as Germany (even in the depression year of 1931, Germany had exported over one-third of her industrial production and had depended on foreign sources for some 40 or 45 percent of her raw materials). A sizable cut in the gold value of the mark would have been necessary simply to keep pace with foreign devaluations, but considerations of prestige apparently told against this. At least in the panic conditions of mid-1931, furthermore, devaluation might have seemed a sign of weakness and have intensified attempts at capital flight. Still remembering the hyperinflation of 1923, the public tended to associate exchange depreciation with impending collapse of the currency, and businessmen feared demands that wage rates be linked to exchange rates.

The Nazi regime tightened the partial moratorium already in effect on payments of interest and principal on external debts. Effective in mid-1933, interest and dividends on foreign-held German securities could be paid only to the Conversion Office for German Foreign Debts. Up to half the amounts so paid were made available to the foreign creditors in free currency, with scrip issued

[15] "Edward C. Simmons, "Discussion," *Journal of Economic History*, **XV**, December 1955, pp. 413-414.

[16] The sections on Germany draw mainly on Ragnar Nurkse, *op. cit.*, pp. 167-183; Frank A. Southard, Jr., *Foreign Exchange Practice and Policy*, New York: McGraw-Hill, 1940, pp. 192-197; P. T. Ellsworth, *The International Economy*, New York: Macmillan, 1950, pp. 621-625, 631-641; Ralph H. Blodgett, *Comparative Economic Systems* (rev. ed.); New York: Macmillan, 1949, pp. 526-532; and Frank C. Child, *The Theory and Practice of Exchange Control in Germany*, The Hague: Martinus Nijhoff, 1958.

for the blocked remainder. The Golddiskont-bank then offered to buy the blocked marks with free currency at a discount from the mark's official value. In effect, foreigners could collect only about three-fourths of the payments due them. In 1934, when a worsening in the German balance of trade endangered the Reichsbank's gold reserves, official conversion of interest and dividend payments into free currency was suspended completely, effective on July 1. Instead, foreign creditors were offered 10-year bonds in exchange for their blocked marks. Also discontinued at this time was the arrangement whereby German sellers of so-called "additional exports" (exports considered unsalable without subsidy at official exchange rates) had been allowed to use their foreign-currency earnings to buy German securities, trading on foreign markets at severe discounts from their prices as translated at official exchange rates, in order to bring the securities home and resell them at a profit in marks. This arrangement had in effect enabled the favored German exporters to collect subsidies from foreign investors, whose German claims had been depreciated by the inconvertibility of the mark. Now, after mid-1934, "additional exports" were to be subsidized in other ways.

Blocked marks continued to be traded abroad, but only at growing discounts. Various types of blocked mark retained what value they did because the German authorities allowed their use for some purposes, primarily tourist travel in Germany, investment in German securities, and gifts to Germans, as well as for purchase of German exports when bilateral agreements with foreign countries so stipulated. The German tourist industry benefited from the cheap marks available to its foreign customers.

Not only capital movements but also trade in goods and services came under tightening control. Even before the Nazis took power, exporters had been required to sell their foreign-exchange earnings to control authorities, who supervised export transactions and export prices to prevent hidden capital transfers. Foreign exchange was rationed among importers, the allotments initially being specified percentages (successively reduced) of the amounts of foreign exchange bought by each importer in a 1930–1931 base period.

In 1932 and 1933, particularly, "private compensation" served as a means of trading under conditions of currency overvaluation and exchange control. Barter deals were at first undertaken chiefly by firms regularly engaged in both import and export business or by German firms trading with foreign subsidiaries. German exporters soon began accepting payment in foreign commodities, which they would then sell to import firms. In 1932, dozens of private and semi-official information agencies sprang up to bring firms together and arrange these transactions. Private compensation trade required government permission, since exports bartered away would not yield foreign exchange for compulsory sale to the authorities. Permission was generally granted only if the exports were considered unsalable in the regular way at official exchange rates and if the imports to be received were considered advantageous to the German economy. The government itself presumably took part in some of the larger deals, such as the barter of coal for Brazilian coffee and of fertilizer for cotton owned by the Egyptian government. In 1934, when importers' rations of free foreign exchange were drastically cut and when demand, strengthened by the return of prosperity at home, was also raising the scarcity value of German imports, private compensation changed in character. Importers rather than exporters now took the initiative. They offered exporters premium prices in marks for foreign goods against which German goods had in effect been bartered. In this way the importer paid more marks for his purchase than corresponded to its foreign-currency value translated at the official rate of exchange, and the exporter received more marks for his merchandise than corresponded to its translated foreign value. Transactions of this sort amounted to a selective devaluation of the mark. Official permission was of course required.

In mid-1934 rationing of foreign exchange according to official judgments about the national importance of various imports replaced rationing according to the base-period purchases of individual importers. The so-called

New Plan took formal shape in September with the establishment of numerous commodity control boards, each responsible for detailed licensing and regulation of trade in a particular group of products. German manufacturers requiring a variety of foreign raw materials had to deal with several separate bureaucracies. Detailed control extended to trade both with free-currency countries and with Germany's partners in bilateral clearing agreements. Before long, the controls were supplemented by a program of direct but secret export subsidies financed by a gross receipts tax levied on German businesses. The subsidy scheme discriminated very flexibly among products, firms, and markets. Selective offsets to the overvaluation of the mark spurred the export of commodities considered relatively dispensable in order to pay for imports considered relatively essential. By maintaining the overvaluation of the mark for certain commodities and markets and neutralizing it for others, the German planners were acting like a discriminating monopolist on the international market. The general purposes of the New Plan were to exploit national bargaining power (and foreign weaknesses) in order to exchange exports for imports on the most favorable terms possible, to achieve a degree of national self-sufficiency, and to cultivate import sources most likely to remain dependable in wartime. Increased bilateralism in trade was one method of pursuing these aims. The German authorities openly abandoned any efforts to restore free exchange markets; they preferred to bolster and exploit their bargaining power by discriminatory controls.

Clearing and Payments Agreements

Bilateral clearing supplemented exchange control in pursuit of the objectives of the New Plan. Some bilateral agreements had been in effect before then. Germany's first, the agreement with Hungary, had been signed even before the Nazi era, in April 1932. (This agreement had a forerunner in the agreement of November 1931 between Austria and Switzerland.) It provided that German importers would pay the Reichsbank in marks

for imports from Hungary, while the Hungarian National Bank would pay Hungarian exporters in pengos. The marks received from German importers were to be used, in part, to pay German exporters to Hungary, while Hungarian importers of German goods would provide the pengos paid to exporters. The agreement evidently envisaged a German import surplus in trade with Hungary, since about 10 percent of the marks paid by German importers were to be released to the Hungarian National Bank in convertible funds, and three-fourths and one-fourth of the remainder were to be used, respectively, to pay for current exports to Hungary and to pay Germans holding old blocked commercial claims on Hungary. In general, exchange clearing was a device for bypassing the foreign-exchange market and diminishing the trade-hampering effects of two countries' exchange controls and artificial exchange rates. Each country maintained an agency to which importers of goods from the other made payment in home currency and from which exporters of goods to the other received payment in home currency. Clearing agreements could cover trade in services as well as in commodities and, as in the German-Hungarian agreement, could even provide for the liquidation of old debts. An important part of a clearing arrangement was the rate of exchange to be used in translating into one currency or the other the value of the trade in each direction and thus in computing the debt that might currently develop between the two national agencies. Except as imbalance in bilateral trade was deliberately provided for, such arrangements tended to promote a downward-biased[17] bilateral balancing of imports and exports: if one of the two countries was underimporting, its importers would not be paying enough money into the home clearing agency to satisfy the claims of exporters; and exporters, meeting delays in being paid, would have an incentive to curtail their shipments.

By the mid-1930s, Germany had bilateral

---

[17] Downward-biased in comparison with trade under equilibrium exchange rates. Actually, bilateral agreements served to promote trade by partially overcoming the impediments of disequilibrium rates.

trade agreements of this or variant types with almost all European countries and a few Latin-American countries. In the Balkans, particularly, the Nazis used clearing agreements and barter deals for economic domination. With the overvaluation of their own currencies and depression and trade barriers in other countries hampering exports through normal commercial channels, many producers in Southeastern Europe welcomed any chance of greater trade with Germany. Exporters thus unintentionally became something of an "economic fifth column" for Germany, prodding their governments to accept German proposals and to make the concessions necessary from time to time to prevent interruption of bilateral trade. The Germans, for their part, were clever in increasing and exploiting the economic dependence of their small trading partners. Often, for example, Germany imported more than its partners than it exported to them; the Balkan countries developed clearing-balance claims which, as long as they went unspent, represented forced loans to Germany from countries poorer than itself. This situation has been called "double exploitation"—exploitation in addition to that achieved by manipulating the terms of trade.[18] The Nazis seem to have realized that a country gains by what it imports rather than by what it exports and that exports are simply the necessary payment for imports. The governments of Germany's economic satellites, rather than let their claims acquired by export surpluses go unused, had an incentive to control trade so as to divert purchases toward Germany, even though the desired goods might be priced lower elsewhere. Despite all this, it has been argued that the countries of southeast Europe did reap a net gain from their economic relations with Germany. Something is better than nothing in overcoming the trade-throttling effects of wrong exchange rates. Furthermore, given the depression and the "orthodox" attitudes that blocked vigorous monetary-fiscal remedies, trade with Germany on otherwise unfavorable terms may have been beneficial, after all, in providing employment and expansionary multiplier effects on national income.[19] Inadequately requited exports to Germany may have served the countries of Southeastern Europe as makework projects; "leaf-raking" in the export sector served as an antidepression measure in the absence of better policies.

Germany's bilateral agreements with West European countries differed from its agreements with its small economic satellites. The West European countries generally took the initiative in seeking agreements. Normally having import surpluses in trade with Germany and so being net sources of free exchange, they saw a bargaining advantage and an opportunity to prod the Germans into making payments on existing blocked debts. By the end of 1933, the Germans had made so-called Sondermark agreements with practically every West European country except the United Kingdom. Apparently these agreements were intended to govern only a small portion of the trade between the partners. Germany agreed to allow importers who had used up their ordinary foreign-exchange allotments to make purchases in the partner country, anyway, provided its clearing agency would accept payment in mark balances of restricted usability. The typical agreement also mentioned the intention of the two countries to keep the import-export ratio in their mutual trade the same as it had been in 1931. Since Germany had had an export surplus with most of its West European partners, maintenance of this ratio would keep import concessions from impairing Germany's ability to repay old debts. Part of the payments into the clearing accounts in creditor countries were, in fact, earmarked for debt service. After 1933, however, the creditor countries saw their import surpluses in trade with Germany shrinking. Some of them, like France, restricted exports to Germany rather than tolerate further delays in collecting debt payments.

In July and August 1934 the British finally

---

[18] Child, *op. cit.,* esp. pp. 83, 139, 207. The Greek government, for example, once yielded to the political pressure of export interests and floated a bond issue to get the drachmas needed to meet the claims of exporters, since Greek importers of German goods were not providing enough of them.

[19] *Ibid.,* pp. 165-168, 229.

signed debt-service and Sondermark agreements with Germany, only to find blocked
mark balances piling up. In November 1934
these arrangements were replaced by a payments agreement. The Anglo-German agreement was a notable example of a device
sometimes worked out between exchange-
control and free-exchange countries, princi-
pally to promote payments on debts due to
residents of the free-exchange creditor country. (A well-known precedent was the payments agreement concluded between Great
Britain and Argentina in May 1933.) The
Germans agreed to earmark 55 percent of
the proceeds of their exports to Britain to
pay for imports from Britain, reserving most
of the remainder for debt service, though
some sterling might remain available to the
Reichsbank as free exchange. This arrangement differed from bilateral clearing of the
type already described in that the controls
over trade and payments necessary to maintain the agreed import-export ratio were to
be exercised by the German authorities alone.
From the British viewpoint, traders could
make and receive payments in sterling bills
of exchange and avoid the vexations of a full-
fledged clearing system.

Aski Marks

For some trade with countries with which
she had no clearing or payments agreements
(such as the United States and some South
American countries and British dominions),
Germany adopted another device for selectively overcoming the trade-throttling effects
of overvaluation. German exchange-control
regulations first mentioned Aski marks in
December 1934. *Aski* was an abbreviation
for *A*usländer-*S*onder*k*onten für *I*nlandszahl-
ungen, meaning "foreigners' special accounts
for inland payments." For imports unobtainable at world-market prices translated into
marks at the overvalued official rate and yet
judged of special importance to the German
economy, German firms were allowed to offer
foreign suppliers premium prices in marks.
Payments were credited to the foreign supplier or to his bank in a special account with
a German bank. The foreigner could either

use these marks himself to buy specified German goods or else sell them to a fellow countryman; they were not generally transferable.
A great variety of Aski marks arose, each
identified with the particular commodity for
which and particular country to which Germans had made payment, as well as with the
kinds of purchases in Germany it might be
used for. German imports from the United
States gave rise chiefly to "cotton marks" and
"copper marks," the former being usable for
a somewhat wider range of German goods
than the latter. Brazilian exporters earned
cotton marks, coffee marks, and so forth,
each usable for purchase of different German
products.

Trading at different degrees of discount
from the parity of the regular mark according to the particular commodities and foreign
countries involved, Aski marks in effect provided a selective or discriminatory system of
German import duties and export subsidies
or a selective or discriminatory system of partial currency depreciation. The United States
Treasury recognized the export-subsidy aspect
of the system in June 1936 by imposing
countervailing import duties on a long list
of German goods. To remove this disadvantage, the Germans renounced subsidies on
exports to the United States and made the
special marks paid to American suppliers
completely nontransferable; only the original
recipient could use them. The United States
Treasury rescinded its countervailing duties
in December 1936. In March 1939, the United
States Treasury again ruled that the German trading arrangements were export subsidization and again imposed countervailing
duties. Even before this time, however, the
Nazi authorities themselves were coming to
realize that the Aski system was not so
much creating "additional" trade as diverting "normal" trade, including export trade
that would otherwise have earned free exchange. Changed German restrictions themselves caused Aski trade to decline in 1936,
1937, and 1938.

Nazi trade policy was not, as sometimes
supposed, contrived above all to prepare for
war. Evolving out of earlier expedients to
check panicky flights of capital and palliate

difficulties stemming from too high a foreign-exchange value of the mark, the policy aimed at maximizing national gain from trade as German planners conceived it. Though the planners may not have thought of the matter in this way, they were seeking to create and exploit monopoly and monopsony positions in foreign markets in order to achieve an approximation to "optimum" terms of trade.[20]

Sterling and the Dollar in the Last Five Prewar Years

While the gold-bloc countries were struggling and ultimately failing to maintain their old exchange parities and while Nazi Germany and a number of less important trading countries were experimenting with exchange controls, the British Exchange Equalisation Account kept the dollar-sterling rate fairly stable but not rigid. Over the four-year period from mid-1934 to mid-1938, the rate averaged fractionally above $4.95 per pound. Its monthly average stayed within 5 cents of this figure about two-thirds of the time and broke out of the range of 10 cents on either side for only three months (August 1934, when it was higher, and February and March 1935, when it was lower). (During the four-year period, the sharpest change from one monthly average to the next occurred at the time of the gold-bloc devaluations of 1936, when the pound depreciated against the dollar by 2¾ percent.) A final breakout from this range of mild fluctuation foreshadowed the end of the entire prewar exchange system.

From mid-April to the end of June 1937, rumors circulated that the United States might cut the dollar price of gold, with other countries perhaps following suit. During this "gold scare" the demand for dollars strengthened and a wave of gold selling occurred. This reversed itself into a "dollar scare" later in the year, when the stock market and business activity slumped in the United States and some fear arose that the dollar might be devalued as an antirecession measure. The speculative outflow of funds from the United States continued through the first half of

1938 and in the ten months up to July amounted to nearly $1 billion. Nevertheless, President Roosevelt's declaration in February that there was no question of devaluing the dollar had helped to restrain the flight from dollars into gold. In the summer of 1938 prices recovered on the New York stock market. Apprehension turned toward sterling, especially as political tension heightened in Europe. During the acute phase of the international crisis in September, before the Munich conference, a violent outflow of capital from Europe began, and in two months, some $600 million came into the United States. Never before, perhaps, had an international hot-money movement changed direction so abruptly. The flow continued at a slackened rate in November and December and regained intensity early in 1939.[21]

Even before then, as early as the first quarter of 1938, sterling had shown signs of receding from the strength displayed during the period of greatest bearishness on the dollar. Commodity prices fell on the average somewhat further and more rapidly in the United States than in Great Britain during the 1937–1938 recession, and the American balance-of-payments surplus increased while the British current account was in deficit. A number of countries accustomed to holding sizable fractions of their international reserves as sterling balances in London suffered from declines in the prices of their raw-material exports during the recession and began drawing on their London funds to meet deficits with other countries. Withdrawals by India, Australia, New Zealand, Ireland, Norway, Sweden, Finland, and other countries tended to weaken the British position. Authorities in Sweden, Norway, and Ireland, for example, were even converting parts of their sterling reserves into gold and dollars. After the franc apparently was stabilized at last in 1938, French funds shifted home from London, particularly in May and again in the autumn. The international crisis over Czechoslovakia motivated transfers to New York also, more so by foreigners holding funds in London

---

[20] *Ibid.*, esp. pp. 53, 78-79, 226-228.

[21] Bank for International Settlements, 8th *Annual Report*, 1937–1938, pp. 19-20, and 9th *Annual Report*, 1938–1939, pp. 23-24, 76.

than by the British public itself. The weakness of sterling produced something akin to the speculation through leads and lags familiar since World War II. Foreign exporters, and even some exporters in sterling countries themselves, apparently began quoting prices and writing invoices in sterling less often than before. As a result, merchants were inclined to reduce their working balances of sterling. Alternatively, exporters pricing and granting credit in sterling as usual were inclined to borrow sterling from the banks in order to sell it for dollars or gold at once.[22]

Under these pressures, the British Exchange Equalisation Account let the pound slide gradually down from its level of almost $5.02 in February 1938. By late summer the rate had definitely broken out below the channel that had so long been maintained of 5 or 10 cents on either side of $4.95. The slide continued evenly (except for a very brief dip to $4.60 at the end of September) down to a low of around $4.67 in December and January. The Equalisation Account had apparently been resisting the decline, but without pegging the rate. But now, and until late August 1939, the Account held the rate practically rigid at fractionally above $4.68.

Various measures to defend sterling were adopted in December 1938 and January 1939. The Bank of England transferred gold worth £350 million to the Exchange Equalisation Account. An embargo was tightened on floating security issues in the United Kingdom if their proceeds were to be transferred abroad. An unofficial embargo on forward dealings in gold and on loans secured by private holdings of gold had been relaxed the previous spring but was now tightened again. The objective was to curb speculation in gold and currencies while not hampering ordinary trade requirements. The London Foreign Exchange Committee advised banks that while no scrutiny of spot operations was necessary, they should be sure, in forward operations, that their customers were covering normal trade requirements only. Forward transactions undertaken merely to protect one's capital were not to be permitted.[23]

The first seven and one-half months of 1939 saw remarkable, if rather artificial, exchange-rate stability. Never since 1931 had currencies fluctuated so little. Yet large movements of funds continued, connected particularly with the repatriation of capital to France, the shift of foreign central-bank reserves out of London, and transfer of safety-seeking funds to New York. In addition, the pound remained under the pressure of an adverse balance of payments (due partly to imports for armaments) and of a continued weakness in the demand for raw materials produced in the overseas Sterling Area.

Pressure against sterling made heavy demands on the Exchange Equalisation Account. When international tensions increased after mid-August, the strain became too great. On the 25th, the Account withdrew from the market. The rate fell from $4.68 to $4.40 in one day and to $4.27 by the end of the month. On the 26th, an official ban was imposed on foreign security dealings. England declared war on September 3 and established exchange control the next day. The exchange rate was pegged in a range of $4.06-4.02, later narrowed to $4.03½-4.02½, or 14 percent below the previous support level.[24]

Sterling-Area countries within the British Empire (all parts of the Empire except Canada, Newfoundland, and Hong Kong) kept their currencies linked with sterling. Most non-Empire members of the Sterling Area dropped out; a number of them, including the Scandinavian countries, did so before their currencies had depreciated against the dollar by more than a few percent. France kept its link with sterling (in fact, an Anglo-French monetary and economic agreement of

---

[22] BIS, 9th *Annual Report*, p. 85.
[23] *Ibid.*, p. 27.

[24] On free markets abroad, however, sterling quotations moved under the influence of private supply and demand. The supply in these markets came from payments in sterling for imports into the U.K. and from existing balances in the U.K. held by nonresidents and transferable to residents or other nonresidents. (Foreigners were thus still able to withdraw funds from London, but not at an officially supported rate.) The demand came from nonresidents having to make sterling payments for which "free" sterling was allowed. Quotations in these free markets fluctuated considerably, briefly touching below $3.20 in May 1940. Free markets and discount sterling never accounted for more than a small percentage of total transactions, however; and they were gradually extinguished after the middle of 1940.

December 1939 hopefully provided for keeping the sterling-franc rate unchanged for the duration of the war and until six months after the signing of peace). Most countries not employing exchange controls before the war now followed Britain and France in adopting them; and by the end of March 1940, only four of the world's major currencies—the dollar, the guilder, and the Swiss and Belgian francs—were still substantially free of controls.[25]

The 1930s in Review

Severe depression, recurrent waves of exchange depreciation, and intensified economic nationalism characterized the 1930s. Some countries, including the United States and France, never did fully recover from the depression during peacetime. Eventually the painful deflation of the early 1930s was to bring a general reaction in favor of expansionary financial policies. At first, however, preoccupation with the inflations of the previous decade, as in the gold-bloc countries and Germany, hindered adoption of expansionary policies and realistic exchange rates. Just as generals are said always to be fighting the last war, policy-makers were often treating economic disorders that had already given way to their opposites.

Monetary nationalism, though tempered by rudiments of international cooperation, was bolstered by quotas and increased tariffs, by preferential trade agreements, and, still in a minority of countries, by exchange controls and bilateral clearing. Productive international lending and investment, as distinguished from speculative or panicky transfers of capital, remained far below predepression levels. Under the circumstances, it is hardly surprising that the recovery of international trade lagged badly behind the recovery of production. From 1850 to 1929 the growth of world trade (as well as the decline during World War I and from 1929 to 1932) had proceeded at much the same rate as the growth (or decline) of world industrial production. From the trough in 1932 to the peak in 1937, however, the estimated physical volume of world trade

rose hardly more than 50 percent, in contrast to a rise of approximately 85 percent in estimated world industrial production. At the highest point in 1939, when recovery from the recession of 1937–1938 was still incomplete, trade and production were slightly more than 40 and 70 percent, respectively, above their troughs of 1932.[26]

The epidemic of exchange depreciation started in late 1929 and early 1930 as the currencies of several primary-producing countries weakened. It gathered momentum with the crisis of 1931 and the depreciations by Great Britain and the other members-to-be of the emergent Sterling Area. As late as the spring of 1933, a considerable body of opinion regarded the international gold standard as only temporarily suspended, but the American depreciation and final devaluation of 1933–1934 and the failure of the London Economic Conference blasted hopes of an early return to gold. After the painfully delayed collapse of the Continental gold bloc in 1936, almost every currency in the world had been affected. Only one currency avoided both depreciation and exchange control—the Albanian franc—until it too was devalued when pegged to the lira after the Italian occupation of Albania in April 1939.

Paper standards came unwanted into existence when the gold standard had clearly failed. Some conditions predisposing the world economy to the Great Depression can plausibly be blamed on the precarious pegging of currencies to gold in the middle and late 1920s. Exchange depreciations came about under pressure of balance-of-payments deficits due to weak export markets or else were undertaken to permit or aid financial policies for recovery from the depression. Sometimes depreciation was a "predatory" measure, adopted more or less intentionally to win a price advantage in export markets, even though this meant "exporting unemployment" to other countries. The world pattern of exchange rates in the 1930s was haphazardly determined and was repeatedly subject to haphazard changes. It was the product neither of unhampered free-market forces nor of conscious international planning. Some

[25] BIS, 10th *Annual Report*, 1939–1940, pp. 18-25.   [26] *Ibid.*, p. 41.

governments clung to hopelessly high parities for their currencies; others deliberately sought to depress their currencies on the exchanges. Almost everywhere, if not always with consistency, governments sought a freedom for domestic monetary management that was incompatible with earlier traditions of exchange-rate fixity.

Many a devaluation in the 1930s was larger than "objective" long-run economic conditions would have called for. Panicky flights of hot money were largely to blame—that is, speculation against currencies whose parities had come under suspicion. Yet paradoxically, by the end of 1936, despite all the upheavals in the meanwhile, exchange rates among the chief currencies still free of exchange control had returned to a pattern not far different from the one prevailing in 1930.[27]

However much the successive depreciations may have reversed each other's effects on exchange rates, they did spell lasting increases in the price of gold in national currencies. This, together with increases in the purchasing powers of the currencies themselves, more than doubled the goods-and-services value of gold. World gold production responded. Including the estimated output of the Soviet Union, it was 1.8 times as great in the four years 1935–1938 as in the corresponding period a decade earlier and was twice as great in 1938 as in 1928. Reported gold reserves of central banks and governments (not counting certain stabilization funds) were half again as large in 1938 as ten years before. These figures refer to physical quantities of gold. Taking account of an average markup of 70 percent or more in terms of national currencies, the money value of world gold production was about three and one-half times as great in 1938 as in 1928, and the money value of central gold reserves was more than two and one-half times as great. Because of general price

deflation, the *commodity* value of gold production and gold stocks had increased even more.

Available stocks of international liquidity or international means of payment did not increase in similar degree. The rise of the Sterling Area did not completely take the place of the gold-exchange standard of the 1920s as a means of "economizing" on gold. Furthermore, ownership of gold stocks became increasingly concentrated. In the six years 1934–1939 gold imports added some $10 billion worth to the American hoard. About $6 billion came from new production outside the United States, $1 billion from the hoards of the Orient, and $3 billion largely from central-bank holdings. At least four-fifths of this total gold gain corresponded to a capital inflow of unprecedented nature and size. The rather unwelcome movement of capital into the United States reached its climax in 1939, when some $2 billion was transferred from abroad. (At intervals, however, as during the "dollar scare" of 1937–1938, the capital movement had been in the opposite direction.) In the five-year period 1934–1938 the American share of the world's monetary gold stock rose from 34 to 57 percent. In 1939, the share of the United States and six other leading holders of gold had risen to 88 percent of the world total, as compared to 62 percent ten years before. The functionless excess gold holdings of the United States practically went out of circulation as international means of settlement.[28]

At the start of the 1930s total American investments abroad probably amounted to roughly $15 billion (not counting war-debt claims), offset fractionally by foreign investments in the United States. During the decade the United States repatriated money invested abroad and served as a haven for foreign flight capital to the extent of becoming the world's largest capital *importer*. By the end of the decade the net international creditor position of the United States had

---

[27] The net change in the exchange rate against the U.S. dollar amounted to not more than a very few percent for Argentina, Sweden, India, the United Kingdom, Canada, and Italy; it amounted to larger percentages, ranging hardly above 20 percent, for Brazil, Australia, Czechoslovakia, France, and Belgium. Nurkse, *op. cit.*, p. 129n.

[28] Most of these figures are taken or computed from *ibid.*, pp. 17-19, 26, 90, 132-133, 233, and Bank for International Settlements, 10th *Annual Report* (1939–1940), p. 83.

shrunk below $2 billion. The shrinkage had been averaging more than $1 billion a year; at this rate, if wartime developments had not intervened, the United States would have become a net international debtor (though still the largest gold-holder) some time in 1940 or 1941.[29]

The flight of funds to the United States, bringing the "Golden Avalanche" with it, was only one example of an abnormal mobility of funds generally prevalent during the 1930s. With liquid deposits earning little or no interest at a time of depressed economic activity, their holders were mainly preoccupied with protecting their capital. When a country's balance-of-payments position seemed to foreshadow either further currency depreciation or the imposition of exchange restrictions, large balances promptly sought refuge elsewhere. Rumors and capital transfers fed on each other. A rise in a central bank discount rate often served less as an inducement for funds to remain in or to enter the country than as a confirmation of financial trouble. Sometimes, after an expected depreciation had taken place or after the crisis had abated without one, the outflow of capital would reverse itself. (As the threat of war increased toward the end of the decade, political considerations replaced purely financial ones as the chief motive of hot-money transfers.) Capital inflows and outflows produced internal as well as international disturbances by alternately flooding and draining the capital markets, and resistance to internal repercussions was one of the chief tasks of exchange equalization accounts. A country sheltering hot money could not well employ it for productive investment for fear of its sudden withdrawal. Externally, capital transfers were often "disequilibrating," adding to rather than cushioning imbalances between imports and exports. Gold became a vehicle for hot money.[30]

---

[29] BIS, 11th *Annual Report,* 1940–1941, p. 98.
[30] Capital movements of this type accounted for the great bulk of the changes in French, British, and American official gold reserves in the years 1933–1938. Nurkse, *op. cit.,* p. 16.

Lessons of the 1930s

There is no denying the historical association between hot-money transfers and exchange-rate variations by uncoordinated national action. They intensified each other. From this and related facts, observers have drawn certain lessons:

. . . the system of flexible exchanges in the 'thirties was associated with disturbances not very different from those associated with freely fluctuating exchanges.

If there is anything that inter-war experience has clearly demonstrated, it is that paper currency exchanges cannot be left free to fluctuate from day to day under the influence of market supply and demand.

. . . any system of exchange rates reached by international consultation will be better than one in which exchanges are determined either by isolated acts of national sovereignty or by markets subject to speculative transfers of funds. To let the exchanges "find their own level" would almost certainly result in chaos.[31]

Now, historical associations, by themselves, never teach lessons. Lessons derive from history as *interpreted* in the light of theories. One theory or assumption apparently underlying the views just quoted is that governmentally managed flexible rates and freely fluctuating rates are essentially the same thing, at least in provoking speculative capital movements. Actually, the supposed lesson of the 1930s requires a more neutral phrasing: Flexible management of exchange rates by uncoordinated national action seems to work badly. History does not prove that management by intergovernmental collaboration is the only workable alternative. The 1930s can-

---

[31] *Ibid.,* pp. 123, 137. Cf. W. M. Scammell, *International Monetary Policy,* p. 94, and Thomas C. Schelling, *International Economics,* Boston: Allyn and Bacon, 1958, p. 294. Scammell notes it as a fact "that neither of the pure unmanaged systems," the gold standard and freely fluctuating rates, "has been successful in operation. . . . after nearly a decade of competitive depreciation, we found we had no stomach for free rates. . . ." Schelling refers to "the experience in the 1930's . . . with freely-fluctuating exchange rates" and clearly implies that the experience was unsatisfactory, especially in the violence of rate fluctuations and of speculative capital movements.

not directly provide any lesson about freely fluctuating exchange rates because

freely fluctuating exchanges were far from common in those years. Exchange rates changed indeed; but the changes were usually controlled. For considerable periods at a time, rates were "pegged" or kept within certain limits of variation. . . . [This was a] system of managed though flexible exchanges. . . .

Wide and sudden changes took place in foreign exchange rates. Yet one of the facts that stands out from this experience is that monetary authorities in most countries had little or no desire for freely fluctuating exchanges.

During the 'thirties, exchange rates changed frequently. But *freely* fluctuating exchanges were by no means common. The changes were either controlled or, after brief intervals of uncontrolled fluctuation, were followed by measures of stabilization at a new level.[32]

The emergence of currency blocs, loose and of doubtful durability though they were, is further evidence that exchange rates were not abandoned to market forces. The completely nationalistic management of rates was far from general as a sustained policy. Numerous governments aligned their currencies with sterling or the dollar, or, in the Far East, with the yen. Even the chief fluctuating rate, the dollar-sterling rate, was held within a narrow channel for several years.

As this last example reminds us, exchange stabilization funds were active. The British fund was originally meant to smooth out speculative and seasonal fluctuations, leaving the longer-term course of the rate responsive to private supply and demand. In practice, it had trouble in distinguishing speculative from nonspeculative movements and could hardly avoid influencing even the general trend of the rate. The American and French funds were meant from the start to influence rates actively rather than just passively to smooth their fluctuations. The American fund sought to "defend" the dollar against competitive depreciation by sterling and other currencies. The British authorities, for their part, seemed unwilling to allow much appreciation of sterling against the dollar. Yet a system of substantially free exchange rates requires, according to one persuasive interpretation, that *all* countries of major financial importance allow commercial forces to work freely. If the government of one important country tries to dominate the exchange rates with other currencies, the other countries must either accept the leadership of the first or else seek international collaboration in management of the exchanges. Management thus tends to spread and to necessitate international cooperation. "These," according to one alternative interpretation, "are the main lessons of the middle and late thirties."[33] The Tripartite Monetary Agreement of 1936, concerned with cooperation among the British, French, and American exchange funds, may be interpreted as a partial and imperfect recognition of these lessons and even as a forerunner of the International Monetary Fund.

---

[32] These passages come, significantly, from the same authoritative source as the "lessons" being considered: Nurkse, *op. cit.*, pp. 8-9, 122, 211.

[33] A. C. L. Day, *Outline of Monetary Economics,* Oxford: Clarendon Press, 1957, p. 511. Cf. pp. 503-504.

Wartime and Early Postwar Financial Developments

✐ 18

Allied Financing

In foreign-exchange policy, World War II brought stricter rate pegging, tightened controls, and further displacement of ordinary commercial practices by intergovernmental arrangements. Sterling was rigidly pegged at $4.03. The Sterling Area became more clearly defined. (Before the war, it had been so loose that it is hard to say whether certain countries belonged or not.) Its wartime membership included the British Commonwealth except Canada and Hong Kong and also, eventually, a few foreign countries such as Egypt, Iraq, and the Free-French overseas territories. Most of the non-Commonwealth members dropped out. Member countries adopted exchange controls to restrict their residents' payments outside the Area while allowing freedom within it.

The British government mobilized privately owned foreign assets to help pay for wartime purchases overseas. By the end of the war, the country had sold nearly £600 million worth of investments in the Sterling Area and about £1.1 billion of foreign investments in all, or nearly one-third of the prewar total. Furthermore, the balances of the sterling countries in London had grown by nearly £3 billion, of which amount the United Kingdom had spent less on supplies for itself than on its defense of India, Burma, and the Middle East. Deferred payment for supplies was also arranged with Canada and some of the neutrals, most importantly Argentina. By the end of the war, the short-term claims on the United Kingdom of other countries in and out of the Commonwealth—the so-called sterling balances—had been built up to over £3½ billion, including the £½ billion or so of balances already outstanding before the war.[1]

Laws passed in the mid-1930s hampered American aid to the Allies at first: the Johnson Act forbade American citizens to grant loans to foreign governments in default on their obligations to the United States government, i.e., their debts from World War I; and the Neutrality Act embargoed sales of war goods to belligerents. Congress soon repealed the arms embargo, however, and allowed cash-and-carry sales to the Allies. An urgent need for supplies frustrated the desire of the British and French governments to use their gold and foreign exchange sparingly. At first the Allied governments sought to meet their spending by an export drive that trenched on home civilian consumption. After the fall of France, the desperate British had to buy supplies almost without regard to their financial future. By the end of 1940, orders had been placed in the United States that, when paid for, would leave Britain practically without dollars. Despite sales of privately owned dollar investments, the financial situation had become acute. Speaking in November 1941, Prime Minister Churchill said: "... this time last year we did not know where to turn for a dollar ... the end of our financial resources was in sight, nay, had actually been reached."[2]

President Roosevelt outlined the American response to the British plight in December

---

[1] William Ashworth, *A Short History of the International Economy*, London: Longmans, Green, 1952, p. 225, and Bank for International Settlements, *The Sterling Area*, Basel, 1953, pp. 18-19.

[2] Bank for International Settlements, 12th *Annual Report*, 1941–1942, p. 103.

1940: when your neighbor's house is on fire, you lend him your garden hose to help put the fire out. The Lend-Lease Act became law in March 1941, nine months before Pearl Harbor. Lend-Lease put a great variety of goods at the disposal of the Allies, with settlement to be worked out later. (As it turned out, the goods used up during the war were regarded as an American contribution to the common effort; goods on the way at the end of the war and installations of peacetime value were sold at bargain prices and on credit.) Because of Lend-Lease, interallied trade in ordinary commercial channels shrank. The British were able to abandon their export drive and devote the resources saved to war purposes. By 1944, British exports (apart from munitions) were under one-third of their prewar volume.[3]

Thirty-eight countries, including several not involved in the actual fighting, eventually received some Lend-Lease aid. The total amounted to some $48.6 billion through September 1946 (straight Lend-Lease had ended a year earlier, but there were some delayed deliveries and some continued aid to China). Of this total, about 65 percent went to the British Empire, 23 percent to Soviet Russia, 7 percent to France and her overseas possessions, and some to China. The United States received about $8 billion in "reverse Lend-Lease," chiefly as goods, services, and facilities provided to the American armed forces in the British Empire; reverse Lend-Lease from Russia was negligible. The United States also eventually received returns of surplus goods and repayments totaling about $4 billion. The net outflow of Lend-Lease in excess of recoveries of all kinds amounted to about $37 billion, valued at prices averaging perhaps half of present-day levels.[4] Besides giving military and civilian aid, the United States government spent about $15 billion abroad from mid-1940 through September 1945 for supplies and other military purposes, mostly in the British Commonwealth and Latin America.

American policy dominated balance-of-payments trends. During a first phase, mostly coinciding with the period of cash-and-carry sales, the large U.S. merchandise export surplus brought a heavy inflow of gold. From the end of August 1939 to the end of October 1941 (when the movement reversed itself) the gain totaled $5.7 billion. (This followed upon net purchases of foreign gold amounting to $3.5 billion in the 13 months before the start of the war.) Toward the end of 1940 foreigners began supplementing and later replacing gold sales by liquidating their dollar bank deposits and securities. From October 1940 through February 1942 this liquidation amounted to over $700 million, not counting sales of foreign-owned businesses besides. During a second phase of balance-of-payments trends, Lend-Lease largely covered the net exports of the United States and relieved the strain on Allied holdings of gold and dollars. With most war material moving under Lend-Lease and few civilian goods available for export, the heavy overseas wartime expenditures of the United States began rebuilding the gold and short-term dollar reserves of foreign countries. By the end of the war, the total holdings of all foreign countries except Russia had risen above the prewar level by $6.2 billion, or 45 percent. The net losses of the European belligerents were more than matched by the gains of Latin America, South Africa, and the European neutrals in particular. Late in 1945, after the war and most Lend-Lease aid had ended, foreign countries again began running down their reserves.[5]

At the height of the war the chief Allied belligerents were devoting half of their national incomes, more or less, to war spending. By the summer of 1945, the total direct war cost borne by the various national treasuries was estimated at at least four times as much, in real terms, as the cost of World War I.[6]

---

[3] Ashworth, *op. cit.*, pp. 226-227.

[4] Bank for International Settlements, 15th *Annual Report*, 1944–1945, p. 121, 17th *Annual Report*, 1946–1947, p. 98, Thomas C. Schelling, *International Economics,* Boston: Allyn and Bacon, 1958, pp. 420-421. Different sources give slightly different figures covering slightly different time periods, but the general picture is the same.

[5] Federal Reserve Bank of New York, *Annual Report* for 1945, New York: 1946, pp. 28-33.

[6] Bank for International Settlements, 15th *Annual Report,* 1944–1945, pp. 27, 35.

Divergent Production and Price Changes

The war intensified world economic disparities. Industrial and agricultural production in the first year or so after the war was only three-fourths or one-half or less of prewar levels in Japan, Greece, Austria, Germany, the Netherlands, France, and elsewhere. On the other hand, production gained ground outside the combat zones, notably in Canada, Sweden, and the United States. During the war the United States recovered from the lingering depression of the 1930s and increased its productive plant by nearly 50 percent and its annual physical output of goods and services by more than 50 percent. At the end of the war over half of the world's manufacturing and one-third of total world production of all goods was estimated to be taking place in the United States. Though European countries had lost nearly 40 percent of their merchant shipping tonnage, the world total had risen by 6 or 7 percent; and of this total, the United States owned half, in comparison with 14 percent in 1939. Even two years after the war, the United States was providing one-third of all the world's exports and taking only one-tenth of the imports.[7]

Despite the far greater financial and material costs of World War II than of World War I, the upheaval in prices was smaller. At any rate, controls over prices and exchange rates concealed it better. Episodes of hyperinflation, in particular, were fewer after the second war than after the first; only in Hungary, China, Rumania, and Greece did price levels get quite out of control. Prices were multiplied about 25-fold in Italy, more than 10-fold in Japan and Thailand, and nearly 10-fold in Lebanon. Early postwar prices were about five or six times prewar levels in Finland, France, Iran, and the Philippines and about double, triple, or quadruple prewar levels in Peru, the Netherlands, Portugal, Spain, Mexico, Czechoslovakia, Chile, Paraguay, India, Brazil, Egypt, Belgium, Bolivia, and Turkey (listed in approximate order of least to greatest inflation). Prices rose by about 50 to 100 percent in New Zealand, the United Kingdom, Sweden, Norway, Denmark, Argentina, Switzerland, Ireland, and Costa Rica and only by about 30 to 45 percent in Canada, Australia, the United States, Venezuela, and the Union of South Africa. These figures compare prices in 1946 or at the end of 1945 with levels of 1938 or 1939; inflation in almost all countries continued longer into the postwar period. Furthermore, any international comparison of inflation can be only impressionistic at best; price controls and rationing make figures deceptive.

International Transmission of Inflation

No country escaped inflation during World War II, not even any neutrals. Several countries, including some in the British Empire, apparently suffered a monetary and price inflation of chiefly external rather than domestic origin. Some of the inactive belligerents provide good examples. Cuban price inflation was unmistakable despite the lack of comprehensive statistics. The index of food prices outside Havana rose by 162 percent between September 1939 and September 1947. Rough estimates suggest that the total cost of living rose some 80 percent from September 1940 to September 1944 and some 125 percent from September 1939 to the end of 1947. The Cuban money supply, consisting of currency and demand deposits in both pesos and U.S. dollars, was multipled by 4.6 between the ends of 1939 and 1945 and by 6.7 between the ends of 1938 and 1947. Government deficit financing played very little part in this expansion; the inflation of prices and incomes raised tax revenues practically in step with expenditures. Bank credit expansion likewise played only a small part. Up to 1945, in fact, its influence was technically negative, in the sense that the growth of bank loans and investments amounted to less than the public's acquisition of time and other nonmonetary deposits. During 1946 and 1947 a sharp expansion of bank credit did accommodate the postwar avalanche of imports, but even then, it accounted for only 15 percent or less of the further growth in currency and demand deposits. Throughout

---

[7] Ashworth, *op. cit.*, pp. 227-228; Bank for International Settlements, 18th *Annual Report*, 1947–1948, p. 15.

the war and early postwar period, the dominant source of inflation was an intensely
active balance of international payments. Repatriation of Cuban funds held abroad (and
curtailment of new capital exports), partly
stimulated by a tax of 0.15 percent a month on
Cuban funds held abroad, was an aggravating factor. The main one was a sugar export
boom: the peso value of total Cuban exports
in 1947 was more than six times the level of
1940. The origins of the money supply can
be classified under two headings: (1) domestic credit origin (bank credit and seigniorage
on Treasury issues) and (2) international
origin (the bullion value of coin, gold bullion and dollars backing silver certificates,
dollars in circulation, and dollars in banks
and net balances abroad). The international
part of the total increase in the money supply
amounted to 101 percent between the ends
of the years 1939 and 1945, 94 percent between
1938 and 1947, and 85 percent between 1945
and 1947. The Cuban inflation thus occurred
under a negative policy of passively tolerating
the inflow of money into domestic circulation
that accompanied an export surplus.[8]

The fact that Cuba was technically at war
may seem, however irrelevantly, to discredit
its experience as an example of imported
inflation. For this reason it may be worthwhile to consider a couple of outright neutral
countries as well. The Bank of International
Settlements reported as follows in 1944:

> Portugal is one of the few countries in the
> world to-day in which the abundance of mone-
> tary purchasing power has in no way been de-
> rived from internal state financing, the Portu-
> guese budget remaining in good order. The
> plethora of money has been due to large ex-
> ports, wolfram and tin being the two most con-
> spicuous commodities for which very high prices
> have been charged.[9]

Switzerland provides a less clear-cut but
better documented example. Despite extensive
price controls and rationing, the Swiss whole-

sale price index in 1945 averaged 107 percent
above and the cost-of-living index 52 percent above the level of 1938. Between the ends
of these two years, the banknote circulation
increased by 119 percent, or by 2084 million
Swiss francs. The total net money supply, as
defined by the International Monetary Fund,
rose by 73 percent, or 3783 million francs.
The increase in the gold and foreign-exchange
holdings of the Swiss National Bank over the
same period amounted to 1770 francs, or 56
percent of the initial holdings.[10] Actually,
these figures for the Bank show only part of
the official acquisitions of gold and foreign
exchange: the Swiss government also shoul-
dered some of this burden and, despite sales
of gold bullion to industry and of gold
coins on the market, it had acquired 1030.2
million francs' worth of gold at the end of
1945 and 1239.1 million francs worth at the
end of 1946.[11] These facts indicate a creation
of Swiss money to finance official purchases of
the country's surplus foreign earnings. In
peacetime, Swiss commodity exports had almost always fallen far short of commodity
imports; the deficiency in value had been 18
percent in 1938 and 31 percent in 1939. But this
deficiency shrank throughout the war and
finally turned into a surplus of 20 percent in
1945. The quantum indexes of imports and
exports in 1945 had fallen to 31 and 57 percent
respectively of their 1938 levels.[12]

There is no denying that the Swiss wartime
inflation resulted partly from real rather than
purely from monetary factors. Some manpower had gone into active military service,
and imports became less available and more
costly to buy and to transport. The government subsidized domestic production of staple
foods, even at the expense of some shrinkage
in milk and meat production; and the Swiss-
grown portion of food consumption rose

---

[8] Henry C. Wallich, *Monetary Problems of an Export Economy*, Cambridge, Mass.: Harvard University Press, 1950, esp. pp. 151-161. Some of the figures cited above are computed from Wallich's tables.

[9] Bank for International Settlements, 14th *Annual Report*, p. 83.

[10] Eidgenössisches Statistisches Amt, *Statistisches Jahrbuch der Schweiz, 1951*, Basel: Verlag Birkhäuser, 1952, pp. 554-555; Swiss National Bank, *44me Rapport*, 1951, Bern: 1952, pp. 56-57; *International Financial Statistics*, December 1948, p. 114.

[11] Swiss National Bank, *39me Rapport*, 1946, pp. 13-14, *38me Rapport*, 1945, p. 11, *Geschäftsbericht*, 1944, pp. 10-11, *Schweizerische Nationalbank 1907-1957*, Zürich: 1957, p. 143.

[12] *Statistisches Jahrbuch der Schweiz, 1951*, pp. 165, 170.

from 52 percent in 1934–1936 to 70 percent in 1943–1945. Real national income per person fell by an estimated 10 percent between 1939 and 1945.[13]

The smallness of this decline in available goods and services in comparison with the percentage rise in prices suggests, however, that real economic deterioration by no means entirely explains the inflation. Real causes were abetted by monetary expansion, which, as already suggested, was not mainly of domestic origin. Though tax increases fell far short of increases in defense spending, the resulting large deficit in the federal budget was met by relatively noninflationary borrowing; and the financial positions of the cantonal governments strengthened notably.[14] "Even in the last year of the war, the National Bank had to place financial means at the disposal of the Confederation only temporarily and never in the form of permanent credit." Furthermore, "Because of the considerable liquid resources at the disposal of the banks, the private economy had recourse only in a slight degree to credit from the bank of issue during the second world war." The continued growth of the monetary circulation "could not be attributed to a more important resort by the State or by the private economy to credit from the bank of issue; it stems above all from the acquisition of foreign exchange arising from exports." "Liquidity did not cease to reign on the Swiss money market . . . the continuous acquisition by the bank of issue of export proceeds and of foreign gold furnished it an uninterrupted supply of available funds."[15]

The troublesome afflux of gold and foreign exchange did not originate in ordinary commercial transactions alone. In addition, for instance, the British and U.S. governments needed Swiss francs to meet diplomatic and other payments, including payments to Japan by way of the Red Cross for the care of prisoners of war. They were able to obtain francs up to specified limits for sterling, dollars, or gold at official rates of exchange.

During the war the Swiss franc became "the currency most readily accepted in Europe for international settlements, notwithstanding the fact that the Swiss monetary authorities have deliberately sought to discourage its use for other settlements than those directly connected with the economic life of Switzerland itself."[16]

In trying to discourage these other uses, the National Bank adopted a policy in the latter part of 1940 of requiring information on the origin of foreign exchange offered to it for sale. The Bank wanted to impede the inflow of unstable foreign funds and to keep dollar balances blocked by the American authorities from being liquidated through the Swiss market. It continued, however, to accept all foreign exchange resulting from Swiss exports or from repatriation of Swiss-owned funds.[17] In September 1941 the National Bank worked out a gentlemen's agreement with the commercial banks whereby only the surplus foreign exchange arising from commodity trade and certain other specified transactions would be acquired at the official rates of exchange. Later on during the war the Bank set monthly limits to its purchases of foreign exchange arising from exports of watches and from exports of textiles and certain other products to the Near East. Occasionally dollars arising from nonprivileged transactions were quoted at heavy discounts on the Swiss market. The Swiss authorities strove to have importers make use of officially acquired dollars to pay for their imports. But no full remedy was found for the growing glut of gold and foreign exchange. Some efforts were made to sell gold coins and bars to the Swiss public as a kind of anti-inflationary open-market operation; and the Swiss government acquired some of the gold itself, paying with funds borrowed out of circulation rather than simply created. The government thus incurred heavy costs in an effort to restrain monetary expansion.[18]

---

[13] *Schweizerische Nationalbank, 1907–1957*, pp. 36-37.
[14] *Ibid.*, p. 67.
[15] These quotations are translated from the Bank's *Rapports* for 1945, p. 13, and for 1943, pp. 11, 13.

[16] Bank for International Settlements, 14th *Annual Report*, 1943–1944, pp. 36, 38.
[17] Bank for International Settlements, 11th *Annual Report*, 1940–1941, p. 38.
[18] Swiss National Bank, *Rapports* for 1943, p. 10, for 1945, pp. 10-11, for 1946, pp. 13-14; *Schweizerische*

The wartime experience is nicely summarized in the National Bank's Annual Report for 1946:

After the United States had blocked Swiss assets in June 1941, inflows of dollars to the bank of issue became ever larger, since the exports of certain industries were growing ceaselessly, while opportunities to import goods were diminishing. Gold and foreign exchange arising from various sources thus began flowing to the bank of issue. This state of affairs entailed a continuous creation of means of payment that implied a danger of inflation in spite of price control and rationing. The exigencies of economic policy and of monetary policy obliged Switzerland to use restraint in the creation of francs corresponding to acquisitions of gold and foreign exchange. The measures taken for this purpose consisted in putting quotas on exports consigned to certain countries and in postponing the payment of a part of the equivalent of dollars derived from sales abroad. In general, the transfer of claims on countries using the dollar was ruled out when interest and capital were concerned. This regulation, considered as a makeshift, was to last throughout the whole conflict.[19]

As already shown, these makeshift measures were far from completely successful. As early as 1942 some people were proposing an appreciation of the franc as a more effective kind of partial insulation from foreign developments. A low enough franc price of foreign currencies would have warded off surplus supplies of foreign exchange clamoring for conversion into newly created Swiss francs. Though imports of goods and services could hardly have been maintained at prewar levels, an appreciated exchange rate could have rectified the trade balance by discouraging unrequited exports. Not even a complete current balancing of trade would have been necessary; for at some raised value of the franc, Swiss businessmen might have regarded foreign exchange as abnormally and temporarily cheap and might have accumulated it for postwar use, relieving the authorities of the burden of absorbing it.

After Sweden and Canada revalued their currencies upward in the summer of 1946, the Swiss authorities were increasingly urged to follow their example. But by this time, doing so would have been belatedly locking the barn door. The Swiss authorities never did consider revaluation a suitable weapon. For one thing, it would have involved writing down the franc value of the National Bank's gold and foreign-exchange reserves. Also, revaluation might have provoked a troublesome capital outflow by causing expectations of some subsequent devaluation.[20] Perhaps just tolerating imported inflation really was the least bad of the courses open.

The examples just considered should not give the impression that monetary expansion connected with a balance-of-payments surplus was *typically* the dominant source of wartime inflation. In most countries, government deficit spending was of course more important. Even in the international transmission of inflation, more than one mechanism was at work. Quite apart from any balance-of-payments surplus, a rise in the real cost of a country's imports because of reduced foreign supplies and increased shipping and insurance rates can begin to percolate through the domestic economy, abetted by practices of pricing goods in accordance with costs and of adjusting wages with the cost of living. A rise in export prices tends to spread similarly. Even apart from any intervening steps, price increases on the world market may lead to a change of market expectations within a country and thus to price markups and to attempts to draw down cash balances. For an inflation transmitted in either of these ways to become general and to carry far within a country, an accommodating expansion of the local money supply is of course necessary; but this is not unusual when money and banking systems are responsive to the "needs of trade."[21]

Nationalbank 1907–1957, pp. 140-145; Bank for International Settlements, 14th *Annual Report*, 1943–1944, pp. 36-38.

[19] Translated from Swiss National Bank, *Rapport* for 1946, p. 12.

[20] *Schweizerische Nationalbank 1950–1957*, pp. 128-129.

[21] According to A. J. Brown, the worldwide spread of the wartime and postwar inflation was due more to a push from increased import and export prices and to linkages involving expectations than to monetary expansions by way of the balance of payments. See his *The Great Inflation, 1939–1951*, London: Oxford University Press, 1955, especially pp. 70-71, 251-257.

The Cuban, Portuguese, and Swiss examples of inflation largely transmitted through the balance of payments are admittedly selective. Their merit is in bringing further historical evidence to bear on the analysis of possible conflict between domestic stability and exchange-rate stability. No reference to the war can validly dismiss this evidence as irrelevant unless one can show in what specific respects war overrides the usual economic principles relating to foreign trade, exchange rates, money, and prices. The authorities of the Swiss National Bank grasped part of the lesson to be drawn from their experience:

From the long-run point of view, Swiss economic policy is equally interested in stable exchange rates and in the maintenance of the purchasing power of the franc. As experience teaches, however, these objectives cannot always be simultaneously attained.[22]

Early Postwar Difficulties

Physical destruction was far greater during World War II than during World War I. The fighting lasted longer and covered a wider area, and the instruments of destruction were more highly developed. Hidden erosion of productive capacity did probably even more total damage than actual shooting and bombing. Wartime urgencies caused postponement and neglect in maintaining and repairing capital equipment: vehicles and railroad cars had been run to ruin, much farm land had gone underfertilized, and many factories and machines were in sorry shape. Inventories of raw materials and goods in process, of consumer durable goods, and of farm livestock had been run down. Populations had been displaced, peacetime productive skills had become rusty, and normal trade and business connections had lapsed or loosened. Years of industrial research and development had been lost, and use of military discoveries for peacetime purposes would take time.

Reconstruction, reconversion, and general economic recovery seemed well under way during the first postwar year in most of the

world except for parts of Asia and the East Indies and the devastated industrial regions of Germany and Japan. Before the middle of 1947, however, a number of threats to continued recovery became apparent in Europe. Bilateral trade and payments agreements were having only limited success in moving trade past barriers thrown up to conserve dwindling national reserves of gold and dollars. An unusually cold and snowy winter in Western and Central Europe hampered transportation and production and intensified needs for imported fuel and food. An inclement spring gave way to a dry summer, causing crop failures and curtailing hydroelectric generation, which intensified the coal problem. For the first two and a half years after the end of the war, as in the period just after World War I, probably the most troublesome bottleneck was the shortage of coal, still the primary industrial commodity and needed for power, for heating homes, and as an industrial raw material. In early 1947, British coal production was still some 13 percent below the 1935–1939 level (because of losses in productivity and in the number of miners), and British coal exports had virtually ceased. The coal output of the German Ruhr was 40 percent below the prewar level. Not until the following year, 1948, would the combined effects of abundant rainfall for hydroelectricity, revived coal production, and continued imports from the United States overcome the coal bottleneck. Steel production lagged. Strikes plagued France and Italy. German recovery was foundering on scanty food rations, political unrest, uncertainty about how much industrial activity the occupying powers would permit, and a suppressed inflation that was crippling the operation of the market mechanism. Rising import prices were damaging European terms of trade and balances of payments.

In the 17 countries that later formed the Organisation for European Economic Co-operation, the index of gross national product at constant prices had regained 93 percent of the 1938 level in 1947; population growth kept real per capita gross national product still 13 percent below the prewar level. Consumption and investment expendi-

[22] *Schweizerische Nationalbank 1907–1957*, p. 103.

tures totaled an estimated $148 billion, about $7 billion in excess of the value of aggregrate production. This $7 billion of excess "absorption" corresponded to an equal excess of imports of goods and services over exports. The imbalance did not stem from any spurt in imports: controls kept West European imports down to 90 percent of their prewar physical volume, though inflation had approximately doubled their dollar value. Commodity exports had likewise fallen in physical quantity but risen in money value. A large increase in the prewar volume of exports would have been necessary to make up for the drop in European earnings from foreign investment and from services such as shipping, insurance, and tourism. Europe's trade-balance problem was particularly acute in relation to the United States, since many goods sought for reconstruction were not immediately available elsewhere, since reduced supplies of some goods from customary sources (food from Eastern Europe, for example) increased Europe's dependence on the United States, and since damage had occurred to the multilateral trade in which Europe had formerly earned dollars by net sales to dollar-earning countries of the Far East. To the $7 billion external deficit on current account was added another $2 billion on capital account, including subscriptions to the International Monetary Fund and International Bank, other intergovernmental payments, and private capital transfers. The gross European deficit of about $9 billion was financed mostly by American and Canadian loans and other foreign aid but also by a further loss of some $2½ billion from gold and dollar holdings. At the worst during 1947, exhaustion of the reserves seemed possible within a few months. In August, the British convertibility experiment failed after six weeks, emphasizing how serious the external payments situation was.[23]

Europe's $7 billion current-account deficit

in 1947 represented an excess of total absorption over total production of only about 5 percent and an excess of goods-and-services imports over exports of about 65 percent. The contrast between these two percentages reflects how small external transactions were in comparison with Europe's domestic production and consumption.[24] The 5-percent figure perhaps suggests that the Europeans faced no hopeless task in readjusting to live within their shrunken means; even the estimated 13-percent deficiency of real gross national product per capita below the prewar level does not exactly spell catastrophe. Was the apparently critical disequilibrium of 1947 really due to inexorable physical realities? Or was it partly due to a greater degree of inflation in Europe than in the United States, whether suppressed by controls, as in the United Kingdom, the Netherlands, and Scandinavia, or openly shown in prices, as in Greece, Italy, and France? Exchange rates exaggerated the purchasing power over imports and export-type goods of the money incomes received by individual persons and businesses. Distorted prices did not correctly indicate how much austerity Europe's real economic deterioration required. From their own points of view, individual decision-makers appeared able to afford a level of consumption and investment that nevertheless exceeded the means available from an overall point of view.

Considering how small a further cut in absorption would have brought it into line with production and restored external balance, one wonders whether the simplest way out might not have been to stop distorting the price signals. The objection that too many "nonessentials" and not enough "essentials" would then have been imported makes little sense except as a worry about income distribution: poor persons might have suffered unduly as rich persons outbid them for scarce goods; "rationing by the purse" was unwelcome; controls were needed to distribute effective purchasing power more equally than money incomes. Other relatively respectable worries were that exchange depreciation

---

[23] On the British convertibility experiment, see Chapter 21 below.

The figures in the text are drawn from OEEC, *A Decade of Co-operation*, Paris: 1958, pp. 22-23, 159-160, and Robert Triffin, *Europe and the Money Muddle*, New Haven: Yale University Press, 1957, pp. 31-32, 43-44, 313.

[24] Triffin, *op. cit.*, pp. 43-44, 313.

would worsen the international distribution of incomes by turning the terms of trade against Europe, or that it might worsen European inflation. These standard theoretical arguments need not be reexamined here.

For some countries, the burden of bringing absorption into line with production would have been much heavier than the overall figure of 5 percent suggests. Germany, Austria, Greece, and Italy, in particular, had already suffered cuts in production and consumption far worse than the average (while Switzerland and the Scandinavian countries had already regained or surpassed prewar levels). Another familiar doubt concerns the feasibility of cutting absorption into line with production in just such a way as to reduce imports and free additional resources for production of exports. Perhaps short-run physical rigidities in the economic structure ruled out a workable realignment: it was common to speak of Europe's incompressible import "needs" and limited export "capacity" in the early postwar period. Conceivably, pricing was almost irrelevant to the problems of the short run. But this seems doubtful. It is practically a denial of economics to speak of "needs" and "capacities" as objective physical magnitudes unrelated to prices.

References to Europe's urgent need for imports and rigidly limited capacity to export might most sensibly have been interpreted as meaning that adjustment through market mechanisms would have been painful and undesirable. The European Allies had made disproportionate sacrifices in the common war effort, had earned the gratitude of the United States, and were entitled to continue living beyond their own resources for the time being. Humanitarian and political considerations called for similar treatment of defeated enemies. A consistent argument for economic aid would not have had to cite balance-of-payments statistics. Ideally, perhaps, countries should have received aid according to some sort of appraisal of their wartime sacrifices, modified by humanitarian and political considerations. It was questionable to earmark aid partly for pegging disequilibrium exchange rates—for that is what

linking aid to the balance-of-payments position amounted to.

American Aid Programs

Assuming continued American aid, it was becoming obvious by mid-1947 that the piecemeal approach was inexpedient. The United States had furnished about $2⅔ billion to liberated countries through the United Nations Relief and Rehabilitation Administration. It had lent $3¾ billion to Great Britain on easy terms. Sizable loans went to liberated Europe and the Far East through the Export-Import Bank and otherwise. Countries under American occupation, chiefly Germany and Japan, got nearly $3½ billion worth of civilian supplies. Congress voted $400 million in May 1947 for aid to Greece and Turkey under the Truman Doctrine. Nearly $600 million was appropriated later that year for interim aid to France, Italy, and Austria. From just before the end of the war until the start of the Marshall Plan in 1948, the worldwide total of piecemeal American aid came to almost $16 billion, about half in grants and half in loans.[25]

In his famous Harvard speech of June 1947, Secretary of State Marshall hinted at American support for a coordinated reconstruction program to be worked out jointly by the European countries. Taking the hint, representatives of 16 countries (not including Soviet satellites) met in Paris the following month, set up a Committee for European Economic Co-operation, and drafted a report for presentation to the United States in September. The report envisaged surpassing prewar levels of industrial and agricultural production and achieving reasonable balance-of-payments equilibrium within four years. Measures to liberate intra-European trade would be a vital part of the program. The report also emphasized that an import surplus would be necessary to achieve the production targets. The necessary balance-of-payments deficit with the Western Hem-

[25] Schelling, *op. cit.*, pp. 417, 421; Lorna Morley and Felix Morley, *The Patchwork History of Foreign Aid*, Washington: American Enterprise Association, 1961, pp. 12-16.

isphere cumulated over four years was estimated at \$22.4 billion, of which about \$16.5 billion would be a deficit with the United States.

The Marshall Plan got under way with the Foreign Assistance Act of 1948, passed in April, establishing the Economic Cooperation Administration to operate the aid program, and followed by an appropriations act in June and by subsequent annual appropriations. In April 1948 the 17 European countries (now including West Germany but still not Spain) signed a Convention for European Economic Co-operation, promising to work together for recovery and growth. Among the methods mentioned were a loosening of trade and payments restrictions and maintenance of internal financial stability and "sound rates of exchange." The Convention also promoted the earlier Committee into an Organisation for European Economic Co-operation. One of its purposes was to help in allocating American aid.

The European Recovery Program was originally supposed to last four years, until the middle of 1952. At the beginning, the executive branch of the U.S. government estimated that the program might call for appropriations of \$17 or \$18 billion over the entire period. Congress eventually voted a little over \$13 billion. The outbreak of the Korean War in 1950 interrupted the original program and shifted the emphasis in American aid from economic recovery to rearmament. The newly created Mutual Security Agency absorbed the functions of the Economic Cooperation Administration in 1951. By the end of that year, aid under the European Recovery Program had amounted to nearly \$11½ billion, of which about 10 percent had been in the form of loans and 90 percent in the form of grants.

At its peak, the aid program was providing most recipient countries with additional goods and services worth only about 3 or 4 percent of their own total production. Even after adjustment for the fact that local-currency prices, distorted as they were by rationing and price and exchange-rate controls, probably understated the importance of the aid goods, American aid still seems

not to have amounted to more than 5 to 10 percent of Europe's own production.[26] In comparison with imports alone, the aid seems larger. It paid for one-fourth of Europe's total imports of goods and services in the period 1947–1950 and for almost two-thirds of its merchandise imports from the dollar area.[27] For particular commodities of crucial importance, such as cotton, the aid program provided half or more of the imports; but this fact means little, for if aid had not been available, the Europeans would presumably have exercised especial restraint in buying relatively nonessential goods in order to be able to pay for the relatively essential ones. Only if one believes in urgent and incompressible import "needs" and inexpansible export "capacities" does the fraction of imports financed by the aid program serve as a meaningful indicator of how large and important the aid was. Actually, the great bulk of the recovery effort had to come from the Europeans themselves, as is clear from the smallness of aid compared with local production. According to the OEEC, however, "American aid played the crucial role . . . in financing essential import needs, accelerating investment and reconstruction, and permitting tolerable consumption levels."[28] Partly, perhaps, by providing psychological assurance as well as actual supplies, the program enabled European consumers to tolerate allocation of nearly 20 percent on the average of gross national product into investment. This was about one-third above the average prewar rate.[29]

During the first year of the Marshall Plan, food, animal feed, and fertilizers accounted for over half of the aid shipments. Some aid even went in the form of tobacco (a fact echoing the realities of American politics). Later on, as the emphasis shifted from relief to industrial reconstruction, raw materials, semifinished products, and machinery dominated the shipments. It is not generally possible, however, to judge the purpose or

---

[26] Schelling, *op. cit.*, pp. 431-433.

[27] OEEC, *op. cit.*, p. 33.

[28] *Ibid.* All OEEC countries received American aid except Switzerland. Sweden received a loan but no grants.

[29] Morley and Morley, *op. cit.*, p. 23.

emphasis of an aid program merely by knowing the types of goods provided. If an official program provides certain goods, less of these and more than otherwise of other goods may be bought in ordinary trade channels. Furthermore, when certain goods arrive in foreign-aid shipments, resources are freed for other types of production in the recipient country. It can be quite rational to assist a country's investment in factories, machinery, roads, harbors, and other fixed capital by giving it consumer goods; it depends on the pattern of comparative advantage and the opportunities for gain from specialization and trade.

A reminder is in order, incidentally, that the individual Europeans who received goods under the Marshall Plan—the consumer of American wheat, the farmer who received an American tractor, the manufacturer who received an American machine—were not themselves receiving free gifts. They paid local currency to their own governments for the aid goods, enabling the governments to meet the American stipulation that they set aside local funds equal in value to the grants received. Five percent of these "counterpart funds" were reserved to the United States for covering the expenses of administering the aid program and for buying materials to be stockpiled in the United States. The remaining 95 percent could be used as agreed upon between the recipient government and the American authorities—for financing public investment projects, for example, or in ways equivalent to cancelling the money as an anti-inflationary measure.

Of the aid provided under the Marshall Plan through 1951, five countries—the United Kingdom, France, Italy, Germany, and the Netherlands—received almost three-fourths. Nearly one-fourth of the total went to the United Kingdom alone, and about one-fifth to France. Decisions on dividing up the American aid apparently took into account such things as the part that each country's own economic recovery could play in the general recovery of Europe, the degree of Communist menace in the various countries, the "requirements" for maintaining "adequate" levels of consumption and invest-

ment, and the forecasted balance-of-payments position of each country, especially with the United States. The last criterion is particularly questionable, for reasons already mentioned. Yet when the members of the Organisation for European Economic Cooperation made the first two annual allocations, "The basic criterion for determining the aid allocation to any particular country was the prospective size of its deficit with the dollar area, but if this had been the only criterion it would not have provided incentives to close the dollar gap, for the bigger the gap the bigger the aid would have been."[30] The Organisation tried to lay down some principles to limit the consumption and investment targets used in assessing the probable size of each country's dollar gap. But agreement was difficult, and the OEEC eventually adopted the proportions set in the second annual allocation as the basic guide for the future. This nearly frozen formula gave countries greater incentives to remedy their balance-of-payments deficits than when aid allocations had illogically been subject to adjustment in accordance with balance-of-payments changes.

Accounts of the Marshall Plan customarily try to judge how successful it was in providing relief, promoting industrial and agricultural recovery, restraining inflation, encouraging European unity, aiding political stability, and countering the Communist threat. But no one knows how things would otherwise have worked out, and any judgment must rely heavily on historical intuition. No such attempt is necessary here, since the Marshall Plan has been mentioned at all only to prepare for surveying postwar monetary developments. In considering figures on European economic recovery and growth, it is helpful to recall that 1947 was the last year before the Marshall Plan and that 1951 was the year when the emphasis in U.S. foreign aid shifted away from European recovery.[31]

---

[30] OEEC, *op. cit.*, p. 33.

[31] For a good explanation of the reservations that must accompany the use of industrial-production indexes and of why such indexes may exaggerate increases in economic well-being, see Bank for International Settlements, 22d *Annual Report*, 1951–1952, pp. 38-44.

The Special Example of German Recovery

The remarkable economic recovery and growth of West Germany in particular is worth a closer look. In the immediate postwar years, the German economy labored under heavy physical destruction, political and economic division, displacement of millions of persons, Russian removal of industrial plant and equipment as reparations, and uncertainty due to proposals for permanent de-industrialization to stifle future war potential. A further handicap was a severe wartime expansion of the money supply whose effects on prices were still being suppressed by cumbersome controls. Paradoxically, perhaps, the victorious occupying powers retained the Nazi wartime system of a thoroughly controlled economy, except that, to make matters worse, the national economy of the Hitler period had been split up at the borders of the states into a number of miniature controlled economies. Trade between these was subject to a panoply of controls similar to those over international trade. The internal lines of demarcation became "harder to cross than any ordinary customs barrier."[32] The low level of production burdened not only the Germans but also the occupying powers, which had to stand the costs of the occupation and of relief to their defeated enemies.

For some time after the war, attempts were made to keep wages at least nominally the same as during the war. Wartime wages in turn had been more or less frozen since the wage and price stop of 1936. Apart from some special consideration for workers in key industries such as iron and coal, most wage increases had to take unofficial forms: employers might offer apartments or houses to good workers at low rents and might serve meals in factory canteens. A worker might still be receiving only 150 marks per month, for example, while the cost of the food allowed by the meager monthly rations might be only 12½ to 25 marks per person. At the same time, a single meal at a black-market restaurant might easily cost as much as his monthly wage. A black-market price of as much as 120 marks for a kilogram of butter was not unusual. With the official prices of "essential" items rigidly controlled, relative prices were curiously distorted: a woman's hat might cost as much as several tons of wheat. Since controls held prices and wages far below the equilibrium levels that would have corresponded to the swollen money supply, the typical family had ample cash balances and found ration coupons more meaningful than money as a limit on its purchases. The effect was twofold: on the one hand, workers lost incentive to stay diligently on the job earning money, since money was not, as in a normal price system, the key to obtaining goods and services; on the other hand, workers had good reason to stay away from work frequently and travel around the countryside in search of food obtainable by bartering with the farmers. Favorite barter articles included cigarettes, nails, small tools such as scissors and screwdrivers, cameras, household effects, and, among miners, coal. Travel on the government-owned railroads was one of the relatively few goods readily available for money at the low official prices. Trains were full of people, even sitting on the roofs and hanging on the sides, traveling to the countryside to engage in barter.[33]

The prevalence of absenteeism and of travel to conduct barter emphasizes how badly the normal channels of internal trade had withered up. Suppressed inflation had undermined coordination by prices. Not only normal domestic trade but also production lagged. In 1946, industrial production in the British and American occupation zones stood at only one-third of the 1936 level; in 1947, it was still under 40 percent.[34] At the beginning of 1948, Wilhelm Röpke, an economist who gave decisive advice on the subsequent economic reforms, was still able to say, "Germany is annihilated and transformed into chaos in a degree that no one can imagine

---

[32] Bank for International Settlements, 17th *Annual Report*, 1946–1947, p. 25.

[33] *Ibid.*, pp. 25, 36-37; Jacques Rueff, "Natürliche Erklärung eines Wunders," in A. Hunold (ed.), *Wirtschaft ohne Wunder*, Erlenbach-Zürich: Rentsch, 1953, esp. p. 208.

[34] Ludwig Erhard, *Prosperity through Competition*, London: Thames and Hudson, 1958, p. 11.

who has not seen it with his own eyes." In April 1948, another observer could write, "It appears as if the economic disorganization is continuing and will persist for an unforeseeable period of time."[35]

Then, after June 20, 1948, everything suddenly changed. Previously hoarded or black-marketed goods appeared, overnight, in store windows. Traffic filled the streets. All economic indicators "shot up steeply." Between the second and fourth quarters of 1948, total industrial production rose 45 percent and consumer-goods production 53 percent. The yearly average industrial production index rose 53 percent between 1947 and 1948, 44 percent between 1948 and 1949, and 25 percent between 1949 and 1950. In the period 1950–1957, gross domestic fixed capital formation amounted to one-fifth or more of gross national product; yet despite this heavy emphasis on investment, real private consumption in Germany rose at almost twice the average rate for all OEEC countries.[36]

It would be wrong to credit this dramatic recovery to one single cause. Various things presumably played a part—American economic aid, a zeal for hard work said to be a national characteristic of the Germans, an influx of competent workers, professional men, and business men from the Soviet zone, and moderation in union wage demands. But the most notable event, the one that most definitely invites a "before-and-after" comparison, is the currency reform of June 20, 1948, together with the other reforms directly dependent on it.

Monetary Reforms

These reforms ended the suppressed inflation that had been sabotaging the price mechanism. There are two main ways of doing this. The first is to let the suppressed inflation become an open one: relax or abolish controls and let prices and wages rise into line with the swollen money supply. France and Italy fairly well illustrate this approach. Germany took the second approach: bring the "equilibrium" price level down more or less into line with the existing controlled level by drastically shrinking the quantity of money. The old Reichsmark currency was abolished and a new Deutschemark currency introduced. Initially, at the time of the reform, individuals were entitled to exchange 600 old marks for 60 new marks, and business firms were entitled to a 600-for-60 exchange per employee. The remaining currency and bank-account Reichsmarks were blocked, to be subsequently released and exchanged for the new Deutschemarks. The terms of exchange eventually worked out to be 100 old for 6.5 new. Debts contracted in old marks were written down to one-tenth of their nominal amount in new marks.[37]

For the reform to have the best chance of success, it had to be, and was, accompanied by the almost complete abolition of price controls and rationing. Economics Minister Ludwig Erhard courageously took these steps despite general skepticism and opposition. Severe reduction in the money supply, not controls, was to be relied upon to keep prices from soaring. Money again represented purchasing power. Goods were available to whoever had it. City dwellers no longer had to make barter expeditions into the countryside; they now had the incentive to stay diligently on the job earning money. Businessmen had the incentive to concentrate their energies on producing the items most in demand rather than, as before, producing the items subject only to relatively lax price controls because the authorities considered them nonessential.

Germany's was the most spectacular but by no means the only currency reform in postwar Europe. The reforms fall into three general categories: (1) conversion of old money into lesser amounts of new, without

[35] Both quoted by Rueff, *op. cit.,* p. 204.

[36] *Ibid.,* pp. 204-205; Erhard, *op. cit.,* p. 26; OEEC, *Industrial Statistics, 1900–1957,* Paris, 1958, p. 9; U.S. Congress, Joint Economic Committee, *Economic Policy in Western Europe* (1959), p. 19. The production indexes cited should probably be regarded with even more than the usual reservations.

[37] John G. Gurley, "Excess Liquidity and European Monetary Reforms, 1944–52," *American Economic Review,* **XLIII,** March 1953, p. 87; Dagmar von Erffa, "Währungsreform," in *Wirtschaftslexikon,* Frankfurt: Humboldt-Verlag, 1954, p. 180.

any blocking of funds in the meanwhile, (2) blocking of funds in special bank accounts pending later release (or, in a few reforms, partial cancellation), but without any conversion, and (3) a mixture of conversion and blocking, as adopted by Germany. The mixed reforms occurred only in West and East Germany, Rumania, and Yugoslavia. The pure-conversion reforms were most typical of Eastern Europe, while the blocking reforms occurred in several Western countries, including Austria, Belgium, and the Netherlands. Several countries, including Great Britain, Switzerland, Sweden, France, and Italy, adopted currency reforms of the sort mentioned here either to a negligible extent or not at all.[38]

---

[38] See Gurley, *op. cit.*

The International Monetary Fund

 19

Background and Purposes

Before continuing with a survey of post-war international monetary experience, we should look at the structure of institutions and ideas within which events unfolded. The core of this "Bretton Woods system" is the International Monetary Fund. Transactions with the Fund will figure prominently in the survey to follow of the experiences of particular countries.

The IMF resulted from lengthy discussions of separate American, British, Canadian, and French proposals drafted during World War II. The British "Keynes Plan" envisaged an international clearing union that would create an international means of payment called "bancor." Each country's central bank would accept payments in bancor without limit from other central banks. Debtor countries could obtain bancor by using automatic overdraft facilities with the clearing union. The limits to these overdrafts would be generous and would grow automatically with each member country's total of imports and exports. Charges of 1 or 2 percent a year would be levied on both creditor and debtor positions in excess of specified limits. This slight discouragement to unbalanced positions did not rule out the possibility of large imbalances covered by automatic American credits to the rest of the world, perhaps amounting to many billions of dollars. Part of the credits might eventually turn out to be gifts because of the provision for cancelling creditor-country claims not used in international trade within a specified time period. The rival American plan took its name from Harry Dexter White of the U.S. Treasury. White rejected the overdraft principle and the possibility of automatic American credits in vast and only loosely limited amounts. Instead, he proposed a currency pool to which members would make definite contributions only and from which countries might borrow to tide themselves over short-term balance-of-payments deficits. Both plans looked forward to a world substantially free of controls imposed for balance-of-payments purposes. Both sought exchange-rate stability without restoring an international gold standard and without destroying national independence in monetary and fiscal policies. According to the usual interpretation, the British plan put more emphasis on national independence and the American plan on exchange-rate stability reminiscent of the gold standard. The compromise finally reached resembled the American proposal more than the British.

The Articles of Agreement of the International Monetary Fund (and also the articles of its sister institution, the International Bank for Reconstruction and Development) were drafted and signed by representatives of 44 nations at Bretton Woods, New Hampshire, in July 1944. By the end of 1945, enough countries had ratified the agreement to bring the Fund into existence. The Board of Governors first met in March 1946, adopted by-laws, and decided to locate the Fund's headquarters in Washington, D.C. One year later the Fund was ready for actual exchange operations.

According to its Articles of Agreement, the purposes of the International Monetary Fund are to promote international monetary cooperation, facilitate the expansion of international trade for the sake of high levels of employment and real income, promote exchange-rate stability and avoid competitive depreciation, work for a multilateral system of current international payments and for elimination of exchange controls over current transactions, create confidence among member nations and give them the opportunity to correct balance-of-payments maladjustments while avoiding measures destructive of national and international prosperity, and make balance-of-payments disequilibriums shorter and less severe than they would otherwise be.

Recognizing that these goals could not all be achieved promptly, Article XIV of the Agreement provided for a postwar "transitional period" during which the member countries might violate the general ban on exchange controls over current-account transactions. No definite length for the transition period was stated, but countries maintaining exchange controls more than five years after the start of Fund operations (that is, beyond 1952) were expected to consult the Fund about them every year.

The "purposes" mentioned above are vague. More specifically, the Fund provides international drawing rights (in effect, loans) to help its members meet temporary deficits without resort to exchange controls, exchange-rate adjustments, or harmful internal deflation. Member countries are supposed to "live with" or "ride out" purely temporary deficits, drawing on the Fund when necessary to supplement their own accumulated reserves of gold and foreign exchange. The Fund is not meant to use up its resources, however, hopelessly palliating "fundamental disequilibrium" (a concept examined later on). A country faced with a "fundamental" deficit in its international transactions may be expected to seek a remedy in devaluing its currency. An opposite situation of "fundamental" balance-of-payments surplus would presumably call for upward revaluation. Such adjustments were expected to be infrequent.

Quotas and Par Values

The rights of member countries to draw on the Fund, as well as their contributions and voting power, are based on their *quotas*.

During 1959 most members agreed to increase their quotas to 50 percent beyond their original sizes.[1] Several countries, including Germany, Japan, Canada, and Australia, agreed to even larger increases either to reflect their world economic positions more accurately or to have greater access to the Fund's resources. At the end of February 1965, the quotas totaled $15,885 million, of which the largest were those of the United States ($4125 million, or 26.0 percent), the United Kingdom ($1950 million, or 12.3 percent), France and Germany (each with 5.0 percent), India (3.8 percent), Canada and China (each with 3.5 percent, the Chinese subscription being almost entirely unpaid because of Communist occupation of the Mainland), and Japan and Italy (each with 3.1 percent). At that time, 102 countries belonged to the Fund. The chief countries neither belonging nor applying for membership were Switzerland and the countries of the Soviet bloc. As a general rule, but with an exception in favor of countries with low international reserves, each member contributed 25 percent of its quota to the Fund in gold or U.S. dollars and 75 percent in its own currency (or in non-interest-bearing demand notes payable in its own currency).

Each member of the Fund is supposed to have not only a quota but also a par value of its currency in relation to the gold content of the U.S. dollar in 1944. Very few countries have not declared par values, and most even of these maintain *de facto* parities. The par values chosen in 1946 were the exchange rates then in effect. Many of these initial rates were quite unrealistic, as emphasized by the fact that except for the United States, Mexico, Panama, El Salvador, and Guatamala, all members announced their intentions to maintain exchange controls

---

[1] "The general increase in quotas, which in 1959 added the equivalent of some $5 billion to the Fund's resources, was mainly designed to adjust the quotas to compensate for the increase in the level of prices by about 50 per cent which had taken place in terms of gold or dollars since the Fund began its operations in 1947." Per Jacobsson, *International Monetary Problems, 1957–1963*, Washington: International Monetary Fund, 1964, p. 271.

A further general increase in quotas came under active consideration in 1964.

for the time being under the "transition-period" clause. Between the initial choice of parities and the wave of devaluations in September 1949, however, only two countries, Colombia and Mexico, established new official parities with the Fund. France also devalued during this period but did not declare a new par value.

Transactions between member countries and the Fund are based on the official par values. These values are also supposed to prevail in private transactions: the Articles of Agreement oblige each member to permit spot transactions involving member currencies to take place within its territory only at exchange rates not more than 1 percent above or below parity. (A member whose monetary authorities freely buy and sell gold for the settlement of international transactions at prices within margins prescribed by the Fund is deemed to be fulfilling this obligation.[2]) In other (e.g., forward-exchange) transactions, the deviations shall exceed those for spot transactions by no more than the Fund considers reasonable. In short —and this point deserves emphasis—the International Monetary Fund embodies an international agreement to enforce fixed exchange rates even in private transactions.

A member government may propose a change in the par value of its currency only to correct a "fundamental disequilibrium" in the country's balance of payments. The Fund may not object if the proposed change will not move the exchange rate more than 10 percent away from its initial party. A country making a larger change without permission may be ruled ineligible to draw on the resources of the Fund and may even be expelled. The Fund may not veto an exchange-rate adjustment necessary to correct a "fundamental disequilibrium," however, even though it may dislike the internal social or political policies of the member country. Changes in parities, when made, call for corresponding changes in the Fund's holdings of the member currencies involved. Incidentally, the Fund may propose (though not impose) uniform percentage changes in the par values of all member currencies. The purpose of such a proposal, which has never been officially made, might be to revalue gold uniformly in terms of all currencies.

Exchange Transactions

The Fund's chief financial operations consist of buying currencies from and selling currencies to the treasuries or central banks of member countries. These purchases and sales might better be recognized as loan transactions: when a member "buys" some foreign currency from the Fund, it is borrowing it against the deposit of its own currency; and when the member buys back its own currency with gold or foreign exchange, it is paying off the loan. From the Fund's point of view, its "sale" of a particular currency constitutes a loan, except that when it sells a country its own currency, it is thereby ordinarily receiving repayment of an earlier loan to that country.

Transactions are subject to certain rules. Within any 12-month period, no member may buy (borrow) foreign currency in an amount causing the Fund's holdings of its currency to increase by more than 25 percent of its quota.[3] The Fund has authority to waive this restriction, however. It first

---

[2] It has been argued that this provision offers a legal loophole for junking the fixed-exchange-rate system, if so desired, without renegotiation of the Articles of Agreement. The Articles say nothing about how narrow the spread between official buying and selling prices of gold must be. The Fund might conceivably prescribe such wide margins that each currency's gold parity became meaningless. Yet by merely standing ready to buy and sell gold at these ridiculously far-apart prices, a member government would be "deemed" to be fulfilling the equivalent of its fixed-exchange-rate obligation. See Robert A. Mundell's remarks in *The United States Balance of Payments,* Part 3, "The International Monetary System: Functioning and Possible Reform," Hearings before the Joint Economic Committee, November 1963, esp. pp. 547-548, 590-591.

[3] This limit of 25 percent within 12 months applies only after the Fund's holdings of the member's currency have reached 75 percent of its quota. This would correspond to the initial position of a member whose currency had not been involved in Fund transactions, since the member initially subscribes 75 percent of its quota in domestic currency and the rest in gold or dollars. The logic of the 75-percent-of-quota qualification is to allow a country whose currency had been lent to others to borrow heavily from the Fund if necessary until its accompanying deposits of its own currency have restored the Fund's initial holdings of it.

granted such waivers in 1953 and thereafter has granted them with increasing liberality, most notably in making massive resources available to Britain and France during the Suez Crisis late in 1956 and to Britain in mid-1961. Another restriction, also subject to waiver, is that no member may cause the Fund's holdings of its currency to exceed 200 percent of its quota. In other words, considering the 75-percent initial position, a country may not be in debt to the Fund for foreign exchange worth in excess of 125 percent of its quota. The implicit counterpart of these flexible limitations on borrowing is a limitation on the lending obligations of countries with balance-of-payments surpluses. Each member deposits the amount of its quota, partly in domestic currency and partly in gold or dollars, and that is all. No matter how large its trade surpluses become or how small the Fund's holdings of its currency, a country cannot be required to furnish any more money (except in return for gold). It may be requested but cannot be required to make a loan to the Fund. In 1962, however, ten major industrial countries agreed to a plan whereby they stand ready to lend the Fund their own currencies to a total equivalent of $6 billion if the Fund should need any of this money for relending to any of the ten countries in an emergency.

The Fund levies interest and service charges on its sales (loans) of foreign exchange. These charges rise according to the size of the Fund's holdings of the borrowing country's currency in excess of its quota and according to the duration of this excess. The twofold progression of these charges emphasizes the expectation that a member country which has drawn on the Fund will reverse the transaction as soon as possible by buying back its own pledged currency. The complicated "repurchase" rules require, in effect, that the member buy back its own currency in the amount of half of any increase in its international reserves or in the amount of half the difference between an increase in the Fund's holdings of its currency and a decrease in its reserves, though it need not do so if its reserves are less than its quota. (Details are given in Section 7 of Article V

and in Schedule B of the Articles of Agreement.) According to a policy statement issued in 1952, the Fund expects a borrowing country to buy back its own pledged currency within at most three to five years.

Regardless of the particular foreign currency originally borrowed, the debtor must repurchase its own currency with (repay the loan in) either gold or *convertible* currency. (Loosely speaking, a country is considered to have a convertible currency if it has given up the postwar-transition-period excuse for exchange controls and has accepted the normal obligations of Article VIII of the Articles of Agreement.) The unattractive prospect of having to repay even soft-currency loans in hard currency[4] is one of the chief reasons why fully 85 percent of gross drawings from the Fund from the beginning through February 1961 were in U.S. dollars, with sterling, marks, guilders, French francs, Argentine pesos, Canadian dollars, Belgian francs, Italian lire, and Danish crowns, in that order, lagging far behind. The major European currencies had become externally convertible *de facto* at the end of 1958, however, and became convertible as defined by the Fund's rules in February 1961. This development, together with the beginning in 1958 of large deficits in the U.S. balance of payments, lessened the overwhelming dominance of the dollar in IMF operations. From the beginning of 1961 through February 1965, only 26.0 percent of all drawings were of U.S. dollars. Drawings of marks, French francs, guilders, and sterling amounted, respectively, to 25.5, 15.4, 6.4, and 6.3 percent of the total; and smaller drawings, listed in order of size, were also made in lire, Belgian francs, Canadian dollars, yen, Swedish crowns, pesetas, Austrian schillings, Argentine pesos, and Mexican pesos.

The Fund's first loan was a sale of $25 mil-

---

[4] A "hard" currency might be defined as one whose gold or foreign-exchange value is genuine—whose value, that is, does not require bolstering by special restrictions on the currency's salability or usability. "Hardness" thus pretty much coincides with "convertibility," not necessarily in the technical sense of the IMF's rules but in the broad sense of unrestricted salability and usability. A "soft" currency, conversely, is one whose supposed value is somewhat artificial or is impaired by restrictions on use of the currency.

lion to France in May 1947. After a burst of activity during the first two years, mainly for the benefit of West European borrowers, the Fund's operations shrank to a small scale. In 1950 the Fund made no new loans at all. Disequilibriums in balances of payments throughout the world so overshadowed the Fund's resources that American aid was allowed to carry the burden instead. Really large-scale lending did not resume until late in 1956, when the Fund responded to the balance-of-payments strains stemming from the Suez crisis. In the five months starting in mid-October, the Fund provided a total of over $1.7 billion for immediate withdrawal or as "standby credits," chiefly to Britain, France, and India. This figure was about half a billion dollars larger than the total amount of IMF transactions from the beginning through the fiscal year ending in April 1956. The Fund was also especially active in the fall of 1957 during the crisis caused by rumors of impending European exchange-rate adustments. The sterling crises of 1961 and 1964 brought further heavy activity.

The standby credits just mentioned were arranged under a system that the Fund had developed during its period of relative inactivity in the early 1950s. A standby arrangement gives a member a nearly (but not perfectly) iron-clad guarantee of being able to draw specified amounts of assistance as necessary within an agreed period of six months to a year (or more, if the arrangement is renewed). This system first went into effect on a small scale in 1952 and 1954 for the benefit of Belgium, Finland, Mexico, and Peru, but only a small fraction of the amounts made available by these early standbys actually had to be drawn. In fact, of the $7884 million of standbys agreed from the beginning through April 1964, only $1948 million, or one-fourth, had been used by that date.

Even in the absence of a formal standby agreement, the Fund's practice as it has evolved allows a member country to count on being able to draw assistance equivalent to its own gold subscription (normally 25 percent of its quota) virtually on demand[5] and to count on having its request for a further 25 percent considered very sympathetically if it can show reasonable efforts to solve its own problems. Requests for aid beyond these limits require "substantial justification" but "are likely to be favorably received when the drawings or stand-by arrangements are intended to support a sound program aimed at establishing or maintaining the enduring stability of the member's currency at a realistic rate of exchange." Members applying for aid ordinarily make "declarations of intent as to the programs that they intend to follow."[6]

The power to withold or limit its assistance gives the Fund a considerable amount of informal leverage over its members' domestic financial policies affecting their balances of payments. Its arrangements with the United Kingdom at the time of the Suez crisis gave strong support to the principle that even major sovereign countries must put up with "strings" attached to large-scale aid. Especially in dealing with underdeveloped countries in recent years, the Fund has typically fitted its financial aid into a comprehensive stabilization program that includes simplification of exchange rates and controls, fiscal and banking reform, and other anti-inflationary measures. The first such program was arranged for Peru in 1954, and most but not all of the later ones have also been for Latin American countries. On several occasions the Fund has joined with other international organizations, U.S. government agencies, and American commercial banks in providing financial support for stabilization programs. These "parallel arrangements" have been made not only for Latin American countries but even for Britain in 1956 and France in 1958. Both in connection with stabilization programs and separately, the Fund has often provided technical as well as financial assistance to under-

---

[5] To emphasize this point (and probably as a piece of self-advertising, also), the Fund recently began adding the amount of this so-called "gold tranche position" to holdings of gold and foreign exchange to arrive at the figures on member countries' "international liquidity" reported in *International Financial Statistics*. Unfortunately, this sort of change of concept causes annoying little problems for people concerned with the comparability of figures in time series.

[6] 1961 *Annual Report*, p. 17.

developed countries, whose government officials are reportedly more willing to discuss exchange and trade controls and domestic financial policies with international civil servants than with representatives of private banks or individual governments. The Fund also conducts a training program for officials of member governments, teaching courses in its own operations and in the preparation and use of monetary and balance-of-payments data.[7]

Table 19.1 summarizes the direct financial operations of the IMF and gives an impression of fluctuations in its activity over time. The figures include amounts drawn both in the regular way and under standby arrangements, but not unused amounts of standbys.

Table 19.1. Loans by the International Monetary Fund

Year	Gross Actual Drawings *(Millions of U.S. Dollars)*	Repayments
1947	468	6
1948	208	11
1949	101	2
1950	0	24
1951	35	74
1952	85	102
1953	230	320
1954	62	210
1955	28	232
1956	693	113
1957	977	64
1958	338	369
1959	180	608
1960	280	681
1961	2479	770
1962	584	1490
1963	333	267
1964	1950	820
Cumulative total through 1964	9029	6163

Repayments include both repayments by the drawer's repurchase of its own currency and by others' drawings of its currency. The addition is not exact because of rounding.

SOURCE: *International Financial Statistics,* April 1965 and earlier issues.

[7] Cf. Brian Tew, *The International Monetary Fund: Its Present Role and Future Prospects,* Essays in International Finance, No. 36; Princeton University, 1960, esp. pp. 3, 6, 7, 17-19, 22.

The Fund's largest borrowers in terms of cumulative amounts actually drawn since the beginning of its operations through the end of 1963 were, in order, the United Kingdom (alone accounting for 33 percent of the total), India, France, Brazil, Argentina, Canada, Japan, and Australia. The members with the largest debt to the Fund still outstanding at the end of 1963 were India (15 percent of the total), Argentina, Canada, Brazil, the United Arab Republic, and Colombia; in contrast with earlier recipients of especially heavy assistance, most of these are underdeveloped or semideveloped countries. A drawing of $1 billion in 1964, however, again made the United Kingdom the largest debtor.

Other Activities

The Fund's chief powers may be summarized as follows. It has authority to limit any member's use of its resources when it considers that they are being improperly used. It may declare members ineligible to draw on the Fund (or even expel them) for unauthorized exchange-rate changes, for use of its resources to finance unauthorized capital transfers (the Fund can permit or even request a country to impose exchange controls against capital outflows),[8] or for failure to remove "transition-period" exchange controls over current transactions when advised to do so. It may veto proposed changes in members' exchange rates beyond 10 percent away from the initial parity if it finds that "fundamental disequilibrium" does not call for such changes. It may invoke the scarce-currency clause to be described below. It may require members to consult with it about any exchange restrictions they may be

[8] Doubt persisted for some years whether the Articles of Agreement permitted the Fund to lend to countries whose balance-of-payments deficits were largely attributable to capital movements. In July 1961 a decision of the Executive Directors confirmed the Fund's practice as it had been evolving: such use of the Fund's resources *was* permissible. This decision makes sense in view of the "difficulty in separating current and capital payments under a system of convertible currencies." Jacobsson, *op. cit.,* pp. 247, 285.

As for the original idea in the Articles of Agreement concerning control over capital-account but not current-account transactions, the doubts developed in Chapter 7 above seem decisive.

maintaining. It may and does provide technical assistance to members and prospective members, particularly underdeveloped countries whose government officials lack experience. It may determine the quotas and terms of admission of prospective member countries not represented at the Bretton Woods conference. It may suspend certain provisions of the Articles of Agreement when it considers this necessary.

Besides its activities and powers already mentioned, the IMF has some further functions widely considered of real importance. It provides facilities for semicontinuous consultation among member governments about controls and financial policies and similar matters of mutual concern, presumably fostering compromises and informal understandings. Its annual meetings, in particular, provide forums for momentous declarations, including denials of rumored adjustments in exchange rates. Through its reports and research studies and in other ways, it exerts influence on policies and even on world opinion. Particularly under the leadership of Per Jacobsson, Managing Director from December 1956 until his death in May 1963, it has practiced moral suasion to combat inflation and promote sound or orthodox finance.[9]

The Fund shares with the CONTRACTING PARTIES to the General Agreement on Tariffs and Trade (GATT) the job of supervising and seeking to relax restrictions (including bilateral arrangements) that impede international trade and payments.

The term CONTRACTING PARTIES (in capital letters) refers to the signatories of what is basically an international trade agreement, conceived of not as individual countries but as a loose sort of international organization. The CONTRACTING PARTIES operate(s) through annual meetings, *ad hoc* committees, and a secretariat borrowed from the United Nations; several attempts to establish a more formal organization have failed. GATT today consists of arrangements for international consultation and compromise on trade policies and for negotiation of reciprocal but multilaterally generalized tariff reductions. It is also a body of rules for nondiscriminatory policy (with exceptions in favor of customs unions and historically recognized preferential economic relations), for avoidance of quantitative trade restrictions (with exceptions, particularly concerning balance-of-payments troubles, economic development, and agricultural programs), for moderation in the use of export subsidies, for simplification of customs procedures, for the freedom of transit trade, and, in general, for the liberalization of trade policies and equivalent internal measures.

Ultimately, GATT derives from proposals initiated by the U.S. State Department during World War II for international trade-liberalization agreements and for an organization to administer them. Postwar negotiations for both went forward in parallel. At Geneva, Switzerland, in 1947, pairs of countries negotiated about individual products of which each country was the other's principal supplier. The "concessions" so agreed on were then to be extended to all members of the negotiating group. During the bilateral stage of negotiations, each country was presumably willing to grant its trading partner "concessions" whose benefits would spill over onto third countries because it realized that it would at the same time reap some of the benefits of "concessions" initially negotiated between other pairs of countries. The results of 123 sets of negotiations among 23 countries were incorporated into a single General Agreement on Tariffs and Trade, signed in October 1947. It became provisionally effective the following January 1 among the United States and seven other countries. This agreement contained not only schedules of "concessions" on individual products but also numerous rules of trade policy, broadly the same as those to be administered by a proposed International Trade Organization. The final version of that Organization's charter was drafted at a lengthy conference in Havana and was signed by representatives of 53 nations, including the United States, in March 1948. To obtain such widespread agreement, the ITO charter included so many exceptions, loopholes, and deliberate ambiguities that even its friends could muster little enthusiasm; and only two countries ever ratified it, Australia conditionally and only Liberia unconditionally. The GATT, which was to have been absorbed into the ITO, remained to carry on alone. Since then, officials of the CONTRACTING PARTIES have regularly consulted with member countries maintaining questionable trade restrictions, exercising moral suasion for their removal. The Geneva confer-

---

[9] *Ibid.*, p. 37 and *passim*.

ence of 1947 has been followed by further general conferences at Annecy, France, Torquay, England, and again at Geneva. Additional reductions and simplifications of tariffs have been negotiated on a reciprocal basis. (All along, the President has hinged American participation in GATT, without ratification by the Senate, on authority claimed under the Trade Agreements Act of 1934, as extended and amended every few years, although Congress has explicitly and repeatedly refused either to confirm or repudiate this interpretation of Presidential authority.)

By mid-1964, GATT membership had grown to 62 countries, not counting several others taking part as associates or on an interim basis. Tariff "concessions" in the General Agreement include commitments to reduce, eliminate, or not increase or impose specified duties. At successive annual sessions of the CONTRACTING PARTIES, an increasing range of issues has come under discussion, including not only agricultural protectionism and the export problems of primary-producing countries but also the rise of regional economic arrangements such as the European Economic Community, the European Free Trade Area, and the Latin American Free Trade Association.

The Fund has chief responsibility for campaigning against restrictions on *payments* (i.e., on private transactions in foreign exchange), while GATT concerns itself with *trade* restrictions, such as quantitative import limitations and discriminatory tariffs. This division of responsibility is rather artificial, and is largely due to historical circumstances,[10] since exchange controls and import barriers often serve the same end, differing only in administrative detail. (There need be little difference between strict rationing of foreign exchange made available to *pay* for foreign automobiles and strict allocation of licenses actually to *im-*

---

[10] For one thing, GATT carried on as a substitute for the stillborn ITO, which was to have operated in tidy parallelism with the IMF. Furthermore, as Tew suggests (in the pamphlet cited, pp. 11-12), voting procedures and degrees of willingness to surrender parts of national sovereignty are involved. In GATT, each member has an ostensibly equal vote; but in the IMF, members have voting power according to (though not strictly proportional to) their quotas. The IMF could hardly have attracted its present near-universal membership if import restrictions for balance-of-payments purposes had been made subject to decisions voted on this basis.

port the automobiles.) Member countries are not supposed to use exchange controls to frustrate the intent of the General Agreement or to use trade policy to frustrate the intent of the IMF Articles. GATT members are authorized, however, to employ trade restrictions to reinforce the effectiveness of whatever payments restrictions the IMF, by exception, does permit. GATT members are required to accept the findings of the Fund on their problems of monetary reserves, balances of payments, and foreign-exchange arrangements. They must either belong to the Fund or conclude special agreements with it. The Fund is sometimes asked to decide whether a country's quantitative import restrictions, which GATT will in principle tolerate only as exceptions on specified grounds, are in fact justified by balance-of-payments troubles (i.e., whether they are needed to prevent a serious decline in the country's reserves or to achieve a reasonable rate of increase in very low reserves). If the Fund finds no balance-of-payments justification and the country can find no other approved excuse, it is supposed to remove the restrictions. In October 1959 the Executive Directors of the Fund decided that there was no longer any balance-of-payments justification for discriminatory features in restrictions maintained by member countries whose current receipts were largely in externally convertible currencies. The Fund communicated its decision to GATT, which then issued a similar statement.

The Scarce-currency Clause

One situation in which the IMF *would* authorize discriminatory controls is worth considering for the further insight it provides into the arrangements contrived at Bretton Woods. The "scarce-currency clause," number VII of the Articles of Agreement, contemplates a situation in which member countries' requests to draw a particular currency exceed the Fund's capacity to supply it. This situation might arise when other countries had exceptionally widespread or severe balance-of-payments deficits with some particular country and were seeking to "ride out" these deficits with the Fund's aid. Unable to meet all of these legitimate calls upon it, the Fund might inaugurate a study of the scarcity and issue a report, seek a loan from the scarce-currency country, or buy the scarce currency with gold. If all else failed, the Fund might formally declare the currency scarce and proceed to ration its available supply among the various applicants. Under the Articles of Agreement, this declaration would authorize member countries to impose discriminatory restrictions on their citizens' expenditures in and payments to the scarce-currency country.

The authors of the scarce-currency clause probably envisaged a situation in which something, probably an American depression, was heavily unbalancing payments between the United States and the rest of the world. Considering all that has been said about "dollar shortage" throughout the postwar period (see the appendix to chapter 25), one might expect the scarce-currency clause to have been formally invoked. Yet it has not been, and for several reasons. First, members' rights to draw on the Fund have never been regarded as fully automatic, so that the Fund has in effect rationed its dollars under normal rather than exceptional procedures. Second, American aid programs have supplied the rest of the world with dollars and so have moderated the demands on the Fund's resources. Third, the kind of discriminatory controls over transactions with the United States that would have been authorized by a formal declaration of scarcity have been practiced under the transition-period provisions, anyway, especially during the Fund's early years.

The scarce-currency clause is of interest, then, not for its application but for its recognition that if the balance-of-payments deficits of numerous countries are the counterparts of one particular surplus, the transactions of the deficit countries with the surplus country rather than among themselves are what require adjustment. Deficit countries should not have to hamstring transactions among themselves for the legalistic sake of acting nondiscriminatorily in their efforts to balance their transactions with some third country. (See the appendix to chapter 7.) Discrimina-

tory controls would then have advantages in comparison with nondiscriminatory controls, but not necessarily in comparison with adjustment by exchange rates.

Balancing of Payments under the IMF System

The broader ideas underlying the IMF system as a whole, even more so than those underlying the scarce-currency clause in particular, grew out of an interpretation of the monetary experiences of the 1930s. These ideas embody horror of fluctuating exchange rates and competitive exchange depreciation and faith in the virtues of deliberate international monetary cooperation. So basic is the insistence on fixed exchange rates that in the few instances of fluctuating-rate systems adopted by its members, the Fund's toleration has been "grudging and frigid."[11] According to its own staff,

If the Fund finds that the reasons advanced by a member for maintaining a unitary fluctuating exchange rate are persuasive, it may say so, although it cannot concur with the action. The Fund has to emphasize that such a measure must be temporary and that it is essential for the member to remain in close consultation with the Fund.

The system of fixed parities

was written into the Articles of Agreement because it emerged from the experience of the world over a period of many years. No one would deny that the maintenance of a given exchange rate is sometimes made very difficult either by a set of internal policies or by the external economic forces with which countries must deal. . . . Nevertheless, it is a striking fact that the maintenance of stable rates of exchange is virtually the invariable objective of all countries at all times; even those countries that have embarked on a policy of fluctuating rates have in practice generally stabilized their rates within narrow limits over long periods of time.[12]

Another of the key ideas underlying the International Monetary Fund is the distinc-

---

[11] W. M. Scammell, *International Monetary Policy*, London: Macmillan, 1957, p. 182.

[12] *The First Ten Years of the International Monetary Fund*, Washington, 1956, p. 14. The second passage is quoted there from the Fund's *Annual Report*, 1951.

tion, never precisely drawn, between "fundamental" and temporary disequilibriums in balances of payments. Temporary disequilibriums, by implication, stem from accidental or random disturbances and will presently disappear of their own accord; the standard example is a crop failure. Such deficits do not call for controls, devaluation, deflation, or any other corrective action; reserves, and if need be the IMF, can properly be drawn upon until the disturbances reverse themselves. Fundamental disequilibriums, as implicitly defined by contrast, presumably reflect deep-seated and persistent maladjustments, as between one country's income or price and cost levels and those in the outside world. Exchange-rate adjustment is a proper remedy for such conditions but is presumably expected to be necessary only rarely.

Still, the recognized possibility of adjustment means that the system drafted at Bretton Woods, unlike the pre-1914 gold standard, is not one of exchange-rate stability intended to be permanent. Rather, it is a system of "adjustable pegs." It attempts to reap the advantages of stable and flexible exchanges both. Except during brief periods of deliberate adjustment in pegged rates, international trade and investment will enjoy the benefits of stability. And on the rare occasions when a change has become advisable, it will be made in an orderly manner, after due consultation among experts, and with safeguards against the selfish nationalistic practice of depreciating excessively in order to "export unemployment" or otherwise obtain an unfair advantage for one's own country at the expense of others. (With postwar inflationary conditions being almost the opposite of those that motivated so many "predatory" depreciations during the 1930s, the Fund in fact has had to restrain unjustifiable devaluations less often than to prod discreetly for adjustments in clearly unrealistic rates.) Actually, the present system comes closer to combining the disadvantages than the advantages of truly fixed and truly free exchange rates. It is questionable whether the Fund has even yet established real confidence in currencies. Rate adjustments sometimes occur; and when they do, they are likely to be much sharper—

20 or 30 percent over a weekend—than those characteristic of fluctuating rates. Even when no adjustment is in fact made, its mere possibility can at times cause disruptive uncertainties, as several crises since World War II amply illustrate. (See chapters 20-25.)

The ideas underlying the Articles of Agreement slide over some crucial distinctions, particularly the distinction between truly free exchange-rate fluctuations, on the one hand, and, on the other hand, either governmental manipulation or unsuccessful pegging of rates, as during the interwar period. Paradoxically, though, the Fund is supposed to make some other, extremely delicate, distinctions. How, for instance, can anyone be confident that a given balance-of-payments disequilibrium is temporary rather than fundamental, except with hindsight, *after* the situation has been dealt with or has run its course? And how plausible is still another original key idea, now eroded—the hope of controlling disruptive hot-money movements while leaving current transactions free? The trouble is that capital can be transferred through changes in the timing or other aspects of normal current transactions. The realities of speculation—on a one-way option and by means of leads and lags if not openly—make the idea of deciding on exchange-rate changes only after thorough international consultation seem particularly wishful. As at the time of the devaluations in 1949, the authorities of a country desiring to change its exchange rate typically make up their own minds on the matter and then simply notify the Fund. Though this notification is phrased as a request for permission, the Fund actually faces the choice only between acquiescing or risking loss of face by seeing its authority flouted and the change made anyway. It may be that the administrative structure of the Fund is not conducive to unhurried deliberation among experts—the executive directors tend less to exercise independent judgment than to act as "glorified messenger boys" for the governments appointing them[13]—but the real difficulty inheres in the idea of the adjustable peg.

With regard to its other original objectives,

[13] Robert Triffin, *Europe and the Money Muddle,* New Haven: Yale University Press, 1957, p. 137.

as well, a verdict that the Fund has been really successful requires either a good deal of generosity or else a set of expectations tempered by the Fund's own unimpressive performance up at least until the time of Suez. (The trend of general opinion on what goals are practical and realistic may itself be one clue about success or failure, more objectively conceived.) Exchange controls under the transition-period excuse lasted many years beyond the time they were originally expected to lapse. Recent years have indeed seen important progress, as the next chapter describes. Still, any judgment whether progress has been sufficiently great and rapid implies a comparison of actual developments both with the expectations that prevailed at Bretton Woods and with the probable course of developments under alternative policies. Even today, most countries are still reluctant to dismantle exchange controls over transfers of funds abroad by their own citizens.

One possible reason for slowness in dismantling controls may be that the Fund (in contrast with the European Payments Union, described in the next chapter) provided no clearing machinery enabling members to use their surplus earnings in trade with some countries to finance their deficits with others. This omission no doubt reflected an optimistic assumption that convertibility of currencies for nonresidents, at least, would rapidly be achieved, making a centralized clearing machinery superfluous.

A more fundamental explanation is that the IMF system lacks any "automatic" international balancing mechanism. The IMF does lend financial resources for "waiting out" disequilibriums hopefully thought fated to go away of their own accord; it does stand "ready to subsidize this breath-holding policy." Unless by exercising moral suasion over its members' domestic financial policies or by authorizing infrequent deliberate adjustments in levels of exchange-rate pegging, however, it does nothing positive to promote equilibrium. It simply helps improvise *ad hoc* solutions for crises.[14] Trade and exchange

controls, which may be sometimes tightened and sometimes loosened and sometimes even hopefully relegated to a standby role, remain as a substitute for a continuously operating adjustment mechanism.[15]

Opinions and Prospects

Some writers have not shrunk from questioning whether the Fund has achieved the aims set forth in its Articles of Agreement. Perhaps more common, however, is the opinion epitomized in *Business Week* for March 30, 1957 under the heading "IMF Wins Over the Skeptics." According to the article, "a decade of prudent management" has wiped out original suspicions in American banking circles of a supposed "device to allow deficit-financing on an international scale." The sudden spurt of lending to meet temporary payments difficulties at the time of the Suez crisis was in line with the Fund's original objectives. Once maligned but now highly respected, the Fund has played an important role in preaching the merits of anti-inflationary policies.

Yet the "doubts and suspicions" wiped out by "prudent management" were not doubts about the key ideas underlying the Bretton Woods system. Little reassurance flows from almost a decade of prudent near-inactivity followed by heavy lending since then. It is only slightly reassuring to cite particular historical occasions when payments difficulties really did prove temporary and when the Fund's aid did let members wait for a crisis

---

14 William R. Allen, "The International Monetary Fund and Balance of Payments Adjustment," *Oxford Economic Papers,* new series XIII, June 1961, pp. 159-

164. As for exchange-rate changes, Allen (p. 152) interprets the Fund's view as that they *"conceivably . . .* should be seriously *considered* when rates are so immensely unrealistic that it would be patently *ridiculous,* if not politically and economically *disastrous,* to maintain them." On the other hand, frequent adjustments in pegged rates are hardly the answer, as the Fund itself has noted (1962 *Annual Report,* p. 62).

15 Robert A. Mundell (in the already-cited Joint Economic Committee Hearings of November 1963, especially pp. 546-547, 568) contends that the Bretton Woods system has fallen into desuetude: "the short-run stability of the adjustable-peg mechanism [has] turned into long-run rigidity"; the world has been slipping back to the inflation-stagnation adjustment rules of the gold standard or to "a system of creeping controls." The emerging system is just too costly in terms of the inappropriate discipline it sometimes imposes on national policies.

to blow over of its own accord. Some such occasions do of course occur. Skeptics simply maintain that not *all* disequilibriums are fated to blow over so easily, that the possibility of occasional self-curing disequilibriums hardly justifies dispensing with a continuous adjustment mechanism, that no one can confidently know in advance whether or not each particular disequilibrium is fated to blow over, and that delay in correcting a disequilibrium not so fated may, through speculation and otherwise, make the crisis unnecessarily serious. Some critics would even question the grounds for preferring a payments crisis that does happen to blow over to the alternative of a temporary and perhaps mild depreciation of the currency under pressure. As for episodes of bold, large-scale, and successful IMF activity in times of crisis, these hardly serve as evidence for the success of the system if the system itself tends to breed the opportunities for display of such heroism.

The management and staff of the Fund have no doubt been conservative, prudent, competent, and wise. But perhaps such talent has been sidetracked into administering questionable principles. Of course, the Fund renders valuable services. It provides "clubrooms," so to speak, for consultations among financial officials of various countries. Its experts give sound advice about domestic as well as international financial policy to some of its economically less advanced member countries, and this advice stands a better chance of being heeded precisely because it comes from a respected international agency rather than from some foreign government. The Fund prepares publications of high quality and great usefulness, such as *International Financial Statistics, Staff Papers,* and the *International Financial News Survey.* Its Annual Reports and Annual Reports on Exchange Restrictions are informative documents. Jointly with the International Bank for Reconstruction and Development, it maintains a specialized research library open to the general public. There is no reason why these services and facilities could not continue even if the ideas underlying the International Monetary Fund were to evolve into something else.

The changes in the Fund that an observer seems safest in predicting, however, are measures to increase its resources for operations of the kind so far pursued, with perhaps minor modifications. These and other proposals for international financial reform are surveyed in the last two chapters of this book.

From Bilateralism through the European
Payments Union to Convertibility

ℳ 20

Early Postwar Bilateralism[1]

Immediately after the end of World War II, a network of bilateral agreements governed European trade and payments. Each of the two parties to an agreement undertook to regulate its own residents' transactions with the other country to avoid any large bilateral imbalance, promote mutual offsetting of obligations, and so minimize the need for settlements by transfer of gold or hard currencies. The governments in exile of the Netherlands and the Belgium-Luxembourg Economic Union signed the first such agreement in 1943. By the spring of 1947 some 200 bilateral payments agreements were in effect in Europe alone. A few years later, almost 400 agreements (not counting those of Soviet-bloc countries) covered almost the whole nondollar world. Lack of an agreement between two particular nondollar countries usually meant either that trade between them was of little importance or that negotiations had somehow fallen through.

What was the purpose of so apparently restrictive a system? Didn't the very impover-

ishment caused by the war call for taking fullest advantage of the gains from multilateral trade? Rightly or wrongly, policy makers thought that desperate conditions called for drastic controls; free markets seemed a luxury for happier times. At controlled prices and exchange rates, shortages were almost universal. Not the least pressing was the shortage of foreign exchange. Almost every European government felt impelled to control trade tightly to make the best of the shortages and save hard currencies for essential imports not otherwise obtainable. In these circumstances, arrangements between countries to favor imports from each other and avoid use of scarce hard-currency reserves might permit rather than restrict trade. In comparison with the alternative of a nondiscriminatory system of controls, bilateralism had a liberal rather than a restrictive purpose.

Bilateral agreements usually came in pairs: a trade agreement sought to determine or forecast the purchases from the other country that each country would undertake or would permit to its residents, while a payments agreement governed the financing of this trade. Trade conducted by government monopolies could be planned rather simply. To regulate private trade, the two governments agreed to issue import or export licenses for specified quantities or values of goods. The results of this permissive rather than positive regulation were inexact; sometimes, for example, one country's purchases from the other would lag behind the forecasted amounts because of unattractive prices. An agreement therefore typically provided for a joint commission to study possible revisions.

---

[1] Some references for this and the next two sections include Robert Triffin, *Europe and the Money Muddle,* New Haven: Yale University Press, 1957, chap. 4; P. T. Ellsworth, *The International Economy,* New York: The Macmillan Company, 1950, pp. 675-681; Raymond F. Mikesell, *The Emerging Pattern of International Payments,* Essays in International Finance, No. 18, Princeton, N.J.: Princeton University, International Finance Section, 1954; Raymond F. Mikesell, *Foreign Exchange in the Postwar World,* New York: Twentieth Century Fund, 1954, chaps. 2 and 5; Merlyn Nelson Trued and Raymond F. Mikesell, *Postwar Bilateral Payments Agreements,* Studies in International Finance, No. 4, Princeton, N.J.: Princeton University, International Finance Section, 1955; and J. Kymmell, *De Ontwikkeling van het Internationale Betalingsverkeer,* Leiden: Stenfert Kroese, 1950, chap. 2.

Besides economizing on transfers of hard-currency reserves, countries also sought to safeguard their own exports from import controls exercised at the unilateral whim of other countries and to obtain essential imports on reasonable terms. Some paradoxes resulted. To win markets for its "nonessential" exports, a country might have to discriminate in favor of certain imports from a bilateral partner and against similar goods obtainable more cheaply elsewhere. Exporting countries were sometimes able to insist on tie-in sales: to get scarce "essentials" such as coal, their partners would have to agree to take "nonessential" imports also. In impoverished immediate-postwar Europe, trade flourished in luxuries such as expensive textiles, cosmetics, perfumes, jewelry, gourmet foods, wines, and vacuum cleaners. Foolish as the resulting pattern of trade may have seemed, each individual country may have been quite rational in bargaining for markets for products in which it had a comparative advantage, even if these were "luxuries."

The payments agreements accompanying postwar bilateral trade agreements differed from the prewar *clearing* agreements typical of Central and Eastern Europe and some Latin American countries in not bypassing the foreign-exchange market by having all payments made in local currency through a clearing office in each country. Instead, the postwar agreements, like the prewar *payments* agreements, allowed use of the normal institutions of the foreign-exchange market. Before the war, one of the two partners in a payments agreement typically had a currency free of exchange control; its currency was used in payments, while the other partner controlled the transactions of its own citizens for the agreed purposes. After the war, both partners, with rare exceptions, had exchange controls and regulated their citizens' transactions.

Degrees of centralization differed widely in the hundreds of postwar payments agreements. Countries with well-developed private-enterprise economies relied on the regular commercial banking systems, which served as agents of the authorities in screening transactions and applying controls. Businessmen dealt with their regular banks to buy foreign exchange for authorized purposes and to sell exchange earned from foreigners. Exports were invoiced and drafts drawn according to normal trade practice. Commercial banks won increasing freedom to hold foreign-exchange balances with correspondent banks abroad, provided they reported fully and promptly. Beginning in 1953, the banks of the main West European countries were even allowed to engage in multilateral arbitrage in spot and forward exchange. (See p. 368.)

Banks running low of foreign exchange demanded by customers for authorized purposes replenished their supply at their country's central bank, where they also sold excess accumulations of foreign exchange. (Reliance on the central bank diminished, of course, as international arbitrage expanded.) Central-bank transactions maintained the exchange rates reaffirmed in the bilateral agreements. Each central bank could supply or absorb the necessary amounts of the other country's money because it maintained an account and enjoyed overdraft privileges with the other's central bank. If necessary, it could draw an overdraft in the other currency and credit the equivalent in its own money to the deposit it owed to its partner. Except for the normal working balances of merchants and commercial banks, each country's foreign-exchange holdings drifted into the hands of its central bank. The central bank ordinarily exchanged any newly acquired deposits in the commercial banks of the partner country for an addition to its account with the partner central bank (or for a reduction in its own deposit liability to the partner central bank).

The net bilateral position developing between partners to an agreement thus tended to show up in the accounts of their central banks with each other. For this reason, discussions of early postwar payments arrangements could personify countries and speak of how much Ruritania owed to Graustark and whether or not Ruritania could use her surplus with Arcadia to cover her deficit with Graustark. Metaphorical language like this requires caution. It can be convenient and harmless only if everyone avoids thinking of countries ˄ monolithic units carrying on trade and finance in great lumps. It is important to understand what actions of individual firms, banks, and government agencies underlie metaphorical references to "countries."

The overdrafts that central banks granted each other made it unnecessary for transactions between two partner countries to balance over short periods of time or to balance exactly. Overdrafts provided a "swing," permitting flexibility in trade and serving much the same purpose as external reserves. Some agreements set no definite limit to the "swing"; agreements with Great Britain, in particular, typically set no limit to the other partner's possible accumulation of sterling. More commonly, though, a limit was set to how much one country might be called on to accumulate of the other's currency. In principle, a balance beyond this limit had to be paid off in gold or in some currency acceptable to the creditor. Alternatively, import and export licensing had to be modified so that altered flows of trade would work off the imbalance. In practice, unforeseen bilateral imbalances became so commonplace that swing limits degenerated from rigid cutoff or gold-payment points to mere "talking points" at which the partners would consult about a remedy. Exporters in a creditor country disliked seeing a debtor partner pressured into balancing its trade by cutting its purchases. Sometimes, instead, traders in the creditor country were allowed to buy goods in the debtor country for resale in third countries. Sometimes the authorities tolerated sales of private balances of debtor currency for creditor currency at depreciated rates. At times, though, reluctance of debtor countries to make settlement in hard currencies and of creditor countries to grant further loans threatened to shrink intra-European trade. This was particularly true during the period of acute "dollar shortage" between the failure of British convertibility in August 1947 and the start of the Marshall Plan the following year. (See pp. 379-380.)

The availability of swing credits with flexible limits shows further how the postwar agreements did not so much force trade into bilateral channels as free it from unilateral and uncoordinated controls. Bilateralism grew looser in several additional ways. Debtor countries sometimes did pay off bilateral imbalances beyond agreed limits in gold or dollars usable as the creditor countries wished. Sometimes bilateral arrangements could be used, officially or unofficially, to finance one country's imports from another for reexport to a third. Bilateral agreements with the United Kingdom, the Belgium-Luxembourg Economic Union, the Netherlands, France, and a few other countries covered their overseas currency areas as well as their home territories and so broadened the scope of multilateral trade. Finally, the transferable-account system set up by the United Kingdom in 1946–1947 and extended and simplified in 1954 enabled foreigners to use pounds earned by exports to the Sterling Area to pay for imports from a wide range of nondollar countries. (See pp. 379-381, 386.)

The Contagion of Bilateralism

The early bilateral arrangements had a more dismal side. Like several other types of economic control, they tended to be contagious. Suppose that Arcadia rejected bilateralism and aimed merely at overall equilibrium. Other countries' bilateralism and currency inconvertibility would interfere with Arcadians' using their surplus earnings in transactions with some trading partners to cover their surplus spending elsewhere. Even though they favored multilateralism, the authorities would have to operate their controls with an eye on Arcadia's bilateral positions with its trading partners. They would, that is, unless they tolerated unpegged exchange rates at which the values of any two foreign currencies in Arcadian currency failed (except by coincidence) to correspond to the official parity between them. In comparison with official parities, Arcadian currency would tend to be strong against currencies of countries with which Arcadia would otherwise have had bilateral trade surpluses and weak in relation to currencies of countries with which it would otherwise have had bilateral deficits. The pattern of broken cross rates would promote a certain degree of bilateral balancing in Arcadia's trade after all.

If, alternatively, the authorities encouraged Arcadians to insist on settling all their foreign transactions in U.S. dollars or other hard currencies, other countries' anxiety to conserve dollars would impede Arcadia's export business and, in turn, her ability to buy imports. Furthermore, if Arcadia did not limit the convertibility of its currency, it probably would see its exports discriminated against as individual foreign countries tried to develop trade surpluses with it to obtain dollars. To defend itself against such victimization, Switzerland, for example, made its franc inconvertible for exchange-control countries, even though it remained convertible for residents of Switzerland and other hard-currency countries.[2] With discriminatory controls and hard bargaining the usual practice, any country failing to join in and use its own bargaining power would suffer from unilateral foreign restrictions. Like Switzerland, some Latin American countries without a dollar problem of their own entered bilateral negotiations largely in self-defense.

The United States was the chief country not drawn into bilateral arrangements. Urgent postwar needs and overvaluation of foreign currencies were spurring its exports. It had no need to bargain in defense of its overseas markets or its foreign-exchange position.

First Steps beyond Bilateralism

The scope remaining for ordinary foreign-exchange institutions and practices and the flexibility offered by credits among central banks provided a point of departure for further liberalization. The next step was to overcome the incentives countries had to discriminate in favor of imports from partners with which they had bilateral trading surpluses even when goods might have been available on more favorable terms from other sources. Prospects for an early start of the Marshall Plan and the establishment of a Committee of European Economic Co-operation (forerunner of the Organisation for European Economic Co-operation) promoted ideas of a European clearing system. With their convertibility experiment having just failed in August 1947, however, the British were in no mood to risk another failure. (See pp. 379-380). A compromise took the form of the First Agreement on Multilateral Monetary Compensation, signed in November 1947, and then two successive Agreements for Intra-European Payments and Compensations, signed in October 1948 and September 1949.[3] Under these arrangements, the participating central banks informed the Bank for International Settlements every month of their bilateral debts to and claims on each other in the hope that a worthwhile volume of mutual cancellation or offsetting could be worked out. The process was far from automatic. The only automatic operations were the "first-category compensations," whereby each country settled its indebtedness to a second country by abandoning its claim on a third country but not by increasing its indebtedness to a third country. These automatic compensations applied in practice only to closed chains in which each country was a creditor of the preceding country and a debtor to the following one. From October 1948 through June 1950, such compensations represented only 2 percent of gross imbalances.[4] "Second-category compensations," in which some countries would exchange debts to or claims on some creditors or debtors for debts to or claims on others, always required the specific authorization of all concerned. In general, these compensations would replace claims on net creditor countries by claims on net debtor countries and replace debts to net debtor countries by debts to net creditor countries. In other words, intermediate countries would find their claims converted into currencies

---

[2] Jacques A. L'Huillier, *Théorie et Pratique de la Coopération Économique Internationale,* Paris: Librairie de Médicis, 1957, p. 206. Canada was another country notably inconvenienced by the bilateralism and currency inconvertibility of others.

[3] The texts of the agreements and supplementary protocols appear in the 18th, 19th, and 20th *Annual Reports* of the Bank for International Settlements, pp. 167-170, 232-254, and 262-286. For discussions, see W. M. Scammell, *International Monetary Policy,* London: Macmillan, 1957, pp. 264-278; Mikesell, *Foreign Exchange in the Postwar World,* op. cit., pp. 100-117; and Triffin, *op. cit.,* pp. 147-160.

[4] Triffin, *op. cit.,* pp. 148-149.

relatively softer than before and their debts converted into currencies relatively harder than before. For this reason, the necessary approval was seldom obtained. In all, compensations of both types cleared only about 4 percent of the positions that would have been cleared under full and automatic multilateral compensation; the remaining imbalance was met by bilateral credits and by U.S.-financed drawing rights.[5]

Under these early schemes, member countries continued to grant each other bilateral drawing rights (lines of credit or overdrafts). American aid under the Marshall Plan was based on advance estimates of each recipient country's deficit in transactions with the Western Hemisphere, but part of this aid was "conditional" on the recipient's grant of equivalent drawing rights to cover other countries' forecasted bilateral deficits with it. (See p. 343.) Besides depending on inaccurate forecasts, this system gave wrong incentives. Each country had reason to forecast deficits and obtain and use drawing rights. It didn't much matter if the imports financed by the drawing rights were less essential or higher in price than goods obtainable elsewhere, since they were, in effect, gifts; and the sale to importers for home currency of foreign exchange provided under the drawing rights had a welcome anti-inflationary effect. Countries with prospective bilateral trade surpluses, on the other hand, had incentives to grant drawing rights sparingly and obstruct their use, since the "conditional aid" came to be largely unconditional in practice; the drawing rights chiefly affected how a given total of American aid was classified into "conditional" and "direct" segments. By offering or withholding drawing rights, creditor countries could wield bargaining power over deficit countries and so strengthen bilateralism as against competition.[6]

Under this system of drawing rights and American aid, deficits and surpluses between each pair of countries were settled every month, even though they might soon have reversed themselves. Furthermore, countries received aid as compensation for granting drawing rights to their deficit partners even when they were already being compensated by drawing rights with other partners with which they had bilateral deficits. Operating on this monthly and bilateral basis, American conditional aid financed only one-third of the total net intra-European imbalance. Yet, according to Triffin, a smaller amount of aid administered on a cumulative and multilateral basis could have financed the intra-European imbalance completely.[7]

The 1949 agreement on intra-European payments moved slightly further toward multilateralism. One-fourth of the drawing rights could cover deficits with countries other than the grantor itself. Conditional aid went to the countries actually called on to honor them. But since the multilateral fourth was not available until the bilateral three-fourths had been used up, bilateralism remained nearly intact. The expansion of European trade before 1950 was perhaps due less to the monetary transferability provided by the compensation agreements themselves, limited as it was, than to American aid.[8]

The European Payments Union

The early compensation agreements were clearly inadequate. Furthermore, the last of them had hardly been signed in September 1949 when the wave of devaluations ruined its balance-of-payments forecasts. A more adequate multilateral compensation arrangement was worked out in 1950. The agreement for the European Payments Union was signed on September 19 but was made applicable retroactively to transactions that had taken place since July 1. The original agreement was to run two years; subsequent renewals were for a year at a time until the Union disbanded in December 1958. The members of the new system were the countries belonging to the Organisation for European Economic Co-operation, and indirectly, the Sterling Area and the overseas monetary areas of Belgium, France, Italy, the Netherlands, and Portugal. (Ireland belongs to the Sterling

[5] *Ibid.,* p. 149n.
[6] *Ibid.,* pp. 153, 157-158. Cf. L'Huillier, *op. cit.,* p. 218.

[7] Triffin, *op. cit.,* p. 155.
[8] *Ibid.,* p. 160, and L'Huillier, *op. cit.,* p. 208.

Area and although a member of the European Payments Union, had no separate position with it. Luxembourg's position in the Union was joined with Belgium's.)

The European Payments Union, though only a temporary arrangement, is well worth fairly detailed study. Since it operated routinely and continuously, clearing the deficit and surplus positions of its members and receiving and making payments and granting and receiving credit every month, an account of its operations serves as a convenient vehicle for surveying European financial history during its existence. This history underscores some noteworthy lessons about balance-of-payments behavior in the absence of a balancing mechanism. The history of EPU operations provides insight into the complexity of multilateral settlements when balances of payments are matters of direct governmental concern; it helps us appreciate, by contrast, what free exchange markets achieve with little fanfare. Furthermore, the EPU continues to serve as a model for proposed regional clearing arrangements in parts of the world where currency inconvertibility continues to prevail, such as Latin America.

The Union's key features were as follows:[9]

Each member's central bank was to continue advancing its own currency to other members as needed for day-to-day stabilization operations in the exchange market. Within months these bilateral credits were practically automatic and unlimited. Every month the Bank for International Settlements, as Agent for the European Payments Union, received reports on each member's bilateral debt to or claim on each other member as a result of the month's transactions. The agent consolidated each member's debts and claims into an overall net debt to or claim on the Union, much as an ordinary clearing house consolidates the items payable and collectable by the various member banks. Each member country's currency was considered equally hard at its official parity against the Union's

unit of account (equivalent to one U.S. dollar). Since each member could use its bilateral claims on some partners to cover its bilateral debts to others and had to settle only its net position with the rest of the group as a whole, the clearing system economized on transfers of reserves. Members no longer had reason to reject clearing arrangements that changed the currency in which a debt or claim was expressed; since the Union itself would be the creditor or debtor of each of its members, all members were in effect jointly guaranteeing the credit risks involved. Only central banks, not private parties, enjoyed this automatic transferability of their claims. Still, it removed monetary or balance-of-payments reasons for discrimination in trade among member countries.

Each member's settlement with the Union depended not just on its latest monthly deficit or surplus but rather on its cumulative position since the start of the Union in mid-1950. Each country's cumulative position was covered partly by automatic credit and partly by payment in "gold" (meaning gold or dollars). Beyond each country's *quota,* further settlement would be made entirely in gold or dollars, unless further credit was arranged by exception. With some modifications, each country's initial quota was set at about 15 percent of its turnover of visible and invisible trade within the EPU area in 1949. The quotas totaled $3950 million, the largest originally being those of the United Kingdom (27 percent of the total), France (13 percent), Belgium-Luxembourg (9 percent), the Netherlands (8 percent), and Germany (8 percent).

A country with a cumulative surplus was to grant credit in full up to the first one-fifth of its quota and was to grant credit and receive payment in gold in equal amounts for the remainder of its quota. A cumulative deficit country was to settle increasingly in gold as its deficit approached its quota limit. According to the originally agreed schedules, either a surplus position or a deficit position that had reached the limit of the quota would have been covered 40 percent in gold and 60 percent in credit. The schedules were simplified in mid-1954 so that all positions within

---

[9] Largely summarized from European Payments Union, *Fifth Annual Report of the Managing Board, Financial Year 1954–55,* Paris: OEEC, 1956, pp. 63ff., and Bank for International Settlements, 21st *Annual Report,* pp. 222ff.

quotas would be met 50-50 in gold and credit. In 1955 the shares became 25 percent of the quota in automatic credit and 75 percent in gold. To keep the absolute size of the credit element within quotas the same as before, the 1954 and 1955 amendments also increased the quotas to 1.2 and then to 2.4 times their original sizes.[10] The EPU paid interest to creditors and collected interest from debtors at rates rising with how long a time the debt had existed.

Early experience with heavily unbalanced trade soon undermined any idea that the quotas rigidly limited credit granted or received. The concept of *rallonges* (extensions) was first applied to creditor quotas and later to debtor quotas also: heavy creditors granted credit in excess of their original commitments and heavy debtors received special loans. The main postquota lenders were Belgium-Luxembourg in the early years of the EPU and Germany later on; France was the chief postquota borrower. At the end of the Union in December 1958, 16 percent of the total credit granted by the Union was by way of rallonge, and 55 percent of the total credit granted to the Union was by way of rallonge (all from Germany).[11]

The new system of partial gold settlements weakened earlier perverse incentives to run up deficits and acquire and use drawing rights. Gold losses would call for policies to cure persistent deficits. Similarly, the obligation to grant credit partially to cover surpluses was an incentive not to let surpluses grow. For merely moderate or temporary deficits, on the other hand, their partial coverage by automatic credit could serve as a reassuring shock-absorber, supplementing gold and dollar reserves. "It was hoped that by drawing on these credit lines Member countries would gain sufficient breathing space to take the steps required to restore their balance of payments without having to withdraw trade liberalisation measures."[12]

Under the original gold-and-credit settlement schedules, imbalances of certain sizes within quotas could have called for larger outpayments of gold to creditors than inpayments of gold from debtors. The EPU therefore needed a fund of working capital, so the United States provided $350 million. Because of initial grants-in-aid to so-called "structural" deficit countries, however, the Union's initial capital in fact amounted to only $271.6 million.

In parallel with the EPU, the Organisation for European Economic Co-operation sponsored a program of intra-European trade liberalization. Building on a start made the year before, the member countries agreed in October 1950 to remove quantitative restrictions in a nondiscriminatory way from at least 60 percent of their imports from one another (most of the calculations were based on private imports during 1948). Various devices for evading this liberalization were ruled out. In the following years the OEEC persuaded members to adopt partially standardized lists of quota-free imports and to increase the percentages of trade represented on these lists. These liberalization measures were qualified in several ways. First, countries could be authorized to backslide from trade liberalization in times of balance-of-payments crisis. Second, member countries retained considerable scope for choosing just which products to free from quotas to satisfy the agreed overall liberalization percentages. Third, measures to free intra-European trade from quotas were not fully reinforced for several years by measures to reduce tariffs, to relax restrictions on service transactions, to liberalize imports from nonmember countries, and to limit discriminatory pricing or subsidization of exports. Some progress was made on each of these matters, though.[13] More generally, the OEEC contributed to a trend in trade policy that helped inspire establishment of the European Coal and Steel Community in 1952, the European Common Market in 1958,

---

[10] Let Q be a country's original quota. Under the original, 1954, and 1955 arrangements, respectively, the credit element within the quota would amount to $.6Q = .5 \times 1.2Q = .25 \times 2.4Q$.

Besides the uniform quota increases just mentioned, the Dutch and German quotas were specially increased in 1951.

[11] Bank for International Settlements, 29th *Annual Report*, pp. 206-207.

[12] Managing Board of the European Payments Union, *Fifth Annual Report*, p. 63.

[13] Cf. L'Huillier, *op. cit.*, pp. 209-217.

the European Free Trade Association in 1960, and the European Atomic Energy Community in 1958.

EPU Operations in the Early Years[14]

The Korean War contributed to wide fluctuations in economic conditions and trade. Intra-European deficits and surpluses rose from the previous average of $200 million a month to $260 million in the 1950–1951 financial year, to $360 million in 1951–1952, and to a peak of $550 million in October 1951. Unexpectedly soon, the EPU faced the problem of abnormally large imbalances.[15]

EPU's first serious difficulty was Germany's import spurt and balance-of-payments crisis of the winter of 1950–1951. During the first half of 1950, expectations of falling prices on world markets had been holding down German imports and the inventories of German firms. When the Korean War broke out, the Germans, sensitized to inflation by two major experiences in a lifetime, were inclined to rush from money into goods. By an unfortunate coincidence, retroactive tax cuts decided upon earlier were swelling the public's spending power. Bank-credit expansion, appropriate earlier, was continuing to feed spending. Germany imported especially heavily from other EPU member countries because their export capacities were continuing to recover, because the 1949 devaluations had made their prices relatively attractive, and because intra-European trade was gradually being liberalized. The current-account deterioration was compounded by capital outflow through changes in ordinary trade credits— another example of leads and lags. By the last quarter of 1950, Germany's foreign-exchange reserves and automatic credit with the EPU were threatening to run out soon. The German authorities adopted internal credit-tightening measures and imposed advance deposit requirements for imports. In December, after approving the German program of seeking balance-of-payments equilib-

rium through tight credit and tax increases, the OEEC Council approved a special EPU loan of $120 million.

After reduced deficits in November and December, a buying wave related to fears touched off by the Chinese Communist intervention in Korea swelled the deficits again in January and February 1951. In March, with foreign-exchange resources at a low level, the German government temporarily suspended import liberalization. The OEEC approved of this step, appointed three independent experts to supervise the distribution of German import licenses, and warned other countries not to retaliate against German exports.

German export trade continued developing favorably, while the monetary and other measures to restrain both imports and speculative capital outflows began showing results. In March and April 1951, Germany ran surpluses with the EPU, and by the end of May the surpluses had grown large enough to permit full repayment of the special EPU credit five months ahead of time. By the end of the year Germany had become a net creditor of the union, had built her dollar reserves up to the highest level in more than 20 years, and had begun progressive removal of the trade and exchange controls restored in March.

The crisis thus ended, but only after drastic changes in financial and import-control policies, after borrowing abroad, and after months of anxiety. According to Triffin, "dynamic and successful handling" of the crisis through national monetary policy and international cooperation gave the young EPU "a prestige and authority far beyond the most optimistic expectations" of its promoters.[16] Speculating on how the situation would have evolved if the exchange value of the German mark had been free to fluctuate all along, Milton Friedman judged that "The whole affair would never have assumed large proportions and would have shown up as a relatively minor ripple in exchange rates."[17] If so, there would

---

[14] The following sections draw on the Annual Reports of the EPU and of its Agent, the Bank for International Settlements.

[15] Triffin, *op. cit.*, p. 180.

[16] *Ibid.*, p. 182. Triffin himself had been the chief architect of EPU.

[17] *Essays in Positive Economics,* Chicago: The University of Chicago Press, 1953, p. 163.

have been no crisis and no opportunity for international economic collaboration to get credit for solving one.

France and the United Kingdom provided further early examples of sudden major reversals of position. Both countries experienced initial surpluses so large that the union persuaded them, early in 1951, to step up their liberalization of trade and payments. A reversal began soon afterwards, in the spring of 1951. During the winter and spring of 1951–1952 France suffered a balance-of-payments crisis related to the inflationary impact of the Korean and Indo-Chinese wars, rearmament, and renewed flight from the currency. The EPU helped with a special credit of $100 million; French dollar receipts from American aid, military spending, and offshore contracts continued large; and France temporarily but totally suspended her import liberalization. The sharp resulting decline in imports kept France from exceeding her EPU quota as a debtor until the last quarter of 1952. From then on, except for moderate improvement from the last quarter of 1954 through the third quarter of 1955, the French cumulative deficit kept generally growing. Progress in trade liberalization was slow after being resumed at the end of 1953, and France resorted to export subsidies and "compensatory" import duties to adjust for an uncompetitive level of prices and costs.

The growing cumulative surplus of the United Kingdom (including the Sterling Area) reached a peak in the spring of 1951 as the largest creditor position in the EPU of any member up to that time. Then it began falling rapidly. By September a series of monthly deficits had shifted the position to the debtor side. By the end of May 1952 the debt had gone beyond the quota and had reached the stage of 100-percent gold settlement. The British response to the problem had already begun late in 1951. It, like the French response, spelled partial reversal of European trade liberalization and temporary frustration of one of EPU's chief objectives.[18] The British cumulative net deficit in EPU

stopped growing in the summer of 1952, and by the late spring of 1955 a series of monthly surpluses had reduced the cumulative deficit to only about one-fourth of its earlier maximum. Thereafter it grew irregularly again, though keeping well within the quota as increased in mid-1955.

Some EPU members exceeded their quotas as creditors for the first time in 1951—Belgium-Luxembourg in August, Portugal in September, and Italy in November. After long and difficult negotiations, each country agreed to grant credit for part of its beyond-quota claims, thus establishing the concept of "rallonges." At the mid-1952 renewal of EPU, a uniform arrangement with major creditors for half-gold-half-credit settlements within beyond-quota rallonges replaced dependence on *ad hoc* arrangements. At the same time, special arrangements were made to reduce Belgium-Luxembourg's beyond-quota cumulative surplus, partly by payment in gold, partly by conversion into a bilateral claim on the United Kingdom, and partly by consolidation into a medium-term debt of the Union.

At the time of this settlement, the troublesome Belgian surplus seemed likely to keep on growing. Like Portugal and Italy, Belgium tried to stimulate imports of goods and services from and exports of capital to other member countries. Belgium and Portugal began temporary partial blocking of export proceeds to discourage exports and lessen the internal inflationary influence of their surpluses. Belgium even resorted to licensing to divert exports from the EPU to the dollar area. These measures, together with antideficit measures in other EPU countries and post-Korea changes in the world economy, kept the monthly Belgian EPU accounts close to balance after mid-1952. Portugal's cumulative surplus, though in excess of her small quota at one time, never was large enough in absolute terms to be really troublesome; and a series of monthly deficits began whittling it away early in 1952. Italy's cumulative surplus also began declining about the same time, turned into a cumulative deficit by the spring of 1953, and had become a beyond-quota cumulative deficit a year after that.

---

[18] International Monetary Fund, *Annual Report*, 1953, p. 13. For details on the crisis and policy responses, see pp. 385-386 in Chapter 21.

The problem of extreme creditors did not vanish, however. The cumulative surplus of the Netherlands reached the limit of the quota around mid-1953 (but did not grow substantially more); and Germany, by this time, had already been experiencing a year of beyond-quota surpluses that were ultimately to grow to mammoth and troublesome proportions.

Increased Scope for Private Exchange Markets

Stabler economic trends in the EPU financial year 1952–1953 permitted further liberalization of imports and financial transactions. A number of members began permitting *multilateral* currency arbitrage: the transferability of member currencies, instead of being carried out solely by central banks and the EPU, could now be carried out on the ordinary foreign-exchange markets also. The United Kingdom had paved the way for this step as early as December 1951 by permitting banks to deal on their own account and no longer as mere agents of the authorities. Forward-exchange rates were allowed to move freely, and the range of possible spot-rate fluctuation within the official buying and selling limits was widened from 0.125 cent to 2 cents on either side of sterling-dollar parity. The British authorities granted freedom for *bilateral* arbitrage transactions with banks in the U.S.- and Canadian-dollar areas and soon extended it to transactions with Switzerland and the French and Belgian monetary areas. In 1952 the Netherlands and Sweden widened their ranges of possible fluctuation in intra-European exchange rates. These changes lessened the need for daily central-bank intervention in the foreign-exchange market and introduced some limited risk into speculative positions. Finally, in May 1953, the authorities of eight EPU members agreed to standardize the spreads between the official buying and selling limits of their currencies at about 0.75 percent on either side of parity and to permit banks to deal with each other in any of the eight currencies. (Previously, this freedom had been limited to bilateral operations.) Much of the multilateral offsetting of balances

previously done once a month by central banks through the EPU could now be done day by day by banks trading in the ordinary market. Much work remained for the EPU, however, in handling balances arising from direct transactions between central banks (for example, direct intervention in support of currencies, intergovernmental payments, repayment of old bilateral debts, and third-currency transfers). Multilateral arbitrage was authorized only for spot transactions at first but was extended to forward transactions in October 1953 and (more fully) in May 1956. The volume of forward arbitrage transactions was still affected by controls over capital movements enforced by most participating countries.

The new arbitrage arrangements were a step toward leaving multilateral compensation to private dealings in ordinary markets, with central banks intervening only to keep spot exchange rates from fluctuating sharply or from going outside of fixed limits. These reforms illustrate the spirit that guided EPU itself. Its managers apparently favored a cautious, gradual return to "normal" conditions in which their own services would no longer be needed.[19]

EPU Modifications of 1954 and 1955

During the 1953–1954 financial year, Germany's cumulative surplus and the cumulative deficits of France and Italy grew markedly (yet Italy had had a troublesome surplus as recently as 1952). Credit granted by surplus countries to deficit countries through the intermediary of the EPU was no longer serving, as originally intended, to meet temporary balance-of-payments fluctuations only; some credits had remained outstanding for three or four years. Persistent creditors faced internal financial problems related to their loans to the union, while debtors worried about their narrowed scope for meeting further deficits. By mid-1954, four of the seven creditor countries had long exceeded their

---

[19] See EPU, *Fifth Annual Report*, pp. 27-28, 67, *Sixth Annual Report*, p. 24; IMF, *Annual Report*, 1953, pp. 66-68, *Annual Report*, 1954, pp. 87-88; and Triffin, *op. cit.*, pp. 212-214.

quotas, and only $70 million out of an initial $1100 million remained available for settlements with the other three. Three of the eight debtor countries had far exceeded their quotas and were having to settle further deficits fully in gold, while only $200 million out of an initial $1350 million of quota credits remained available to the other five debtors.[20]

How could some of this outstanding credit be removed from the framework of the Union so as to reopen lines of credit for future EPU settlements? The renewal of the Union in mid-1954 brought a compromise. Some debts to and claims on the Union were converted into bilateral debts to and claims on particular creditor and debtor countries. Thirty-three separate agreements (and a few more in later years) had to be worked out. Most of them called for partial payment in gold or dollars at once and payment of the remainder in installments over several years. Each bilateral payment, when made, was to cancel an equal amount of the debtor's debt to and creditor's claim on the Union (until then, the amounts were to remain on the books of the Union, subject to its usual conditions and interest rates). The immediate payments plus the obligations for subsequent installments covered about three-fourths of the debts and claims outstanding at the time. Besides sponsoring the bilateral repayment system, the Union itself divided a special repayment of $130 million out of its dollar assets among the seven countries that were creditors in mid-1954. The immediate reduction in debts and claims outstanding within the Union correspondingly rebuilt the credit lines offered to or by the countries concerned.[21]

The arrangements of mid-1954 also extended the total borrowing privileges of deficit countries beyond the regular lines of credit within quotas. Creditor countries, in return for the partial repayment of their claims, agreed to new and higher limits to future

credits to the Union in part settlement of surpluses.

When the EPU was again renewed in later years, some further bilateral agreements similar to those of 1954 were made, but for smaller amounts. All creditors' claims, with the notable exception of Germany's, were brought well below the limits of their lending commitments.

Other important changes at the mid-1954 renewal of EPU were the 20-percent increase in quotas and the already mentioned agreement to settle future imbalances half in gold and half in credit. The latter uniform rule removed any danger that larger payments than receipts of gold or dollars might some time embarrass the Union.

When the EPU agreement expired again at the end of June 1955, it was prolonged for one month and then renewed with important modifications from August 1. The shift from 50-50 to 75-25 settlements moved further toward ultimate full settlement of all balances in gold or convertible currency rather than credit and also cut incentives to keep on discriminating against expenditures in the dollar area. The new settlement percentages were accompanied, as already mentioned, by a doubling of the quotas as adjusted the year before.

The 1955 renewal of the EPU for the first time contained a special termination clause. It remained in subsequent renewal agreements until finally put into effect in December 1958. The EPU was to be disbanded at any time when members holding at least 50 percent of the total amount of quotas requested it and if the standby European Monetary Agreement was brought into force at the same time. If major EPU members were to adopt external convertibility, the Union would no longer be needed to make their currencies transferable; and most settlements would then probably take place through the ordinary foreign-exchange markets. Still, a centralized settlement system was to be kept available for occasional use if members so desired. Under the new system, with settlements made entirely in convertible currency, the automatic credit characteristic of the EPU would no longer apply. Hence the

[20] EPU, *Fifth Annual Report*, pp. 67-68; Triffin, op. cit., pp. 193-194.

[21] EPU, *Fifth Annual Report*, pp. 34-36, 68; Bank for International Settlements, 25th *Annual Report*, 1954-1955, pp. 173ff.

standby agreement provided for loans on a
nonautomatic basis to countries in balance-of-
payments trouble.

Meanwhile, European steps toward convertibility included a pair of arrangements
that, though not actually a part of the EPU,
affected its members and shared its general
purpose. These were the "Hague Club" and
the "Paris Club."[22] The first resulted from
revision in 1955 of the bilateral trade and payments agreements between Brazil and several
EPU members. Brazil would no longer have
a purely bilateral position with each. Brazil-
ians could now collect for their exports and
pay for their imports in the currency of any
of the participants. Taken together with the
existing wide facilities for transferring sterling, marks, and Belgian francs, the new arrangement made Brazilian earnings of any
"club" currency available for expenditure
throughout most of the nondollar world (and,
by way of unofficial markets in sterling and
marks, for expenditure in the dollar area itself). The Brazilian authorities agreed not to
discriminate among the European participants
in controlling imports. A similar arrangement
with Argentina, the "Paris Club," was developed in 1956 and 1957 and eventually expanded to include all but a few EPU members, as well as Finland. It enabled Argentina
freely to transfer its earnings of one member
currency to other members.

Strains and Adjustments of 1955–1958

During the 1955–1956 financial year, four
EPU members had conspicuous imbalances.
After a respite the year before, France and
the United Kingdom again faced growth in
their large cumulative deficits. Among creditors, Belgium-Luxembourg ran a net surplus
almost triple that of the year before, and
Germany's yearly surplus roughly doubled.
These Belgian and German surpluses accounted for over 90 percent of the total net

surpluses and for all of the new credit granted
to the union during 1955–1956. Debtor and
creditor positions changed much more moderately than cumulative deficits or surpluses,
however, because of the new rule for 75-
percent gold settlements within quotas, settlement of certain net positions wholly in gold,
and some repayments outside the regular
monthly settlements.

EPU reports attributed the growth of imbalances during 1955–1956 to differences from
country to country in demand pressures and
price increases and in the effectiveness of
governmental measures. Some exceptional influences also made themselves felt in 1956–
1957—the Suez crisis, which raised fuel and
freight costs, deprived the United Kingdom
in particular of some oil earnings, and
touched off speculation against sterling (see
Chapter 21); frost damage to crops in February 1956, particularly in France; France's
Algerian expenditures, worsening an inflationary budget and credit situation; and the
mobilization of French reservists, which handicapped mine production in particular. The
French deficit and German surplus grew
notably. The gold and dollar assets of the
German central bank rose by about one-
third between mid-1956 and mid-1957, almost
entirely as a result of transactions with other
EPU members. The EPU positions of most
other members tended toward better balance
over the 1956–1957 financial year as a whole.

In the summer of 1956 the OEEC set up a
Ministerial Working Party to study the growing disequilibriums and related internal policies. Its report in November recommended
that debtor countries intensify their anti-
inflation policies and that creditors try to
increase their imports and use their surpluses
so as to avoid strain on other members. In
June 1957 the deputies of the Working Party
agreed that measures taken since the November recommendations had been insufficient
and that France and Germany had special
responsibilities for finding remedies. The deputies regretted that France had reacted to her
balance-of-payments crisis that very month
(June 1957) by completely suspending import
liberalization under the OEEC code. They
urged Germany to consider further unilateral

---

[22] Cf. IMF, 1956 *Annual Report,* pp. 100-101, 1957
Annual Report, p. 100, 1958 *Annual Report,* p. 127;
Bank for International Settlements, 26th *Annual Report*
(1955–1956), p. 140; EPU, *Sixth Annual Report,* pp.
24-25; Triffin, *op. cit.,* p. 217; Rolf Sannwald and
Jacques Stohler, *Wirtschaftliche Integration,* Basel: Kyk-
los-Verlag; Tübingen: Mohr, 1958, pp. 156-157.

tariff reduction, to limit capital imports through EPU channels, to facilitate capital export, and repay some government debt in advance.[23]

Intra-European disequilibrium became critical in the late summer of 1957. In France, the suspension of trade liberalization and restrictive budget and monetary policies were failing to stop foreign-exchange losses. A piecemeal *de facto* devaluation in August and October 1957 changed the rate from 350 to 420 francs per dollar. Speculation against the pound sterling had already been feeding on worries about British labor costs and about weakness of demand for primary products of the overseas Sterling Area. The Dutch guilder also felt some bear speculation. The corresponding bullishness centered on the mark, considered a candidate for upward revaluation. Intensified speculation drove the British government to drastic measures in September. The annual meeting of the International Monetary Fund that month heard firm declarations against exchange-rate alterations. France, Belgium, the Netherlands, Sweden, and the United Kingdom were taking steps to tighten credit. The Germans were easing their monetary policy and making advance transfers to the United Kingdom for debt repayments and arms purchases. The crisis thus blew over. Germany even ran monthly deficits in its EPU account in November and December 1957 and in February 1958.[24]

The measures taken to stem the 1957 intra-European crisis did not prevent renewed growth of Germany's cumulative surplus early the following year or the continued growth of the French deficit. France drew on $655 million of assistance provided in January 1958 by the OEEC, the International Monetary Fund, and the United States, tightened foreign-exchange regulations, and postponed reversing the suspension of trade liberalization. In mid-1958, when the EPU was again extended for what proved to be the last time, the overall degree of intra-European trade liberalization was about the same as it had been a year before. During the final six months of EPU, the German surplus continued growing. The next largest current surpluses were those of the Netherlands, Italy (which continued paying off old debt), and Belgium-Luxembourg. France again had the largest deficits, followed by the United Kingdom.

Western Europe as a whole escaped a repetition in the EPU's 1957–1958 financial year of the exceptional influences (Suez, poor harvests, and so forth) that had halted the growth of gold and dollar reserves the year before. Developments in capital movements and in the prices of several raw-material imports were favorable in 1958, while a temporary slackening of European economic growth occasioned cutbacks in inventories and imports. From mid-1957 to mid-1958 the total official gold and foreign-exchange reserves of all EPU member countries grew by some 14 percent. European reserve gains were especially rapid during the second half of 1958, and between mid-1957 and the end of 1958, they totaled 27 percent.[25] During 1958, Western Europe obtained by far the largest share of the record-breaking increase in total foreign gold and dollar reserves that corresponded to the swollen deficit in the balance of payments of the United States. The much publicized American gold loss of $2.3 billion was more than matched by the gains of West European central banks, which traditionally hold the bulk of their international reserves in gold.

These developments were but the last of a series that had paved the way for a return to European currency convertibility. In earlier years, international commodity markets had been reopened in London and other European centers and EPU currencies made acceptable in payment for reexport even of goods imported from other currency areas. Multilateral currency arbitrage had been restored among most EPU members. Sterling, marks, and some other EPU currencies had become widely transferable even for holders outside the EPU and dollar areas, and sterling had been made practically convertible into dollars by the start of official support operations in transferable sterling in February 1955. (See

---

[23] EPU, *Seventh Annual Report*, pp. 24-30, 33.
[24] EPU, *Eighth Annual Report*, pp. 15-17.

[25] *International Financial Statistics*, May 1959, p. 16.

p. 387.) Increased transferability enabled any EPU member to alter its position with the Union almost at will by using another EPU currency in settlement of non-EPU transactions or by dealing in it against dollars in the unofficial market. Such operations violated the logic of an automatic credit arrangement supposedly designed to settle net imbalances within the EPU area alone.[26]

The End of EPU: A Retrospect

At last, on December 27, 1958, Belgium-Luxembourg, France, Germany, Italy, the Netherlands, and the United Kingdom, holding more than the required one-half of all EPU quotas, announced that they wished to make their currencies externally convertible, terminate the EPU, and bring the European Monetary Agreement of 1955 into effect. All the other members except Greece (no longer an exception after May 1959), Iceland, and Turkey, together with Finland, followed suit in making their currencies convertible for nonresidents. (The Swiss franc had already been fully convertible for residents of Switzerland itself and of other hard-currency countries.) Foreigners currently earning any of the newly hardened currencies could now freely sell it for any other currency, including dollars, at exchange rates maintained within official support limits.

The Bank for International Settlements, as agent, proceeded to liquidate the EPU. Funds corresponding to the Union's capital were transferred to a new European Fund. The Union's small net interest earnings were distributed among member countries as increases in their claims on or reductions in their debts to the Union. The remaining convertible assets of the Union were distributed among its creditors. Finally, each creditor's remaining claim on the Union and each debtor's debt to it were split up among all other member countries in proportion to their respective quotas, and each of the resulting pairs of bilateral positions was then netted. Germany, as the largest creditor (holding more than three-fourths of the total claims against the

Union), acquired claims on all other member countries; and France, as the largest debtor (with 43 percent of the total liability, not counting the special credit of January 1958), incurred debts to all others. In all, 105 bilateral positions were thus established.[27] Repayments were scheduled over periods ranging from a few months to several years.

A description of the system that replaced EPU will follow some remarks in summary and appraisal. Table 20.1 classifies the ways that the cumulative total of the monthly bilateral positions of all members with one another were settled over the entire life of EPU. Explaining each item in the table will review the logic of the system. Item 1 is explained as follows: Each month each participating central bank may have used or granted overdrafts in dealings with each of the other participating central banks, running up a corresponding deficit or surplus (or a zero balance either if no bilateral credit had been used or granted or if any credit had been fully reversed during the same month). In the total, each bilateral position is counted twice, as one country's surplus and another's deficit, and all of the monthly totals are added together for the whole period of operation of the Union. The $46.4 billion figure refers to *net* bilateral transactions only, that is, the total of the balances left on each bilateral account after offsetting all debits and credits that had passed through it during the

Table 20.1. Cover for Total Bilateral Positions in EPU over Its Entire Existence

	Billions of Dollars	Percentages of Total
1. Total bilateral positions (deficits plus surpluses)	46.4	100
2. Multilateral compensations	20.0	43 ⎤ 70
3. Compensations through time	12.6	27 ⎦
4. Effect of special settlements and adjustments	0.5	1
5. Balance (= 1 minus 2, 3, & 4)	13.4	29
Of which settled in —		
6. Gold	10.7	23
7. Credit	2.7	6

SOURCE: EPU, *Final Report*, p. 39.

---

[26] Cf. Triffin, *op. cit.*, pp. 214-219.

[27] Bank for International Settlements, 29th *Annual Report*, pp. 215-220.

month; the value of the underlying commercial transactions was many times greater.

Item 2, "multilateral compensations," refers to bilateral positions cleared through the EPU at the end of the month when they arose. It is the total of the amounts by which each country's surpluses with some members were offset against its deficits with other members. The difference between items 1 and 2 is the cumulative total over the whole period of each member's monthly deficits and surpluses with all other members as a group. The table shows that rather less than half of the bilateral imbalances were multilaterally compensated away; more than half represented members' net imbalances with the rest of the group.

Item 3, "compensations through time," is the amount by which these consolidated deficits or surpluses were later—perhaps very many months later—offset by corresponding surpluses or deficits. (If a cumulative deficit country developed a surplus in some later month or a cumulative surplus country developed a deficit, the current monthly position was settled by repayment of gold previously paid or extinction of credit previously granted.)

Item 4, "effect of special settlements and adjustments," refers to settlements by positions initially allocated as grants, by transfers from initial holdings of national currencies, by the net effect of interest due to or from the Union, and by adjustments in connection with special gold credits.

Imbalances that had not been multilaterally offset, had not reversed themselves over time, and had not been specially settled or adjusted were necessarily met either by credit received or granted within the framework of the Union and not yet repaid or by transfers of "gold" not yet reversed. ("Gold" is not meant in the strict sense; it also includes dollars and other currencies acceptable to creditors.)

As Table 20.1 implies, the cumulative total of members' deficits and surpluses *not* multilaterally cleared each month (item 1 less item 2) was $26.4 billion. Of this total cumulative imbalance of individual members with the rest of the group, only $12.6 billion, or less than half, reversed itself over time. The major

part of the imbalance had to be met either by payments and receipts of gold and foreign exchange drawn from or added to national reserves or earned or spent in opposite imbalances with non-EPU countries or else by credit received or granted within the framework of the Union and not repaid by December 1958. This nonreversal of half of the net intra-Union imbalance emphasizes, for one thing, how little reason there is to expect a country's external accounts to be in balance with any group of trading partners smaller than the entire rest of the world, even over a span of several years, so long as any multilateralism prevails in worldwide trade. Restriction of multilateralism to a limited area would interfere with the international division of labor, as was recognized in the merely temporary status of the EPU.[28]

A second lesson of EPU experience serves once more to discredit the hope that balance-of-payments disequilibriums will prove minor and self-reversing. There were some spectacular reversals of position within the Union, it is true: the deficit crisis of Germany in 1950–1951 gave way to the persistent problem of mounting cumulative surpluses; the Sterling Area's surplus in 1950–1951 switched abruptly into deficits that later became troublesome; the Italian surplus in 1951–1952 later reversed itself; and the early deficits of the Netherlands later yielded to comfortable surpluses. But rather than being mere minor alterations first one way and then the other from a balanced position over the long run, these reversals illustrate how empty the notion is of a long-run equilibrium rate of exchange. Balances of payments are often inconveniently sensitive even to comparatively minor changes in domestic or international conditions. Experience under the EPU also provides several striking examples—notably the German and French—of severe disequilibriums accumulating over several years *without* any major reversal.

Several related aspects of the EPU illustrate the lack of adjustment mechanism. The Un-

---

[28] On this and some of the following points, cf. L. W. Towle, *International Trade and Commercial Policy*, 2nd ed., New York: Harper & Row, 1956, pp. 393-397.

ion was called on to provide emergency credits in time of balance-of-payments crisis, as with Germany late in 1950 and France early in 1958. The concept of rallonges was introduced to palliate the problems of cumulative deficit and surplus positions beyond quotas. For Germany, an unlimited creditor rallonge was established in November 1956 and was renewed up to the termination of EPU. At the termination, though, Germany had the only postquota creditor position; 55 percent of the outstanding total credit granted to the Union was by way of rallonge.[29] The corresponding figure had been only 27 percent in mid-1954, when the persistence of large debtor and creditor positions had nevertheless been considered troublesome enough to call for special bilateral repayments to deal with the problem. Balance-of-payments troubles caused a good deal of temporary backsliding from trade liberalization, as by Austria in 1951, Iceland in 1952, Turkey in 1953, and most notably by Germany and the United Kingdom in 1951 and France in 1952 and 1957.

EPU combined a regional payments scheme with preferential relaxation of trade barriers among the members. One disadvantage is that imbalances may result from differences among member countries in rates of domestic inflation, in degrees of currency overvaluation, and in the stringency of restrictions on imports from outside the area. Businessmen have an incentive to import outside goods into the member countries with the relatively most liberal trading policies for transshipment into the countries whose restrictions against outside imports are among the tightest and whose currencies are among the most overvalued in relation to the degree of domestic inflation. Or, if direct transshipment is effectively controlled, the inducement remains to import outside goods into the relatively least restrictive countries and then sell to other members of the preferential area either locally made substitutes for the imported goods or locally made goods embodying the imports or substitutes for them as ingredients. The relatively liberal intermediary countries thus face a drain of hard currencies in exchange for an accumulation of relatively soft claims on fellow members of the preferential area. Belgium, for example, experienced some of these difficulties until about mid-1952. Transit trade was subjected to licensing and extra restrictions imposed on imports paid for in dollars. The National Bank of Belgium was worried about undue domestic credit expansion based on the financing of the surplus of exports to other EPU countries. The steps taken to meet this danger and promote better balance in intra-European trade included a temporary partial blocking of the intra-European earnings of Belgian exporters.[30]

The EPU felt called upon to concern itself with the relation between balance-of-payments troubles and domestic financial policies. Some remarkably frank passages appear in its Sixth *Annual Report* (pp. 21-22, 30-31):

> With the increasing freedom of intra-European trade and payments, countries have become more vulnerable to the measures taken by their neighbours . . . a disequilibrium in intra-European trade and payments could not fail to become worse if the financial policies of the Member countries were not co-ordinated.

> . . . this increasing and freer flow of trade and of capital between Member countries, together with the gradual extension of the multilateral links with nonmember countries, makes the economy of each country more sensitive to developments in the economy of each of its partner countries and requires to a much greater extent than before that their economies should develop on parallel lines and that all should maintain internal financial stability. . . .

> This situation gives new emphasis to the role already played by the E.P.U. in providing a framework within which Member countries discuss their problems and the co-ordination of their financial and economic policies in the common interest.

A final observation about balance-of-payments adjustment is that although the EPU countries did not tolerate fluctuating exchange rates, some of them did make deliberate rate changes. In October 1950 Austria simplified

---

[29] Bank for International Settlements, 29th *Annual Report*, pp. 202, 206.

[30] Bank for International Settlements, 22nd *Annual Report*, 1951–1952, pp. 108, 198, 200, 24th *Annual Report*, 1953–1954, p. 109.

its multiple-exchange-rate system in a way that amounted to a devaluation of the schilling, and another simplification to a single-rate system in May 1953 amounted to a further devaluation. The French franc was devalued in 1957 and again when the EPU was dissolved in December 1958. The Greek drachma was devalued by 50 percent in 1953, after some earlier modifications of multiple-rate practices. Iceland made several changes in its multiple-rate structure during the life of the EPU. Modifications in the exchange value of the Turkish lira were even more numerous and complicated. EPU members also made numerous modifications in taxes and tariffs and other aspects of commercial policy serving as *ad hoc* measures for coping with balance-of-payments difficulties.

Despite lack of a continuous balancing mechanism, the lapse of 13 years since the end of World War II allowed time to overcome the war-created disorders so often loosely referred to as urgent import "needs" and damaged export "capacities." It allowed time for the financial policies and the price and income levels of the various European countries to become better aligned with one another at established exchange rates. What the EPU itself achieved was not so much a solution of each member country's actual or potential balance-of-payments problem as a simplification of it. Each member no longer had to concern itself with its position vis-à-vis each fellow member separately, but it still had to strive for overall balance.

Unlike the International Monetary Fund, the EPU was based on no ambitious blueprint for an ideal future state of affairs. It was designed as an immediate and temporary palliative for glaring defects in earlier arrangements. It loosened the rigidities of bilateralism and destroyed incentives for discrimination in controlling imports from fellow member countries. By encouraging gradual adjustments in national policies and by twice raising the percentage of gold payments in intra-European settlements, it helped prepare its members for increasingly liberal policies toward hard-currency countries as well.[31]

One may wonder whether the gadgetry and gradualness really were necessary, but by the tests usually applied to international economic institutions, EPU was an outstanding success.

The European Monetary Agreement in Operation

The shift from EPU to the European Monetary Agreement involved few administrative changes. All members of the Managing Board of EPU were initially reappointed as the Board of Management of the new European Fund. The Bank for International Settlements continued as agent for financial operations. The reorganization of the Organisation for European Economic Co-operation in September 1961 as the Organisation for Economic Co-operation and Development (with Canada and the United States added as members) likewise had no practical repercussions; the enlarged organization carried on as sponsor of the European monetary arrangements.

Under the post-1958 system, member central banks make settlements entirely in gold or dollars. The European Fund—something of a European miniature of the International Monetary Fund—replaced the automatic credit facilities of EPU. Its capital, consisting of the original U.S. contribution to EPU and of subscriptions by its members, amounts to $607.5 million (raised from $600 million when Spain joined in July 1959); part of the capital was actually paid in, and the rest remains subject to call as needed. The European Fund has the purpose, expressed in familiar language, of "providing all members with a potential source of short-term credit in order to aid them to withstand temporary overall balance of payments difficulties, in cases where these difficulties endanger the maintenance of the level of their intra-European liberalisation measures."[32] The OECD and the managers of the Fund have wide discretion in granting or withholding credits. They may take account of an applicant country's internal and external financial and economic situation and policies and may make aid conditional on adoption of their recommendations. All

---

[31] On the success of EPU, see Triffin, *op. cit.*, pp. 161-163, 199-200, 208-209, and *passim.*

[32] EPU, *Fifth Annual Report*, p. 50.

loans are drawn and are repayable in "gold" and bear interest. The lending activity of the European Fund has remained very small compared with that of EPU; in fact, only four countries (Greece, Turkey, Spain, and Iceland) had borrowed at all as of 1963.

The only remnant of automatic credit still available under the European Monetary Agreement is "interim finance": each country is required to make its own currency available between settlement dates to any other participant so requesting. The arrangement is the same as under EPU, except that each member has a limit on the total amount that it may draw from or advance to all other members.

The greatest change from EPU operations is that central banks are no longer expected to bring into the monthly settlements all balances acquired during the month. They need bring only balances arising from credit under the very few bilateral payments agreements still in existence or from interim finance not repaid during the month when drawn. This Multilateral System of Settlements is basically a standby with little work to do. Balances not required to be centrally cleared would usually not be, and any interim finance drawn would usually be repaid within the same month. The reason is that a central bank reporting a bilateral balance for centralized clearing must make payment (if a debtor) or accept payment (if a creditor) at the exchange rate which is at the limit of permissible fluctuation most unfavorable to itself; the central bank would almost always do better to deal in the ordinary market at an exchange rate fluctuating *inside* the official support limits. Operations under the new system have in fact borne out these expectations: members have conducted nearly all their foreign-exchange transactions on the ordinary market.

Unlike the EPU, the European Monetary Agreement was meant to be more than a temporary expedient. When the new arrangements were reviewed at the end of their first year, the Multilateral System of Settlements was extended indefinitely. Capital subscriptions of some countries were revised, and an amendment was adopted enabling the Fund to obtain special means of finance from members under certain conditions when wanted to finance larger loans to deficit countries than the ordinary capital subscriptions would cover. In the extent of its actual operations, however, the system has remained relatively unimportant.

The Outlook for Convertibility

How fully convertible did European currencies become? For many years, of course, the word "convertibility" has not had its traditional gold-standard meaning. It now means nothing more than unrestricted salability for other currencies. Even in this sense, most European currencies became freely convertible only for nonresidents of the country concerned; most Europeans still did not regain complete freedom to spend or lend or invest their money wherever they wished.

With all currency acquired by foreigners (in current if not capital transactions, anyway) becoming salable for dollars at officially supported rates, European governments lost any apparent financial reason for continued discrimination against imports from the dollar area. The level of a country's official gold and dollar reserves no longer depended on *where* in the outside world its residents made purchases. One country after another announced further liberalization of import quotas and licensing and an abatement of discriminations against the United States.[33]

Convertibility unified and broadened the markets in spot and forward exchange, made competition in them more keen, narrowed the spreads between buying and selling quotations, and apparently made forward premiums and discounts more responsive than before to international differences in short-term interest rates. The increased interest-sensitivity of short-term capital movements and the reemergence of an international money market was not entirely an unmixed blessing; as will be mentioned in some of the chapters to follow (particularly the one on the United States), heavy and volatile transfers of funds have occasionally embarrassed monetary authorities. Convertibility also increased the

[33] See Federal Reserve Bank of Kansas City, *Monthly Review*, May 1960, pp. 14-15.

attractiveness of the London gold market and contributed to a sharp increase in the volume of transactions in 1959.

Early experience suggested that European countries had moved toward convertibility at an opportune time. In February 1961 nine of them (Belgium, France, Germany, Ireland, Italy, Luxembourg, the Netherlands, Sweden, and the United Kingdom), as well as Peru, joined the United States, Canada, and the eight countries of northern Latin America that had already been operating under Article VIII rather than Article XIV of the International Monetary Fund Charter. By this step, which was more a symbol of liberalization already attained than an immediate step toward further liberalization, the ten additional countries at last waived the postwar-transition-period excuse for exchange restrictions and agreed to impose or maintain them thereafter only with the specific permission of the International Monetary Fund. Practically all currencies used to finance international trade and payments thus became "convertible" under IMF rules and eligible for use in repayment of drawings from the Fund. In March 1965, 26 IMF members had convertible currencies as defined by Article VIII.

It was still too early, however, for complacency. Piecemeal liberalization stretching over the ominously long period of 13 years between the end of World War II and the important measures of December 1958 still left many countries, particularly outside Europe and North America, with controls over trade and payments that on the whole were restrictive not merely in comparison with the period before World War I but even in comparison with the late 1930s. Perhaps currency convertibility will eventually become complete for residents as well as nonresidents; perhaps controls for balance-of-payments purposes will become quite unnecessary. On the other hand, backsliding may occur in the future, as it has in the past. There may have been an element of fortunate historical accident in Europe's early experiences with convertibility. The strength in European balances of payments corresponded to an apparent shift from "dollar shortage" to "dollar glut" in the balance of payments of the United States. Balance-of-payments worries had not disappeared: their focus had simply shifted. This point and others will be developed in chapters on the experiences of several individual countries.

Sterling since World War II

21

Britain's postwar experience is particularly worth reviewing not only because of sterling's role as a key currency but also for the sake of insights into the administration and gradual simplification of exchange controls and into the "stop-and-go" character of an economy in which policy interacts with recurrent external crises.[1]

The Legacy of War Finance

During World War II Britain's balance-of-payments deficit meant a welcome net inflow of goods for maintaining essential consumption and fighting the war. This import surplus was financed mainly by American Lend-Lease aid and by disinvestment and borrowing abroad. Foreign investments estimated at nearly one-third of the prewar total were sold. Most of the borrowing took the form of paying for overseas purchases with sterling deposits or other short-term sterling obligations. During the war, the British added roughly

£3 billion of such debt to the £½ billion or more already outstanding. By the end of 1946, these externally held "sterling balances" had risen to about £3.7 billion. India, Egypt, and the colonies were the chief creditors. Sterling Area countries had tended passively to accumulate sterling because of the linkage of their monetary systems with the British. Sterling earned by exporters in these countries, when sold for local currency at a fixed exchange rate, served as the legal reserve basis for local monetary expansion. The resulting inflations were part of the process of transferring real resources to Britain in exchange for paper or bookkeeping claims.

The end of the war cut off Lend-Lease aid. Britain now suddenly had to balance her external accounts or find new sources of finance. Devaluation of the pound was not seriously considered. Rightly or wrongly, people believed that an early postwar import surplus would be due not so much to wrong prices and exchange rates as to physical limitations on export capacity and to urgent and relatively incompressible import needs. The exchange rate was to remain pegged at $4.03; controls were to continue coping with balance-of-payments problems, and further foreign credits were to be sought.

The American Loan Agreement

A loan agreement signed in December 1945 and ratified by the United States Congress in July 1946 gave Britain a $3.75 billion line of credit, available at any time up to the end of 1951, carrying interest at 2 percent, and repayable in 50 annual installments beginning at the end of 1951 but subject to modification in

---

[1] General references include Judd Polk, *Sterling: Its Meaning in World Finance*, New York: Harper & Row, 1956, chaps. 3 and 4; Philip Bell, *The Sterling Area in the Postwar World*, Oxford: Clarendon Press, 1956, chaps. 2 and 3; Brian Tew, *International Monetary Co-operation, 1945–60*, 6th ed., London: Hutchinson's University Library, 1962, chaps. 10-15; Bank for International Settlements, various *Annual Reports* and also *The Sterling Area*, Basel: 1953; International Monetary Fund, various *Annual Reports*; R. G. Hawtrey, *Towards the Rescue of Sterling*, London: Longmans, Green, 1954, esp. chaps. 1-3; Peter B. Kenen, *British Monetary Policy and the Balance of Payments, 1951–1957*, Cambridge: Harvard University Press, 1960; M. FG. Scott, "The Balance of Payments Crises," chap. 7 in G. D. N. Worswick and P. H. Ady, eds., *The British Economy in the Nineteen-Fifties*, Oxford: Clarendon Press, 1962; and E. Victor Morgan, pp. 404-424 in his revision of Albert Feavearyear, *The Pound Sterling*, 2nd ed., Oxford: Clarendon Press, 1963.

years of severe British balance-of-payments difficulties. Canada lent another $1.25 billion. These loans were originally intended largely to cover the estimated (and, as it turned out, underestimated) British current-account deficit with the dollar world during the first three or four postwar years. The small size of the American loan had, in fact, disappointed the chief British negotiator, Lord Keynes. Besides granting the loan, however, the United States cancelled any British obligation on account of wartime Lend-Lease and provided a further long-term credit of $650 million to cover both civilian goods in the Lend-Lease pipeline at the end of the war and the purchase at bargain prices of American military installations and surplus goods located in British territory.

The loan agreement carried some noteworthy "strings" to prod the United Kingdom back into a multilateral international payments system. Britain promised not to restrict payments and transfers to the United States for current transactions and promised to avoid restrictions on the use of practically all American-owned sterling (but did not forswear nondiscriminatory trade restrictions, as distinct from exchange restrictions, on imports from the United States). Within one year after the agreement went into effect, furthermore, sterling currently earned by foreigners was to be freely convertible into dollars at the official exchange rate for purposes of current spending. Britain was to work out arrangements with Sterling Area countries so that their citizens also could freely convert currently received sterling for current use outside the Area; the agreement intended "that any discrimination arising from the so-called sterling area dollar pool will be entirely removed and that each member of the sterling area will have its current sterling and dollar receipts at its free disposition for current transactions anywhere."[2]

The convertibility provision did not cover sterling balances already in existence. The British and American negotiators hoped that the creditor countries would write off part of their claims in thanks for Britain's great share in the common war effort. Parts of the remaining balances might be blocked by mutual agreement at first and gradually made available in later years. These hopes were in vain. Australia and New Zealand did later write off a token of £46 million of their claims as a gift, but the major creditor countries, poor compared with Britain, were unwilling to scale down their claims. Around £3½ billion of the balances thus remained. The threat of their expenditure was met only by loose short-term blocking arrangements and by the regular practice in some countries of holding sterling as external reserves. Egypt, incidentally, left the Sterling Area because of disagreement over which government was to do the blocking.

The Failure of Convertibility

July 15, 1947, was the date for convertibility to begin under the Anglo-American agreement. Early that year, in preparation, the British authorities began liberalizing their bilateral payments regime by establishing a system of transferable accounts. Residents of specified countries were authorized to transfer sterling among themselves and into the Sterling Area for current transactions, and in February, transfers to residents of the dollar area were also authorized. Between then and July, more and more countries were added to the transferable-account list. To gain this status under the British exchange controls, a country had to agree to report transfers to the Bank of England, to accept sterling from the Sterling Area or from other transferable-account countries without limit or restriction in payment for current transactions, and to prevent capital transfers to nonresident accounts.[3] Finally, on July 15, convertibility was generalized to residents of all but a few countries with which the necessary agreements had not yet been reached. Persons living outside the United Kingdom could now sell currently acquired sterling or officially released old balances at the $4.03 parity for dollars or other currencies needed for current transactions.

---

[2] Quoted in Bell, *op. cit.*, p. 53.

[3] W. M. Scammell, *International Monetary Policy* (1st ed.), London: Macmillan, 1957, p. 425; Raymond F. Mikesell, *Foreign Exchange in the Postwar World*, New York: Twentieth Century Fund, 1954, pp. 43-44.

Actually, the time was not ripe for convertibility on these terms. A very severe winter had been followed in February by a fuel shortage that stalled much of industry and caused heavy if temporary unemployment. The loss of production, together with continuing inflation at home, swelled Britain's external current-account deficit. A hot dry summer now threatened a poor harvest. Quite possibly the pound was not really worth $4.03 in view of the terms on which and the amounts in which the British were prepared to supply exports. It is true that a comparison of British and American price indexes on a prewar base suggests, if anything, an *under*valuation of the pound;[4] but the British indexes remained more distorted by price and other controls than did the American. Lengthy delays in filling foreign orders for British goods further restricted the actual purchasing power of the pound. The countries of the outer Sterling Area were also running an increased dollar deficit. British surpluses in trade with some parts of the world were not convertible to meet the dollar deficit. On the contrary, the aftermath of war left much of the world still dependent on American supplies and anxious to snatch at any source of dollars. Knowing the date when convertibility would become effective, foreigners had an incentive to postpone their sterling receipts until then. A number of countries tightened currency or trade restrictions to increase their net earnings of newly convertible sterling. The segregation of currently earned sterling from old and supposedly inconvertible sterling proved far from airtight.

In short, foreigners leapt at the chance to convert. Britain lost about $1 billion worth of gold and dollars before abandoning convertibility, with American consent, on August 20. These losses contributed to the unexpectedly early exhaustion of the American loan in March 1948.[5]

---

[4] Cf. Lloyd A. Metzler, "Exchange Rates and the International Monetary Fund," *International Monetary Policies* (Postwar Economic Studies, No. 7), Washington: Board of Governors of the Federal Reserve System, 1947, pp. 24-27, 38-41, 44-45.

[5] The debt has not been forgiven; the British are still repaying it in the prescribed installments.

The failure of 1947 colored British attitudes for several years afterward, seeming to demonstrate more than ever the necessity for controls. Actually, what had failed was an exchange-rate-stabilization loan, for this is what the American financing of the supposedly temporary British payments disequilibrium amounted to. American aid might well have proved more constructive if it had been granted without the conditions that bedeviled the 1946 loan.

After convertibility failed, British exchange-control regulations reverted to the earlier type. What a holder of sterling could do with it depended not only on whether he lived in or out of the United Kingdom or Sterling Area but also on *where* he lived in the outside world. *American-account countries* included the United States and its dependencies, Canada, the Philippines, and several countries in northern Latin America. Residents of this "dollar area" could transfer sterling elsewhere with little or no restriction and could sell it for dollars at the official rate. Without these privileges, they would probably have refused to accept sterling altogether. In dealing with other nonsterling countries, the British authorities aimed in general to avoid gold and dollar losses but make sterling widely usable so it would be an attractive currency to hold. With sterling no longer convertible for payments to dollar countries, a number of countries quit the *transferable-account* group. Its relatively few remaining members were countries that were willing to use and hold sterling as an international means of payment, whose transactions with one another and whose sterling receipts and payments could be expected to stay in reasonably near balance, and whose authorities were willing and able to administer the necessary controls. Their residents could use sterling for payments into the Sterling Area and could transfer it for current purposes to residents of other transferable-account countries. More countries now fell into the *bilateral* classification, however, than into any other. With some exceptions, residents of a bilateral country could use their sterling freely only for payments to their fellow coutnrymen or to Sterling Area residents; transfers elsewhere required special administrative permission. For a small group of *unclassified countries,* the British authorities dealt with each proposed transfer as the question arose.

Membership in the transferable and bilateral groups changed from time to time. The progressive simplification of Britain's postwar exchange controls is largely a story of reclassification of bilateral countries into the transferable group. As will be mentioned later, practically all bilateral accounts became transferable in March 1954; and in December 1958, the transferable and American-account classifications merged.

Crisis and Devaluation in 1949

For several weeks early in 1948, after Britain had used up the American loan and until Marshall Plan dollars became available, Sterling Area reserves were without American support. The drain on them was cut during the year, however, by import restrictions and favorable export trends. The improved strength of sterling in world financial centers and the reduced discount on British banknotes in the Swiss and American markets seemed to justify optimism in early 1949. But the position weakened that spring. American exports to the Sterling Area, financed in part by the Marshall Plan, were holding up; but the value of American imports from the Area was being cut in half. A recession had begun in the United States late in 1948 and was still under way. American manufacturers were drawing down their raw-material inventories and currently buying less abroad. Prices of primary products exported by the overseas Sterling Area were softening. With domestic expenditures booming and their international current accounts in deficit, several overseas sterling countries were using their sterling balances to draw on the dollar pool in London. The main trouble did not lie in the United Kingdom itself, since its balance of payments was in approximate overall equilibrium in the year and a half before mid-1949. Surpluses earned in soft currencies or in old sterling balances were not usable, however, to cover a continuing dollar deficit.

As the year went on, sterling weakened further under speculative pressure.[6] Americans paid for larger and larger fractions of their imports from the Sterling Area with "cheap sterling," consisting of sterling bank accounts held by nonresidents of the Sterling Area and supposedly not convertible into dollars. Holders anxious enough for dollars to accept less than the official rate could sell their sterling through "commodity-shunting" or "switch" arrangements. Wool, rubber and other Sterling Area commodities ostensibly destined for nondollar countries could be paid for in non-American-account sterling, yet were in fact delivered to the United States. Sterling suffered in two ways. First, dollars that exports to the United States might otherwise have earned were sidetracked to countries holding supposedly inconvertible sterling. Second, the discounts on cheap sterling that made commodity-shunting attractive strengthened impressions that the pound was definitely overvalued at $4.03.[7] Traders were aware that British exporters were having difficulty competing in price and especially in delivery dates and suspected that the official rate misrepresented relative production costs in Britain and the United States. Though this is not clear from price and wage indexes, speculation did seem to be feeding on something fundamental.

As rumors of devaluation spread, traders sought to shift their borrowing to London in order to owe sterling rather than dollars. Foreign buyers of goods from the Sterling Area delayed their purchases and payments, while importers in the Area hastened to buy and pay before dollars and dollar goods should cost more in sterling. U.S. merchandise imports from the entire Sterling Area fell from $364 million in the first quarter of 1949 to $283 million and $224 million in the second and third quarters, rebounding, after the de-

---

[6] Cf. Samuel I. Katz "Leads and Lags in Sterling Payments," *Review of Economics and Statistics,* XXXV, No. 1, February 1953, esp. pp. 79-80; Bank for International Settlements, 20th *Annual Report,* pp. 149-150.

[7] Quotations on "cheap" sterling during the summer of 1949 varied from $2.80 to $3.20 according to the country of the holder. After April, British banknotes also weakened again on the Swiss and American markets, going to a discount of more than 30 percent by late summer. Bank for International Settlements, 20th *Annual Report,* p. 150 and graph on p. 149.

valuation, to $290 million in the fourth quarter. The ratio of U.S. imports to exports in commodity trade with the entire Area fell from 0.72 in the first quarter to 0.49 and 0.51 in the second and third before recovering to 0.74 in the fourth.[8]

Speculative influences on the timing even of ordinary trade thus show up in statistics despite at least two obscuring circumstances. First, devaluation and the resulting shift in expectations occurred while the third quarter still had almost two weeks to run. Secondly, a number of emergency measures were adopted in the summer of 1949, including tighter import controls designed to cut imports into the United Kingdom from the dollar area to three-fourths of their 1948 level. At a meeting in London in July, all of the Commonwealth finance ministers except the South African agreed to recommend similar measures to their own governments.

As late as September 6, Sir Stafford Cripps, the Chancellor of the Exchequer, made another one of his numerous denials that devaluation was impending, even though he must have had the step under very serious consideration by then and although American officials were confidentially urging it.[9] Cripps's denials failed to stop the speculative drain on London's gold and dollars. This drain, as well as the discounts quoted on banknote, transferable, and forward sterling, cumulatively intensified the distrust. By midyear the reserves were less than half as large as at the beginning of 1938, and less than one-fourth as large in real buying power, in view of the rise in American prices in the meanwhile. In the eleven weeks until September 18, the re-

serves fell nearly 20 percent further to $1340 million, or only about half the end-of-1946 level. The accelerating drain reached an annual rate of almost $1.4 billion. In the picturesque words of R. F. Harrod, "When some low-browed international financier, swirling the brandy around in his glass, uttered his profound thought, 'I don't believe the pound is worth four dollars', there was a run on the bank and all was over."[10]

On September 18, after consultations with the International Monetary Fund so scant as to be hardly more than mere notification, the British government announced a devaluation of the pound to $2.80. Its sharpness, 30.5 percent, came as a surprise. Twenty-three countries followed the British move within one week, and seven more followed later. In all, the wave of devaluations engulfed 31 countries (not counting colonies separately). The devaluing countries accounted for approximately two-thirds of all world trade and included the entire Sterling Area (except Pakistan, which staved off devaluation until August 1955), as well as Canada and most other countries of importance in world trade.[11] The chief currencies not devalued were the U.S. dollar and some Latin American currencies tied to it, the Swiss franc, the Curaçao guilder, and the currencies of Turkey, Brazil, Pakistan, Japan, and the Iron Curtain countries. In Western Europe, Ireland, the Netherlands, Greece, Iceland, Finland, and the Scandinavian countries, all devalued to about the same extent as Britain. (Finland's 30.5-percent devaluation came on the heels of a 15-percent devaluation in July, and Iceland's devaluation was followed in March 1950 by a further 43-percent devaluation.) Austria devalued by more than Britain (by 53 percent), and Belgium-Luxembourg, Germany, Italy, and France devalued by less.

These currency upheavals invite comparison with those of almost exactly 18 years before. (See pp. 295-299 above and Bank for International Settlements, 20th *Annual Re-*

---

[8] In 1950, by contrast, both U.S. imports from the Area and the import-export ratio rose from each quarter to the next. On both merchandise and goods-and-services accounts, U.S. transactions with the Sterling Area showed only a negligible surplus in the first quarter and moved into substantial deficit in the remainder of 1950. Exchange-rate expectations are of course not the sole explanation of these trade shifts; seasonal and business conditions (and Korea in 1950) also played a part. The figures are computed from U.S. Department of Commerce, Office of Business Economics, *Balance of Payments Statistical Supplement,* rev. ed., Washington: Government Printing Office, 1963, pp. 94-95.

[9] According to R. G. Hawtrey, *op. cit.,* p. 34, the decision to devalue was actually made at the end of August. Another British economist, speaking off the record nine years after the decision, dated it in July.

[10] Roy F. Harrod, *The Pound Sterling* (Essays in International Finance, No. 13), Princeton, N.J.: International Finance Section, Princeton University, 1952, p. 28.

[11] Federal Reserve Bank of New York, *Annual Report* for 1949, pp. 32, 36.

port, pp. 148-149.) Both episodes fell within periods of postwar reconstruction. Both involved heavy bearish speculation. On both occasions, the depreciation of sterling touched off chain reactions of exchange-rate adjustment. But there were differences. The commodity price declines that preceded the 1931 episode were severe and general and had been going on for at least two years (and more for wheat and other grains); the price declines in 1949 were of short duration and chiefly affected primary products imported by the United States. The 1931 episode occurred while a worldwide depression was still growing worse. The mild American recession in 1949, on the other hand, was a mere interval in a still generally inflationary period, and an interval already coming to an end at the time. Finally, the chain reaction of devaluations ran its course more quickly on the later occasion.

Recovery after the Devaluation

How effective were the 1949 devaluations? An answer would require knowing how things would have turned out otherwise. In a limited sense, though, the devaluations did work: they met a problem of speculation that would hardly have responded to any other treatment. The controls already in effect were proving inadequate, and additional controls would have had to be drastic and far-reaching indeed to cope with leads and lags and other ways of speculating through legitimate commercial transactions. It is only fair, however, to record the contrary judgment of the leading critic of the decisions of 1949. According to Sir Roy Harrod, The British devaluation was "a disaster of the first magnitude"; it would have been better to freeze every nonresident sterling balance and pay gold out of the reserve down to the last penny; it would have been better to adopt a firm policy of deflation while repudiating any thought of devaluation.[12]

In any case, the gold and dollar drain did stop promptly. Between September 18 and September 30, the British reserves rose from

$1340 million to $1425 million; and by the end of the year, they were 26 percent above the September 18 level. They kept on growing throughout 1950 and in mid-1951 reached almost triple the predevaluation low. The total gold and dollar holdings of countries other than the United States rose from $14.7 billion at the end of September 1949 to $18.2 billion a year later. A net inflow of $341 million of gold into the United States during the first three quarters of 1949 gave way to a net outflow of $150 million in the fourth quarter and another net outflow of $1709 in 1950. Between the first half of 1949 and the first half of 1950, the annual rate of current-account surplus in the United States balance of payments fell from $3.7 billion to $1.9 billion with the OEEC countries and from $7.6 billion to $3 billion with the entire world. After the devaluations, the major European countries enjoyed a "spectacular improvement" in their position.[13] Britain's net trade position within Europe shifted from monthly deficits of over $150 million just before the devaluation to monthly surpluses of from $20 to $90 million in late 1949 and the first half of 1950. Britain agreed to stop receiving Marshall Plan aid at the end of 1950, two years ahead of schedule.

So far, this account of what happened is probably too favorable. In part, the improvements were due to reversal of speculative positions, including resumption of delayed American purchases from the Sterling Area. Imports into the Sterling Area remained subject to the controls that had been tightened in the months before the devaluation. Britain's anti-inflationary measures presumably accomplished some of the intended restraint on imports. Reconstruction in Europe continued boosting the output available for use at home and for export. A business revival had gotten under way in the United States towards the end of 1949. Even before the Korean War broke out in June 1950, but especially afterwards, world demand was strengthening; the dollar prices of most American raw-material imports rebounded to and eventually above their predevaluation

[12] Harrod, *op. cit.,* pp. 28-29; *Policy against Inflation,* New York: St. Martin's Press, 1958, p. 151.

[13] Robert Triffin, *Europe and the Money Muddle,* New Haven, Yale University Press, 1957, p. 160.

levels. (Largely reflecting these price trends, the terms of trade of the United States worsened by about 26 percent between August 1949 and the middle of 1951, while the British terms of trade worsened by about 33 percent.) [14]

These are only some of the influences that almost hopelessly blur a view of how sensitively the flows of trade responded to the price adjustments accomplished by the devaluations. Between the first half of 1949 and the first half of 1950, the physical volume of European exports to the United States did apparently rise by just about enough to offset their reduced dollar prices; the aggregate dollar value of European exports to other markets in the Western Hemisphere actually rose about 10 percent. The European countries that devalued by 20 percent or more generally increased their shares of overseas markets, while countries devaluing little or none suffered relative losses in export markets. The Economic Commission for Europe ventured the conclusion that devaluation did indeed help improve the current-account balances of devaluing countries. [15]

The effect on imports is particularly hard to gauge because of the tariffs and controls already in effect and tightened in mid-1949. Even a highly price-sensitive shrinkage in the volume of *frustrated desires* to import would hardly show up in the statistics. On the export side, also, price was by no means the only determinant of trade volume. Britain was still apparently experiencing over-employment and latent or suppressed inflation; with some industries handicapped less by uncompetitive prices than by difficulties in obtaining factors of production and in making sufficiently rapid deliveries, a failure of devaluation to make exports boom would hardly be surprising. [16] But by the same token, it would

hardly teach any general lesson about the effectiveness of devaluation. Furthermore, the worldwide prevalence of controls explicitly *designed* to hamper the response of trade to price and profit incentives was bound to obscure how price-sensitive trade might be in a more liberal world. Simultaneous devaluation by so many countries in 1949 also made estimating the price sensitivity of any particular country's trade especially difficult.

Although they could not give due weight to the various specific historical influences at work reinforcing and neutralizing one another and obscuring the effects of devaluation, at least two prominent British economists (Harrod and Hawtrey) did imply that the "perverse-elasticities" case characterized the British balance of payments in 1949, at least in the short run. [17] A "colossal and unnatural rise in the volume of exports" strained Britain's manufacturing capacity, but to no avail. The devaluation of their prices in foreign currency shrank the total import-buying capacity of British exports, especially on the assumption that the uptrend of export volume would have continued even without the devaluation. [18] It is true that the dollar value of British exports to the dollar area rose not only above the depressed level of 1949 but also above the level of 1948. On the other hand, the physical volume of total British exports, after rising in 1950, slumped slightly again in 1951–1953.

Actually, the perverse-elasticities interpretation seems a strained one in the absence of any balance-of-payments deterioration and in view of the striking improvement in Britain's gold and dollar reserves.

Another of Harrod's objections to the devaluation was that, through import prices, it unleashed an inflationary cost-push on the British economy whose effects stretched out

---

[14] Mikesell, *op. cit.*, pp. 146-151.

[15] *Ibid.*, pp. 147-148, citing J. J. Polak in IMF *Staff Papers*, September 1951, and *Economic Survey of Europe in 1950.*

[16] For this view, see Hawtrey, *op. cit.*, pp. 30-32, 44; Harrod, *The Pound Sterling*, p. 26, and Harrod, *Policy against Inflation*, p. 132. Even in such a situation, however, a plausible if not conclusive case could be made for devaluation. Devaluation might increase the local-currency prices of export goods, thereby bidding some of them away from home consumers and also making it possible

for the export trades to bid additional factors of production away from production for the home market. Devaluation might be part of a process of opening up a suppressed inflation and correcting the disequilibrium pattern of prices and apparent real incomes that had been accounting for "absorption" in excess of the national means. Compare Chapter 8 above.

[17] Harrod, *The Pound Sterling*, pp. 30, 34; Harrod, *Policy against Inflation*, pp. 147-148; Hawtrey, *op. cit.*, p. 32.

[18] Harrod, *The Pound Sterling*, p. 29.

over several years. This may be true, but the question remains whether an alternative policy of relying on still stricter exchange and import controls could have warded off inflation. The latent or suppressed inflation already existing (and evidenced, perhaps, by delays in filling orders) should not be forgotten.

The Crisis of 1951–1952

The Korean War boom in the raw-material exports of Sterling-Area countries benefited the postdevaluation position of sterling so much that rumors of its impending upward revaluation (as well as revaluation of the Danish and Swedish crowns) circulated in the winter and spring of 1950–1951. Merchants now tended speculatively to delay receipts and hasten payments due in sterling. Traders outside the Sterling Area tended to accumulate sterling in anticipation of commercial needs.[19]

The bullish rumors ceased as the pound rather suddenly came under renewed pressure. The speculative inflow of funds in the first half of 1951 gave way to an apparently even larger outflow in the second half. The London gold-and-dollar pool fell by 40 percent between midyear and the end of 1951. The high prices and incomes previously received by Sterling Area exporters of primary products were having their full impact on imports only after some delay. Further time elapsed before goods ordered abroad were delivered and had to be paid for. Import payments thus peaked after the export boom had already begun to subside. The increased imports during 1951 apparently went mostly for additional private consumption, but increased investment in economic development was also important. To meet growing external deficits, country after country in the overseas Sterling Area drew on the London dollar pool. In the spring of 1952, several overseas sterling countries even developed a sterling shortage and for the first time since the war resorted to significant restrictions on imports priced in sterling.[20]

The United Kingdom was having troubles of its own. Its worsened payments position with the United States and EPU countries in 1951 was not fully offset by its shift from deficit in the first half of the year to surplus in the second in trade with the outer Sterling Area. For 1951 as a whole, import expenditure was 49 percent above the year before, while export value rose only 19 percent. The surge of imports went partly to replenish—and at increased prices—the business inventories run down during 1950, when the tightened import restrictions of 1949 were still in effect. Strategic stockpiling and an expanded rearmament program also absorbed imports. A steel shortage accompanying the defense program and a recession in world textile demand hampered exports. The invisible accounts suffered from the nationalization of British oil properties in Iran, a slump in the profits of companies engaged in the overseas production of commodities whose prices were now receding, an increase in overseas military expenditures, and the start of repayments on the American and Canadian loans. At home, shortages of steel, coal, and skilled manpower dramatized an inflationary atmosphere that affected business decisions. Speculative changes in the timing of import and export payments made matters worse.

Amidst the crisis, the Labor government lost the elections of October 1951. The next month the new Conservative government took several steps toward ending the cheap-money era that had lasted since 1932: it changed Bank rate for the first time since October 1939 by raising it from 2 to 2½ percent, discontinued pegging of the Treasury bill rate at about ½ percent, successfully converted about £1 billion of treasury bills into somewhat longer securities, tightened restrictions on installment buying, and maintained and intensified qualitative controls over new security issues and bank loans. The Chancellor of the Exchequer described a further increase of Bank rate to 4 percent in March 1952 as "an essential part of our campaign

---

[19] Bank for International Settlements, 21st *Annual Report*, pp. 128, 168, and 22nd *Annual Report*, p. 24.

[20] Cf. Bank for International Settlements, 22nd *Annual*

Report, p. 24; Samuel I. Katz, "Sterling's Recurring Postwar Payments Crises," *Journal of Political Economy*, LXIII, No. 3, June 1955, esp. pp. 221–224; and figures in *International Financial Statistics*.

to fortify the currency" and demonstrate readiness to take "whatever firm measures may be necessary, however unwelcome they may be."[21]

At an emergency session in London late in 1951, the Commonwealth finance ministers had already agreed to tighten controls again on imports from the dollar area and to backslide from trade liberalization under the OEEC Code. A 25-percent cut in dollar imports was generally taken as a target. But until tight money and the tightened import controls took hold, the reserves continued falling, reaching a level in mid-1952 some 56 percent below that of just one year before.

The crisis blew over in 1952 for several reasons. The 4-percent Bank rate and an end to rumors of a convertible floating pound had a healthy effect on capital movements. Some elements of the crisis had been inherently temporary, such as the rebuilding of depleted inventories and the speculation through leads and lags. Basically, current-account transactions overshadowed short-term capital movements; the crisis had been largely a gigantic fluctuation in the current account of both the United Kingdom and the outer Sterling Area. A dollar deficit in the first half of 1952 gave way to a dollar surplus in the first half of 1953. The reserves rose in the last quarter of 1952 and throughout 1953 and the first half of 1954.

The Simplification of Controls

Even at the worst of the crisis, around the turn of the year 1951–1952, discussions with the U.S. Treasury and the IMF were exploring how sterling might eventually be made fully convertible. One step, effective in December 1951, was to allow banks to deal in foreign exchange as principals and to hold limited foreign balances for the purpose. (From 1939 until then, banks had dealt only as agents for the Bank of England.) Even now, the banks could buy foreign exchange only for permitted payments to the country concerned; and arbitrage remained forbidden

until introduction of the multilateral scheme of May 1953.

Sterling's strength during 1953 permitted removing some domestic and import controls, as well as most of the restrictions imposed in March 1952 on loans to traders outside the Sterling Area. Sterling fared well even during the 1953–1954 business recession in the United States: easy money there created an interest-rate differential that apparently drew funds to London.

A more notable simplification in British controls came early in 1954. Until then, sterling payments had been largely bilateral (though decreasingly so as time went on; already the Bank of England was usually granting requests for transfers among important bilateral accounts). Officially, the transferable-account group included only the monetary areas of 18 countries agreeing to accept sterling payments for current sales to other transferable-account countries and the Sterling Area and agreeing to permit sterling transfers for current transactions only. Actually, enforcement languished. Transferable sterling changed hands readily and was even salable for dollars on active free markets in New York, Zurich, and other centers. By March 1954 it was quoted at a discount of only about 1 percent. The British authorities now added all bilateral-account countries, with three minor exceptions, to the transferable group. From now on someone living almost anywhere outside the Sterling Area could convert currently earned sterling at the official rate into almost any other currency except dollars. The new regulations even recognized the futility of trying to distinguish between current and capital transactions in transferable sterling. Facilities for holding it were extended to individuals and corporations as well as banks. Sterling's major classes were reduced to three: accounts belonging to Sterling Area residents, "American accounts" (belonging to residents of the dollar area, including Canadians), and the newly liberalized transferable accounts. (In addition there remained the minor category of "security sterling," consisting mostly of funds derived from legacies, sales of capital assets, and the like.) The only important simplifica-

---

[21] Bank for International Settlements, 22nd *Annual Report*, p. 28.

tion not yet undertaken was official convertibility of resident and transferable sterling into dollars.

A new minor category, "registered sterling," was created when the London gold market reopened in March 1954 after being closed or all but closed since 1939. Persons living outside the sterling and dollar areas could obtain registered sterling in exchange for gold or dollars and use it to buy gold or dollars or to make payment into almost any other type of sterling account. Sterling Area residents could buy gold only if they held special licenses as traders or industrial users. All gold transactions had to take place through a small number of authorized dealers (banks and specialist bullion firms).

In the second half of 1954 and at the beginning of 1955, a combination of fundamental and expectational factors weakened the sterling exchange rate and widened the discount on transferable sterling to 2 or 3 percent. In earlier years, such a discount would have been too small to make commodity shunting worthwhile; but since the simplifications of March 1954 had made the transferable-sterling market broader and more dependable, shunting developed again, especially in tin, and deprived the official reserves of some dollar proceeds of Sterling Area exports.

Partly to stop these transactions, the Exchange Equalization Account began, in February 1955, to support transferable sterling on its unofficial markets abroad.[22] It is not certain whether this support cost the official reserves fewer dollars than the discouragement of commodity shunting saved. Anyway, the discount was held to within about 1½ percent at most from then on except for a brief period during the Suez crisis of 1956. In fact, though unofficially, the British authorities were making nonresident sterling convertible into dollars at no more than a slight discount from the rate on American-account sterling. So important was this decision that Harrod dates the postwar restora-

tion of *de facto* sterling convertibility in late February 1955.[23]

Problems of 1955 and 1956

Despite Bank-rate increases from 3 to 3½ percent on January 27 and to 4½ percent on February 24, as well as tighter controls on installment buying, sterling's recovery in early 1955 was short-lived. Unemployment was down and unfilled vacancies up in the United Kingdom, investment was booming, and prices were rising again after a pause. Some overseas sterling countries were also feeling inflationary strains. Rising imports were eating into the gold and dollar reserves. Wage increases during the early months of 1955, an income-tax cut in the April budget, retirement pension increases, uncertainty preceding the elections in May, dock and rail strikes in May and June, and discouraging trade figures for June and July—all helped sap confidence in sterling. Rumors circulated concerning the eventual end of the European Payments Union and possibilities that the pound would be allowed either to "float" or to depreciate within widened support limits. During the third quarter of the year, until the Chancellor of the Exchequer scotched these rumors at the Istanbul meeting of the International Monetary Fund in September, speculation joined with current-account deficits in causing heavy reserve losses. Pressure on the banks during the summer to cut their lending, government budget adjustments in October 1955 and February 1956, and a further rise of Bank rate to 5½ percent in February helped defend sterling. The strain never reached true crisis proportions.

Disinflationary domestic policies, reinforced in the April 1956 budget, helped shrink Britain's current-account deficit with non-sterling countries and expand her surplus with the outer Sterling Area. American-account sterling fluctuated above par during the winter and spring, the discount on transferable sterling remained within 1 percent, and the reserves grew. Increasingly high in-

---

[22] "Shunting could not in practice be prevented by controls; it could only be discouraged by making it unprofitable." Tew, *op. cit.*, p. 147.

[23] *The Pound Sterling, 1951–1958* (Essays in International Finance, No. 30), Princeton, N.J.: Princeton University, 1958, p. 27; *Policy against Inflation*, p. 174.

terest rates in Germany began attracting funds, however. These transfers grew as rumors of an upward revaluation of the mark fed on the German Economics Minister's proposal for "a discussion of the problem of exchange rate parities" at the July 1956 meeting of the OEEC.

Sterling's intra-European troubles developed into something more general after Egypt seized the Suez Canal on July 26. The resulting need for heavier dollar outlays on imports showed how all European countries were vulnerable together. The already weakening rate on American-account sterling now fell close to the $2.78 limit, requiring official support that depleted the reserves by $272 million during the last five months of the year. Without special receipts of $177 million in September from sale of the Trinidad Oil Company to American interests and of $561.5 million in December from the International Monetary Fund, the reserve loss would have amounted to $1010 million in these five months (as a matter of mere arithmetic, not of cause and effect). The net loss for the entire year 1956 would have been $725 million, or slightly more than one-third of the reserves held in January. The deterioration occurred although the United Kingdom continued to run an overall surplus on current account. A number of countries, notably India and Japan, were drawing on their sterling balances. The speculative outflow of funds by way of leads and lags was particularly heavy after fighting broke out at Suez in October, since the closing of the Canal and the resulting switch in sources of imported oil threatened payments problems.

The British finally restored confidence in December by statements of determination to maintain sterling's $2.80 parity and by recourse to international assistance. The International Monetary Fund provided not only the cash already mentioned but also a standby credit for a further $738.5 million. The United States added a $500 million line of credit from the Export-Import Bank and waived the December interest payment due on the loan of 1946. At the end of the year, American-account, transferable, forward, and banknote sterling all were recovering from

several months of weak quotations; and the reserve drain stopped early in 1957, permitting a cut of Bank rate to 5 percent in February. No tightening of controls had proved necessary. The International Monetary Fund had successfully enabled a member to ride out a temporary and nonfundamental crisis; on this occasion, at least, it carried out the intentions of the Bretton Woods conferees.

The 1957 Crisis and 1958 Recovery

Even after the Suez crisis blew over, confidence in sterling suffered from strikes and strike threats in February and March and from worry that prices and wages had a stronger upward tendency in Britain than in competing countries. Long-term capital still escaped through gaps in Sterling Area controls. The British balance of payments continued running a current-account surplus, however, both globally and with the United States; and the overseas sterling countries more than met their current deficit with the United States by dollars received on capital account.

The next crisis was therefore not due to any obvious fundamental disequilibrium. The Rome Treaty for a European Common Market had been signed in March 1957, and negotiations were pending for a Free Trade Area of broader membership. The opinion grew that properly implementing these projects would call for adjusting exchange rates, in particular those of the reputedly overvalued French franc and undervalued German mark. Yet the Germans, whose overall trade surplus masked a heavy deficit with the dollar area, were reluctant to appreciate against the dollar. Any appreciation of the mark would probably have to be *relative* only, by way of a devaluation of sterling and a still sharper devaluation of the franc. A *de facto* devaluation of the franc in August and the persistence of Germany's trade surplus and foreign-exchange accumulations sharpened expectations. Discussions of exchange-rate policy were in prospect at the International Monetary Fund meeting in Washington in September and the OEEC meeting in Paris in October. Speculative transfers became heavy. The International Monetary Fund "estimated that outflows of this kind from official reserves in the third quarter of 1957 were of the order of $600–$700 million in the United Kingdom, and of about $175 million in the Netherlands; the inflow into Germany and into the United States may have amounted to $500 million in each case."[24] The German representative at the IMF meeting stated that more than half of the increase in Germany's reserves during the first eight months of 1957 had resulted from speculative operations. Much of the shift in short-term funds operated through the familiar commercial leads and lags.

Speculative opinion in the summer of 1957 was strikingly reflected in abnormally large spreads between spot and forward rates of exchange. Although German banks were forbidden to pay interest on foreigners' deposits (with a few exceptions not relevant here), the spread became so large at one time that by buying marks spot and selling them forward, an English bank, for example, could obtain a *de facto* interest rate of no less than 17 percent a year. A German firm borrowing at 8 percent in London could similarly earn 9 percent (17 minus 8) by thus going into debt. Another sign of the low confidence in sterling was the drop in the banknote quotation from almost $2.80 in July down almost to $2.56 in September.

At the worst point of the crisis, the official British gold and dollar reserves fell to about $1850 million, 22 percent below the level of just three months before. The loss attained a rate that would have spelled total exhaustion in a matter of months—and the prospect of exhaustion would doubtless have further accelerated withdrawals.[25]

As early as July the British authorities tightened exchange controls by forbidding residents of the United Kingdom to buy foreign securities even from residents of other Sterling Area countries without express permission. This departure from freedom of payments within the Area seemed necessary to check capital outflows operating through free markets in some parts of it, such as Kuwait, where dollar securities could be bought with resident sterling.[26] In August and September, to limit the availability of funds for speculation, the authorities put new restrictions on granting sterling credits to nonresidents. (British banks then resorted to the Eurodollar market—see pp. 467-471 below—and offered dollar credits in place of the prohibited sterling credits.)

The main response to the crisis came in domestic financial policy. Although the current account of the balance of payments posed no immediate danger, foreigners and residents alike were worrying that Britain "had lost control over the internal value of her money. . . . in the summer there were times when even the British Government found increasing difficulty in marketing its longer-term securities."[27] The government announced a pause in the upward trend of investment by central and local authorities and nationalized industries and asked banks to hold loans to the level of the year before. On September 19 the Bank of England raised its discount rate by two points to the highest level since 1921, pushing up the entire structure of money rates along with it. Instead of being seen as "panic action," an interpretation the governor of the Bank later admitted fearing, the "rather sensational"

---

[24] IMF, 1958 *Annual Report*, p. 48.

[25] Lionel Robbins, "Thoughts on the Crisis," *Lloyds Bank Review*, April 1958, n. s. No. 48, pp. 1-26, esp. p. 9.

[26] The "Kuwait gap" had been troublesome for years. To keep the oil-rich Persian Gulf sheikdom in the Sterling Area, Britain tolerated its virtual lack of payments restrictions; Kuwaitis could use their abundant foreign-exchange earnings as they wished. As residents of the Sterling Area, they could also sell securities they owned to residents of the United Kingdom. Arbitrageurs profited by the resale in London of sterling securities bought in New York at a discount roughly in line with the discount on security sterling. Kuwaiti arbitrageurs also bought dollar securities in New York and resold them in London at the prevailing premium. By liquidating blocked sterling balances in London and adding to private British holdings of dollar securities, these transactions diverted foreign exchange from the official reserves. Under the new restrictions of July 1957, the arbitrageurs could operate only in sterling securities.

[27] Quoted from the *First Report* of the Cohen Council (1958), p. 34, in Samuel I. Katz, *Sterling Speculation and European Convertibility: 1955-1958* (Essays in International Finance, No. 37), Princeton, N.J.: Princeton University, 1961, p. 20.

7 percent Bank rate symbolized a determined internal policy.[28]

Solemn British and German promises at the September IMF meeting, together with cancellation of the OEEC meeting scheduled for October, helped restore confidence in existing exchange parities. Britain drew $250 million in October under the line of credit granted by the Export-Import Bank the previous December and renewed her standby arrangement with the International Monetary Fund. Private short-term capital began returning to England. Gold and foreign-exchange reserves rose by September 1958 to 69 percent above the crisis level of one year before.

The external recovery was not without domestic cost. By the summer of 1958 unemployment and excess capacity, slight by prewar but heavy by postwar standards, were breeding some fear of an actual recession. Bank rate, already lowered in three steps down to the precrisis level of 5 percent by June, was further lowered to 4½ and then 4 percent before the end of the year. At the beginning of July the ceiling on bank advances imposed during the crisis was removed, as were installment-purchase restrictions soon afterwards. When the control of the Capital Issues Committee for almost all domestic borrowing was abolished, the banks became free, for the first time since before the war, to make whatever domestic loans then saw fit, subject only to the overall restriction of their cash and liquidity ratios.[29]

During 1958 the British current-account surplus grew with sterling and nonsterling countries alike. Although a continuing fall in primary commodity prices hit the overseas sterling countries, gold production and capital inflows more than covered their deficits with the outside world and so shielded the London reserve pool. Britain and other European countries benefited from improved terms of trade. In December Britain was able to join the other major European countries in establishing nonresident currency convertibility.

Experience since Convertibility

In 1959 British domestic economic activity continued recovering from the slowdown of the year before, and imports rose relative to exports. In contrast to their growth the year before, the gold and foreign-exchange reserves fell, though by less than the amount of debt repayment and additional gold subscription to the International Monetary Fund.

The sharply shrunken current-account surplus of 1959 gave way in 1960 to the largest deficit in nine years. Imports were responding to further trade liberalization of the year before, strong domestic economic activity, and further rebuilding of depleted inventories. Export growth remained disappointing. The trade balance worsened particularly in transactions with the United States. Net invisible earnings suffered from more competitive foreign shipping, greater foreign travel by Britons, larger interest payments on foreign funds in Britain, and rising government outlays abroad for aid and defense. The net outflow of private and official long-term capital, while smaller than the year before, continued above $500 million.

Paradoxically, and even despite accelerated repayment of debt to the IMF, the official gold and foreign-exchange reserves *rose* by 18 percent in 1960. Under the circumstances, this did not indicate an improvement in overall net external liquidity. Overseas sterling countries drew upon their sterling reserves to finance adverse balances of payments of their own, but U.K. sterling liabilities to nonsterling countries rose by considerably more than did the gold and foreign-exchange reserves. An inflow of short-term capital from Continental Europe and North America, partly recorded and partly concealed in "errors and omissions," was masking the more basic payments deterioration. Suggested explanations include an excess of British over foreign money-market interest rates, speculative pressure against the dollar in the autumn,

---

[28] Cf. Paul Einzig, *A Dynamic Theory of Forward Exchange*, New York: St. Martin's Press, 1961, p. 517. Despite appearances in retrospect, says Einzig, speculators were not mistaken at the time in being bearish on sterling, given the financial policy prevailing before their very attack forced action to slow down wage inflation. Scott, *op. cit.*, p. 223, expresses more skepticism about the deflationary measures.

[29] Morgan in Feavearyear, *op. cit.*, p. 412.

and German and Swiss resistance to inflows of funds (mainly from the United States).

The interest-rate differentials reflected British policy. Beginning early in 1960, prospects of excessive domestic demand, as well as the basic balance-of-payments situation, had prompted monetary restraint. Bank rate went up from 4 to 5 percent in January and to 6 percent in June. Installment-credit controls came back in April. Requirements for special deposits at the Bank of England (rather like reserve requirements) were imposed on the commercial banks in April and raised in June. Long- and short-term interest rates were allowed to rise. Whether or not as a result of these measures, growth of industrial production did pause after the first quarter of 1960. Bank rate cuts to 5½ percent in October and 5 percent in December, following interest-rate reductions in the United States, meant no reversal of generally tight policy; the British authorities had become concerned over a possibly excessive interest-motivated inflow of short-term funds.

Early in 1961, seeking other measures to affect demand besides interest-rate manipulation, the authorities relaxed consumer credit terms and encouraged easier bank credit for exports. The expansion of bank lending in the first half of the year occurred only at the expense of a further decline in the banks' general liquidity position. The budget of April scheduled a smaller overall government deficit than in recent years and authorized the Treasury to vary the main customs, excise, and purchase taxes within limits, as well as a surcharge on employers similar to a payroll tax.

Deficits on current plus long-term capital account persisted in the first half of 1961. Narrowing of the interest differential in favor of London and abatement of the speculative pressure experienced by the dollar late in 1960 contributed to reversing the earlier inflow of short-term funds. The British exchange rate was weakening even before revaluation of the German mark in March touched off bearishness on sterling. (See Chapter 23.) During the first week or so after this event, support of sterling on the exchanges cost an amount widely estimated at nearly $300 million, or nearly 10 percent of the total British reserves. (The reported reserve drop of only $174 million for the entire month of March understates the extent of hot-money movements and support operations, since Continental central banks provided much of the support by acquiring and holding on to sterling.)[30] Announcement of cooperation among central banks, together with denial of any intention to devalue sterling and Swiss, French, and Italian denials of any intention to revalue their currencies, helped ease and later reverse the pressure. Still, the British external difficulties were due to more than a speculative episode. Growth of industrial production was reviving and bank loans expanding. By midyear the unemployment percentage had sunk to a four-year low. Some prosperous manufacturers had grown rather indifferent to export markets. A slump in the foreign demand for British automobiles continued, and net receipts from invisibles remained at a low level. In the six months February through July, nearly one-fourth of the external reserves went to support sterling; and the loss would have been worse except for special receipts in connection with American Ford's purchase of the minority interest in its British subsidiary, special debt repayment from Germany, and massive aid from Continental central banks. Spot sterling continued weakening, and in mid-July the three-months forward quotation sank as low as $2.75½. By early summer Continental speculators on a devaluation were reportedly making heavy sales of sterling.

Britain responded with an austerity program. On July 25 the Chancellor of the Exchequer announced a 10 percent surcharge on customs and excise duties and purchase taxes, a 7 percent Bank rate and further increases in the banks' special-deposit requirements to squeeze credit and restrain inventory and other investment, refusal or postponement of wage increases in government and the nationalized industries, and efforts to

---

[30] *Business Week,* 18 March 1961, p. 31; *Wall Street Journal,* 6 April 1961, p. 2; *The Economist,* London, 6 May 1961, p. 572.

stiffen resistance against wage increases in private industry as well. (A widespread opinion blamed wage increases in excess of productivity gains for several years of worsening in Britain's international competitive position.) The government would try to economize at home, hold the line on foreign-aid expenditures for a while, and reduce military spending abroad. Britain drew $1.5 billion in nine currencies from the International Monetary Fund and used some of the proceeds to repay Continental central banks for their earlier support. The Fund made another $500 million available under a standby arrangement. The Treasury toughened its policy on British business investment outside the Sterling Area and tried to improve the rate of remittance of overseas earnings.

Even before its details were announced, the program to defend sterling reversed speculative sentiment. Before the end of July, apparently, speculators began covering their short positions. Leads and lags went into reverse. The spot sterling rate strengthened 3 cents between July and late September. By the end of the year, reserve gains had permitted full repayment to the Continental central banks and partial repayment to the IMF. An improvement in the current account of the balance of payments continued in the first half of 1962.

Apparently worrying about an inflow of undependable hot money from the Continent and the United States, the authorities cut Bank rate to 6½ percent in October 1961. But the unwelcome inflow persisted and apparently even grew in haste to take advantage of high interest rates in London not expected to remain available much longer. Bank rate came down again in November and March and reached 4½ percent in April 1962.

By this time some relaxation of financial restraint seemed wise to help production resume growing after the pause that followed the crisis measures. The April 1962 budget remained cautious, however, so that the government deficit turned out to be smaller than the year before. Not until June were the banks' special deposit requirements reduced. Consumer credit restrictions were eased. Then, with the home economy still sluggish,

the banks were entirely freed from their special deposit requirements and from earlier urgings to be restrained and selective in granting credit. Market rates of interest were allowed to sag further. Late 1962 and early 1963 brought cuts in the purchase tax, some other expansionary fiscal measures, and a 4-percent Bank rate. The strongly expansionist budget of April 1963 raised government spending, liberalized investment allowances, cut personal direct and indirect taxes, and avowedly planned a government deficit for the first time since 1947. By the spring of 1963 the economy showed signs of entering onto a phase of renewed expansion.

On the balance-of-payments front, the underlying position seemed strong enough by mid-1962 to justify paying off the remaining debt still owed to the IMF. Favorable changes in both basic transactions and short-term capital movements, especially in the first half of the year, allowed 1962 as a whole to register a substantial overall surplus, following the deficit of 1961. The strongest features were a continued increase in exports to the Continent, recovery in invisible earnings, and relative modesty of the net capital outflow. The current account showed strength again in the first half of 1963. Nevertheless, General de Gaulle's veto in January of Britain's membership in the Common Market brought brief speculative pressure against the pound, strongly resisted by official intervention. Early March saw a second and stronger movement against sterling, following discussion in the press and elsewhere of the merits of devaluation. A number of Continental central banks aided vigorous official support. Britain's surplus on goods and services practically vanished around midyear. Over the whole year 1963, the gold and convertible-currency reserves sagged some 5 percent, continuing a generally downward drift from 1960 on.

By early 1964, the general picture was one of a booming home economy and a weakening balance of payments. Publication of January figures showing an all-time record monthly deficit in merchandise trade brought speculative pressure against the pound. One response was a boost of Bank rate from 4 to 5 percent on February 27, and further action likely to slow down the rate of economic growth was generally expected.

By October 26 the threat of another balance-of-payments crisis had become serious enough to provoke drastic action. The newly elected Labor government levied supposedly temporary surcharges of 15 percent on all imports except foods, tobacco, and basic raw materials, thus roughly doubling the average tariff level. Partial rebates of indirect taxation were introduced to spur exports. Hopes of thus avoiding the need for restraint on domestic demand proved in vain. Speculation on devaluation of the pound carried the external reserves to a seven-year low in November. A rise of Bank rate to 7 percent on November 23 failed to end the crisis (but was promptly followed by a rise of the Federal Reserve discount rate in the United States). On November 25 the United States and 10 other countries pledged a $3 billion emergency line of credit to supplement a $1 billion standby credit that Britain had already arranged with the International Monetary Fund. This international rescue operation, the largest in history, beat back the largest speculative attack ever mounted against a currency. Renewed bearishness on sterling brought a defensive budget in April 1965. It tightened restrictions on foreign travel and capital export and adjusted taxes and government spending in ways viewed as deflationary. The budget discontinued the tax-deductability of business entertainment expenditures—except, rather comically, expenditures to entertain foreign buyers. Two days later the government outlined a long-expected "incomes policy", which, among other things, called for a voluntary $3\frac{1}{2}$ percent limit on annual wage increases.

Review and Appraisal

After surveying the postwar British crises and recoveries, we may step back to draw some broad impressions. Sterling is one of the two currencies most widely used in international payments and used as a reserve for authorities and banks in other countries. Britain's gold and convertible-currency reserves have ranged widely from hardly more than one-fifth to only about one-third of its net sterling liabilities.[31] Normal as it is for a banker, a fractional reserve system can prove awkward when many depositors wish to cash their claims.

A second characteristic of sterling's postwar position has been the striking variability reflected in exchange-rate fluctuations (of various types of nonofficial and forward sterling and of official spot sterling within the support limits), in the level of the gold and dollar reserves, and in the general tone of anticipation and discussion. Remarkable strength and critical weakness have alternated rapidly. For example, the weakness that brought devaluation in 1949 gave way to strength and rumors of upward revaluation in 1950–1951 and then in turn to the crisis of 1951–1952. The first three postwar crises of 1947, 1949, and 1951–1952 caused much talk of a "biennial pattern" of crises in odd-numbered years and recoveries in even-numbered years. While further experience departed from so systematic a pattern, the variability remained evident. Some observers may prefer to emphasize the autonomous disturbances caused by definite historical events, such as the Korean War, the Suez difficulties, or the German revaluation. But historical events are always occurring and are all too readily available as easy explanations for the jerky operation of economic institutions. As Lionel Robbins has aptly said, "If a car fails to reach its destination, if it is continually running into the side, or if it is continually having to solicit hauls from passing lorries, we should not regard it as a sufficient explanation that the roads are not level and straight, that there are hills to ascend and corners to turn."[32]

A third characteristic, particularly of Britain's early postwar difficulties, was dependence upon import restrictions to meet reserve

---

[31] These are defined as "the UK liabilities in current and deposit accounts, UK Treasury bills, commercial bills drawn on and promissory notes made by UK residents, and the holdings of overseas banks and central monetary institutions (but not of other holders) of long-term British Government securities at nominal value less bank advances to overseas residents, overdrafts, and commercial bills drawn by, and promissory notes and acceptances outstanding in favor of, UK residents." Liabilities to international organizations are not counted. *International Financial Statistics*, February 1964, p. 285.

[32] *The Balance of Payments*, Stamp Memorial Lecture, London: Athlone Press, 1951, p. 16.

drains and a resulting periodic depletion of inventories of imported materials.[33] This accentuated the import fluctuations. At times, controls cut back imports; at other times, imports spurted to make up for previous cutbacks or to anticipate future controls. One clear example is the running-down of inventories in 1950 and their subsequent replenishment as one aspect of the 1951–1952 crisis.

Fourth, the payments positions of the United Kingdom and the overseas sterling countries sometimes tended to be strong or weak together. Speculation played a part. This is hardly remarkable in a system of currencies so closely tied together. Nor is it remarkable that Britain at times tried to persuade the overseas sterling countries voluntarily to adopt import restriction policies paralleling her own.[34]

Fifth, some of the crises were of a more speculative than fundamental nature. Even exchange controls proved nearly powerless to prevent speculation through acceleration and delay of payments and even of actual purchases and sales. In Katz's words, "recurring speculative movements against the pound . . . could make any weakness in the balance of current payments into a serious crisis within a few weeks."[35]

A sixth characteristic was the complex and partly psychological interaction between domestic financial policy and the foreign-exchange situation. Especially during the first few postwar years of cheap money, traders had an extra incentive to borrow in London and postpone payments for commercial transactions when the pound was under pressure. Easy money also facilitated borrowing by overseas sterling countries and tended to reduce pressures on them to bring their current external transactions into balance.[36] The switch to tighter and more flexible monetary policies after the Conservative election victory in 1951 and, most conspicuously, the adoption of a 7-percent Bank rate in 1957 and again in 1961 and 1964 came in response to external

crisis. This source of discipline against a lax inflationary drift may perhaps sometimes be welcome.[37] On the other hand, the responsiveness of short-term capital movements to interest-rate differentials since adoption of convertibility in 1958 has occasionally been a nuisance. At times, furthermore, financial policy seems to have been tighter than purely internal conditions called for. According to one widely held view, "Britain's chronic balance of payments troubles themselves have hampered growth. . . . Successive British governments have been forced to throttle down the economy each time it began to build up steam, in order to restrain inflation, hold down imports, and erase any doubts as to maintenance of existing exchange rates."[38] According to the Bank for International Settlements, "The growth rate for 1955–60 of 2.4 percent a year was unsatisfactory. If the persistent balance-of-payments obstacle to expansion could be overcome, a better record could be achieved. . . ."[39] The fact may be just a coincidence, but investment has been a smaller percentage of gross national product and production has grown more slowly for several years in Britain than in other major industrial countries.

Finally, the rapid reversibility of British policy has been almost comical at times. Balance-of-payments troubles have brought *ad hoc* responses such as exchange devaluation on one occasion, tightening of import and exchange controls, tightening of domestic financial policy, and reversals of these actions. Reliance on such expedients creates dangers of improper timing, of anticipatory private actions, of overshooting the mark, and of intensified instability as a result. As for financial policy, it can impair economic performance not only if it is consistently too tight or consistently too loose but also if it is inconsistently too jerky.

[33] Katz, *Journal of Political Economy*, June 1955, p. 220; cf. pp. 217, 222.

[34] Cf. *ibid.*, pp. 221-222; A. C. L. Day, *The Future of Sterling*, Oxford: Clarendon Press, 1954, p. 82.

[35] *Journal of Political Economy*, June 1955, p. 223.

[36] *Ibid.*, pp. 223-224.

[37] Cf. Katz, *Sterling Speculation and European Convertibility*, pp. 3, 9-10, 13, 14, 25, 29-30. The need for restraints on wage-push inflation has been a recurring theme of recent *Annual Reports* of the Bank for International Settlements, for example, the 32nd, p. 14, and the 33rd, p. 56.

[38] Chase Manhattan Bank, *Report on Western Europe*, August–September 1961, pp. 2-3. Cf. "Britain: Slowdown Bolsters Sterling," *Business Week*, 4 November 1961, p. 116.

[39] 32nd *Annual Report*, p. 13.

The French Franc since World War II

↬ 22

Multiple Rates and Broken Cross Rates

In December 1945, France devalued the franc from its wartime rate of 50 per dollar to 119.107 per dollar. This became the initial French parity registered with the International Monetary Fund in 1946. In January 1948 a complicated system of multiple exchange rates replaced it.[1] As the system evolved during the year, so-called free rates were quoted for the U.S. dollar, Portuguese escudo, and Swiss franc. Fully applicable mainly to tourist and financial transactions in the three "hard" currencies, these rates were "free" only in not being rigidly pegged. Occasional official intervention, together with manipulation of supply and demand by adjusting the stringency of exchange controls and import licensing and the classification of imports as "basic" and "nonbasic," kept the dollar rate in the range of about 305 to 312 francs for most of the year (with equivalent rates on the other two currencies). A new official rate of 214.39 francs per dollar applied to certain favored, or "basic," imports, including coal and wheat. The dollar, escudo, or Swiss-franc proceeds of exports could be sold half at the free and half at the official rate; and except at first, when the free rate alone applied, foreign exchange for authorized "nonbasic" imports from the three currency areas was bought half at each rate. The effective rate for most trade with the three areas was thus an average of the official and free rates. This middle rate on the dollar hovered in roughly the 260-264 range.

For currencies other than the designated three, the rates for all transactions corresponded to the official dollar rate of 214.39. Since the parity of the pound sterling was still $4.03, the French rate for sterling was $214.39 \times 4.03 = 864$ francs per pound. The cross rate for sterling diverged from it: the official rate on sterling and the effective dollar rate of 260 francs implied only $864/260 = 3.32$ dollars per pound. French merchants found it profitable to buy rubber in Malaya with cheap pounds, for instance, and then sell it in the United States for dollars. A Frenchman might buy £1 at the official rate of 864 francs, buy a pound's worth of commodities with it somewhere in the Sterling Area, sell the commodities for $4.03 in the United States, and realize $4.03 \times 260 = 1048$ francs on the transaction (less costs of transportation, administration, and the like). In this way, France could intercept some of the dollar earnings of the Sterling Area. Disorderly cross rates involving the lira made similar commodity-shunting operations profitable for Italians, also. In cheap-sterling deals such as this, Australian wool was resold to the United States through France and Italy, costing Australia some dollar earnings. Britain lost dollars because of furs bought in London on French account and then resold in the United States. American importers bought Indian tea through Italian merchants. Conversely, it was profitable for Britons to buy goods in hard-currency areas and reexport them to

---

[1] Cf. Bank for International Settlements, 18th *Annual Report*, (1947–1948), pp. 91-93, 19th *Annual Report* (1948–1949), pp. 119-122; International Monetary Fund, 1948 *Annual Report*, pp. 36-38, 76-78, 1949 *Annual Report*, pp. 23, 60-61; F. Bloch-Lainé and others, *La Zone Franc*, Paris: Presses Universitaires de France, 1956, p. 325; Emil Küng, *Zahlungsbilanzpolitik*, Zürich: Polygraphischer Verlag, 1959, pp. 594-597; and various issues of *International Financial Statistics*.

France or Italy, so far as controls permitted or could be circumvented. A British merchant might obtain $4.03 for £1, buy American goods and sell them for 4.03 × 260 = 1048 francs in France, and then sell the francs for pounds at the official 864 rate, yielding approximately £1⅕. This sort of operation would eat into the British dollar reserves for commodities going to France. Similarly, French soda manufacturers had an incentive to sell their output to Swiss firms, compelling British users to buy in Switzerland. Britain's hard-currency reserves thus suffered to the benefit of the French. The countries harmed could not stamp out such operations entirely, since the difficulty might stem from combinations of individually legal transactions.

Because it had foreseen this sort of thing and, more generally, because discriminatory multiple exchange rates with broken cross rates ran counter to its basic principles, the International Monetary Fund refused to approve the French system. (It did not object to devaluation of the franc as such and had in fact urged devaluation to a realistic single rate.) The French government went ahead with its own proposal, anyway, whereupon "the Fund considered that France had made an unauthorized change in its par value and had therefore become ineligible to use the Fund's resources."[2]

As French prices rose during 1948, the trade deficit with the Sterling Area grew. For this and other reasons, the government decided to carry out an "alignment of the exchanges" in October 1948. Franc rates for all currencies were brought into line with the average of the free and par rates on the dollar, then about 264 francs. For all currencies except the three directly traded on the "free" market, official rates were fixed once a month at the mean dollar rate multiplied by the dollar parity of each currency in question. Cross rates were no longer disorderly. The free rate remained applicable only to financial and tourist transactions in the designated three currencies. The IMF "welcomed" the unification of French exchange rates for trade transactions but did not get around to restor-

ing France's eligibility to draw on its resources until October 1954.

In the fall and winter of 1948–1949 the discount on French banknotes abroad and on the Paris "parallel" market widened, at one time reaching more than 60 percent from the authorized free rate. Tourists and others had incentives to use this market rather than convert their foreign currency into francs at legal rates. To improve the quotation of French banknotes on the unofficial markets by raising the demand for them, the authorities repeatedly raised the amount that travelers could legally bring into France. A recovery in the parallel rate for franc banknotes to a range of around 350-370 to the dollar in the spring of 1949 and a deterioration of the authorized free rate to about 329 narrowed the gap between these two markets to about 10 percent. Even after the "alignment" of October 1948, the official dollar parity had been kept at 214.39 francs. In mid-1949 the free rate was being kept stable by official operations at around 330 per dollar. The average rate, effective for most transactions and serving as the basis for the official rates on currencies other than the dollar, escudo, and Swiss franc, had worsened to about 273 in the months before the devaluations of 1949.

From 1949 through 1956

The events of September 1949 provided an opportunity to apply a single exchange rate to all transactions again. The new rate of 350 francs per dollar, with properly aligned rates on other currencies, represented a devaluation of about 22 percent from the old average dollar rate but only of about 6 percent from the "free" rate that had still applied to tourist expenditure and financial remittances. Relative to the more sharply devalued pound sterling, the franc appreciated by about 12 percent. At the same time, the unity of the franc area was reestablished by a decision to keep the parities of the overseas currencies and the metropolitan franc in line from then on; the former became mere multiples of the latter.[3]

---

[2] International Monetary Fund, 1948 *Annual Report*, p. 37.

[3] Bloch-Lainé, *op. cit.*, pp. 346-347. This decision particularly affected French colonies in the Pacific, whose

During 1950, France was able to relax foreign-exchange restrictions. Travelers were permitted to take with them out of France twice as many francs in banknotes as before, and restrictions were dropped on bringing French banknotes back into the country from abroad. Forward-exchange regulations were also relaxed. In November 1950, in connection with the newly established European Payments Union, balances in French francs held by residents of other EPU countries were made freely transferable. French authorities noted that each new liberalization measure brought increasing amounts of foreign exchange into France through official channels.[4]

In the first quarter of 1951 France was still gaining gold and dollar reserves. After that, however, a drain set in. It became particularly heavy in the fourth quarter of the year and continued into the first quarter of 1952. A domestic inflationary spurt was being fed by increased spending on the Indo-China war and perpetuated by political obstacles to sufficiently prompt and firm countermeasures. Tightened import restrictions, new tax rebates and other encouragements to exports, and a respite from the inflation all then came to the aid of the situation. During the first half of 1953, however, the overall French balance of payments was again seriously passive. The premium on the one-month forward dollar widened from about 5 to about 11 percent, indicating fear of devaluation. French importers speculated by anticipating their future requirements in foreign currencies, while exporters delayed selling their foreign-exchange receipts. By the early summer of 1953, the French Stabilization Fund's holdings of convertible currencies were badly

depleted. France received special aid from the United States in order to meet its current obligations in the EPU and also obtained an advance of $100 million from the Export-Import Bank in anticipation of later receipts from off-shore contracts with the U.S. government. In the second half of the year the overall balance of payments shifted into surplus, forward quotations on the franc improved, and the French gold and foreign-exchange reserve recovered. The improvement continued into 1954. The French government was able to begin advance repayments on its loan from the Export-Import Bank. Exports grew (most were still subsidized in one way or another), and the franc area as a whole ran a surplus on current account (even excluding all receipts due to foreign aid) in the first half of 1954, in contrast to a deficit in the first half of 1953. During 1954, even after repayment of foreign debts totalling some $300 million, the IMF estimate of France's official gold and foreign exchange holdings rose by over 50 percent. Domestic price stability for more than two years was helping to increase the flow of available saving and was bringing some gold out of private hoards.

The improvement continued in 1955, with estimated reserves again rising more than 50 percent. France benefited from strong European demand for and increased domestic production of its foodstuffs, coal, and steel.

The following year was less favorable. In the winter of 1955–1956 war expenditures in Algeria and frost damage to crops threatened fresh inflationary pressures. Europe's total gain of external reserves was uneven in 1956, and France was an especially big loser. Taking not only gold and dollar holdings but also other items into account, especially France's deficit position within the EPU, French reserves fell by more than 45 percent during 1956 and the first quarter of 1957. They had been equivalent to the value of five months' imports at the end of 1955; at the end of 1956 they were worth only two and one-half months' imports. A boom at home was spurring imports of raw materials, fuel, and equipment, while an expanding government budget deficit was absorbing a bigger share

franc had not followed the various postwar devaluations; and its parity in metropolitan francs was rounded off to 5½. The Djibouti (French Somaliland) franc was something of a curiosity. Its parity was established in March 1949 at 214.392 per dollar (then still the official but scarcely applicable parity of the metropolitan franc). It was fully backed by dollar reserves and was made freely convertible into dollars. French Somaliland abolished exchange controls and became a hard-currency country, outside the franc area from the standpoint of French exchange regulations. The Djibouti franc remained aloof from the devaluations of 1949 and later years.

[4] Bank for International Settlements, 21st *Annual Report*, 1950–1951, p. 137.

of the savings of the economy and leaving other activities more dependent than before on bank credit. Speculation by way of commercial leads and lags, as well as increases in the exchange holdings of banks, also sapped the reserves. In mid-October—even before fighting broke out at Suez—France arranged with the International Monetary Fund to draw up to $262.5 million from the Fund within the following 12 months. Although France did not begin to use this credit until February 1957, $220 million had already been drawn by the middle of May.[5]

Crises and Devaluations in 1957 and 1958

The heavy loss of foreign exchange in 1956 gave little room to relax foreign-exchange restrictions; some (governing French purchases of foreign securities, for example) were even tightened a bit. In February 1957 the foreign-exchange allowance for Frenchmen traveling abroad was cut in half. March brought new measures to restrain imports. Import licenses became valid for only three instead of six months, importers had to make advance deposits at their banks of 25 percent of the value of their licensed imports, and an existing special compensatory import tax was extended to a wider range of goods and was standardized at the previous maximum rate of 15 percent. At the beginning of June, the import predeposit requirement was raised to 50 percent and half of the predeposited amounts were to be transferred to a special account at the Bank of France. On June 18, 1957, the liberalization of imports from quantitative restrictions under the Code of the OEEC was suspended entirely. These measures came too late to keep France's external reserves from practically running out (except for the supposedly "untouchable" gold stock of the Bank of France). Even the credit arranged with the International Monetary Fund in October 1956 and all of the French

entitlement to credit in the European Payments Union had been used. By early August, speculation was pressing heavily against the franc.

The government's response came on August 12. For all transactions except imports and exports of certain specified commodities, a 20 percent surcharge or premium was applied to purchases and sales of foreign exchange at the official rate of 350 francs per dollar. This absorbed the special 15 percent import tax previously in effect and also replaced export subsidies in the form of tax rebates. Various controls were liberalized. The maximum duration of import licenses was again extended to six months and the import predeposit requirement was dropped. As long as certain imports continued enjoying the old 350-per-dollar exchange rate instead of the generally effective new rate of 420, speculative buying mounted. On October 28, therefore, the devaluation was generalized to these commodities also. Meanwhile, the reserves had fallen so much that the French authorities felt they could not wait for the devaluation to take effect and replenish them. Toward the end of the year France sought new foreign credits. Early in 1958 arrangements were made for a total of $655 million from the European Payments Union, the International Monetary Fund, and the United States government.

The year 1958 saw further profound changes in the international status of the franc.[6] Before General de Gaulle came to power early in June, the French economy had been experiencing productive strength but financial crisis. Real gross national product had been increasing at an average rate of more than 5 percent a year since 1953, with industrial production growing even more rapidly. Prices were on the rise again, and

---

[5] The preceding paragraphs draw in particular on Bank for International Settlements, 22nd *Annual Report* (1951–1952), p. 171, 24th *Annual Report* (1953–54), pp. 128-129, 160, and 27th *Annual Report* (1956–1957), pp. 20-21, 180, 183, as well as the *Annual Reports* of the International Monetary Fund.

[6] Cf. Jacques Rueff, "The Rehabilitation of the Franc," *Lloyds Bank Review,* No. 52, April 1959, pp. 1-18; "France Beats Back Inflation," *Business Week,* 16 May 1959, pp. 68ff.; Bank for International Settlements, 29th *Annual Report* (1958–1959), pp. 45-47, 77-81, 140-143, 175-176, 191-193; "The French Stabilization Program," Federal Reserve Bank of New York, *Monthly Review,* January 1960, pp. 11-15; and Michael A. Heilperin, "Accelerating France's Expansion," *The Banker,* April 1961, pp. 247-254.

between the end of 1956 and the middle of 1958, the cost-of-living index had risen about 18 percent. A current-account deficit in the balance of payments was persisting if not growing. Sagging confidence had been worsening the drain on France's foreign-exchange reserves, especially from early 1956 on. Commercial leads and lags when the franc looked particularly weak are thought to have drained several hundred million dollars from the reserves in 1957.[7] At the end of 1955 the gold and foreign exchange reserves had been around $2 billion; by the beginning of June 1958, the reserves (not counting the currency reserve of the Bank of France) had fallen as low as $169 million, with $104 million having been lost in the politically turbulent month of May alone.[8] A loss continuing at this rate would have exhausted the reserves by mid-July.

The formation of de Gaulle's government and the return to the Finance Ministry of Antoine Pinay, known for conservative views, had a healthy psychological effect. The previous massive outflow of funds gave way to a small-scale repatriation. Pinay imposed new taxes and, repeating an operation that had proved successful in 1952, issued a loan with repayment indexed to the franc price of gold and offering tax advantages. To encourage the repatriation of foreign assets, a 25 percent fine on reimported flight capital, in effect since 1948, was removed provided that the repatriation took the form of gold to be promptly offered for sale on the Paris market. The loan raised about 300 billion francs, including about 60 billion in foreign exchange or gold. A slight industrial slowdown under way since the spring of the year also presumably helped the balance of payments. But the problem was not fully solved: a worsening of the psychological climate could easily have touched off a new exchange crisis.

In September 1958 the government appointed a committee of financial experts headed by Jacques Rueff. The committee's report of early December stressed France's vicious circle of inflation. A shortage of genuine saving coming onto the loan market—itself largely due to fear of inflation—had left the government unable to borrow enough funds to cover its chronic budget deficit in a noninflationary way. Fiscal expedients that fed inflation had been intensifying this problem. Large private hoards of gold symbolized the attitude of the public. No one really knew their aggregate size, but it was often estimated at several thousands of tons, worth some billions of dollars.

The Rueff committee recommended cutting the French government budget deficit to a level that could be financed by borrowing the genuine savings of the public. Increased excise and income tax rates and withdrawal of certain exemptions were to expand budget revenue. On the expenditure side, the committee recommended cutting subsidies, including those paid on food, fuel, and public utilities in struggles to hold down the cost-of-living index. Reorganization of the social services and increased prices of postal and other services supplied by the government were to achieve further economies.

Unfortunately, some of these economy measures—especially the removal of subsidies—would directly tend to raise some prices and indirectly tend to raise wages and other payments linked to the cost-of-living index. Therefore, the committee recommended and the government decreed an end to all arrangements tying wages and agricultural prices to a price index. The only exception was the continued indexing of the minimum wage rate. The decree did not cut all connection between wages and prices, of course, but only the most mechanical one. Further to check price increases, the committee recommended opening French markets to intensified foreign competition. Most of the import quotas reimposed during the 1957 crisis were to be taken off and France was to proceed with its obligations under the Code of Liberalization and the Common Market Treaty.

To make renewed import liberalization possible, something else had to be done to keep the balance of payments in order, and on December 27 the franc was devalued by 17.55 percent to 493.7 per dollar. At the same

---

[7] *Wall Street Journal*, May 1, 1959, p. 8.

[8] These are Rueff's franc figures converted into dollars at the 420 rate then in effect.

time, along with most other West European currencies, it became freely convertible for nonresidents. A so-called "new franc" was also announced and was finally introduced in January 1960. Two zeros were lopped off all prices, including the price of the dollar, and the exchange rate became 20¼ U.S. cents.

Initial Success of the Reforms

According to its author, Jacques Rueff, the financial reform had a breadth, coherence, and systematic character unprecedented in French history. The de Gaulle government had the advantage of operating under emergency powers. For the first time a devaluation was undertaken "in cold blood" and accompanied by associated measures needed for success.

The financial rehabilitation did indeed seem to stop endless inflation and recurrent external crisis. The annual indexes of wholesale and consumer prices rose by an average of only about 5½ percent between 1958 and 1959 and less than 3 percent between 1959 and 1960—not too bad a record in comparison with the 13-percent rise between 1957 and 1958 and considering price increases in the nationalized industries and the removal of subsidies that had been falsifying the cost-of-living index. In 1961 prices averaged 3⅕ percent higher than the year before, and the following year the rise averaged 3½ percent. The weakening of inflationary expectations encouraged saving by households and was reflected in a decline in long- and short-term interest rates. The growth of production did slow down at first (hardly surprising when an ingrained inflation is brought under control), but forecasts of an actual recession were not borne out; and production soon surged ahead again. The balance of payments improved even though the removal of quotas on intra-European trade, which France had suspended in June 1957, was restored in December 1958 and made almost complete soon afterwards, even though liberalization of imports from the dollar area was reintroduced and extended, even though travel allowances

and other aspects of exchange control were liberalized, and even though the 10-percent tariff cuts and the quota enlargements made in favor of the other five members of the European Economic Community at the beginning of 1959 were extended to other countries during the year. Both in dollar value and in physical volume, total imports actually fell between 1958 and 1959. French exports fell about 7 percent in yearly average dollar price (higher franc prices partly offsetting the cheapening through devaluation) and rose about 10 percent in total dollar value and 20 percent in physical volume. The balance of merchandise trade thus shifted from a deficit of nearly $300 million in 1958 to a surplus of about $435 million in 1959. The invisibles account improved also, especially because of a rise in tourist earnings. The capital account benefited from reversal of the previously adverse leads and lags, a return of French funds held abroad, and an inflow of foreign investment (apparently attracted in part by the relaxation of exchange restrictions). For France and the rest of the franc area together, the total balance on current and private capital accounts swung from a deficit in 1958 to a surplus of $1.3 billion in 1959. Despite heavy repayments on debts to the EPU, the IMF, and other creditors, the French official reserves and the foreign assets of the commercial banks combined were able to rise almost $1 billion during 1959.[9] Part of this early improvement stemmed from lucky coincidences or temporary responses, including recovery from the 1957–1958 recession in the United States and other customer countries, an immediate postdevaluation shift in leads and lags and an initial cutback of imports previously stockpiled to beat devaluation or tighten restrictions, and a heavy repatriation of private long-term capital. With these influences spent, the recorded surplus shrank in 1960; otherwise, the basic balance would have risen then and again in 1961. From $645 and $1050 million at the ends of 1957 and 1958, the gold and convertible-currency holdings

[9] Bank for International Settlements, 30th *Annual Report*, 1959–1960, pp. 47-48, 122-124, 142-144, 157; and *International Financial Statistics*.

of the monetary authorities rose to $1720 million at the end of 1959, continued growing every year, and reached $4457 million at the end of 1963. In 1961 France displaced Germany as the country with the world's biggest balance-of-payments surplus and biggest gain of official external reserves.

The first four years after the reforms of 1958 brought a growth of $4.7 billion in France's *net* external assets, counting the official reserves, the net IMF position, and the prepayment of debt. External surpluses over the four years totaled $1.4 billion on trade account, $1.7 billion on invisible account, and $1 billion on ordinary long-term capital account.[10] Imports rose moderately in relation to the uptrend of production, while exports grew strikingly. Autonomous factors were partly responsible, such as growing supplies of petroleum and petroleum products and natural gas from inside the franc area and the export success of the new Caravelle airplane. Reequipment and capacity expansion in capital-goods production and modernization of farm techniques promoted export growth in these sectors. Foreign capital flowed in, partly for investments previously postponed.

Nevertheless, the evidence permits supposing that the correction of the franc's overvaluation did work as standard theory envisages. The devaluation of 1958 may even have been excessive.

France began learning the German lesson: large and persistent external surpluses can cause trouble. The French authorities took advantage of their opportunity to relax controls further. They raised the foreign travel allowance for residents in June 1961 and February 1962. In April 1962 they authorized Frenchmen to make portfolio investments abroad via the official exchange market. At the end of 1962 they further relaxed rules concerning the surrender of export proceeds for francs. Early in 1963 they even adopted one measure against capital imports by forbidding interest payments on the franc accounts of nonresidents.

Renewed Inflation

These and other measures were designed not only to help the international payments situation but also to resist a tendency toward imported inflation.[11] They fell short of what was needed. Perhaps the continuing monetary expansion caused demand-pull inflation; perhaps it came as the mere passive support of wage-push inflation. Anyway, it occurred. Its relation to the balance of payments is suggested by the fact that the domestic monetary reserve base in the form of currency and bankers'-deposit liabilities of the Bank of France expanded by very roughly as much as the Bank's net foreign assets. (In earlier postwar years, in contrast, expansion of its *domestic* assets, including loans to the commercial banks, had matched expansion of its monetary liabilities.) From the end of 1958 to mid-1963, the net foreign assets of the Bank of France grew by 27 percent more than its liabilities serving as the domestic monetary reserve base. Over the shorter period from the end of 1959 to mid-1963, it is true, this "high-powered" money grew by 23 percent more than the Bank's net foreign liabilities.[12] Apparently a massive sterilization of foreign-asset acquisitions in 1959 was partially undone in the following years.

The ordinary money supply (demand deposits and currency, as distinguished from its reserve base) grew by *larger* percentages *after* the famous Rueff reform, and especially after 1959, than in the several preceding years. (The percentages of growth each year averaged 10.2 and were falling in 1954 through 1958 but averaged 14.3 and were generally

---

[10] Bank for International Settlements, 33rd *Annual Report*, 1962–1963, p. 103.

[11] Advance repayments of government external debt are sometimes listed among these measures. Actually, though, any anti-inflationary effect from them depends on the accompanying domestic financial policy. The effect would be strongest if the government bought foreign exchange for debt repayment with francs raised by taxation or noninflationary borrowing at home. So far as the authorities continue buying up the surplus foreign-exchange receipts of the private sector with newly created francs, the effect of these open-market operations (which is what they amount to) remains expansionary whether the authorities repay foreign debt with the foreign exchange bought or simply hold it.

[12] These and the figures to follow are computed from *International Financial Statistics*.

rising from then through mid-1963.) This monetary expansion was by no means fully matched, of course, by growth of the foreign assets of the central and commercial banking system as a whole. As usual, its main counterpart was loans to domestic business (while, for a change, bank loans to cover the government budget deficit were *not* an important factor).

So much creation of ordinary money would hardly have been possible, however, without an expanding reserve base of new high-powered francs. French official reports explicitly recognize that while expansion of bank credit to domestic borrowers was the chief immediate source of new money, the banks enjoyed the necessary liquidity because the Bank of France was buying up foreign exchange yielded by the balance-of-payments surplus.[13]

Another expansionary factor was the French public's growing willingness to hold demand deposits. Currency fell from 50 percent of the demand-deposit-and-currency total at the end of 1953 to 47 percent at the end of 1958 and to 39 percent by mid-1963. Not only the total stock of high-powered francs was growing, but also the fraction of it held by the banks as reserves rather than held by the public.

The unfamiliar—to Frenchmen—basis of the monetary inflation perhaps helps explain why the process was not more generally understood and resisted. The moderate—for France —pace of price rises in the first few years after 1958 may have contributed to complacency.

In comparison with a 90 percent monetary expansion from the end of 1958 to October 1963, the home-and-import-goods price index rose only 18 percent and the cost-of-living index only 28 percent. The explanation (on the level of mere arithmetic) involves not only the continued growth of real output but also a decline in the velocity of money: the ratio of gross national product to money supply (average of beginning- and end-of-year money) fell from 3.30 in 1958 to 2.93 in 1962 and 2.79 in 1963. In the opinion of the French authorities,[14] the apparent success of monetary stabilization was encouraging the public to demand larger stocks of money and other liquid assets in relation to income. Furthermore, the authorities seemed timid about resisting a process that they could describe as spontaneous rather than as due to any unsound positive actions of their own. After all, growth of population and incomes and increased wages and costs and prices were supposedly creating a *need* for more money. "The development of the money supply is linked to these different movements by such diverse relationships that it seems to be their effect as well as their cause." "Brutal" measures of monetary restriction, unaccompanied by other anti-inflationary policies, would have risked jeopardizing the expansion of the economy.[15] Monetary policy, by itself, was inadequate to reconcile the goals of price stability, "expansion, full employment, a sufficient volume of investments, and the saving necessary to finance them."[16]

As the rise in prices became less gradual, concern about creeping inflation revived. The authorities continued wanting both easy medium-term and long-term credit for industry and commerce and some mild restraint on the growth of liquidity. In January 1961 they imposed on the banks a new required ratio of liquid assets (cash, Treasury bills, and certain specified paper) to demand and time deposit liabilities. The new ratio was first set at 30 percent, raised to 32 percent a year later, and raised again to 35 and 36 percent in

---

[13] Cf. Conseil National du Crédit, *Dix-Septième Rapport Annuel, Année 1962*, Paris: Imprimerie Nationale, 1963, esp. pp. 35-36, 44-46, 62, 77; Banque de France, *Compte Rendu des Opérations*, 1962, Paris: Imprimeries Paul Dupont, 1963, esp. pp. 5-6, 25-26. For other comments on the inflationary impact of the French external surplus, see Bank for International Settlements, 32nd *Annual Report* (1961–1962), pp. 28, 30, 64, and 33rd *Annual Report* (1962–1963), pp. 11, 13; International Monetary Fund, 1962 *Annual Report*, p. 96, and 1963 *Annual Report*, pp. 108-109; and *The Economist*, 6 April 1963, p. 77. According to Professor Fritz Machlup, inflation in France and some other European countries during this period was due "entirely" to purchases of foreign-exchange reserves at pegged exchange rates. *The United States Balance of Payments*, statements submitted to the Joint Economic Committee, November 1963; Washington: Government Printing Office, p. 308.

[14] Bank for International Settlements, 33rd *Annual Report* (1962–1963), p. 60.
[15] Conseil National du Crédit, *op. cit.*, pp. 217, 218.
[16] Banque de France, *op. cit.*, p. 27.

March and May 1963. Meanwhile, attempts continued to manipulate the structure of interest rates so as to promote the development of the capital market and encourage medium- and long-term lending at the expense of short-term lending. When prices and liquidity continued rising into 1963, the banks were asked to hold the expansion of credit to the private sector down to 12 percent in the ensuing 12 months (about two-thirds of the rate of increase of recent years), while discriminating in favor of export credit and medium-term investment credit. The different strands of policy were not fully consistent with each other.[17]

As early as April 1963 the authorities began controlling the prices or retail mark-ups of many manufactured consumer goods. In September the government announced further measures against inflation. These were to include requiring government approval for price increases on industrial products, controlling factory prices of nearly all manufactures, controlling some retail prices and limiting distributors' profit margins, cutting some gasoline and cigarette prices for symbolic effect, lowering import duties on many consumer goods, taking a tough line (without an actual freeze) on wages in the public industries and using a profit and credit squeeze to pressure private employers into tough wage bargaining, advancing the discharge dates of Army draftees and stepping up the recruitment of foreign workers to ease the labor market, further reducing the government budget deficit, tightening the

limit on bank credit expansion, and floating a bond issue to drain off bank funds. Further tightening of credit restrictions and price and profit controls was scheduled for early 1964, as well as continued resistance to wage increases. As so often in recent French history, suppressing inflation seemed to get at least as much emphasis as stopping it.

By this time inflation seemed again to be undermining French international competitiveness. Valued to include insurance and freight costs, merchandise imports had already overtaken exports in 1962. The current-account surplus shrank in 1962, shrank further in 1963, and had apparently vanished by 1964. In 1963 and 1964, private capital inflows and net surpluses earned by the overseas franc area were accounting for the continuing overall balance-of-payments surplus and further growth of French external reserves. (By the end of 1964, official holdings of gold and convertible currencies reached $5.1 billion.) How long such a situation could last in the face of growing merchandise trade deficits, and whether a dramatic change might occur, had become a live question. By French standards, a relatively restrictive domestic monetary and fiscal policy was having some success by then in slowing the pace of price inflation, but at the cost of slowing down or even stopping the growth of production.

French experience since 1958 may turn out to illustrate again how something like the gold-standard mechanism may still operate under fixed exchange rates: balance-of-payments surpluses tend to cure themselves sooner or later by inflating the domestic economy if a passive policy permits, but this rather unhealthy cure comes with lags and with the danger of going too far.

---

[17] Bank for International Settlements, 32nd *Annual Report* (1961–1962), pp. 6, 67; 33rd *Annual Report* (1962–1963), pp. 13, 60-62; International Monetary Fund, 1963 *Annual Report*, p. 109.

The German Struggle against Imported Inflation

 23

The German Balance of Payments

Germany's external disequilibrium after 1950 offers an instructive contrast to the experiences of other countries. Tracing it will give some fresh slants on how internal and external conditions can interact and on how well or how poorly various expedients can succeed in reconciling internal and external policy objectives. The story of primarily German events also helps describe the environment in which the experiences of other countries unfolded.

Earlier chapters have already mentioned German developments up to the time when emergency measures stemmed a balance-of-payments crisis early in 1951. The shift within a few months from a critical deficit to an eventually troublesome surplus illustrates how sensitively trade and capital movements can respond to changes in expectations and to even rather small changes in objective conditions when no "automatic" adjustment mechanism is at work.

Let us first broadly survey the German balance of payments from that time until the end of 1960 (after which its development was interrupted). As measured by the annual growth in official reserves of gold and foreign exchange,[1] the overall surplus rose between

1951 and 1953 to a level equaling over one-sixth of the value of merchandise exports. The continuing gain of gold and foreign exchange shrank in 1954 and 1955, rose again to peak levels in 1956 and 1957, and shrank in 1958. An actual decline in the reserves in 1959 was due to special circumstances and policy expedients and is misleading by itself, especially since the surplus from trade in goods and services remained not far below its peak levels. In 1960 the gain of reserves again set a new record.

The largest single contribution to the surplus on current account and to the growth of reserves was an excess of merchandise exports over imports. It even exceeded the growth of reserves in most of the years of the decade. This trade surplus grew without much interruption.

Between 1950 and 1960, German exports rose at average annual rates of 19 percent in money value and 16 percent in physical volume.[2] This rapid export growth would hardly have been possible without rising total industrial production and real gross national product (GNP in current marks deflated by the cost-of-living index); their growth rates averaged $9\frac{1}{2}$ and not quite 9 percent a year respectively over the same period. Among the suggested explanations of such rapid economic advance[3] are an expanding labor force fed by refugees from the East (which, incidentally, helped keep wage demands moderate), the legendary German industriousness,

---

[1] The concept used here corresponds to line 10 in issues of *International Financial Statistics* of 1961 and earlier. The continuity of this series is broken by the exclusion, from the beginning of 1959, of net bilateral claims arising from liquidation of the European Payments Union. Where it makes any difference in discussion of changes in reserves during 1959, these net bilateral claims have been added back in to preserve continuity with the figures reported for the end of 1958. A conceptual change first adopted for line 10 in *International Financial Statistics*, August 1961, should also be noticed.

[2] If $8.35x^{10} = 47.93$, $x = 1.19$, where the 8.35 and 47.93 are exports in 1950 and 1960 in billions of marks. Other growth rates mentioned in this first section are similarly computed from figures in *International Financial Statistics*.

[3] See Federal Reserve Bank of New York, *Monthly Review*, December 1960, p. 207.

and a sustained rise in productivity, based in part on restoration of an efficient price system after June 1948 and in part on a higher ratio of saving and investment to national income than in most other countries. Fiscal measures encouraged accelerated depreciation and the plowing-back of profits. The smallness of the drain of national resources into defense contributed to the export supply capacity of the German economy as well as to investment; and a lag of defense spending even behind appropriations enabled the Federal government, until late in 1956, to run budget surpluses. This fiscal restraint, coupled with anti-inflationary monetary policy, contrasted with strong demand throughout most of the rest of the world and so helped promote German exports of machinery, automobiles, and other highly fabricated products. German industry promoted exports aggressively through trade fairs and otherwise and flexibly adapted its wares to foreign requirements. Tax incentives and government export credit insurance played a part. German capital goods especially appealed to businessmen in countries whose balance-of-payments controls still discriminated against imports from the United States.

Imports rose not quite as strongly as exports, though still at annual rates averaging 14 percent in money value and 15 percent in physical volume between 1950 and 1960. Decades of tariff protection and other policies to promote a large measure of self-sufficiency may have somewhat restrained a rise in the fraction of German income spent on imports. Also, the postwar emphasis on production of capital goods with a relatively low content of imported materials helped restrain the growth of total imports.[4] (These observations do not, of course, justify any notion that the German export surplus has been of "structural" origin. So-called structural conditions that apparently predispose a country to an export surplus at one set of domestic and foreign price relations would not do so at another.)

In comparison with merchandise trade, the net position from ordinary services (including travel, transportation, and investment income,

among others) fluctuated more widely. This balance was negative except in 1957; and though apparently in an unsteady trend toward still larger deficits, it remained too small fully to offset the positive trade balance. Its component parts showed opposed trends during the 1950s, including a shift from surplus to deficit in foreign travel, a shift from deficit to surplus in transportation, rising net outpayments of foreign investment income, and a growing deficit in other nonmilitary services.

Sales of services to NATO forces stationed in Germany grew year to year without interruption. This military item ranked second only to the merchandise export surplus, and was gaining ground on it, as the biggest contributor to the net surplus on current account and so to the growth in external reserves. About four-fifths of these services were sold to United States forces and the remainder to British and other NATO forces.

Among net debit balances, the one ranking second only to nonmilitary services from 1955 on was official donations. Germany's earlier heavy net inflow of foreign aid had almost vanished by 1953, and after then Germany became a net donor on a growing scale. German unilateral transfers consisted mainly of indemnification payments to Israel and to victims of Naziism living in other countries, but aid to underdeveloped countries promised to become an increasing share of the total.

The long-term capital account usually but not always showed a negative balance, particularly because the government was repaying its external debt in installments and because private Germans were generally net buyers of foreign securities. Short-term capital movements, whether recorded or concealed in "errors and omissions" and whether undertaken by the government, the banks, or other firms and individuals, fluctuated widely.

The net imbalance from all the items just surveyed made the official reserves of gold and foreign exchange grow not only in every year from 1951 through 1960, with the sole exception of 1959, but even in every single month from early 1952 until October 1957. Even thereafter, monthly reserve losses occurred only in October 1957 through Febru-

---

[4] *Ibid.*

ary 1958 and in January through April and June through September 1959. No further losses occurred until after the exchange-rate adjustment of March 1961. The increase in reserves from $274 million at the end of 1950 to $7199 million at the end of 1960 amounts to an average annual growth rate of 39 percent.

Monetary Expansion in Germany

A balance-of-payments surplus tends to withdraw goods and services from the home economy, expand money income through the foreign-trade multiplier, and expand the home money supply as reserves grow. One way to throw light on this last aspect of the problem is to compare increases in the net foreign assets and other assets and in the monetary and other liabilities of the consolidated monetary system. A paradox, however, bedevils the comparison. In a fractional-reserve banking system, the normal tendency (unless counteracted by deliberate policy) is for central-bank purchases of foreign exchange to expand the volume of bank reserves and the ability of the commercial banks to acquire additional domestic loans and investments through additional deposit creation. Growth of the consolidated system's foreign assets amounting to only a small percentage of money-supply growth might suggest, on the one hand, that external factors had been relatively insignificant. On the other hand, this very smallness might suggest that external factors had had a strong *multiple* impact in the way just mentioned. Table 23.1, superficially inspected, would understate the role of foreign-exchange acquisitions in monetary expansion. Even so, it is noteworthy that over the period considered, the change in net foreign assets accounted directly for more than one-fourth of the change in total net assets,[5] more than

___

[5] How large the change in foreign assets looks in relation to the change in total assets depends very much, of course, on the degree of netting done. For example, the change in total assets is smaller, and therefore the change in foreign assets looms larger relatively, if claims on the government are taken net of liabilities to the government (as seems appropriate and as is done here) than if claims on the government are considered gross.

Table 23.1. Relations between Changes within Calendar Years in Net Foreign Assets and Other Balance-sheet Items of the Consolidated German Monetary System

Change in Net Foreign Assets Expressed as Percentage of Change in—	1952	1953	1954	1955	1956	1957	1958	1959	1960	Entire Period Between Ends of 1951 and 1960
Total net assets	35%	31%	22%	20%	43%	36%	30%	−2%	36%	26%
Money+quasi-money	50	46	32	33	70	46	36	−3	57	38
Money	138	157	84	70	219	134	89	−9	207	107

NOTES: All figures refer to *changes* within the periods indicated and have been computed from end-of-year figures published in *International Financial Statistics*, February and April 1961, which may be consulted for detailed definitions. The consolidated monetary system comprises the central bank (called the Bank deutscher Länder at first, later reorganized as the Deutsche Bundesbank), the Reconstruction Loan Corporation, the deposit money banks, and the Treasury coin circulation. Net foreign assets are the foreign assets minus foreign liabilities of the central bank and the deposit money banks. Other assets include loans to and investments in the private sector of the economy and net claims on government. Claims on all levels of government and some government agencies are recorded net of government deposits, counterpart funds (which originated in connection with receipts of U.S. aid in earlier years), and government loans made to certain types of banks for relending to the private economy. Other assets include the country's net position with the International Monetary Fund, as well as unclassified assets. Nonmonetary liabilities include bonded indebtedness of banks, which is much more common in Germany than in the United States, as well as unclassified liabilities and capital accounts. Money is coin, currency, and sight deposits held by the public; quasi-money is time deposits.

the full amount of the monetary expansion, and nearly two-fifths of the expansion in money plus time deposits.

The likelihood of multiple expansion of monetary liabilities and domestic assets on the basis of additional reserves suggests examining separately, apart from the rest of the monetary system, the institution that issues the "high-powered" deposit liabilities and currency usable as bank reserves. Table 23.2 considers certain key assets and liabilities of the central bank with two different degrees of netting. Shown first are changes in gross foreign assets, total assets (equaling total liabilities), and total monetary liabilities, including central-bank notes and deposits held by the banks, the private sector of the economy, and government units. Also shown are changes in foreign assets net of foreign liabilities, total assets net not only of foreign liabilities but also of both monetary liabilities to government and counterpart funds, and currency and deposit liabilities to banks and the private sector only. In most years and over the entire period, the change in foreign assets, whether gross or net, was actually larger than the changes in the other items with which comparisons suggest themselves. Evidently the central bank sought, in its domestic operations, to counteract rather than reinforce the expansionary effect of its foreign-exchange acquisitions.

No one single comparison—no one single percentage—will unambiguously measure the domestic monetary importance of the balance-of-payments surplus and the growth in foreign-exchange reserves. Nevertheless, the unmistakable impression emerges that external influences have been large and significant. A survey of how often balance-of-payments considerations have dominated decisions about monetary policy will reinforce this impression.

The Issue of Imported Inflation

Granted that acquisitions of gold and foreign exchange were large in relation to domestic monetary changes, one still might question whether this posed any problem. It might even have been a fortunate coinci-

dence that balance-of-payments developments helped create the money needed by a rapidly growing economy. On the other hand, expansionary external influences narrow the scope for the monetary system to acquire domestic assets. Avoiding inflation may even call for actually shrinking domestic assets. (In Germany between 1951 and 1960, the consolidated monetary system reduced its net claims on the government, and the central bank reduced the aggregate of its domestic assets.) Furthermore, acquiring foreign-exchange reserves represents passively giving foreigners loans that might not have been attractive in their own right. Without such passive lending abroad, noninflationary extension of credit and therefore real capital formation at home could presumably have been all the greater.

In questioning whether the theory of imported inflation did actually apply to Germany, one might point out how mildly German prices rose. Between 1950 and 1960, the deutschemark lost purchasing power over consumer goods and services at a compound average rate of only 2.1 percent a year, compared with 3.9 percent for the pound sterling and 5.4 percent for the French franc. Money lost purchasing power at about the same rate in Germany as in the United States, and very few countries (Portugal, Switzerland, and Belgium, in Europe) recorded slower rates of depreciation.[6]

An answer to this skepticism about imported inflation has at least three strands. First, the money supply *did* expand rapidly in Germany between the end of 1950 and the end of 1960; compound annual growth rates averaged 10.8 percent for currency plus demand deposits and 15.5 percent for currency plus demand and time deposits. Had not Germany enjoyed conditions permitting real production to grow very rapidly, such rapid monetary expansion could hardly have failed to breed unmistakable price inflation. Secondly, an "identification problem" is involved: Whether or not we expect to find inflation associated with a balance-of-payments surplus depends on the direction of cause and effect

---

[6] First National City Bank of New York, *Monthly Letter*, May 1961, p. 59.

Table 23.2. Growth of Monetary Liabilities of the Central Bank in Relation to Other Annual Changes

	1951	1952	1953	1954	1955	1956	1957	1958	1959	1960	End of 1951 Through End of 1960
Change, billions of deutsche-marks, in											
Gross foreign assets	1.0	2.8	3.4	3.0	1.8	5.0	5.7	2.7	−2.4	7.9	29.9
Net foreign assets		3.3	3.6	2.8	2.0	4.6	5.0	3.0	−2.1	8.2	30.4
Total assets (= total liabilities)	0.2	0.3	0.8	1.3	3.5	3.2	5.3	2.0	−0.1	6.4	22.7
Total assets net of selected liabilities		1.5	1.4	1.3	1.7	1.8	4.1	2.3	2.8	5.3	22.2
Total note and deposit liabilities	0.8	1.3	1.2	1.4	3.8	2.8	4.4	2.1	0.2	6.5	23.7
Note and deposit liabilities to banks and the private sector	1.2	1.6	1.3	1.5	1.7	1.7	3.8	2.4	2.5	5.1	21.6
Change in gross foreign assets expressed as percentage of change in											
Total assets	500%	933%	425%	231%	51%	156%	108%	135%	(2400%)	123%	132%
Total note and deposit liabilities	125	215	283	214	47	179	130	129	−1200	122	126
Note and deposit liabilities to banks and the private sector	83	175	262	200	106	294	150	113	−96	155	138
Change in net foreign assets expressed as percentage of change in											
Total assets net of selected liabilities		220	257	215	118	256	122	130	−75	155	137
Total note and deposit liabilities		254	300	200	118	164	114	143	−1050	126	128
Note and deposit liabilities to banks and the private sector		206	277	187	53	271	132	125	−84	161	141

NOTES: The figures are derived from *International Financial Statistics*, February and April 1961. Net foreign assets is gross foreign assets minus foreign liabilities. Total assets (=total liabilities) is the balance-sheet total as printed in IFS. Total assets net of selected liabilities is this last figure minus foreign liabilities, monetary liabilites to government, and counterpart funds. Total note and deposit liabilities include monetary liabilities to government.

considered. The surplus, as a cause, tends to produce inflation as an effect. On the other hand, the surplus itself may be largely the effect of having less inflation than other countries, if any. Since the surplus merely *tends* to undermine the freedom from inflation that was one of its causes, the absence of conspicuously rising prices is no disproof of inflationary tendencies. (Had these tendencies been allowed full scope, they might have kept the balance-of-payments surplus from persisting, as the theory of the adjustment mechanism under international monetary linkage explains; and *imported* inflation would again have been difficult to demonstrate "empirically" because no balance-of-payments surplus would be persisting as its obvious source.) A third reason for recognizing the danger of imported inflation as a real problem is that the German authorities were continually preoccupied with it and were continually experimenting with various expedients to cope with it. The mildness of the uptrend in prices may mean not that the problem was nonexistent but rather that policy dealt with it more or less successfully—dealt with it, however, at the cost of imposing tighter domestic financial conditions than would otherwise have been necessary. Landing on one horn of a dilemma rather than the other does not disprove the dilemma.

Foreign criticism of the German choice between horns further suggests that the dilemma was genuine. Sir Oliver Franks, reporting to the stockholders of Lloyds Bank Limited at the end of 1957, criticized Germany's monetary and credit policies as inappropriate for a surplus country with big reserves; they threatened "to disrupt the whole system of European payments." The proper policy, observed Sir Oliver with excessive ingenuity, would be to fight inflation not by raising interest rates and restricting credit but by "expand[ing] incomes and allow[ing] the external account to swing back into balance again, thus obtaining additional real resources on which the larger money incomes can be spent." Moreover, lower interest rates would influence capital flows appropriately. If Germany could not avoid pressure on the exchange reserves of other countries by making

long-term foreign loans, and if she remained unwilling to appreciate the mark, then "The only remaining recourse, if the surplus continued, would be to allow money incomes and the standard of living to rise, even if that meant abandoning the dogma of absolute stability in internal prices." No loyal member of an international system, said Sir Oliver, could reject *all* of these possible remedies.[7]

The Danger Recognized

Until some time around 1955, the payments surplus and related monetary problems had persisted for too short a period to arouse serious worry. From 1953 through 1955, in fact, the current-account surplus and the annual growth of external reserves had been shrinking under the influence of import liberalization, rising domestic demand, and increased capital outflows. The earlier absence of worry about the surplus shows up in maintenance until 1954–1955 and even later of exchange controls typical of a country with *deficit* troubles. These controls concerned the use of old blocked mark balances owned by foreigners, the transfer of earnings on foreign-owned capital in Germany, the export and reimport of German currency, limits on foreign travel expenditure by Germans, the obligation to surrender earnings of foreign exchange, and restrictions on German ownership of foreign bank accounts and investments.[8]

Other evidence besides tardiness in relaxing controls shows an early lack of worry about imported inflation. Increases in the liquidity of the German money market were allowed to lead to cuts in the official German discount rate in May and August 1952 and January and June 1953. A final cut to 3 percent came in May 1954. Market rates of interest also sagged. The money supply, defined as currency plus demand deposits, was allowed to grow somewhat more rapidly in 1952 and 1954 than at the average rate for the decade; defined as currency plus demand and time

---

[7] Sir Oliver Franks, in *The Economist*, vol. 186, January 25, 1958, pp. 352-353.

[8] See Bank for International Settlements, 24th *Annual Report*, pp. 129-130; 26th *Annual Report*, p. 129.

deposits, it grew at considerably above the average rate in each of the three years 1952, 1953, and 1954. In its annual report for 1954, the Bank deutscher Länder explained that its policy corresponded

not only to the internal monetary position but also to the rules of the traditional gold-standard mechanism, as determined by the balance of payments, when it had not only refrained from intervening by employing the instruments of credit policy to curb the expansionist tendencies connected with its purchases of foreign exchange but had rather admitted these tendencies by the reduction in its discount rate in May 1954.[9]

In 1955, concern about credit expansion, rising wages and prices, and a possibly excessive boom finally crystallized into a shift toward restriction. The Bank deutscher Länder rearranged the rediscount quotas of the commercial banks early in the year and undertook contractive open-market operations. In August it raised its discount rate from 3 to 3½ percent and raised bank reserve requirements. In March and May 1956 the Bank raised its discount rates in full-point steps to 4½ and 5½ percent. Monetary expansion slowed down in 1955 and 1956. The tightening of money and credit drew criticism as a threat to continued economic growth, but the central bankers justified it as a timely action to safeguard the mark and preserve the basis for continued and orderly economic expansion. The Bank deutscher Länder felt that unfortunate repercussions on the desired revival of the capital market should not deter it from safeguarding the currency.[10]

A Federal government budget surplus sup-

plemented monetary restraint. It had prevailed since 1952 and had been growing. Taxation was geared to defense appropriations in excess of actual expenditures. This "leakage" out of the domestic spending stream luckily tended to offset the "injection" from the active balance of payments. The bank deposits of all levels of government grew throughout the decade. The deposits corresponding to unspent defense appropriations and accompanying the growth of the country's gold and foreign-exchange reserves came to be known as a modern Julius-Tower, in allusion to the tower in Spandau where the Imperial Government had accumulated treasure for future war purposes. Surpluses continued accruing until late in 1956. When the budget position then shifted into deficit, the increased expenditures that were responsible went largely for increased purchases of or for prepayments for imported defense materials and to that extent were not additional direct injections into the domestic spending stream.

By this time various observers were pointing out how internal measures to counteract liquidity of external origin tended to be self-defeating. Effectively resisting internal inflation, explained Wilhelm Röpke, makes the balance-of-payments surplus and its expansionary effects all the more stubborn. If countries such as Germany, Switzerland, or Belgium were denied the possibility of protecting themselves against imported inflation, the fate of their currencies would become dependent in the last analysis on "the steel workers of America, the election tactics of the Republican Party, the trade unions of England and the confusion of parties of France."[11]

Writing in a similar vein, L. Albert Hahn likened internal measures against external inflation to

the activity of the Danaids with the opposite algebraic sign. As is well known, the Danaids

[9] Quoted in Bank for International Settlements, 25th *Annual Report*, p. 45n. The Bank for International Settlements found the German monetary expansion appropriate both to match the rapid growth in German production and to promote international equilibrium. Even in its following annual report (the 26th, pp. 52-53), the Bank continued to describe the German current-account surplus and reserve growth as an "entirely satisfactory" situation. The balance of payments did not give "any cause for concern"—almost as if only a deficit could be considered a "cause for concern."

[10] Cf. Dr. Wilhelm Vocke, then president of the Bank deutscher Länder, writing in a supplement to Federal Reserve Bank of New York, *Monthly Review*, June 1959, and his Bank's annual report for 1955, paraphrased in Bank for International Settlements, 26th *Annual Report*, pp. 54-55.

[11] "Das Dilemma der importierten Inflation," *Neue Zürcher Zeitung*, July 29, 1956, Handelsteil, sheet 11. Röpke sympathized with the German authorities for behaving in the reverse of the way that a balance-of-payments surplus would have called for under the international gold standard, since it was precisely the absence of that standard that permitted other countries to have the inflation whose contagion menaced Germany.

sought to fill a bottomless barrel with water, which they didn't succeed in doing because of the outflow of water. The B.d.L. seeks to hinder the rise of the water level in a barrel into which water again flows from all sides as soon as the water level sinks a bit.[12]

Internal measures to mop up liquidity of external origin, far from preserving a neutral situation, involved tighter credit and higher interest rates than would otherwise be appropriate. On the one hand, Hahn argued, this tended to attract capital, perpetuating the inflationary acquisitions of foreign exchange. On the other hand, deflationary credit policy hampered the development of the German capital market and so tended to restrict the production of investment goods in favor of consumption goods and of excess sales to foreigners. By involuntarily lending to foreigners at zero or low rates of interest through passive accumulation of external reserves— something hardly compensated for by interest- and speculation-motivated transfers of short-term funds into Germany—the Germans were actually subsidizing foreign economic growth at the expense of their own.[13] (That this situation was not generally recognized and condemned is presumably due to the fact that *other* conditions were so favorable to German capital formation and economic growth.)

In its faithfulness to fixed exchange rates, the German central bank (like the International Monetary Fund) would not admit, said Hahn, "that a single country must either howl along with the others, so to speak, or break out of the international currency-zoo. It seeks to remain in the currency-zoo without howling along. It wants to remain in the water of currency stability without getting wet with the inflation of other countries."[14]

As the analyses just mentioned would suggest, the newly intensified policy of restraining domestic demand may have contributed to reversing the 1953–1955 shrinkage of the balance-of-payments surplus. In 1956, exports rose 20 percent while imports rose roughly

13 percent above the previous year's value. Exports benefited from the especial German restraint in the investment-goods sector, while foreign demand remained strong. The surpluses in merchandise and goods-and-services trade grew so much between 1955 and 1956 that the gain in external reserves rose by about 170 percent. The German reserve gain in 1956 was more than triple that of Western Europe as a whole.

Contributing to this overall surplus was the virtual disappearance of net capital exports. Expanded German long-term (mostly direct) investment abroad was outweighed by foreigners' greater long-term investment and short-term lending in Germany. The swollen "errors and omissions" item probably reflected such short-term capital inflows as prepayments for German export deliveries.[15] The tightened credit and increased level of interest rates in Germany, relative to rates abroad, was an important attraction to foreign capital, especially in the first half of the year. While short-term interest rates and the central-bank discount rate turned downward in the second half of 1956, bond yields continued to rise for a while. Speculation on possible exchange-rate adjustments also contributed to capital inflow through leads and lags. Funds were already flowing in from Britain in May, June, and July, and the Suez crisis made itself felt in the fourth quarter.

Policy in 1956–1958

The German authorities adopted several measures in 1956 to resist growth of the external surplus and also to help stabilize prices. In June they freed imports from the dollar area from quantitative restrictions to about the same extent as they had already done for intra-European trade. Various tariff cuts followed, both unilaterally and under the General Agreement on Tariffs and Trade. The duty on most manufactured imports was lowered to a maximum of 21 percent *ad valorem,* and duties on fuel oil and machine tools were suspended altogether in order to hold down prices in the investment sector.

---

12 *Autonome Konjunktur-Politik und Wechselkurs-Stabilität,* Frankfurt/Main: Knapp, 1957, p. 12.

13 *Ibid.,* esp. pp. 13-15, 23-24.

14 *Ibid.,* p. 11.

15 International Monetary Fund, 1957 *Annual Report,* pp. 44-45.

In the two years 1956–1957, the tariffs on most industrial products were lowered by nearly 50 percent. Partly as a result, imports of finished products rose in 1959 to 138 percent above their level of 1955, and their share in total imports rose from 19 to 31 percent, though these effects were obscured by the sluggishness of food and raw material imports and the continuing export boom. In August 1956 the official export-credit-guarantee agencies began narrowing their protection of German exporters. Official imports of defense materials and payments on foreign debt were accelerated somewhat, and measures were taken to discourage short-term capital inflow and further to relax restrictions on private capital exports.[16]

Begun earlier, an easing of domestic financial policy was symbolized in September by a half-a-point cut in the 5½ percent discount rate prevailing since May. The change continued towards the end of the year with tax reductions, increases in public spending, and a shift from surplus to deficit in the government budget. The continued growth in external reserves prompted the change in policy, and so did some signs of a slowdown in the investment boom and of an impending seasonal winter decline in economic activity. When the central bank cut its rate again to 4½ percent in January 1957, it explained that external conditions called for the change and internal conditions did not bar it.[17]

The shift toward easier credit continued into 1959. The initial discount-rate cuts in September 1956 and January 1957 were followed by further one-half-point cuts in September 1957 and January and June 1958 and a final cut to 2¾ percent in January 1959. These and other measures of monetary ease presumably contributed to the faster rate of money-supply growth recorded in 1957

through 1959 than in the relatively tight years 1955 and 1956 and than over the decade as a whole. (Currency plus demand deposits grew by 12.1, 13.1, and 11.8 percent in 1957, 1958, and 1959, while currency plus demand and time deposits grew by 18.0, 15.7, and 16.3 percent. The average annual rates for the two concepts of money over the entire decade were, to repeat, 10.8 and 15.5 percent respectively.)

Monetary ease during this period was by no means unambiguous. If the apparent inconsistency among various strands of policy does not indicate an imperfect understanding of how the interest-rate, bank-reserve, and money-supply aspects of monetary ease or tightness are interrelated, it at least provides further evidence of the conflict of objectives that perplexed policy-makers. Despite repeated discount-rate cuts, the central bank continued relatively heavy open-market sales of securities. On repeated occasions—five times during 1957 alone—it arranged with the government for conversion of some of the "equalization claims"[18] it held into government securities salable on the open market. So reequipped, the central bank could continue trying to mop up bank liquidity. Other exceptions to the general policy were the measures of May 1, 1957: bank reserve requirements were raised so as to sterilize over half a billion marks of the banks' resources; rediscount quotas were lowered; and the banks' borrowings abroad, except for the financing of imports, were deducted from these rediscount quotas. In May and September 1957 the reserve requirements applicable to the deutschemark deposits of nonresidents were raised to the highest level allowed by law. In December, as a feeble weapon against the boom in commodity exports, the Bundesbank excluded export bills from rediscounting privileges altogether.

---

[16] Bank for International Settlements, 27th *Annual Report* (1956-1957), pp. 143-144; International Monetary Fund, 1957 *Annual Report*, p. 33; Federal Reserve Bank of New York, *Monthly Review*, December 1960, p. 208.

[17] Samuel I. Katz, *Sterling Speculation and European Convertibility: 1955–1958* (Essays in International Finance, No. 37), Princeton, N.J.: Princeton University, 1961, p. 13; Federal Reserve Bank of New York, *Monthly Review*, February 1957, p. 17.

[18] The reforms of 1948 cancelled government debts and scaled down claims on other debtors. Financial institutions holding large amounts of claims on the government would have been made insolvent if they had not been given amounts of equalization claims sufficient to equate assets and liabilities in their first post-reform balance sheets. The equalization claims were essentially government bonds subject to special restrictions.

The measures taken for the sake of the balance of payments did not operate strongly or promptly enough to keep the surplus on goods-and-services account from rising a further 36 percent between 1956 and 1957. The most notable shift was from deficit to surplus on transportation account. The larger surplus on goods and services was offset, however, by larger government advance payments for military imports and transfers for restitution and indemnification. The flow of private long-term investment capital was more heavily outward; and in 1957, for the first time since the war, the German banking system made loans to the governments of other European countries. Other short-term capital moved heavily inward during most of the year, however, especially as rumors circulated of impending depreciation of certain European currencies and appreciation of the mark. As measured by "errors and omissions," this movement amounted to about half a billion dollars in the third quarter of the year alone, and the Bundesbank estimated that about two-thirds of the exceptionally large $800-million net increase in its external reserves during that quarter could be attributed to the speculative capital inflow. Much of the funds apparently came from London.[19] This hot-money flow partially reversed itself toward the end of the year, after declarations at the International Monetary Fund meeting in September had helped calm down speculation. For 1957 as a whole, the overall effect on the external reserves was an increase little if any larger than the year before. Germany took the bulk of its reserve gain in gold and again, as in 1956, acquired more than the estimated world total increase in official gold holdings.[20]

Measures taken to resist the balance-of-payments surplus in 1957 included the increased government outpayments already mentioned; a notable example, helpful to the United Kingdom in its balance-of-payments difficul-

ties, was German acquisition of £68 million in sterling to hold against future repayments of debt to the United Kingdom. Private capital exports were encouraged by removal of the last remaining restrictions on foreign investment by German residents, but high long-term rates in Germany remained a deterrent. Imports of manufactures were already running above the year before when duties on them were further reduced in September, and in the last quarter of the year their value was 40 percent above that of 1956. The proportional impact on total imports was much less because finished and semifinished goods still accounted for hardly more than one-fifth of the total value and because German agriculture continued to enjoy extreme protection against import competition.

In 1958, for the first time since World War II, estimated total industrial production in the free world fell below the level of the year before, and the dollar value of world trade declined for the first time since a slight dip in 1952–1953. Germany, by exception, recorded continued (though smaller) growth in both production and trade. Imports grew more than exports as a percentage of the previous year's physical volume but grew less in absolute money value, so that the merchandise export surplus actually rose. A large increase in sales of services to foreign troops failed to outweigh a still larger shift from surplus to deficit in ordinary services, and the net change in the overall balance on goods and services was small, though still positive. The modest rise in this balance was far outweighed by an increase in net capital exports. It is true that official capital exports in the form of advance payments for military imports were temporarily stopped and reversed, but other official capital exports rose by way of subscription to the capital of the European Investment Bank (one of the institutions of the European Economic Community) and German participation in international loans to France and Turkey. Recorded and unrecorded private capital shifted outward, partly in response to a continued decline of German relative to foreign interest rates and the liquidity of the German financial system. Trade

[19] Federal Reserve Bank of New York, *Monthly Review*, January 1958, pp. 12-13; International Monetary Fund, 1958 *Annual Report*, p. 97; Katz, *op. cit.*, p. 21.

[20] International Monetary Fund, 1958 *Annual Report*, pp. 56, 147.

financing by German exporters continued to revive; in fact, the decline in German interest rates promoted a lengthening of payments terms and in turn facilitated commodity exports. Other short-term foreign lending had resumed late in 1957, foreign direct investment by German industry continued to develop, and long-term lending to foreigners began on a small scale. Success in reviving the German capital market was symbolized in September 1958 when a South African corporation floated the first foreign industrial bond issue in Germany since before World War I. An Austrian power loan followed early in 1959. In addition to these capital exports, the "errors and omissions" item for 1958 included a large outward shift, partly reflecting a continuation into the early months of the year of the hot-money reversal that had taken place late in 1957 after abatement of the speculative crisis. The net effect of all transactions so far mentioned was that the external reserves still grew during 1958, but by only half as much as the year before. They had fallen, in fact, in the five months from October 1957 through February 1958 but began rising again in March and by early June had regained the peak level of the previous autumn.

Despite the smaller growth in external reserves, the increase in the German money supply was slightly larger in 1958 than in 1957 (13 as against 12 percent). Medium-term and long-term bank loans and investments in both the public and private sectors played a part in this monetary expansion. On the one hand, the authorities were continuing (though less vigorously than before) to offset the effects of reserve gains by open-market operations; on the other hand, they were continuing to reduce official discount rates and permit the continued expansion of bank liquidity. A cash deficit in the Federal budget continued at a reduced size and corresponded to official payments abroad; domestic cash transactions continued in substantial surplus.[21]

When the major European countries adopted external currency convertibility late in December 1958, Germany merged the lim-

ited-convertibility mark accounts with the freely convertible accounts that had already existed. Next month virtually full convertibility privileges were extended to residents and nonresidents alike. With minor and temporary exceptions, exchange control vanished. Actually, all of this did little more than formalize arrangements that had prevailed *de facto* for some time. As early as 1956, the obligation to surrender foreign-exchange receipts after a certain period had been abolished. In 1956 and 1957, the rationing of foreign exchange for travel abroad had been discontinued and restrictions on holding foreign portfolio and direct investments and bank accounts had been greatly relaxed. Various steps to liberalize gold transactions culminated in January 1959 with an end to the remaining German restrictions on domestic and international trade in coined and uncoined gold.[22]

The 1959 Interlude

By early 1959, the policies for influencing capital movements were apparently succeeding so well, in comparison with previous (and subsequent) experience, that the official reserves fell by $879 million, or 14 percent, in the first four months alone. For the year as a whole, net exports of long-term private capital were much larger than in 1958, official capital movements for debt settlement and advance payment for military imports were again heavily outward, and Germany paid an additional gold subscription of 480 million deutschemarks to the International Monetary Fund. The surplus on goods-and-services account persisted in 1959 but was 9 percent smaller than before, mainly because of heavier German tourist spending abroad and larger earnings paid on foreign capital invested in Germany. Germany displaced the United Kingdom in 1959 as the world's second largest merchandise exporter. A sharp recovery of international reserves toward the

[21] International Monetary Fund, 1959 *Annual Report,* pp. 67-68, 94.

[22] See Bank for International Settlements, 27th *Annual Report,* p. 190, 29th *Annual Report,* p. 193; International Monetary Fund, 1959 *Annual Report,* pp. 127, 129, 157, 1960 *Annual Report,* p. 154; Federal Reserve Bank of New York, *Monthly Review,* February 1959, p. 27.

end of 1959 was not enough to keep them from declining by 8¾ percent over the year as a whole.[23]

This first annual decline in reserves, instead of indicating a solution to the balance-of-payments problem, reflected some untypical influences. The burden of accumulating external assets had not been shed altogether but just temporarily shifted from official to private shoulders, which later proved inconvenient. During the first nine months of 1959, while the official reserves were falling by almost $1 billion, the net foreign-exchange assets of the commercial banks grew by $540 million. Over the full year, the gold and dollar holdings of German banks and official institutions *combined* actually rose by about 1 billion marks' worth.[24] Especially during the early months of 1959, the private institutions had been responding largely to a changed pattern of international interest-rate differentials. The official discount rate went down to 2¾ percent in January, and in April the Bundesbank reduced the interest rates at which it sold money-market paper, bringing the German equivalent of the Treasury bill rate to its lowest level since the war.

As far as the German authorities could tell in the spring of 1959, without knowing what the future held in store, their policies were working well in influencing capital movements. In fact, the discriminatory features of bank reserve requirements and rediscount quotas that had been introduced in May 1957 to discourage speculation in favor of the mark no longer seemed necessary. From April 1, therefore, the Bundesbank lowered the reserve requirements for foreign-owned deposits to the same level as for domestic deposits. From May 1, for the first time since the war, German banks were permitted to pay interest on foreign-owned deposits. At the same time, sales of German money-market paper to nonresidents were permitted, and restrictions on

loans from nonresidents to residents (such as that the loans had to be of at least five years' maturity) were removed.[25]

The removal of these special discouragements to capital inflows proved premature; the conflict between internal and external considerations of policy soon returned to prominence. Internally, low interest rates stimulated construction and helped promote the continued revival of economic growth in 1959 after the slowdown of 1958 (while briefer and less marked than in most other industrial countries, the slowdown had nevertheless been appreciable by recent German standards). By early 1959 production was expanding again at a rising rate. Market rates of interest rose in the second half of the year. These domestic developments prodded the authorities into increasingly restrictive credit policies from September on. At first the Bundesbank raised its discount rate by one-fourth of a point, to 3 percent, and then, in October 1959 and June 1960, by full points to 4 and finally 5 percent. The rediscount quotas of the commercial banks were cut in October 1959 and cut again in March. An increase in bank reserve requirements was announced in October, became effective in November, and was followed by further increases in January, March, and June 1960. In late 1959 and early 1960 the Bundesbank repeatedly warned about upward pressures on wages and prices, threatened still stricter credit controls if demand should continue excessive, and urged noninflationary budgets at all levels of government. Money-supply growth slowed down in 1960 to 6.8 percent for currency plus demand deposits and 11.2 percent for currency plus demand and time deposits, well below the annual growth rates for the preceding years and for the decade as a whole.

Domestic considerations were overriding the desire to promote capital exports. The Bundesbank regretted but "deliberately accepted the possibility" that German funds might return from abroad and that the growth of foreign-exchange reserves might "again

---

[23] This figure, like those in the next paragraph and the first sentence of this one, refers to reserves defined as including net EPU claims. With reserves defined to exclude these claims, the decline is 4 percent.

[24] The last two figures are from Bank for International Settlements, 30th *Annual Report* (1959–1960), p. 145; International Monetary Fund, 1960 *Annual Report*, p. 93.

[25] Bank for International Settlements, 29th *Annual Report*, p. 193; International Monetary Fund, 1959 *Annual Report*, p. 63; Federal Reserve Bank of New York, *Monthly Review*, June 1959, p. 84.

cause . . . headaches."[26] Events did bear out these fears. During the last quarter of 1959, the commercial banks reduced their foreign-exchange assets by well over $100 million and increased their deutschemark liabilities to foreigners by about twice the amount of their decline during the nine preceding months. These trends continued far into 1960. The external assets of the Bundesbank (excluding EPU liquidation claims) grew by almost one-seventh during the last quarter of 1959 alone.

Policy Changes in 1960

Though the repatriation of German capital seemed practically unavoidable, the authorities hoped at least to restrain the inflow of foreign capital. They reinstated discriminatory reserve requirements. Effective the first day of 1960, the Bundesbank raised to the legal maximum the reserve requirements against increases in foreign-owned bank deposits above their end-of-November levels. Effective July 1, German banks were again, as before May 1959, forbidden to pay interest on foreign-owned sight and time (but not savings) deposits and were also forbidden to sell money-market paper to nonresidents. The Bundesbank also withdrew an earlier exemption of foreign-owned deposits from reserve requirements to the extent that they were matched by foreign-currency assets.

These expedients apparently did work to some extent; the growth of foreign deposits in German banks paused after May 1960. On the other hand, the "net errors and omissions" item in the balance of payments switched from negative in 1958 and 1959 to increasingly positive in the first three quarters of 1960. In large part this apparently reflected the repatriation of German capital and German borrowing of foreign capital through either unrecorded financial transactions or shifts in the timing of commercial payments. Widespread rumors of an exchange-rate adjustment intensified the demand for marks, especially in mid-June. Some transactions during a long holiday weekend were actually made at rates

on the mark stronger than the official support limit of 4.17 per dollar,[27] and the premium on forward marks rose. A clear-cut denial by the Bundesbank and the government of any intention to revalue the mark helped shrink the inflow of funds at the end of June and in July. Another helpful factor was that the German banks were apparently at last nearing the end of their short-term foreign investments available for repatriation. But in the 13 months between the ends of August 1959 and September 1960, the banks did draw down their foreign short-term assets by $530 million, returning them to just about their level of late 1958, when the Bundesbank had begun to encourage the outflow of short-term funds. Over the same period, the German banks also increased their outstanding short-term foreign debt from $67 million to $257 million.[28]

The inflow of funds tended to replenish domestic liquidity, feeding the boom. The Bundesbank responded, as already mentioned, not only by raising the discount rate to 5 percent in June 1960 and by discriminating further against foreign-owned deposits but also by again tightening domestic reserve requirements. In August the Bundesbank reached an agreement with the commercial banks under which the banks agreed to buy DM1 billion of nonnegotiable two-year 5½ percent government notes; this had the effect though not the form of a further increase in required reserves.[29]

Attempted restraints on capital inflow apparently had their main effect in merely changing its *form*. Foreign buying of German stocks and bonds spurted during the second half of 1960. Borrowing abroad by German banks and corporations continued despite a further deterrent adopted late in August. From time to time the Bundesbank had already sought to promote German lending abroad by providing forward cover for short-term money-market investments abroad;

---

[26] The President of the Bundesbank, quoted in Federal Reserve Bank of New York, *Monthly Review,* February 1960, p. 32.

[27] Federal Reserve Bank of New York, *Monthly Review,* July 1960, p. 134.

[28] Federal Reserve Bank of New York, *Monthly Review,* December 1960, p. 208.

[29] Federal Reserve Bank of New York, *Monthly Review,* September 1960, p. 162.

that is, it had repurchased dollars forward when selling them spot to guarantee German institutions against exchange risk. The Bundesbank now extended these "swaps" of spot for forward dollars to transactions connected with the financing of import and transit trade. The Bank would agree to forward maturities ranging from 15 days to 6 months. Furthermore, it would buy the forward dollars at a premium above the rate charged in the spot sale. In effect the Bundesbank was now not only subsidizing short-term German investments abroad but was also subsidizing the lending to importers of dollars that commercial banks would buy from its own swollen external reserves. In effect it was trying to encourage German importers to borrow foreign exchange from itself, through the intermediary of the commercial banks, rather than to borrow abroad, as they had recently been doing in large volume. International competition in import financing had become keen; Italian and Swiss banks in particular were offering funds to German importers on terms that German banks had been unable to match, especially in view of the domestic tight-credit policy. Even the Bundesbank's 1½ percent swap premium was probably too small to have the full effects desired, especially on short-term capital exports, since it still did not bring the yield on short-term funds transferred to the United States up to what could be earned in Germany.

The measures adopted during 1960—the prohibition of interest on and the discriminatory reserve requirements for foreign deposits and the swap-premium system—dealt more with the symptomatic and aggravating element of short-term capital movements than with fundamentals. Exports of goods and services in 1960 still exceeded imports by $1.9 billion, or almost as much as the record set two years before. By the autumn of 1960 mere palliatives were clearly failing to offset the double pull on short-term capital of the excess of German over foreign interest rates and of recurrent exchange-rate rumors. The first three quarters of 1960 contrasted sharply with the same period one year before: recorded capital movements and those concealed

in "errors and omissions" turned heavily inward. Official reserves grew by $1805 million, or nearly 40 percent, from January through September 1960. The German government had to consider more basic correctives. Larger contributions to NATO would go some way toward reducing or offsetting Germany's large foreign-exchange receipts from NATO troop expenditures. The Reconstruction Loan Corporation, owned jointly by the Federal government and the states, might lend abroad for development purposes; and some part of the state government budget surpluses might also be used for foreign aid. The government might further hasten repaying foreign debts. (But on the theory involved, see page 401, note 11.) Domestic policy might shift emphasis from monetary to fiscal tightness.

As part of this "new look" in policy, the Bundesbank cut its discount rate on November 11 from 5 to 4 percent—"solely in the light of the external monetary situation," as its announcement said, and not because of any lessened domestic need for restraint. Discount-rate reductions abroad had made a similar step in Germany "unavoidable." Special reserve requirements that had been introduced in June were dropped on December 1. As German financial commentators noted, "Although it would be desirable for domestic reasons to continue a policy of tight money, experience has shown that it is impossible to achieve both aims, cheap and tight money, for any length of time."[30] Further cuts in January and May 1961 brought the discount rate down to 3 percent, where it remained for several years afterwards. Additional credit-easing steps included reduced reserve requirements against domestic bank deposits, larger rediscount quotas for the banks, and reduced interest yields on money-market paper sold by the Bundesbank. During the first six months of 1961, German credit institutions were able to expand their loans and their deposit and other liabilities by roughly half again as much as in the same period the year before, yet they were able to turn their net short-term liability to foreigners into virtual

---

[30] *Frankfurter Allgemeine Zeitung*, editorial of 3 December 1960, summarized in *International Financial News Survey*, 9 December 1960, pp. 597-598.

balance.[31] After the banks' liquidity began
coming under strain in August, the authorities pushed their earlier measures further and
also removed the obligation imposed on banks
the year before to hold 1 billion deutschemarks worth of special Treasury notes.
By the beginning of 1962, the yield on three-
month Treasury bills had reached its lowest
level since the war.[32] The switch from monetary tightness to ease after November 1960,
like the switches from ease to tightness in
1955, back to ease in 1956, and back again to
tightness in 1959, was one more example of
thrashing back and forth in efforts to reconcile internally and externally oriented strands
of policy.

Revaluation and Its Immediate Aftermath

The reorientation of financial policy got
early support from something more dramatic.
After repeatedly disavowing any such intention,[33] the government revalued the mark
upward. Effective Monday, March 6, 1961,
its parity went from 4.2 to 4 per dollar. This
meant a 5 percent rise in the dollar price of
the mark and a 4.76 percent cut in the mark
price of the dollar. Commentators saw political and economic motives combined. The
alternative proposed by Economics Minister
Erhard, discontinuance of both the refund
of turnover tax on exported goods and the
"equalization" tax on imports, had drawn
too much protest from industry. Germany's
gold and foreign-exchange reserves, then
second only to those of the United States and
over twice the size of the British, had widely
if not logically been seen as evidence of Germany's capacity to carry a still larger share
of defense and development-aid burdens,
especially in view of recent American balance-
of-payments troubles. Yet the Adenauer government, facing an election in September,
was wary of tax increases to pay for foreign

aid; and Erhard was unenthusiastic.[34] By
revaluing, the Germans would seem to be
doing something about their embarrassing
international imbalance and their bloated
reserves. The step might lighten foreign
pressures on them and leave them more
nearly free to decide for themselves on the
size of their defense and aid contributions.
Inside Germany, furthermore, the new exchange rate would tend to cheapen imports
for consumer-voters. More broadly, the revaluation might help resist the inflationary
danger of the new policy of easier money.

One day after Germany acted, the Netherlands revalued the guilder by the same percentage. As the Dutch finance minister
explained to parliament, the country had
been running substantial current-account surpluses in most years since 1951. Recent capital
flows had been heavily inward. The gold and
foreign-exchange holdings of the Netherlands Bank had climbed 23 percent in 1960
alone to a record level of $1.8 billion. Failure
to follow the German lead would have intensified inflationary influences by spelling
devaluation of the guilder against the currency of the country accounting for more
than one-fifth of all Dutch foreign trade.
The Dutch authorities hoped that a reduction in the payments surplus and cheaper
imports would slow down price increases
expected in 1961 and temper wage demands.[35]

At first the two revaluations boomeranged.
Their very occurrence, especially without due
international consultation in advance, reminded speculators not to trust official
denials of impending exchange-rate adjustments. Their smallness suggested possible
repetition, especially when a statement
by the U.S. government welcomed the German revaluation as "a useful but modest
step" only. As German officials complained,
the word "modest" incited speculation on a
further change. (American officials later interpreted the word as a call for bigger aid
and defense contributions and emphasized

[31] Computed from BIS, 32nd *Annual Report*, p. 69.
(The institutions' foreign liabilities grew, but their
claims on foreigners grew more.)

[32] *Ibid.*, p. 71; IMF, 1962 *Annual Report*, p. 93.

[33] Disavowals dated back six years or so, the most
recent explicit one coming on 18 October 1960. *Wall
Street Journal*, 6 March 1961, p. 3.

[34] *Ibid.*; (anonymous), "Sterling after the Storm,"
The Banker, April 1961, pp. 235-237.

[35] Federal Reserve Bank of New York, *Monthly
Review*, April 1961, p. 63.

that they were "entirely satisfied" with the extent of the revaluation.) Germany's merely "modest" adjustment also suggested that the dollar and sterling, still supposedly overvalued in terms of the mark, would contribute their share by devaluing. Hot money surged violently from London and New York into Germany. As one international banker put it, "The speculators have tasted blood, and no matter what you say, they won't believe that another revaluation isn't in the wind."[36] The Bundesbank absorbed $125 million worth of gold and foreign exchange during the week including two trading days after the revaluation, and $206 million more in the following week.[37] During the month of March as a whole, the German reserves rose by $362 million, or about 5 percent.

The initial burst of bullish speculation extended to other currencies, especially the Swiss franc and to a lesser extent the revalued Dutch guilder, the French franc, and the Italian lira. An official statement on March 6 ruled a Swiss revaluation "out of the question" because there was "no similarity" with the German situation; yet almost $300 million moved into Switzerland during the next nine or ten days, according to an estimate by the Swiss National Bank. For Switzerland as for Germany, the growth in reserves during the second week of March set a new record for so short a period.[38] The chief currency weakened by the corresponding outflows of funds was sterling (as detailed in Chapter 21).

At their regular monthly meeting for March at the Bank for International Settlements in Basel, the governors of eight leading European central banks issued a joint statement emphasizing that rumors of further currency adjustments had "no foundation." They emphasized their own close cooperation in the exchange markets to discourage speculation and cushion the impact of hot money on reserve positions. As President Blessing

of the Bundesbank later argued when urging inclusion of the United States in a broadened scheme of cooperation, the speculator would have no chance against "an association of central banks operating in unison," and the sooner this was realized, the quicker speculative money movements would lose force. The European central bankers agreed, specifically, not only to make short-term loans of needed currencies but also to hold each other's currencies more extensively than before, instead of converting them at once into gold or dollars. In fact, they agreed to hold one another's currencies (including short-term securities) in unlimited amounts in order to meet hot-money movements. The British reserves would escape depletion by speculative attack, for example, to the extent that Continental central banks were willing to keep holding sterling acquired with their own currencies in pegging operations on the exchange market. The United States would benefit so far as the European banks were willing to absorb dollars without converting them into gold. These procedures were to be temporary, pending a more fundamental reform of methods for dealing with short-term capital movements and financial disequalibriums in general.[39]

Whether because of these pronouncements and actions or just of its own accord, speculation did die down by the end of March. Meanwhile, however, events had shown again how unsettling an official realignment of a major currency can be. Outright speculators had not made a real killing but had not been defeated, either. "As a British official put it, 'they've hurt us as much as we've hurt them.' "[40] The events of March had brought a change in market psychology. Before then, growing confidence in currency convertibility and the pattern of exchange rates had caused much international business to be conducted without forward-exchange protection. Afterwards the practice became more general of

[36] *Business Week,* March 18, 1961, p. 31.

[37] Federal Reserve Bank of New York, *Monthly Review,* April 1961, p. 63.

[38] *Ibid.;* Bank for International Settlements, 31st *Annual Report* (1960-1961), p. 147. According to another estimate, the Swiss took in $350 million in a single week. *Business Week,* April 22, 1961, p. 48.

[39] *International Financial News Survey,* April 7, 1961, p. 97; Federal Reserve Bank of New York, *Monthly Review,* April 1961, p. 64; *Business Week,* April 8, 1961, p. 76, and April 22, 1961, pp. 45-50; *U.S. News and World Report,* April 3, 1961, p. 113; *The Economist,* May 6, 1961, p. 572.

[40] *Business Week,* April 22, 1961, p. 50.

arranging forward cover for foreign-exchange positions.[41]

The Shift to an External Deficit

German trade took a while to show a clear response to the revaluation, partly because of a backlog of unfilled export orders. The commodity export surplus reached an all-time record level for the year 1961 as a whole, though it shrank after the first quarter and in the fourth quarter was smaller than a year earlier. The surplus on services (including services sold to foreign troops in Germany) disappeared after the first quarter because of increased spending abroad by German tourists, increased remittances by foreigners employed in Germany, and increased payments of interests, profits, and dividends. Outward governmental transfers (mainly indemnification payments) and private transfers also rose. The surplus on goods and services fell from DM7.6 billion in 1960 to DM6.5 billion in 1961; the surplus on goods, services, and transfers fell from DM4.6 billion to DM2.8 billion. The net inflow of long-term private capital shrank slightly between the two years and actually turned negative in the second half of 1961 (under the influence of the Berlin crisis). The "basic" balance on account of all these ordinary transactions was still in surplus for the year as a whole, though slightly in deficit for the second half. Movements of short-term capital and some special government transactions were large enough to make the Bundesbank's gold and foreign exchange reserves start shrinking after the revaluation and register a decline over the year as a whole (though the total reserves, counting Germany's IMF position, did not quite fall back to their end-of-1960 level). The special transactions included advance debt repayments to the United States, United Kingdom, and France, military purchases abroad, and credits and contributions to the World Bank, International Monetary Fund, and the underdeveloped countries.

The move away from balance-of-payments surplus continued in 1962. Imports rose more strongly than exports, cutting the merchandise export surplus roughly in half. Further growth in German tourist spending abroad and in remittances by foreigners working in Germany pushed the balance on services (even including sale of German services to foreign troops) into deficit, after near-evenness in 1961 and surpluses in earlier years. The surplus on goods and services together was approximately half as large as in 1961. Defined as also including private and government transfers, the current account registered a deficit in both halves of 1962 and Germany's first deficit for any calendar year since 1950. A slight net inflow of long-term capital was too small to prevent an overall "basic" deficit.

Mirroring these and all other items, including short-term capital movements, the Bundesbank's reserves of gold and foreign exchange fell by $87 million in 1962. This fall of only 1.3 percent, unlike the 2.9 percent fall of 1961, reflected a "genuine" overall deficit. In fact, the reserves would have fallen considerably in 1962 but for repayments collected on earlier loans made through the International Monetary Fund and sales of foreign assets by the banking system. (International liquidity, counting the IMF position along with gold and foreign exchange, fell by $207 million.) In 1961, by contrast, changes in the net IMF position and in the foreign position of the banking system (excluding year-end window-dressing) had more than offset the decline in gold and foreign exchange. A more important difference is that special compensatory government transactions such as advance debt repayment were unnecessary in 1962, whereas, without them, the reserves would have shown a big rise the year before.[42]

Was the revaluation really responsible for the shift in the balance of payments? A change in price-competitiveness was indeed one influence at work, among others. Import prices in marks fell to annual averages of 3 percent in 1961 and 4 or 6 percent (depending on the index used) in 1962 below their level of 1960, while German industrial and agricultural wholesale prices and the cost of

---

[41] International Monetary Fund, 1961 *Annual Report*, pp. 6-7.

[42] Bank for International Settlements, 33rd *Annual Report*, p. 130.

living continued rising mildly and reached 1962 averages of 3, 4, and 7 percent, respectively, above their 1960 levels. German export prices in dollars averaged 6 percent higher in 1962 than in 1960, while over the same period the indexes rose only about 1 percent for Western Europe as a whole and 2 percent for the United States.[43] According to one authority, "the gradual evaporation of the large surpluses" was "clearly," if only "partly," a result of the revaluation, "which had cut into the competitive margin enjoyed by exporters . . . while also making imports cheaper." The Bundesbank noted some effects of revaluation—a prompt decline in export *orders* if not in shipments and some apparent restraint on imports, especially of finished goods.[44] Largely, though, the change in the current account after so small a revaluation resulted from the continuation of tendencies already at work.[45] One of these was the continued rise of incomes and of demand pressing on domestic resources. The slow-down in growth of German real national income from its unsustainable earlier pace to about the Continental European average of 5 percent between 1960 and 1961 was due not to financial tightness but rather to physical constraints such as labor scarcity, further accentuated in 1962 by a shortening of the average work week, longer paid vacations, and greater difficulty in recruiting foreign workers as skilled labor enjoyed full employment practically throughout Continental Europe. German expenditures abroad on "invisibles" were rising in a partially autonomous trend.

Perhaps the most notable influence on the balance of payments was the shift toward an easier domestic monetary policy that had already begun a few months before the revaluation. The external deficit of 1961 did not neutralize this shift, since the official transactions responsible for the deficit—debt prepayments and contributions and government expenditures abroad—were of a sort that allowed other parts of the balance of payments to continue actually adding liquidity to the domestic banking system.[46] As a combined result of the balance of payments and reinforcing domestic policy, then, the German money supply grew by 14.8 percent during 1961. (This relatively large increase contrasts with average and maximum annual increases of only 10.2 and 13.1 percent over the previous five years and 10.6 and 13.2 over the previous nine.) At the end of 1961, interest rates on the German money market were actually lower than in most other international financial centers.[47]

With the balance of payments no longer in either overall or basic surplus in 1962, the German authorities could pay more attention again to the problem of rising wages and prices. As the Bundesbank reported,

Continuance of the previous year's policy of relaxation aligned to the balance-of-payments situation was . . . not required. The Bundesbank was on the contrary able to cease applying the pressure, which it had exerted on the money market from the end of 1960 to the end of 1961 so as to reduce the inflow of foreign moneys or to inhibit its resumption and could thus in many respects give a different inflection to its monetary policy.[48]

A housing and construction boom, a return to a Federal government budget deficit, and wage-push were seen as the main inflationary pressures and, operating unevenly over the economy, were considered less effectively subject to money and credit restraints than to fiscal and direct restraints. The authorities took some direct measures to curb governmental and other construction. The Bundesbank left both its discount rate and bank reserve requirements for domestic liabilities unchanged in 1962. It did, however, at least passively allow the liquidity positions of the banks to tighten as the demand for bank credit continued strong, as the total of required reserves grew in step with deposits, as the public drained currency into circulation, and as the government budget absorbed

---

[43] Computed from *International Financial Statistics.*

[44] Federal Reserve Bank of New York, 1962 *Annual Report*, p. 35; Bundesbank, *Geschäftsbericht für das Jahr 1961*, Frankfurt: 1962, p. 430.

[45] Bundesbank, *ibid.*, p. 421.

[46] *Ibid.*, pp. 29, 31, 34-35.

[47] See Bundesbank, *Report for the Year 1962*, Frankfurt: 1963, p. 14.

[48] *Ibid.*

loanable funds. The Bundesbank raised the interest yield on short-term securities it sold. Money-supply growth fell to 6.6 percent in 1962, a smaller rate than in any of the preceding ten years.

The Old Story Once Again

This comparative restraint presumably had something to do with bringing on another balance-of-payments reversal. In 1963 merchandise trade recorded an export surplus larger than in any previous year except only 1961; the surplus on goods and services was twice as large as the shrunken surplus of 1962, and 1962's deficit on account of goods, services, and private and governmental transfers gave way to the more familiar surplus. After declining slightly in 1961 and 1962, the Bundesbank's holdings of gold and foreign exchange rose by $0.7 billion in 1963, or by 10 percent of their amount at the beginning of the year. The restored balance-of-payments surplus grew with particular vigor in the fourth quarter. Early 1964 brought further heavy reserve gains. An inflow of hot money into Germany was both feeding and feeding on rumors of another upward revaluation of the mark.[49]

What explains this return to earlier conditions? For one thing, prices were rising much more moderately in Germany than in neighboring countries (in France and Italy, price inflation had come to arouse actual anxiety). The rise in German wages slowed down noticeably in 1963. German dollar export price indexes had held steady (or had even declined slightly) since being raised by the 1961 revaluation, and export prices in marks had been steady for several years, while competitors' prices had risen. The German surplus was in notable contrast with the growing external trade deficit of all six Common Market countries considered together.

Germany's spectacular export gains were threatening to transmit inflation into Germany by both reducing the supply of goods on the home market and increasing the supply of money. (The rate of money-supply growth recovered in fact to 7.2 percent in 1963 and 10.9 percent in 1964.) In March 1964, as a measure of resistance, the Bundesbank began granting domestic commercial banks forward-exchange protection on favorable terms to encourage them to invest funds in U.S. Treasury bills. Soon afterwards, the authorities again forbade payment of interest on foreign-owned bank deposits and doubled the reserves required against them. The government also introduced a 25 percent withholding tax on income from foreign-owned German fixed-interest securities, which not only checked the inflow of long-term capital but also caused foreigners to liquidate a considerable part of their holdings of German securities. Earlier surpluses on trade account also shrank as the year went on. Over 1964 as a whole, official reserves of gold and foreign exchange fell by about 1.8 percent. January 1965 brought a cut in income taxes and a rise to 3½ percent in the Bundesbank's discount rate.

Off and on again, it seems, Germany was facing her familiar problem of how to reconcile policies aimed at internal and external balance and cope with their troublesome lagged interactions.

---

[49] *Wall Street Journal,* February 27, 1964, p. 14, and April 9, 1964, p. 12.

Canada's Fluctuating Exchange Rate

∽ 24

The Pegged-rate Background

Canada adopted a fluctuating exchange rate in 1950 after several years of trouble with pegging. During 1945 and the first half of 1946, a growing opinion that the Canadian dollar was undervalued at its wartime rate of 90.9 U.S. cents led Americans to buy Canadian securities heavily, while Canadians cut their holdings of American securities. The resulting rise in official Canadian holdings of U.S. dollars, together with hopes of checking the contagion of American price inflation, led the Canadian government to revalue its dollar to parity with the U.S. dollar on July 6, 1946.

Revaluation soon proved a mistake. Canada's current-account deficit with the United States had traditionally been met by a surplus with the United Kingdom and Western Europe, but in the early postwar years these impoverished customers were unable to pay fully in gold or convertible currencies. Canada was in effect making foreign loans and grants out of her reserves of U.S. dollars. While her overall balance on current account remained positive (though shrunken), her pent-up demand for imports led to unprecedentedly large current deficits with the United States in 1946 and 1947. Another difficulty was that the inflow of capital from the United States fell off after the revaluation of 1946 and reversed itself in 1947. Official Canadian holdings of gold and U.S. dollars fell from US $1667 million in May 1946 to only US $480 million in November 1947. A loss continuing at the same average monthly rate would have wiped out the remaining reserve by the early summer of 1948. Instead of devaluing to meet the crisis, in November 1947 the government imposed severe restrictions on imports from and travel in the United States and other countries. The controls were discriminatory in fact though not in form. Canada also cut its foreign lending and borrowed from the U.S. Export-Import Bank. This program stemmed the crisis. Still, inconvertible pounds earned in trade with Great Britain did not satisfactorily meet the continuing (though much shrunken) deficit with the United States. In the summer of 1949 (a year of American recession), Canada's Acting Prime Minister warned that tighter austerity measures might again be necessary. And when the worldwide devaluations of September 1949 threatened Canadian exports with intensified competition, Canada responded with a 10 percent devaluation against the U.S. dollar.

People soon felt that the Canadian dollar was now undervalued. Expectations of revaluation crystallized under the influences of a boom in exploration and development of Canadian natural resources and of external inflationary pressures resembling those that had led to the revaluation of 1946. Rumors gained support from the Commerce Minister's statement in Parliament on June 5, 1950—*before* the Korean outbreak and the resulting boom in raw materials—that the discount on the Canadian dollar might not last much longer. Of the roughly C$1 billion of net capital inflow in 1950, only about one-fourth was for direct long-term investment; most of the remainder represented speculation.[1] Foreigners acquired Canadian banknotes, bank

---

[1] Samuel I. Katz, "The Canadian Dollar: A Fluctuating Currency," *Review of Economics and Statistics,* **XXXV**, August 1953, pp. 236-237.

deposits, and government and corporation securities, either for cash or on margin. The item "other capital movements" in the Canadian balance of payments swelled tremendously: many U.S. companies with Canadian affiliates delayed taking their profits out of Canada and delayed paying for things bought in the United States for use in Canada; foreigners due to receive payments in Canadian dollars were glad to wait, while Canadians due to make payments in foreign currencies were anxious to stall.

The fixed exchange rate forced the Foreign Exchange Control Board to meet this speculative capital inflow by buying all U.S. dollars offered—still at a 10-percent premium in terms of Canadian dollars. Official Canadian holdings of gold and U.S. dollars rose from $1117 million at the end of December 1949 to $1255 million at the end of June 1950 and, by a further 43 percent in the third quarter of 1950 alone, to $1790 million at the end of September. The monthly increases amounted to $73 million in June, $65 million in July, $184 million in August, and $285 million in September. The sharp peak for September dramatizes the snowballing speculation.

Finding the Canadian dollars to buy the foreign exchange offered to the Control Board became a serious problem. The government had to supplement funds from its budget surplus by borrowing from the chartered (commercial) banks and by turning to the Bank of Canada for help in absorbing foreign exchange. Like a giant open-market operation, these purchases of foreign exchange provided the chartered banks with reserves and the public with Canadian money. The Bank of Canada tried to offset these inflationary effects by selling government securities on the open market. As the Governor of the Bank later told a parliamentary committee, these sales, relative to the size of the Canadian economy, constituted the largest open-market operation in the history of central banks. Still, they did not suffice to keep the reserves of the chartered banks from rising during 1950.

Toward the end of September 1950, official holdings of gold and U.S. dollars had climbed to nearly $1.8 billion. Announcement of this figure, due early in October, was sure to spur speculation still more as long as the Canadian dollar stayed pegged at 90.9 U.S. cents. The Finance Minister felt there was "no telling how much further this movement might have gone so long as the fixed rate of a 10% premium on U.S. dollars was maintained and people believed in the possibility or probability of an official change to another fixed rate such as parity."

The Minister went on to say that "an influx of funds on this tremendous scale would, if continued, be likely to exercise an inflationary influence in Canada at a time when government policy in all fields is directed to combatting inflationary developments."[2]

Something had to be done. But what? Raising the Canadian dollar to parity with the American dollar would probably have reversed the capital movement as speculators took their profits at the expense of the Canadian authorities. The Finance Minister emphasized that adoption of parity or any other fixed rate "would not necessarily be justified by fundamental conditions and might be found to require reversal or further adjustment within the not too distant future."[3] Emerging weakness in trade and service items in the balance of payments made the problem still more delicate. With all alternatives open to serious objection, Finance Minister Douglas Abbott persuaded the cabinet to try a fluctuating rate. The government tried to make the free rate palatable to the International Monetary Fund by giving lip-service to the idea that it was tentative and experimental and that fixity might be reimposed in more appropriate circumstances.

On Friday evening, September 29, the government instructed Canadian banks to suspend foreign-exchange dealings and invited the chiefs of their foreign-exchange departments to a briefing in Ottawa the next morning. There the authorities announced

[2] Bank of Nova Scotia, *Monthly Review,* September 1950, p. 4.
[3] Raymond F. Mikesell, *Foreign Exchange in The Postwar World,* New York: Twentieth Century Fund, 1954, p. 162.

their surprise decision.[4] Over the weekend the banks reshuffled their personnel, established departments for free-market exchange trading, and installed extra telephones. The free market opened on Monday morning, October 2.

The immediate results were gratifying. Though American investment funds kept moving into Canada, the heavy speculative inflow ceased without giving away to a speculative outflow. For a while Canada cautiously kept its general structure of control over international transactions (though not over the exchange rate itself). Finally, after 14 months of progressive relaxation, exchange controls were completely abolished on December 14, 1951. Canada then notified the International Monetary Fund and so became the first member country that had imposed exchange controls during and after World War II to give up the "transition-period" excuse for them. These results contrast with the unsatisfactory conditions that had led to upward revaluation of the Canadian dollar in July 1946, to a tightening of trade and exchange controls in the fall of 1947, to the devaluation of September 1949, and finally to abandonment of rate-pegging at the end of September 1950.

Fluctuations

The free Canadian dollar was first quoted at about 93½ U.S. cents. It reached parity with the American dollar on January 22, 1952 and, apart from dipping briefly back to parity late in 1955, remained at a premium until the end of the free-rate period. The end came in June 1961, though with hindsight one might perhaps date the first steps away from the free rate as early as December 1960 (the relevant events will be described below). The first and last full calendar years, full quarters, and full months of the free-rate period are therefore 1951 and 1960, the fourth quarter of 1950 and the first of 1961, and October 1950 and May 1961.

Over the whole period, the Canadian dollar fluctuated in a range of fractionally more than 13 U.S. cents, reaching a low of 93 cents in the very first month of free rates and a high of nearly 106.2 cents on August 20, 1957. Much of this fluctuation can readily be explained by "objective" economic conditions. As was to be expected, however, the state of the balance of payments on current account bore no clear relation to the level of the rate; each was partly a cause and partly an effect of the other, creating an "identification problem" akin to that found in statistically deriving demand or supply curves for individual commodities. The rate was positively correlated with purchasing-power parity (calculated with wholesale price indexes) and with the excesses of Canadian over American long-term and short-term interest rates.[5]

If the theory of perversely low price elasticities of demand had been applicable to Canada, or if seriously destabilizing speculation had taken place, the exchange rate would presumably have fluctuated sharply. Yet the fluctuations were mild and orderly. Rarely were they as large as a full U.S. cent during a single day. Samuel I. Katz found that during 1955 the daily high and low quotations in New York diverged by one-fourth of a cent or less on 223 days and by more on only 26 days; the average daily high-low spread was only 0.07 of a cent.[6] Even within months and years the range between highest and lowest quotations was small. In only 6 of the 128 months of free rates—October 1950, December 1951, November 1952, February 1955, and May and De-

---

[4] The *Financial Post*, in its last issue before the announcement (September 30, p. 2) had characterized "reports of imminent revaluation" as "completely unfounded."

[5] For the period up to mid-1957, details, figures, and calculations concerning these relations and others to be mentioned below appear in "Some Facts About the Canadian Exchange Rate," *Current Economic Comment*, XX, November 1958, pp. 39-54. Constraints of time and space made presenting updated versions of all these computations here seem hardly worth while, especially since students of the Canadian experience hardly disagree any longer about the broad facts themselves (as distinguished from the general lessons they may or may not teach). On speculation, in particular, see the studies cited in footnotes below, especially the two by Rudolf Rhomberg.

[6] *Two Approaches to the Exchange-Rate Problem: The United Kingdom and Canada* (Essays in International Finance, No. 26), Princeton; N.J.: Princeton University, 1956, p. 6.

cember 1960—did the high Canadian quotation on the U.S. dollar exceed the low by more than 2 cents; and in no month was the range larger than $2^{11}/_{16}$ Canadian cents. The range stayed below 1 percent of the monthly average rate in more than two-thirds of the months and averaged only 0.87 percent over the entire period. The largest high-low range within a full calendar year was 5.82 percent of the annual average rate (in 1951); the smallest, 2.47 percent (in 1954); the average of the ten yearly ranges was 4.17 percent.[7]

Official Intervention in the Free Market

How much credit for this orderliness belongs to the Exchange Fund Account, managed by the Bank of Canada? Would the record have been worse or better without the Fund? The Canadian authorities repeatedly stated that they allowed the rate to respond to the normal play of economic forces; the Fund made no attempt to resist persistent trends and dealt in the market only to dampen whatever excessive short-run wobbles might otherwise have occurred.[8] According to no less an authority than the International Monetary Fund, "From October 1950 to June 1961, the Canadian exchange rate was permitted to fluctuate freely, being determined by market forces and with a minimum of official intervention. . . ."[9] Details of the Exchange Fund's operations were not made public, for obvious reasons, but published figures on official Canadian holdings of gold and U.S. dollars at the end of each month offer some clues suggesting that the Fund's influence was indeed peripheral. In the 123 months of free rates through the end of 1960 (thus not counting the five following months of possible transition to a new system), net monthly changes in official reserves did not exceed $20 million in over five-eights of the months and

remained under $40 million in 87 percent of the months. The net change was (slightly) over $100 million in only two months (August 1951 and May 1960). The average monthly change was US $21.0 million, or well under 5 percent of the size of monthly total balance-of-payments credits or debits on current account.

This restrained Fund activity contrasts sharply with average monthly reserve changes of $54.5 million in 1946 through the third quarter of 1950, even though the volume of Canada's international transactions had expanded greatly since then and even though direct controls over trade and payments and two deliberate adjustments in the pegged exchange rate had supplemented use of reserves in that earlier period. In the possibly transitional first five months of 1961, the average change in reserves amounted to $24.0 million. In the 12 following months, during all or part of which the authorities were avowedly manipulating a flexible exchange rate, the monthly change amounted to $75.1 million on the average and to over $175 million in two months (October 1961 and February 1962).

A further clue to policy during the free-rate period is the fact that the Exchange Fund was usually acquiring gold and U.S. dollars (that is, tending to restrain or depress the Canadian dollar) during months when the Canadian dollar was generally rising and drawing down its reserves (that is, tending to support the Canadian dollar) during months when the Canadian dollar was generally falling. Such passive resistance occurred in 100 out of the 123 months from October 1950 through December 1960; in only 23 months did Exchange Fund operations appear to be reinforcing or determining the trend. (For the period through May 1961, the corresponding breakdown is 104 months and 24 months.) Another way of considering intervention was to correlate the monthly changes in official reserves from October 1950 through December 1960 with the average daily change in the Canadian dollar rate as computed by fitting a least-squares straight-line trend to the daily New York quotations within each month.[10] (Uptrends in the rate and intervention tend-

---

[7] Computed from various issues of Bank of Canada, *Statistical Summary*, and annual *Supplement*.

[8] See, for example, statements by Finance Minister Abbott on February 19, 1953, and Finance Minister Harris on April 5, 1955, printed in House of Commons, *Parliamentary Debates* for these dates, pp. 2120 and 2729, respectively.

[9] 1962 *Annual Report*, p. 56.

[10] Details on procedure followed appear in my article in *Current Economic Comment*, November 1958.

ing to support the rate—i.e., reserve losses—counted as positive, the opposites as negative.) The resulting correlation coefficient of − 0.66 (derived from 123 monthly "observations" and significant at better than the .01 level if the usual test is applicable) also suggests that the Fund's practice was indecisively to resist rather than to intensify or determine rate movements. A further experiment was to correlate the two sets of figures just mentioned without regard to algebraic sign. If large Fund operations went with small exchange-rate trends, yielding a negative correlation, this would suggest that the rate was stable or unstable according to whether the Fund was especially active or inactive and would favor giving the Fund considerable credit for the observed exchange-rate stability. If, on the other hand, large operations went with large rate trends and small operations with small trends, this would suggest that relatively large Fund activity occurred primarily in response to but was not dominant enough to suppress rapid change in the market and that steadiness when it occurred was due primarily to private supply and demand rather than to heavy intervention. The latter interpretation receives some support from a correlation coefficient of + 0.41 (also significant at the .01 level).

The foregoing evidence of mild resistance to short-run trends in the exchange rate does not cast doubt on the Fund's announced policy of refraining from intervention except to counter excessive short-run wobbles. For the Fund could not know at once whether a given change was only a brief wobble. It apparently tried to steady the rate but stopped trying when a continuing market tendency showed the change to have been more than random. If the general tendency of the exchange rate during a particular month turned out to have been mainly in one direction, the Fund's continual "testing" of the market produced an unintentional net gain or loss of reserves and appeared, misleadingly, to indicate deliberate resistance to the trend.[11] In

summary, the managers of the Exchange Fund Account showed remarkable restraint. Until the government set a new policy in 1961, they apparently avoided determining the rate and limited themselves to trying to moderate minor short-run wobbles. The managers avoided the market disorder likely to result from giving speculators "one-way options" under a system of actively managed rates. It is an open question, however, whether exchange-rate instability would have been greater or still slighter than what was actually observed if there had been no Fund and no official practice of first countering rate movements and then abandoning resistance to them when they proved more than random.

Speculation

We may infer something about speculation not only by observing whether the exchange market behaved in an orderly manner but also by studying capital movements as classified into two categories: (1) investment capital movements—direct investment and new issues and retirements of securities, and (2) short-term capital movements—transactions in outstanding securities and changes in Canadian-dollar holdings of foreigners, as well as the "other capital movements" listed in the

writers have reached similar conclusions. In *The Canadian Dollar, 1948–1958*, University of Toronto Press, 1960, p. 123, Paul Wonnacott notes that the Fund's stabilizing activity usually seemed greater shortly after the rate movement had changed direction than some time later. In *Bank of Canada Operations and Policy*, University of Toronto Press, 1958, p. 208, E. P. Neufeld notes the Fund's policy of "backing away" from the market when the rate movement persisted in one direction. In "Canada's Foreign Exchange Market: A Quarterly Model," IMF *Staff Papers*, **VII**, April 1960, p. 447, Rudolf R. Rhomberg notes the relative smallness of official intervention and its apparently much smaller influence than stabilizing speculation exerted in limiting rate fluctuations. In "The Canadian Exchange Rate, 1950–57," *Southern Economic Journal*, **XXVI**, January 1960, p. 207 and footnote, James C. Ingram mentions the apparent smallness of Exchange Fund transactions and finds it reasonable "to treat the Canadian dollar as if it were a freely fluctuating currency." R. E. Artus found little evidence that the Fund intervened any more actively between 1952 and December 1960 than to smooth day-to-day fluctuations, "and the movement of the rate seems to have been determined wholly by the play of demand and supply in the market." "Canada Pegs its Dollar," *The Banker*, **CXII**, June 1962, p. 362.

[11] Cf. Samuel I. Katz, "Le dollar canadien et le cours de change fluctuant," *Bulletin d'Information et de Documentation de la Banque Nationale de Belgique*, 30th year, vol. I, May 1955, pp. 7-8. Several later

Canadian balance of payments. These "other" movements include changes in international commercial indebtedness associated with hastening or delaying payments for Canadian imports and exports, changes in balances owing between corporate affiliates, loans between unaffiliated parties, changes in the foreign-exchange holdings of banks, various capital movements not directly recorded, and other errors and omissions. No one supposes that the capital movements in the first category are entirely nonspeculative and those in the second category entirely or even overwhelmingly speculative; the distinction between nonspeculative and speculative actions is unavoidably loose. Still, it does seem that the second category is more likely than the first to contain a significant speculative element. The rather obvious *a priori* reasons for this belief are supported by the heavy short-term capital inflows in the summer of 1950, when upward revaluation of the pegged Canadian dollar was generally expected, and by the rather opposite events of the second quarter of 1962, when the flexible rate was again pegged. During the free-exchange-rate period, also, the two types of capital movements behaved in characteristically different ways.[12]

It would be interesting to know how, if at all, movements of short-term capital and the exchange rate were related. By the same method as already described for trends within months, a daily average rate change was computed to measure how sharply the Canadian dollar was rising (+) or falling (−) on the average over each quarter-year. Short-term capital movements were taken from quarterly balances of payments, a plus sign indicating an inflow and a minus sign an outflow. Simple correlation of the two sets of figures yielded coefficients of − 0.17 for the 42 quarters from the fourth of 1950 through the first of 1961 and of − 0.21 for the 41-quarter period through the fourth of 1960. These coefficients are too small to be statistically significant, but they do have the same sign as some others to be mentioned. The same short-term capital movements correlated to the

extent of − 0.55 with indicators of the strength of the Canadian dollar in relation to the recent past, that is, with quarterly average exchange rates expressed as percentages of each preceding quarterly average, for the 41 quarters from the first of 1951 through the first of 1961. (The fourth quarter of 1950 was not included because the ratio of its exchange rate to the preceding rate would have involved a quarter when the Canadian dollar was not yet unpegged.) The corresponding coefficient for the 40 quarters through only the fourth of 1960 was − 0.53. Small as they seem, these last two coefficients are statistically significant at better than the 1 percent level for the 41 or 40 "observations" involved if the usual criterion is applicable. Apparently, short-term capital movements generally tended to resist exchange-rate movements. Familiar qualms about correlation of time-series data apply here with less than the usual force because none of the series is dominated by obvious trends; the short-term capital movements and the indicators of exchange-rate behavior often changed sharply from one quarter to the next.

Whether quarterly movements of short-term capital and of the exchange rate generally went in the same or in opposite directions is hardly a complete test of whether speculation was destabilizing or stabilizing. Even if capital movements did sometimes tend to reinforce or even cause rate movements, they might still have tended to iron out deviations from a longer-run average rate, provided that the current rate at those times was still below average though rising or still above average though falling. The third quarter of 1957 provides an example. For the quarter as a whole, the trend of the Canadian dollar was definitely downward; a continuing mild rise that carried the rate to an all-time peak of over $1.06 on August 20 was followed and outweighed by a sharp depreciation that continued throughout the rest of the quarter (and year). Yet short-term capital moved out of Canada to the extent of 72 million for the quarter as a whole. An English financial columnist, writing in mid-September, commented on "a wave of bear speculation" and detected signs of profit-taking by former

---

[12] For details and statistics and other variants of the approach to assessing speculation used here, see the article cited in footnote 5.

bulls and of bearish delays in making payment by buyers of Canadian goods. (Interestingly enough, the columnist attributed the bear speculation to growing expectations of "a basic change in Canadian exchange rate policy" designed to force down the premium on the currency.[13] Although no such policy change in fact occurred until 3¾ years later, expectations were able to feed on the common knowledge that an Exchange Fund existed and was in the market to at least some extent.) Although the Canadian dollar was falling at this time, its quarterly average quotation was still higher than ever before and higher than in any succeeding quarter until the fourth of 1959. It is thus by no means clear that the capital outflows must be called destabilizing; after all, they were tending to *lessen* the deviation of the exchange rate from its longer-run average.

This episode suggested another approach to the statistics. To measure the strength of the Canadian dollar in each quarter in relation to both the recent past and near future, each quarter's rate was expressed as a percentage of the average of itself with the rates of the two preceding and two following quarters. These percentages were correlated with short-term capital movements in the 38 quarters from the second of 1951 through the third of 1960. (Use of this shorter period avoided having any of the five-quarter moving averages involve quarters before or after the free-rate period.) The coefficient turned out to be − .43, significant at the 1-percent level for the 38 "observations" by the usual criterion. Yet this coefficient seems surprisingly low when one sees a time-series chart of the underlying figures. Ordinary correlation is perhaps too exacting a test. Perfect inverse correlation would require not merely that capital movements were inversely related to exchange-rate deviations from a longer-run average but they were related in size by a definite linear formula. Any departure from a rigid linear relation would hold down the computed coefficient, even if capital movements were always in the "stabilizing" direction. Exchange-rate changes and speculative

capital movements were each undoubtedly subject to many influences besides the other. While the statistics hardly indicate any close rigid connection between the two series, they do at least definitely fail to support the standard theoretical worries about destabilizing speculation. On the contrary, they suggest, if anything at all, that speculation tended to buoy up the Canadian dollar when it was falling or relatively low and to restrain it when it was rising or relatively high.

In one way or another, several scholars have reached pretty much this same conclusion.[14] At least one observer, though, dissents from the usual implied interpretation of the equilibrating capital movements.[15] The so-called "other capital movements" form a usually dominant, though highly variable, part of total short-term capital movements. These "other" movements are thought largely to reflect changing balances of commercial indebtedness. In an almost mechanical way, then, these movements were likely to be inward into Canada when the Canadian dollar was weak or falling and outward when the Cana-

[13] Lombard, "About Turn for Canadian $," *Financial Times,* London: September 17, 1957, p. 3.

[14] See, for example, R. Craig McIvor, *Canadian Monetary, Banking and Fiscal Development,* Toronto: Macmillan, 1958, p. 218; L. Albert Hahn, *Autonome Konjunktur-Politik und Wechselkurs-Stabilität* Frankfurt: Knapp, 1957, p. 34; Ingram, *op. cit.,* esp. pp. 213, 215; Rhomberg, *op. cit.,* esp. p. 447; and Rhomberg, "A Model of the Canadian Economy under Fixed and Fluctuating Exchange Rates," *Journal of Political Economy,* LXXII, February 1964, esp. p. 12. Rhomberg's econometric model for the period 1952–1959 implies that a 1-U.S.-cent depreciation of the Canadian dollar would tend to attract approximately the same *inflow* of short-term capital into Canada as a 1-percentage-point excess of Canadian over U.S. short-term interest rates. Artus, *op. cit.,* p. 363, commented on the "very effective equilibrating mechanism associated with short-term capital flows" and concluded that "As regards stability . . . , the floating rate performed eminently satisfactorily." Wonnacott, *op. cit.,* pp. 128-130, 139, found evidence on short-term capital movements less persuasive than these other students; yet he too judged that on balance they were more stabilizing than destabilizing. Even the 1953 *Annual Report* (p. 70) of the International Monetary Fund, surveying the earlier period when the exchange rate had behaved less stably on the average than it proved to do over the remainder of the free-rate period, observed that "capital movements, on the whole, have been equilibrating rather than disturbing. Canadian trade and normal capital movements have accordingly not lost the important benefits that are commonly associated with rate stability."

[15] Harry C. Eastman, "Aspects of Speculation in the Canadian Market for Foreign Exchange," *Canadian Journal of Economics and Political Science,* XXIV, August 1958, esp. pp. 361-365, 368-372.

dian dollar was strong or rising. Weakness of the Canadian dollar, Harry Eastman suggests, seemed typically due to a sluggishness of Canadian exports (and other independently motivated credit or plus transactions) relative to imports (and other independently motivated debit or minus transactions). This then meant, incidentally, that the volume of short-term credit extended to foreign buyers of Canadian exports dropped relative to credit extended to Canadian importers by their foreign suppliers. Strength of the Canadian dollar, on the other hand, was likely to result from strength of export demand relative to import demand, and the difference between commercial credit granted by and received by Canadians then shifted in the direction of a capital outflow. This interpretation raises doubts whether the capital movements had been motivated by exchange-rate expectations. Few businessmen had enough faith in their rate-forecasting ability. Firms with large foreign transactions, despite their presumed access to expert opinion, generally found it best to deal in exchange as their ordinary business required, without hastening or delaying transactions in hope of profiting from moves in the rate. More active forms of speculation were also unimportant, partly because of the disapproval of the banks. Professionals most familiar with the market reportedly believed that deliberate speculation, at least after the first two or three years of the fluctuating rate, had been sporadic, on a small scale, and without significant influence.

This line of interpretation invites four comments, not necessarily dissenting. First, it is not clear that the trade balance was closely related to the exchange rate (the "identification problem" looms again). Second, it is doubtful whether the "other capital movements" always reflected nothing more than normal commercial credit; the massive surge of "other" capital into Canada in the summer of 1950, when people expected an upward revaluation of the pegged Canadian dollar, is striking evidence of this. The actual speculative character of commercial leads and lags has also often been clear in the postwar experience of other countries. Third, regardless of the motivation behind the equilibrating

capital movements, the fact remains that they apparently did occur. If they were largely automatic, rather than dependent on speculators' forecasts and moods, their implications are in some respects still reassuring. Fourth, even if conscious speculation actually was negligible, this fact itself fails to bear out the usual theoretical worries.

All this forms just one reason why we cannot unequivocally cite the Canadian experience as an example of speculation that was unquestionably equilibrating in the sense of being based on a correct diagnosis of objective market conditions and prospects. Another reason hinges on a theoretical point. Speculation might be considered equilibrating, even when intensifying rate movements, if it hastened reaching the rate appropriate for emerging price-level and interest-rate relations and for other "fundamental" supply and demand conditions in international trade. On the other hand, it might be considered disequilibrating if, by delaying rate movements in accordance with "fundamental" conditions, it made adjustments all the sharper when they finally occurred. Speculation could conceivably stabilize an exchange rate "too much" and so hamper adjustment to changed conditions. The Canadian experience is significant only in a modest sense: it fails to bear out standard worries about speculative intensification of functionless fluctuations. Furthermore, the Canadian free rate did what it was originally intended to do: it solved the earlier problem of exchange crises and hot-money movements.[16]

Trade and Investment

Did the risk of exchange-rate fluctuations impede Canada's international trade and

[16] After emphasizing this "overwhelming advantage" of the free-rate policy, the President of the Royal Bank of Canada took note of the argument that hot money is no longer a problem and that changed conditions require new policies. "But hot money is no longer a problem for Canada precisely because we *have* the free exchange rate." He went on to draw a contrast with the way that inflows and outflows of hot money had plagued European countries and even the United States. W. Earle McLaughlin, address at the annual meeting of his bank's shareholders, Montreal, January 12, 1961, p. 3.

capital movements? Their larger size after the unpegging of the rate than before in large part simply reflects general economic growth. A more meaningful comparison is of the *rates* of year-to-year growth in the postwar period before and after the unpegging. Because the war continued through most of 1945 and because the exchange rate remained fixed only during the first three quarters of 1950, some doubt exists about just which "before and after" periods to consider. Table 24.1 shows the various possibilities for the physical volume of exports plus imports, both of goods and services and of commodities alone.

Table 24.1. Growth of Canadian Exports Plus Imports before and after 1950

| Period | Average Yearly Percentage Increase | |
	Quantum of Commodity Trade	Value of Trade in Goods and Services at Constant Prices
1945–1949	−1.74%	−2.60%
1945–1950	−1.00	−1.47
1946–1949	+1.06	−0.30
1946–1950	+0.99	+0.39
1950–1960	+4.26	+4.16
1951–1960	+3.73	+3.77

NOTES AND SOURCES: A quantum index of commodity exports *plus* imports was obtained by averaging separate export and import quantum indexes (given in various issues of *International Financial Statistics*), using base-year money values as weights. Goods-and-service trade in "constant (1949) dollars" is given in Bank of Canada, *Statistical Summary, 1960 Supplement*, pp. 124-125. The yearly average percentages of increase (or decrease) were obtained by fitting exponential trends to the trade figures for the years indicated (i.e., by fitting linear trends to their logarithms).

Another clue may lie in the total of Canadian imports and exports expressed as a percentage of total world imports and exports. This figure averaged 5.56 percent in 1947 through 1949, 5.53 percent in 1947 through 1950, and 5.63 percent in the ten years 1951 through 1960.[17] Although Canada and the United States together supplied a share of world exports in the early postwar years that was considered abnormally large and was ex-

pected to decline[18] and although the growth in Canadian trade did slacken in the late 1950s, comparison of the entire "before and after" periods is not unfavorable to the fluctuating rate. Another impression emerges from seeing whether the growth of imports and exports of goods and services has kept pace with general economic growth, as judged from their total expressed as a percentage of Canadian gross national product. This figure averaged 49.7 percent from 1946 through the third quarter of 1950 and 44.7 percent from the fourth quarter of 1950 through the first quarter of 1961. In the light of the other before-and-after comparisons, it is uncertain whether this difference shows interference from exchange-rate fluctuations; to suppose so would be to rule out, among other things, any possible connection between growth of gross national product (especially during the early part of the free-rate period) and the freedom from exchange and other controls permitted by a free exchange rate. It seems probable, however, that other particular historical circumstances had much more to do with the growth both of trade and of the Canadian economy in general than did exchange-rate policy.

How badly did exchange-rate fluctuations impede international investment? As already explained, capital movements by way of foreign direct investment in Canada, Canadian direct investment abroad, and new issues and retirements of securities are less likely to reflect mere speculation than are short-term capital movements. These investment capital movements were heavier after than before the exchange rate was freed in 1950, whether one considers their net inflow into Canada or —as seems more appropriate for detecting the possible influence of exchange risk—one considers the items reported in the balance of payments totaled without regard to algebraic sign. The same is true of a before-and-after comparison of growth—if growth rates are meaningful for such widely fluctuating magnitudes.[19]

---

[17] The underlying figures are from *International Financial Statistics*, December 1961, pp. 38-39, and earlier issues. Comparable figures for 1946 are not available. In 1938, the Canadian share of world imports plus exports was 3.85 percent.

[18] Cf. Ivar Rooth in International Monetary Fund, *Summary Proceedings of the Tenth Annual Meeting of the Board of Governors*, September 1955, p. 11.

[19] See the reference in footnote 5.

For movements of investment capital as also for trade, it is probably true that their size and growth depended less on exchange-rate policy than on other influences, including particular historical circumstances (for example, continued exchange-rate pegging and the slow removal of controls in other countries, close economic ties with the United States, the Korean and cold wars, and Canada's own boom in natural-resource development). No one knows, of course, "what would have happened" to Canada's international trade and capital movements if the exchange rate had been kept fixed in the 1950s. What can be said is that any damage in accordance with the standard theoretical worries was slight enough to be covered up by other influences.

Abandonment of the Free Rate

"On the whole, the Canadian experience with a flexible exchange rate has been a happy one"—to use the words of a Canadian economist who appears to have reached this conclusion without enthusiasm and who would regret seeing his country's example widely followed. Canada in the 1950s enjoyed "one of the most remarkable periods of rapid and relatively stable growth" in its history. The flexible exchange rate did not *cause* Canadian prosperity, of course, but neither did it appear to dampen it significantly[20]—not, at

least, until towards the end of the decade. Yet Canada abandoned its free rate in 1961. Had it proved unsatisfactory after all?

Before judging, we must look at the background of economic developments and policy proposals. Unemployment, in particular, had become a conspicuous problem. As a percentage of the labor force, it had reached 10 percent early in 1958, had averaged 6.7 percent over 1958–1960, and had averaged above 11 percent in the first three months of 1961. It still stood at 7 percent in May. In part the trouble supposedly stemmed from a continuing rapid rise in the labor force as the wartime crops of babies grew up, as people left the farms, and as refugees from Hungary migrated into Canada after the events of 1956. A shortage of vocational training schools and the influence of a heavy demand for unskilled labor some years before, when the primary industries had been growing so rapidly, left an excess of unskilled labor.[21] In addition, the problem seemed partly cyclical and partly related to an apparent slowdown in economic growth. Over the ten years from 1950 to 1960 as a whole, Canadian gross national product in constant prices had increased 45 percent (compared with 39 percent for the United States), but the growth had been less rapid in the last four years of the decade than in the first six. Table 24.2 summarizes some contrasts.

The total of construction and other investment had been declining since 1957. Pro-

---

[20] Wonnacott, *op. cit.*, p. 130. Numerous scholars could be cited who agree on the success of the Canadian experiment, but few dissenters. Perhaps the most skeptical is Jacob Viner, who sees "no important lesson to be drawn from it, given the relevant circumstances of the period, except that in some circumstances the adoption of a floating currency does not lead to disaster—or does not lead to it quickly." "Some International Aspects of Economic Stabilization," in Leonard D. White, ed., *The State of the Social Sciences,* Chicago: University of Chicago Press, 1956, p. 296.

The most prevalent reason for seeing little general significance in the Canadian experiment is the idea that Canadian circumstances were so untypically favorable. The fact that the Canadian and American currencies are both "dollars" may have bred a stabilizing "parity psychology." (Egon Sohmen persuasively questions this widespread notion, however, in *International Monetary Problems and the Foreign Exchanges,* Princeton, N.J.: Princeton University, 1963, pp. 27-28.) Canada had relatively sound monetary and fiscal policies and a relatively slight bias toward inflation, a fine record of economic growth, abundant natural resources to be

developed, and good prospects for the future. Her international current-account balance adjusted relatively easily to changes in long-term capital movements because of the tendency to import a sizable fraction of the capital goods used. Canadian corporations and governments had easy access to the American capital market. (Wonnacott, *op. cit.,* pp. 130, 140, makes these points.) In other respects, too, Canada had very close economic ties with the United States (though it is uncertain whether this dependence was more an advantage or a disadvantage).

For all these reasons, it is interesting to compare the operation of a free exchange rate under quite different circumstances. Austria-Hungary in the late nineteenth century, for example, lacked most of Canada's special advantages, yet her exchange rate was if anything *less* unstable than the Canadian.

[21] Some facts here and later come from Alfred Zänker, "Centralbankkonflikt och expansionssträvanden i Kanada," *Ekonomisk Revy,* **XVIII,** September 1961, pp. 483-492, and "Canada's New Economic Measures," Federal Reserve Bank of New York, *Monthly Review,* February 1961, pp. 22-24.

Table 24.2. Canadian and U.S. Economic Growth, 1950–1956 and 1956–1960

	Real Gross National Product		Total Industrial Production		Physical Volume of Total Exports	
	Canada	U.S.	Canada	U.S.	Canada	U.S.
Total percentage increase						
1950–1956	36.3%	26.7%	44.9%	33.3%	37.2%	48.9%
1956–1960	6.6	9.9	8.1	8.8	9.3	8.8
Arithmetic mean of year-to-year percentage increases						
1950–1956	5.4	4.1	6.4	5.1	5.6	7.4
1956–1960	1.6	2.4	2.0	2.4	2.3	2.9

NOTES AND SOURCES: Bank of Canada, *Statistical Summary, 1960 Supplement,* pp. 124-125, 128, 152; *Economic Indicators,* November 1961, pp. 1, 14; and various issues of *International Financial Statistics.* Canadian GNP is given in 1949 prices; U.S. GNP in 1960 prices. U.S. exports exclude military aid goods.

duction was lagging in such labor-intensive industries as transportation equipment, machines, electrical goods, clothing, rubber, and leather goods. Total exports set new records in 1959 and 1960, but longer-term prospects seemed doubtful. Canada's postwar boom had largely concentrated on export-oriented basic industries, such as wood and pulp products, oil, and uranium and other metals. Overestimation of future demand and prices at the time of the Korean War had prompted construction of what later proved to be excess capacity. Exports of wheat, forest products, and some metals and other minerals were already reflecting a weak world demand or the intensified competition of rival suppliers. Good trade with Britain and Western Europe was helping to offset the relative stagnation of exports to the United States, but the European Common Market threatened discrimination against Canadian goods; and if Britain joined, most Canadian exports would probably lose their duty-free entry into the British market.[22] Even in the home market, Canadian producers of finished goods faced competition not only from the United States but also from Germany, Japan, and other countries.

One more factor impairing Canadian competitiveness was the high exchange rate. The premium on the Canadian dollar had oscil-

lated around an average of 2.7 U.S. cents over the years 1952–1960 inclusive. The combination of these various real and monetary factors gave rise to a current-account balance-of-payments deficit averaging about C $385 million a year in 1951–1955 and C $1343 million in 1956–1960 (that is, about 7 percent of total current-account credit items in the first half of the decade and 20 percent in the second half). A persistent deficit in transactions with the United States far overshadowed a usual positive balance in overseas trade. Numerous categories of goods and services, together with net outpayments of interest and dividends, contributed to the overall current deficit. Ordinarily one might have expected depreciation of the free exchange rate to cure or prevent this deficit, but a heavy inflow of investment capital kept sustaining the rate. Funds flowed in, mostly from the United States, to establish or expand Canadian operations of American firms, to buy corporation stocks and other outstanding securities, and to buy new bond issues that corporations and provincial and local governments floated in the American market in response to the interest-rate differential. This was nothing new; foreign funds had traditionally fed every major expansion in Canada's history.

Despite some intimations in the financial press, the state of the balance of payments did not demonstrate a failure of the exchange-rate mechanism. The rate did maintain equilibrium between *total* supplies of and *total* demands for foreign exchange. The current

---

[22] More than 95 percent of Canada's exports entered Britain duty-free; under Common-Market tariff policy, only about 25 percent would. *Business Week,* December 9, 1961, p. 36.

account deficit and the capital-account surplus were the real and the financial sides of interwoven developments. Worry could not logically center on the current-account alone.

The capital account did receive critical attention. In the 15 years since the end of World War II, the gross total of foreign capital invested in Canada had more than tripled; net of Canadian capital invested abroad, the figure had more than quadrupled. Net outpayments of interest and dividends on these investments had reached a level of nearly $½ billion a year and were still growing. Besides this, American corporations might some day decide to bring home the earnings that they had been leaving in Canada. Pessimists foresaw an awkward day of reckoning when the capital inflow on which Canada had come to depend should dwindle; the country's natural-resource industries were already losing some of their attractions as fields of investment. Some saw too much reliance on foreign capital as the root of the country's economic difficulties: foreign capital had pushed efforts to do much too fast, had contributed to unbalanced expansion, and, by discouraging exports and promoting imports through the exchange premium, had aggravated unemployment.[23] From this point of view, the strengthening of the Canadian dollar in 1958 and 1959 seemed particularly untimely.

Some critics even blamed the heavy capital inflows on the exchange-rate system. Yet one can hardly have one's criticism of the free rate both ways: if it fostered too heavy a capital movement, then the risk of fluctuations in it was not too great an interference.[24] Before passing judgment, one should also consider the two alternative exchange policies. If the Canadian dollar had been kept pegged *below* the free-market level for the sake of the current account and employment, the inflow of

private capital might have been even heavier (entailing awkward official accumulations of foreign exchange); the reasons had already been well illustrated in the summer of 1950. Pegging *above* the free-market level would probably have restrained the capital inflow, but at the cost of a current-account response opposite to the one desired for the sake of employment and at the risk of a balance-of-payments crisis. Two ways of restraining capital imports are vastly different: artificial exchange appreciation, and either direct obstacles or domestic cheap money to get free-market depreciation as a desired by-product.

A more optimistic view saw the productive contribution of venturesome foreign capital as well worth the interest and dividends paid on it. Relative to export earnings, the burden of debt service had not greatly increased since the war. Over half the foreign investment in the country consisted of direct investment that would probably never have to be repaid. If Canada ever should become a mature debtor country, with interest, dividend, and amortization payments exceeding new receipts of capital, the free exchange rate, still equating *total* supplies of and demands for foreign exchange, would automatically solve the supposed problem of providing enough foreign exchange for the foreign remittances. Besides, asked the optimists, if an eventual cessation or reversal of the capital inflow is something to fear, why do anything to hasten the evil day, especially as long as foreign capital is still finding constructive employment?

Further reasons for worrying about the inflow of foreign capital—thus indirectly promoting the eventual shift in exchange-rate policy—were as much political and emotional as economic. Critics played on fear of foreign domination. They cited such facts as that U.S. investments in Canada amounted to over $17 billion and were growing by about $1 billion a year. Foreigners owned or controlled more than one-half of Canadian manufacturing, nearly two-thirds of all mining and smelting, and more than three-fourths of the petroleum and natural-gas industry. American corporations and their subsidiaries were accused of discriminating against Canadians in various ways. Though the best customer

[23] Federal Reserve Bank of New York, *Monthly Review,* February 1961, pp. 23-24, summarizes some of the opposing views. A good example of the pessimistic view is Wm. Stix Wasserman's pamphlet, "A Study of the Canadian Dollar," New York: Wm. Stix Wasserman & Co., Inc., February 1961. Mr. W. Earle McLaughlin's speech already cited, pp. 9-14, is a good example of the optimistic view considered below.

[24] It is hard to see, furthermore, why the system should have especially promoted capital movements in one direction only. Sohmen, *op. cit.,* p. 26.

for U.S. manufactures, Canada was exporting much of its own produce in a raw or semifinished state for processing abroad. American investment was allegedly stifling industrial development, keeping Canada a mere "hewer of wood and drawer of water."

The Diefenbaker government felt heavy pressure to embrace economic nationalism and ward off further foreign capital, thereby presumably causing exchange depreciation as an easy answer to unemployment and other problems. The revised budget of December 1960 made mild—but only mild—concessions to this pressure. It withdrew the existing preferred tax treatment for earnings on foreign loans and investments in Canada and adopted tax incentives for private domestic investment. The Dominion government had already been exhorting provincial and municipal governments to reduce their bond issues in New York, and from early 1960 until late 1962, this type of borrowing virtually dried up.[25] Hindsight makes one suspect a more direct though quiet alteration in exchange-rate policy, also, around the end of 1960: a $120 million rise in the official reserves during the first five months of 1961 —a change exceeded (slightly) in only one of the full calendar years of the free-rate period —points to official intervention as what was keeping the premium on the Canadian dollar from rising more than fractionally above 1 U.S. cent.[26]

The most prominent advocate of more vigorous action against foreign investment was James E. Coyne, Governor of the Bank of Canada. Among other things, he proposed an increase in withholding taxes on foreign earnings. Measures to promote domestic saving and investment, including heavier taxes on luxury consumption and establishment of a National Development Corporation, would partially displace American capital, and higher tariffs would protect Canadian manufacturing. As for unemployment, Coyne felt that it was "structural." Monetary expansion

and cheaper credit would not solve the problem but would promote inflation.[27] Any remedial increases in spending would have to be selective. The Bank of Canada had accordingly allowed the money supply to sag after the summer of 1958 and to recover by two years later to only just about the earlier level.[28] "With Mr. Coyne it appeared to be an article of faith that Canada's unemployment problem was not amenable to correction through an expansion of the money supply."[29] Many Canadian economists took a dimmer view of tight money, and a number of them sent a rather vaguely worded petition to the Finance Minister in December 1960 calling for Coyne's resignation. By the end of May 1961, Finance Minister Fleming apparently had concluded that Governor Coyne's many politically tinged public speeches advocating tight money and economic nationalism had invaded the government's prerogatives, and he called for Coyne's resignation. Coyne delayed resigning until July, after the Canadian Senate had given him what he considered a clean bill of health for his personal integrity in conducting the Bank's affairs.

Meanwhile, on June 20, the Finance Minister introduced his delayed budget for the fiscal year ending March 31, 1962. It eliminated the excise tax on automobiles, boosted depreciation allowances on new plant and equipment, and gave tax incentives for scientific research. Altogether, the budget cut taxes by some $101 million annually and increased government spending. Canada was to run an administrative deficit of $650 million in fiscal 1961–62, almost double that of the year before, and the cash deficit was to be about $1 billion, or more than triple the preceding year's. Further to stimulate business activity

---

[25] Bank of Nova Scotia, *Monthly Review,* March 1963, p. 3.

[26] Artus, *op. cit.,* p. 362, also infers that "the Canadian authorities . . . moved away from a true floating rate" after the latter part of 1960.

[27] Facts on Coyne's views and his controversy with the government have been taken from Bank of Canada, *Annual Report* for 1960 (Ottawa: 1961) and from the already cited articles by Zänker and in the Federal Reserve Bank of New York's *Monthly Review* of February 1961, as well as from press items.

[28] Plus or minus one or two percent. The ambiguity lies in the definition of the Canadian money supply held by the general public: holders of personal savings deposits are in practice allowed to write some checks against them. Money defined as including these deposits rose somewhat more than money defined as excluding them.

[29] Artus, *op. cit.,* p. 367.

(as well as to discourage capital inflow), interest rates were to be brought down. Fleming saw no danger of inflation as long as heavy unemployment persisted, along with excess capacity in several industries. Further adjustments were made in taxes on foreign investment earnings, but the budget included no provisions for direct restrictions on foreign capital or for general tariff increases. It rejected outright economic nationalism.

In his budget speech, the Finance Minister also announced the government's intention to push the Canadian dollar to an unspecified but "significant" discount. Not only interest-rate cuts but also direct intervention by the Exchange Fund Account would be the method. Instead of just embarking on expansionary monetary and fiscal policy and letting the free exchange rate adapt, the government hoped to stimulate employment and production by artificially pressing the currency down. A new example was apparently at hand of the "competitive exchange depreciation" so widely practiced in the 1930s.

Developments on the Manipulated Market

Even before Finance Minister Fleming confirmed the new policy, growing awareness of his controversy with Governor Coyne had affected the exchange market. The Canadian dollar had already been weakening fractionally during the first week and a half of June 1961. On Tuesday the 13th, when the controversy broke into the open, the market closed with the premium at ¾ of one U.S. cent, down from 1.2 cents the day before. By the end of the week the Canadian dollar was practically down to par for the first time since December 1955; in fact, it dipped briefly below par in the Montreal market on Friday the 16th. Prospects of Coyne's departure and the drop already begun in interest rates apparently prompted a rush to sell Canadian dollars, as well as pressure from leads and lags.[30]

A more dramatic change occurred the morning after Fleming's budget speech of Tuesday the 20th. The Canadian dollar

dropped slightly more than 3 cents overnight. Its discount ranged from 3½ to 2¼ cents during the morning alone. Quotations rose on stocks of companies selling in export markets, particularly pulp and paper and gold companies.

Speculation continued to aid the new policy for a while; but the authorities did not rely on announcement effects alone, and over the entire month of June (two-thirds gone at the time of the change) official holdings of gold and U.S. dollars rose by $36 million. From July until late September, however, these reserves actually fell (mostly reflecting Canada's contribution to a British drawing on the International Monetary Fund), suggesting that no further official intervention was necessary to maintain the discount. Difficulties began late in September. Investors and merchants who had been waiting to see where the discount would settle apparently felt that the time had come to move funds into Canada. Official intervention kept the rate practically rigid at 97⅛ U.S. cents during almost all of October, and the external reserves rose $186 million during the month. On October 27, false rumors that the rate would be allowed to float back to par forced the Exchange Fund Account to spend an estimated $50 million buying up U.S. dollars to maintain the discount.

This decisive intervention, together with a reminder from the Finance Minister that the rate might be pushed still lower, turned the tide.[31] From then on, in fact, the Canadian dollar sagged from an average of 97.1 U.S.¢ in October 1961 to an average of 95¼¢ the following April. Preventing any larger depreciation cost $516 million, or practically one-fourth of the official reserves, between the end of October and the end of April. Around the turn of the year, when the Canadian dollar stood at a discount of slightly more than 4 cents, the Canadian government would apparently have liked to see the rate stabilize on its own. The government's silence about how low a rate it wanted contributed, however, to reduced demand for and in-

---

[30] *New York Times,* June 17, 1961, pp. 25, 32.

[31] In addition to the usual statistical sources, see *Wall Street Journal,* November 7, 1961, p. 13, and *Business Week,* November 11, 1961, p. 138.

creased supply of Canadian dollars. Experienced bankers saw signs of bearish leads and lags.[32]

Early in April 1962, at the time of the annual budget message, the government reaffirmed its intention not to set a fixed rate through "any hasty action which might prove premature or impossible to sustain."[33] The speculative outflow of funds continued. What had begun early in 1961 as an operation to depress the Canadian dollar had changed, one year later, into an uncomfortable support operation. "The decisive and most devastating blow" came from short selling by Canadians rather than Americans. When Canadians' confidence in their own currency weakened, a "marked reduction in the exchange rate became inevitable."[34] On May 2, the Canadian government devalued its currency by 2.9 percent from the prevailing market rate to a new fixed parity of 92.5 U.S. cents. Finance Minister Fleming noted that the move had been precipitated by speculative pressures and by the International Monetary Fund's urging that Canada peg its dollar.[35]

Significance of Fixing the Rate

The IMF "warmly welcomed" the action, and the U.S. Treasury expressed agreement with the Fund's view.[36] Respectability had triumphed. *Business Week*'s issue of May 12 (p. 44) saw the abandonment of fluctuating rates as a confession that "Canada's experiment has proved a failure." What is the supposed proof? The much-deplored persistent current-account deficit during the free-rate period was actually the real counterpart of the inflow of foreign capital that had been contributing to Canadian development. The free rate had not been balancing the current account alone—nor does theory suggest that it should have—but it had been equilibrating *total* supplies and demands on

the exchange market. Worry about the current account in particular is more relevant when the exchange rate is fixed and its tenability uncertain; it is hardly logical to appraise a free-rate system by criteria appropriate only to a different system. The worry about a future crisis when capital inflow might dwindle in the face of continuing interest and dividend outpayments was an *a priori* worry about the future, not a defect of the system already "proved" by experience. Political and emotional worries about excessive dependence on foreign capital certainly received much attention in Canada but were hardly relevant in appraising the performance of the exchange market.

As for problems related to unemployment and slow economic growth, expecting any particular exchange-rate system to solve them by itself was almost as naïve as expecting it to prevent alcoholism or juvenile delinquency. The main thing a free exchange rate can be expected to do is to avoid balance-of-payments crises, without controls, and so clear the way for whatever policies seem best on domestic economic grounds. But doing that is doing a lot. Failure to make good use of this opportunity is essentially what the economist critics of Governor Coyne's tight-money policy were complaining about.

A troublesome and unusually large spread of Canadian over U.S. interest rates towards the end of the free-rate period, though not actually intended, was partly a result of deliberate policy. A major refunding operation to lengthen the average life of the outstanding government debt had been attempted at an unfortunate time, in mid-1958. The bond market became demoralized; Coyne and the Bank of Canada, fearful of inflation, ceased cushioning bond prices in the open market; and for a year or so afterwards, the market appeared unresponsive to any official attempts to reduce interest rates significantly.[37] The resulting impact on capital flows and the exchange rate made it seem superficially plausible to blame "inadequate demand for domestic output . . . on foreign investment or foreign competition." The

---

[32] *Wall Street Journal*, April 16, 1962, pp. 1, 6.
[33] *Ibid.*, p. 1.
[34] George H. Chittenden, speech reprinted in *Morgan Guaranty Survey*, April 1963, p. 8. Cf. Bank for International Settlements, 32nd *Annual Report*, p. 150.
[35] *Wall Street Journal*, May 4, 1962, p. 20.
[36] *Wall Street Journal*, May 4, 1962, p. 20.

[37] Artus, *op. cit.*, pp. 364-365, 367.

uneven incidence of weakness in demand, including the quite normal incidence of general unemployment on the least skilled workers in particular, lent plausibility to emphasis on structural maladjustments and inadequate training of labor. In the words of one observer, "errors in Canadian monetary policy [were] the sole (and insufficient) justification for the abandonment of the floating rate of exchange. . . ."[38]

Easier money and credit would have expanded the demand for Canadian goods and services and labor not only in the usual direct way but also through the effect of exchange depreciation on the current account. Instead of spelling manipulation, this depreciation would simply have meant a free-market balancing of exchange supply and demand in the light of the total economic situation, with domestic policy one of its facets. Recognizing this is not to hail easy money under free exchange rates as a cure-all. The Canadian trouble with unemployment and slackened growth may indeed have been partly "structural," possibly involving the pattern of the labor supply and the country's vulnerability to shifts in foreign demand because of its close gearing into the world economy and particularly the U.S. economy. The important freedom to manage the overall level of demand cannot, after all, make shifts in the *composition* of demand harmless, nor can it dispel any domestic dilemma of having to choose between unemployment and inflation.[39]

As for the performance of the exchange market itself, narrowly considered, the evidence already shown for the period up to early 1961 is reassuring. The speculation and crises and alternation of heavy gains and losses of external reserves that followed in the eleven

months before adoption of the new fixed parity occurred under a regime of officially manipulated flexible rates, *not* of free rates. This distinction is crucial, yet often missed.[40] Once again, as in France in 1936–1938, experience showed the absurdity of classifying the two flexible-rate regimes together and comparing this blurry hybrid concept with fixed rates. In important respects, on the contrary, a rate manipulated to the extent of actually being fixed and a flexibly manipulated rate have more in common with each other than either has with a free rate. It is important to be clear about *what* system had "failed" by May 1962.

Experience under the New Parity

Canada was not yet out of the woods. The exchange rate was permitted to fluctuate in a narrow range around the new 92.5-cent par. By the middle of May it stood below 92 cents. Only support from the official reserves, which shrank $102 million in May alone, kept the rate from sinking below 91¾¢. During just three weeks of June the government had to spend over a third of its remaining unborrowed reserves to buy Canadian dollars unloaded by speculators.[41] Another ironic example was at hand of official action to depress the Canadian dollar overshooting the mark through its effect on expectations; the authorities were having to struggle to keep the rate from falling further than they had desired. Even the International Monetary Fund, hardly likely to exaggerate the difficulties of a return to its fold, described "the speculative flow of funds out of Canada" as the "most serious instance of a disequilibrating movement of short-term funds" occurring during the period covered by its 1963 *Annual Report* (p. 5).

---

[38] Harry C. Eastman, Review of Harry G. Johnson, *Canada in a Changing World Economy,* Toronto: University of Toronto Press, 1962, in *American Economic Review,* LII, December 1962, p. 1172. As Harry Johnson put it, "the Canadian return to a fixed exchange rate . . . involved a failure of governmental competence, not of the floating rate system. . . ." "The International Competitive Position of the United States and the Balance of Payments Prospect for 1968", *Review of Economics and Statistics,* XLVI, February 1964, p. 28.

[39] McIvor, *op. cit.,* p. 249, mentions some of the special limitations on Canadian monetary autonomy.

[40] Belief in stabilizing speculation could find little support, wrote Hal B. Lary, in Canada's experience before May 1962. "Its difficulties, first in depressing the Canadian dollar from a level deemed too high and then in preventing the fall, once it had started, from becoming excessive, show how drastically private evaluations and behavior can shift." *Problems of the United States as World Banker and Trader,* Princeton: Princeton University Press for the National Bureau of Economic Research, 1963, p. 112.

[41] *Wall Street Journal,* December 7, 1962, p. 1, puts the drain during these 3 weeks at $US400 million.

The June 1962 elections kept the Conservatives in office precariously, without an absolute majority in Parliament. Immediately afterwards the government took emergency action. It cut the duty-free exemption on purchases brought home by returning Canadian tourists from $300 to $75 a year and imposed surcharges ranging from 5 to 15 percent on about half of Canada's imports.[42] Fiscal and monetary policy tightened. Cuts in government spending amounting to $250 million in the fiscal year were scheduled. The Bank of Canada strove for higher interest rates to attract a big enough capital inflow to cover the current-account deficit and help rebuild reserves. Its discount rate, which since November 1956 had been set every week at ¼ of 1 percentage point above the market-determined fluctuating tender rate on Treasury bills, was raised on June 24 to a fixed 6 percent. This and other measures caused a conspicuous upward bulge for several months in the time-series chart of yields on government securities of various maturities. To keep yields from coming down again too far and too quickly when their high levels began stimulating nonbank security purchases, the authorities let the tightening of liquidity force banks to run down their own security holdings.[43] Another indicator of relatively tight money in 1962 was the mere 3½ percent growth in the money supply (more or less, depending on whether or not personal savings deposits are included); this compares with growth rates of either 8.7 or 12.4 percent in 1961 and either 6.8 or 7.2 percent in 1963 (depending on the same matter of definition).

In September, amidst signs that the emergency program was affecting the balance of payments as desired, monetary policy shifted toward ease. The authorities began replenishing bank liquidity. A series of cuts carried the Bank of Canada's discount rate down to 4 percent in November 1962 and 3½ percent in May 1963. (It went back to 4 percent in August 1963 in response to developments in the United States—a rise in the Federal Reserve discount rate and threats of other measures to discourage capital outflow.) Meanwhile, Canada had seen the ironic adoption of *contractionary* monetary and fiscal policies to cope with an emergency stemming from official action to depreciate the Canadian dollar, in turn undertaken in hopes of *expanding* employment and production.

Besides resorting to special tariffs and financial tightness, Canada obtained $1050 in foreign credits at the time of the crisis in June—$300 million worth of European currencies from the International Monetary Fund, a $400 million line of credit from the Export-Import Bank, and credits of $250 million and $100 million under reciprocal currency arrangements with the Federal Reserve System and the Bank of England.

The package of measures brought confidence in the devalued Canadian dollar. The flows of both long-term and short-term capital turned heavily inward, far exceeding the deficit on current account and causing Canada's external reserves to increase by more during the second half of 1962 than they had fallen in the first half. (This contrast holds true whether or not changes reflecting the foreign credits are counted.) The bilateral credit arrangements (as distinguished from the IMF drawing) made in June were all terminated or converted to stand-bys by the end of 1962.

The emergency had been very largely psychological, involving speculation first on official manipulation of a flexible exchange rate and then, in May and June, on the possible collapse of a new parity. Fundamentally, the 92.5-cent parity was more probably an undervaluation than an overvaluation. (Most of the time since the 1962 crisis blew over, the Canadian dollar fluctuated in the upper range of its support limits against the U.S. dollar.) The new parity, together with the staggered depreciation that had already been under way since late 1959 or early 1960, does seem to have "improved" the merchandise and current-account balances. Recovering from the sharp drop due largely to the emergency surcharges of mid-1962, imports rose

---

[42] These surcharges were temporary and were finally removed in April 1963, after being gradually relaxed.

[43] Bank for International Settlements, 33rd *Annual Report* (1962–1963), pp. 70-71.

only moderately in relation to Canadian incomes. Exports of manufactures rose 85 percent over the three years 1961–1963, wheat exports gained from sales to Communist countries, and exports of other products rose almost 15 percent over the three-year period. Governmental defense-sharing and export-credit programs and other special influences played a part in this performance, but so did improved price competitiveness. In relation to merchandise imports, the value of exports (as defined in balance-of-payments figures) rose from 92 percent in 1959 to 97 percent in 1960, 103 percent in 1961, 103 percent in 1962, and 108 percent in 1963. In the remainder of the current account, tourist trade showed notable changes: foreign spending in Canada continued to rise, while Canadian spending abroad fell markedly from mid-1962 to mid-1963. Total current-account receipts in relation to payments rose from 82 percent in 1959 to 85 percent in 1960, 89 percent in 1961, 90½ percent in 1962, and 94 percent in 1963. These changes were accompanied, naturally enough, by successive declines in the annual totals of net long-term capital inflow.[44] (Identification of cause-and-effect relations between the exchange rate and the capital account must, however, await further experience with the pegged rate.) Official reserves of gold and U.S. dollars, after falling sharply toward the end of 1961 and in the first half of 1962 and then recovering in the second half, remained fairly steady in 1963 and 1964 at several hundred million dollars above the level of the free-rate period.

On the domestic scene, industrial production had averaged practically the same in each of the three years 1956, 1957, and 1958. It had risen about 7½ percent between 1958 and 1959, less than 1 percent between 1959 and 1960, and about 3 percent between 1960 and 1961. It rose about 7½ percent between 1961 and 1962 and about 5½ percent between 1962 and 1963. Gross national product in current prices rose in comparison with the preceding year by 4.3 percent in 1957, 3.1 percent in 1958, 5.7 percent in 1959, 3.3 per-

cent in 1960, 4.2 percent in 1961, 8.0 percent in 1962, and 6.6 percent in 1963. What happened to prices before and after the depreciation and devaluation? Comparison of the average indexes for 1963 and 1960 shows rises of 5.9 percent in wholesale and 3.9 percent in consumer prices; between 1957 and 1960 the rises had been 1.5 and 5 percent. Manufacturing employment had fluctuated generally downward from 1956 and 1957 to early 1961 (seasonally adjusted) and did not regain the 1956–1957 level until early 1963. Overall unemployment, which had averaged 6.7 percent over 1958–1960 and 7.2 percent for 1961 as a whole, declined to average rates of 5.9 percent in 1962 and 5.5 percent in 1963. Some before-and-after contrasts can thus be detected, perhaps, but are hardly striking. It seems reasonable to suppose that the exchange depreciation-and-devaluation, by itself, could not have greatly stimulated the home economy unless it had either permitted or actually promoted growth of the money supply. Apparently this did happen: we have already noted the contrast between the money-supply growth rates in 1961 and 1963 (1962, the year of the balance-of-payments crisis, was an exception), on the one hand, and in the immediately preceding years of Governor Coyne's policy. Of course, the authorities could have had faster monetary growth, if they had wanted it, without abandoning the free-rate system.

The clearest contrast concerns the foreign-exchange market itself. The free-rate period was notably free of the troubles experienced both before October 1950 and again after official manipulation began in June 1961 and after the repegging of May 1962. It is not even clear that the changed policy deserves better marks for rate stability. In the 12 months after May 1961, the Canadian rate fell 9½ percent. The spread between calendar-year highest and lowest Canadian quotations on the U.S. dollar (expressed in relation to the yearly average) reached 6 percent in 1961 (larger than the spread in *any* of the full years of free rates) and 4.4 percent in 1962 (larger than the average of the spreads in the ten full free-rate years).

---

[44] Bank of Nova Scotia, *Monthly Review,* January 1964, and computations from various issues of Bank of Canada, *Statistical Summary.*

The United States Balance of Payments

✍ 25

From Dollar Shortage to Dollar Glut

The large gains of gold and dollars that helped Western Europe back to external currency convertibility at the end of 1958 mirrored a deterioration in the balance of payments of the United States. After many years of worry about a supposed "dollar shortage" (reviewed in the appendix to this chapter), its opposite began causing alarm.

Confusion even over definitions hampers diagnosis. The Department of Commerce has traditionally defined the *overall deficit* or surplus as the difference between total credits and total debits on account of all transactions except those in foreign liquid claims on the United States and gold (and, recently, official U.S. holdings of convertible foreign currencies). These "below-the-line" items are considered the means of settling or financing an imbalance in other transactions. (Because of their ready marketability, foreign-held U.S. government dollar securities of all maturities, as well as bank accounts and other short-term liabilities, are counted among the foreign liquid claims.) The concept of *basic deficit* keeps "below the line" not only these traditional settlement items but also movements of U.S. short-term capital, commercial credits received by Americans from foreigners, and errors and omissions. Transactions in these categories are supposedly more volatile and less meaningful than the "basic" transactions in goods and services, aid, and long-term capital. In some recent years the basic deficit has been smaller than the overall deficit, understandably making the Administration prefer that concept. Various concepts of *adjusted deficit* or of *deficit on "regular"*

(as distinguished from special) *transactions* usually give a less cheerful impression: they put "below the line" certain special official transactions designed to lessen resort to traditional means of financing a deficit on ordinary transactions.[1] Unless otherwise indicated, the figures in this chapter will refer to the traditional concept of the overall deficit.

So defined, the deficit amounted to $3.5 billion in 1958. It was matched by a $1.3 billion increase in short-term liabilities and an all-time record gold loss of $2.3 billion, or about 10 percent of the gold held at the beginning of the year. In thus choosing to accumulate almost two-thirds of their balance-of-payments surplus in gold and only one-third in dollar claims, foreigners broke sharply with their earlier practice. In 1950 (the year of the largest previous gold loss, $1¾ billion) almost half of the U.S. deficit had been with non-European countries, which are traditionally willing to accumulate reserves largely in foreign exchange, but in 1958 the United States incurred over 85 percent of its deficit with European countries, which traditionally prefer gold. The deficit grew to $3.7 billion in 1959 and $3.9 billion in 1960. Thanks partly to special government transactions, it shrank to $2.4, $2.2, and $2.7 billion in 1961, 1962, and 1963.[2]

---

[1] Several concepts of the deficit are well described in Wilson E. Schmidt, *The Rescue of the Dollar*, Washington: American Enterprise Institute for Public Policy Research, 1963, pp. 16-24.

[2] By including "above the line" *all* special government transactions of kinds devised since 1958, including even the sale to foreign authorities of special *convertible* U.S. government securities, one could report the 1963 deficit to be as small as slightly under $2.0 billion. The distinction between convertible and nonconvertible securities

The new development is not the deficit itself but its size and apparent persistence. A deficit had appeared every year from 1950 on, except 1957. But apart from the $3.6 billion recorded in 1950, under the influence of the 1949 devaluations and the Korean War, the deficits had been moderate, averaging only $1.2 billion a year over the period 1951 through 1956. The change from surplus to deficit between 1957 and 1958 reflected normalization of trade after reopening of the Suez Canal. The deficit increased as recovery

is explained in a survey of policy expedients later in this chapter.

Aside from conceptual difficulties, undoubted inaccuracies call for skepticism about the figures in this chapter. Most of them are Commerce Department figures as reproduced, with various rearrangements, in innumerable publications.

from business recession came earlier in the United States than in some of its chief export markets. It shrank in 1961 as the United States still felt the effects of another recession while other industrial countries continued to enjoy rapid expansion.[3] By then, remedial policies were showing some results.

The Arithmetic of the Deficit

Looking unanalytically at the bare figures and glossing over year-to-year changes, we can resolve the deficit into military expenditures overseas, government aid grants, and net outflows of government and private

[3] International Monetary Fund, 1963 *Annual Report*, p. 119.

Table 25.1. U.S. Balance of Payments, Summary, 1950–1963

	Annual Average 1950–1956	1957	1958	1959	1960	1961	1962	1963
Credits								
Merchandise exports	13,576	19,390	16,264	16,282	19,459	19,913	20,479	21,902
Military sales		375	300	302	335	402	660	632
Income on foreign investments	2,078	2,817	2,845	3,043	3,222	3,844	4,322	4,565
Other services sold	2,724	3,899	3,658	3,849	3,958	4,152	4,329	4,504
Net inflow of foreign non-liquid capital	287	487	22	863	366	728	1,020	802
Debits								
Merchandise imports	10,975	13,291	12,952	15,310	14,723	14,497	16,145	16,962
Military expenditures	2,144	3,216	3,435	3,107	3,048	2,934	3,028	2,880
Other services bought	2,993	4,245	4,474	4,925	5,434	5,436	5,791	6,276
Remittances and pensions	572	702	722	791	672	705	736	812
Net outflow of U.S. private long-term capital	1,183	3,301	2,625	2,298	2,544	2,609	2,766	3,440
Net outflow of U.S. private short-term capital	217	276	311	77	1,348	1,541	507	642
Outflow of U.S. government grants and capital, net of repayments	2,485	2,574	2,587	1,986	2,769	2,782	2,998	3,558
Errors and omissions (Credit +, Debit −)	+373	+1,157	+488	+412	−683	−905	−1,025	−495
Settlement of imbalance by change in U.S. reserves and liquid liabilities (Credit = Settlement of Deficit, +; Debit = Settlement of Surplus, −)	+1,530	−520	+3,529	+3,743	+3,881	+2,370	+2,186	+2,660

NOTES: Figures exclude military grants and exports supplied under them and U.S. subscriptions (in 1959) to the International Monetary Fund. Foreign-investment income includes government as well as private earnings. Income on foreign investments in the U.S. is included in "other services bought" in the debits list.

SOURCES: Department of Commerce figures as reproduced in *Economic Report of the President and Annual Report of the Council of Economic Advisers*, January 1964, pp. 297-298, and *Economic Indicators*, April 1964, pp. 24-25. For the 1963 balance of payments in greater detail, see Chapter 3, Table 3.2.

capital totaling more than a surplus of earnings over expenditures in commodity trade, income on foreign investments, and transactions in some services. Because of this large surplus on commercial account, the President's Council of Economic Advisers was able to stress that the payments problem "does not reflect any over-all tendency for the United States to 'live beyond its means.' Americans collectively do not spend more than their real incomes permit and therefore do not absorb goods and services, on balance, from the rest of the world." Nor does the deficit "reflect a reduction in net worth in relation to the rest of the world. In fact, U.S. assets abroad—in the form of private equity investment, short- and long-term credits, and government loans—have in general been increasing faster than U.S. liabilities. The U.S. deficit does reflect a loss of liquidity in the form of a reduction in gold reserves and a build-up of liquid liabilities to foreigners."[4]

Of course, transactions interact. If the net debits on military, aid, and capital account had been smaller than they were, the goods-and-services surplus would also have been smaller. And anyway, equilibrium does not require balance in each separate category of a country's international transactions. As compared with putting the blame on the particular categories in deficit, it might not be much less reasonable to blame particular surplus categories for not being still larger. Not even seeing which deficit categories have grown most or which surplus categories have shrunken most yields a conclusive diagnosis; it might not be downright illogical to put some blame even on growing surplus categories for not growing still more. From when should analyst start measuring changes? What past period was "normal"? Another trouble with emphasizing changes is that temporary influences of one sort or another are often conspicuous and may sidetrack attention from more enduring influences. Finally, the causes of a deficit do not necessarily coincide with the conditions that "ought" to be eliminated to restore equilibrium. If expenditure on urgently needed surgery threatens a deficit in an individual's personal balance of payments, it hardly follows that he "ought" to avoid this deficit by canceling his plans for the operation.[5]

Even though it cannot pinpoint "causes," surveying some broad categories of transactions may prove useful. The export surplus in ordinary merchandise trade ranged between $1 and $3 billion a year from 1950 through 1955. It rose exceptionally to $4.6 billion in 1956 and $6.1 billion in 1957 (when the Suez repercussions temporarily stimulated petroleum exports, in particular). It fluctuated in a more normal range of between $3.3 and $5.4 billion a year after that, except for a fall to slightly below $1 billion in 1959 only. The annual surplus on ordinary services (including income on foreign investments) fluctuated rather widely around an average of about $2 billion from 1951 on, rising to almost $2.5 billion in 1957 and to $2.6, $2.9, and $2.8 billion in 1961, 1962, and 1963. This surplus on ordinary services was outweighed by American military expenditures abroad, which rose above $3 billion in 1957 and fluctuated around that figure afterwards. (The figure includes spending by both the government and American servicemen and their families overseas.)

For the total goods-and-services account (including military spending and foreign-investment income), the export balance averaged $2.3 billion a year, or 14 percent of the import side, over the period 1950–1956. This surplus rose to $5.7 billion (28 percent) in 1957, fell to $2.2 billion (11 percent) in 1958, nearly vanished in 1959, and recovered to $3.8, $5.4, $4.8, and $5.5 billion (16, 24, 19, and 21 percent) in 1960–1963.

Government economic aid grants (as distinguished from military aid) declined from over $3 billion a year in 1950 and 1951 and fluctuated below $2 billion since then. Government loans net of both regularly scheduled repayments and special repayments fluctuated widely from year to year, ranging between a small net inflow in 1954 and a net outflow of

---

[4] *Economic Report of the President and Annual Report of the Council of Economic Advisers,* Washington: Government Printing Office, January 1964, p. 122.

[5] Schmidt, *op. cit.,* pp. 25-33, esp. p. 28.

$1.1 billion in 1960 and again in 1962. Including minor additional categories lumped together with loans and grants and military expenditure, government transactions showed annual deficits trending generally upward from below $5 billion in the early 1950s to ocacsionally almost $6 billion in the years since then.

The net outflow of private U.S. long-term capital spurted from an annual average of slightly under $1 billion over the six years 1950–1955 to averages of $2.8 billion in 1956–1958 and of $2.6 billion in 1959–1962 and to a level of $3.4 billion in 1963. These figures include capital newly transferred abroad for both portfolio and direct investment, but not local reinvestment of profits earned abroad by American-owned businesses. In considering policy questions later on, we should perhaps remember that earnings on existing private American loans and investment abroad remitted to the United States have exceeded the new capital outflow. These earnings (already counted among exports of goods and services) averaged $2.9 a year over the period 1956–1962 showed an uptrend, and reached $4.1 billion in 1963. As for foreign-owned private capital (other than liquid funds), its net inflow into the United States fluctuated widely from year to year, but in the general range of several hundred million dollars.

As for private U.S. short-term capital, its recorded net outflow fluctuated widely around an average of only $0.2 billion a year in the decade of the 'fifties but reached $1.3, $1.5, $0.5, and $0.6 billion in the four years 1960–1963. In addition, the item "errors and omissions" (or "unrecorded transactions") is usually supposed to consist largely of unrecorded flows of short-term capital, American and foreign. This inference is supported by its being a net credit item throughout the postwar period, except for a small debit in 1950 and debits (outflows) of $0.7, $0.9, $1.0, and $0.5 billion in the four years 1960–1963.

Divergent Diagnoses and Prognoses

If these figures reveal no clear picture, it is understandable that experts should disagree on diagnosis.[6] The authors of the Fairleigh Dickinson study of 1963 concluded that the "deficits since 1957 have not resulted from any serious imbalance within the private sector of this country's international accounts." If any single factor could be singled out, it appeared to them "to be military expenditures abroad." They called for a "critical reexamination" of foreign aid and military spending.[7] According to Professor James W. Angell, however, "the essential character of the . . . disequilibrium is simple. Our transactions in merchandise on private account show large and continued export surpluses, and our service transactions come fairly close to equilibrium, but we are very heavy net exporters of capital, both on private and governmental account. These capital exports are where our international deficits chiefly come from."[8]

When the merchandise and goods-and-services export surpluses had fallen from several billion dollars in earlier years to $1.0 billion and $0.1 billion respectively in 1959, attention centered on the question whether American business had become seriously less competitive than before in the world market and even at home. "Responsible observers have expressed views that range from extreme alarm to rather surprising complacency."[9] Alarmists could easily point to declines in the U.S. shares of total exports from the industrialized to the nonindustrialized countries and of manufactured exports from the industrialized countries to all markets (including each other's). While overall indexes of American wholesale and export prices had been rising only moderately in comparison with those of leading competitor countries, it was possible—and remained possible for some years afterwards—to cite relative price

---

[6] Furthermore, the disease may not have remained of the same nature ever since 1958. Capital movements, for example, have gained in importance since then in the arithmetic of the deficit.

[7] Nasrollah S. Fatemi, Thibaut de Saint Phalle, and Grace M. Keeffe, *The Dollar Crisis,* Fairleigh Dickinson University Press, pp. 293, 251, 295.

[8] *The United States Balance of Payments* (Statements on the Brookings Institution study submitted to the Joint Economic Committee), Washington: Government Printing Office, November 1963, p. 32.

[9] Federal Reserve Bank of New York, 1959 *Annual Report,* p. 41.

rises in certain categories of American exports, such as vehicles, steel, and machinery. Barring really major and obvious differences between the price trends of different countries, broad indexes can hardly settle the question of competitiveness. They can hardly allow for nonprice competition, such as shifts in quality, variety, novelty, availability, and promptness of delivery of products, in credit terms, and in sales promotion. They can hardly sort out the influences of business-cycle developments and of special historical circumstances such as the brief American vogue for compact foreign cars, the abatement of post-Suez abnormalities, or the reduction in the cotton export subsidy and the switchover to jet aircraft production that temporarily burdened U.S. exports in 1958–1959. Comparing individual commodity prices instead of indexes, or collecting examples of lost export sales, can hardly settle the question, either, since it is in the very nature of comparative advantage and of a dynamic economy that some American sellers should find themselves beaten by the competition at any given time.[10]

In a broad sense that need not imply business sluggishness or inflationary laxness in the United States, however, the American position has worsened *relatively*: remarkable postwar recoveries have turned Western Europe and Japan into formidable suppliers on world markets. Their recoveries had been a leading goal of American policy; its success should hardly count as an American failure.

A still broader argument might urge that regardless of price and market-share statistics and of the surplus earned in ordinary transactions, the overall balance-of-payments disequilibrium itself shows that American goods and services are not competitive *enough* for the situation facing the country (including its defense and aid burdens).[11] According to a view shared by several competent observers, an overvaluation of the dollar of probably "some 15 or 20 percent with respect to most European currencies . . . is at the heart of the American balance-of-payments problem. It can be traced to the European

devaluations of 1949, which turned out to have been excessive. The existence of overvaluation is evident not only from price comparisons (whether static or dynamic), but also from the joint appearance of domestic unemployment and an international deficit in the United States."[12]

The experts disagree not only about balance-of-payments experience so far but still more strongly about the outlook for the next few years.[13] What will happen depends not only on employment, price, and productivity trends in the United States and abroad and on the defense, aid, trade, and anti-inflation policies of the various governments but also on what historically unique developments will emerge in the future—perhaps further oil discoveries in Europe, or European advances in aircraft design and production, or cost-cutting developments in Japanese shipbuilding, or, most characteristic of all, quite unforeseeable political and other events. Balance-of-payments policy designed to deal with historical combinations of circumstances as they occur or are expected to occur will continue proving in practice to be a series of *ad hoc* expedients, expedients that add up to what Professor Gardner Patterson has aptly called a "back-door devaluation" of the dollar.

Events and Policy, 1958–1961

A chronicle of recent developments affecting the balance of payments and gold reserves, as well as of how policy responded to them, will help document this assessment. Between 1957 and 1958, the dollar value of U.S. merchandise exports fell 16 percent. The stimulus of the Suez events had ended, recession had developed abroad as well as in the United States, and temporary conditions

---

[10] Schmidt, *op. cit.*, p. 31.

[11] Cf. *ibid.*, p. 33.

[12] Hendrik S. Houthakker in *The United States Balance of Payments, op. cit.*, p. 217. This last interpretation, if correct, reminds us again of the bias toward overadjustment in the adjustable-peg system, once delayed changes are at last forced, and of the will-o'-the-wisp character of any long-run equilibrium rate of exchange.

[13] A convenient sampling of opinion appears in *ibid.*, which contains the comments of some 68 economists, bankers, and others on Walter S. Salant and others, *The United States Balance of Payments in 1968*, Washington: The Brookings Institution; Joint Economic Committee print, 1963.

hampered exports of fuel, automobiles, air-craft, and cotton. At the same time, merchandise imports fell only about 2½ percent in value. The inflow of foreign capital, partially offsetting the American outflow, was much smaller in 1958 than before. This change in the capital accounts seemed due partly to the low recession-year interest rates in the United States and to stoppage and partial reversal of the capital inflows from Europe that had occurred during the 1957 exchange crisis. Military expenditures abroad, net of sales of military goods, continued rising.

Merchandise exports continued shrinking in early 1959 as recovery from the recession abroad generally lagged behind recovery in the United States, but exports turned upward before midyear. For the year as a whole, their dollar value and physical quantity were both about the same as in 1958. As recovery from the recession proceeded, total imports rose about 19 percent in both value and quantity; the merchandise export surplus fell further and drastically. Some special factors, such as strikes in the steel and copper industries and an unusually large rise in coffee inventories, were also at work. Thanks partly to changed interest-rate relations and to liberalization of European controls, the net outflow of capital from the United States shrank and held the increase in the overall deficit between 1958 and 1959 to only about $0.2 billion.

The overall deficit again grew slightly in 1960 despite a very strong recovery in the merchandise trade balance (exports rose almost 20 percent in total value, while imports fell 4 percent). The great worsening came in the capital account. The explanation apparently involves a drop in interest rates as the United States slipped into recession while several other industrial countries were tightening their credit policies to restrain inflation. Europe's move to convertibility in 1958 had given increased scope to the influence of interest-rate differentials.[14] The inflow of foreign capital (other than "below-the-line" liquid funds) fell by $½ billion, the outflow of American capital for direct investment in-

creased more than $0.3 billion, and the recorded outflow of short-term capital rose by almost $1.3 billion. In addition, the "errors and omissions" item deteriorated by $1.1 billion, switching from the net credit almost always previously recorded to the net debit recorded ever since. The country's "basic" deficit (not counting recorded and unrecorded short-term capital movements), in contrast to the overall deficit, was actually lower in 1960, at $1.9 billion, than it had been in the two preceding years. (An opposite divergence had appeared in 1959, when the overall deficit of $3.7 billion fell short of the basic deficit of $4.2 billion.)[15] This contrast between basic improvement and overall worsening emphasizes how changeable and unpredictable balance-of-payments items are. The last few months of 1960 showed this to be especially true of short-term capital movements.

Speculation on a possible devaluation of the dollar may have been linked then with uncertainty over the impending Presidential election and the policies of a new Administration. The drain of gold from U.S. reserves accelerated during the summer and fall and amounted to $1.7 billion for 1960 as a whole. A "gold rush" developed on the London free market. Ever since the market reopened in 1954, the price of gold had remained within a few cents of the U.S. Treasury's buying and selling prices of $34.9125 and $35.0875 per ounce. Late in October, however, the price shot to a brief peak of over $40 an ounce. Additional demand from banks and hoarders outside the Sterling Area was hitting the ordinarily thin market. The West German ban of interest on new foreign deposits and the Swiss *charge* of 1 percent a year on foreign deposits had presumably helped make gold itself more attractive relative to dollars. Speculators enjoyed a "one-way option," hoping for a rise and confident of no cut in the official price of gold. (To restrain speculation by means of some two-way uncertainty

---

[14] Federal Reserve Bank of New York, 1960 *Annual Report,* pp. 32-33, 38-40.

[15] *Economic Report of the President and Annual Report of the Council of Economic Advisers,* Washington: Government Printing Office, January 1963, p. 96. For a slightly different concept of the basic deficit, the figures are $1.8 billion in 1960 and $4.7 billion in 1959. Salant, *op. cit.,* p. 281.

about gold, some academic economists then recommended that the United States stand ready to make occasional moderate cuts in its official price.)

After first uttering mere words about the strength of the dollar, the U.S. Treasury soon reportedly began feeding gold to the London market through the intermediary of the Bank of England in order to beat down the price and disappoint the speculators. The price sank and remained below $36 but continued for a while to fluctuate in a wider range than before October 1960.

In 1961 the central banks of England and six continental countries joined the United States in an informal "pool" to coordinate their price-stabilizing interventions on the gold market. The Bank of England acted as agent for this group and, within limits, both sold and bought gold for its members. At first the pool was a gold-selling operation. By early 1962, however, the market had been stabilized and all the gold previously sold bought back. Later, when an oversupply of gold began to develop, the members of the pool were apparently able to take gold off the market, which helps explain why U.S. gold losses fell off, especially in 1963.

The United States took some independent action to help check the private demand for gold. Shortly before leaving office in January 1961, President Eisenhower issued an order forbidding persons subject to U.S. jurisdiction from holding gold abroad. (Private gold holdings within the United States had been forbidden ever since 1933.) Americans already holding gold abroad were ordered to get rid of it by June 1.

President Kennedy reaffirmed this and some other of Eisenhower's orders.[16] He pledged to hold the $35 gold price and emphasized that the entire U.S. gold stock and IMF quota stood behind his pledge. He promised there would be no exchange controls over trade or investment. He furthered the "tying" foreign economic aid to pur-

chases in the United States, a policy increasingly emphasized since October 1959, when the Development Loan Fund was directed to see that its loans were spent in the United States. He supported export promotion through bigger commercial staffs attached to U.S. embassies abroad, fuller participation in foreign trade fairs, dissemination of more information about sales opportunities abroad, and extension of the export credit insurance facilities of the Export-Import Bank. A revision of tax depreciation schedules begun in 1961 was designed to stimulate business investment that would raise productivity and thereby improve the international competitiveness of American products. In hopes of partially offsetting American spending abroad, tourist visa formalities were simplified and other steps taken to promote foreign travel in the United States. A law effective in September 1961 "temporarily" reduced from $500 to $100 the duty-free allowance on purchases brought back by returning American tourists. Kennedy did depart from Eisenhower's approach, however, in rescinding an order of November 1960 that would have cut the number of wives and children living with American servicemen stationed abroad; he directed the Secretary of Defense to achieve equivalent savings on expenditures abroad by other, less drastic, means.

The basic deficit disappeared from the U.S. balance of payments early in 1961, when the low phase of the business recession was depressing imports while continuing expansion in industrial economies abroad was benefiting exports. Although it reappeared as business recovered, the basic deficit remained much smaller for the year as a whole than it had been in 1960. The overall deficit was only three-fifths as large in 1961 as in the year before. As a matter of arithmetic, this improvement was attributable to further growth in the surplus on goods-and-services account and to special advance debt repayments to the U.S. government; other flows of capital, including those concealed in "errors and omissions," remained on balance heavily outward.

Among policy measures reflecting official concern with short-term capital flows, the most prominent in 1961 was abandonment

---

[16] A further order of July 1962 banned private American holdings abroad even of rare gold coins. Those already owned had to be either sold or imported into the United States. New purchases and imports of gold coins were forbidden without special Treasury license, rarely granted. IMF 1963 *Annual Report*, p. 180.

of "bills-only." Even shortly before the 1960 election, the Federal Reserve had bought some short-term certificates, notes, and bonds, as well as Treasury bills. The announcement of a deliberate change in open-market policy came in February 1961; and the Federal Reserve made a significant portion of its purchases during the year outside the short-term area, even buying some over-ten-year bonds. The new policy, continued in the following years and known as "Operation Twist," aimed to keep up short-term interest rates to deter capital outflows while holding down long-term interest rates to aid domestic economic growth. At times, resistance to downtrends in the bill rate required selling bills and buying longer issues almost simultaneously. To supplement Federal Reserve efforts, government trust funds and investment accounts bought long-term securities with currently accumulated funds and sometimes in replacement of short-term holdings sold.[17] How well the "twist" was succeeding, however, remained open to rival interpretations. One minor measure to make U.S. government securities more attractive relative to gold was a tax exemption extended to all foreign central banks on their U.S. interest income; before 1961, only some of these banks had enjoyed the exemption.[18]

Events and Cooperation in Policy, 1961 and 1962

In foreign-exchange policy specifically, some notable developments followed closely upon the German and Dutch revaluations of March 1961. During the speculative flurry that ensued, foreigners expecting to receive dollars were especially anxious to sell them forward to guard against possible further exchange-rate adjustments. The resulting discount on the forward dollar became so wide that some foreigners found it cheaper to obtain protection by shunning the forward market and instead borrowing dollars at once (which they would repay out of their ex-

pected future receipts), selling the borrowed dollars spot for their own currencies, and investing the proceeds. The wide forward discount also made it unprofitable for some foreign investors to hold dollars. Dollars flowed into European official reserves. In these circumstances the Federal Reserve Bank of New York, as agent for the Treasury, began dealing in foreign exchange. It dealt in several currencies during 1961, mainly German marks and Swiss francs, seeking the greatest effect by concentrating its intervention in the comparatively "thin" forward markets. The Federal Reserve collaborated closely with foreign authorities in these operations and joined regularly in the monthly meetings of central bankers at Basel. The new policy apparently did slow down the movement of dollars into foreign official reserves and reduce potential demands on the U.S. gold stock. Furthermore, the market's awareness of continuous intervention by cooperating central banks supposedly helped quiet distrust of existing exchange rates.[19] Incidentally, the Treasury had obtained some Swiss francs for its operations by issuing short-term obligations denominated in that currency. The modest initial accumulation of official foreign-exchange reserves by the United States illustrated the possibilities of a shift toward a *multiple-key-currency* system as an improvement on existing international monetary arrangements. (Chapter 27 discusses this idea further.)

Besides coordinated intervention on the foreign-exchange and gold markets, other kinds of international cooperation gained ground in 1961. While the United States tried manipulating interest rates to check capital outflow, several surplus countries, notably Germany, eased credit to check capital inflow. Several official transactions helped reduce the liquid dollar holdings and potential gold purchases of foreign authorities. Germany made a $587 million advance debt repayment; the United States took part of this amount in marks and used them in its exchange-market operations. Some other countries made smaller advance repayments. The In-

---

[17] Federal Reserve Bank of New York, 1961 *Annual Report*, pp. 20-21, 1962 *Annual Report*, p. 20.
[18] Federal Reserve Bank of New York, 1961 *Annual Report*, p. 34.

[19] *Ibid.*, pp. 31-33.

ternational Monetary Fund increasingly encouraged its borrowers to draw the currencies of countries with large or growing international reserves. Consultations within the IMF and the newly reorganized Organization for Economic Cooperation and Development aided these cooperative measures.[20]

The trend of the U.S. deficit in 1962 defies quarter-by-quarter interpretation because changing special circumstances were at work. In the first half of the year the Canadian exchange crisis affected many figures in the U.S. balance of payments favorably; the Canadian recovery in the second half had an unfavorable influence. Dock strikes in October and December distorted trade patterns.[21] Viewed as a whole and compared with 1961, the year 1962 provided another example of opposite changes in the "basic" and "overall" U.S. deficits: the former rose while the latter fell slightly. The most important single "adverse" development was an 11-percent rise in the value of merchandise imports accompanying a rise in domestic business activity. Merchandise exports rose less than 3 percent, partly because of such special factors as Japanese and Canadian measures to deal with their own balance-of-payments troubles. While the balance on services (including investment income) improved, the balances worsened on account of ordinary government capital and grants and private American long-term capital. (The capital outflow for direct investment held steady or even slackened, but portfolio investment rose again as the large and efficient U.S. capital market continued attracting bond-issuers from around the world.) Advance repayments of debt to the U.S. government, though totaling almost $0.7 billion, were no larger than the year before.

The slight improvement nevertheless observed in the overall balance of payments was due, as a matter of arithmetic, mainly to three components. First, the recorded net outflow of U.S. short-term capital shrank by $1 billion. (This happened despite occasional interest-motivated transfers of funds abroad and some speculative transfers after the stock-

market break in May. On the other hand, net short-term lending to Japan shriveled up, partly because domestic restraint was shrinking that country's payments deficit and the need to finance it.) The second main item of apparent improvement was nearly $½ billion of advance military payments by foreigners. The third was the sale of some $¼ billion worth of special nonmarketable medium-term U.S. government securities to the Italian and Swiss authorities.

Until the autumn of 1962 liquid claims on the United States had consisted entirely of foreign holdings expressed in dollars. Then, however, the United States began to issue nontransferable obligations expressed in the currency of the foreign central bank or government buying them. Their maturities usually ranged from 15 to 24 months. The first of these "Roosa bonds" (so called in reference to Under Secretary of the Treasury Robert V. Roosa) were nonconvertible. Later on, to accommodate legal portfolio requirements of some foreign central banks, new issues were made convertible at short notice into quickly redeemable claims. Holders could then obtain cash quickly to help meet some unexpected drain on their own reserves. By holding a U.S. Treasury obligation denominated in its own currency instead of dollars, the foreign authority enjoys a guarantee against loss in the event of an American devaluation; yet the obligation, unlike gold, pays interest. The "Roosa bonds" provided a way for surplus countries in effect to lend to the United States their otherwise excessive accruals of international reserves.

Several observers objected to the mere "prettying up" of the U.S. balance of payments achieved by counting sales of Roosa bonds "above the line" as an inflow of medium-term capital into the United States rather than "below the line" among the settlement items. Commerce Department statisticians stressed the liquid-liability character of these bonds, drawing, in rebuttal, accusations of being statistical masochists.[22]

[20] *Ibid.,* pp. 34-35.

[21] International Monetary Fund, 1963 *Annual Report,* p. 120.

[22] Cf. *Wall Street Journal,* October 31, 1963, p. 16. For remarks about the classification of special bond transactions in 1963, see Chapter 3, Table 3.2, and the accompanying discussion.

In February 1962 the Federal Open Market Committee authorized the Federal Reserve, for the first time since before the war, to resume foreign-exchange operations on its own account, while continuing to serve as agent for the Treasury. To acquire foreign currencies for this purpose, the Federal Reserve began negotiating a series of "swap arrangements" with foreign central banks. These arrangements provided for reciprocal lines of credit, that is, for the creation of deposits in each other's favor. On request, each party would exchange its own currency for the other's up to an agreed maximum amount. When the agreed time period (such as three to six months) had elapsed, the swap of currencies was either reversed or renewed. Both parties were protected against exchange risk, since the reversal occurred at the original exchange rate, regardless of what devaluation or revaluation might have taken place in the meanwhile.

By the end of 1962 the United States had arranged lines of credit totaling $900 million with the Bank of Canada, the Bank for International Settlements, and eight European central banks. The Federal Reserve and Treasury drew on these credits throughout the year to resist fluctuations in both spot and forward exchange rates. They sold spot marks to support the dollar when the mark was unusually strong. They also dealt in several other Continental currencies, both on the market and in direct transactions with the respective central banks. Currencies obtained by swaps thus mopped up dollars that would otherwise have flowed into foreign reserves and become convertible into gold. By the end of the year the Federal Reserve was able to reverse some of its operations and either partially repay currencies drawn under swaps or rebuild depleted balances of those currencies. In June, Canada used U.S. dollars obtained under a swap arrangement to defend its currency against speculative attack.[23]

In October 1962 the supplementary borrowing arrangements of the International Monetary Fund came into effect. Ten major industrial countries had agreed to lend the Fund up to a total of $6 billion worth of their own currencies in case of need. By calling on the pledges of the other nine, the Fund would be able to accommodate even a massive drawing by the United States.

On the domestic policy front, efforts continued to "twist" the interest-rate structure up at the short end and down at the long end. To expand usable bank reserves without open-market purchases that would have put direct downward pressure on short-term interest rates, the Federal Reserve lowered reserve requirements against time and savings deposits in October 1962. To reduce incentives for foreign conversion of dollar claims into gold, Congress suspended the interest-rate ceilings on time deposits held by foreign and international monetary authorities. Closer alignment of European and American interest rates during 1962 reduced the scope for purely interest-motivated short-term capital movements. Toward the end of the year, however, "the freedom and ability of monetary policy to do more to spur the domestic economy further were increasingly brought into question. The balance-of-payments situation ruled out actions that would flood the economy with liquidity, since the odds were strong that a policy of even greater ease would aggravate the payments problem and raise doubts in the minds of foreign holders of dollars as to our willingness to defend the dollar."[24]

Developments in and after 1963

In 1963 the United States achieved a merchandise export surplus about $0.6 billion larger than the year before. Exports benefited from temporary conditions such as bad weather, poor crops, interruptions to coal production in Europe, and removal of the remaining import restraints imposed by Canada in 1962. In addition, longer-term factors seemed to be working toward an improvement, including export-promotion programs and a slower pace of wage and price inflation

---

[23] Federal Reserve Bank of New York, 1962 *Annual Report,* pp. 7, 31-33; Robert V. Roosa, "Reforming the International Monetary System," *Foreign Affairs,* **XLII,** October 1963, pp. 118-119.

[24] Federal Reserve Bank of New York, 1962 *Annual Report,* p. 7.

in the United States than elsewhere. Nevertheless, the overall deficit rose to $2.7 billion (or to $3.3 billion on the conservative interpretation of special government transactions as "below-the-line" settlement items.)

The deterioration was concentrated in the first half of the year. The outflow of private U.S. capital spurted. Direct investments abroad and recorded short-term capital outflows were heavy, but the most notable spurt came in foreign security issues in New York. Most of the issues originated in Canada and Japan and European countries where borrowing costs were generally higher than in the United States. Paradoxically, "the unique size, strength, and accessibility"[25] of its capital market was proving troublesome for the United States.

Policy responded shortly after midyear. On July 16 to the Federal Reserve raised its discount rate to 3½ from 3 percent and raised the maximum allowable interest rates on time and savings deposits. The domestic business situation allegedly permitted this further monetary tightness.[26] In a special message to Congress on July 18, President Kennedy called for a supposedly temporary "interest-equalization tax" on American purchases from foreigners of new or outstanding foreign securities of three or more years' maturity. (The tax was to apply to securities originating in any industrial country, as distinguished from underdeveloped countries, although an early understanding modified the application of the proposed tax to Canada.) The measure would amount to an ad hoc tariff on capital exports, that is, on imported securities. It would add about 1 percentage point to the effective annual interest rate paid by foreign borrowers. The President also announced other measures, including further economies in government spending overseas, further tying of foreign aid to exports, further efforts to sell American goods, securities, and tourist services to foreigners, and negotiation of a $500 million standby credit with the International Monetary Fund. This last action was partly designed to emphasize the

availability of the Fund's resources in defense of the dollar. Largely, though, it was a technical measure recommended by the fact that the Fund's holdings of dollars had risen to just about the limit normally permissible under its rules. Debtor countries wanting to use dollars for repayments to the Fund would have first had to buy gold from the United States or else sell their dollars in the foreign exchange markets for currencies acceptable to the Fund. The standby arrangement enabled the United States to draw such currencies for sale to countries needing them for repayments. (The United States did not make its first actual drawing—$125 million worth of German, French, and Italian money —until February 1964.)

These measures and announcements helped improve the balance of payments sharply in the second half of 1963. Since the interest-equalization tax, if finally enacted by Congress, was to take effect retroactively as of the day after the President proposed it, the volume of new foreign security issues in the United States shrank dramatically. (Even so, the heavy volume of issues already floated or arranged for carried American purchases of new foreign securities to a new annual record, and direct investment abroad was also higher than the year before.) Part of this impact was presumably temporary. Potential borrowers had reason to wait in hopes of selling their issues at better prices if the tax should definitely fail to be passed and its threat should vanish. Even if the tax should pass, foreign issues might then increase because the reason for postponing them would have passed. By early 1964, furthermore, increased bank lending abroad seemed to be partly offsetting the shrinkage in American portfolio investment.

One year later, in February 1965, President Johnson invoked his standby authority to extend the interest-equalization tax (which had finally been enacted in September 1964) to bank loans abroad with maturities of one year or more. The President announced a campaign for voluntary restraint on shorter-term bank loans abroad also, as well as on foreign investment and spending by business corporations. His immediate reason was apparently

[25] Federal Reserve Bank of New York, 1963 *Annual Report*, p. 11.
[26] *Ibid.*, pp. 7, 24, 25, 33-38.

a sharp deterioration in the private capital account of the balance of payments in the fourth quarter of 1964. (Preliminary estimates for 1964 as a whole put the overall deficit at some $3 billion, using the definitions that count special government transactions "below the line.")

In the realm of international cooperation, further foreign purchases of U.S. Treasury securities denominated in foreign currencies carried the total outstanding at the end of 1963 to the equivalent of $760 million. During that year, reciprocal currency or swap arrangements had been extended to cover eleven foreign central banks and the Bank for International Settlements. An initial $50 million arrangement with the Bank of England had been increased to $500 million; and the total amount of swap facilities had risen above $2 billion, mostly still on a standby basis. Use of these facilities countered strains during the year in the markets between dollars and the British, German, Swiss, Dutch, Italian, and Canadian currencies. When Britain failed to gain entry to the Common Market, the Bank of England counteracted the resulting speculative outflow of funds by drawing on its swap line with the Federal Reserve Bank of New York and also obtaining funds from several European central banks. During the spring and summer and again in November, when the German mark was under buying pressure, the Federal Reserve intervened heavily by selling marks obtained under a swap agreement, acting in close coordination with the Bundesbank. In the hours and days immediately after the assassination of President Kennedy, the Federal Reserve and some foreign central banks maintained orderly conditions in the foreign exchange markets by offering foreign currencies for dollars at the existing rates.[27]

The Gold Position

At $461 million dollars, the U.S. gold loss in 1963 was smaller than in any other year after 1958. Even this relatively small loss was offset to the extent of $113 million by a rise in official U.S. holdings of convertible foreign currencies. The smallness of this net loss was partly due to foreign cooperation with the United States in intervening on the gold and foreign exchange markets and in buying Roosa bonds. Behind the scenes, the United States was presumably pressuring foreign authorities not to draw gold. Increased Free World production and Soviet sales of gold also benefited the U.S. gold stock. Finally, some more fundamental balance-of-payments improvements may have been at work.

Still, the gold drain had only slowed, not stopped. At the end of January 1964 the U.S. gold stock, standing at $15½ billion, was smaller than at any time since before World War II. Of this amount, approximately $12½ billion was immobilized to meet the 25-percent legal reserve requirement against note and deposit liabilities of the Federal Reserve Banks. (However, the Board of Governors had legal authority to suspend this requirement and keep renewing the suspension, subject to levying a tax on the deficiency.) The difference, the "free" gold reserve, amounted to some $3 billion only, and against it stood some $23.1 billion of liquid liabilities of the government and the banks to foreigners and international agencies.[28] Foreign authorities held more than half of these claims; commercial banks and the private sector held some 40 percent. Slightly over half of the total liability took the form of deposits in U.S. banks and more than one-third took the form of government securities.

A 13-percent ratio of free gold to foreign liquid claims is perhaps not as alarming as it might seem at first. Simply repealing the reserve requirement against Federal Reserve notes and deposits would raise the free-gold percentage (for deposits, in fact, the requirement was repealed in March 1965, freeing some $5 billion of gold to meet the resumption of heavy foreign demands). And anyway, holding only fractional reserves is quite normal for international as well as domestic banking. Not all of the foreign funds are in practice subject to immediate withdrawal; foreign banks and business firms hold most of their

---

[27] *Ibid.*, pp. 43-45, 51.

[28] This is the figure reported in *International Financial Statistics*. Other sources give somewhat different figures for somewhat different concepts.

dollars as working balances and could not part with them without gravely inconveniencing their regular business.[29] The United States could draw up to more than $5 billion worth of foreign currencies from the International Monetary Fund to meet a run on the dollar (and more by special waiver). Supplementary borrowing arrangements under and outside the aegis of the Fund provide further means of defense against critical drains.

Other considerations are less reassuring. First, reserves that might be ample with a balancing mechanism in operation are less so without one. Second, precisely because so many official agencies and commercial banks throughout the world hold dollars as a uniquely important international reserve currency and means of settlement, these holders will remain alert to signs that the dollar is losing the characteristics that had previously made it desirable. International cooperation may not withstand really serious suspicion that a devaluation or a suspension of convertibility into gold is at hand. For this reason, the dollar is more vulnerable than, say, the Venezuelan bolivar or even the Swiss franc. Third, the reassuring comparison with a fractional-reserve domestic banking system is questionable because, for one thing, neither the International Monetary Fund nor any other organization is truly comparable to the Federal Deposit Insurance Corporation as a rescuer in time of trouble and as a reassurance to claim-holders in the first place.

A fourth point deserves emphasis. The distinctions between officially held and privately held dollars and between foreign-held and American-held dollars are not especially important. Neither private foreigners nor private Americans can redeem their dollars in gold at the U.S. Treasury. But any of them, when they saw fit, could hasten to sell dollars for foreign currencies on the ordinary exchange market. Foreign central banks, to keep their own currencies from appreciating against the dollar in violation of the policy of fixed exchange rates, would absorb the abnormal offerings of dollars. As official holders, the foreign central banks could then redeem the dollars in gold. The chief restraint on flight from the dollar is whatever need for working balances might persist even despite mounting distrust.

A Broader View of the Problem

Standing back from details about exports of cotton and airplanes, interest-rate differentials, and palliatives tried and remedies proposed, let us ask what lessons the balance-of-payments problem teaches. Since 1958, the size and make-up of the deficit has varied sharply. While some items have improved from one year to the next, others have worsened—sometimes trade in goods and services, sometimes long-term capital movements, sometimes short-term capital movements. These facts are trite but important; they emphasize how changeable economic conditions are. Balances of payments can react sensitively to slight differences among countries in rates of economic growth or price rise, to changes in so-called "structural" conditions, and to special historical circumstances.[30] A trade surplus or deficit is a difference between differences, since imports and exports are themselves differences between domestic production and domestic use. A search for stable functional relations between balance-of-payments positions and their innumerable determinants is practically hopeless; forecasts can be little better than short-run extrapolations. A sensible policy would not have to depend on them.

The volatility of a balance of payments is not the same thing as an alternation of deficits

---

[29] As a partial offset to foreign claims, furthermore, American banks held short-term foreign assets amounting to $6.1 billion at the end of January 1964. Counting American long-term investments abroad also, total American claims on foreigners are of course far in excess of foreign claims on the United States. Barring drastic government requisitioning of foreign investments, however, the size of private American holdings has little relevance to the problem of meeting foreign withdrawals of short-term funds.

[30] Consider the Brookings study (by Salant and others) of *The United States Balance of Payments in 1968*. The authors worked with two different sets of assumptions about U.S. and European prices and real gross national products in that year. Those of the figures that differed at all between the two sets of assumptions differed by only a few percent at most. Yet the discrepancy between the two resulting projections of the "basic" U.S. payments position was practically as large as the average actual "basic" deficit over the years 1958–1962.

and surpluses around a longer-run equilibrium. In the absence of an equilibrating mechanism, balance-of-payments troubles are likely to persist or recur; instead of vanishing, they are at best likely to give old victims a respite as they turn to plague new countries. Worry about a supposedly chronic and almost intractable "dollar shortage" remained fashionable until it gave way to an opposite worry about a stubborn U.S. deficit. Although the term "dollar glut" has come into semiserious use, no one yet seems to have "explained" and dignified a chronic glut with any such ingenious theories as used to dominate the dollar-shortage discussion. Still, the two opposite worries do illustrate what, in another context, Professor Haberler has called the "Konjunkturgebundenheit" of much economic thinking[31]—the urge to read deep-seated, "structural" significance into the current state of economic affairs, whatever it may be.

Remedies for the Gold and Payments Problems

What should be done? At one extreme, the advice boiled down to: Nothing.[32] It is usually possible to find some signs of spontaneous change for the better. By early 1964, the impression was gaining ground in the United States that inflation was eating away any competitive advantage European producers might have enjoyed in world markets. From 1960 to 1963, wages had risen two or three times as much as productivity in manufacturing in the big European countries, whereas unit labor cost in manufacturing had if anything shown a slight decline in the United States.[33] While neither the relative position

of U.S. industry in world markets nor even the relative movement of export price indexes had yet shown a definite change in favor of the United States, underlying cost changes seemed to be working in these directions.

To put it bluntly, this line of thinking recommended that the United States cheer for inflation in Europe and Japan, hope foreign antiinflationary measures fail, and hope any foreign efforts take the form of fiscal tightness rather than of the monetary and interest-rate tightness that would tend to draw funds out of the United States. Note, for example, the following colloquy during a Joint Economic Committee hearing on November 14, 1963:

CHAIRMAN DOUGLAS. . . . We should encourage the Europeans to raise their prices. You have spoken of the cooperation of the European central banks in being so kind as to hold American dollars. I would say the greatest contribution would be to let their price level rise so that we could increase our exports. Instead of people being afraid of the European central banks, we ought to urge them to join in international cooperation as we have cooperated with them for many years.

SENATOR PROXMIRE. The answer to that, of course, is that they have been doing that in the last year. They had a substantial inflation, far more than ours, about four times more than ours.

CHAIRMAN DOUGLAS. Let them continue.[34]

Besides being passive and unneighborly, such thinking was a reminder of the inflationary bias of whatever remained of an international balancing mechanism in the contemporary world.

One strand in a related line of thinking actually recommended fiscal ease for the United States: greater domestic prosperity would result, bringing brighter profit prospects and higher interest rates and giving American capital greater inducement to stay at home rather than flow abroad. Some writers even judged that the capital account of the balance of payments would improve

---

[31] Gottfried von Haberler, *Prosperity and Depression,* London: Allen & Unwin, 1958, p. 471n. (Other examples are the "stagnation" doctrines of the 1930s and the more recent doctrines about an "age of inflation.")

[32] This, essentially, was what Salant and his associates advised in the government-commissioned Brookings report of 1963. Its authors' "best guess" was that the payments deficit would vanish of its own accord within a few years. They did recommend some reforms in the international monetary system, but not specifically as remedies for the U.S. deficit.

[33] "Are Cost Catching Up with Europe's Exports?" *Morgan Guaranty Survey,* March 1964, pp. 9-15, esp. p. 10.

[34] *The United States Balance of Payments, op. cit.,* Hearings, Part 3, Washington: Government Printing Office, 1963, p. 524.

enough to outweigh the tendency of higher incomes to promote larger imports.[35] Some such idea probably influenced some votes in favor of the tax cut enacted early in 1964 (along with the hope that reduced business taxes and growing consumer demand would promote investment in cost-cutting plant and equipment and so strengthen the competitive position of American products). The idea may not be patently fallacious, but it certainly does contain an element of wishful thinking.[36]

An opposite line of thinking has been made familiar by the many bankers, columnists, and conservative economists who welcome the "discipline of the balance of payments" and urge heeding it. In their view, the payments deficit results from a surplus of domestic monetary liquidity. Surplus liquidity slops over the country's boundaries, being spent, for example, on foreign securities. Putting the blame on specific types of transactions, say these observers, is like wanting to stop an overflow from a bathtub by building up "the low spots around the edge where the water is running over. The tub, they insist, will continue to overflow somewhere unless the faucet of monetary liquidity is turned off after the tub is full."[37]

Taking a rather different view of the implications for monetary-fiscal policy, a majority of the Joint Economic Committee found it intolerable that balance-of-payments deficits of the order of magnitude of $2 to $3 billion a year should, for an extended period of time, cause a $600 billion economy to pursue policies that aggravate serious domestic problems, particularly when the surplus countries are not adequately meeting their responsibilities in the adjustment process. So minute a tail must not be permitted to wag such a large dog. Monetary policies that lead to higher interest rates to restrain domestic inflation are one thing. But it is another thing to pursue such policies for a period of substantial duration solely to protect the balance of payments when unemployment is high, prices are relatively stable, and countries in balance-of-payments surplus not only fail to adjust with appropriate vigor, but continue to rely on policies which intensify the forces of disequilibrium.[38]

None of the above-mentioned views on financial policy for the balance of payments necessarily clashes with also welcoming miscellaneous expedients. We have already chronicled many examples of this approach—the "tying" of foreign aid, clamping down on overseas military spending, such discouragements to imports as the cut in the duty-free allowance on tourist purchases, schemes to promote exports and encourage visits by foreign tourists, the taxation of foreign bond issues, a tightened ban on American ownership of gold, pressures on foreign authorities both to get rid of their countries' payments surpluses and meanwhile to accept settlement in media other than gold, and the arm-twisting of American bankers and industrialists to obtain "voluntary" restraint on foreign lending and spending.

Such measures are questionable. Tying U.S. foreign aid somewhat reduces its usa-

---

[35] See, for example, the Brookings report (Salant and others), esp. pp. 21-23, and Paul M. McCracken in his and Emile Benoit's *The Balance of Payments and Domestic Prosperity,* Michigan International Business Studies, No. 1: Ann Arbor, Bureau of Business Research, University of Michigan, 1963, pp. 25-26.

Beryl W. Sprinkel apparently favored even money-supply as well as fiscal ease, expecting that after the initial impact, better economic growth would raise rather than lower interest rates and so help keep capital at home. See his "Relative Economic Growth Rates and Fiscal-Monetary Policies," *Journal of Political Economy,* LXXI, April 1963, pp. 154-159, and his testimony in *Recent Changes in Monetary Policy and Balance-of-Payments Problems* (Hearings before the House Banking and Currency Committee, July 1963), pp. 189 ff.

[36] Hendrik S. Houthakker, in *The United States Balance of Payments,* statements for the JEC, 1963), pp. 218-219, commented on what slender evidence supported this optimistic view and on how interwar American and postwar Japanese experience rather supported the usual view that domestic prosperity tends to weaken a country's balance of payments.

[37] McCracken in McCracken and Benoit, *op. cit.,* pp. 11-12. McCracken is of course summarizing, not endorsing, this view.

[38] *The United States Balance of Payments, Report,* March 1964, p. 10.

Professor Gottfried von Haberler, notably enough, expressed similar views about U.S. domestic policy in his presidential address to the American Economic Association. He blamed the recent slackness of employment and growth in the American economy on the balance-of-payments deficit, both directly and "indirectly via somewhat tighter monetary and fiscal policies than otherwise would be necessary. . . ." Without the deficit, "our economy would expand substantially. . . ." *American Economic Review,* March 1964, p. 13.

bility and so its real purchasing power and lends some plausibility, however unjustified, to hostile charges that the real purpose of American loans and grants is to shore up a shaky capitalist economy. Furthermore, it impairs the consistency with which the United States has traditionally championed multilateralism and nondiscrimination in international trade. This inconsistency is especially awkward at a time when the United States is pressing foreign countries to remove the remaining quotas, import licensing systems, and bilateral arrangements that they still (though to a much reduced extent) employ to restrict their citizens' imports from and spending in the United States. In deciding where to deploy its bases and troops and where to buy supplies to support them, the United States government lets essentially irrelevant balance-of-payments considerations get in the way of straightforwardly weighing dollar costs against defense and foreign-policy benefits. The United States puts pressure on foreign governments to take on bigger shares of the common defense and foreign-aid burdens not merely in the name of fairness but also on balance-of-payments grounds; it also asks them to order and pay in advance for American military goods, or to repay debt ahead of schedule, or to acquire special nonnegotiable bonds instead of gold. "Moreover, U.S. officials have to choke back their wrath at such things as de Gaulle's flirtation with Red China; France is already the biggest buyer of U.S. gold, and could mightily embarrass the U.S. by buying much more. 'You wouldn't want to insult the guy who holds the mortgage on your house, would you?' one official sighs."[39]

Professor Milton Friedman has incisively deplored the adoption of

one expedient after another, borrowing here, making swap arrangements there, changing the form of loans to make the figures look good. Entirely aside from the ineffectiveness of most of these measures, they are politically degrading and demeaning. We are a great and wealthy Nation. We should be directing our own course, setting an example to the world, living up to our

destiny. Instead, we send our officials hat in hand to make the rounds of foreign governments and central banks; we put foreign central banks in a position to determine whether or not we can meet our obligations and thus enable them to exert great influence on our policies; we are driven to niggling negotiations with Hong Kong and with Japan and for all I know, Monaco, to get them to limit voluntarily their exports. Is this posture suitable for the leader of the free world?[40]

On more strictly economic grounds, *ad hoc* expedients are objectionable because they are selective and so tend to distort international trade out of line with comparative advantage. They tend—subject to the same familiar qualifications—to impair efficiency just as protective tariffs do. (Protectionists have not hesitated to add the balance-of-payments problem to their repertoire of arguments and to latch onto the prestige that the government's examples add to their own recommendations.) Perhaps the most obvious of the higher costs appear in buying military and foreign-aid goods in the United States even when they could be bought more cheaply abroad. Effectively paying higher interest rates to foreigners than to domestic savers also involves a cost to the country in real goods and services. Incurring special costs of export promotion are open to the same sorts of objections as export subsidies generally are. Nonselective measures of adjustment, in contrast, would work by way of either the general price level or the exchange rate.[41] Few observers recommend painful outright deflation for the United States, but some do recommend devaluation of the dollar (assuming foreign countries would agree not to frustrate this step by equiproportionate devaluations against gold of their own).

Objections of the sorts raised against the selective measures already mentioned would apply even more strongly to outright, avowed controls over trade and payments.[42] Some of

---

[39] *Wall Street Journal*, March 20, 1964, pp. 1, 22.

[40] *The United States Balance of Payments*, Hearings before the Joint Economic Committee, Part 3, November 1963, pp. 458-459.

[41] Cf. Schmidt, *op. cit.*, esp. pp. 75-77.

[42] ". . . if the U.S. deficit is not sharply reduced soon," Professor James W. Angell, for example, recommends controls over capital exports, together with what-

them—restrictions on foreign travel, for example—could even tend to impair personal freedom. Might not such a cure be worse than the disease? If worst came to worst, might it not be a lesser evil simply to let the deficit continue until it exhausted the U.S. gold stock? Meanwhile, we could have finished repealing the domestic gold reserve requirement.

Would that outcome really be a calamity? On the contrary, wouldn't we Americans be acquiring useful goods and services in exchange for our stockpile of an industrially rather unimportant metal? Wouldn't we benefit from unloading gold onto unwary foreigners at its current price, a price kept artificially high so far by governmental demands for gold as a monetary reserve? Would the American economy really collapse if the link between money and gold were cut? On the contrary, wouldn't freedom from

that troublesome link simplify the job of monetary management?

The usual answer to such questions warns against knocking out the key pin of the existing international monetary system. ". . . international trade and lending could just about halt, toppling many nations, and perhaps the whole Free World, into depression."[43] American prestige would supposedly suffer.

Whatever the correct view on these questions may be, it is true that the conditions of the U.S. balance of payments and of the international monetary system are linked together. Even if the U.S. deficit somehow vanished of its own accord or were cured in some acceptable way but no deeper reform accompanied this change, problems would remain. The largest postwar source of growth in the "international liquidity" of foreign countries would have been cut off.

At this point, the problem of the U.S. deficit blends in with the more general issue of world monetary reform. The last two chapters will examine this issue.

---

ever "exchange control over all purchases abroad by Americans" may be necessary to make the capital controls effective. *The United States Balance of Payments* (statements submitted to the Joint Economic Committee, November 1963), p. 33.

[43] *Wall Street Journal*, March 20, 1964, p. 1.

❧ Appendix to Chapter 25: The Dollar Shortage

An Assortment of Ideas

The balance-of-payments troubles of many countries for several years after World War II suggested the diagnosis of a "dollar shortage" that, with hindsight, could be traced back several decades. Most of the world outside North America supposedly suffered from a persistent or recurrent tendency to spend more than it earned (or borrowed at long term) in dealing with North America. Its reserves of gold and dollars seemed in continual danger of running out unless protected by direct controls over international trade and payments and by resort to loans or grants from the United States or from American-financed international agencies.

Writings on the dollar shortage kept piling up even in the late 1950s, years after the gold and dollar reserves of foreign countries as a whole had begun a sustained rise, years after the external position of the United States had actually shifted from surplus to slight deficit, and right up to the time when the fashion shifted toward worry about an American *deficit* and a dollar *glut*.[1] If the whole discussion now seems hopelessly dated, this very fact suggests an object lesson worth emphasizing. Fashionable and excessively ingenious theories that read deep-seated significance into temporary conditions do not deserve quiet oblivion as soon as brute facts crush them; they should be remembered to permit recognizing their counterparts in the future. Continuity is of value in scientific disputes.

No amount of chronicling the balance-of-payments troubles of particular countries could illuminate the dollar shortage unless these troubles could be shown to share common characteristics and causes. Rather than a thing or a series of historical events, the dollar shortage was a theoretical concept. It was the idea of a long-term imbalance in international payments stemming not from remediable errors of policy but from deep-seated objective circumstances. Kindleberger, for example, spoke of tendencies rooted in "climate, geography, causes of war, the growth of productivity and consumption, the distribution of income, etc."[2]

More nearly specific explanations were legion: a secular tendency for a greater degree of economic stagnation or lesser degree of inflation in the United States than elsewhere (Kindleberger, Bollier, de Vries); low elasticities of demand and supply in international trade (Balogh, Harrod); a great shrinkage of international liquidity relative to international trade because of the failure of the price of gold to rise in step with the prices of other things (Harrod); America's great size and strength, leading to greater dependence of the rest of the world on the United States than conversely (Williams, the London *Economist,* Crowther); various kinds of "deep-seated structural changes in the world economy" (Zupnick, who, with particular reference to British problems, mentions among other things American dominance in the world petroleum industry, increasing industrialization in the overseas Sterling Area, and Britain's failure to adapt basic changes in the world's economic structure); an international demonstration effect prodding foreigners to live beyond their means in an attempt to imitate the American standard of living (Kindleberger);

---

[1] For surveys of the literature in the late 1950s, see Charles P. Kindleberger, "The Dollar Shortage Re-Revisited," *American Economic Review,* XLVIII, June 1958, pp. 388-395, and Raymond F. Mikesell's refreshingly iconoclastic note on "Dollar Shortage: A Modern Myth," *Journal of Political Economy,* LXVII, June 1959, pp. 307-309.

[2] Charles P. Kindleberger, *The Dollar Shortage,* New York: The Technology Press of MIT and John Wiley & Sons, Inc., 1950, pp. 170-171.

a more rapid pace of innovation of productivity growth in the United States than elsewhere or in some sectors of the American economy than in others (Hicks, Balogh, de Vries, Croome, Williams, Crowther); or asymmetry in trade adjustments because the United States specializes in research-intensive commodities and the rest of the world in traditional commodities (Hoffmeyer).[3]

Wary of sweeping insights, at least one writer scrutinized the American balance of payments item by item and projected the probable future size of each item under various assumptions. His method is epitomized by his observation, in discussing U.S. raw-material imports, that successful efforts were being made to reduce the use of tin in tin cans.[4] He concluded that structural developments were likely to keep

the foreign demand for American goods growing more strongly than the American demand for foreign goods; only under improbably optimistic assumptions would a long-term dollar problem fail to persist. This approach is reminiscent of W. Stanley Jevons's fears, in the last century, of impending shortages of coal and paper.[5] Once one has become convinced that a shortage of something or other is or is not likely, diligent study and thought can produce almost innumerable "considerations" in support of that opinion.

Some of the arguments contradicted each other. The argument about America's superior dynamism in innovation and productivity ran counter to the one about America's greater tendency towards economic stagnation. Emphasis on the ability of efficient American producers to undersell foreigners almost all across the board ran counter to the supposition of low price elasticities of demand in international trade. The apparent contradictions might have been reconciled somehow, but this was not really necessary. The notion of dollar shortage actually thrived on the many kinds of supporting considerations, even mutually contradictory ones, that kept coming forth. "Dollar shortage" was a label that lumped together a vaguely defined *range* of conditions or developments that might lessen countries' gains from international trade, or that might impose awkward internal economic readjustments, or that might tend to create balance-of-payments deficits, or that might hamper adjustment mechanisms. The rise of a dollar-shortage fad—a fashionable topic for books, articles, and doctoral dissertations—gave economists a positive incentive to devise new products marketable under that label and to devise new "explanations" for the range of problems it so vaguely suggested. The billowing academic smoke strengthened belief in a real-world fire.

Growth of Productivity

A particularly influential line of argument emphasized differential rates of growth in productivity. Even within this line, contradictions abounded. Harrod worried about especially rapid productivity growth in the export sectors of the more progressive economy, Hicks about

[3] The references are to Kindleberger, *Dollar Shortage,* esp. pp. 170, 181; René D. Bollier, *Die These einer chronischen Dollarknappheit,* Zurich: Polygraphischer Verlag, 1956; T. de Vries, "De theorie van het comparatieve voordeel en het dollartekort," *De Economist,* vol. 104, Jan. 1956, pp. 1-39; T. Balogh, *The Dollar Crisis,* Oxford: Basil Blackwell, 1949, esp. pp. 229, 8-9; Roy F. Harrod, "Imbalance of International Payments," IMF *Staff Papers,* III, April 1953, pp. 1-46; John H. Williams, *Economic Stability in the Modern World,* Stamp Memorial Lecture, London: Athlone Press, 1952; *The Economist,* Vol. 145, 4 December 1943, pp. 750-751; Geoffrey Crowther, *Balances and Imbalances of Payments,* Boston: Harvard University, Graduate School of Business Administration, 1957, esp. p. 48; Elliot Zupnick, *Britain's Postwar Dollar Problem,* New York: Columbia University Press, 1957, esp. pp. 183, 226; J. R. Hicks, "An Inaugural Lecture," *Oxford Economic Papers,* n.s. V, June 1953, pp. 117-135; Honor Croome, "The Dollar Siege," *Lloyds Bank Review,* July 1950, pp. 30, 37, quoted in Zupnick, *op. cit.,* pp. 206-207; Erik Hoffmeyer, *Dollar Shortage and the Structure of U.S. Foreign Trade,* Copenhagen: Ejnar Munksgaard; Amsterdam: North-Holland Publishing Co., 1958.

R. F. Harrod's participation in the discussion is interesting because of his earlier much-quoted remarks that "dollar famine" is "one of the most absurd phrases ever coined" and that the "allegation of a 'world dollar shortage' is surely one of the most brazen pieces of collective effrontery that has ever been uttered." *Are These Hardships Necessary?,* 2nd ed., London: Rupert Hart-Davis, 1947, pp. 42-43. Hoffmeyer, *op. cit.,* pp. 27, 38-39, refers to Harrod's "conversion" to belief in the dollar shortage.

[4] Donald MacDougall, *The World Dollar Problem,* London: Macmillan, 1957, p. 193 and footnote. Similarly, Hoffmeyer, to bolster his thesis about the special research intensity of American production, provided historical-statistical surveys of various categories of U.S. foreign trade—wool, sugar, shipping, newsprint, copper, oil, and business machines. He also reviewed developments in trade policy. This sort of thing gave an unwarranted air of specificity and empiricism to the idea of dollar shortage.

[5] Cf. John Maynard Keynes, *Essays and Sketches in Biography,* New York: Meridian Books, 1956, pp. 128-133.

productivity growth concentrated in import-competing sectors, Balogh about random increases in productivity, and Williams even about uniform productivity growth in the more progressive economy.[6] Whether or not wage levels rose in step with productivity also entered the discussion. If productivity kept growing in the United States faster than abroad and faster than American wage levels, then the American price level would fall, tending to stimulate exports relative to imports. Foreigners would have import surpluses unless they endured deflation or unless the dollar were allowed to appreciate on the exchanges. The foreigners would probably share in America's increased productivity by way of improved terms of trade. This outcome could occur without major changes in exchange rates or foreign price levels if American wage levels did rise along with productivity in such a way that the price level held roughly steady.

J. R. Hicks took a dimmer view. His "Inaugural Lecture"[7] had a remarkable influence in keeping the whole discussion respectable and topical. He saw American productivity growing more rapidly in import-competing industries than in export industries. To hold their American markets, foreigners would have to accept ever lower prices while enjoying only slightly cheapened American exports. If foreigners resisted the necessary decline in their terms of trade and their real incomes, as by delaying devaluation relative to the dollar, balance-of-payments equilibrium would develop.

A stronger argument, perhaps, pointed to constant American dynamism not only in cutting the real-input production cost of existing products but also in developing improved products or entirely new products not soon available from other sources. In both ways the pattern of comparative advantage kept changing. Foreign countries might have a comparative advantage in certain industries one year, a comparative disadvantage the next. The smaller and poorer countries, with their industries continually becoming obsolete, kept on having to retreat into specialization in less and less advantageous lines of production. American dynamism set a killing pace of adjustment. Painful adjustments would be undertaken only under the pressure of actual balance-of-payments deficits; and even so, the foreign economies might not succeed in

adjusting fast enough. Adaptations were likely to be obsolete even before they could be completed.[8]

The differential-productivity-growth arguments were open to questions of fact[9] and also of analysis. The various hypothesized patterns of productivity growth would not necessarily, without further assumptions, intensify foreign eagerness to trade relative to American eagerness. And even if this result did occur and did, rather implausibly, tend to shrink foreigners' gain from trade with the United States, this still would not be the same thing as turning their gain into actual loss. As for continual American development of new and improved products not available elsewhere, one wonders why the job only the American machine could do had to be done. If foreigners would buy American goods at whatever cost, something was peculiar and in need of explanation about their overall propensity to spend, and not merely about their propensity to import.[10] If the pessimistic theories were correct, incidentally, why were the less dynamic regions of the United States not suffering from a conspicuous dollar shortage in their trade with the more dynamic regions?

These questions fail, however, to press the main objection. Much ingenuity went to waste demonstrating possibilities no one ever doubted: *of course* changes in wants, resources, and technology can shift the pattern of comparative advantage and reciprocal demand to the benefit of some countries and the harm of others. (Most obviously, one country could suffer from new and cheaper competing supplies of the things it exports and from new and intensified competing demands for the things it imports.) What remained to be shown was that such changes had decisively characterized the decades of dollar shortage and were fated to keep on doing so in the future. It especially remained to be shown—depending on just what the dollar-shortage thesis was, anyway—either that these changes unavoidably caused intractable external

---

[6] See Zupnick, *op. cit.*, p. 208.

[7] *Oxford Economic Papers*, June 1953. Cf. the discussion in de Vries, *op. cit.*, pp. 11-14.

[8] This paragraph combines points raised in Balogh, *op. cit.*, pp. 8-9; Croome, *loc. cit.*, Dennis H. Robertson, *Britain in the World Economy*, London: Allen & Unwin, 1954, and de Vries, *op. cit.*, esp. pp. 15-16, 23-24, 28-30, 32.

[9] Cf. J. Kymmell, "Het dollar probleem; duurzame realiteit of tijdelijk fenomeen?," *Economisch-Statistische Berichten*, **XLI**, March 14, 1956, esp. pp. 216-217; and J. M. Letiche, "Differential Rates of Productivity Growth and International Imbalance," *Quarterly Journal of Economics*, **LXIX**, August 1955, pp. 371-401.

[10] Kindleberger, *American Economic Review*, June 1958, p. 393.

deficits or else that their harmful effects could largely be avoided by controls to replace market adjustment mechanisms.

Adjustment Mechanisms: The Crucial Question

Here was another fundamental ambiguity in the dollar-shortage thesis. Did it contend that no "automatic" market processes *could* work to equilibrate balances of payments? Or that reliance on controls was preferable? Or that political realities made acceptance of market processes unlikely? Apart from terminology, there would have been nothing basically new or particularly disturbing in either of the two latter contentions. What was disturbing was the denial, on the first interpretation, of the theory of self-regulation of the balance of payments by way of changes in incomes, prices, and exchange rates. What, exactly, was wrong with standard economics?

Ridicule was one way of dismissing this question. Kindleberger found wrong exchange rates responsible for disequilibrium only in the sense that "there is never a shortage of anything, but merely wrong pricing." Eisenhower's troops in World War II never ran short of ammunition; "the price was merely too low."[11] Vagueness supplemented quips. Standard analysis was called static, while reality is dynamic.[12]

A matter of sheer public relations handicapped the traditional analysis. Any simple explanation of dollar shortage seemed *too* simple. See how many laws and regulations had been promulgated to deal with it, how many crises experienced, how many international conferences held, and how many loans arranged. See how many books and articles had appeared with complex and impressive theorizing, massive statistical tabulations, learned historical surveys, and detailed technological investigations (penetrating even to the fabrication of tin cans). Criticism emphasizing adjustment mechanisms was damned for its simplicity—for its very merit of abstracting the relevant main truths from the incidental details. It was orthodox or classical, furthermore, and thus behind the times practi-

cally by definition.[13] Finally, disparagement of orthodox analysis had the same sort of strength as the positive case for dollar shortage: it had so many strands to it, even vague and mutually contradictory strands, that it could hardly be pinned down.

If what the dollar-shortage theorists had in mind was the *disadvantages* of automatic adjustment mechanisms, their saying so openly would have helped bring their opinions into relation with the existing literature on the issue.[14]

Some of the dollar-shortage literature did explicitly acknowledge the central question of whether "automatic" equilibrating tendencies could work. The answer often implied was "no." One writer saw the problem as primarily the result not of "wilful policies" but rather of "basic forces which have transformed the nature of the world economy . . . and precluded adequate adjustment. . . ."[15] On another page, however, he defined a dollar shortage as existing when more dollars were demanded than supplied "at an acceptable level of employment, real income, and import restrictions. . . ." The key word was "acceptable," whose imprecision was frankly recognized by the remark that an acceptable level of real income is one below which "tensions" would "threaten the stability of the social and political equilibria." This minimum acceptable level of income might be ascertained in a general way by knowing "a country's history, customs, traditions, and institutions. . . ." The problem of dollar shortage was "one of restoring equilibrium without in-

---

[11] Kindleberger, *Dollar Shortage*, pp. 175-176.

[12] E.g., Balogh, *op. cit.*, p. 229; Balogh, "The Dollar Shortage Once More; a Reply," *Scottish Journal of Political Economy*, II, June 1955, p. 151; Williams, *op. cit.*, pp. 13-14.

As Machlup and Samuelson have noted, the term "static" often is little more than an epithet to disparage other people's theories while describing one's own, and the world they supposedly refer to, as "dynamic."

[13] De Vries, *op. cit.*, pp. 1-2, implies that refusal to take the dollar shortage seriously is reminiscent of the classical economists' insistence on Say's Law and refusal to worry about depressions and unemployment.

[14] De Vries, whose dollar-shortage argument is one of the most nearly plausible known to me, recognized that fluctuating exchange rates might perhaps be a solution. He dismissed this possibility, however, as too complex a topic for the scope of his paper. *Op. cit.*, pp. 30, 39.

[15] Zupnick, *op. cit.*, p. 226. Similar passages occur in Williams, *op. cit.*, p. 7, and Crowther, *op. cit.*, p. 52. Crowther thinks (p. 50) that exchange-rate adjustments, no matter how large, might not provide equilibrium; even a 50 percent devaluation of the pound would not balance Britain's international payments. Similarly, but in a more general context, Seymour E. Harris, *International and Interregional Economics*, New York: McGraw-Hill, 1957, p. 440, insists on the possibility "that at *no* value of a currency will there be equilibrium. . . ."

Perhaps the denial of equilibrating processes stems from a vague idea that equilibrium is a Good Thing by definition, coupled with the judgment that reliance on market processes would be a Bad Thing in the modern world. Cf. F. Machlup, "Equilibrium and Disequilibrium: Misplaced Concreteness and Disguised Politics," *Economic Journal*, LXVIII, March 1958, esp. pp. 13-14.

ducing an intolerable decline in the levels of
real income and employment."[16]—Such statements slide from a denial of market adjustment
mechanisms to a judgment that their operation would be intolerable.

Policy Arguments

Other writers frankly accepted the latter interpretation. Thomas Balogh, for instance, emphatically recognized that equilibrium in international payments could easily be achieved
without controls. He predicted the consequences:
worsened terms of trade, diminished real income,
worsened maldistribution of income in the
poorer countries, worsened prospects for a decrease in international inequality, a need for
periodic further readjustments by the poorer
countries, and probably even "mass unemployment and starvation."[17] Unfortunately, the fact
that a country's trading opportunities have
changed adversely does not necessarily mean
that controls and tariffs could do much about
it. What if the country lacks any great monopoly-
monopsony power on the world market? If
anything, the thesis about the overpowering
economic strength of the United States and
about how one-sidedly the rest of the world depended on trade with it suggested little opportunity for the rest of the world to twist the
terms of trade in its favor. The two strands of
argument do not mesh well.

By now the implication is out in the open
that the dollar-shortage thesis sometimes served
as a vehicle for policy arguments. Balogh developed a sizable list of arguments against free or
freer trade. Crowther predicted, and quite apparently recommended, that in the future trade
between the dollar world and the sterling-EPU
world would be balanced only "by the brute
force of control and restriction." Williams found
the world more than ever "in need of close cooperation looking toward the conscious development of an integrated pattern of trade. . . ."
Hoffmeyer pleaded for a more liberal U.S.
import policy. Zupnick listed numerous recommendations, including measures to modify the
structure of the British economy, the screening
of British capital exports to the overseas sterling
area as well as to the outside world, a rise in
the dollar price of gold, cuts in American tariffs,
continued temporary toleration by the United

States of currency inconvertibility and of discrimination against itself, and continuance of
U.S. foreign aid. On this last point, the dollar-
shortage thesis did often seem to convey tacit
approval of international imbalance so far as it
meant that the rest of the world was obtaining
more goods and services from the United States
than it sent in return. This would be a sophisticated variant of the view that balance-of-payments difficulties are in themselves an argument
for American aid. As the main conclusion of his
Dollar Crisis, Balogh frankly called for "the
international development of the poorer, financed
out of *free* contributions of the richer, countries. . . ." De Vries argued that convertibility
of European currencies would probably have
to be supported for a few years by American
military grants and special dollar expenditures
in Europe.[18]

One could reject the dollar-shortage thesis, of
course, and still agree with some recommendations made in its name. The most forthright
and ultimately most persuasive way of stating
the case for aid, for example, would seem to be
to show that the recipients are poor and deserving.

Confusion of Value Judgments
and Positive Analysis

Despite occasional openness about policy preferences, the entire texture of the dollar-shortage
discussion made these preferences appear to
have been imposed by inexorable developments
that had destroyed or seriously impaired the
traditional adjustment mechanisms. Normative
judgments and policy proposals thus took on
the prestige of positive propositions of fact and
logic.

If a writer purporting to analyze dollar shortage really meant that many foreign countries
were so desperately poor as to have an understandable and forgivable tendency to try to live
beyond their means; or if he was comparing
the relative merits of rival balance-of-payments
adjustment mechanisms; or if he thought he
had found some crucial flaw in the traditional
analysis of those mechanisms; or if he had in
mind some political or other reason why no
otherwise-workable mechanism would be toler-

---

[16] Zupnick, *op. cit.,* pp. 3-6.

[17] Balogh, *Scottish Journal of Political Economy,* June
1955, p. 154; *Dollar Crisis,* p. 136; "The Dollar Crisis
Revisited," *Oxford Economic Papers,* **VI,** September 1954,
pp. 276-277.

[18] See the following works already cited: Balogh,
Scottish Journal of Political Economy, June 1955, pp.
153-154; Crowther, p. 35; Williams, p. 33 (and cf. p. 26
for musings about a fundamental reshaping of British
production and trade); Hoffmeyer, p. 206; Zupnick,
pp. 227-232; Balogh, *Dollar Crisis,* pp. xxxiv-xxxv and
chap. 6; de Vries, p. 39.

ated; or if he was calling for tariffs and other trade controls to improve terms of trade, safeguard home employment, affect income distribution, foster infant industries, or promote economic diversification and so reduce vulnerability to changes in world markets; or if he was discussing some other familiar matter, he should have said so openly. Unnecessary new terminology appearing to deal with a new and distinct topic only interferes with bringing to bear on a topic any analyses and arguments that are already familiar. If these precautions had been taken in the first place, the dollar shortage would never have seemed to be a distinct reality requiring explanation by distinct and novel theories.

Existing Arrangements for International Liquidity

ᕲᕿ 26

The Gold-exchange Standard

The existing international monetary system has grown up haphazardly. Countries tie their currencies to gold or to the dollar, which is in turn tied to gold. In their official external reserves, a few countries hold gold almost exclusively; but many hold key currencies—sterling or dollars—in addition to or even almost entirely instead of gold. For this reason the system is commonly called a "gold-exchange standard."

Its defects have long been clear both from theoretical analysis and from historical experience, especially in the late 1920s and early 1930s. But only recently, and especially since about 1958, have events again forced widespread attention to these defects. These events have been recurring balance-of-payments and foreign-exchange crises, the swollen deficits of the United States in particular, and the heightened mobility of short-term funds among countries with externally convertible currencies.

Not all observers emphasize the same defects and not all insist on more than minor remedies, but a remarkable consensus has arisen that *something* is wrong and that *something* should be done. Several of the proposed reforms are compatible with one another, and some are likely to be adopted partially and in piecemeal fashion over the next few years. These partial reforms will draw still closer attention to the overall problem and to diagnoses indicating a need for more sweeping reforms. The really radical proposals will take time to become practical politics; they are unlikely either to be adopted or to be conclusively dismissed from con-

sideration over the next few years. International monetary reorganization will remain a live issue for years to come.

One much-mentioned feature of the system since the return to convertibility is the mobility of short-term funds in response to interest-rate differentials among financial centers and to changing opinions about the strength or weakness of currencies.[1] In some ways and under some conditions, unhampered international movements of short-term funds are a healthy thing: they can lubricate the international flow of goods, services, and long-term capital and accomplish the currency and interest arbitrage and the stabilizing

---

[1] See the observations in *International Payments Imbalances and Need for Strengthening International Financial Arrangements,* Hearings of May and June 1961 and papers contributed to the Subcommittee on International Exchange and Payments of the Joint Economic Committee; Washington: U.S. Government Printing Office, 1961, by Douglas Dillon, p. 28; Walter W. Heller, pp. 46-47, 53; David Rockefeller, p. 138; Harry G. Johnson, p. 173; Peter B. Kenen, pp. 179-180; Emile Despres, p. 280; and Charles P. Kindleberger, p. 284. (*International Payments Imbalances* . . . is hereafter cited as "1961 Hearings," and the Subcommittee's Report of the same title is hereafter cited as "1961 Subcommittee Report.")

For more recent and generally more skeptical studies of the influence of interest rates on capital flows, see Philip W. Bell, "Private Capital Movements and the U.S. Balance-of-Payments Position," in *Factors Affecting the United States Balance of Payments,* studies compiled for the Subcommittee on International Exchange and Payments of the Joint Economic Committee; Washington: Government Printing Office, 1962, pp. 395-481; Peter B. Kenen, "Short-Term Capital Movements and the U.S. Balance of Payments," and Benjamin J. Cohen, "A Survey of Capital Movements and Findings Regarding Their Interest Sensitivity," the latter two studies both in *The United States Balance of Payments,* Part 1, "Current Problems and Policies," Hearings before the Joint Economic Committee, July 1963, Washington: Government Printing Office, 1963, pp. 153-191 and 192-208.

speculation necessary for efficient spot and forward foreign-exchange markets. But on the other hand, they can be the vehicle for destabilizing speculation and can sometimes make countries pursue different monetary and credit policies than domestic conditions call for. With no "automatic" mechanism balancing international transactions on current and long-term-capital account, changing assessments of the soundness of different currencies have wide scope.

Triffin's Diagnosis

Professor Robert Triffin has vigorously publicized one notable "absurdity"[2] of existing arrangements. As world income and trade continue to grow, countries will need more and more reserves to finance temporary deficits in their balances of payments. The worry is not that this liquidity has already become unduly scarce, or even that liquidity requirements are sure to grow in full proportion to trade,[3] but that the need will continue to grow in the future and that the sources which have met it in the past will become increasingly unsatisfactory as time goes on. Experience punctures any hope that gold production alone can fully meet the need (assuming no price-level deflation and no repeated increases in the price of gold).

---

[2] Triffin, *Gold and the Dollar Crisis*, New Haven: Yale University Press, 1960, p. 67. Triffin offers his diagnosis and remedy in this book and in numerous articles and Congressional hearings, including the 1961 Hearings, pp. 300-311.

[3] The analogy between "needed" sizes of world reserves of gold and foreign exchange and a country's domestic money supply is faulty because while the latter serves as the everyday medium of exchange, the former serve only to fill in gaps between ordinary supply and demand on the foreign-exchange market at pegged rates. How large these gaps are depends on many circumstances, especially on how effective a mechanism for balancing international payments is in operation. Some reasons for expecting imbalances and the need for reserves to grow even in relation to the volume of trade, under likely policies, are listed in Walter S. Salant and others, *The United States Balance of Payments in 1968*, Washington: Brookings Institution, 1963, pp. 236-238 of the Joint Economic Committee print, and in J. M. Culbertson, "U.S. Policy and the International Financial System," in *Recent Changes in Monetary Policy and Balance-of-Payments Problems*, Hearings before the House Banking and Currency Committee, July 1963, Washington: Government Printing Office, 1963, p. 346.

For decades, many countries have been "economizing" on gold by also holding sterling or dollars as reserves. Since World War II, only a small fraction of the growth of gold and foreign-exchange holdings (whether official holdings or official and private holdings combined) has come from current gold production in Western countries. A still smaller fraction has come from Soviet gold sales. The major part has taken the form of liquid claims on the United States. Of the total increase between the ends of 1949 and 1963 in official gold and foreign-exchange holdings of all countries for which the International Monetary Fund has figures, only one-third took the form of gold. For all countries other than the United States, the part of the total increase in official reserves over this same period that consisted of gold other than gold lost from U.S. reserves amounted to only 19 percent. In 1958 and 1959, all but 8 percent of the growth came from net U.S. reserve losses.[4]

"Key currency reserves increase or decrease in supply, depending on whether the key currency countries happen to be running balance-of-payments deficits or surpluses and quite independently of the growth in need or demand for international liquidity."[5] Such a system hardly provides a safe basis for expanding the supply of reserves to accommodate a growing world economy. Over the long run, the key-currency countries must have deficits to expand the reserves of other countries. Yet the key-currency countries thereby incur ever larger liquid liabilities to foreigners; as a percentage of these liabilities, and perhaps in absolute amount also, their gold reserves become smaller and smaller. While there simply is not enough gold for all countries to hold their international reserves in gold alone, the monetary authority of any individual country, acting by itself, is free to hold as much of its reserve in gold as it wishes. The only real incentive (apart from international cooperation and the like) for holding

---

[4] Computed from *International Financial Statistics, Supplement to 1963/64 Issues*, pp. iv, v, and June 1964 issue, pp. 16-17, except that the last percentage cited is from Triffin in 1961 Hearings, p. 301.

[5] Tibor Scitovsky in 1961 Hearings, p. 176.

some or most of the reserve in key currency instead is its convenience and interest yield. Precisely because of its reasons for holding any international reserves in the first place and because of its own sophistication, a national monetary authority will actively consider getting rid of a key currency whose gold parity seems shaky. If more key currencies than one serve as international reserves, the rush may be from the weaker to the stronger. If the threatened key currency has no rivals, the rush will be into gold. ". . . the gold-exchange standard . . . is a fair weather standard, which tends to break down and has in the past repeatedly broken down as soon as confidence in a key currency is shaken."[6] The 1931 monetary collapse shows how history might some day repeat itself.

In summary, Triffin and his followers find that under existing arrangements, long-run balance-of-payments deficits of key-currency countries are both necessary yet alarming. This haphazard system becomes more and more precarious as time goes on.

A Conservative Diagnosis

It is remarkable how similar an analysis has been put forth even by conservative commentators who are presumably shocked at the type of reform that Triffin proposes. Probably the most prominent member of this school is Jacques Rueff, General de Gaulle's architect of French economic and monetary stabilization. He sees the present system repeating the gold-economizing practices adopted during the 1920s partly under the inspiration of the Genoa Conference of 1922. Countries acquiring sterling or dollars through current-account surpluses or returns of flight capital did not demand their full redemption in gold, as they would have done under a genuine gold standard. They left the funds on deposit in the countries of origin; the international monetary system became a "childish game" in which the winners returned their marbles to the losers; the key-currency countries learned "the marvelous secret of the

deficit without tears."[7] Balance-of-payments adjustment ceased being quasi-automatic and came to depend on *ad hoc* measures of credit or trade-control policy. Growing claims of surplus countries on deficit countries could serve as a basis for credit expansion in the former without imposing contraction on the latter. Imbalances in trade or even capital movements (such as repatriation of capital that had previously taken flight) could therefore promote inflation in some countries without promoting deflation in others. But this duplication of the credit pyramid on a relatively narrow gold base cannot go on indefinitely. The house of cards gets shakier and shakier and eventually collapses, as in 1929–1931. Essentially the same danger exists nowadays. It has developed not because the United States has lost so much gold since 1950 but because it has lost so *little*, unduly postponing correction. The existing system "is the product of a prodigious collective error"; it "will go down in history as cause for stupefaction and scandal." It will end in crisis and panic unless it is deliberately and carefully dismantled. Deep study and discussion are needed.[8]

Some Grounds for Optimism

One prominent dissenter from this pessimism was Per Jacobsson, late Managing Director of the International Monetary Fund. For the following reasons, he thought the currency breakdowns of the early 1930s were unlikely to recur: (1) Widespread deflation

---

[6] *Ibid.*

[7] One might add that by acquiring bank accounts, government securities, and similar liquid claims on a relatively rich key-currency country, relatively poor foreign countries grant free or cheap loans to that country and thus move capital in the perverse direction.

[8] "The West Is Risking A Credit Collapse," *Fortune*, LXIV, July 1961, pp. 126-127, 262, 267-268. A very similar article by Rueff, "Gold Exchange Standard a Danger to the West," is reprinted in Herbert G. Grubel, ed., *World Monetary Reform*, Stanford: Stanford University Press, 1963, pp. 320-328. Professor Michael A. Heilperin of the Graduate Institute of International Studies in Geneva gives a similar conservative analysis in "Monetary Reform in an Atlantic Setting," in 1961 Hearings, pp. 331-340, and in "The Case for Going Back to Gold," reprinted in the Grubel volume, pp. 329-342.

caused currency failures then; nowadays, monetary authorities know how to prevent deflation and would do so. (2) Many European countries had then acquired much of their exchange reserves by large-scale short-term borrowing; nowadays, most countries are the true owners of their reserves. (3) Nothing like the International Monetary Fund then existed.[9] The first point calls for noting that the currency failures of the early 1930s were not simply *caused by* deflation. The two troubles interacted with and intensified each other; unsatisfactory monetary systems, along with other things, predisposed the world economy to deflation. Nowadays, a collapse of currencies is less likely to bring on intensified deflation than widespread controls and devaluations. But the fact that a collapse of the system would be less disastrous now than before does not disprove the analysis of its weakness. As for the second point, reserve arrangements then and now differ more in detail and degree than in fundamentals; a pyramiding of currencies onto a narrow gold base is the feature common to both sets of arrangements. Gold, the "first-class international money," becomes scarcer over time in relation to the "second-class" moneys that eke out its inadequate supplies.[10] As for the International Monetary Fund, it patches up some cracks in the system—it serves, in Heilperin's words, as "a sort of first-aid station for temporarily disabled currencies"— but hardly changes the system's basic nature.

Pyramiding and "Eurodollars".

Without being alarmist or implying that the rise of "Eurodollars" is on balance an unhealthy development, we may view this phenomenon as an example of certain features and tendencies of the existing gold-exchange standard. It is also fascinating in its own right.[11] Though by no means new, it has become important since the establishment of convertibility in 1958.

The term *Eurodollars* is hard to define because it so often serves as a loose label for a wide range of operations rather than as the name of a specific type of asset or liability. The general tone of writings on the subject suggests defining *Eurodollars,* in the strictest sense, as short-term deposits held with British or Continental banks but expressed in dollars instead of the local currency.[12] Actually, banks headquartered in Canada, Japan, and other countries have also been accepting deposits denominated in U.S. dollars; and deposits denominated in sterling, marks, lire, Swiss francs, and guilders are accepted by some banks outside the country where each of these currencies circulates. Still, "Eurodollar"—or "Eurocurrency"—remains the usual term for operations of this sort.

---

[9] *International Financial News Survey,* September 29, 1961, particularly p. 301.

[10] The troubles of having two or more classes of international money have been much emphasized by J. M. Culbertson; see his article cited in footnote 3. This concept will prove crucial in appraising several proposed reforms.

[11] Facts and some of the analysis for the interpretation given here, though not the full interpretation itself, come from Alan R. Holmes and Fred H. Klopstock, "The Market for Dollar Deposits in Europe," Federal Reserve Bank of New York, *Monthly Review,* XLII, November 1960, pp. 197-202; Bank for International Settlements, 31st *Annual Report* (1960–1961), p. 138; the special West European correspondent of the *Eastern Economist,* New Delhi, "Euro-Dollars Versus Triffin," XXXVII, 21 July 1961, pp. 111-112; Paul Einzig, "Statics and Dynamics of the Euro-dollar Market," *Economic Journal,* LXXI, September 1961, pp. 592-595; Oscar L. Altman, "Foreign Markets for Dollars, Sterling, and Other Currencies," "Canadian Markets for U.S. Dollars," and "Recent Developments in Foreign Markets for Dollars and Other Currencies," in IMF *Staff Papers,* VIII, December 1961, pp. 313-352, IX, November 1962, pp. 297-316, and X, March 1963, pp. 48-96; "Euro-Dollar," *Farmand,* 15 September 1962, pp. 17-21; Curt Carnemark, "Euro-dollarmarknaden," *Ekonomisk Revy,* XX, January 1963, pp. 40-47; M. P. Gans, "Van Eurodollars en Yankee-yens," *De Economist,* CXI, March 1963, pp. 193-213; and Reinhard Kamitz, "Ein neuer internationaler Geldmarkt," *Der Österreichische Volkswirt,* XLIX, 15 November 1963, pp. 1-2.

[12] In its 34th *Annual Report* (1963–1964), which came to hand after this section had been written, the Bank for International Settlements defines a Eurodollar "as a dollar that has been acquired by a bank outside the United States and used directly or after conversion into another currency for lending to a nonbank customer, perhaps after one or more redeposits from one bank to another" (p. 127). The Bank then expands this definition in such a way as to leave it quite unclear what specific thing, if any, the term refers to.

A hypothetical example will help explain the arrangement. A European exporter has received payment in the form of a dollar check or a deposit in a New York bank. For some reason he wants to continue holding dollars for a while, not yet spending them on American goods or converting them into his home currency. But instead of having to hold them on deposit in New York, he may, if he wants, hold them in the form of a dollar claim on his bank in Europe, to which he transfers ownership of the deposit in New York. The European bank can in turn transfer this deposit to someone who wishes to borrow immediately spendable dollars. The European bank will hold such positions with many customers at the same time—owing dollar liabilities to many depositors and holding dollar claims on many borrowers. The bank will probably not lend out the full amount of U.S. bank balances transferred to it; it will keep a fraction of them in reserve to honor the demands of depositors who may wish to cash their claims into dollars actually spendable in the United States. (While some Eurodollar deposits are repayable only after a specified number of days or months, some are repayable on demand.) Suppose the European bank has dollar deposit liabilities of $1 million, reserve balances in New York of $200,000, and outstanding dollar loans of $800,000. The borrowers or those to whom the borrowers have made payments (Americans, typically) actually have the $800,000 in the form of balances in U.S. banks. Yet the depositors of the European bank still have their $1 million, only now in the form of their claim on that bank. The bank has intermediated transfers of balances in the United States from its depositors to borrowers while still leaving its depositors holding claims that they regard as dollars. One million dollars has become $1,800,000; in a sense, the European bank has taken part in *creating* $800,000. When we consider European banks in the aggregate or as a system, we realize that their multiple creation of Eurodollars on the basis of additional reserves of U.S. dollars must be much more narrowly limited than the multiple creation of demand deposits on the basis of additional reserves by the

American banking system. The reason is that since Eurodollars do not circulate as an actual medium of exchange, the drainage of U.S. dollars out of the possession of the European banking system as ultimate borrowers spend them is relatively much larger than the analogous drainage of reserves out of the American banking system. In this respect, the operations of European banks in creating Eurodollars and serving as intermediaries in loans of U.S. dollars are analogous to the operations of nonbank financial intermediaries in the United States in creating liquid (but also noncirculating) claims against themselves and serving as intermediaries in loans of money. Still, the point remains that European banks do take part in creating Eurodollars on the basis of merely fractional reserves of U.S. dollars.[13]

What motivates this system? Why should anyone care to hold Eurodollars? The chief reason seems to be that a depositor can earn a competitive interest rate on his Eurodollar account, whereas in the United States, the Federal Reserve forbids interest on demand deposits and limits interest on time deposits. The European bank's motive is that it can relend the deposited dollars at a somewhat higher rate of interest than it pays. The source of the interest-rate advantage shared between the European bank and its borrowing customer is basically the opportunity to borrow dollars relatively cheaply from a depositor whose alternative would have been to hold his demand or time deposit at no interest or low interest in the United States. Related to this is the gain from operating on a fractional-reserve basis. Furthermore, the familiar advantages of financial intermediation enter into the explanation. A European without regular American banking contacts can borrow dollars from his own bank. Ultimate lenders of dollars—and these are often American banks—can let better-qualified European banks bear the trouble and risk of lending to ultimate European borrowers.

These reasons also explain transactions in "Eurosterling" and in deposits of Continental

---

[13] The dollars serving as the reserve base of the pyramid have no special nature. They are the same as other dollar deposits in U.S. banks.

currencies outside their home countries. A foreign bank, not bound by the regulations and practices of the country where a currency circulates, may be able to operate on smaller margins, paying higher rates of interest on deposits of it and charging lower rates on loans of it. Foreign transactions are a way of getting around unofficial limits on interest on sterling deposits in Britain, for example, and the ban that Germany and Switzerland have at times imposed on interest payments by their banks on mark or franc deposits owned by foreigners.

The foregoing description only begins to indicate the complexity of the Eurodollar system. Actually, foreign banks not only trade spot and forward dollars against local currencies but also actively borrow and lend dollar balances among each other. Some Eurodollar activity begins with the borrowing of other currencies that are then sold for dollars on the exchange market. Canadian banks have borrowed heavily in the Continental dollar market to relend to securities dealers and brokers in New York, where their agencies are in a favorable position to supervise the loans. Curiously enough, many of the published descriptions of the Eurodollar market put almost their entire emphasis on transactions among banks, with little attention to the ultimate supply and ultimate use of dollars at the two ends of what may indeed be a rather long chain of interbank transactions. This complicated intermediation reflects specialization, the tailoring of terms to the wants of participants, the sharing or reallocation of risks, and so forth. For example, a bank may borrow dollars on call and relend them on time, relying on fractional-reserve principles to protect it from embarrassment when asked to repay call money. The spread between borrowing and relending rates in interbank Eurodollar transactions is small, but the participating banks get other advantages besides an explicit profit margin, such as the opportunity to pave the way for other types of business by cultivating contacts with correspondents and by keeping their names familiar in the international banking community.

Business firms and commercial banks are not the only holders of Eurodollars. Banks of communist countries have acted on their supposition that dollars are safer from legal attachment or restriction when on deposit in a European instead of an American bank. The central banks of some 20 to 25 countries are said to have fed the market by holding parts of their external reserves in this new form. They have either handed over dollar balances to commercial banks or to the Bank for International Settlements in return for a dollar deposit claim or have sold dollars to commercial banks for local currency under repurchase agreements. The motive (besides, in some cases, the desire to influence capital movements) is a better yield on Eurodollars or Eurosterling than on U.S. or U.K. bank deposits or Treasury bills. More than $1 billion—an estimated 45 percent—of the total increase in foreign-exchange reserves of national monetary authorities in 1960 reportedly took an untraditional form, largely dollar and sterling deposits in banks outside the United States and the United Kingdom.[14] The central banks of the main financial centers, however, have placed few if any funds on the Eurodollar market, and total central-bank placements fell off after about 1961 or 1962. As for the total amount of Eurodollars held by holders of all types, little can be said with confidence. The Bank for International Settlements estimated its net size (excluding interbank deposits) at about $7 billion in 1963, consisting of about $5 billion in dollars and about $2 billion in other Eurocurrencies.[15]

How is this new development to be appraised? For good or ill, it is a long step toward a keenly competitive and unified international money market and the narrowing of discrepancies between interest rates in different countries. Some European bankers have hailed the system as disproof of worries about an inadequate growth of international liquidity and as an example of how liquidity can adapt itself to the needs of trade through increased velocity of circulation. It has helped

---

[14] Kamitz, *op. cit.;* IMF, 1961 *Annual Report,* pp. 112-114.

[15] Bank for International Settlements, 34th *Annual Report,* 1963–1964, pp. 132-133, 130.

meet the growing demand for credit to finance international transactions. Expanded holdings of foreign exchange by banks and business firms increase the scope for the financing of international payments to take place outside of official reserves, leaving the latter freer for absorbing fluctuations in balances of payments.[16] So far as the Eurodollar market gives foreign private holders attractive alternatives to selling their dollars to their central banks or gives central banks attractive alternatives to converting their dollars into gold, the U.S. gold reserves are spared. (The extent to which international liquidity is created or stretched in these ways, however, must be haphazard and difficult to assess.) Less welcome, perhaps, is the impairment of official restraint on outflows or inflows of short-term hot money. What good does it do a country like Germany or Switzerland to forbid interest on foreign-owned deposits in its banks if holders of noninterest-bearing mark or franc balances can collect interest after all by redepositing them with foreign banks? By linking the money markets of different countries more closely together, the system intensifies some features of international borrowing and lending in general. For good or ill, national policies must become less independent of each other. For example, business firms and banks have become more able than before to weaken or circumvent a domestic anti-inflationary tight-money policy by borrowing abroad and forcing their country's central bank to create additional "high-powered" domestic bank reserve funds as it buys up the borrowed foreign money to keep the exchange rate pegged.[17]

In countries whose currencies incur the competition of deposits created by foreign banks, the monetary authorities may have a slightly trickier job of gauging the appropriate regulation of the home money supply.

Applied to the United States, this worry remains rather far-fetched unless the volume of Eurodollars should ever become sizable in relation to the ordinary domestic money supply and unless asset-holders should come to regard dollar deposits in foreign and American banks as close substitutes. As they affect U.S. monetary management at present, Eurodollars would appear analogous to the liquid liabilities of a relatively unimportant class of nonbank financial intermediaries. A still more conjectural worry is that the chance to escape from the interest prohibition and reserve requirements applicable to banks in the United States might bring Eurodollars into use as a medium of exchange, being transferred by check in payments among Americans. While not actually used in this way, Eurodollars—a sizable fraction of the total—have already been acquired by U.S. residents and companies and European branches of American companies.

Critics of the gold-exchange standard may view Eurodollars as a new basis for their fears. They form a new layer in the inverted monetary pyramid (though it is still relatively very small and though, as already explained, the drainage of dollars spent by ultimate borrowers restrains the pyramiding). Financial practice has now evolved beyond a mere pyramiding of deposit money in U.S. banks onto Federal Reserve funds, which in turn are pyramided onto gold. We now have the pyramiding of dollar deposits in European banks onto a fractional reserve of ordinary deposits in American banks, which are pyramided onto a fractional reserve of deposits in the Federal Reserve banks, which in turn are pyramided onto a fractional reserve of gold. And this is not all. Insofar as some foreign authorities peg their currencies to fractional reserves of foreign exchange consisting partly of Eurodollars rather than entirely of ordinary dollars, foreign currencies are pyramided onto a fractional reserve of Eurodollars, which are pyramided fractionally onto ordinary dollar deposits, which are pyramided fractionally onto Federal Reserve deposits, which in turn are pyramided fractionally onto gold.

All this underlines how precarious the ex-

[16] *Eastern Economist, op. cit.;* International Monetary Fund, 1963 *Annual Report,* p. 43.

[17] Presumably for this reason, among others, the United Kingdom, Italy, France, and other countries maintain some restrictions on borrowing abroad by their residents. BIS, 34th *Annual Report* (1963–1964), pp. 139-140.

isting system of international liquidity is. It is quite true that all is well as long as confidence in dollars and sterling remains absolute and unquestioned—and as long as changed international interest-rate differentials do not motivate a large move out of either. But should confidence ever weaken, the scope for a destructive chain reaction is greater than before the development of Eurodollars.[18]

18 Holmes and Klopstock, *op. cit.*, p. 202, and Einzig, *Economic Journal*, September 1961, pp. 593-594, do allude briefly to vulnerability and the importance of confidence. Even the basically complacent *Eastern Economist* correspondent, *op. cit.*, p. 112, while denying any problem over the quantities of dollars and sterling, insists on the importance of maintaining pre-eminent confidence in them. This calls for the classic monetary remedies, says the article, and not world monetary plans.

Moderate Proposals for International Monetary Reform

ᘒ 27

The purpose of reviewing some of the many reform proposals put forth in recent years is not to pay homage to their authors' ingenuity. Rather, it is to gain further insight into the strengths and weaknesses of existing arrangements and further insight into the alternatives open to policymakers. This chapter and the next consider proposed reforms in approximately the order of least to most radical or ambitious, though such a ranking cannot be perfectly clear-cut.[1]

Extension of Credit Facilities

Ad hoc mutual support arrangements among central banks or national treasuries could lessen the need for growth in reserves. The various authorities would agree among themselves to acquire and hold the currency of a country coming under exceptional balance-of-payments strain; they would not demand immediate settlement in some other currency or gold. The country could ride out its deficit by building up liabilities in its own currency that would, in effect, be temporarily blocked by agreement. Alternatively, the arrangements might permit a deficit country to borrow foreign currencies or gold. Informal precedents for such support extend back into

the heyday of the international gold standard before 1914. More recent examples have already been described in earlier chapters: the "Basel arrangements" whereby European central banks cooperated to defend sterling against speculation touched off by revaluation of the German mark in 1961, the international defense of sterling in November 1964, and the network of inter-central-bank swap arrangements that the United States began establishing in 1962.

Under the more formalized of such arrangements, a country equips its currency with a "gold guarantee" or "exchange guarantee." Its authorities guarantee that in the event they devalue the currency, they will credit designated foreign holders of it with enough additional amounts of it to keep the total gold or foreign-exchange value of each guaranteed foreign holdings as large as before. The suggestion is often made that the United States should guarantee foreign-held dollar assets in this way, even apart from any particular international credit arrangements. In restraining purely speculative runs from dollars into gold, the proposal has much to be said for it. But a guarantee would do little if anything toward solving problems of balance-of-payments adjustment and international liquidity. The prospect of large and incalculable dollar costs would in some ways awkwardly tie the hands of the authorities giving a guarantee. Problems would arise of deciding what types of dollar asset and what types of foreign holders should be covered. It might be difficult to confine the guarantee as decided. What, for example, would keep dollars from swarming into the guaranteed holdings of foreign authorities as private

---

[1] For details on most of the reform schemes surveyed in this chapter and the next, and some others, as well as for identification of their authors, see the "1961 Hearings," the "1961 Subcommittee Report," and the book edited by Grubel, all three cited in the last chapter, as well as *Economic Report of the President and Annual Report of the Council of Economic Advisers*, Washington: Government Printing Office, January 1964, pp. 133-148, and Fritz Machlup, *Plans for Reform of the International Monetary System*, Special Papers in International Economics, No. 3, 2nd ed., Princeton, N.J.: International Finance Section, Princeton University, 1964.

Americans fled into foreign currencies in anticipation of a devaluation of the dollar? What would keep Americans from transferring dollar assets to foreigners entitled to the guarantee with the understanding that the Americans and the cooperating foreigners would share in the nominal dollar profit when the guarantee came into effect upon devaluation? In connection with specific credit arrangements, though, guarantees make sense.

Several years ago Edward M. Bernstein and other experts proposed channeling mutual support through either the International Monetary Fund or a special IMF account to be created for the purpose. These proposals bore fruit in October 1962, when, as already mentioned in Chapter 25, ten industrial countries put into effect a $6 billion pool of lines of credit. The Group of Ten is likely to be strengthened by additional members or in other ways. Some such arrangement is probably better than relying exclusively on increases from time to time in members quotas in the International Monetary Fund. That approach, by itself, tends to load up the Fund still further with "cruzeiros, bolivianos, rupees, rupiahs, bahts, kyats," and other internationally useless currencies, all to obtain more of the few major currencies that really are in demand.[2] Furthermore, paying 25 percent of any additional subscription to the IMF in gold, as is normally required, could be awkward for countries already worried about gold losses.

"The availability of loans from the IMF," says Scitovsky, "differs as much from international reserves proper as a person's access to a moneylender differs from a credit balance on his bank account."[3] Authorities will presumably resort more quickly to trade and exchange controls to safeguard the balance of payments when they have to eke out skimpy reserves in their actual possession by borrowing than when they own adequate reserves outright. Partly to meet such objections, the IMF has recently been urging its members to regard their rights to draw on it as nearly the same as reserves. In reporting the typical member's "international liquidity" in *International Financial Statistics,* the Fund has recently begun counting not only its gold and foreign-exchange reserves but also its IMF "gold tranche position" (loosely speaking, the member's gold subscription plus or minus the amount of the equivalent of negative or positive drawing from the Fund). Bernstein has urged that countries integrate their IMF drawing rights with their owned reserves, that the Fund free rights to draw on it from existing restrictions, and that drawings be regarded as normal rather than emergency measures. So interpreted and used, IMF quotas would come to be practically the equivalent of owned deposits, or so Bernstein has agreed.[4]

Reciprocal Holdings of Reserves

In 1962, by starting to acquire some official reserves in foreign currencies, the United States took a small step towards adopting a proposal once made by Under Secretary of the Treasury Robert Roosa.[5] Under the Roosa Plan, the United States could work to cure its balance-of-payments deficit—a separate problem, requiring a separate solution—without endangering the growth of international liquidity for foreign countries. The United States could buy foreign currencies with dollars, which foreign central banks could accumulate as reserves. When balance-of-payments developments appeared to threaten a drain of gold, the United States could use some of its previously accumulated foreign currencies to buy back dollars and thus reduce foreign holdings of claims redeemable in gold. As time went on, international reserves could keep on rising: foreign countries would be holding more dollars, and the United States would be holding more foreign currencies. U.S. reserves would no longer have to shrink as a percentage of external liabilities, only they would no longer consist of gold alone.

The plan is ingenious in a rather zany way. *Business Week* once called it "monetary incest." While the United States and the aver-

---

[2] Robert Triffin in the 1961 Hearings, p. 304.

[3] 1961 Hearings, p. 176.

[4] See his testimony reprinted in Grubel, *op. cit.,* esp. pp. 401-402.

[5] See his paper reprinted in *ibid.,* pp. 261-274.

age foreign country would each see its external reserves growing over time, it would also see its liquid liabilities growing. How much if any *net* liquidity the process would create would depend on how asymmetrical a view national authorities took of their assets and their liabilities. This is a psychological matter, subject to sudden change. The plan would not stretch the world's limited supply of gold in a very satisfactory way. The dollar and other reserve currencies would remain second-class international moneys in relation to gold, which would become relatively ever scarcer.[6]

The Multiple-key-currency System

National authorities might develop the habit of holding their external reserves not only in gold and dollars or sterling but also in a number of other important currencies.[7] Growth in international liquidity would then no longer depend particularly on a U.S. deficit. To encourage foreign acquisition of their currencies as reserves, the new key-currency countries would stand ready to sell gold at a fixed price to foreign monetary authorities on request, just as the United States now does. There would be no need to create new international institutions or expand the functions of existing institutions.

Against its advantages stands the fact that the multiple-currency system would complicate the job of obtaining an appropriate supply of international liquidity, since not merely the payments deficit of the United States but rather the aggregate deficit of all key-currency countries with the rest of the world would become relevant. Self-interest would impel reserve-holding authorities to choose among key currencies according to the interest obtainable on them and according to their ap-

parent security against devaluation. The different key currencies would be competing for status and would have to be defended not only against gold but also against each other. Prudent reserve percentages would be larger than otherwise; this fact counters the hope that giving key status to additional currencies already backed by gold would bring additional gold into the basis for international liquidity.[8]

Multiple Key Currencies Backed by Each Other

The systems of multiple key currencies and reciprocal reserve holdings could be combined. Having each of the several key currencies backed in part by the others would supposedly economize on gold. However, the amount of net liquidity thus created would depend on a changeable asymmetry of outlook towards assets and liabilities and would defy quantitative measurement and control. The system would be unhealthily dependent on professional courtesy among central bankers.

A plan suggested by Professor Posthuma, a director of the Netherlands Bank, would formalize the combination system just mentioned. Each of the ten or so major countries taking part in the proposed arrangement would agree to keep gold down to some fixed maximum percentage (perhaps 60 percent) of its reserves and of additions to them; it would hold the remainder in the currencies of the other participants.

Edward Bernstein made the idea still more definite by suggesting how to make countries hold currencies other than dollars in their reserves.[9] To specify a fair and proper proportioning of the different currencies in the foreign-exchange reserves of each participant, a new reserve unit would be created. It would be equal in value to a gold dollar and would consist of about 50 cents in U.S. money and smaller amounts of sterling, francs, and other

[6] J. M. Culbertson has elaborated a criticism along these lines in "U.S. Policy and the International Financial System," in *Recent Changes in Monetary Policy and Balance-of-Payments Problems,* Hearings before the House Banking and Currency Committee, July 1963, Washington: Government Printing Office, 1963 (hereafter cited as *Recent Changes*), esp. pp. 337-338.

[7] Probably the most prominent advocate of this system is Friedrich A. Lutz. His paper explaining it (No. 41 in the Princeton Essays in International Finance) is reprinted in Grubel's volume, pp. 238-252.

[8] Cf. Culbertson, *op. cit.,* pp. 338, 339, 368-369.

[9] "A Practical Program for International Monetary Reserves," *The United States Balance of Payments,* Part 3, Washington: Government Printing Office, 1963, pp. 525-533.

moneys as determined by their relative importance in international trade and so forth. At the start, each participating country would deposit its own currency with the International Monetary Fund and receive credit on the Fund's books for the equivalent reserve units. Reserve units would increasingly displace dollars as the medium for holding reserves in addition to gold; and ultimately, countries would agree not to hold or acquire gold in amounts more than double their holdings or acquisitions of reserve units. The maximum permissible ratio of gold to reserve units and the proportioning of the various currencies in the reserve unit would lessen the danger of speculative shifts from key currency into gold and from one key currency into another. Restrictions on its eligibility to be held and used would downgrade gold and weaken the troublesome distinction between first-class and second-class international moneys.

The Stamp Plan

Sir Maxwell Stamp has proposed that the International Monetary Fund create additional international liquidity by issuing certificates denominated in gold but not convertible into gold.[10] The issue would be limited to perhaps $3 billion a year. Aid-coordinating agencies would distribute the certificates to underdeveloped countries, which would be pretty sure to spend most of them. The certificates would thus come into circulation among central banks as international reserves and would be considered practically equivalent to gold, dollars, and sterling. The plan would kill two birds with one stone —expand international liquidity and help the underdeveloped countries. (Stamp subsequently modified his plan to try to make it more acceptable: the issue of certificates and the amount of them any country would be expected to absorb would be more tightly limited than in the original plan.)

Unfortunately, the real resources transferred to underdeveloped countries under the plan would not be coming out of some fourth

dimension; they would be inflated out of the possession of countries absorbing the certificates. Furthermore, the plan would not replace but merely supplement the gold-exchange standard.

This last is in fact the fundamental objection to several of the palliative plans reviewed so far. They deal indirectly at best with the problem of second-class key currencies. They reduce the need for any particular key-currency country to run deficits but do not cope directly with inadequate growth of gold stocks in relation to money supplies, trade, and total external reserves.

The Triffin Plan

Most of the plans reviewed so far seem to have come forth as reactions to the Triffin Plan, already proposed. They reflect an apparent unwillingness to follow the logic of Triffin's diagnosis of existing arrangements all the way to its logical conclusion. They apparently represent attempts to offer reforms that will seem less radical and will be less difficult to sell to policy-makers. Many authors have hastened to supply their own ingeniously differentiated products on the market for reform plans that Professor Triffin had created.

The Triffin Plan itself goes pretty far toward fundamental reform. Except for the sake of keeping the numbers of pages from being too unequal, it might well belong in the next chapter instead of this one. It is too far-reaching to win general support quickly, yet the persuasive arguments in its favor will probably keep it alive over the next several years as a standard of comparison for more temporary and timid reforms. It could conceivably be adopted on an exploratory, gradual, piecemeal basis. At first the International Monetary Fund might accept purely voluntary deposits from its members of some of the gold, dollars, or sterling that they had already been holding. In addition, the Fund might create deposits in its lending operations; deficit countries could borrow newly created deposits from the Fund and use them to make settlements with surplus countries willing to accept them. These deposits would

---

[10] See the 1961 Hearings and Stamp's paper reprinted in Grubel, *op. cit.*, pp. 80-89.

be usable for buying any currencies needed for international settlements, would bear interest, would carry a guarantee of their gold value, and would therefore probably be more attractive than dollars as an international reserve and settlement medium.

The full-fledged Triffin Plan would require instead of just permit countries to hold parts of their international reserves on deposit with the Fund. As time went on, the requirements would become tighter. We need not consider the suggested details of negotiating and carrying out a gradual transition; we can best understand and appraise the plan logically extended to its final form. Ultimately, countries would hold almost all of their official international reserves—beyond some small maximum allowable gold percentage—in the form of deposits with the "XIMF" (as Oscar Altman has suggested calling the expanded International Monetary Fund). The XIMF could pay its members interest on their deposits because it would be earning interest on the foreign-exchange assets initially transferred to it and on the other loans and investments that it would acquire later. International settlements nowadays made by official transfers of gold and key currencies would be made, under the new system, by transfers of deposits at the XIMF. Central banks could draw on their XIMF deposits to obtain currencies actually needed for their stabilizing interventions in the foreign-exchange markets.

Deposits at the XIMF would constitute a new international money, perhaps known as "bancor" (the name suggested by Keynes in his plan of 1943 for an international clearing union). The XIMF would be a central bank for central banks, adjusting the total supply of bancor to the liquidity needs of the world economy. It could expand the bancor supply gradually over time by making loans and acquiring securities, just as a national central bank can expand the national stock of currency and commercial-bank reserve funds. Under the new system, the total supply of bancor, and therefore of bancor plus gold, could be subjected to a rational management impossible for gold alone or for gold and foreign exchange.

Gold would play a peculiar role. National currencies, bancor, and gold would all be pegged together. The needed long-run growth of international liquidity would make gold become an ever smaller fraction of bancor deposits. Two things would avoid the otherwise obvious danger: a so-called gold or exchange guarantee would prevent any loss of confidence that might touch off a run from bancor into gold, and anyway, the convertibility of bancor into gold for hoarding purposes would be narrowly limited. One wonders though, what could conceivably happen that could force the XIMF to devalue bancor in terms of gold and yet leave it able to honor its gold guarantee. The real answer, apparently, is that members would be restricted to holding ever smaller fractions of their total international reserves in gold. The Fund's ability to satisfy all legitimate demands for conversion of bancor into gold would be safeguarded by defining "legitimate" demands very narrowly and ultimately even by requiring national monetary authorities to turn over to the Fund most of any new gold they might acquire. These restrictions on gold ownership by monetary authorities would almost certainly require an accompanying ban on private gold ownership in all member countries. The fixed gold content of money units would retain very little operational meaning. Only in the degree of subsidy to gold mining is there any real difference in saying that a dollar is worth $\frac{1}{35}$ of an ounce of gold but that no one can have the gold and saying that a dollar is worth $\frac{1}{70}$ of an ounce of gold but that no one can have the gold. As rights to redeem XIMF deposits in gold become ever more narrow, the gold guarantee of the bancor unit would become ever more completely empty. Under the Triffin Plan, bancor displaces gold as the ultimate international currency. It is an unnecessary complication to have rules about defining and guaranteeing money units in terms of gold, about restricting official and private ownership of gold, and about tightening these restrictions from time to time. Gold becomes a mere appendage, apparently serving as nothing more than a costly public-relations device.

Because the scheme ultimately depends on

requiring member countries to hold no more than a specified small percentage of their total reserves in gold, liquidating it and repaying the depositors would be awkward. If one or more important members wanted to withdraw, the XIMF might find itself in trouble. Even if countries did commit themselves irrevocably never to withdraw, some government of some important country might still repudiate the commitment. The Triffin Plan is no stopgap to be tried pending invention of something better. As a practical matter, its adoption would block any fundamentally different solution to the world liquidity problem. It is much more fully true of the plan than of economic reform proposals generally that we cannot afford to experiment, hoping to guide ourselves by how the plan works out in practice. It is necessary to reason out, in advance, how it is likely to work.

One objection to Sir Maxwell Stamp's plan for the issue of IMF certificates applies also to the Triffin Plan as well: it accomplishes international transfers of real resources that are incidental to the creation of liquidity rather than deliberately chosen on their own merits. The creation of bancor apparently rewards balance-of-payments deficits; for precisely the countries to which the XIMF lends are ones running deficits, and those in which it invests on its own initiative are presumably those expected to put most of their new bancor reserves into international circulation by using them to finance deficits. The XIMF will presumably lend and invest more on the basis of supposed "need" and less on the basis of prospective productivity than do ordinary commercial banks. This conjecture is supported by the suggestion that the XIMF make investments largely in underdeveloped countries, either by buying their securities directly or by buying World Bank bonds. Of course, deficit countries do not get new bancor as an outright gift; but the way it is issued suggests that they enjoy cheaper and fuller access to capital than they would otherwise have. The surplus countries will earn interest on their bancor; but this is no proof that their loans of real goods and services, corresponding to their accumulations of bancor, are wholly voluntary. Central banks will sometimes accumulate bancor involuntarily in stabilizing exchange rates, rather than solely according to the ordinary motives that guide ordinary individuals and business firms in managing their cash balances and their investments.

The Triffin Plan goes even further than any of its rivals yet mentioned in perpetuating international monetary linkage. No excessively rigid version of the purchasing-power-parity doctrine is necessary to show that price levels in different countries will have to move roughly in parallel if their currencies are to stay linked together at fixed rates in substantially free markets and without a panoply of controls. A country that inflates too fast will incur balance-of-payments deficits; a country that lags behind in a general inflationary procession will find the danger of imported inflation thrust upon it. Somehow, actively or passively, monetary conditions within the various countries will have to be more or less coordinated.

Coordinating national monetary managements among themselves and with the international management of bancor will be a delicate task. The quantity of bancor in existence at any given time and the quantities and purchasing powers of national currencies must be connected. One reason is that the volume of bancor "needed" to lubricate the flow of trade depends largely on the price level of internationally traded goods. National inflations can thus increase the quantity of bancor needed and the quantity presumably provided by the XIMF. Causation runs the other way, too: by allowing some countries to have larger or more persistent deficits than they could otherwise have afforded, creation of bancor will strengthen demand and raise prices in the world markets for their imports and exports.

International liquidity management cannot follow some simple criterion of stabilization, for the purchasing power of bancor consists of the purchasing powers of the national currencies tied to it; and national price levels are subject to domestic policies. The difficulty is that under the Triffin Plan, money-supply management would be taking place on two levels—the international and the national.

This problem of two levels would be absent only if countries gave up their monetary independence and oriented their domestic monetary conditions above all towards keeping their international transactions balanced. A country's monetary supply, price level, and state of business activity would be related to its holdings of gold or bancor. A world gold or bancor shortage would then be unambiguously deflationary. But when, as nowadays, countries orient their policies toward maintaining full employment (or even toward financing government budget deficits) and refuse to accept deflation to keep in step internationally, liquidity need not always be deficient or excessive on the national or international levels both at the same time. In particular, a shortage of international liquidity need not mean a deflationary shortage of domestic liquidity. An international liquidity shortage may breed restrictions on international trade, but ordinarily not deflation. As the early years after World War II amply illustrate, inflationary abundance of domestic liquidity can coexist with impediments to international trade that might somewhat plausibly be blamed on a shortage of international liquidity available for riding out deficits (although the deficits themselves stemmed partly from divergent degrees of inflation within countries).

In such situations, remedying an international liquidity shortage would mean creating more bancor even when it was not needed to avoid any price-level deflation. The point is not that liquidity is inherently "bad" or "inflationary," but simply that creating additional liquidity even when there would otherwise be no deflationary deficiency of it does tend toward inflation. Triffin counters the fear of inflation by suggesting some conservative percentage limit to the annual increase in the supply of bancor. But then, as just shown, the supply of bancor might sometimes fall short of what was needed.

Is the opposite sort of conflict also possible —too much liquidity to lubricate international trade but not enough to prevent deflation within countries? This is unlikely. An excess of international liquidity hardly has any meaning, apart from its effect on price levels;

and domestic policy can avoid domestic deflation. The conflict is asymmetrical: the needs of international trade may sometimes promote but never restrict the creation of liquidity when an opposite policy is advisable on domestic grounds. The inconsistencies of trying to manage liquidity on two levels at the same time shake the hope that international liquidity would never be created in inflationary excess, but always created only to stave off a deflationary deficiency.

Let us consider this inflationary bias further. New international liquidity would seldom be created to prevent deflation of prices and business activity; domestic policies would be taking care of that, anyway. Controls or devaluation, not deflation, are the ultimate response to balance-of-payments crises. Domestic policies nowadays tend to err more on the inflationary than on the deflationary side. The supply of bancor does not significantly restrict domestic money supplies, yet this in no way means that creating additional bancor will not expand them. New bancor adds new spending power even to not-otherwise-deflationary situations. Its purpose is to let deficit countries avoid or postpone or mitigate the controls or devaluations otherwise necessary, financing larger or longer-lasting deficits than if new bancor had not been created. The hope that payments surpluses will alternate with deficits provides little reassurance, for the alteration will take place at generally higher levels of spending.

When some countries are financing larger or longer-lasting deficits than they could have done without the new bancor, other countries will be experiencing correspondingly larger or longer-lasting surpluses and facing correspondingly stronger pressures of imported inflation. Later balance-of-payments reversals do not undo inflation imported earlier; well-known "ratchet effects" are at work. This problem besets not only the Triffin plan but any or almost any arrangement for the more ample financing of international imbalances.

Inflationary biases could even make the Triffin Plan partially self-defeating. Higher prices would make more international liquidity needed to peg exchange rates at any given real flow of trade. If the XIMF expanded the volume of bancor to meet these needs, the process could proceed for another round. If on the other hand, the XIMF was determined to avoid feeding price-level inflation—if it operated according to liquidity requirements on the national level—only coincidence could assure adequate liquidity on the international level as well. A further complication is that liquidity requirements even on the national level would diverge among countries. It would be beyond the power of the XIMF to guarantee adequate but not excessive liquidity for all countries at the same time.

Proposals for Thoroughgoing Reform

28

A Genuine Gold Standard

Return to a *genuine* gold standard would count among the more radical or thorough-going of the reforms currently under discussion. The emphasis on *genuine* is necessary, since "gold standard" means very different things to different persons.[1]

The historical association between economic freedom and the international gold standard in the late nineteenth century makes going back seem appealing. Progress in science and

[1] A brief survey cannot report the arguments and proposals of various advocates of the gold standard in the detail and with the nuances that they themselves would want. To avoid unfairness, therefore, it seems best not to attribute particular views to particular persons but simply to list a sampling of the highly diverse writings consulted in preparation of the gold-standard sections of this chapter. In addition to the articles by Heilperin and Rueff already cited in the two last chapters, see, for example, the lectures by Murray Rothbard and Arthur Kemp in *In Search of a Monetary Constitution*, Cambridge: Harvard University Press, 1962; the remarks of W. J. Busschau, Donald H. McLaughlin, Philip Cortney, O. Glenn Saxon, James Washington Bell, Philip M. McKenna, and Henry Hazlitt in the National Industrial Conference Board Economic Forum, *Shall We Return to a Gold Standard—Now?*, New York: NICB, 1954; W. J. Busschau, *Gold and International Liquidity*, Johannesburg: South African Institute of International Affairs, 1961; Walter E. Spahr, "The Gold Standard and Its Significance," *Modern Age*, Summer 1960, pp. 297-301; E. C. Harwood, *Cause and Control of the Business Cycle*, 5th ed., Great Barrington, Mass.: American Institute for Economic Research, 1957, esp. Chap. IX and Appendix D; Ludwig von Mises, *The Theory of Money and Credit*, new ed.; New Haven: Yale University Press, 1953, part four; Charles Rist, *The Triumph of Gold*, trans. with an introduction by Philip Cortney, New York: Wisdom Library, a division of Philosophical Library, 1961; Wilhelm Röpke, *International Ordnung—heute*, Erlenbach-Zürich: Rentsch, 1954, pp. 30-31, 110-112, 219-220, 278, 334-335, 314-350; and the monthly *Monetary Notes* and occasional other publications of the Economists' National Committee on Monetary Policy.

technology, in economic well-being, in individual freedom, and in political democracy then seemed fated to continue indefinitely. People could cross almost all boundaries with few restrictions or formalities. Trade in goods and services was practically free from quantitative restrictions and from all but moderate tariffs. International investment took place with little interference and was conspicuously beneficial to the host countries. Exchange-rate risk was almost absent. Use of coins with different names and sizes in different countries was a mere detail and did not keep gold from being the international money. Nationalistic governmental manipulation was kept away from money as from other human affairs. Monetary internationalism seemed to be the condition and corollary of internationalism in all policies affecting the movement of goods, services, capital, persons, and ideas.

Actually, this happy association may have been more a coincidence than a matter of cause and effect. (On the contrary, something besides coincidence may explain why the worldwide trend toward freer trade began to run down and give way toward renewed protectionism at just about the time the gold standard was becoming truly international in the 1870s.) But whether historically and logically warranted or not, the idea does have widespread appeal that monetary and other kinds of internationalism naturally go together, as do their opposites. Some people even call monetary nationalism the worst kind of nationalism and the root of all other kinds.

Some advocates of the gold standard build their case at least as much on political philosophy as on economics. Government is an actual or potential enemy. It is a necessary evil—necessary because anarchy would be intolerable, evil because it tends to push its coercive powers beyond their proper sphere. Government, on this view, is no mere committee appointed by ordinary citizens to administer their common concerns, no mere body of public servants, no mere instrument passively recording and implementing the desires of the voters. On the contrary, it is a group of officials seeking power for themselves. Throughout the ages, the state has used inflation of the money supply to wrest resources from its subjects and build up its own power at their expense. The gold standard can help fight this statism. Excessive issue of fiduciary money or expansion of government spending will alarm the ordinary citizen into presenting his paper money for redemption. To restore confidence and save its dwindling gold reserve, the government must quickly return to financial prudence. The citizens hold the purse strings and control their government more directly and effectively than they could do at the ballot box alone. Furthermore, gold coins promote human freedom by providing a durable but liquid form of wealth, high in value in relation to bulk, that can easily be hidden and protected from confiscation. It is no accident, some of its advocates are fond of stressing, that the gold standard and classical liberalism flourished together.

The entire contemporary discussion—not just the present review of it—suffers from vagueness about what "the gold standard" means. This vagueness gives the proposal much of whatever appeal it has. It serves as a slogan or rallying point for opposition to the long record of government mismanagement of money and especially for opposition to the generally inflationary mismanagement of the last 25 or 30 years. To many people, it symbolizes automaticity as opposed to governmental discretion. The gold standard enjoys the advantage of being a negative position; its features and operating properties are not carefully examined and its own defects do not come to the fore. Of course, its supporters do not neglect its operating properties completely. They talk quite a bit about

how the genuine gold standard, in contrast to the present-day sham, provides balance-of-payments discipline and an adjustment mechanism. But it is doubtful whether its typical supporter—even its typical academic supporter—has gone much beyond sloganizing and has considered in detail and welcomed with understanding the deflationary process of removing an external deficit, particularly as it would operate in the world of today, where conditions are less favorable than in the nineteenth century.

Different Varieties of Gold Standard

Perhaps it is not quite fair, after all, to say that the gold-standard proposal is vague. A minority of supporters do say rather clearly what they want, how they propose to achieve it, and how it will work. But because it does mean so many different things to different people, the gold standard retains the tactical advantage of being an ambiguous rallying cry for opposition to "things as they are." Simply to illustrate this diversity of opinion and not to make detailed appraisals, it is worthwhile to mention a few of the varieties of gold standard that have been proposed.

A small minority wants a 100 percent gold standard. Gold would be the only money. Government issue of any other kind would be forbidden, and even private issue of banknotes, demand deposits, or other liabilities usable as media of exchange would be suppressed unless they were fully backed by gold. Supporters deny that enforcing these prohibitions would bring totalitarian governmental intervention in economic life; government would simply be doing its traditional duty of preventing force and fraud (for the issue of demand obligations that could not all be honored at once is fraudulent, on this view). The total supply of a pure gold money would grow slowly and without erratic variations; the economic system could adjust to an impersonal and dependable monetary framework. Of course, adopting this proposal would massively shrink countries' money supplies and require tremendous price-level deflation unless the gold contents of money units were drastically reduced. The same is true, though to a lesser degree, of the proposal to forbid governmental fiduciary money but tolerate the private creation of money on a fractional-reserve basis. Some proposals would impose reserve requirements on banks; others would subject them to no regulations beyond those governing all business, including the obligation to honor contracts. The gold reserve ratios that banks would voluntarily adopt to be safe and to guard their reputations for soundness would, it is hoped, gear the total supply of money in a satisfactorily stable manner to the unmanipulated total stock of gold.

Still other proposals would tolerate issue of fiduciary media not only by commercial banks but also by governments or central banks. The official fiduciary issue might be limited to some definite size, with all additional issues requiring full gold backing, or the law might require some definite reserve percentage. The legislature might even allow the monetary authorities to choose their own reserve ratio in the light of evolving experience. One well-known American group objects not to fractional reserves but rather to the dishonesty of the meaningless promises to pay that appear on U.S. paper money. Honesty requires that promises be honored in gold and that the gold content of the dollar be inviolate. And the time to start being honest under a restored gold standard is at the very beginning. This principle forbids another devaluation of the dollar. Even with the dollar continuing to be $\frac{1}{35}$ of an ounce of gold, existing gold stocks should be adequate, on this view, to avoid severe deflation and to sustain prices at close to their present levels. Government-issued and bank-created fiduciary media will continue abundantly to supplement gold money. Although redeemability is vitally necessary for honesty and soundness and to check the inflationary propensities of government, people will not in fact exercise their right of redemption extensively enough to keep the monetary system from working well even with gold reserves of less than 10 percent. As long as people know they can get gold whenever they want it, they will not want it; they will prefer the convenience of

paper money and bank accounts. The monetary authorities will even have scope for using traditional central-bank weapons to dampen the business cycle and to correct balance-of-payments disequilibriums. (The use of Bank rate in pre-1914 England has considerable nostalgic appeal.) The smallness of fractional gold reserves would actually be an advantage if the authorities should show signs of deviating from sound policies: even a small rise in demands for redemption on the part of uneasy holders of fiduciary media would promptly compel the authorities to mend their ways. In short, a fractional-reserve gold system is safe, on this view, *if* monetary policy is sound—and *only* if it is sound, which itself is a welcome restraint on government. But other advocates of a gold standard are much less sanguine about narrow fractional reserves. While recognizing a 100 percent standard as impossible, they would seek a comfortable cushion of reserves.

All this emphasizes a great diversity of opinion as to how high, how rigid, and how automatic the gearing should be between the quantity of money and the quantity of gold. At one extreme, the advocates of a 100-percent standard want a completely automatic and rigid one-to-one linkage. Many more persons, at the other extreme, envisage a rather high and flexible gearing under central-bank management. The chief virtue of the gold standard in their eyes is not that it avoids monetary management (they know it doesn't) but that it requires the managers to behave so as to preserve unshaken confidence in the perpetual redeemability of money in gold at a fixed ratio. The view that would be satisfied with redeemability in gold bullion is more completely at the extreme of belief in high and flexible gearing than the view that insists on redeemability in and actual circulation of gold coins.

One of the leading arguments for the gold standard is that it provides a closer approach than we have known for several decades to a state of affairs in which the economy must adjust itself to an objectively given quantity of money, largely immune to conscious human will and to influence by politicians and self-seeking economic interests. It seems odd, then, to set about loosening the link between the quantities of gold and money by devising or tolerating methods of "economizing" on gold. The present state of the gold-exchange standard has resulted from an increased pyramiding of money onto a gold base by such measures as the withdrawal of gold coins from circulation in favor of a bullion standard, by the spread during the 1920s of the practice of basing domestic money on a fractional reserve of foreign exchange, in turn only fractionally based on gold, and by prohibition of private gold ownership since the 1930s. Inconsistently, nations have tried both to preserve and to escape the linkage of money to gold. They have tried to preserve an appearance while destroying its meaning. Just one of the many difficulties with a highly geared gold standard is that shrinkage in gold reserves (caused, for example, by a balance-of-payments deficit) can require awkward multiple variations in the total money supply if redeemability is to be preserved. Some advocates of a gold standard insist, nevertheless, that the distinction among varieties of gold standard is less important than the distinction between being or not being on a gold standard at all. In fact, they "resent" any distinction between "real" and "pseudo" gold standards.[2] Yet the distinction remains a crucial one.

The Gold Link versus Other Rules

Gold-standard advocates should recognize their dilemma. The tighter and more unchangeable the link is between a country's gold stock and money supply, the more fully sheer accident determines whether or not the money supply grows in step with the aggregate demand for real cash balances (as determined mainly by growth in population and productivity). A faster or slower growth of the money supply than of the demand for it burdens the economy with price inflation or with deflation. As Sir John Clapham once

wrote, "A currency system which in difficult times depends on the chance occurrence of nuggets in gulches and gold dust in river sands lacks stability."[3] These considerations speak in favor of only a loose and adjustable link between the gold stock and the money supply. But the looser this link, the more the money supply loses the objective-fact-of-nature quality that was supposed to be the key advantage of a gold standard.

Perhaps we do want discretionary management, but within limits. But if so, can't we devise some better rule for limiting discretion than keeping money redeemable at a fixed rate in an industrially rather unimportant metal? Is this what we really want? Or, instead, do we want money of stable value that does not generate economic disturbances? It would seem more sensible to aim at what we really want rather than hope for what we want as a by-product of an indirect approach. The rules that make the best economic sense should have the best chance of eventually commanding public respect and of becoming a new "monetary religion."

As this remark suggests, rules of economic policy are not self-enforcing. How durable a rule is depends ultimately on whether or not it operates satisfactorily. If the gold standard is a poor rule for regulating the money supply, then its results impair its durability. In historical fact, the gold standard has not proved durable. Governments can and do go off it when they are forced to or find its restrictions inconvenient. No mythical or religious aura will do much to prevent departures from the rules of a restored gold standard.

Internationally as well as within countries, the gold standard does little to provide an appropriate quantity of money. It does nothing to make international liquidity grow as needed over the long run to finance disequilibriums between expanding flows of international trade. As already noted, gold production alone will not even come close to satisfying the growth in demand for international liquidity.

---

[2] Milton Friedman makes this distinction in a paper of that title, *Journal of Law and Economics*, **IV**, October 1961, pp. 66-79.

[3] *The Bank of England*, Cambridge: Cambridge University Press, reprinted 1958, **II**, pp. 222-223.

An Increase in the Price of Gold

Some people advocate doubling or more than doubling the price of gold to permit returning to a genuine gold standard. Otherwise, they feel, gold production and gold stocks would be inadequate to support not only 100-percent standard and not only a fractional-reserve standard with gold coins in circulation but even just a gold-bullion standard with foreign exchange eliminated from countries' reserves. Some who hold this opinion would set a new price of gold after studies by experts; others would establish a temporary "free" gold market, watch what level the price settled at, and then freeze this price and redefine money units in gold accordingly.

It is easy (if not quite fair) to make fun of gold-standard supporters who would adjust the price of gold. They allegedly ignore the essence of a gold standard—the supposedly fixed and permanent gold content of each money unit. In effect they are saying: Give us just this one last opportunity to tamper with the gold contents of money units and we promise never to do it again. (In fact, though, a few would not even make this promise; they would keep open the possibility of further but infrequent gold price increases.) A critic might ask: If you really believe in a *fixed* relation between money and gold and really believe that the economy should adjust to an unmanaged quantity of money, when is a better time to put your belief into practice than at the very beginning? Money units are *already* defined in terms of gold; the task is to make these definitions meaningful. How can you hope to reestablish a quasi-religious taboo against tampering with the relation between money and gold when you propose to start off with just such tampering? Gold-standard supporters could reply that precisely because we have *not* been on a genuine gold standard for several decades, price levels have *already* gotten too far out of line with the price of gold to permit avoiding an adjustment. In making an adjustment that would indeed be subversive of an already existing gold standard we are only realistically facing up to the conse-

quences of our not having been on one. We should not start out burdening a restored gold standard unnecessarily with the consequences of our not having been on it all along. After the restoration, the continuous discipline of economic adaptation to the available quantities of monetary gold will prevent further disproportionalities between gold stocks and price levels and will forestall any need for further tampering.

Another school of reformers proposes an increase in the price of gold without a return to a full gold standard. This step would increase supplies of international liquidity and give key currencies more adequate backing while leaving the existing features of the gold-exchange standard qualitatively unaffected. It would hardly be a fundamental reform; but a discussion of it fits in conveniently here, while we are also considering an increase in the price of gold as part of a more ambitious program. Much can be said against it. The increase would have to be steep—just how steep depending on how big a role gold was to have in international liquidity and national money supplies, but probably at least a doubling or tripling. The benefits would accrue haphazardly. A price increase would be least beneficial precisely to those countries that had been particularly short of gold reserves. The chief gainers would be private gold hoarders, gold-mine owners, Russians, South Africans, and "any countries which had previously been 'rocking the boat' by switching out of dollars and pounds into gold."[4] The old joke about paying people and wasting resources to dig up gold in one place and rebury it in another would become even more apt. An impending increase in the price of gold could not be kept completely secret and would be preceded by one-way-option speculation.[5] If gold were still to be heavily relied on for national

[4] Brian Tew in 1961 Hearings, p. 289.
[5] For one thing, an increase in the dollar price of gold would require an Act of the U.S. Congress, whose deliberations could hardly go unnoticed. It is true that speculation against the dollar could be forestalled by a sudden and unexpected Presidential order blocking foreign-owned dollar balances before the gold-price issue even came up in Congress. This would be too drastic an action to take against friendly foreign countries in peacetime.

moneys and international liquidity, the reasons that called for the initial price increase would develop again in later decades and require further increases. Variability in the price of gold would undermine even the *pretense* of linking currencies to gold. It would heighten the danger of flights from national currencies into gold and discredit their use as international reserves (which would be less of a disadvantage, however, if the intention were to abandon the gold-exchange standard *completely*). Unless the price of gold were to increase continuously, day by day or at least month by month, either at a specified rate or according to some formula, the price changes would come in discrete jumps. This way of keeping the effective supply of liquidity in step with the growing demand for it over the long run would mean that liquidity was inadequate before every price increase and temporarily excessive afterwards (causing inflationary tendencies that would not be completely reversed later on). Gold price increases as a way of creating international liquidity are subject not only to the special disadvantages just listed but also to the general disadvantages bedeviling any *ad hoc* creation of international liquidity. (These disadvantages have to do with the contradictions involved in trying to manage liquidity on two levels, national and international, at the same time. They have already been discussed in connection with the Triffin Plan.)

Financial Integration

Gold would not necessarily play any part in thoroughgoing international financial integration. If the integration proposed by James Ingram[6] could be put into effect, it would largely solve or sidestep all problems of balance-of-payments adjustment and

liquidity among the countries taking part. Individuals, firms, banks, and government agencies would have complete freedom to trade in securities and other financial claims across national boundaries. All legal barriers to transfer or repatriation of principal or interest and dividends would be removed. Local and foreign securities would become thoroughly intermingled in the portfolio of the typical insurance company, bank or other financial institution. A substantial portion of the entire stock of financial claims held by a country's residents could potentially enter into international payments adjustment, and the adequacy of a country's external reserves in the traditional narrow sense would become a question of relatively slight importance. The pressure of an external imbalance would be widely diffused through the financial markets. Exchange rates would require little central-bank support because commercial banks in a deficit country would themselves sell off internationally acceptable claims or otherwise arrange foreign-exchange cover. Such sales would marginally raise interest yields in the deficit country, attracting purchases by foreign financial institutions. International movements of capital and securities would be highly sensitive to differences among countries in yields.

Suppose the United States developed an external deficit. As their customers drew down their deposits, U.S. commercial banks would individually feel the pressure in the form of adverse clearing balances and would act to replenish their reserves by selling securities. Incentives operating on the banks individually would bring into play the adjustment process just described.

Ingram emphasizes several key conditions or policies required for the necessary degree of financial integration: (1) Completely rigid exchange rates, with no range of fluctuation around par and no possibility of change (for only then would capital movements be sufficiently sensitive to interest rates); (2) removal of restrictions on international payments; (3) removal even of *de facto* impediments to capital movements (such as tax provisions and other legal discriminations in favor of local securities in the portfolios of

---

[6] "A Proposal for Financial Integration in the Atlantic Community," *Factors Affecting the United States Balance of Payments,* studies compiled for the Subcommittee on International Exchange and Payments of the Joint Economic Committee, Washington: Government Printing Office, 1962, pp. 177-207. See also Ingram's *Regional Payments Mechanisms: The Case of Puerto Rico,* Chapel Hill: University of North Carolina Press, 1962, and the section on interregional adjustment in Chapter 5 above.

financial institutions); and (4) development of an efficient and unified market in securities and claims.

A single country could no longer pursue a separate national monetary policy in the sense of making its level or structure of interest rates diverge appreciably from those of its partners. Yet, according to Ingram, the required *additional* sacrifice of monetary independence would be small. The independence prevailing nowadays is largely illusory anyway in view of the fixity of exchange rates, the trend toward fuller currency convertibility and freer commodity trade, and the repeatedly demonstrated need to adjust national financial policies in response to balance-of-payments pressures. Furthermore, some room would remain for autonomous fiscal policy: a government could still engage in countercyclical deficit financing if it borrowed at competitive interest rates. (Yet this last point is not convincing if what it does to the money supply is the essence of effective fiscal policy.)

Ingram doubts the need for a common currency and supranational monetary and fiscal authorities. But the required coordination of national policies would amount to much the same thing. Ingram's entire case really concerns avoiding speculative crises in the absence of fundamental disequilibrium; but something else, that is, financial coordination, is necessary to avoid fundamental disequilibrium.

Such proposals for integration are a valuable contribution to the discussion because they shun weak eclecticism. Starting from their analysis of the inconsistencies of existing hybrid arrangements, they logically follow through to a consistent policy conclusion.

In a discussion of financial integration, the question naturally arises of monetary and balance-of-payments policies within a common market such as the European Economic Community. The Rome Treaty of 1957, which established the EEC, provided for no genuine and continuous adjustment mechanism. It only called vaguely for financial coordination and established a Monetary Committee to make studies and give advice. Further committees were established later to promote consultation among central-bank governors and consultation on budgetary and business-cycle policies. In April 1964, in an atmosphere of growing concern about inflation—and divergent degrees of inflation— in the member countries, the Council of Ministers of the EEC adopted a set of recommendations to member governments about anti-inflation policy. The recommendations concerned making stabilization of prices and production costs an overriding economic objective, further liberalization of imports within the EEC and from the outside world, limitation of increases in public spending and in government and private construction activity, tax measures to dampen demand, reduction of the deficits of nationalized enterprises, and stricter enforcement of antitrust laws. The Ministers made some special recommendations for Italy, with its relatively large degree of inflation, and for Germany, with its relatively slight degree. Still, the recommendations remained just that, lacking legal force.

In the early years of the Common Market, an easy balance-of-payments position (matching the deficits of the United States) made it possible to overlook problems connected with the near-absence of adjustment mechanisms. By the spring of 1964, however, the time for making some forthright decisions seemed to be drawing close. Already in its *Report* for 1962 (p. 37) the German Bundesbank had aptly remarked that monetary union among the member countries would require much more than bringing part of their monetary reserves into a common pool. Such a union

cannot be conceived until there is not only a common trade policy but also a common (or jointly and bindingly agreed) financial and budgetary policy, a common economic and cyclical policy and a common social and wage policy, that is a common policy *tout court*—in a word, until there is a Federal state with a European Parliament which has power to legislate for all the member states.

Is monetary unification—a common currency or firm fixity of exchange rates—necessary or even conducive to economic integration in the sense of fully reaping the advantages of geographic specialization? It would be a shame to let a mere verbal association of ideas prejudge this question. A price system is, among other things, a network of communications linking together the different sectors of a national economy and the international economy. Flexible prices serve as signals in this process of communication and economic linkage. It is far from clear that freezing some of these signals, namely exchange rates, necessarily does more to help than hinder this process.

Obviously, there is such a thing as too extreme a degree of monetary fragmentation. An independent currency for an economically very small area would not satisfactorily fulfil money's role as a highly *liquid* asset and as a vehicle for hedging against the risk of relative price changes if its management aimed at stabilizing its purchasing power only in terms of the narrow range of goods and services produced locally. If its managers were to have it taken seriously as a genuine money, they would have to tie its value to that of other currencies and thus sacrifice independent control over the local money supply.[7] It hardly follows, however, that the greater the range and tightness of monetary integration, the better. Quite conceivably there can be such a thing as too much sacrifice of the opportunity to compartmentalize monetary disturbances and too much sacrifice of functional flexibility of prices translated at flexible exchange rates. Questions of economic performance and optimum currency areas call for economic analysis and should not be foreclosed by the mere sloganistic or verbal identification of monetary unification with economic integration. (See pp. 97-99 above.)

A Non-gold Key Currency

We now turn from monetary unification to a reform almost as extreme in degree but almost the opposite in nature. This is true for the United States, anyway, which could make the change easily. The American authorities could simply ignore the country's balance-of-payments deficit and keep on paying out gold until it was all gone, incurring "that ultimate and unmentionable calamity whose consequences are the more dreaded for never being described."[8] The United States would then stop buying as well as stop selling gold. The link between gold and the dollar would lapse, and in the United States, anyway, gold would revert to the status of an ordinary commodity.

Foreign authorities might then stop pegging their currencies to the dollar and holding dollars as reserves. On the other hand, they might continue using the dollar as a key currency, just as many countries forsook gold and clung to sterling when Britain abandoned the gold standard in 1931. The crucial flaw in present-day arrangements is not really the use of key-currency reserves, as such, but the use as international liquidity of key currencies precariously pegged to gold on a fractional-reserve basis. With no official gold reserve remaining whose shrinkage could sap confidence, with gold demoted and the problem dispelled of having both first-class and second-class international moneys, and with no possibility remaining of one-way-option speculation on a devaluation of the dollar, the precariousness of today's system would be gone. (If more key currencies than one served as international liquidity, however, and if they were pegged together at fixed rates, the possibility would remain of flights from relatively distrusted to relatively trusted key currencies. The system works best when there is only a single key currency.)

Any run from the dollar would then have to be a run into American goods and services (if some foreigners unloaded their dollars onto other foreigners, this would not be a run from the American point of view). Unlike a run from a gold-standard dollar, this could cause no crisis for the United States; the capital outflow would finance itself by and coincide with surplus exports of goods and services. Even this development would be limited, to the extent that the dollars were

---

[7] Cf. R. I. McKinnon, "Optimum World Monetary Arrangements and the Dual Currency System," *Banca Nazionale del Lavoro Quarterly Review*, no. 67, December 1963, esp. p. 371.

[8] The phrase, though not necessarily the recommendation, is James Tobin's. "Europe and the Dollar," *Review of Economics and Statistics*, **XLVI**, May 1964, p. 123.

held by foreign monetary authorities and banks rather than by business firms, for it is hardly conceivable that central and commercial banks would fly on any large scale from dollars into commodities. To persuade residents of their own countries to take dollars off their hands and use them for purchases in the United States, the foreign authorities might relax import and exchange restrictions previously in effect or sell the dollars at a reduced price (that is, revalue the local currency upward against the dollar). The only devaluation of the dollar against foreign currencies to worry about would have to come at the initiative of foreign authorities, since the United States would not have been pegging the dollar in the first place.

Fears of continuing American inflation might conceivably motivate a flight from foreign-held dollars into American goods and services. This would differ little from a flight out of domestically held dollars. Foreign and domestic flight would occur together, if at all, developing gradually as a continuing inflationary drift in American monetary policy undermined confidence in the purchasing power of the dollar. In a key-currency country as in a non-key-currency country, the monetary authorities might either succeed or fail in recognizing and stopping such an inflationary drift. But with the key currency unpegged from gold, the domestic and external criteria of monetary policy could not clash. With its objectives made fewer and simpler, monetary management in the key-currency country would have a better chance of success.

Exchange rates would not necessarily fluctuate. Foreign authorities might peg their own currencies among themselves and with the dollar and even to gold as well, thereby indirectly linking the dollar and gold. Any distrust of this link—any fear that the dollar might lose value relative to gold—would imply expectations of either an upvaluation of foreign currencies against the dollar while leaving the foreign-currency price gold unchanged or an increase in the foreign-currency price of gold while leaving exchange pegging against the dollar unchanged. If private parties were acting on expectations of the first alternative, foreign authorities

would have to absorb dollars to keep exchange rates fixed until, if ever, they made the expected decision to change the level of pegging. For reasons already mentioned, an official flight from dollars is unlikely. Expectations of the second alternative would motivate a flight into gold from dollars and foreign money alike. In neither case would the American authorities face any crisis, since it is not they who would have been doing any pegging and worrying about drains on reserves in the first place. The foreign authorities would meet difficulties (akin to those of bimetallism) in trying to peg their currencies to each other, the dollar, and gold all at the same time; but the difficulties would be theirs, not American. The nongold key-currency system is most coherent, of course, when gold is demonetized everywhere.

Even under this system, individual foreign countries would occasionally face deficits, reserve losses, and one-way-option speculation on devaluation, or surpluses and unwanted large accumulations of dollar reserves. These are difficulties of exchange-rate pegging as such rather than of the choice of a particular international reserve medium. For the United States, balance-of-payments problems would be less serious, though a conceivable run out of dollars into goods and services, meaning an export surplus, would presumably be more nearly troublesome than a deficit. Even such a surplus would be nothing worse than repayment of real resources previously lent especially cheaply by foreigners.

Over the long run, a deficit would be more likely as foreigners accumulated dollar reserves. Far from being troublesome for the United States, this would mean receipt of cheap loans. From the foreign point of view, this "coals-to-Newcastle" capital flow is a defect of the nongold key-currency system, but no worse than the present system of in effect exporting capital by accumulating not only gold-pegged dollars but also gold itself.

No Official Reserves

If American abandonment of all remnants of the gold standard led foreign authorities to stop pegging their currencies to the dollar, gold, or anything else, exchange rates would become flexible. This restoration of an international balancing mechanism would pretty much dispel the liquidity problem as well. One feels apologetic in emphasizing anything so obvious as the relation between non-self-correcting disequilibriums and the need for international liquidity, but the point is crucial.

Let us suppose that national and international authorities stop concerning themselves with international liquidity, external reserves, or foreign-exchange operations. Foreign balances would be held only by individuals, commercial banks, and other business firms and private organizations (as well as by government agencies solely in connection with their regular international transactions rather than to influence the exchange market). Holders would determine and manage their foreign bank balances according to the same sorts of motives that govern their domestic bank balances and their inventories of ordinary commodities. (For private business, foreign exchange is indeed a kind of intermediate good, like fertilizer, office supplies, pig iron, or cloth; it is an "ingredient" in the process of "producing" imported goods and services; it is itself "produced" by domestic labor and resources in the export industries.)

Even under the Triffin Plan, which seeks to rationalize official reserves only, private holdings of foreign exchange would remain substantial. With only *official* ownership of other countries' currencies forbidden, private holdings of foreign exchange could still become subject to one-way option speculation from time to time; for Triffin's XIMF could hardly guarantee all national currencies, as well as bancor, against devaluation. A private flight from dollars into sterling, for example, could force the Bank of England to accumulate dollars in its exchange-stabilization operations. Since the Bank would be forbidden to continue holding these dollars, it would require the United States to redeem them in bancor. The drain on the bancor reserves of the United States could be quite as serious as a gold drain nowadays. The United States might borrow from the XIMF, but this would not so much prevent as palliate the dangers of one-way speculation.

Avoiding official reserves and intervention and relying exclusively on privately owned foreign-exchange reserves, by contrast, would enlist the Law of Large Numbers on behalf of a resilient national and international monetary structure. But nowadays, the Law of Large Numbers is inapplicable in two ways: one or two currencies alone make up the great bulk of foreign-exchange reserves, and a small number of national authorities hold the bulk of the total. When just one leading currency comes under suspicion, a large fraction of all international reserves is by that token under suspicion and particularly dependent for its fate on the decisions of a relatively few authorities. But if all foreign-exchange holdings were private, there would be no dominant holders of particular currencies. Thousands of merchants and banks would hold foreign exchange and no one of them would hold more than a very small percentage of the total amount of any currency. Furthermore, no one currency would fully retain its present-day dominance as an international reserve medium. Each merchant would probably hold bank accounts in the currencies in which he ordinarily made and received payments. Each bank, similarly, would hold foreign balances in many currencies. Speculative opinion would be diffused over a large number of currencies and among many holders, none of whom would be of dominant size. In contrast with the present system, only a widespread realignment of opinion could seriously strain international monetary relations.

This distinction needs some qualification. As bank runs illustrate, distrust may spread and destroy the independence of decisions necessary for the Law of Large Numbers. A similar linkage of opinion might affect private holdings of international reserves, though presumably less than when attention had been concentrated all along on one or two key currencies largely held by a few dominant holders. The absence of exchange-rate pegging is more important. Incipient distrust of a currency can express itself by a slight weakening of its exchange quotation, producing a new alignment of speculative opinion. An exchange rate determined by truly free private supply and demand almost by definition cannot be lopsidedly expected to move in one particular direction rather than the other. There is no one-way option.

With the pricing of currencies as free from official intervention as the pricing of ordinary commodities, the profit motive could usually be trusted to keep inventories of foreign exchange, as of any ordinary commodity, tending toward a level appropriate to the needs of its holders and to the cost of tying up resources in that form. Foreign exchange even contrasts favorably with flour, paint, salt, and other ordinary commodities in that large amounts of it could, at a price, be "produced" quickly if necessary. Banks could borrow abroad; balances in one money can turn instantly into foreign exchange by mere change of ownership. Severe inflations or deflations may conceivably distort holdings of foreign exchange away from a socially optimum level, defined in any plausible way. But these distortions, stemming from price-level instability and the resulting expectations, would be similar for inventories of foreign exchange and ordinary commodities alike. This consideration strengthens the case for aiming at domestic monetary stabilization.

Under the system outlined here, there could be no such thing as a shortage of international liquidity apart from deflationary shortages of domestic currencies within countries. Anyone who wanted to obtain more than he already held of some particular foreign currency could always do so at some price, a price at which its total quantities supplied and demanded were equal. Of course, adding an intensified foreign demand onto the domestic demand for cash balances of a particular country's currency would exert a deflationary tendency on that country. (The deflation can be understood either in terms of the demand for and supply of cash balances or in terms of appreciation of the affected currency on the exchange market and a resulting import balance of goods and services, with the foreign-trade multiplier operating to contract domestic income.) Far from being burdensome, the opportunity to create additional domestic money to meet the intensified foreign demand for it would allow the country to acquire real goods and services on in-

definite loan at zero or low interest from the foreign holders of its money or near-moneys. In any country, stable economic growth requires satisfaction, somehow, of the growing demand for real cash balances that accompanies long-run growth of population and production; and the fact that foreigners account for part of the growth in demand for cash balances need cause no particular complications. Changing demands for cash balances (changing velocity) may pose problems in managing a country's money supply; but the changes are of many kinds, and the state of foreign demand for the currency is by no means the most troublesome. The exclusively private holding of foreign exchange at least avoids the especially troublesome conflict between domestic and international considerations caused by the existence and management of a separate international money in addition to the various national currencies. Monetary stabilization has a better chance of success when it can be pursued in accordance with fairly simple criteria on the national level and for national objectives alone than when the task is complicated by liquidity management for international objectives as well.

The Need for Choice

In summary, general reliance on flexible exchange rates to equilibrate balances of payments would simplify the liquidity problem: if money supplies were not excessive or inadequate from national points of view, they could not be excessive from the international point of view either. Of course, this system has defects; no system of national and international monetary organization ever tried or conceived of has advantages only. We have to choose among total packages, trying to give due weight to all the advantages and disadvantages of each.

A point developed in Chapter 6 is relevant to this choice: to achieve a definite number of policy goals, an equal number of policy weapons are necessary. Specifically, achieving both internal and external balance requires using mutually compatible measures for pursuing each goal. If a country is using expenditure policy for internal balance, then either *ad hoc* controls or exchange rate flexibility are required for external balance. Many writers have expressed this necessity as a conflict between three things, each of which is desirable in its own right: (1) freedom for each country to pursue a monetary and fiscal policy for full employment without inflation (or for the best domestically attainable compromise), (2) freedom of international trade from *ad hoc* controls wielded to *force* equilibrium in balances of payments, and (3) fixed exchange rates. Any two of these are possible together, but not all three. With controls ruled out, a country can maintain a fixed exchange rate only by sacrificing its monetary independence and allowing its domestic business conditions and price level to keep in step with foreign developments. Unless the outside world remains perpetually stable, a country must choose between domestic stability and exchange-rate stability.

Sometimes this so-called Doctrine of Alternative Stability is questioned.[9] A country with abundant external reserves and large enough to sway world economic conditions has some leeway for a full-employment policy, for example, even in the face of world depression. Use of this leeway counts as temporarily dropping the goal of external balance (or, alternatively, as adding the weapon of variability in reserves), so that goals and weapons remain equal in number. But this qualification to the doctrine is a clearly limited one. Another qualification of limited importance refers to a country trading in an economically stable world environment but beset by an inflationary or deflationary impulse of domestic origin; the deficit or surplus that would develop in its trade would contribute to the country's economic stability while it acted to put its own house in order. It would benefit by diluting its instability onto the outside world. The Doctrine of Alternative Stability is not wrong but simply irrelevant for a country with such lax domestic finances that internal instability and

exchange-rate instability react upon and intensify each other. Nobody supposes that exchange fluctuations themselves generate domestic stability.[10] The doctrine states not that each of the two kinds of instability rules out the other but that each of the two kinds of stability rules out the other (unless the world economy is stable). The Doctrine is relevant for countries that have reasonable hope of doing better in monetary and fiscal policy than the general range of other countries.

If countries do not openly choose which one to sacrifice among monetary independence, external balance without controls, and fixed exchanges, the choice gets made unintentionally. Under the pre-1914 international gold standard, monetary independence was sacrificed to fixed gold parities. In the early years after World War II—the "transition period" of the IMF Charter—freedom from controls was sacrificed to national pursuit of full employment. In more recent years, the choice has become fuzzier; many countries seem to be seeking a compromise in the merely partial sacrifice of each of the three objectives. In the economically developed countries, the progressive dismantling of controls has become an important goal, and indeed an accomplishment. But the accomplishment is not really secure. Balance-of-payments difficulties sometimes bring tightening or reinstatement of controls or import duties, as illustrated by France in the late 1950s and Britain in 1961 and 1964. Even the United States adopted certain *ad hoc* measures as balance-of-payments worries developed from 1958 on; witness the tightening of "Buy American" rules for foreign-aid agencies and the armed forces, the cut in the duty-free import allowances of returning travelers, and proposed tax changes to make foreign investment less attractive. While not sacrificed, national financial independence has also been modified, and keeping not too far out of financial step with other countries has become fashionable. At times France and

---

[9] Wilhelm Röpke, *Crises and Cycles* (adapted from the German by Vera C. Smith), London: Hodge, 1936, pp. 164-173; Röpke, *Internationale Ordnung,* Erlenbach-Zürich: Rentsch, 1945, pp. 246-253.

[10] John T. Walter, *Foreign Exchange Equilibrium,* Pittsburgh: University of Pittsburgh Press, 1951, esp. pp. 38-39, however, makes quite a point of refuting this unavowed supposition.

more clearly Great Britain have adopted tight-money measures more out of regard for the external than the internal situation. Balance-of-payments considerations played a part in American abandonment of the "bills-only" policy in 1960–1961. In Germany, policy seems to have vacillated back and forth between efforts to resist the inflationary impact of a chronic balance-of-payments surplus and defeatist acquiescence in this impact. Exchange-rate fixity, finally, has also been compromised with. Without adopting flexible rates, a number of countries, notably including France, have adjusted their pegs often enough to jeopardize whatever advantages fixed rates may offer. Small and tardy though it was, the German rate adjustment of March 1961 seemed like a significant straw in the wind precisely because it was not a forced change but instead came in response to a merely annoying external surplus. The exchange speculation provoked by this step dramatized a general recognition that exchange fixity is not an overriding policy goal, and the evidence is relevant even though no further rate adjustments except the Dutch one were in fact made on that occasion. Even continuous exchange-rate flexibility has become less rare than in the earliest postwar years; Canada and several South American countries provide examples.

Historical evidence illustrates, in short, the logically inexorable need to sacrifice one of three objectives completely or two or three of them in part. Considering that the necessity for choice is the most fundamental principle of economics, it seems odd that economists should even yet not have reached near-unanimity on the need, in framing international monetary policy, to sacrifice one or more individually desirable things. We cannot have all good things at once. The only choice that has not been tried by numerous countries over a considerable period is to hold to national monetary independence and freedom from controls and frankly sacrifice exchange-rate fixity. Saying this, however, is by no means to recommend free exchange rates for all countries under all circumstances. As is clear from the growing literature on the theory of optimum currency areas, some coun-

tries may have persuasive reasons for tying their currencies together and coordinating their domestic monetary and fiscal policies. The chief recommendation here is simply that policy-makers choose with their eyes open.

The adjustable-peg system is one obvious example of trying to wriggle out of the necessity for choice. Another is the idea of leaving exchange rates free to fluctuate, but only within limits of, say, 10 percent above and below parity.[11] As long as free-market supply and demand keep a rate well within them, the two limits are unnecessary. And if the rate should come to press against one limit or the other and be held there only by official support operations, the disadvantages of exchange-rate pegging, including the danger of one-way-option speculation, again appear. A somewhat less irresolute idea is that of letting the rate fluctuate without limit but having an exchange equalization account smooth out erratic fluctuations in the very short run. If the managers can avoid blundering or being tempted into resistance to longer-run trends, they will not do much damage and may conceivably even do some good. But the idea of such intervention often betrays a reluctance to make clear-cut choices.

Counterarguments

Before concluding, I should repeat what seems to be the strongest argument *against* the policy endorsed here. It does not concern perverse elasticities, speculation, exchange risk as a deterrent to trade and investment, and the other standard objections considered at length in earlier chapters. Instead, it is the financial-discipline argument. What if the government finances spurts of expenditure by creating money? What if wage pushes and upward pushes on import prices generalize and support themselves through monetary expansion? What if the money supply accommodates itself to every little inflationary shock? What if the authorities react calmly

---

[11] For a view of this idea more sympathetic than mine and for a description of its several variants, see George N. Halm, *The "Band" Proposal: The Limits of Permissible Exchange Rate Variations,* Special Papers in International Economics No. 6, Princeton, N.J.; International Finance Section, Princeton University, 1965.

to a rise of a few per cent in the money supply or the price index? With no balance-of-payments crisis to force prompt action, inflation remains a problem to tackle *mañana*.[12] If this is the attitude, a persistent inflationary bias makes the requirement of internal and external balance both generally point in the same direction. If the country is somehow unable to follow the discipline of a price-level rule for monetary management or a rule limiting the growth of the money supply, the discipline of reserve losses at a fixed exchange rate is a welcome substitute.

A second reason for opposing free exchange rates is partly related to this one. It rarely if ever sees print in a clear-cut version; even in conversation, it lurks as an undertone. It seems to be a vague distaste for automaticity in balance-of-payments adjustment. This distaste may stem from uneasiness about the wide and unfathomable repercussions of market adjustments.[13] Somehow, the consequences of a country's balance-of-payments position should not spread themselves out inconspicuously in time and scope. They should remain concentrated and visible as a signal that changes are needed in economic

policy, as a pivot for consultations, and perhaps even as an argument for international cooperation and aid from abroad. An occasional balance-of-payments crisis may even provide welcome excitement and an opportunity to engage in expertise. With some people, opposition to free exchange rates stems from nearly ultimate value judgments.

Economy in Value Judgments

This sort of opposition is found, for example, among many supporters of the gold standard. They intimate that morality requires fixity in gold as the only really sound, decent, and honest monetary basis.

Another approach shuns ideological considerations in a choice among rival policies. Of course, it does not dispense with value judgments entirely; no policy whatever can rest on purely scientific grounds alone. Most of us presumably prefer a kind of society in which individuals can follow their own ideals and pursue their own goals with as little clash as can be arranged among their respective pursuits, with opportunity for effective cooperation in pursuing goals requiring common action, and with no unnecessary private or governmental coercion. This implies a preference for an economy coordinated by free markets and, in turn, for whatever monetary arrangements promise, *on purely technical grounds,* to be most workable. No detailed ethical premises are appropriate in appraising, say, fiat money against a gold standard or fluctuating against pegged exchange rates. Ideology properly relates to general pictures of a good society, but what sort of monetary arrangements are most conducive to the operation of a market economy in a free society is a technical matter. People who share common ultimate values ought to be able to discuss monetary issues among themselves on this technical plane, without bandying about suspicions of ethical deficiency. An Occam's Razor can be applied to value judgments as well as to analytical concepts: value judgments are not to be multiplied beyond necessity.

---

[12] Lionel Robbins's emphasis on this argument has already been mentioned in an earlier chapter. Jacob Viner also values a commitment to exchange-rate fixity because in many countries, he believes, this "seems to be the only factor of any strength which puts a brake on inflation." "Some International Aspects of Economic Stabilization," in Leonard D. White, ed., *The State of the Social Sciences,* Chicago: University of Chicago Press, 1956, p. 294; cf. p. 296.

[13] On November 15, 1963, Senator Douglas told the Joint Economic Committee: "For years I have urged the Federal Reserve, the Treasury, and our representatives on the IMF, to consider the flexible exchange rates, and I have been deeply disappointed by their refusal even to consider or study the matter. It has been an automatic reaction and, to tell the truth, I have not seemed to generate any real argument. It has been a sort of tropismatic response, even below the level of instinct. . . . I have been unable to get any lucid discussion on this subject from any representative of the Federal Reserve Board. . . . as this question has been put time and time again . . . there has only been a bland parry." *The United States Balance of Payments,* Part 3, "The International Monetary System: Functioning and Possible Reform," Washington: Government Printing Office, 1963, pp. 576, 581.

INDEXES

Index of Names

Index of Subjects